Working Boats of Britain

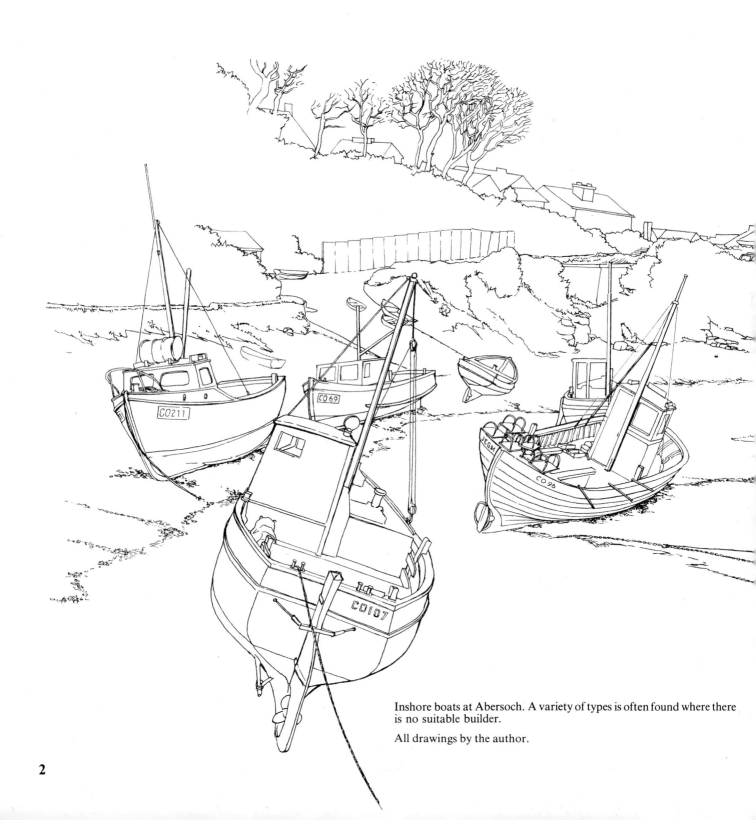

Inshore boats at Abersoch. A variety of types is often found where there is no suitable builder.

All drawings by the author.

Working Boats of Britain

THEIR SHAPE AND PURPOSE

Eric McKee

CAIRD RESEARCH FELLOW
NATIONAL MARITIME MUSEUM
OCTOBER 1973 TO JUNE 1978

INTRODUCTION BY
Dr Basil Greenhill

DIRECTOR
NATIONAL MARITIME MUSEUM

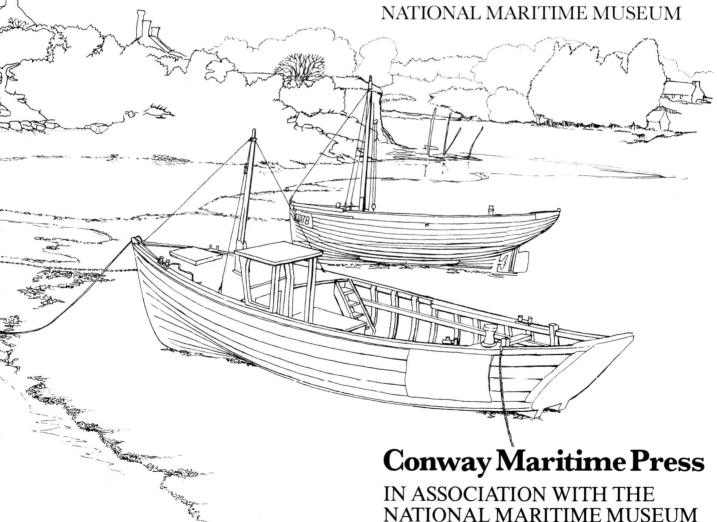

Conway Maritime Press

IN ASSOCIATION WITH THE
NATIONAL MARITIME MUSEUM

To Betty,
for all her patience, help and encouragement

First published in Great Britain 1983 by
Conway Maritime Press Ltd
24 Bride Lane
Fleet Street
London EC4Y 8DR

Designed by Geoff Hunt

Typesetting and artwork by Witwell Ltd, Liverpool

Printed and bound in Great Britain by
Butler & Tanner Ltd, Frome

Contents

Introduction

by Dr Basil Greenhill CB CMG FSA FRHistS

For many years the detailed study of working boats has gone on in Sweden, Denmark, Norway, Finland, Italy, Portugal and the United States. The work of Eskeröd, Christensen, Faerøyvik, Törnroos, Filgueiras, Chapelle, Gardner and many others has ensured that a great deal of information about the boats of their countries is now on record in published form.

The work of these men has had interesting side effects. In Scandinavia, Finland and the United States there has been a great widening of public interest in traditional wooden boats and boatbuilding. Many copies of old boats have been built and they are used for leisure purposes. Rallies and regattas for these boats are regularly held. You can see examples of most of the beautiful traditional working boats of the United States around the New England coast in summer. In northern Europe you can see shallop-rigged fishing boats all through the summer on the east coast of Gotland, church boats forty feet long with many oarsmen and -women on Finnish lakes, sprit-rigged boats of the type that used to attend upon shipping in the Sound between Denmark and Norway, and many more old and beautiful types of working boat brought back to life. Rowing, other than competitively, has been reborn both in American and Baltic waters as a leisure occupation, often in wooden boats of traditional forms.

Fifty years ago the Society for Nautical Research, with the aid of a grant from the Pilgrim Trust, employed the late Philip Oke to travel round Britain collecting information on some of the surviving boats and small craft. His work was invaluable, but it was never properly published. The late H Oliver Hill for thirty years recorded the social and working background to boats on many parts of the British coast, but again his work was never published. The late Edgar J March exhaustively studied the larger sailing trawlers and drifters and published the results in his two great books on these vessels in the early 1950s. But since then, despite the work which has gone on abroad, there has been a long period of almost total neglect of original research into small British working craft and there has been no phenomenon to compare with the revival of interest in working boats which has taken place in the Baltic and on the east coast of the United States.

For some years, with its displays in the New Neptune Hall, through publications and by providing a Boatbuilding Shop for public use, the National Maritime Museum has been endeavouring to stimulate interest in this country in this important and interesting part of our maritime heritage. But the Museum's most important contribution has been to finance, assist and encourage the work of Eric McKee, here presented in what is certainly the most comprehensive single study of the working craft of a country ever published. It is indeed a great pleasure when a Research Fellow produces work which at one bound advances the study of a subject to sudden full maturity, as does *Working Boats of Britain*. It is to be hoped that this publication will mark the beginning of a new era in the study in this country of that most delightful tool of man, the working boat.

Basil Greenhill

7

Preface

In the theory of the Art there are no fixed and positive principles established by demonstration and confirmed by use. There is hardly a rule sanctified by common consent, but the Artist is left to the exercise of his own opinion, and this generally becomes so rooted in habit, as to resist innovation, however specious. Undoubtedly there is reason for caution on one hand as there is for enterprize on the other. We ought to be as anxious to preserve the merits that are determined, as to overcome the acknowledged insufficiencies.

Marmaduke Stalkartt, 1791

This book is about simple boats and not complex vessels. It is about their many shapes, as they are found in Britain, and is concerned with how the waters, landscape and climate of this land, together with its inhabitants and their motivations and talents, have influenced them. Finally, it is about the fashion or way in which these boats have been built and used, in so far as this also affects their shape.

Brought up in the flat part of Somerset, I got to know how well simple boats, which by all accounts had not changed in ages, suited their surroundings and the task they had to do. Naval service was an introduction to boats all over the world, but hampered further study of those in Britain. Retirement at last gave me the opportunity to look at the Somerset boats more carefully, and, by way of comparison, those in Dorset and south Devon too. It soon became evident that if anything comprehensive was to be achieved before the time of wooden boatbuilding ran out, a more concentrated effort was essential.

Explaining the situation, I asked the Trustees and Director of the National Maritime Museum for help. This they gave in the form of a Caird Research Fellowship. This fellowship included assistance with travelling costs on top of financial aid to cover initially three, ultimately extended to five, half-yearly periods, when the extent of the project and progress made became clear. The reason for the half-years was that winter weather and summer crowds restricted field work for those parts of the year, and also I needed some time to raise funds by other means. A further requirement was that by the end of the fellowship there was to be a typescript suitable for publication as a book.

Initially, the intention was to find out what remained of the traditional types of British boat and why they differed so widely in shape. In the event the outcome of the study was rather different from this, as the text will show. The study took the form of a combination of activities, which occurred as the opportunity arose, rather than in this more logical order:

Stage I. Consolidating earlier work.

Stage II. Establishing and maintaining correspondence.
Stage III. Touring Britain, keeping a diary and photographic record.
Stage IV. Finding and measuring local types of boat.
Stage V. Recording boatbuilding and handling techniques.
Stage VI. Developing systems for this account to be written.

The end of the five-period fellowship saw the completion of Stage III with only a start made on Stage VI and the writing of the text. As boatmen do not live for ever, Stages II, IV and V are a continuing occupation.

An early personal reaction was that this study should not have been attempted in this way, but that it might have been better to have recruited a team of researchers, each with an area to examine in depth. It was realised, on reflection, that the administration of such a scheme would prove the harder task, if a balanced response was to be obtained in time. It is hoped instead that this more overall approach may encourage other investigators to examine the findings here in the light of their more detailed knowledge of their own local boats.

Some details of the various stages of the study may be of interest. The first stage has meant reading books and studying pictures, models and draughts, both before as well as during the period of the fellowship. Information first began to be published about one hundred and fifty years ago. In spite of the size and value of these contributions, they are not comprehensive, owing to a tendency to repeat studies in those places which had been described by the earlier writers and to neglect those which had not. While there is continuity in some places, interesting boat populations in others have been missed. There has been a preference for the larger sailing boats, especially those suitable for conversion into yachts, rather than the simpler small workboats that often retain more primitive features. There has also been a disregard for the recent changes that have taken place following the introduction of engine-powered propulsion and man-made boatbuilding materials. As this last period now spans almost a century some of the earlier evidence is already hard to find. To bring all this information together would be a task beyond the scope of a single fellowship, though there is a clear indication where it might be most useful to search.

Writing and reading letters have proved a worthwhile research tool. A wide circle of correspondents provide information and leads, criticism and encouragement, and in this case particularly invaluable local knowledge on the places to visit and people to see when planning trips. While most boatmen only pick up pens with reluctance, the few that have done so have been rewarding sources of information, particularly when establishing the manner and order in which boatbuilding and fishing were performed.

The tour of Britain was spread over the whole fellowship period. A major trip of two or three weeks was arranged twice a year, one in the early spring and the other in the late autumn. A timetable was worked out, but as it was impossible to foretell which places would require more or less time, this was kept flexible. While boatyards would be open on weekdays, fishing boats would only be in port over the weekend and their crews home, which today is seldom one of the old fishermen's cottages. A motor caravan was used to make the tours, as in addition to providing transport it guaranteed an office, a meal and a bed wherever one happened to be. The Caravan Club guide was a great help in finding overnight sites even out of season. As a result of these trips it was necessary to make short follow-up visits to consolidate lines of investigation that could not be included without disrupting the programme. These visits generated more informative relationships. Revisiting was seldom possible in the more distant parts of Scotland, where happily letters are still written. A diary and photographic record were kept. The former shows that just under 16,000 miles were covered, about 400 places visited – many several times – and about twice that number of photographs taken. As well as looking at boats and boatyards, harbours and beaches, it was possible to improve my knowledge of the topography of the coast of Britain. While it was possible to make useful contacts with many boatbuilders, far less was achieved with working boats' crews as opposed to older men who had retired.

The frequency with which little-known or -recorded boats were found was encouraging. Many of these were out of sight, in barns or yards, and were only found by following up leads. There are probably far more boats laid up like this than were ever discovered. Whenever possible the boat was fully measured, generally on a follow-up trip. On return home a draft was made as soon as possible to identify errors and omissions. These could only be put right by yet another visit. Returns had to be avoided, unless they could be combined with further research, so care was given to developing a system of measurement that minimised error. It was found that orthogonal measurements led to trouble, especially when the boat was out of true, as it was difficult in such circumstances to establish a datum. The use of a liquid level for vertical measurements and triangulations for the rest has proved satisfactory. Though this saves time on site, it adds to the time spent on the drawing board as the boat may have to be drawn twice, once askew as found, then again upright, if a conventional draught is required. Finishing drawings has been a bottleneck and clearing the backlog has delayed the completion of this written report.

So as to describe and compare their shapes in the light of their work and surroundings, it was necessary to have a method that could be applied to all known British planked boats. While it is thought that this system may well be capable of expansion to include those from other countries, this was not the objective. With this and new designs in view, it would be surprising if this classification could not be improved upon, but, as it stands, it does provide a means of handling a wide range of shapes. Other innovations are those used in describing the aspect of the coast to the prevailing wind and distribution patterns.

Getting the material together for this book has been far from a single-handed effort. As well as my wife and family, who have put up with this preoccupation, there have been a great number of others who have contributed. In the first place there are the writers like Keble Chatterton, H Warrington Smythe and R C Leslie who first showed me how fascinating small boats were. Subsequently there were other writers who widened my interest as did early membership of the Society for Nautical Research. In addition to the British ones mentioned throughout the work, there have been many foreigners: Americans – Howard I Chapelle, John Gardner, William Baker, Attwood Manley and M V Brewington; and Europeans – Manuel Leitao and O L Filgueiras of Portugal, François Beaudouin, Jean le Bôt and Bernard Cadoret of France, Lucien Basch of Belgium and a whole school of

Scandinavians, of whom Arne-Emil Christensen Jr and Ole Crumlin-Pedersen have shown me how this subject might be tackled and the standards to be expected.

Certain persons because of their early or prolonged contact have influenced my thoughts and conclusions. While deeply grateful to them for those results that are sound, only I am at fault for those that are not. From early school days there was John Coates, who shared with me what must have seemed a rather eccentric hobby. Encouraged by Graham E Farr, we preferred scrambling round the old trows at Redcliff Back and sailing models on the pond at Beggar's Bush to cricket. Not long after this, Harold Kimber, the boatbuilder at Highbridge, and Mr Haddock, the Warrant Shipwright in HMS *Swiftsure*, showed me their trade, the latter letting me help to build a clinker dinghy onboard. I stayed in touch with Harold Kimber, earning his just rebukes up to the end for anything said, written or done that was not good enough for him. While at school, I had read an article, 'The Forgotten Harbours of Somerset' by another Bristol boy, but it was not until many publications later that I was to meet in person the present Director of the National Maritime Museum, Dr Basil Greenhill. This work was started largely at his instigation and would not have been finished without his practical advice and insistence.

In every way the financial and professional help given by the Trustees, Director and Staff of the National Maritime Museum at Greenwich has been of the utmost value. Captain T L Martin, the former Secretary of the Museum and of the Caird Fund, Dr Alan McGowan, Head of the Ships Department, together with Neville Upham and David Lyon of the Draught Room, G A Osbon, formerly of the Historic Photograph Section, Ursula Stuart Mason, Dr J F McGrail and David Proctor, amount to impressive support. Mrs 'Tricia' Palmer's ability to keep wheels turning smoothly has been specially appreciated. George Naish and Professor Ralph Davis, the latter my mentor for this fellowship, both gave me invaluable advice and encouragement at the outset of the study, and both were sadly missed at its conclusion.

A great many more have given me help during the study. While space might suggest otherwise, I am sure their names should be given, not only to acknowledge their worth, but to show others how widespread and generous assistance like this can be.

Taking the boatbuilders first, for their forbearance, though it is doubtful if all they have shown and told me could be included, it is hoped that they have not been misinterpreted in any way. To avoid any suggestion of merit, they are listed alphabetically:
Clifford H Adams, East Looe; Stanley Baker, West Hay; Sam Bennet, Hayne's of Itchenor; N J Benny, St Just-in-Roseland; Alec Blagdon, Devonport; John Caddy, Weymouth; Frank Castleton, King's Lynn; Crossfield's successors, Arnside; Dawson brothers, Seahouses; R Dixon, Exmouth; Tom Eaton, Montrose; Bob Frederick, Burne's of Bosham; Hector Handyside, J & J Harrison's of Amble; Mr Hutton, Southwold; Joe R Gelsthorpe, Hornsea; C A Goodall, Sandsend; George Jarvis, Devonport; Mr Kelly, Shaldon; Percy Lee, Berwick Salmon Fisheries Ltd of Spital; Douglas M Lindsay, Kerrara; R Lower & Son, Newhaven; J N Lowther, Whitby; 'Algee' Marks, Cawsand; H J Mears, Seaton; Bert Merrit, Ferrybridge; James Miller, St Monance; Garry & Brian Mitchell, Portmellon; Alexander, Peter & John Noble, Girvan; Alan Pape, West Looe; Ron Parkin, Devonport; Harry Philips & son, Rye; Mr Prosser, Minsterworth; Percy Roberts, Wyke Regis; Russel brothers, Exmouth; Tom Sandell, Devonport; Lester Southerland, Brancaster Staithe; J C Toms, Polruan; Bill Ward, Lowestoft; Mr Woods, Nottage Institute of Wivenhoe; L H Walker, Leigh-on-Sea; and Gerald & Bill Worfold, King's Lynn.

The list of boatmen is shorter but no less valuable, as the discussion often took place while mussels were being sorted, a trammel was being untangled or pots were being baited. More time and people are needed to tap this source properly.
Mr Arnold, Abbotsbury; Mr Bayliss, Gatcombe; The Beseleys, Doniford; Mr Boyne, Teignmouth; Mr Browning, Longney; Mr R Crabb, Lyme Cobb; Dennis & Robert Emmerson, Flamborough; Mr Tom Greening, Minsterworth; Mr Bill Hardy, Bullo Pill; Mr Hobbs, Henley-on-Thames; Mr J O Hudson, Chepstow; Mr Albert Hutchings, Beesands; John MacNeil, Castlebay; Levi Northover, Chickerell; Mr Clifford O'Brien, Weston-super-Mare; Mr Reynolds, Hope Cove; Mr Stone, Torcross; John W Stone, Chiswell; Arthur Southerland, Brancaster Staithe; Fred Thomas, Paull; and Alfred White, Bosham.

Further help came away from the immediate waterfront, mostly from other researchers:
Richard Barker of Burrowash, whose scholarly reading and many long letters have given me useful leads to follow

up; the Rev John H Cormack of Campbeltown, who has kept me supplied with local press cuttings, history and contacts, but better than that, encouragement; Les Harris, for his twice-yearly accounts of his own spare-time investigations along the English north-east coast; J W Holness of Southampton, a Chartered Naval Architect, whose draughtmanship is flawless; John Murdo Macleod of Stornoway, descended from a line of sgoth builders (though he has written at length to me, it will be his own book about the boats of Lewis that will be worth waiting for); Adrian Osler, now of the Tyne and Wear Museums, who has studied the Shetland boats but is now taking a closer look at the coasts and rivers of Northumberland and Durham; and Edward Paget-Tomlinson, who in addition to finding answers to many queries, has, by publishing his classic *Canal and River Navigation* provided me with a most welcome inland boundary.

While all of these were helping over most of the study, there were others who assisted in a more specialised way, such as providing access to books and exhibits, showing how they did their work or helping to measure a boat: Mrs Ann Bayliss, Gatcombe; Jim Bellchambers, Dartington Amenity Research Trust; Alan Binns, Paull; Maureen Boddy, Weymouth Libraries and Museum; Dr N C A Bradley, Topsham; Michael M Cobbold, Newnham Park, Plympton; Pip Corin, St Keynes, Liskeard; Odile and Gerard Cey, lugger *Erin*, Paimpol; Philip Draper, Arne; Mrs Valerie Fenwick, Highgate; R S Glover, Institute of Marine Biological Research; Major D R Goddard, Exeter Maritime Museum; W A King-Webster, Innerwell Fishery, Garlieston; David R MacGregor, Barnes; David Phillipson, Zetland Museum, Redcar; Captain Francis Poole, once of Hartlepool now of Montreal; John Rawson, Hampstead; James Richard, Henleaze; Sir Eric Smith, Marine Biological Laboratory; M K Stammers, Merseyside County Museums; F W Tresidder, Penrose's, Falmouth, and Carl Olof Cederlund, Stockholm.

I am also grateful for the volunteered or requested information that the following men and women supplied: Malcolm Adkins, Wanstead; K M Anderson, Berwick Salmon Fisheries; Frank Argall, Truro; L Athay, Tewkesbury; G S Bagley, Rye; John R Baldwin, Lothian Regional Council; Margaret Blackburn, Ironbridge Museum; Sandy Boyle, Finchley; Howard Brinkwell, Frampton-on-Severn; G D Campbell, Lochgilphead; Guy Cockerell, Barrachan; Ian Cooper, Bowness-on-Windermere; J Corin, Clevedon; George A Dunn, Mevagissey; Rev Alex Fraser, Furnace, Argyll; Crispin Gill, *The Countryman*; Mrs Hodgson, Goole library; Margaret Holmes, County Records Office, Dorset; Mr Hunter, Maidstone Museum; Mr Johnston-Stuart, Joseph Johnston & Sons, Montrose; R J Julyan, Tretheake Manor, Veryan; Martin Langley, Wells; Mr Lee, Tudweiliog; Arthur Littlewood, Scottish Country Crafts Museum, Auchindrain; Mr Matthew, J & J Harrison's, Amble; Naomi Mitchison, Carradale; Angus Martin, Campbeltown; Cdr C J H Moles, Norleywood; Colin Moore, Leigh-on-Sea; W H A Pearce, Salcombe; A E Readman, Saltburn-by-the-Sea; J F Reed, Berwick Salmon Fisheries; Mr Searle, Emsworth; Mr Small, Christchurch; G Sterne, Scottish Fisheries Museum, Anstruther; A I B Stuart, Campbeltown; Tom Swanson, Scrabster; R C Todd, Bristol; A E Truckell, Burgh Museum, Dumfries; Gray Usher, Clevedon; Ivor Waters, Chepstow; J A C West, Weymouth Libraries and Museum; F S Woodford, Meteorological Office of Bracknel, and A J Miller-Williams, Plymouth.

PART I
The Factors
affecting Boatshape

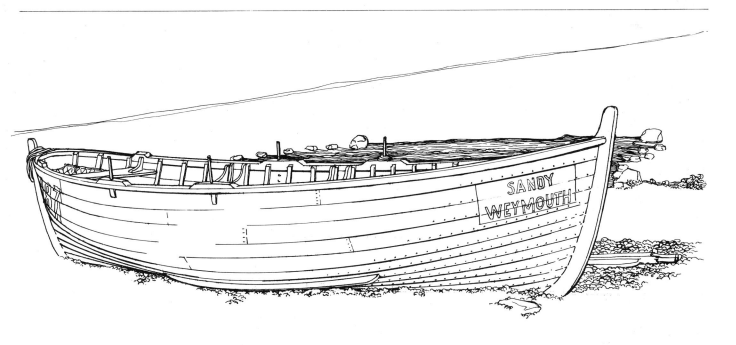

Fig 1: Lerret at East Beckington.

1.
Definition and limits of the study

Professor Filgueiras starts his work *No crepusculo das embarcacoes regionais* with these words: 'If, in broad terms, the study of Man's implements of work gives a fair measure of his technological and social development, then boats are a particularly important source of material for such evaluation.' While the truth of this observation can be demonstrated in both primitive and emerging societies, it seems harder to do so in the case of rapidly developing ones and harder still when studying simple boats that are still being used by people who have reached a high technological and social level. Even in societies such as these, implements like spades keep their ordinary shape and usefulness, long after elaborate earth-moving devices like bulldozers have become available.

This book will try to examine this extension of Professor Filgueiras' observation through a study of the shapes of boats in Britain only; for what is true in this country may be so elsewhere. The matter is worth looking into, for what should be a standard-shaped implement – like the spade mentioned above – comes in many shapes and sizes. The reasons for these differences, unless they are accidental, should be discovered. Once Man has developed an implement for a set purpose, he does not alter it, even if he has the means to do so, until a situation occurs that proves that it is inadequate. This static state of affairs is not to be confused with an outwardly similar one, in which, though the implement is unsatisfactory, it stays the same because the means of improvement are absent. On the other hand, where one finds implements being improved, one may be sure that they have been found unsuitable in some way or other; and, what is more, that their users have had the means of doing something about it. As a great number of changes have been made in the shape and structure of some British boats in the last century or so, while others have remained unchanged, both states of affairs are available for investigation.

For this study, Britain has been taken as being the largest of the British Isles – the one that contains England, Scotland and Wales, together with the islands close to it. Ireland has not been included – not because there are not many interesting and relevant boat types there, but because there has neither been a great deal written about them, nor has the writer yet had the chance of seeing them for himself. For similar reasons the Shetlands, the Isle of Man and the Channel Islands have been excluded. While this is to be regretted, it is as well, for one of the problems has been how to handle the wide variety of British boats,

not only varied in form, but owing to the introduction of new materials, methods of propulsion and operation. With this forbidding number of types to deal with, it was essential that their limits should be defined. Within the geographical boundary already given, the historical period has been taken as from the present day to as far back as the sequence of development is clear. This has never been less than a hundred years but rarely more than two hundred.

As the investigation has been confined to boats alone, one has to try and define the term 'boat'. Firstly, one has to consider the term 'implement' when applied to those water-borne implements collectively known as vessels, craft, ships and boats. Implements are those items which Man collects around himself so as to live what he believes would be a better life than he could without them. It could be said, in the material sense, owning implements raises Man above the animals. Implements include tools, furniture, utensils, weapons and the means of moving people and their belongings about. The means of moving that relies on flotation is what James Hornell called 'water transport'. What is carried in this way determines whether the vessel is a fishing vessel, a warship, a house boat, a pleasure craft or so on. It is hard to think of any sort of vessel that is in herself some other category of implement than that of water transport.

Just as land transport terms like 'cart', 'carriage' and 'waggon' once had precise meanings, which have become blurred by slack usage, so too had those of water transport. It is a pity, as correctly used the terms 'vessel', 'craft', 'ship' and 'boat' span the whole spectrum of water transport, and so provide the study's limits.

While any object that is hollow may be called a 'vessel', it is normal to keep the term for larger forms of water transport, smaller forms being called 'craft'. These two terms overlap. It is right, however, to say that no ship can be a boat, as the greatest boat must be less than any ship. Where, then, does the overlap of vessels with craft and the gap between ships and boats occur? It is not possible to be precise, but one can get close enough to an answer to meet the needs of this work.

The Concise Oxford Dictionary describes a 'ship' as a 'sea-going vessel of considerable size'. This would seem to mean that a 'ship' has to be able to stay at sea in all weathers until she reaches her destination, while a boat can only make short trips when the weather allows. Both ships and boats have crews, who need shelter, rest and food. Ships provide these all the time and have to have some form of deck, sleeping spaces, cooker and provisions to do so. Boats, without these, have to return periodically for their crews to recuperate ashore. Boats can be open- or part-decked and, unencumbered by deadweight, can have a greater part of their design devoted to their real task. For example the lerret of Chesil Bank is an oared seine net boat which is almost entirely a platform for rowers and nets, with only a tiny locker aft (Fig 1). By comparison a modern frigate has to give up a great deal of space to messes, galleys, storerooms and ventilation if her crew is to remain efficient. All boats, even those that work well offshore, depend on having a refuge that can be reached in bad weather. This may be a harbour or even a beach if the boat is of the right shape.

Craft on board larger vessels are usually boats on ships. While quite small craft may have to have a small boat to work the gear or ferry the crew ashore daily, a tender like this is rarely brought inboard, but is towed astern or left behind on the mooring. North-east coast cobles carried their corfs onboard when long-lining, but this did not make them ships as they could not stay at sea for long. Ship's boats get less regular use, for example in an emergency or for some special task when the ship herself is stationary.

Vessels and, even more rarely, ships are not the sole property of any one person who works on board. Ships more often belong to some shore-based organisation, which gives the crew wages or a share of the profits. Craft are often user-owned, while boats are almost always owned by one or more members of the crew or their relations. There are places where there is a history of men who have owned and operated several boats and run them with the aid of relations and paid hands (see p184).

The *International Collision Regulations* can give us some idea of the actual sizes. Though arbitrary, these rules differentiate between sailing and powered vessels and rowing boats, and group vessels above or below 150ft, 65ft and 40ft length overall (LOA). These lengths come close to the divisions in the figure, namely, 150ft being the lower limit for a ship, 65ft being the mid-figure of the overlap between vessels and craft, and 40ft being the upper limit for a boat. While this seems to suit the present situation well, whether it does so for the past is doubtful. The *Golden Hind* though between 70ft and 80ft LOA must be counted as a ship, while 45ft naval launches, being open and carried onboard, were boats. A diagram like this (Fig 2) would need to be tailored to match its period, and even then taken as a guide rather than a rule.

This book will be using the terminology of the diagram in Fig 2, but this is not to say that people found round and about water transport were exact or consistent in their use of terms. It was found throughout the study that both local terms and meanings given to a term differ from place to place and even from person to person. While these complications are confusing, the use of dialect words and meanings are often informative, so have been retained. Even the colloquial use of 'ship' and 'boat' calls for some care. Owners or crew members often refer to their ship as a 'boat', which is a case of an intimate using an affectionate

Fig 2: Water transport

WATER TRANSPORT

CRAFT— — — — — — —		
	— — — — — — —VESSELS	
BOATS— — — — — —		— — — — —SHIPS
Small	Medium	Large
Local Haven		Ports at Destinations
Range Limited	Specific Trips	Ocean Voyages
Weather Limitations		Unrestricted
Little or no Shelter	Minimal Accommodation	Full Housing
Open Part Decked		One or more Full Decks
Carries no Tender		Carries Lifeboats
or is a	May Tow or Carry a Tender	or
Tender to a larger Vessel		Servicing Craft
Owner Operated	Locally Owned	Remote Owners
Supports her Crew	Profits Shared with Owner	Owner Pays Crew

diminutive. Modern submariners serve in 'boats' although nowadays they are 7000-ton capital ships. The reverse also applies for, as A Noble points out[1], a steam drifter if only 80ft long was still called a ship.

There is a further feature which identifies boats, and this is the persistence of their designs. This helps research in a field that is less documented than that of ships. When one considers their comparative sizes, one might suppose that the smaller artifact was easier and more liable to change. However it is ships that change, from one replacement to the next, because the need for improvement is more pressing. Ships represent a bigger proportion of a society's resources, so cannot be military or commercial failures. As ships travel further than boats, their crews can compare them with those from other lands. Performance if not in conflict eliminates poor designs and a sea-going nation which cannot modify their own must copy those of others. Comparative improvement like this has brought about a closer resemblance, in any period, between ships of the same class than between boats a few miles apart on the same coast.

Boatmen have less chance to make these comparisons. Even when fleets of sailing fishing vessels from different places worked together they still retained their identity. Their comparative performance on the fishing grounds must have counted for less than the local conditions that had brought about the design in the first place. Even when the advantages of iron and steam became evident, few boatmen would have had the resources to change a boat into a small ship without capital from elsewhere. What is often put down as the conservatism of boatmen might also have been lack of local finance, material or technology. In the case of iron-built steam trawlers, Brixham was badly placed for building them compared, say, with Grimsby.

Ship's boats, recreational, and ceremonial boats have been excluded from the study as their shape was not much influenced by local conditions. All these three categories have tended to follow more or less standard patterns throughout Britain. They cannot be dismissed altogether, however, as all of them have some features which have come from, or have been adopted by, working boats. Taking each category separately, these features may be recognised.

Ship's boats, being part of a ship's inventory, are, it would seem, outside the scope of this investigation – that is, until their building and disposal is considered. Such boats were included in a new ship's contract, so were built in the shipyard, if not bought from a workshop specialising in ship's boats. In the first case there was a preference for shipyard processes like lofting and rib-before-shell structure, and in the second for designs that could be batch-produced. In both cases there had to be a specification, possibly even drawings, and an inspection to check that all the conditions had been met. Contemporary models and drawings of ship's boats were being made long before those of local working boats, which supports this view. Ship's boats became available to a wider public

either when the parent ship was broken up, or when they were unfit for service at sea but still able to fossick inshore. When trade booms and wars have expanded shipping, small boatyards have been pressed into building some of the additional ship's boats and so have had to learn shipyard methods. In these several ways the design and way of building ship's boats have influenced more traditional boatbuilding methods.

This sort of influence can be as positive as that from overseas. There is every sign that where there have been concentrations of ships – the Downs and the Fal for example – there has been a resemblance between the local and ship's boats. It cannot be said which came first. It is possible, however, to trace how some of the beach types seem to have originated this way, and, after some improvements, have been re-adopted to work out of ships again.

There was a mutual interaction between working and recreational boats as well. Taking to the water for pleasure is older than the occasions described by Evelyn or Pepys and drawn by the Van de Veldes. Given fair weather, much of the time spent in a working boat can also be enjoyable, in much the same way as walking, riding or driving can be, between one job and the next. So it is hard to imagine when or where a boatman did not occasionally use his boat for the sheer pleasure of it, nor lay on a coat of paint as much for looks as preservation. Only a man enslaved by the poverty of his existence or the drive of his own or master's ambition could fail to find the time for this.

The invention two hundred years ago and subsequent growth of seaside holidays have not only spruced up the working boats used for pleasure trips but have introduced new types as well. Though examples may be seen on many beaches and waterways, they have attracted comparatively little attention. Fortunately, if largely accidentally, they have been recorded in the picture postcards issued by Valentine, Frith and Judges from the latter part of the nineteenth century onwards, and the National Maritime Museum hold comprehensive collections of these. Though these boats were often used and built for no better purpose than to be let out on hire to inexperienced visitors, they do reflect the local traditions in their build and decoration. One can, or could, find small round-sterned double-ended skiffs on Brodick beach, punts at Christchurch and a variety of double-ended skiffs and surf-boats on the beaches and harbours of north Wales and Yorkshire, being offered for hire (Fig 3). The numbers of boats on inland waterways are as prolific; even the artificial lakes in urban public parks have fleets of corporation boats, like those built in wood and GRP by Salter Brothers of Folly Bridge, Oxford, McNulty & Sons, South Shields, or one of the many other kinds built in other yards all over the country.

The search for pleasure has produced as many, if not more, distinct types of recreational craft as there have been working ones. There are seven sorts of shell, three dozen large classes of racing dinghy, and many more of motor

Fig 3: Rowing boats at Bridlington Quay are called skiffs when fitted for only one pair of oars.

and sailing cruisers, ocean-racing boats and luxury yachts. Though some never seem to leave their moorings, the majority of these enable thousands of men, women and children to carry on the sea-going tradition. Though these people may be motivated by a desire for solitude, adventure, competition, fitness or respite from regimentation, rather than making a living, at least the experienced is first-hand and not second-hand from a book, film or model.

The designs of many recreational boats were derived from one kind of working boat or another. From time to time designers and writers appeared to have made a systematic search through all the local types to see which of them might prove satisfactory for racing or cruising. Dixon Kemp was one of these and gave no less than twenty examples[2]. Allowing for deformities that stemmed from current rating rules and fashions, a scientific approach coupled to higher skills and finer materials made for a more rapid improvement in the performance of yachts than for working boats. However the working boatman has been quick to spot which of these might both benefit him and be within his reach. There is another rapidly growing class of boat that deserves mention. This is the working boat used by amateur fishermen. Sometimes she will be hired out by the day to clubs or individuals, or be owned outright by a spare-time boatman, who fishes for gain when his real job allows. In both cases, the existence of local types have been extended, so they have been included in this study.

It is hard to draw a line between luxury yachts and ceremonial vessels. Graves in Egypt, Scandinavia and even this country show that these have been one of the more important trappings of a maritime ruler. The ceremonial vessel often takes the form of a large galley, in which the number of oarsmen reflect the power of the ruler, and the richness of the decoration his wealth[3]. Apart from a few comments, exalted vessels like this are outside this work's scope. The adornment of some river craft and even lesser yachts reflect this influence; so does the use when racing of more oars than would be normally practical in a river. Multi-oared boats can be justified sometimes – for life-saving, moving numbers of men from ship to shore, towing a becalmed ship or laying out her ground tackle. In landlocked channels, where the wind blows straight up or down, if at all, an oared vessel with a down-wind sail ensures movement. The birlinn or galley of the north-west coast of Scotland was like this, while the number of oarsmen provided the offence or defence required. The study of boats on inland waterways has been limited to those that have survived in a nearly primitive form, as these can show how simple boats may develop. The specialised barges used on canals and river navigations have not been studied as these have been so well described elsewhere.

Certain conditions have to be met before water transport can develop. There has to be a need for it, and there must be appropriate waters and boatbuilding skills and materials. There are two design extremes: either there is an ingenious craftsman, but one that has no boatbuilding experience; or there is a boatbuilder who knows what to build. These extremes – independent invention or diffusion – equate to complete absence of, or fully effective, communication, and approximate to the conditions found in the least and most fully developed societies. There are stages in between, depending upon whether it has been the surroundings, the materials or the need for the boat that has changed. Modified diffusion occurs when previous shapes and structures have to be altered to suit a new situation, and modified invention when a change enforces a break from the old designs.

Except for independent invention, which is unlikely with improving communications, there are two factors at work on a boat design. There is the influence of what is already there (the native one), and the influence that comes from elsewhere (the foreign one). The influence of native conditions are unrelenting, but the locally available solutions may be unable to deal with them. Foreign influences become weak if the conditions that gave rise to them no longer apply, but strengthen if they offer a better solution. The boat design that will last will be the one that proves itself in daily use, and there are examples of successful native, foreign and combined solutions in Britain.

The coracle has been an example of a long-lasting native solution which has not been bettered for fishing in rivers made up of pools joined by rapids or falls. The Shetland sixern is an example of a foreign (Norse) solution, which either filled a previous void or replaced an earlier foreign (Pictish or Celtic) solution, where the lack of suitable materials hampered native inventions[4]. The English coble seems to be a combined solution, adapted over the centuries until she was suitable for most of the work along a long stretch of varying coast.

Many of the boats seen during this study were initially strange to me. To get to know them I looked at them in three ways: from the point of view of their shape, to work out how they might behave; internally, to see how they were put together; and then in context, to find out about the people, tasks and landscape that generated them. Though one has to separate out the component elements, like climate, tide, fish, timber and so on, for discussion, in reality they are interlocked in various mixtures peculiar to particular places. The order in which these elements have been taken is arbitrary, as, if no change is taking place in a boat, it is fair to assume that within the resources of that society all the elements are being satisfied, and that no one of them is dominant. Yet, should one element change and the boat not come up to this new requirement, this is the element that counts for most. When study shows that shape has changed, one tries to find the element responsible. Few boat types are static. This is due, when all other possibilities have been ruled out, to Man's drive for a bit more speed, capacity, endurance or power than his colleagues.

Working Boats of Britain is in two parts, the first of which deals with the influences that change boats. These are the surroundings, the use to which the boat is put, and the personality of the boatmen. This is followed by an explanation of the method used to describe the shape and structure of the boats. The findings of the study form the second part, with chapters on building and propulsion methods, type definition and distribution, culminating in the conclusions reached.

2.

Influence of surroundings

A boat's surroundings are made up of a number of mainly natural phenomena, which, though they may be changing slowly, are generally beyond the ability of boatmen to alter to any extent. Before a boat can operate, she must have come to terms with the limitations imposed by the climate, land and seascape.

The climate of Britain has not materially altered during the period being studied, from two to three hundred years ago until the present day. The warm climax of the thirteenth century was followed by a period of increasing cold that reached its low towards the end of the seventeenth century. Since then there has been a gradual increase in warmth broken by a cool spell at the start of the nineteenth century and, for the last twenty-five years, another gradual cooling. It is too early to say if this current tendency is a fluctuation or the start of a longer-lasting change. For the most part we are concerned with the overall warmer conditions that have developed since the 'Little Ice-Age'. This term is somewhat of an exaggeration, as, although this period saw the depopulation of the Norse settlement of Greenland and the freezing over of major rivers in Britain during the more severe winters, the weather does not seem to have had an effect on the shape of British boats. What must be taken into account is that the annual variation in temperature, from summer to winter, is far greater than the overall change that has occurred over the centuries. The average lowest surface temperature now experienced on the east coast in January is 40°F(4°C) rising to 44°F(7°C) in the extreme south-west.

The reason for the temperature falling from west to east rather than from south to north is mainly due to the warming effect of the North Atlantic Drift, which favours the northern end of the island, and also to the Scandinavian mountain ranges diverting the upper air stream. Over the same 10° of latitude as Britain in January the west coast of the European mainland experiences a range of temperatures from 24°F(–4°C) up to 40°F(4°C). In July the gradient is more south to north, being 60°F(16°C) down to 56°F(13°C) all over the western parts of Europe.

The winter in Britain is still too cool to permit domestic cattle to forage unaided, and this has made fish an important source of winter protein. This combination of a mild winter and cool summer is relatively rare in the world as a whole. In the Northern Hemisphere it occurs between Brittany and south Norway on the Atlantic seaboard, Iceland and the Pacific Coasts of Oregon, Washington and British Columbia, and in several places in the Southern Hemisphere.

The North Atlantic Drift keeps the sea water itself within even narrower limits than that of the land surface, say between 32°F(2°C) and 55°F(13°C). Even in summer this does not allow men to work immersed in the sea for any time. Even if we were to go back as far as the early Neolithic Period when the average surface air temperatures are thought to have been some 35°F(3°C) warmer than today, the hardiest boatman would have preferred a water-free boat to one that let water flow in like a raft or bundle boat. In winter (when clothing must have been needed by Neolithic Man), the importance of keeping dry is the factor that limits the endurance of men in open boats. While they can put up with wet outer clothes, boatmen cannot support life for long once soaked to the skin.

Through most of our period the prevailing wind direction over Britain can be said to have been from the southwest. In the last quarter century however the winds have had a more northerly component and the frequency of westerlies has become less. On the coast the prevailing wind can blow very strongly and from time to time harder than boats can withstand in open water. In winter the gap between successive gales may be only a day or two. Gales can occur even in summer, especially in August. The winds from other directions can be strong to gale force at any time during the year, but tend to be more widely spaced, of varying duration and give less warning of their arrival than the south-westerlies. These are known as dominant winds when they blow onshore over a long stretch of open sea; and as such can be a greater threat to a boat than the prevailing wind that has been slowed down after crossing the width of the country.

The frequencies, directions and strengths of the wind are recorded in the form of tables and wind roses on weather maps. These apply to only one place and at least four are needed to indicate the seasonal changes. Given enough data a wind rose can be drawn to show how the strength of the wind varies, but in Britain the weather changes so much from year to year that the wind rose cannot be relied upon for prediction. In the days of sail the boatman was concerned with those winds that let him work, that is those that were neither too little nor too much. Looking at the column headed 'Coastal Criterion' in Beaufort's notation this would be equivalent to Force 1 to 6 inclusive for decked smacks, but proportionately less for smaller open and light-handed boats. Though the prevailing wind would give most of the working days, the danger of over-strong dominant ones had also to be considered. Lacking a predictable seasonal weather pattern, the British boatman

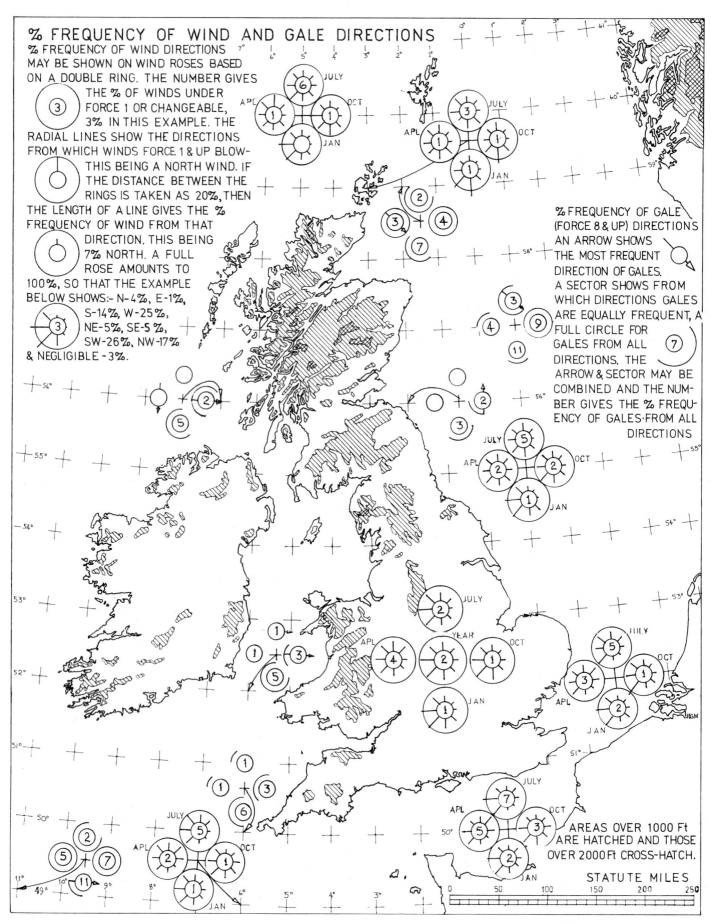

% FREQUENCY OF WIND AND GALE DIRECTIONS

% FREQUENCY OF WIND DIRECTIONS MAY BE SHOWN ON WIND ROSES BASED ON A DOUBLE RING. THE NUMBER GIVES THE % OF WINDS UNDER FORCE 1 OR CHANGEABLE, 3% IN THIS EXAMPLE. THE RADIAL LINES SHOW THE DIRECTIONS FROM WHICH WINDS FORCE 1 & UP BLOW – THIS BEING A NORTH WIND. IF THE DISTANCE BETWEEN THE RINGS IS TAKEN AS 20%, THEN THE LENGTH OF A LINE GIVES THE % FREQUENCY OF WIND FROM THAT DIRECTION. THIS BEING 7% NORTH. A FULL ROSE AMOUNTS TO 100%, SO THAT THE EXAMPLE BELOW SHOWS:- N-4%, E-1%, S-14%, W-25%, NE-5%, SE-5%, SW-26%, NW-17% & NEGLIGIBLE - 3%.

% FREQUENCY OF GALE (FORCE 8 & UP) DIRECTIONS AN ARROW SHOWS THE MOST FREQUENT DIRECTION OF GALES. A SECTOR SHOWS FROM WHICH DIRECTIONS GALES ARE EQUALLY FREQUENT, A FULL CIRCLE FOR GALES FROM ALL DIRECTIONS. THE ARROW & SECTOR MAY BE COMBINED AND THE NUMBER GIVES THE % FREQUENCY OF GALES·FROM ALL DIRECTIONS

AREAS OVER 1000 Ft ARE HATCHED AND THOSE OVER 2000 Ft CROSS-HATCH.

STATUTE MILES

0   50   100   150   200   250

Fig 4: Frequency of wind and gale directions.

has, until recently, had to rely upon his own ability to foretell the short-term weather. Failing this his life rested on whether his boat could get him home or not.

Fig 4 sets out how a wind rose can be drawn, giving a simple form which only indicates those winds above and below Force 1, with a separate diagram to show the comparative frequencies of gale (that is Force 8 and over) directions. The direction of a gale matters most when this prevents a return home or endangers boats already in harbour or beached. The same figure also illustrates the overall seasonal wind pattern using both wind roses and gale diagrams, the central rose being an expression of the annual pattern for the whole island. Due to local topography and annual variation the information on a map like this can only be a point of departure when investigating the weather at any one place or time.

A few generalisations however, can, amplify a map like this. The further one goes offshore, the stronger the winds become. Most gales come from the south to south-west sector in the south west, from the south-east to south-west sector in the North Sea and from the north-west in the Irish Sea. The proximity of land masses reduces the frequency, strength and duration of gales; for instance, they occur twice as often and last twice as long at the western end of the English Channel as in the Straits of Dover. Gales are more frequent in winter than summer, in autumn than in spring, to ratios of 8:1 and 5:3 respectively, except that in the crossroads of winds off Aberdeenshire, north-westerly summer gales occur more frequently. Even on exposed British coasts, steady winds over Force 10 are exceptional, though gusts of hurricane force are to be expected. Though passage over land reduces wind strength they become dangerously gusty if they pass over high ground before reaching the far coast. High ground on any coast diverts the direction of onshore winds. Generally south-westerly gales are short-lived, not more than 4 to 5 hours at full strength in exposed places. South-easterly gales in the North Sea can blow for days, and, where the fetch is large, raise large waves. Similarly north-westerly gales blowing into the Irish Sea through the North Channel can, in combination with the tide, raise big seas as well. About Easter there is usually a period lasting a few weeks when easterly winds persist in the English Channel, and sometimes re-occur later in the year. While these winds are dangerous to havens sited primarily to give shelter from the prevailing wind, these periods once assisted westward-bound shipping and fishing fleets. Otherwise boats might lie weatherbound by alternating calms, westerlies and gales for weeks.

At longer intervals, sometimes as far apart as a quarter of a century, there are freak gales, hurricane in force. They can affect the whole island or be concentrated on a relatively short section of coastline. Both are capable of destroying boats at sea and in harbour. As storms like this bring about loss of life and property they were well recorded and motivated improvements in both the boats and their harbours. Just a few examples can illustrate the

magnitude of these disasters. On 22 November 1824, the Chesil Bank was overswept in a storm; 26 inhabitants of the village of Chiswell were drowned and all the boats and seine nets from Portland to Wyke destroyed. According to an eye-witness account, 'Twern't a sea at all – not a bit of it – t'wer the great sea hisself rose up level like, and come on right over the ridge and all, like nothing in this world'[1]. On 16 July 1832, a four-day hurricane struck the Shetlands from the north-west, and 31 boats and 105 men were lost. Then on 19 August 1848, there was a great gale along the whole of the east coast of Scotland. The widespread loss of life and boats was attributed to the suddenness of the storm, the poor state of many of the harbours and lack of life saving equipment. As a result Captain Washington made his investigation and wrote his often-quoted report[2]. Though his recommendations were not readily accepted in Scotland, this disaster marked the start of a general improvement in the fishing industry.

Taking Professor H Lamb's figures for gradient winds over London from 1729 to 1879, it can be seen that the prevailing surface wind was south-westerly, even though the decade averages vary a great deal, from 124 days a year down to 59, with the lower frequencies occurring over the middle of this period[3]. A rather more general picture can be had if one consider the winds grouped into three sectors, namely the south-westerly (S + SW + W), the northerly (NW + N + NE) and the smaller easterly (E + SE). Averaged out over the whole period the surface wind blew from the south-westerly sector 180 days a year, from the northerly about 100 days and from the easterly about 50. North-east and east winds had the most predictable frequencies of 40 and 20 days a year. Though south winds also averaged about 40 days a year they were liable to considerable fluctuations (Fig 4). Exceptionally the pattern broke down during the last decade of the eighteenth century when easterly and southerly winds averaged 88 and 70 days a year respectively, which were in excess of the 60 days each with south-westerly and westerly winds.

This 200-year or so pattern has been changing during the middle of the twentieth century. The frequency of the winds from the south-westerly sector have decreased while those from the northerly sector have increased, especially in the south of England where the figures for the two sectors are much the same. Motorised fishing boats have not been so affected by this change as the sailing ones would have been. It is however worth noting that there have been previous periods, notably in the middle of the eighteenth century when the winds from these two sectors were also much the same over a decade. As harbours and beaches in Britain have always had to contend with a proportion of winds from the northerly sector, they were able to withstand higher frequencies. Nevertheless examination of Appendix I and III and Fig 7 will show that there are shores which have changed their aspect to these new prevailing winds and where this is also in a direction of fetches over 100 miles, there will be more days on which inshore conditions will be unsafe even for motor boats.

In late spring, all summer and early autumn, 3 or 4 days a month may be without wind at all. The effect of this might be lessened by the sea and land breezes which come up in the forenoon and late afternoon on cloudless days. Unfortunately these differential heating and cooling rates of land and sea can act so as to modify light overall winds to calms, strong breezes and sudden changes in direction.

Fig 6 is a table to show the number of days of calms, working winds and gales that might be expected in a selection of places round Britain during the months of January, April, July and October. It will be seen that a boatman might be expected to be at sea 8 days out of 10 throughout the year, except off the east coast of Scotland where it might only be 6 or 7. In the winter months, he might get 7 out of 10 good days along the more sheltered coastlines, but only 5 off Buchan Ness. In summer however, except once more for the east coast of Scotland, only 1 day in 10 is lost to lack of wind.

While the figures allow for some time for days lost in harbour because of gale warnings and aftermaths, no allowance has been made for days lost when a succession of gales kept boats in for many more days than when the gales were actually blowing. The table probably errs towards giving too many working days for sailing boats in winter, but should be correct for motor boats having the benefit of good weather forecasts. No account has been taken of Sundays, which were rarely worked, or of public holidays.

The situation of the British Isles in relation to the Continent alters the simple tidal system set up by the sun and moon. Strong winds blowing up or down tapering channels further change the time and height of the predicted tide, while a combination of gales and very high spring tides can still prove disastrous.

The time of slack water varies so much that at any time of the clock it will be taking place somewhere in Britain. This no current state coincides with high and low water at

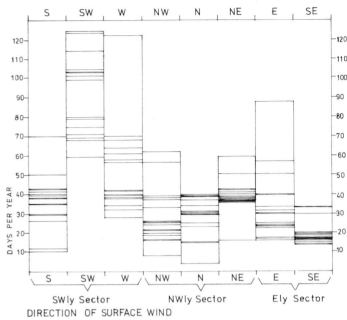

VARIABILITY OF SURFACE WIND DIRECTION
DECADE AVERAGES OVER LONDON BETWEEN 1723 AND 1879 A.D. PLOTTED AS SUPERIMPOSED HISTOGRAMS BASED ON H.H. LAMB'S PROVISIONAL FIGURES IN HIS "CLIMATE" VOL. 2, p. 647.

BRITAIN % FREQUENCY

N	JAN	APR	JUL	OCT	YEAR
N	8	14	11	10	11
NE	6	12	9	7	8
E	5	9	6	8	7
SE	10	8	8	10	10
S	14	11	11	15	13
SW	21	14	18	20	19
W	22	14	19	18	19
NW	13	14	16	11	11
C&V	1	4	2	1	2

C & V = Calm & Variable

Fig 5: Variability of surface wind direction.

Fig 6: Table to show the number of days each month when the wind is suitable for work boats.

TABLE TO SHOW THE NUMBER OF DAYS EACH MONTH WHEN THE WIND IS SUITABLE FOR WORK BOATS

		ENGLISH CHANNEL WEST	ENGLISH CHANNEL EAST	EAST ANGLIA	NE COAST ENGLAND	E COAST SCOTLAND	W COAST SCOTLAND	IRISH SEA
JAN.	Becalmed	1	2	2	1	1	1	2
	Working(%)	21(68)	23(74)	25(81)	22(71)	16(52)	23(74)	22(71)
	Stormbound	9	6	4	8	14	7	7
APR.	Becalmed	2	3	2	2	2	1	2
	Working(%)	26(87)	25(83)	27(90)	25(83)	22(73)	28(93)	27(90)
	Stormbound	2	2	1	3	6	1	2
JUL.	Becalmed	3	5	3	3	3	2	3
	Working(%)	27(87)	26(84)	27(90)	27(87)	24(77)	29(94)	27(87)
	Stormbound	1	0	0	1	4	0	1
OCT.	Becalmed	1	2	1	2	1	1	2
	Working(%)	26(84)	26(84)	27(87)	22(71)	18(58)	27(87)	25(81)
	Stormbound	4	3	3	7	12	3	4
YEAR	Becalmed							
	Working(%)	298(82)	298(82)	317(87)	284(78)	236(65)	317(87)	298(82)
	Stormbound							

the heads of estuaries and inlets, but occurs at intermediate times along the coast and offshore. The time of slack water changes rapidly over short stretches of coast in some straits like those between the Isle of Purbeck and the Cherbourg Peninsula, East Anglia and Holland, Wales and Ireland and again between Kintyre and Antrim, but not in those of Dover, where the tidal systems of the North Sea and the English Channel meet to create a co-tidal stretch from Selsey to Harwich with the same times as at Greenwich. There are other co-tidal zones from Liverpool to Campbeltown and again from Colonsay to Cape Wrath. Everywhere else it is found that about 70 miles of coast brings slack water one hour earlier westward of Portland or northward of Cromer.

The greatest range of tides is experienced at the heads of large estuaries. The greatest can be well over 25ft between high and low water springs; this occurs in the Severn and river mouths along the north west of England, and up to this figure in the Kyle of Lochalsh, Moray Firth, Humber, Wash, Thames and East Sussex. In some places like the Sound of Jura, off Yarmouth and Dorset the range does not exceed 8ft. An 18ft spring tide range can be taken as usual around our coasts, but it is the exact amount which matters and these are given in the last column of Appendix II for one place in each section of the coast.

Boatmen are much concerned with the state and amount of the tide. Though the depth of water is important where it affects harbours and channels, it is less critical for boats than ships. Tidal streams in the Pentland Firth and Menai Straits can run faster than boats can row or sail, and in most major estuaries currents of 4 knots are usual at times, so it will be this which dictates when and in which direction trips are made. While a tide can be made to serve, it can also become a peril when trying to make harbour before it dries out. While a tide may help to get boats from one harbour to their fishing grounds at the proper time of day, it may as easily keep those from another in port. Tides and winds can set up races and overfalls off headlands and over shoals, where the current tends to run fastest. These two places are where fish are found and boats will go in settled weather. When the weather deteriorates such places must be skirted, which adds to the time before harbour is reached.

Britain being an island has a coastline which presents itself at every possible angle to the prevailing or dominant winds. Disregarding for the time being local features, like the lesser headlands and inlets which only affect a short stretch of coast, let us consider the general orientation of the shoreline to these winds and how it influences the boats that have to work there.

Before the introduction of engines, most types of boats could be rowed or sailed, either method having some limitations. Although rowing will propel a boat directly into the wind, this tires out the rowers quickly and progress is discouraging as the boat slows down or even stops during the recovery stroke. Long, light and narrow boats like the Cornish gigs and Deal galleys overcame this

disadvantage by having many oars, but not many working boats could support such large crews legally. In their favour, it must be said that oars are a most effective way of getting clear of trouble, keeping warm and, of course, getting back when the wind fails. However, rowing can interfere with other forms of work, such as shooting nets and hauling pots.

A boat under sail cannot make better progress to windward than when she is pointing at a certain angle to the wind. This angle is optimal, that is to say, if she tries to go higher than this she will slow right down; if sailed further off the wind, though she may be going faster through the water, she will be making good less windward gauge. The ability to point well is a function of both the sail and the hull. Some sails will hold a better wind than others while some hulls will make less leeway. There is neither benefit from fitting close-winded sails to a shallow keel-less hull, nor from putting baggy sails over the hull of a racing yacht. The sail and the hull should be matched to each other.

Most sailing working boats were modest performers to windward compared to what is now possible. Though there have been plenty of views expressed as to their comparative performances, there are too few facts of figures. The very best boats are claimed to have been able to sail within 5 points ($56\frac{1}{4}°$) of the wind with favourable sea conditions. There were others that were only just able to better a broad reach. For the purpose of this discussion we will assume that an average boat could be relied upon to sail within 6 points ($67\frac{1}{2}°$) off the wind. This leaves a $136°$ sector of the sea to windward that she could not reach without a change of tack.

With a boat like this there are four coastlines to be taken into account: the lee shore, the exposed shore, the sheltered shore and the weather shore. Assuming a south-west prevailing wind, Fig 7 shows which of these the various coasts of Britain are, and Appendix III lists them with their features. It can be worked out from this that there are about 350 miles of lee, 875 miles of exposed, 1100 miles of sheltered and 500 miles of weather shore, giving some 2825 miles in all.

The lee shore is the one that lies across and facing up into the wind. If the general inclination is less than the boat can point, she will be able to clear the shore safely on one tack only, but can sail roughly parallel to it on the other (Fig 8). This would be risky as the broken water and backwash close into a lee shore adversely affects a boat's ability to point well and may stop her carrying her way through on to the other tack when she decides to do so. There is however a safe sector between the land down wind and the best course to windward out to sea. In this sector there is a margin of safety as the boat can go out and return with the sheets slightly eased, a trim suitable for most working boats. Once clear of land, especially after several changes of tack, the boat is sure of a commanding wind home. The weather-beaten nature of lee shores make rockbound cliffs or long beaches backed by sand dunes the

Fig 7: Aspect of coast to south westerly winds and population distribution.

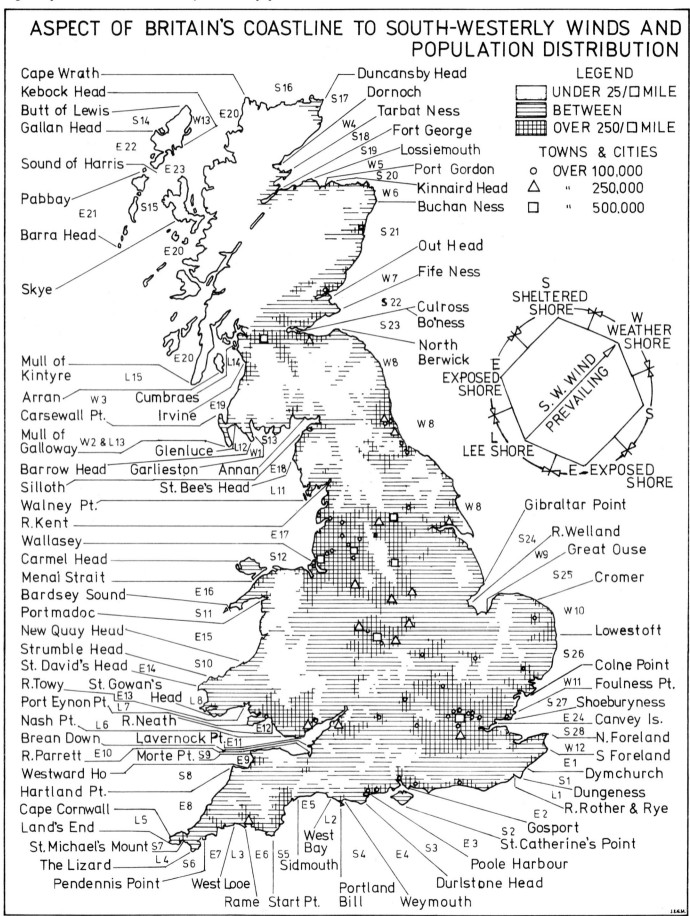

ASPECT OF BRITAIN'S COASTLINE TO SOUTH-WESTERLY WINDS AND POPULATION DISTRIBUTION

LEGEND

UNDER 25/□ MILE
BETWEEN
OVER 250/□ MILE

TOWNS & CITIES
o OVER 100,000
△ " 250,000
□ " 500,000

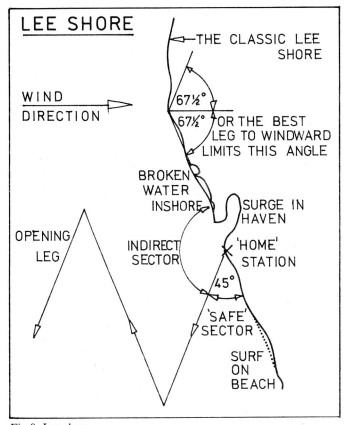

Fig 8: Lee shore.

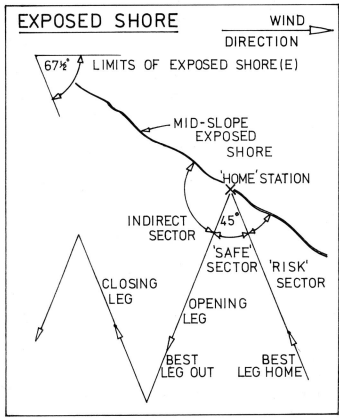

Fig 9: Exposed shore.

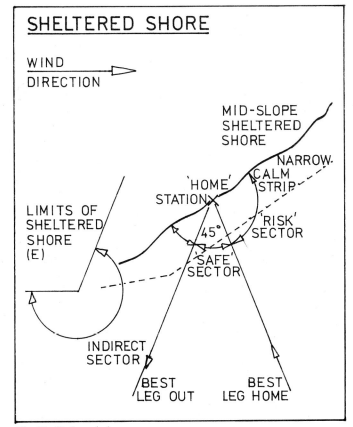

Fig 10: Sheltered shore.

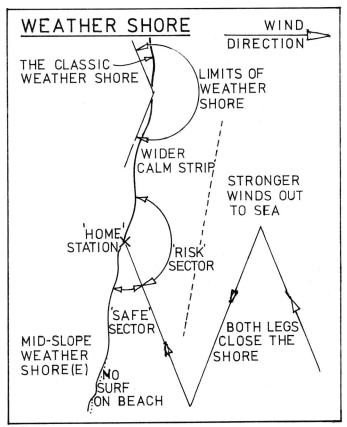

Fig 11: Weather shore.

normal scene, so there are not many beach stations in creeks or beaches there. The deepwater natural harbour of Milford Haven opening into one of these stretches is an exception, though there are several artificial harbours like those at Porthleven, Port Talbot and Ardrossan and one improved natural one at Portpatrick. It has been seen that high ground close to lee shores deflect the wind along one of its flanks; this may alter such a shore into an exposed one.

The exposed shore is one that lies between the best pointing angle and dead down wind (Fig 9). There are three sectors available on setting out: the larger, safe one of 45° which lies between the best points of sailing on the inward- and outward-bound legs, the indirect sector between that and the shoreline to windward, and finally the risky sector between the safe one and the shoreline downwind. Providing the wind is steady in direction, and this tends to be more so with prevailing than other winds, a boat which stays in the safe sector is sure of an easy trip out and home. It follows that a fishing community is well placed if there are good fishing grounds in this sector, but will need weatherly boats if these grounds are in either the indirect or risky sectors. This may be one of the reasons why two adjacent ports on the same stretch of coast may have different sorts of boats, if the grounds lie between. It can be seen from Appendix III that, in addition to being approximately three times the length of the lee shores, the exposed ones links many of them together and occur in longer stretches. As might be expected they are largely on the western and southern sides of Britain. The coasts are indented with access to beaches, rivers and estuaries and are well supplied with boat stations except where the human population is small.

The sheltered shore is the one that lies between dead down wind to the best point of sailing homeward, that is to say when the windward leg of the safe sector corresponds with the general run of the shoreline (Fig 10). While this type of shore enjoys the shelter of land close inshore, there is a much larger sector of open sea from which returning home means working to windward. Once again the benefits of remaining in the safe sector are evident. From Appendix III it can be seen that this coast is somewhat longer than the last and is of a very different nature, because very long stretches are found all the way round the island and these may contain many kinds of landscape. Even more boat stations are found along these shores.

The weather shore is the one that lies, as it were, with its back to the wind, from one best point of sailing through to the other (Fig 11). This shore gets even greater shelter from the prevailing wind and calm water will tend to stretch even further out to sea. There will be less surf during launching and beaching, and winds may be gusty if the hinterland is hilly. There is not however a safe sector, and the further one goes offshore the harder it will be to regain the shelter of the land. Unless the boats are kept close enough to be rowed home, they have got to be weatherly. More than half this coastline lies in a single stretch between the Forth and the Wash, but is made up elsewhere of relatively short lengths.

This account of the British coastline is much simpler than in reality. There are two modifying considerations. Firstly, short stretches of coast, which, due to bays or headlands, do not follow the general run of the coast, have been discounted if they are less than 8 miles long. This figure has been taken as the distance a boat can cover out and back in a working day, one third of which would be spent handling her gear. The second is the effect of fetch during both prevailing and dominant winds, as the presence of land masses a short distance to windward greatly reduces the height of storm waves. Ireland and the Outer Isles shorten the fetch of prevailing winds for much of the west coast of Britain, whereas the continent does far less to soften the dominant north-easterlies on the east coast.

Whatever aspect a shoreline may have to the wind, the fetch or distance of open water over which it has blown governs the height of the waves generated. This is proportional to the square root of the fetch. This means that a thousand mile fetch could produce more than three times the height of waves than if the fetch was only one hundred miles, or ten times for ten miles, with the same wind strength. The larger figures are only found after storms with a duration normally only experienced in the land-free latitudes of the southern hemisphere.

In addition to preventing boats from using their beaches or harbours, waves can damage the coastline for boats in other ways, even after the wind that created them has dropped. Waves attack cliffs and override natural and artificial sea walls, the first being a continual and generally gradual process, while the latter can be sudden and unforeseen. The impact of great storms moves vast quantities of sand or shingle along the coast, destroys masonry and sets up waves in normally sheltered harbours. Beaches which are steep-to after spells of settled weather may be flattened out by storms, while spits may be extended so that leading marks become a hazard. The harbour wall at Wick has been shifted time after time due to the north-easterly fetch of 300 miles[4], while the harbour at Trevaunance in North Cornwall facing due west into the Atlantic was built and rebuilt five times before being finally abandoned[5].

Appendix I lists some fifty places from which boats have operated. In each case, the aspect of the shore to the south-westerly prevailing wind, the type of haven and the fetch in each of the main wind direction is given. It should be noted that the information on fetch only applies to the place named and does not necessarily relate to any places in between. Nor should it be taken that, because the direction of the greatest fetch is sometimes the same as the prevailing wind, the other wind directions can be disregarded. Instead, it is usual to hear boatmen say that they find storms from other than the south-westerly sector the more treacherous. South-easterlies with a hundred miles or so of fetch are particularly disliked in south Devon and Cornwall.

Two further features of onshore waves can trouble boatmen. The first of these is that wave fronts are altered by a headland so that both the flanks are attacked as well as the point. Not only does this extend the area of platforms and rockfalls near the headland, but also it restricts the sites for havens close by. Secondly, waves striking cliffs fall back into oncoming waves to produce a confused sea capable of swamping an open boat. As such rocky bottoms are likely places to find crabs and lobsters, fleets of pots may only be shot there in settled weather and have to be relaid elsewhere when storms are foretold.

If, as it would seem, landscape can influence boatshape in many ways, then an interest in geology is necessary. Rock formation and how it has moved and weathered determines the nature of our coastline, whether it is steep-to or shoal, open or indented, rocky or sandy and so on. The inland masses also affect the coast, as these give rise to the rivers and whether they run fast or slow. If the masses are large they may have caused the coast to sink or emerge. Some landscapes seem to encourage the development of boats, while others, a long surf-beaten beach for instance, discourages it utterly in our cold climate. Furthermore, landscape is what determines the purpose to which boats may be put and of what she is built.

Interesting and rewarding as the study of how rocks and boats may be related could be, no more space can be given to this than to indicate that it exists and is significant. For its size this island has a wide range of rock formations, which for the most part cross it diagonally north-east/south-west, so that one tends to find the same sorts of rocks on both the lee and weather shores. The rocks between Filey and Whitby are similar in origin to those between Swanage and Eype, near Bridport, but, subsequently, have undergone quite different wear and tear. In this way the coastline may be conveniently divided according to the age of the rock formations.

A line from the Tees taken along the valleys of the Swale, Trent, Avon and Severn then across the Somerset flats to the south Devon coast make this division. The rock to the south-east of this line is relatively young, secondary formations or less, with rolling coastal plains for the most part with open coastlines and featureless estuaries. To the north-east of this line the rocks are much older, primary or pre-cambrian, which, facing into the prevailing wind, give indented coastlines, cliffs with mountains and deep water often close to the shore. The coastline is mainly under 1500ft, and even in the most mountainous regions rarely over 3000ft.

The main exception to the general division is that the major estuaries both sides of this line are of the most recent formation of all. Appendix II lists the nature of all the coastal rocks together with an indication of what the immediate land and seascape is like. The mouths of the smaller rivers all round the island often provide the site for a harbour. Generally speaking these harbours on the younger side of the dividing line have undergone rapid and recent changes, due to land reclamation, silting or changes in the course of the river. North and west of the line however, especially when the river valley is the result of glacial or later sinkage, these are deep and cannot be seen to have changed during the period that they have been known to have been harbours.

The wide variety of terrain listed in the landscape column of this table has ensured that many species of trees have grown in Britain. Quite a few of these are suitable for boatbuilding. Most of these are deciduous, so-called hardwoods, and are truly native, growing on the flatter parts of the country. The evergreen softwoods, which prefer slopes, are more recent introductions.

The timber used in boats is less standardised than that used in ships, both availability and durability governing the type chosen. If a boat is small and its design simple, the labour cost of a replacement may well be less than that of procuring a more durable but distant alternative. In this way English elm, a widely distributed hedgerow giant, though preferably limited to parts which will be always wet, like a keel, or dry, like an apron, might be used for other components, like the sides of a Parrett flatner or all of turf boat, as neither had to last very long. The wych elm, which grows in woods in the southeast and southwest of England, has a more pliant and durable wood. For these reasons it was chosen for planking, as the longevity of the Cornish and Scilly pilot gigs goes to prove.

English and sessile oak, together with their hybrids, can also provide material for every part of a boat, if the crooked and straight stuff is seasoned to an appropriate degree. Oak once grew as part of vast forests sited mainly to the east of the Tees/Axe line, until iron smelters and shipbuilders almost obliterated them. Where its weight can be tolerated the wet flexibility of oak is suitable for stringers, bent timbers and planking, yet when dry its strength is ideal for frames, beams and backbone components. Care has to be taken to avoid splits when drying.

Other native trees, like ash for oars and bent timbers, Scots pine for spars and board-work and crack willow for poles, are used along with whatever else is available locally in sufficient size. European larch has been here since the middle of the eighteenth century, so is now taken as being a native timber. In Scotland and the north east of England it is the preferred material for planking. In the first half of the nineteenth century, Sitka or silver spruce, used for fine planking, oars and spars, and Douglas fir or Oregon pine, used for decks, heavy spars and stringers, were both introduced into this country. The spruce has become the most common of all our plantation trees, whilst the Douglas fir does best in deep well-drained soil.

The need to convert trees into a form in which they could be used in a boat restricted the choice of timber up until the time sawing and transport was mechanised. When felling and conversion were dependent on the whip-saw and horses, as much work as possible had to be done at the site of the felling, which of necessity could not be far away. Mechanisation in addition to bringing the log to the saw has resulted in standard timber sizes for all forms of wooden structures and not for boatbuilding in particular. Crooks for instance are often left for firewood and, unless a boatbuilder establishes a steady demand for them, they become hard to find. Right up to the present day there are still a few boatbuilders who buy growing trees and personally supervise their conversion in sawmills prepared to take on this jobbing work.

More and more timber arrives in this country from overseas, and much of it already converted. Some of the types are well established, such as Honduras and Spanish mahogany, which is as versatile as oak but lighter, Canadian rock elm for sprung keels, stringers, rubbers and bent timbers, Archangel whites for high quality board-work, flat bottom planking, thwarts and flooring, teak and pitch pine for durable planking. Many of these woods have in turn become unobtainable, and since the start of this century have been progressively replaced by timber from West and East Africa, Malaya, Borneo and Australasia. Where boatbuilders have access to timber shipping ports, it is found they will be using exotic sounding woods like Iroko, Utile, Sapele, Yakal, Meranti, Changal, Kauri and Jarra, because local timber is either too dear or no longer available. Except in Scotland where the availability of larch and oak has been maintained, boatbuilding in wood is declining in favour of other materials such as metal, cement and petrochemicals, which have no local character.

The next aspect of a boat's surroundings is that of population which during the period of this study has seen a great change in total numbers and distribution. Fig 7 shows the situation in the early 1920s at about the time power replaced sail as the means of propelling a boat. Only the least populated areas, which coincide fairly closely with those over 1000ft, have barely changed, and those that have are mostly holiday and retirement centres. The present densely populated zones are the product of industrialisation and are sited largely inland. Though some of the large cities like London, Bristol, Liverpool and Edinburgh pre-date this expansion, by far the greater number of them and much of the subsequent growth of all of them do not.

Population density may determine whether a boat is used for commerce or subsistence. Along lightly populated coastlines it will be the latter, with the boatman using her for part-time fishing and carrying. In well populated coasts with good land transport and heavily populated areas, boats tend to be used full-time commercially, and become specialised for particular kinds of fishing, cargoes, pleasuring or other occupations. In the areas between, those with 25 to 250 persons to the square mile, one finds full-time boatmen with more general purpose boats. This gives patterns of boat distribution that provide the subject of a later chapter.

In Britain a boat's surroundings may be peculiar to quite a small area, in which all the constituent elements have to be considered, if the shapes of the boats there are to be fully assessed. Though this chapter has had to be too generalised for immediate practical application, it should serve as a guide as to how surroundings may be observed.

3.

Work for boats

Fig 12: Severn long net salmon boat, near Elmore at 6pm, 1 July 1975, and at Tewkesbury at 7.30am, 21 April 1804 (detail from drawing in Tewkesbury Town Council Chamber).

As boats are found from well inland to far out to sea, it is convenient to divide their areas of operation into inland waterways, estuaries and landlocked and open coasts. Oceans are not included here as the only boats out there will be ship's tenders. These areas have a close bearing on the type of work the boats there may have to do, and this in turn affects shape. A boat has to be really needed if the effort of building her is to be justified, nor will she be replaced once the need ends. It is the initiation, alterations and ending of these needs that has, does and will change the shape of a boat. Finding out what these needs might be in Britain should help us understand her boats.

The inland waterway boats we are interested in are simple in form when used for rural purposes on rapid-free rivers. The turf and withy boats of Somerset, the trows used as ferries on the Fleets in Dorset, the salmon punts in

Christchurch Harbour, the gun punts of Essex and elsewhere and the long net salmon punts of the Severn are examples (Fig 12). These boats all have flat bottoms and sides with square or pointed ends. They are within the skill of the owner or the local carpenter to build. The flat bottom lends itself to work inland, the square-ended ones for crossing and the pointed ones for longer trips up and down stream. In either case the flat bottom has the advantages of small loaded draft and the greater weight a man or a horse can move afloat than ashore.

Crossing ferries often appear in artist's sketches and finished work. They are one of the earliest types of boat to be drawn, but do not seem to follow any regular pattern. They are also well documented from medieval times as their operation and ownership was often a matter of legal dispute or inheritance. As roads improved and bridges

Fig 13: Bodinnick ferry.

Fig 14: Bridgwater barges.

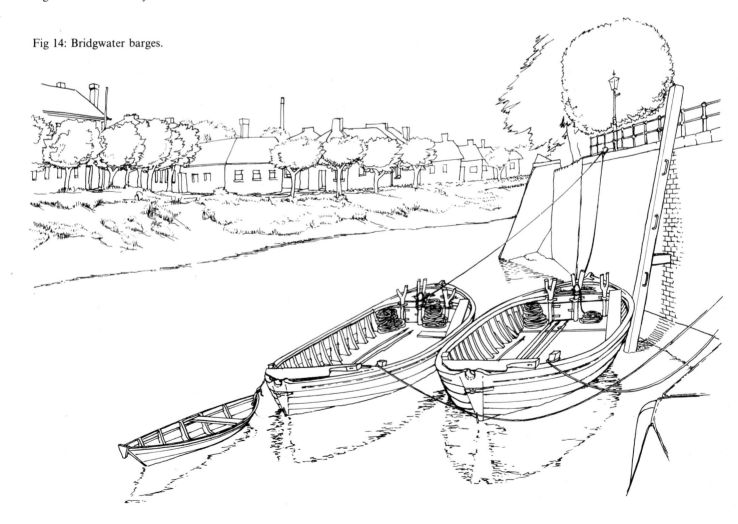

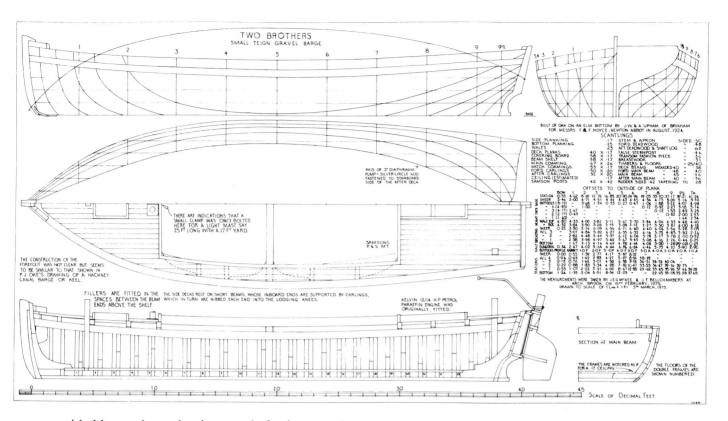

Fig 15: *Two Brothers*, small Teign gravel barge – lines and construction.

were provided lower down the rivers, only ferries over the longer stretches of water survived. Even these came to be built of steel and had to be powered so that they could handle cars and lorries. There are a few wooden ferries remaining, like those at Bodinnick and Kingswear, which are dumb and rely on a motor launch to take them across (Fig 13). There are still purely passenger ferries like the one at Felixstowe Ferry, but none that have kept their sails like those that once crossed the Lynher at Forder or Old Mill Creek on the Dart. The stronghold of crossing ferries for vehicles is on the west coast of Scotland; but even here the once famous one at Ballachulish has recently been replaced by a bridge.

Traffic along rivers has produced distinctive types of vessel, many of them having survived well into this century. The Fenland barge, Teign keel and Bridgwater barge were all flat bottomed and little more than large examples of a smaller rural type (Figs 14 & 15). They depended on the tide or tracking for movement, only using poles or sweeps to manoeuvre. If used at all sails were set on jury poles, which could also serve as quants or boathooks. Some rivers carried more advanced designs with round bottoms, external keels and other features that hinted at influences from shipbuilding. These are hard to separate from estuarine craft. If the types that made coastal trips are excluded, one can list the Tyne keel and wherry, the Norfolk keel and wherry, the Rye and Arun barges and the Severn up-river trow as examples (Fig 16). All of these had more or less permanent arrangements for setting sails as well as poles, sweeps and tow-ropes. Above bridge lighters like these were made as large as the bridge arches and seasonal depths of water would allow. Later

these limitations were to include the length of locks and the width of their gates. In the river navigations dumb lighters and barges had to be pulled upstream from the tow path when the tide no longer served. Both men and horses were used for tracking, whichever was the cheaper. Keeping open a right of way along a tow path set up friction between landowners and bargemen, who had no common aims. The bargemen got and probably earned an evil name for trespass, poaching, damage to fencing and rowdiness. Certainly the men employed tracking stood on a low rung of the wage ladder, though the masters of the larger barges on the Thames, Severn and Trent, being in charge of valuable goods for long periods, were men of some status.

Where, on lakes, forks and marshes, there was no tow path sweeps, poles or sails had to be used. All kinds of sailing rigs were fitted: square, some with topsails, on the Severn, Tyne and Humber tributaries; sprit on the Thames and Arun and gaff on the Broads. One has to look at the landscape to realise why the Norfolk wherry had the more handy gaff on the open reaches of the Broads rather than the high square rig of the up-river trows running with the prevailing south-westerlies when travelling upstream through the Severn gorges.

The place where a river is bridged nearest to the sea provides a boundary between inland waterway and estuary. This bridge is important, because not only does it eliminate a crossing ferry, but also the place becomes a junction between land, fresh and salt water traffic. One cannot exaggerate the role bridge-towns have played in the

Fig 16: Severn up-river trow, 1804 (detail from drawing in Tewkesbury Town Council Chamber).

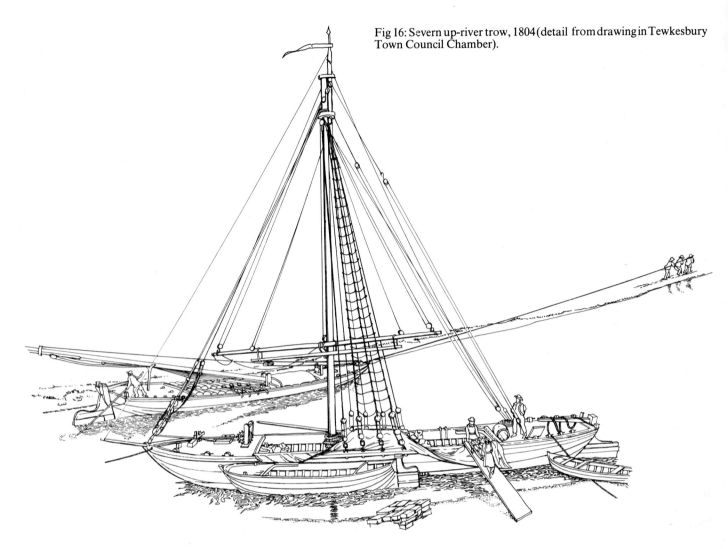

development of all these forms of transport and how they have given work for boats. The site for the bridge was, apart from the civil engineering problem, influenced by military and economic considerations. These favoured places some miles inland from the open sea: Arundel was 8 miles, Bristol 11, Chester 25, Dumfries 10, Exeter 11, Fareham 7, Glasgow 21 and so on through the alphabet to York at 53. This kept down the size of vessel that could reach the bridge-town and as ocean-going ships grew created a need for entry ports with dock facilities closer to the sea, like those at Littlehampton, Avonmouth, Kingston-upon-Hull, Goole and so on. The arms of the City of Bristol show a sailing ship half way under a fortified bridge. This precisely illustrates the role of a bridge-town, which, though it gives protection to the sea-going vessel, also stops her going further up-river. If this marks the inner extremity of an estuary, the outer limit may be taken as being in the vicinity of the entry ports, where ships might lie when working cargoes, weather bound, taking on stores or pilots or waiting for orders. As ships and entry ports became larger, the bridge-towns diminished as seaports. This created new work, for boats and boatmen found that they could benefit from offering ships a quick turn-round, based on reliable pilotage,

trustworthy watermen and readily available towage and lighterage. On the busier rivers like the Thames there was also passenger traffic along the river, met by pair-oar wherries for the well-to-do or by tilt boats plying between the Pool and Gravesend, while on the Severn market boats ran once or twice a week between Chepstow and Bristol since 1680[1].

It is not possible to differentiate exactly between the various classes of boats employed serving shipping, as the move away from bridge-town to entry port was often only partial. In broad terms only it is found that there were boats for pilots, watermen and lighterage. In the busiest places any of these could be further sub-divided to take account of specialisation.

As long as ships have been 'going foreign', the inward-bound ones in particular have depended upon local knowledge, even before sighting land. Speaking a pilot might be the first indication a master might have of the accuracy of his navigation or safety of his landfall. Just sighting a pilot boat gave one a position, as her rig alone would tell from where she came even before the number on her sail or her red and white pilot flag could be seen. Up-to-date information was essential; shoals and their marks might have been moved, and wind and tide predictions would help decide how best a sailing ship should make her approach. When proceeding in poor visability, simple guides like which fields were under grass or plough and the nature of the bottom after heavy rain might mean the difference between an early safe arrival, a missed tide or worse. Ships need pilots, who in turn have to have boats to get onboard.

A pilot's boat varies depending on how often and far out to sea or inland his services are required. They seem to have undergone at least four changes to reach their most advanced stage. The first stage occurs in the smaller places where the pilotage is only occasional. One or two local fishermen or watermen act as a pilot whenever a ship signals for one. Such a man would use his own boat but, if this were too large, then her punt. A fee would be agreed before boarding, after which the boat would generally be towed astern during the ship's passage in. Lug-rigged Clyde skiffs, sprit-rigged Southport skiffs, gaff-rigged north-west coast nobbies and sprit-rigged Portishead yawls were examples of local types that were also used by pilots with little or no modification. The list is a long one and includes Cornish gigs, Falmouth quay punts, Solent or Itchen ferry boats, Gravesend goozieboats, East Coast smacks, Humber gold-dusters, the double-ended Tees cobles and the Tyne and Wear foyboats. Even where the pilot boats were rigged the same as local craft, they tended to have smaller spars and sails, especially during the winter months.

The second stage was reached when there was sufficient work and fees to justify a number of full-time pilots in selected or specially built boats going well out to sea to find ships to bring in. This led to regulation of the numbers of pilots and the necessity of ensuring that each one of them had the standard of knowledge and behaviour expected before he was licensed[2]. This duty usually fell to the port authority, which varied from one place to the next, but all of which laid down the fees as well as when and where pilotage was obligatory. Within these rules the licensed pilots competed keenly with each other and this encouraged improvements to their boats, which could involve a marked departure in size and shape from the

local prototype if they were to search well out to sea. Before anything else the boats had to be able to cruise on station whatever the weather, and this is some cases meant in the unsheltered south-west approaches. Only just less important was the need to have a boat that could be sailed back home short handed, or if the waters were sheltered and a smaller boat could be used, capable of being towed astern safely. Speed and close-winded performance were less important, however much they might have been prized in places where competition was high. The Bristol Channel pilot cutter or skiff, the Swansea Bay pilot schooner, the Liverpool pilot cutter and schooner and the large Falmouth, Plymouth and Solent pilot cutters fall into this category. Except where towing home remained a necessity a pilot cutter had much the same draft limitation as the ship being piloted. This allowed deep-keeled designs which were both able to stand up to a press of sail and yet lie-to in comparative comfort during gales. Both these qualities were looked for by cruising and ocean racing yachtsmen and this has helped to extend the life of some examples of this type.

In the larger ports the individually operated sailing cutter came to an end when it was recognised that rivalry benefited no one. The third stage was entered when the pilots combined to buy larger vessels, often choosing this time to change over to steam. Not only could a steam cutter be on station and stay there longer; without competition and to ensure safer re-embarcation of fresh pilots, she could now cruise closer to where pilotage became compulsory. This extended the usefulness of boatmen or unlicensed pilots who still undertook to bring ships up channel to the desired station. Though these pilot cutters were small ships rather than large boats in smaller but busy ports like Fowey, where the capital expenditure on a large cutter could not be supported, a small fleet of three local boats is kept for the use of pilots instead (Fig 17).

Wireless telegraphy and radio position fixing together have brought about the change to the final stage in most of the larger ports today. Incoming ships with these much surer ways of knowing their position must signal their

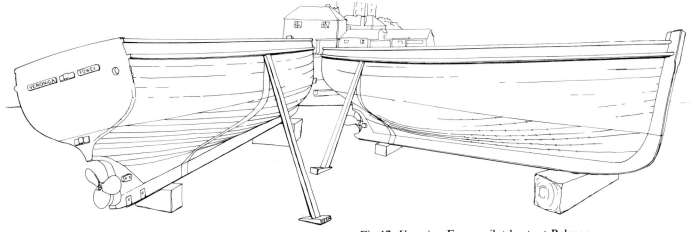

Fig 17: *Veronica*, Fowey pilot boat, at Polruan.

estimated time of arrival several days ahead and confirm the exact time a few hours before. This enables a small but powerful motor boat to come out to meet the ship at a spot sheltered enough to allow the pilot to board in safety. These boats are built by specialists, Brooke Marine of Lowestoft, Cheverton Workboats of Cowes and Fairey Marine of Hamble being some of the better known.

In England, Scotland and Wales together there are 162 places listed where some form of pilotage can be obtained. 92 of these make the use of a licensed pilot compulsory, and will levy fines if other than these are employed. As might be expected these include the Thames ports and provide for pilots being embarked as far away as Brixham or Cherbourg even though one is not essential until off Harwich or Folkestone. The Clyde, Humber, Mersey, Fal and Bristol Channel are also amongst the compulsory pilotage areas. What might not be expected is that it is not compulsory to take on a pilot for the ports from Bridlington to Blythe, nor for any of the ports in South Wales except Neath, although they are available and would of course be used. There are still 18 pilot vessels which cruise on station, more or less continuously with pilots for the ports in that district. 18 of the places that do not make pilots compulsory recommend that all craft however small should employ one; 5 more places can go no further than suggest the services of a local man. It can be seen from this that three out of the four stages outlined above for the development of pilot boats are still to be found – only the specialised cutter owned by the pilot searching and competing for work has vanished. In place of this there is one pilot station that is within one mile of the harbour, to where if it turns rough the pilot vessel will return to wait for incoming ships. Although this is the extreme example, conditions are changed from those when pilot cobles from the same Tyne river met their ships off Flamborough Head ninety miles down the coast.

In addition to the licensed pilots working within the fixed stations, there were deepwater boatmen keen to put a man on board homeward-bound ships long before they had reached the limits of any of the compulsory zones. While such men might not yet or ever be licensed, they gave a real service before there were electronic aids to help ships get up channel in unfavourable weather. The unlicensed man was bound to hand over to a licensed pilot the moment he made contact. As the official pilot was more expensive, some masters were not above making a confused signal to the genuine pilot vessel. Apart from risking a fine up to double the due, this master would be badly placed in the event of an accident. The unofficial pilots used their own local types of boats, of which the Deal lugger, searching as far west as the Lizard, was the oldest and best known. For one of these to pick up a Dundee-bound ship was to earn the most lucrative fee of all.

Closely allied to pilot work was hovelling, which involved the transport of all manner of necessities out the ships lying off, namely men, mail, food, ground tackle and general ship's chandlery. While in many cases one type of boat might do all this, elsewhere special types evolved for the different tasks. This was true of the Downs, where the large concentrations of ships assembled called for a degree of specialisation. As well as the pilots, the Deal luggers recovered and supplied ship's anchors and cables, while the smaller galleys, galley punts and punts, depending on the state of the weather, took care of the less bulky stores and passengers.

Once in a roadstead or port approach a sea-going ship looked to the watermen, sometimes even before she came to rest. There were agents to be brought off, pilots to be landed and health, custom and immigration formalities to be observed.

As port facilities have improved, both naval and merchant ships spend more time alongside and less in anchorages. Before the Second World War warships in commission lay at buoys when in home ports, alongside berths only being required for such events as refits, re-commissioning and major re-storings. Out in the stream the warship's own boats undertook all ceremonial and routine trips, official calls, mail and libertymen at set times. On top of this dockyard craft ran services for topping up fuel and water frequently, and replenishment of victualling and armament stores occasionally. Some of these craft were cut-down coasting smacks like the *Marie* of Salcombe (Fig 18) rather than specially built port auxiliary craft. Civilian watermen met all needs for transport after this and plied for hire when embarking canteen and wardroom stores, and ferrying both officers and men between routine trip times, especially during working hours and late at night. Since 1945 the number and size of warships has decreased and their equipment has become so complex that it has to be shut down partially for maintenance in harbour with the lost service provided from shore. With the ample berths now available all major warships can go alongside and be connected up to the dockyard electrical, steam, telephone, and fresh, salt and chilled water systems. The watermen are not needed and though their boats have been dispersed, examples of them can still be recognised (Fig 19).

Merchant ships at anchor would make less use of their own boats than warships, but rely even more on watermen. As well as the services already mentioned, local tradesmen like ship's chandlers, outfitters and runners from the less respectable establishments would use the watermen's boats to tout for custom, often bringing samples along with them. Roadsteads like those of Carrick off Falmouth and Spithead off Portsmouth, though sheltered for a ship, could give brisk going for small and mostly open watermen's boats, who were expected to carry on in all weathers without getting their passengers and luggage too wet. When a merchant ship picked up a buoy or came alongside the watermen were needed to take out the cables or berthing hawsers, and after all was secured they might be given employment cleaning and painting topsides after the crew had been paid off.

Fig 18: *Marie*, of Salcombe, victualling yard lighter, at Devonport.

Fig 19: *Parson Gay*, Tamar waterman's barge.

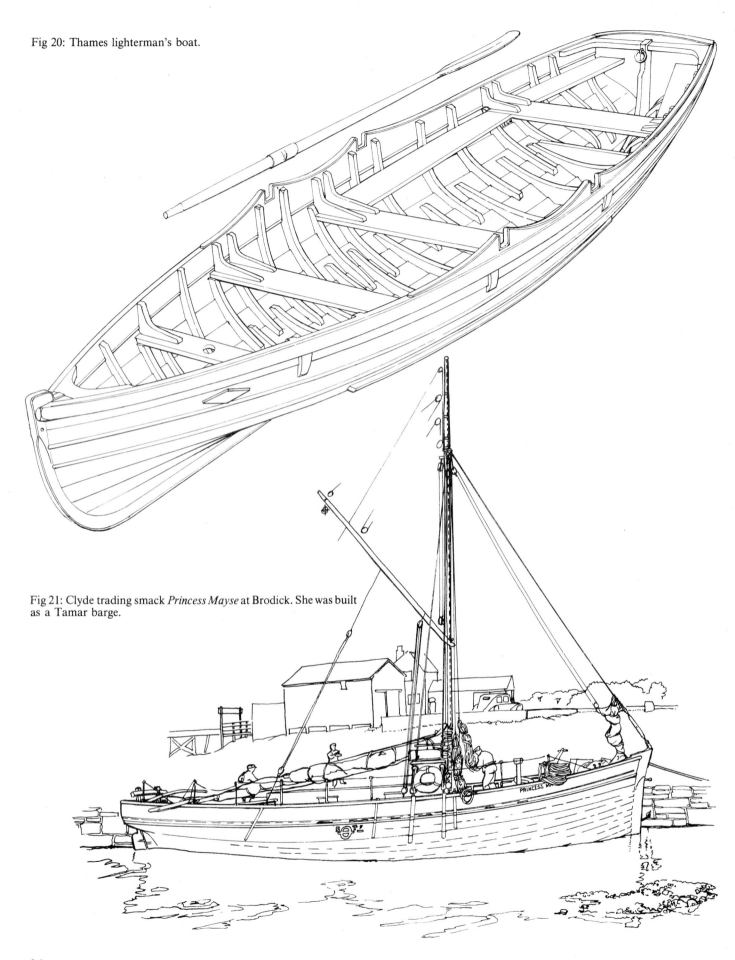

Fig 20: Thames lighterman's boat.

Fig 21: Clyde trading smack *Princess Mayse* at Brodick. She was built as a Tamar barge.

Merchantmen mostly go alongside now to handle their cargoes and other union labour paints the side, so there are fewer calls on watermen. Almost living in his boat, a waterman handled her mainly under oars, sometimes under sail with the minimum waste of effort. The passenger-carrying boats were usually spotless, combining capacity with speed in a way that has attracted amateur ownership.

In the days of sail, and in certain classes even today, merchant ships were able to handle their cargoes and stores without going alongside a wharf. Unless the distance by land was short, transportation by waterway would be cheaper than rail. Lying out in the stream brought two advantages; lighters could lie on both sides of the ship and pilfering, endemic in dockland, was a little harder. The other need for a lighter was, as her name says, to reduce the ship's draft so that she could carry the balance of her cargo upstream to the bridge-town. Lighters also assembled cargoes for outward bound ships by reversing the distribution process.

Examination of lighters suggests they can have two origins: either they are versions of above bridge types, or they are developed from cut down sea-going vessels. Furthermore lighters can be given many different sorts of work to do. Below the bridges this group of vessels was anything from a dumb barge to a self-propelled sailing or motor barge. Each estuary developed its own distinctive types. The dumb lighter, perhaps because at first she looks featureless, has not had a lot written about her. She depends on tide or tug to move her on her proper job of transferring cargoes between ship and shore. She may also be used as a floating warehouse or for freighting on the wider canals. Though they follow fixed patterns on some waterways, dumb lighters are generally found as a mixture of types and are a study in themselves. Scientifically designed lighters are produced on the Thames and other major rivers, and their shapes are worth studying for their ease of towing at all states of loading and, in the case of the Thames swim barge, to see how a much earlier shape had been refined.

The arrival of steam tugs greatly benefited the operation of dumb lighters, as one set of engines would enable a few lightermen to handle a relatively large fleet without being ruled by the tide. The lighterman's skiff is used to ferry the men between the normally unmanned lighters. These boats are quite large and heavy looking, being of necessity robustly built entirely of oak. In spite of this they are said to row well and are quite distinct from the other rowing boats on this river (Fig 20).

The Humber keels and sloops, the Thames sailing barges and tilt boats, the Solent barges and Cowes ketches, the Severn trows, the Mersey flats and the Clyde gabbarts are all examples of the sailing lighters that have been well described by others. All had well developed sailing rigs, many of which could still be taken down to pass under bridges. Their hull shapes show that though consideration had been given to their sailing qualities, cargo space was more important. The Thames barge had a flat bottom, but only amidships as her ends took on rounded sections. As all the estuaries were tidal with deep channels between mud or sandbanks, draft was less critical. The deeper hulls lent themselves to motorisation, which extended their useful life long after steel motor lighters were being built.

The need to import raw materials to and then export products from the new factories of the nineteenth century brought about an expansion of the ports close to the navigable estuaries and a building boom. The demand for sand, gravel, stone and clays for bricks and cement, all of which were to be found in and around these quaternary estuaries, gave more work for lighters. Those that did not have to go into deep water, like Chapman's Thames chalk barge, the Taw gravel barge, and the Fal and Tamar inside stone barges were quite simple in shape, structure and rig; but those, like the Clyde gravel smacks, which had to work in open water were more like small coasters (Fig 21).

Some estuarine vessels were able to make regular coastal passages. These were the Thames boomy barges, the West Country outside barges, the Severn box trows, the Mersey jigger flats, and the Clyde trading smacks. Though, by the earlier definition, these in many respects were ships rather than boats, they earn our attention as they are clearly recent developments from smaller local models. They were all round bottom designs built mainly in wood but also in iron or steel. They generally had statutory cruising limits, but their two- or three-man crews sailed them all the year round, helping with upkeep and cargo handling. They carried tall rigs until they were cut down, bit by bit, as auxiliary engines became more reliable. Added to this list should be the small powered cargo carriers. These first appeared at an early date; the *John* for instance was built of iron at Neath Abbey in 1840 and was still afloat in 1939, hence steam and sailing lighters were running side by side for almost a hundred years (Fig 22). This suggests that, even where steam and coal were plentiful, there was little to choose between the two, if there were also soldier's winds and twice daily four-knot tides as there were in the Bristol Channel. On the Clyde and the west coast of Scotland with less helpful winds and tides, the steam lighter or puffer rapidly replaced the gabbart and sailing smack and this in an area where there was little overland transport.

While railways and commercial fishing were mutually good for each other, railways and waterways, inland and coastal, were more often than not in direct competition. In our long narrow estuaries where the sea routes are shorter than those by land, the railways were at a disadvantage to start with until they had acquired many of the small harbours and only maintained those which contributed to their own traffic. In spite of this it took diesel lorries and better roads to outdate most forms of water traffic by the middle of this century. Since then the pruning of branch lines from the railway system has been matched by indications that small ports and the building material trade are reviving.

The large areas of shallow water and flats in the estuaries provided the conditions in which shrimps, small fry, oysters and other shellfish thrive. These, when cheap, were eaten in great quantities as part of the diet of the new populations of the industrial expansion. The fisheries gave work to fleets of specialised craft designed to catch and transport this food to the nearest market or railhead. Thus bawleys, shrimpers and oyster dredgers developed into fast weatherly craft capable of working and often processed their catch onboard throughout the winter months. Overfishing, land reclamation and pollution separately or together cut down the size of the catches without destroying the appetite for them. What once was a vulgar commodity turned into a rare delicacy, so prices rose and this has kept some of the old small boat fisheries going, unlike those for coarse fish which have been largely taken over by larger craft. As stocks have to be conserved, restrictive rules generally banning innovations have been introduced. This has kept many distinct types of boats, especially those engaged in commercial oyster and salmon fisheries, in existence longer than their once more profitable, numerous and powerful sisters.

The only real extent of landlocked coastline in Britain is from Cape Wrath to Kintyre. Here headlands and sea lochs alternate, having many islands close to seaward, which provide sounds or sheltered channels up much of this coast. A further forty miles out into the Atlantic lie the Outer Hebrides, nearly unbroken for one hundred and thirty-five miles. In spite of the presence of Ireland, the eastern shore of the Irish Sea has sufficient fetch to be regarded as an open coast.

The Scottish west coast and its fish would seem to be ideal for boats, but gives little work for local ones. The scarcity and isolation of the population only justifies small boats suitable for subsistence fishing and some inter-island carriage. The bulk of the freight and passengers are carried by ships of the nationalised company of David MacBrayne, while the commercial fishing has been mainly done by nomadic fleets. The following table may help to explain the difference between this coast and that of the rest of Scotland. The five largest ports – Granton, Aberdeen, Peterhead, Fraserburgh and Buckie – have been shown separately as many of their vessels are almost ships.

To express the difference in another way: there was the equivalent of three 26-ton boats every mile along the east coast at that time, against one 7-tonner a mile in the south west. They were not, of course, spaced out like plants in a kitchen garden, but were for the most part centred on well built harbours and used for commercial fishing. In the Outer Isles there was the equivalent of four 4-tonners a mile, but only one of them every 1½ miles along the west coast. After the larger harbour-based boats have been extracted the other smaller boats are spaced more evenly between the waterside crofts. These open boats may be found in ones or twos in bays and creeks, and where there is no beach the rocks on the foreshore have been cleared to

SCOTTISH FISHING BOATS JUST AFTER WORLD WAR 2

	East Coast Burnmouth to Cape Wrath		West Coast Cape Wrath to Carradale	Outer Isles Butt of Lewis to Barra Head	The South West Loch Fyne and Clyde & Solway Firths
	Big Five	Others			
Number of Boats	700	1300	800	940	400
Total Tonnage	33,500	19,500	3000	3750	3000
Average Tonnage	50	15	3¾	4	7¼
Places of over 100 Fishermen	5	22	2	8	3
Places of under 100 Fishermen	0	85	64	18	50
Total Fishermen	5200	6600	560	340	950
Total Crofter/ Fishermen	0	180*	920	2140	0

*All from Caithness or Sutherland.

form a narrow launching slip and heaped on the weather side to make a line of stepping stones out to the boat, almost like a jetty. The difficulty of obtaining boatbuilding materials in the Outer Isles in particular has resulted in the import and encouraged longevity of their boats. Though there were local builders once, few of their creations can now be found. Instead, there are good examples of other Scottish types, some in use long after the last one has gone from the port of origin (Fig 23).

The ever-changing work and appearance of modern Scottish harbour-based fishing boats is much the same all over that country. The crofter's boat however is more distinct and seems to be static. They are mostly one-man boats for lining and potting for home consumption, and seaweed is also harvested. In the latter case the boat will have to take considerable wear and tear from the rocks; and for this, ferro-cement construction has been tried with encouraging results. Where fish processing plants have been established some of the crofters take up full-time fishing in larger boats (p 204).

Along the open coastlines the majority of boats are engaged in one or other kind of fishing. Hovelling and pleasuring are lesser occupations. The type of fishing gear used influences the boat's design and will fix her shape, size and propulsion. These in turn will often determine whether the boat in any sort of fishery operates from an open beach, a sheltered creek or a harbour. Fishing gear and how it is worked can be a study on its own. It is constantly being altered to keep in step with the variations in the available fish stocks and market demands. There are good books on the subject and new ones get written

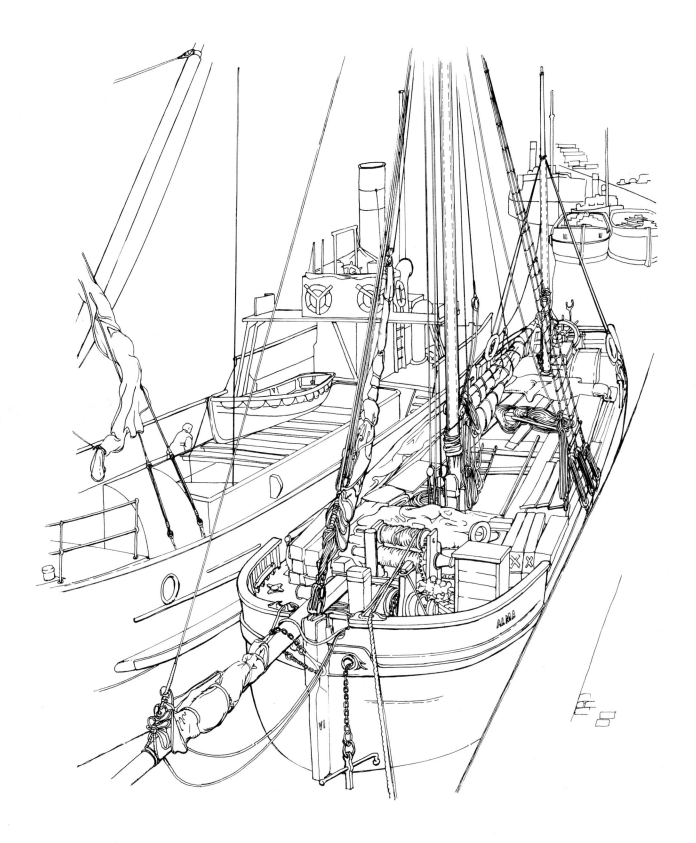

Fig 22: Trow *Alma* and ss *Tanny* at Bristol.

yearly[3]. Fishing methods will not therefore be described in any more detail than is necessary to show how they affect boatshape. Changes in gear can even make classes of boat obsolete. At Filey, for example, where once there were separate classes to suit the seasonal fishing pattern, there is now a range of round-the-year boats. Nowadays more attention is given to producing versatile designs capable of managing several types of fishing gear.

Fishing gear may be grouped according to whether it is shot by the vessel when she is stationary or under way, whether it has to be towed to make it fish or whether it can be left and picked up later.

In the first instance the boat's main work is to transport nets or traps out to the grounds. Here they are put over the side and stretched out by anchors, stakes or by the boat herself lying attached to the downwind end. The nets may vary from small but complicated ones either designed to tangle up the fish like the trammel, or small mesh funnels to guide the fish into a trap, like the stow-net, or they may be very long ones with the mesh the right width to hold the desired size and sort of fish by the gill cases, like the drift-net. In all cases the net is left in position for some hours before it is hauled inboard with the catch. The boat needs to be big enough to accommodate the wet nets, warps, anchors, catch and crew large enough to handle all this gear. Speed under way is an advantage both in securing good pitches and getting the catch home fast. As much time is spent stopped, firm bilges and lowering rigs help cut down rolling and drag.

The second group employs the movement of one or more boats to extend the net into the desired shape, then contract it until the fish are surrounded and guided into an area where they can be taken out of the water by some other means. These basically are all forms of seine or ring nets, having a mesh smaller than the fish being caught. The seine has been developed in a number of ways, all of which depend on a boat that can be manoeuvered precisely. For this reason they once had to be rowed, but now can be engine driven. In all nets that are shot under way, there must be nothing to snarl the gear while it is moving. In small seine-net boats there must be ample buoyancy in that part of the boat, normally aft, where the wet net is stowed. Each time the net is hauled a great deal of water is brought into the boat with it, and there must be some sure way of bailing this out as free surface water destroys stability. Some of the up-to-date seining arrangements require the loaded net to be hauled while the boat herself is going ahead. This calls for an even larger main engine as the winch takes its power from it. Unless the boat is a lot more stable than one that hauls her nets at rest, there is a risk of swamping through open hatches, either by girding herself during hauling or due to the capsizing moment of the catch as it comes clear of the sea at the end of a derrick. Ample beam and avoidance of topweight are desirable.

Boats which fish by dragging nets or grabs over the bottom or at set depths, with or without the help of the tide or a second boat, do so on a steady course. Bottom trawling calls for considerable power, which under sail

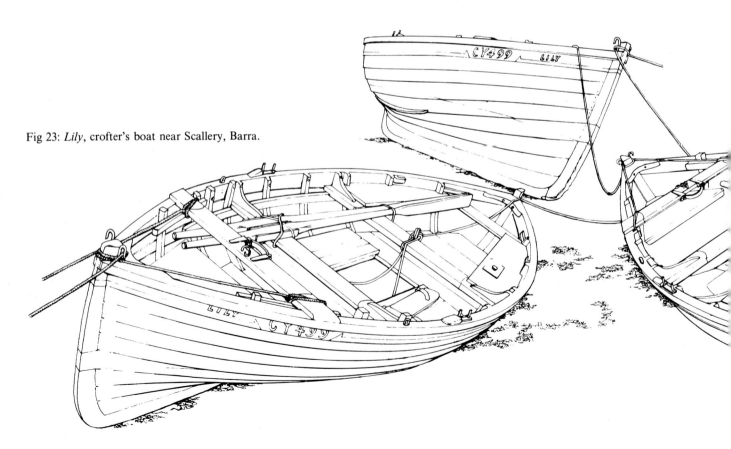

Fig 23: *Lily*, crofter's boat near Scallery, Barra.

meant large areas of it balanced by a heavily ballasted hull. Whatever the form of propulsion the large power available for trawling ensured a good turn of speed out and back. This encouraged hulls with fine lines, there being not the same demand for capacity as there was in a drift-net boat. Though the net of the trawl was much smaller, the beam that spread it was about the same length as the vessel, and with its heavy trawl heads at either end was tricky to manhandle in a sea-way. While a sailing boat would not have the speed in light winds to rely on otter boards she could only use a beam to spread her trawl. The power boat could and did use otter boards, and much simpler deck lay-outs leading to stern trawling resulted. As well as bottom fish, oysters, scallops and shrimps are taken in dredges. These highly priced catches have to be controlled to prevent overfishing, sometimes by short seasons and even by banning engines or too effective gear.

In all methods of fishing which require heavy or awkward gear to be brought inboard, the height of the rail or gunwale above the sea has to be kept small with the low point preferably well aft. This has produced the sloping sheerline with an abrupt turn up of the stern seen in many offshore craft. This low freeboard constitutes a danger from swamping in an open boat and favours a deck, certainly for harbour-based craft. The open-beach boat does not take kindly to a deck for several reasons. First and foremost it puts up weight and so reduces the capacity and performance of a boat whose size is limited by launching considerations. The cost is greater and it is hard

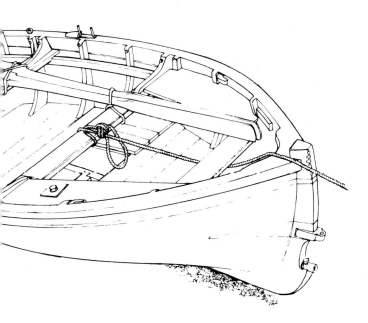

to devise a way of rowing her unless a large well is left undecked, or an engine or a hauling-off rope is provided to get her through the surf. Lastly, unless the boat is large, it is rarely possible to raise the bulwarks enough to keep men on deck from going over the side without making the topsides disproportionately high. A man standing on the bottom boards of an open boat is safer and has less distance to lift. It can be seen that an open boat is better for work off a beach, while a sizeable decked trawler generally has to work out of a harbour.

While in the past most fish were caught either near the surface or at the bottom, it is now possible to find and catch them in between. This is done under way using underwater detection devices both to locate the fish and to position the trawl at the same level. Instead of working nets hopefully in areas where fish might be expected, one finds the fish before using the gear, which ashore would be the difference between firing at a target blindfold or not. The use of powered sheaves wide enough to haul the net as well as the warp has made gear recovery much quicker and is now seen in quite small boats (Fig 24).

The use of baited traps calls for a boat large enough to carry a fleet of pots. The deeper the water the fewer the pots in a fleet, as, if they are to be hauled by hand, one does not want more than one coming up at a time. In summertime when there is a sure market for crabs, many more pots will be laid and bigger boats needed to manage the larger fleets. Lobsters which have a ready market at any time have been overfished and apart from a few out-of-the-way places such as north Wales and the Outer Isles they are rarely the main catch. The attraction of potting lies in that it has the least initial outlay of any type of fishing and can be worked from the smallest boats. This was specially true when the pots were made locally, as occasionally they still are, from material freely available. The same pots will generally serve for both crabs and lobsters. Prawns, eels and whelks however are taken in specially shaped traps.

The most demanding requirement of pot work is the desirability of serving the fleets the day after they have been laid. If bad weather intervenes, the catch gets away and the pots are broken. Crab and lobster pots are best laid on rocky bottoms, which may be close to cliffs, ledges and outlying rocks. A pot boat needs to be handy in broken water and able to look after herself while the crew clears and rebaits the pots. When continuing bad weather prevents pots being laid, shellfish may still be taken during lulls using hoop nets or variations of the baited net, which have to be hauled before the quarry has time to abandon its meal. The crudest form of this trap is the eel blob, which is just a bundle of worsted and worms; but once the eel has bitten into it with its long incurving teeth, it is unable to let go. It is hard to see how potting influences shape, when round the coast it is carried out in every kind and size of craft. Generally these are small local types from creeks and beaches, with larger less localised kinds of vessel from the harbours. This suggests that, apart from the seaworthiness, stability and handiness expected from most inshore working boats, it is landscape rather than the work that is the principal factor.

The boat using baited hooks has very similar requirements, with the reservation that long lines with a great number of hooks are laid mostly on flat bottoms in usually more open water. The size of the boat was governed by how far she had to go, the number of lines carried, and, once again, whether she was beach- or harbour-based. As large boats tend to be too heavy to be hauled up to their lines without breaking them, small boats were carried for hauling. The classic example of this was the lining for halibut and cod off Greenland, Iceland and Newfoundland between the sixteenth and twentieth centuries. Though much has been written about the dories used by the French, American and Portuguese fishermen, little is known about the British boats used for the same purpose in these fisheries. The Parrett flatner, which was superficially like the dory, was used in a different way, serving stake-nets in the estuary and for dip-netting in the river, but not as far as can be found out for ship-borne long-lining (p 209). Shorter varieties of long lines were set by crabbers from isolated bases to catch pot-bait as well as food though harbour-based ones could buy the unmarketable fish. As much of the bait for lines had to be found along the shore by the women and children, the siting of stations close to sources of bait was an advantage. Long-liners based on harbours looked partly to the railway as a supplier of bait, the whelks used in Yorkshire for example coming from north Norfolk. The long line was doubly vulnerable to the trawl, as not only could it be dredged up by the trawl, but also the fish stocks were more likely to be exhausted by this more effective method.

Hand lines with relatively few baited hooks may be worked from any sound sort of boat, whether in the form of a bottom line or a troll. The former is a weighted line lowered from a stopped boat. Depending on the place and season this can be a selective method of fishing if the bait and hook arrangement is right. It is a subsistence rather than commercial method. The latter, also called whiffing, has baited hooks or lures towed astern and weighted to run at a set distance below the surface. Apart from knowing where to fish, this requires less skill, and, equipped with line haulers, this is a successful way of inshore fishing for mackerel. Both bottom and towed lines can be attached to rods but not by professional fishermen in this country as they are too unproductive and fragile for everyday work. Where boats are used for giving amateurs with rods a day's fishing, it is observed that as large an open space as possible is provided aft.

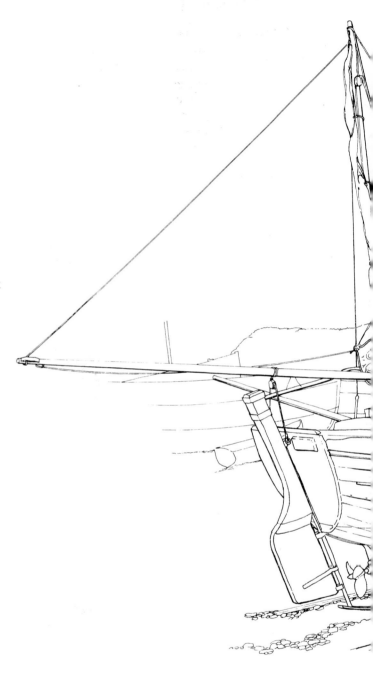

Fig 24: Hastings beach punt with power block.

4.

Personality of boatmen

The shape of boats must depend a great deal upon the personality of the men who build and use them. As it is unusual to find a boatbuilder who is also a part-time user, these two kinds of boatmen may be considered separately. Another variable is the racial background and this affects both builders and users. This aspect, which is tempered by local history and landscape, shows itself in dialect, religion, buildings and occupation; but, like boats, these have to be looked at in depth if anything of value is to emerge. It is unlikely that any one person could do this properly for the whole of Britain, much less in this one chapter. Nevertheless, the different natures and racial backgrounds of the boatmen were evident in my journey round Britain.

Britain has been an island for so long that most of its population changes must have been by sea. These changes are still taking place, but how and when the early ones occurred is far from clear. Some of the new races came from different climates and landscapes, some in flight and some to rule. In so far as their boats are concerned the reactions of the boatmen to their changed circumstances must be considered. It should not be assumed that, because they only built in a certain way at their place of origin, they would continue to do so wherever they settled.

BOATBUILDERS
The builder of a boat can no more be said to come before her user than a hen before an egg. Not forgetting that a boat is the outcome of user's experience, the personality of boatbuilders will be discussed first, as one has to start somewhere.

There are three ways material can be formed into a vessel: reduction, junction and moulding. Each can be used on its own or in various combinations and degrees with the others. Reduction, or cutting a large piece down to a smaller one of the desired shape, though no longer much used for making dug-outs, is still the way of shaping stems, aprons and deadwoods. Junction, or assembling a number of small parts to form a larger unit, can be done by weaving or fastening them together. Weaving implies the pre-stressing of components so that their attempt to regain their unstressed shapes holds them together. Fastening implies the components do not have to be stressed for assembly but depend entirely upon bolts, lashings, fits, mortices or glues to hold them in place. Together they cover a wide range of structures from baskets to edge-positioned plank boats. Edge-fastened plank boats often rely on a degree of pre-stressing of their strakes and timbers for resilience, so are a combination of the two techniques. Moulding, or altering the shape of a material but not its volume, is employed by potters, smiths and founders. The difference here lies in the heat needed to make the material first malleable then stable. This had not been used in this country as a way of making boats until the recent introduction of GRP and ferro-cement. GRP involves the subsequent junction of moulded components and internal strength members and ferro-cement the preliminary weaving and fastening of the reinforcing frame, so neither are examples of pure moulding.

As described above briefly, the various races introduced and practised these basic techniques when fashioning stone, wood, fibres, clay and metal into buildings or implements. To this extent they are more or less inherent in a boatbuilders make-up. It rests largely with the boatbuilder which he will choose to use, tempered of course by his own abilities, local practice, materials to hand and the requirements of the user.

There have to be enough boats in a given area to justify a full-time boatbuilder. With less, there are still several ways of getting boats built. If the local work and conditions combine to require a large or elaborate design, then the prospective user will have to look outside his normal area for a builder. If however the boat is quite small and simple he has a choice. Either he can build his own boat if his seasonal programme allows or he can go to his local woodworker, who will be able to build such a boat as well as a roof truss, wheel barrow or a coffin if necessary.

Given sufficient work, one-man firms are common, both for building and repairing boats. This boatbuilder is able to carry out all the operations involved, unaided except for an occasional second pair of hands, which may belong to his wife, neighbour or new owner. In addition to building the single-hander has to supply his own materials and manage the funds and paperwork of his business, the latest of which nowadays can be considerable. The boatbuilder may have learnt his trade either as an apprentice or he may have taught himself. This is not unusual and occurs when a boat user, finding himself in an area without a boatbuilder, first does his own repairs and then progresses from undertaking repairs for others to building a boat completely.

A boat can be built with no more than a chest full of hand tools. This allows a single-hander to be quite mobile and up to the end of the last century it was common for young men just out of their time to move from yard to yard often agreeing to build a number of boats on contract. However a shed with a bench and some power tools will double the boatbuilder's output without any reduction of quality. Though the one-man firm with such low overheads is potentially profitable, it lacks the flexibility to cope with sickness, too much or too little work. This together with ambition, sons to place and the slowing down that comes in old age can persuade the single-hander to become a master.

The master boatbuilder is one who while supervising others still works with his tools. As well as employing journeymen he may take on a lad and show him how to build every part of a boat. When the lad is fully trained he may have to leave and strike out on his own if the firm cannot afford the full wages of a man. In either case a new lad will have to be found as a replacement. Many small yards depend only on apprentices for their skilled labour with perhaps one unskilled man, often a retired seaman, for general yard duties.

Larger yards will employ both apprentices and journeymen, but as their numbers grow the master boatbuilder will have to spend a greater proportion of his time finding the work, supplying materials, overseeing the output and dealing with customers.

There are still many firms like this, seldom static but in a state of growth or decay. They seem to reach a critical point when the master has to decide whether to stop using his tools altogether so as to concentrate on managing his firm as a business. If he does not the yard will stagnate and his better hands will move on. If he becomes a successful manager, the boatyard will become like a shipyard with the men specialising more and more in certain aspects of the work and becoming less capable of building a complete boat. For these reasons yards are constantly appearing and shutting down, so that it is rare to find many that survive under one name for more than three generations.

For the most part boatbuilders are individualistic, working as they do alone or apart. It is hard to recall a single instance of a boatbuilder praising another's work, unless it was that of the master who taught him or, more rarely, of an outstanding apprentice. This is not through any lack of generosity of spirit on the part of the boatbuilder, but seems to grow out of a need to believe that the way that he builds a boat is the ideal way, with the rider that any other way is not. In pursuit of this ideal, boatbuilders are less set against change than is sometimes claimed. What really governs how a boatbuilder works is what he can sell and whether the boat will earn the reputation that will bring him more customers. There are very few shoddy boatbuilders, as such yards seldom last for long. If the designs of working boats have changed so slowly, it is because of the reluctance of the users to rely upon anything that has not already shown itself safe throughout many years of service.

A boatbuilder leads a comparatively regular life, and as he works for the most part indoors he can expect to see a predictable amount of progress when he knocks off work at the end of the day. A builder's skills are manual and are based on procedures the scope of which can be measured by the range of boats he is prepared to build. He will have an exact idea in his mind's eye of what the finished boat will be like. Once he has chosen a design and started, the work must proceed to plan and any departures from it can only be minor ones.

BOAT USERS

The man who has to work in the completed boat leads a very different existence, and needs another set of qualities to do so successfully. A fisherman, in particular, is not often able to say just what he will be doing even a few nights or days ahead. Even when he can, there is no way of telling whether he will catch many fish, or if he were to, whether there will be a good market for them. His skills are less ordered and depend on his knowledge of how fish are affected as the seasons, weather and grounds change. Even though electronic aids help him to locate and catch fish, they cannot tell him where to look in the first place.

The uncertainties of the occupation seems to act as both an attraction and a deterrent to becoming and remaining a fisherman and this helps to indicate the sort of men they are. Each time they set out, there is a chance of a catch that will pay well and another that there will be no catch or one that may have to be dumped. Irrespective of whether the boat is singly or collectively owned, it is probable that a large proportion of the capital used to purchase it was in the form of loans, so a bad season can end in dispossession. With a run of good catches loans can be paid off and steps taken to move up to a better boat. While a readiness to take such chances appear to be an essential part of a fisherman, he is not prepared to take any chances when it comes to the seaworthiness of his boat. Though much less so now than in the days of sail, sea-fishing still carries considerable risks from severe weather and other shipping, causing loss of gear, vessels and life. A fisherman needs stamina, strength, adaptability and dexterity. There seems to be a higher proportion of big men, especially those in boats that have to be rowed, than in any other industry. Not unlike farmers, fishermen are wary of strangers and are slow to admit to a good season. They tend to be superstitious and to follow a code of behaviour, much of which would not be acceptable on land. While they are prepared as lifeboatmen to risk their own lives to save those of others, they have a more flexible attitude towards other people's waterborne property, almost bordering on piracy. While all but a few respect what belongs to the other local fishermen, there is a sliding scale which operates adversely for foreigners, amateurs and divers. Commercial fishing boats and yachts are seldom found sharing the same harbour or part of it.

The eclipse of sail was accompanied by a fall-off in the number of fishermen, both the older ones whose hard-earned skills became redundant and the younger ones who could see no future in such a hard life at that time. Since the Second World War, however, there has been a steady return to fishing, which attracted men with qualities described above rather than those with paper qualifications. The life is far less hide-bound than most others, with the possibility but no certainty of prosperity, and this attracts men who probably could not progress beyond being a labourer ashore.

With hovellers and watermen a rarity, most boatmen now are fishermen. Like the boatbuilders they can vary from part-time to full-time and from those that employ to the employed. The part-timers, of whom the crofter-fishermen is the classic example, may be a landed farmer who keeps one or two boats for seasonal fishing or transport, or, at the other extreme, a fisherman, who works a small plot. A growing section of part-timers have no land, but instead work in factories and offices often well inland, yet still run boats and market their catch. There are still large numbers of full-timers. Depending upon the size of their vessels and extent of their voyages, some of them have to be in possession of certificates of competency as Skippers or Second Hands before being allowed to go to sea. Conveniently the regulations concern much the same ranges of vessels as exists between boats and ships. If the boat is less than 25 tons (*ie* about 40 to 45ft long) and does not go beyond 61°N, 12°W or 48°30'N, neither the Skipper or Second Hand has to have a certificate. This area is large and includes all the North and Irish Seas, the English Channel, the Atlantic up to the Shetlands and up to 100 miles from the west coast of Ireland. This, it will be noticed, more than covers all the old approaches to Britain except the direct one from Spain. Larger boats up to 50 tons (*ie* about 60ft long) and fishing in the same limits are obliged to carry at least one man with a Second Hand's (Special) Certificate. Larger vessels going outside these limits must have a Skipper and Second Hand with full certificates. To qualify for examination for certificates a man must have had 4 or 5 years' seatime, some of which may be spent in a recognised training establishment or as an indentured apprentice, though the latter is only likely in a deep-sea trawler. In these larger vessels, as in the larger boatbuilding firms, there is a place for some unskilled labour, but with powered winches and complicated gear this is not to be compared with the numbers of pierhead capstan hands that were once needed in sailing drifters[1].

5.

Structure

Both reduction and junction of material will have to be amplified before boat structures can be properly described. The techniques used to build wooden boats vary a lot and many of them have the appearance of being related to much earlier practices. It is not claimed that there has been an unbroken line of development with any of these methods but that under certain conditions, depending upon the materials and skills available to him, a boatbuilder may revert to or re-discover a primitive technique or borrow a practice from another trade, such as a cooper or saddler.

There are several rudimentary types of vessel, which have been listed and described often enough to need no repetition. Of these, this work may ignore bundle boats and inflated skins as being too wet for our cold climate,

ceramic boats as too fragile and bark boats as there are no suitable trees[1]. This leaves only three seminal methods from which the more elaborate boats of this country could have developed. These are skin-covered frames, log rafts and shaped logs. Even in their simplest form each method requires a different set of tools and skills to build.

For building coracles, edged tools are needed to cut withies and wedges to split laths, together with the skill to weave or tie them into the shape of a vessel. The builder has also to be able to preserve and sew animal skins into a covering. For rafts, axes or fires are needed to fell and dress trees into logs, transport is needed for moving them to the water's edge and some means of lashing or pegging them together. For dugouts, edged tools or fire are needed to shape a log inside and out. In spite of the initial

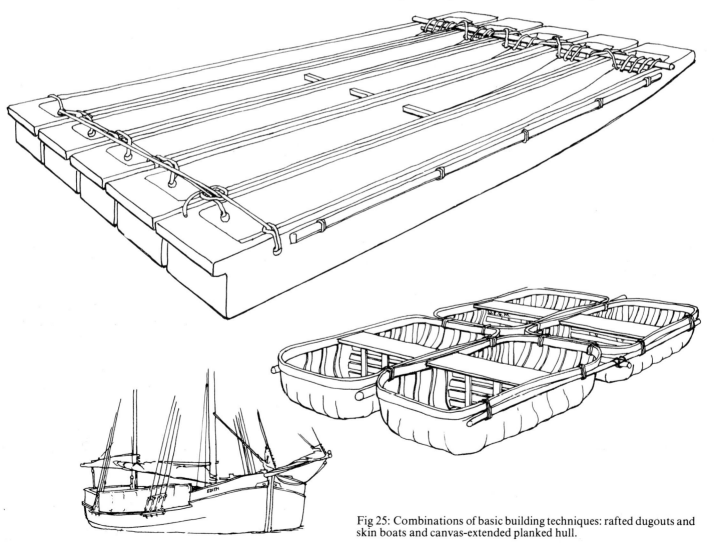

Fig 25: Combinations of basic building techniques: rafted dugouts and skin boats and canvas-extended planked hull.

SHORT GRAIN — NAIL TEST TO INDICATE SAFE ZONE

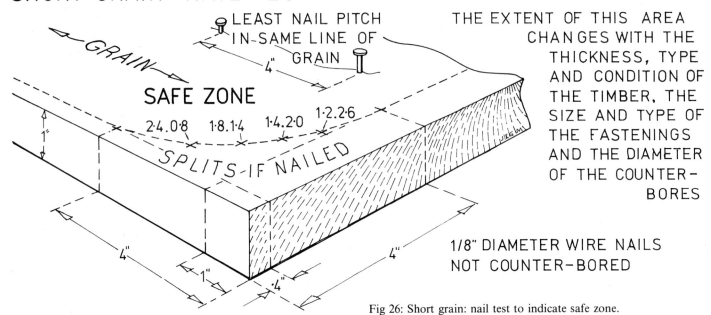

LEAST NAIL PITCH IN SAME LINE OF GRAIN

THE EXTENT OF THIS AREA CHANGES WITH THE THICKNESS, TYPE AND CONDITION OF THE TIMBER, THE SIZE AND TYPE OF THE FASTENINGS AND THE DIAMETER OF THE COUNTER-BORES

GRAIN

SAFE ZONE

2·4·0·8   1·8·1·4   1·4·2·0   1·2·2·6

SPLITS — IF NAILED

1/8" DIAMETER WIRE NAILS NOT COUNTER-BORED

Fig 26: Short grain: nail test to indicate safe zone.

conception being so different, there are similarities between them. There is a common use of fastenings in the first pair, the use of whole logs by the last pair and the realisation of an entire boat with bottom, ends and sides in the first and last methods. In all three, their builders would have been aware that unless both sides were alike, the boat would not run true and thus would be hard to propel. These common features suggest that there is no hard and fast division between them. In Britain all three types and their hybrids have co-existed in the past, just as they still do worldwide. Classifications therefore are for convenience rather than reality.

In their pure forms, the skin boat, raft and dugout are design conceptions limited respectively by size, weight and girth, the last of which gives more stability or freeboard but not both. Long ago, the three seminal methods were taken to their utmost limits, beyond which there was no further progress without combination or addition of new methods. On the Severn side cloths were fitted to open trows and in Poland rafts were made from dugouts[2]. It was, however, the use of planks more than anything else which overcame the inherent limitations of skin boats, rafts and dugouts (Fig 25). Boats built with planks cannot be counted as one of these seminal types, as they are evidently either derivations or combinations of skin boat, raft or dugout practices.

Unlike stone and metal, wood is not homogeneous; although otherwise strong and resilient, it is weak in tension perpendicular to the direction of growth. The discovery that wood splits was probably accidental, and probably an unwelcome one if it occurred while a joint was being fastened. Boatbuilding and many other trades show that splitting can be exploited to turn straight-grained timber into square baulks, flat boards, battens, laths, staves and trenails, thus giving woodworkers a choice of shapes

and structures they could build.

A risk of immediate or subsequent splitting is incurred any time wood is perforated, whether by driving nails or boring for fastening or lashing. It is well known that a nail too close to the butt of a plank or another nail in the same line of grain may start a split, but it may not be appreciated that the safe distance progressively increases as the plank edge is approached. This is because it is not only the length of grain that matters, but also the amount of wood present either side to take up the stresses without undue distortion. Where there is a concentration of stresses and parts to be joined a greater volume of wood is needed if the fastenings are to be adequately spaced (Fig 26). A carpenter instinctively provides this and spaces and bores for his fastenings on the safe side. Once a split forms the stresses concentrate to act on the end of it and this propagates the failure, which though desirable when cleaving, is not when fastening.

Technical advance depends on a good idea working in practice, and this may mean waiting until some other, apparently unrelated, branch of technology has reached a stage when it can be used to overcome an obstacle. Boatbuilding methods may also be put aside for centuries and then re-adopted when a new use is found for them. A coracle cannot be enlarged much beyond the size of a curragh, unless the frame can be strengthened and the skin be made to contribute to the structure's strength. The British skin boat did not develop this way or it might have turned into an edge-positioned plank boat. Instead the new work disciplines necessary to bring this about probably came from abroad in the form of a proven ship design, the carrack. The coracle went on developing slowly and gave rise to other types of boat.

There are building techniques and terms in use, which suggest skin boat practices. The overlapping joint between

Fig 27: Square-ended boat shapes:

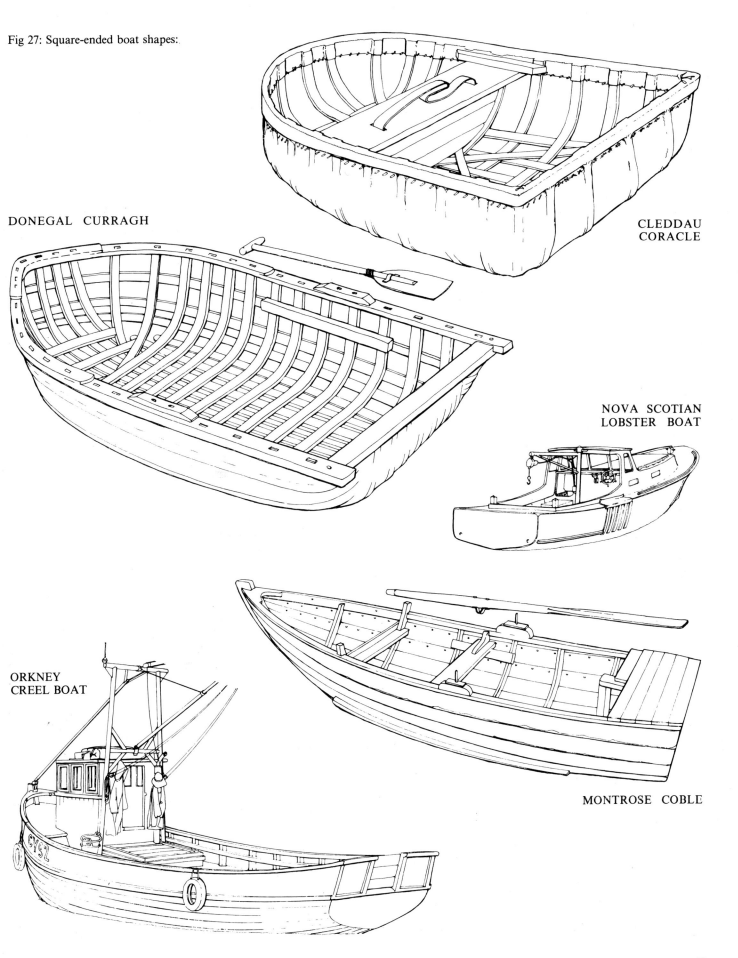

DONEGAL CURRAGH

CLEDDAU CORACLE

NOVA SCOTIAN LOBSTER BOAT

ORKNEY CREEL BOAT

MONTROSE COBLE

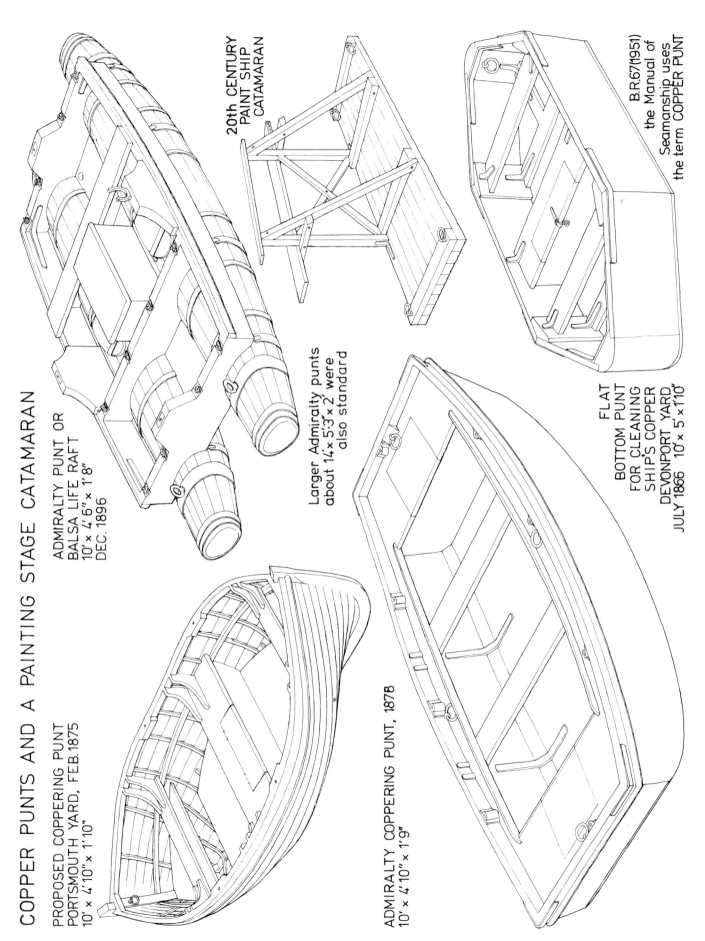

COPPER PUNTS AND A PAINTING STAGE CATAMARAN

ADMIRALTY PUNT OR
BALSA LIFE RAFT
10' × 4'6" × 1'8"
DEC. 1896

20th CENTURY
PAINT SHIP
CATAMARAN

Larger Admiralty punts
about 14' × 5'3" × 2' were
also standard

B.R.67(1951)
the Manual of
Seamanship uses
the term COPPER PUNT

FLAT
BOTTOM PUNT
FOR CLEANING
SHIP'S COPPER
DEVONPORT YARD
JULY 1866 10' × 5' × 1'10"

PROPOSED COPPERING PUNT
PORTSMOUTH YARD, FEB.1875
10' × 4'10" × 1'10"

ADMIRALTY COPPERING PUNT, 1878
10' × 4'10" × 1'9"

Fig 28: Copper punts and painting stage.

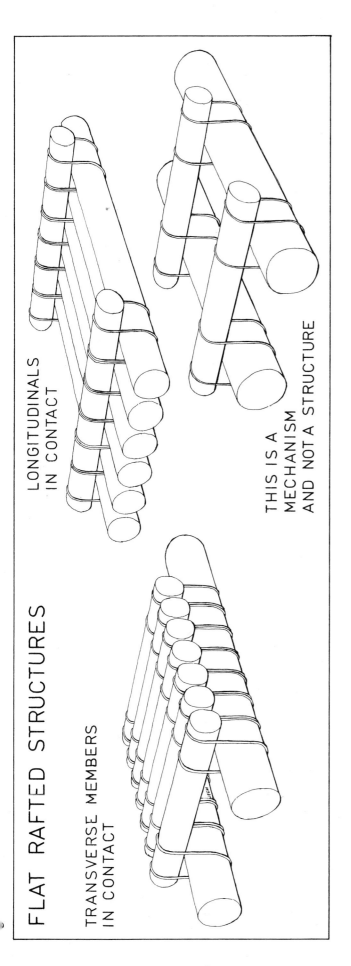

FLAT RAFTED STRUCTURES

LONGITUDINALS IN CONTACT

THIS IS A MECHANISM AND NOT A STRUCTURE

TRANSVERSE MEMBERS IN CONTACT

two planks, the shaping of which is known as 'hemming home' in the south-west of England, and the use of the word 'skin' when talking about the boat's planking are examples of this. The use of flexible steamed timbers in place of solid grown ones became common early in the nineteenth century, and looks like a return to lighter weaving practices. When thin strakes are used for edge-positioned planking, they run slackly and unfairly over their moulds but when the timbers have been bent and nailed in, the whole structure stiffens and the undulations vanish. Apart from the reduced gaps between the longitudinals, the resulting structure is the same as a woven or pinned lath framework. Terms like apron, hood, seam and tuck sound more like the work of a tailor than a carpenter. Some of the ways of working the gunwale of a modern boat have parallels in coracles[3], while the use of struts and bulkheads to distribute local loading will be dealt with later in this chapter. The placing and spacing of ribs, braids and bands in coracles to give strength and hold shape for the least weight at least showed the wooden boatbuilder what could be done even if he did not copy them exactly. Making lobster pots and creels keeps alive many of the coracle builder's skills.

Both the Cleddau coracle and the most primitive of the Donegal curraghs have square almost truncated sterns while their bows are hardly pointed at all[3] (Fig 27). The shape is only slightly different from the Scottish form of the coble. This shape has been further developed into the Orkney creel boat, and was probably the original form of the round bottom lobster boats of the Maritime Provinces described by Greenhill[4]. The framework of some coracles was formed on a mould, a method used by Harold Kimber of Highbridge to build clinker yacht tenders in the 1930s. Ribs and braids in a moulded coracle were no longer woven once metal fastenings became available. The covering, acting more like the cross wires in a braced lattice girder than the stressed skin of a monocoque fuselage, does not add much strength to a skin boat. Some of the lighter plank boats described later are between the two, while some of the recent curraghs are closer to being planked than skin boats, since the covering only prevents the seams from leaking.

The only examples of raft-like vessels that come to mind today are the massive 'cats' placed between the thin side plating of modern warships and the dockyard wall and the smaller ones used as paint stages. 'Cat' is short for catamaran, which is a fair use of the term as they are made up of several layers of cross-laid baulks bolted together. The service copper punt is another form of raft, being a pair of long casks held apart by a platform on top. It was used for painting boot-topping, hence the name which was handed down from an earlier plank boat[5] (Fig 28).

A raft can be put together in two ways, either as a platform of long logs joined across by a few spaced out short ones, or several long logs spaced apart and joined by many short ones. Either the long or the short logs have to be continuous in order to form a rigid structure and not a

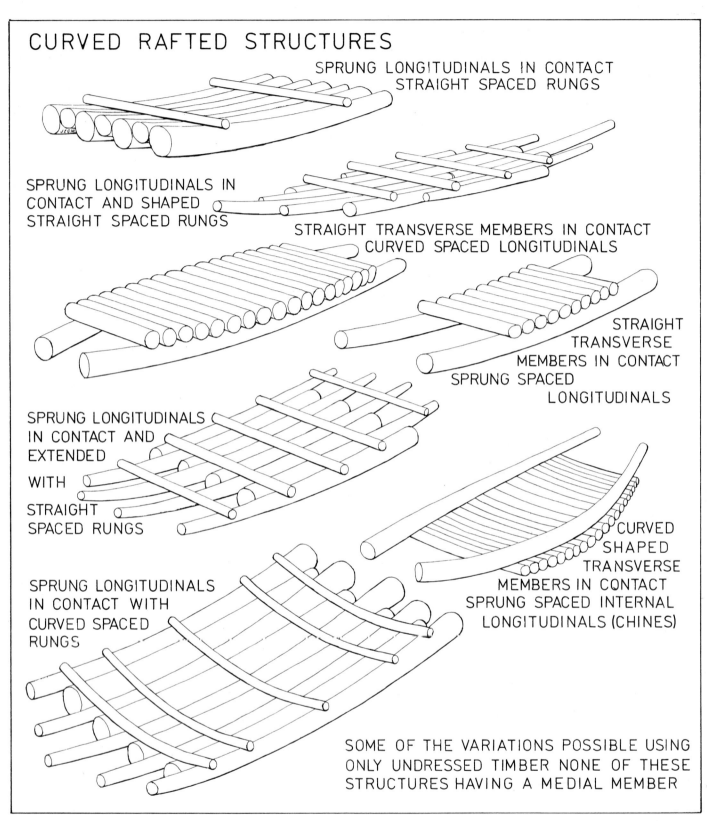

CURVED RAFTED STRUCTURES

SPRUNG LONGITUDINALS IN CONTACT
STRAIGHT SPACED RUNGS

SPRUNG LONGITUDINALS IN
CONTACT AND SHAPED
STRAIGHT SPACED RUNGS

STRAIGHT TRANSVERSE MEMBERS IN CONTACT
CURVED SPACED LONGITUDINALS

STRAIGHT
TRANSVERSE
MEMBERS IN CONTACT
SPRUNG SPACED
LONGITUDINALS

SPRUNG LONGITUDINALS
IN CONTACT AND
EXTENDED

WITH

STRAIGHT
SPACED RUNGS

CURVED
SHAPED
TRANSVERSE
MEMBERS IN CONTACT
SPRUNG SPACED INTERNAL
LONGITUDINALS (CHINES)

SPRUNG LONGITUDINALS
IN CONTACT WITH
CURVED SPACED
RUNGS

SOME OF THE VARIATIONS POSSIBLE USING
ONLY UNDRESSED TIMBER NONE OF THESE
STRUCTURES HAVING A MEDIAL MEMBER

Fig 30: Curved rafted structures

Opposite:
Fig 31: Narrow boat – mid-section.

Fig 32: Thames sailing barge – mid-section

lattice, which is a mechanism. The first arrangement uses the most wood so would be a better way to move timber, while the second uses less and is preferable if the raft is to carry a load (Fig 29).

Flat rafts have very little reserve of buoyancy for their total weight, which makes them large and cumbersome for the small extra load they can carry. Though they may be suitable for sea crossings, they perform better on rivers where the traffic is downstream. Fig 30 shows how the natural shape of longitudinal logs can be used to alter the outline of a raft, especially when it is the short logs which are continuous. If the joining surfaces of the logs are fayed the raft will be drier, more compact and easier to handle.

Both these raft arrangements are found in flat bottom plank boat construction, the use of continuous longitudinals being the usual method found in this country. The longitudinals are boards, normally edge-positioned by a number of transverse members, which will be called 'rungs' to differentiate them from 'floors', which are associated with keels and composite frame structures. The continuous transverse arrangement, where the bottom is cross-planked under chines, with or without a keelson along the centre line, is uncommon in Britain, but it is found in the once numerous narrow canal boats[6] (Fig 31). Here the lowest strake of the side accepts the end fastenings of the bottom planks and so acts as a chine as well. After the sides the next important longitudinal strength member is the keelson, which is not much greater in section than one of the bottom planks and, like them, rests flat on one side. The planks of flat bottoms are thicker than they would have to be in round bottom hulls. This is because they provide all the strength in one direction or the other and take the chine fastenings in short grain.

Although she does not have a true flat bottom from end to end, the Thames sailing barge is an example of a rafted structure (Fig 32). Both the inner and outer bottoms are planked longitudinally, sharing the same set of rungs between them. The outer bottom has a central plank which is almost a keel as it may be rebated for, and thicker than, the planks on either side of it. The inner and outer bottoms have chines outside the bottom planking. The outer chine is not much larger in section than the side plank, but the inner chine is twice as thick, while the keelson is twice as thick again. The side frames are secured between these two chines and the side structure is a repetition of that of the bottom.

Longitudinally curved or sprung flat bottoms can be worked in either type of rafted bottom by using curved logs or planks. Transversely curved or cambered bottoms are not so easy. In a cross-planked bottom this would call for a considerable number of matched and curved components, and no example can be given. In longitudinally run bottoms, camber can be obtained by fitting curved rungs, and, where planks are used, by placing them so that their annual rings follow the desired arc. Natural warping can be induced if the outside of the plank is kept wet while the inside is heated over a fire, as was once the practice

when building a Parrett flatner.

The combination of spring and camber produces a dished bottom, the component longitudinal planks of which have the same outline as a barrel stave. A dished raft, even if the curvature is slight, is drier and easier to propel and turn than a flat one. If correctly pre-shaped, quite thin planks can be sprung and held in position by their rungs to give a dished shape. The locked-in stresses in both the planks and rungs combine to form a rigid structure. The fragment of a small boat found close to the ancient vessel in the river Rother in 1822 used this construction[7].

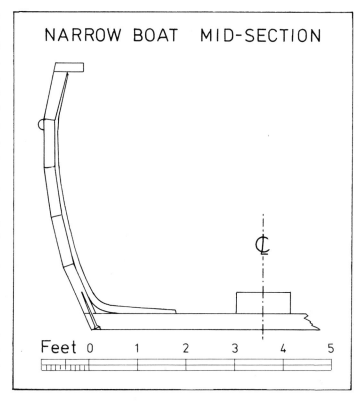

NARROW BOAT MID-SECTION

Feet 0 1 2 3 4 5

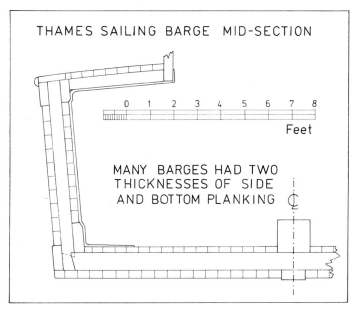

THAMES SAILING BARGE MID-SECTION

0 1 2 3 4 5 6 7 8

Feet

MANY BARGES HAD TWO THICKNESSES OF SIDE AND BOTTOM PLANKING

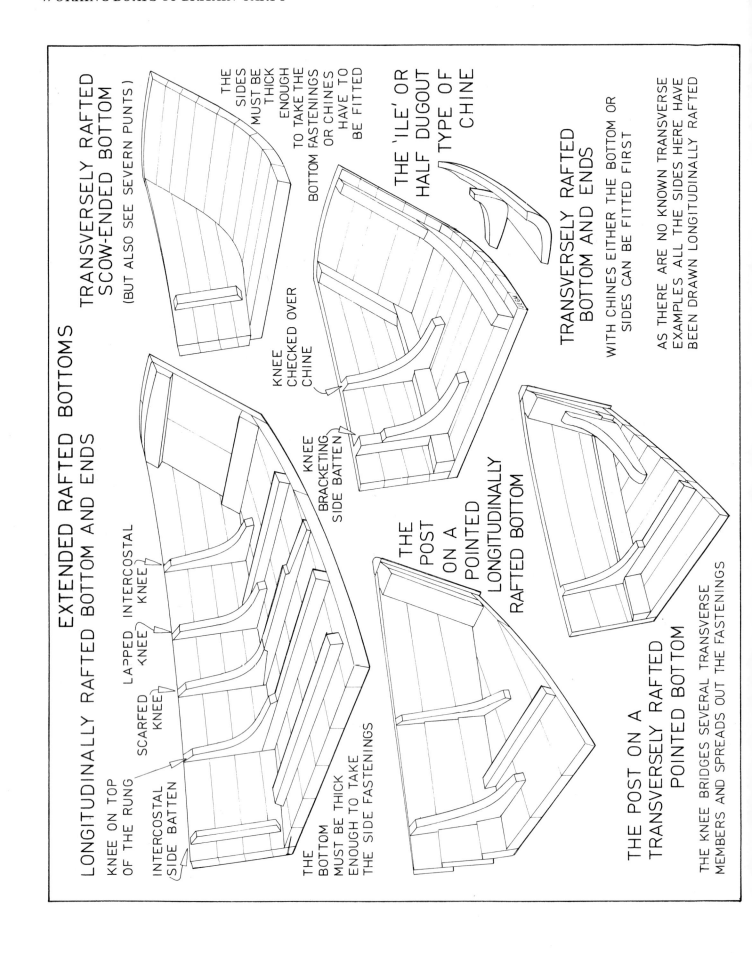

EXTENDED RAFTED BOTTOMS

TRANSVERSELY RAFTED SCOW-ENDED BOTTOM
(BUT ALSO SEE SEVERN PUNTS)

THE SIDES MUST BE THICK ENOUGH TO TAKE THE BOTTOM FASTENINGS OR CHINES HAVE TO BE FITTED

THE 'ILE' OR HALF DUGOUT TYPE OF CHINE

TRANSVERSELY RAFTED BOTTOM AND ENDS

WITH CHINES EITHER THE BOTTOM OR SIDES CAN BE FITTED FIRST

AS THERE ARE NO KNOWN TRANSVERSE EXAMPLES ALL THE SIDES HERE HAVE BEEN DRAWN LONGITUDINALLY RAFTED

KNEE CHECKED OVER CHINE

KNEE BRACKETING SIDE BATTEN

LONGITUDINALLY RAFTED BOTTOM AND ENDS

KNEE ON TOP OF THE RUNG

LAPPED INTERCOSTAL KNEE

INTERCOSTAL KNEE

SCARFED KNEE

INTERCOSTAL SIDE BATTEN

THE BOTTOM MUST BE THICK ENOUGH TO TAKE THE SIDE FASTENINGS

THE POST ON A POINTED LONGITUDINALLY RAFTED BOTTOM

THE POST ON A TRANSVERSELY RAFTED POINTED BOTTOM

THE KNEE BRIDGES SEVERAL TRANSVERSE MEMBERS AND SPREADS OUT THE FASTENINGS

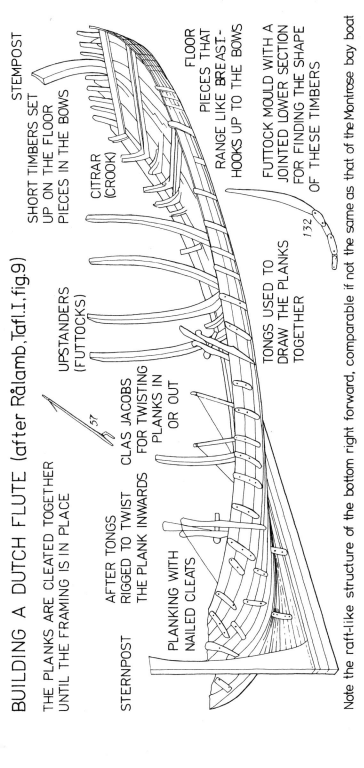

BUILDING A DUTCH FLUTE (after Rålamb,Tafl.I,fig.9)

THE PLANKS ARE CLEATED TOGETHER
UNTIL THE FRAMING IS IN PLACE

STEMPOST

SHORT TIMBERS SET
UP ON THE FLOOR
PIECES IN THE BOWS

CITRAR
(CROOK)

FLOOR
PIECES THAT
RANGE LIKE BREAST-
HOOKS UP TO THE BOWS

FUTTOCK MOULD WITH A
JOINTED LOWER SECTION
FOR FINDING THE SHAPE
OF THESE TIMBERS

UPSTANDERS
(FUTTOCKS)

CLAS JACOBS
FOR TWISTING
PLANKS IN
OR OUT

TONGS USED TO
DRAW THE PLANKS
TOGETHER

AFTER TONGS
RIGGED TO TWIST
THE PLANK INWARDS

PLANKING WITH
NAILED CLEATS

STERNPOST

Note the raft-like structure of the bottom right forward, comparable if not the same as that of the Montrose bay boat

Opposite:
Fig 33: Extended rafted bottoms.

Above:
Fig 34: Rafted into round bottom: building a Dutch flute (after Rålamb).

A raft has no need of a centreline keel to increase its strength as thicker bottom planking would do this more efficiently. If a flat bottom has keel it will be for some other reason, such as distributing a local loading, taking wear on beaching or for the attachment of further components. Nor do pure rafts need pointed ends for hydrodynamic reasons, as, floating as they do so close to the surface, more flow takes place under the hull than around it. Pointed ends are more difficult to work than springing square ones clear of the water in a cross-planked raft.

Both types of raft are improved by the addition of ends and sides. This is done is four ways, depending upon whether the raft was longitudinal or transverse in the first place, and, then, whether a raft or dugout practice followed. Fastening an end or side to a square-ended raft of either sort presents no problems as long grain is available for fastenings in either the upper or lower timbers. It is usual to rake square-ends to help them pass over waves. If an end is pointed, an additional upright member or post is needed for the plank-end fastenings. This is simpler to arrange in a longitudinally rafted bottom than a transverse one with chines, where there are more timbers coming together, making it necessary to fit knees (Fig 33).

If raft techniques are used for the sides, longitudinal strakes with transverse stiffeners permit curvature in two planes. These side stiffeners are generally integral, with a knee acting as a bracket where the bottom and the side meet at an angle. The horizontal limb of the knee can lie on top of or be scarfed into the end of a rung, or be alongside it or part-way between a pair of them. In the first case some hold depth is lost, whilst the second and third involve a concentration of fastenings; the last, however, spaces the fastenings well and adds to the battening and strength of the bottom.

There are two, what appear to be dugout-inspired, devices used to extend a rafted bottom. The first is an L-shaped chine, which is like a dugout split in two. This has been recently termed an 'ile'[8]. A full length ile can furnish a corner for the bottom, side and each end, though scarfs may be necessary. Though effective, iles are extravagant in their use of labour and material. The heavy chine-like bilge strakes (*meginhufr*) of some Scandinavian finds come close to being a form of ile[9].

Even with the chine angle fully retained, an extended raft may have a variety of shapes with square and pointed ends and sprung bottoms. With a dished bottom and curved sides, it is even possible to have a fully round bottom form[10] (Fig 34). As well as knees, bulkheads and decks are used to strengthen these angular hulls. A flat bottom with sides and ends can be loaded much deeper than a raft, but this makes her harder to move. Several things are done to improve this; the flat bottom is narrowed, the sides flared, the ends sharpened and the dish of the bottom increased, all of which tend to reduce capacity and increase draft. In the end it is hard to realise that boat such as this is based on a rafted structure.

There is ample evidence that dugout techniques are still

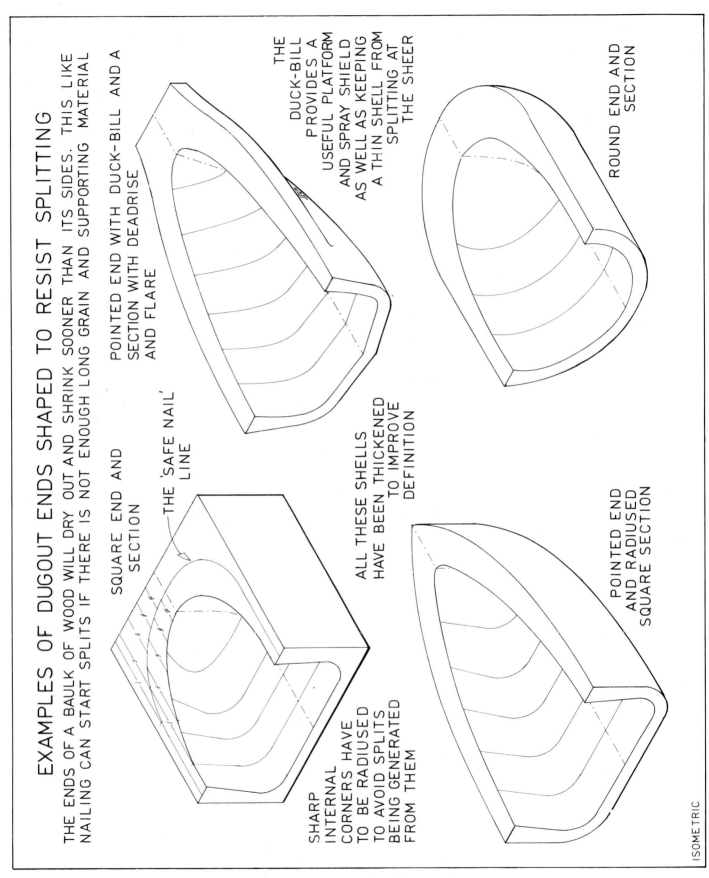

EXAMPLES OF DUGOUT ENDS SHAPED TO RESIST SPLITTING

THE ENDS OF A BAULK OF WOOD WILL DRY OUT AND SHRINK SOONER THAN ITS SIDES. THIS LIKE NAILING CAN START SPLITS IF THERE IS NOT ENOUGH LONG GRAIN AND SUPPORTING MATERIAL

POINTED END WITH DUCK-BILL AND A SECTION WITH DEADRISE AND FLARE

THE DUCK-BILL PROVIDES A USEFUL PLATFORM AND SPRAY SHIELD AS WELL AS KEEPING A THIN SHELL FROM SPLITTING AT THE SHEER

ROUND END AND SECTION

SQUARE END AND SECTION

THE 'SAFE NAIL' LINE

ALL THESE SHELLS HAVE BEEN THICKENED TO IMPROVE DEFINITION

SHARP INTERNAL CORNERS HAVE TO BE RADIUSED TO AVOID SPLITS BEING GENERATED FROM THEM

POINTED END AND RADIUSED SQUARE SECTION

ISOMETRIC

Fig 35: Dugout ends that resist splitting.

Opposite:
Fig 36: Planked boat and expanded dugout, related central structures.

used in boatbuilding – mainly for components that have to be cut to shape from the solid. The resemblance is strong in parts which have been hollowed out in one or more planes or shaped to form a curved portion of the backbone or shell. Dugout thinking is less apparent in some transverse members that cross the keel to maintain the shape of the bottom.

Though both rafts and dugouts start as logs, they make use of them in quite a different way. In a raft the log is used as a module to produce a variety of shapes and sizes; in a dugout it is a blank to be cut into any shape. The size of the blank limits the boat's dimensions, but not her shape. On top of this the dugout builder must have a greater knowledge about the properties of wood than the raft assembler.

A plain log is not even a satisfactory flotation much less a boat. Being round it offers no resistance to rolling. As the centres of buoyancy and gravity are always one above the other, there can be no righting moment. Even if a man rode a log like a bicycle and put up with the wet and the cold, there would be little useful he could do with it. Whether it was a series of accidents or deduction that led Man to hollow out a log, it was a stroke of genius as it gave him a vessel that had both capacity and stability. Tapering the ends and removing as much wood as possible were improvements that led to splits and shapes had to be found that would resist splitting (Fig 35). While these have no relevance any longer, the shapes that worked well then still look right now, though they may be unsuitable to reproduce in GRP, ferro-cement or cold-moulding.

The great classic authors of books about boats have described how dugouts can be expanded beyond their limited beams[11]. This technique involves care in the choice of timber, knowledge of its behaviour and strict process control. Once mastered, this is one of the more elegant boatbuilding methods. Sadly, it is like a clipper's skysail or a turbo-supercharger on a piston engine, in that it is a clear indication that the limit of the design conception is close. In this case it is the limit of what can be done with just one piece of wood. What now concerns us are the pieces of wood that had to be left in an expanded dugout to keep her spread out. If one observes how the garboards of a plank boat are held upright at each end while being forced outwards by the floors in the body of the boat, one realises that this resembles the spreaders in a dugout more than the rungs on a raft (Fig 36).

The expanded dugout, like the dished raft, is only part way towards a fully-formed hull as both lack sides. The dugout has to undergo further changes before she has these and there are several possibilities. Strakes can be added to the sheer, the dugout can be split down the middle and planks inserted between the two halves, or it can be divided transversely and rejoined with strakes fore and aft. All these methods have been used, but none recently in Britain; however, clinker planking and chine construction are examples of developments of the first two possibilities.

The struts used to force out the sides of a dugout during expansion are of little permanent use. They exert too concentrated a pressure on the boat's side and will, sooner or later, force a split. To avoid this, floors are fitted snug to the dugout's bottom, where they can still hold the sides apart and distribute any stresses over a greater area of the shell. Not only are these floors less of an obstruction but their weight is lower. Expansion outward reduces freeboard, so more girth is needed to restore the hull's reserve of buoyancy. The use of basket-work and skin would be enough to do this for a boat with paddles, but solid wood becomes essential if the raised sheerline has to

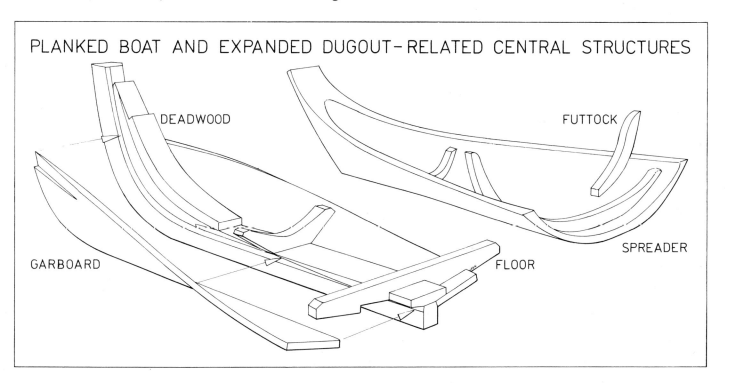

PLANKED BOAT AND EXPANDED DUGOUT–RELATED CENTRAL STRUCTURES

DEADWOOD

FUTTOCK

GARBOARD

FLOOR

SPREADER

pivot oars or locate stays. If the extension were only needed to eke out a deficiency in the log, it would be reasonable to accept flush seams and longer floors, however contrived. A lapped joint, however, offers a more straightforward way of adding a complete strake, and for just one pair ribs are hardly necessary. With greater extensions and loadings some transverse stiffeners are needed, not so much to support the joint but to transmit stresses to the rest of the hull. The placing of these stiffeners is related primarily to the point of application and direction of the loads and secondarily to the existing stiffening in the bottom of the boat.

It is necessary to locate the ends of full length strakes. Mitres at the plank ends give too little wood for safe direct fastening, so a third component has to be fitted, and one that is extended downwards and secured to the rest of the dugout or hull. This is an apron, which differs from the post found in the sharp-ended flat bottom boats. This is because an apron is fastened to the inside of the timbers forming the extremity of the boat, while a post, in addition to being part of that extremity, is also fastened to the bottom or the keel, whichever is present (Fig 37).

Neither the apron or the post is satisfactory alone, if the end grain of the side strakes are left exposed to the

Fig 37: Pointed ends of planked boats – components.

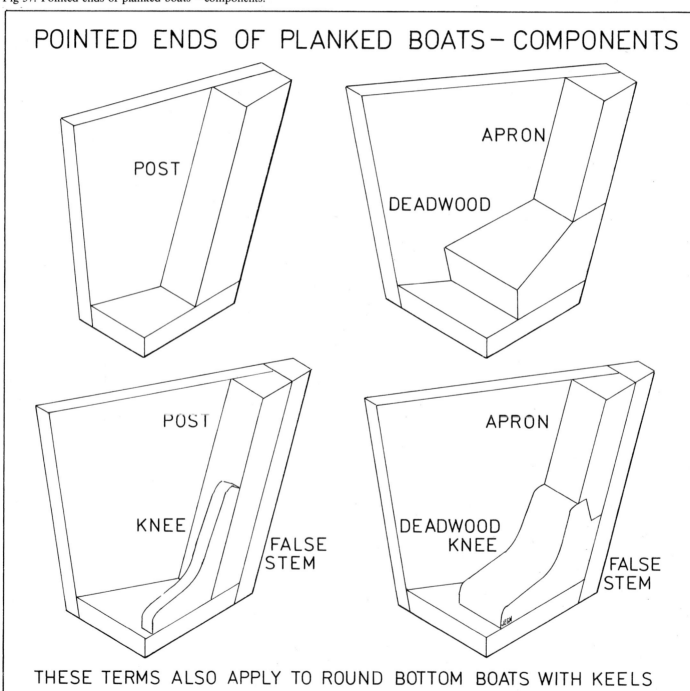

POINTED ENDS OF PLANKED BOATS— COMPONENTS

POST

APRON

DEADWOOD

POST

KNEE

FALSE STEM

APRON

DEADWOOD KNEE

FALSE STEM

THESE TERMS ALSO APPLY TO ROUND BOTTOM BOATS WITH KEELS

Fig 38: Stemposts with rabbets.

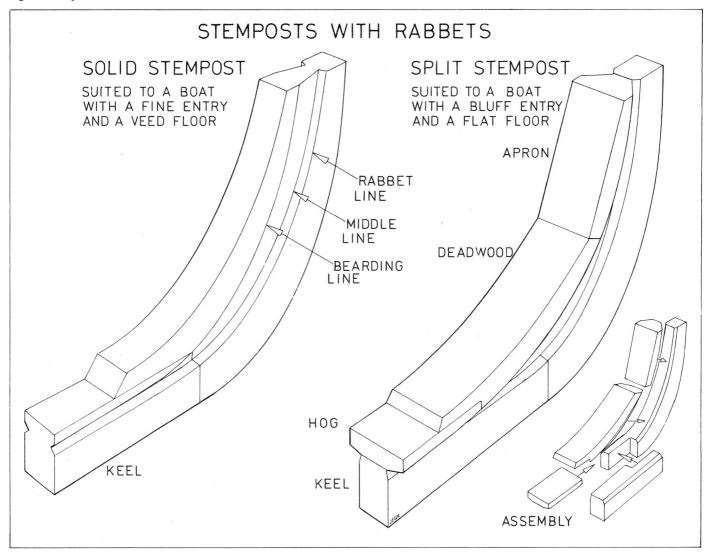

STEMPOSTS WITH RABBETS

SOLID STEMPOST
SUITED TO A BOAT
WITH A FINE ENTRY
AND A VEED FLOOR

SPLIT STEMPOST
SUITED TO A BOAT
WITH A BLUFF ENTRY
AND A FLAT FLOOR

APRON

RABBET
LINE

MIDDLE
LINE

BEARDING
LINE

DEADWOOD

HOG

KEEL

KEEL

ASSEMBLY

weather. In this critical position, being dry and wet in turn, the plank ends are liable to split and rot, especially at the forward end, where it is harder to avoid damage and keep painted. The plank ends can be cut off flush and square with the outer face of the apron or post and a fourth piece of wood fitted externally. A false stem like this provides protection, nips the plank ends and helps fasten them. This serves boats with short lives, like the Parrett flatner, well enough, but hinders plank replacement in more durable types. The disadvantage is overcome by bevelling the inner edge of the false stem to fit plank ends that have been left square. This forms a true rabbet with the apron or post with the join coinciding with the middle line (Fig 38). This kind of stem is called a split rabbet stem and is the commonest form seen in Britain today. It has many advantages: it can be constructed with little or no lofting, crooks for the component parts are not too hard to find and the renewal of any one part need not disturb the others.

If the sides have fair sectional curves, there are two features in extended rafts and dugouts as well as planked keel boats which go a long way to determining the ultimate shape. These are the outline and hemming of the centreline foundation and the profile of the ends. If attempts are made to force wooden strakes away from the natural shape initiated by these surfaces, the fastenings will be strained and the seams, especially near the ends, will open up. This does not stop large angles being employed between strakes, when there are only a few broad ones, if extra care is taken over shaping and hemming. Providing the profile and garboard surfaces relate well to each other, a round bottom boat is more easily stiffened transversely than one with a chine.

Transverse stiffening can be by bent or solid timbers, irrespective of whether the planks are edge-fastened or -positioned. Steam or cold bent timbers may run from one gunwale right across the boat to the other, or from the keel to the gunwale if the angle at the centreline is too acute for bending. Any flexible wood may be used, providing the grain is coaxial and resists splitting. Timbers bend and take nails more readily when hot, but there is a limit to their cross-sectional size. This is a maximum of about $2\frac{1}{4}$in moulded and sided, which is about right for a 45ft MFV.

Solid timbers may be grown or sawn to shape, the use of

Fig 39: Zones of transverse stiffening in a frame.

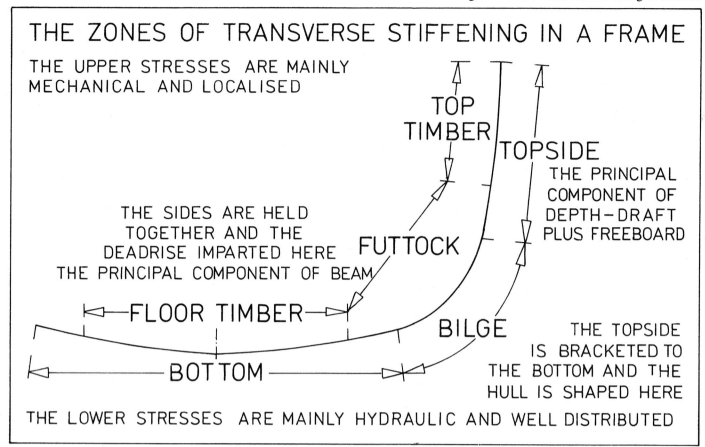

THE ZONES OF TRANSVERSE STIFFENING IN A FRAME

THE UPPER STRESSES ARE MAINLY MECHANICAL AND LOCALISED

TOP TIMBER

TOPSIDE

THE PRINCIPAL COMPONENT OF DEPTH – DRAFT PLUS FREEBOARD

THE SIDES ARE HELD TOGETHER AND THE DEADRISE IMPARTED HERE THE PRINCIPAL COMPONENT OF BEAM

FUTTOCK

FLOOR TIMBER

BILGE

BOTTOM

THE TOPSIDE IS BRACKETED TO THE BOTTOM AND THE HULL IS SHAPED HERE

THE LOWER STRESSES ARE MAINLY HYDRAULIC AND WELL DISTRIBUTED

straight grown stock being acceptable where the curvature is small. If the cross section of the solid timber is small, scarfed joints are difficult to make and, unless the material and workmanship are excellent, become a site for damp spots and rot. If, instead, two components are overlapped along a common station a stronger, if heavier junction, results. Although hit-or-miss frames look untidy, they make good use of the available timber, ventilate well and are easy to fit. Thoughtlessly installed they can lead to weak areas and observation of sound discontinuous framing systems usually shows that a rough plan of action has been followed, which allows for shifts in the plank butts as well as those in the other timbers. The frame components in lofted vessels are mostly worked to one of several more systematic patterns, not unlike one of the bonds used by bricklayers as opposed to the more haphazard random courses. The best known form of framing divides into three overlapping zones, each of which has a special task. The first zone of stiffening is across the bottom or the keel, where the floor timbers maintain the twist in the garboard strakes and hold the two sides of the boat together (Fig 39). In the next zone, that of the bilge, the futtocks connect the bottom to the sides and shape what is usually the most curved part of the hull. The topside zone is stiffened by the top timbers, which, being higher in the structure, need to be kept light. Though the topsides are less subject to hydraulic stresses, they are liable to local stresses from waves, stays, oars and impact. Though top timbers can be placed where these stresses are

predictable, they may also need to be joined together by longitudinal members to distribute shocks that are not. Thicker sheer strakes, gunwales, risings and rubbers (rubbing strakes or bands) are the more common methods of doing this in a boat.

Framing methods are more varied than other parts of British boats. While this is not governed by whether the planking is edge-joined or -positioned, the larger the boat, the heavier the planking and the more continuous the frames will tend to be, and thus the more likely that she will have edge-positioned planks. In addition, there are still preferences for one system or another in certain localities. Fig 40 and the following show the variety of methods in use:

Hit-or-miss
As described above, an apparently haphazard and discontinuous arrangement of sawn or grown solid timbers.

Zoned discontinuous
An organised pattern of discontinuous solid or bent timbers, or mixtures of them in the various zones.

Single continuous frame
From gunwale to gunwale and made up from a number of components all on the same station. The parts may be scarfed, chocked, dowelled, butted or strapped together so that they are disposed in a random, asymmetric or

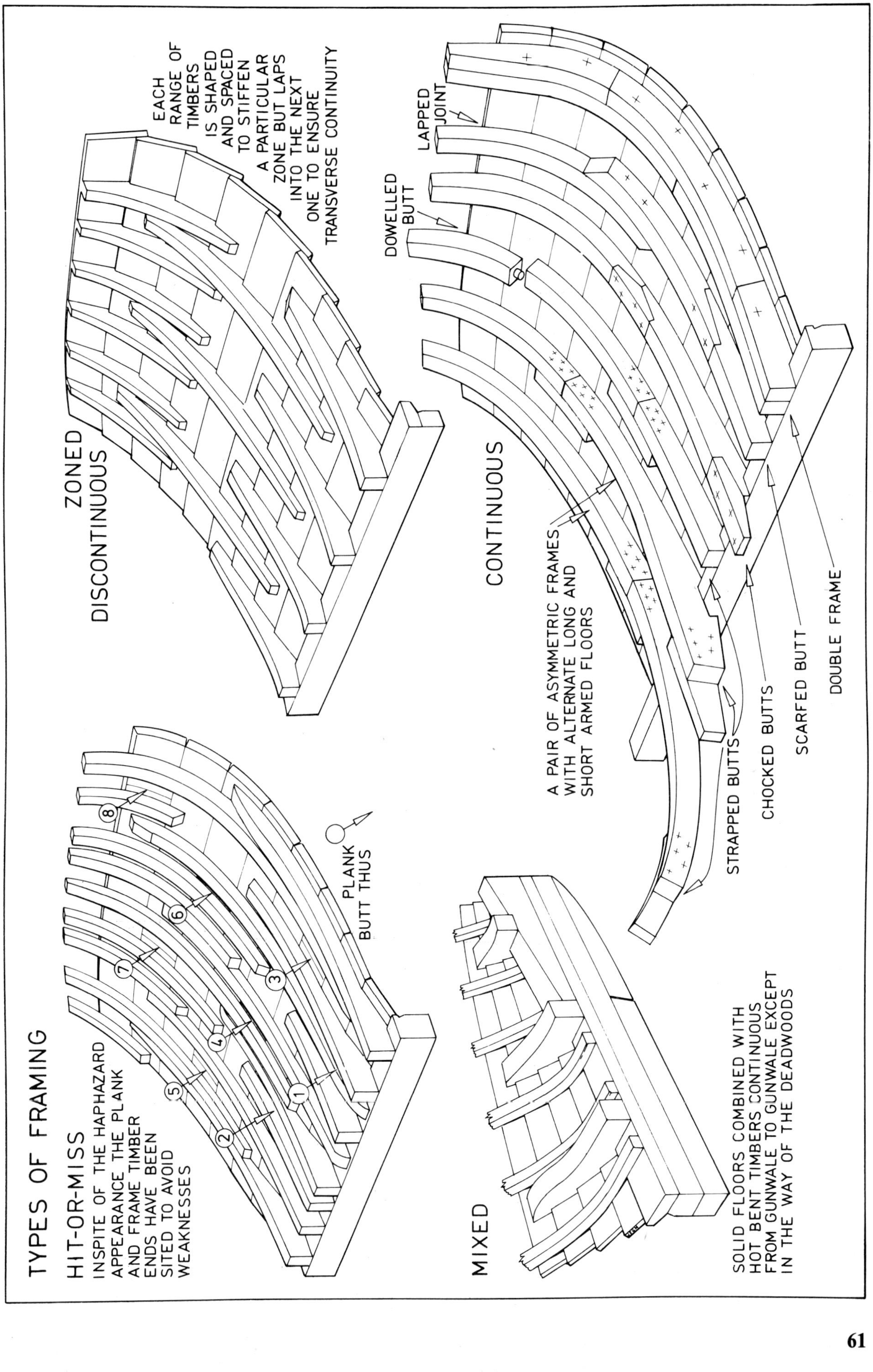

Fig 40: Types of framing.

TYPES OF FRAMING

HIT-OR-MISS

INSPITE OF THE HAPHAZARD
APPEARANCE THE PLANK
AND FRAME TIMBER
ENDS HAVE BEEN
SITED TO AVOID
WEAKNESSES

PLANK
BUTT THUS

ZONED
DISCONTINUOUS

EACH
RANGE OF
TIMBERS
IS SHAPED
AND SPACED
TO STIFFEN
A PARTICULAR
ZONE BUT LAPS
INTO THE NEXT
ONE TO ENSURE
TRANSVERSE CONTINUITY

CONTINUOUS

DOWELLED
BUTT

LAPPED
JOINT

A PAIR OF ASYMMETRIC FRAMES
WITH ALTERNATE LONG AND
SHORT ARMED FLOORS

STRAPPED BUTTS

CHOCKED BUTTS

SCARFED BUTT

DOUBLE FRAME

MIXED

SOLID FLOORS COMBINED WITH
HOT BENT TIMBERS CONTINUOUS
FROM GUNWALE TO GUNWALE EXCEPT
IN THE WAY OF THE DEADWOODS

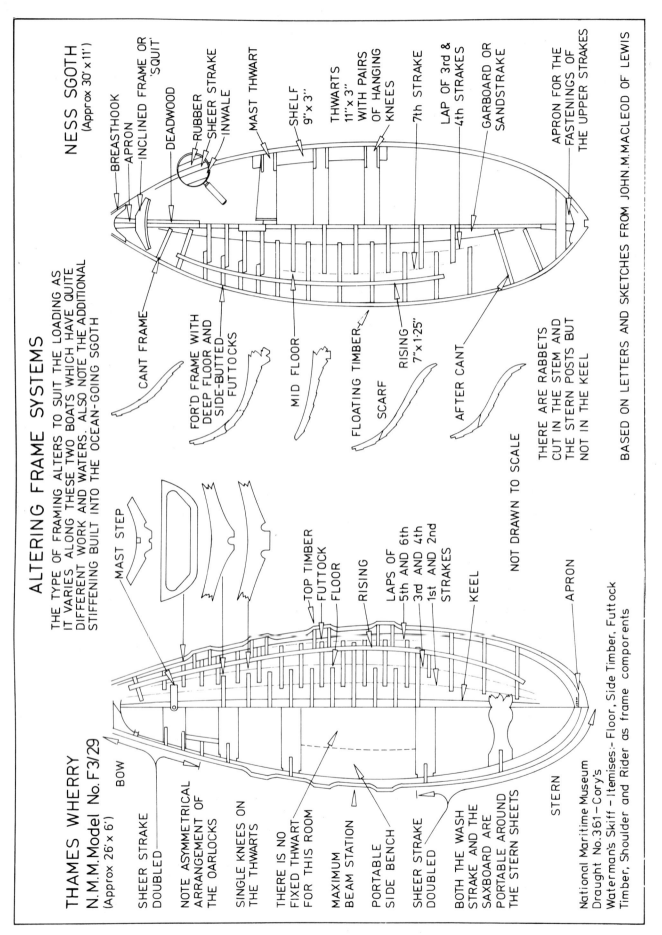

ALTERING FRAME SYSTEMS

THE TYPE OF FRAMING ALTERS TO SUIT THE LOADING AS IT VARIES ALONG THESE TWO BOATS WHICH HAVE QUITE DIFFERENT WORK AND WATERS. ALSO NOTE THE ADDITIONAL STIFFENING BUILT INTO THE OCEAN-GOING SGOTH

NESS SGOTH
(Approx 30′ x 11′)

BREASTHOOK
APRON
INCLINED FRAME OR 'SQUIT'
DEADWOOD
RUBBER
SHEER STRAKE
INWALE
MAST THWART
SHELF 9″ x 3″
THWARTS 11″ x 3″ WITH PAIRS OF HANGING KNEES
7th STRAKE
LAP OF 3rd & 4th STRAKES
GARBOARD OR SANDSTRAKE
APRON FOR THE FASTENINGS OF THE UPPER STRAKES

CANT FRAME
FOR'D FRAME WITH DEEP FLOOR AND SIDE-BUTTED FUTTOCKS
MID FLOOR
FLOATING TIMBER
SCARF
RISING 7″ x 1·25″
AFTER CANT

THERE ARE RABBETS CUT IN THE STEM AND THE STERN POSTS BUT NOT IN THE KEEL

BASED ON LETTERS AND SKETCHES FROM JOHN.M.MACLEOD OF LEWIS

THAMES WHERRY
N.M.M. Model No. F3/29
(Approx 26′ x 6′)

BOW

SHEER STRAKE DOUBLED

NOTE ASYMMETRICAL ARRANGEMENT OF THE OARLOCKS

SINGLE KNEES ON THE THWARTS

THERE IS NO FIXED THWART FOR THIS ROOM

MAXIMUM BEAM STATION

PORTABLE SIDE BENCH

SHEER STRAKE DOUBLED

BOTH THE WASH STRAKE AND THE SAXBOARD ARE PORTABLE AROUND THE STERN SHEETS

National Maritime Museum
Draught No.361-Cory's
Waterman's Skiff – Itemises:- Floor, Side Timber, Futtock Timber, Shoulder and Rider as frame components

MAST STEP

TOP TIMBER
FUTTOCK
FLOOR
RISING
LAPS OF 5th AND 6th 3rd AND 4th 1st AND 2nd STRAKES
KEEL

NOT DRAWN TO SCALE

APRON

STERN

Fig 41: Altering frame systems – Thames wherry and Ness sgoth.

Fig 42: Some stem designs.

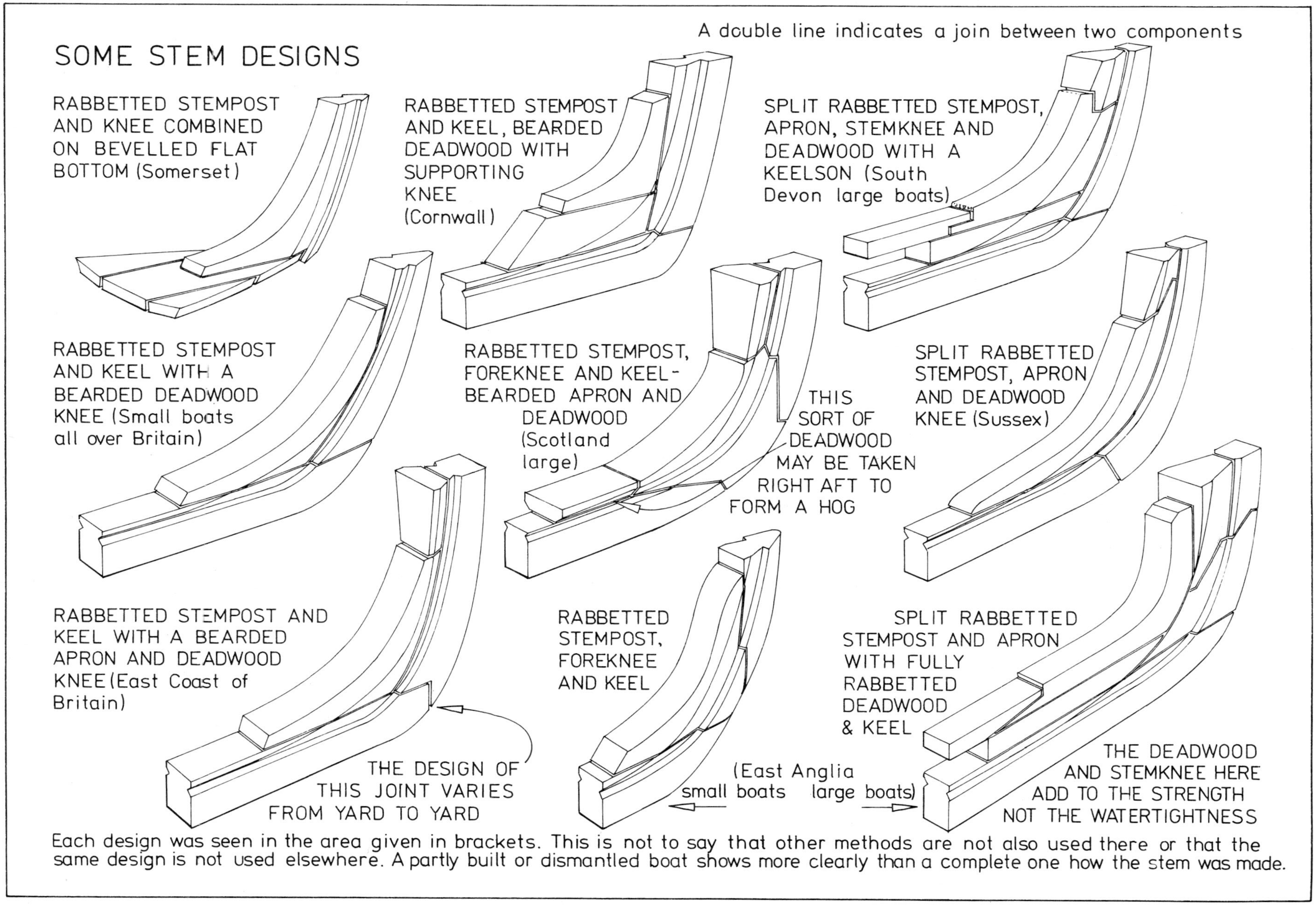

SOME STEM DESIGNS

A double line indicates a join between two components

RABBETTED STEMPOST AND KNEE COMBINED ON BEVELLED FLAT BOTTOM (Somerset)

RABBETTED STEMPOST AND KEEL, BEARDED DEADWOOD WITH SUPPORTING KNEE (Cornwall)

SPLIT RABBETTED STEMPOST, APRON, STEMKNEE AND DEADWOOD WITH A KEELSON (South Devon large boats)

RABBETTED STEMPOST AND KEEL WITH A BEARDED DEADWOOD KNEE (Small boats all over Britain)

RABBETTED STEMPOST, FOREKNEE AND KEEL – BEARDED APRON AND DEADWOOD (Scotland large)

THIS SORT OF DEADWOOD MAY BE TAKEN RIGHT AFT TO FORM A HOG

SPLIT RABBETTED STEMPOST, APRON AND DEADWOOD KNEE (Sussex)

RABBETTED STEMPOST AND KEEL WITH A BEARDED APRON AND DEADWOOD KNEE (East Coast of Britain)

THE DESIGN OF THIS JOINT VARIES FROM YARD TO YARD

RABBETTED STEMPOST, FOREKNEE AND KEEL

SPLIT RABBETTED STEMPOST AND APRON WITH FULLY RABBETTED DEADWOOD & KEEL

(East Anglia small boats ⟷ large boats)

THE DEADWOOD AND STEMKNEE HERE ADD TO THE STRENGTH NOT THE WATERTIGHTNESS

Each design was seen in the area given in brackets. This is not to say that other methods are not also used there or that the same design is not used elsewhere. A partly built or dismantled boat shows more clearly than a complete one how the stem was made.

symmetric pattern to avoid lines of joints in adjacent frames.

Asymmetric continuous frame
In the Scottish manner, this is reversed successively so that the long and short legs of the floor fall on the alternate sides of the boat.

Double continuous frame
Made by bolting two continuous frames side by side. The butts in each are staggered to eliminate scarfs, chocks or straps.

Mixed framing
A few lofted continuous frames act as controls or permanent moulds. Some or all of the rest of the frames, which may be of any kind, are fitted to ribbands, which are removed as planking proceeds on completion of which any remaining frames are put in.

Lofted frame
Made from a mould picked up from full sized lines drawn on the loft floor. The exact shape and correct bevel is applied to the frame before it is placed on the keel, reducing dubbing and trimming to a minimum.

As bent timbers are least satisfactory where they cross the keel, especially if it is ballasted, the combination of solid floors with bent timber is often seen. This introduces a zone of rigid structure into what otherwise would have been a pliant hull. Unless the two zones are blended, stress concentraion breaks bent timbers, opens up seams and splits planks along this boundary. Some boats alter the methods of framing from forward to aft, so that rigid frames are placed in way of the mast with more flexible ones in the bow and stern. The Ness sgoth is an example, while the Thames wherry is another which has three different patterns from forward to aft (Fig 41).

Hulls which have been built as if they were rafts, with sides above a chine or an ile, may terminate in a flat, as opposed to a pointed, bow or stern. The opening in this ending is closed by planking up one side of a continuous frame, which is usually sloping like the stern of an English coble. The planking may even be carried beyond the frame to avoid short grain. This is a square end and has no need of either stiffening or bracketing at the centre line, especially if the bottom is flat with no keel. As a hull structure, it differs from a transom in that it is a truncation of the hull shape and not an addition to a sternpost. Though this ending may have been unsatisfactory in a dugout due to short grain and cutting pitfalls, it is a satisfactory arrangement in a planked boat's stern and in the bow, if well inclined and made small in proportion to the midship section, and the combination is found in the pram form.

If the ends were to be cut off a dugout and then re-joined by longitudinal planks, a larger boat would emerge than would be possible from a single log. The bow and stern of such a boat have been termed block stems[12]. In conception such stems are the same as a stempost with rabbets once the side planks are let in to improve flow and to cover the plank ends at the same time. A further advance occurs when the block stem is tilted or cut from stock that has grown to the same shape as the profile, and together they help a builder to plank up a boat with sharp ends and full midships. There are regional and ancient examples of stems partially or entirely made up from dugout-like components, just as there are many ways of attaching the plank ends to them. Both these features have been described fully by Greenhill[13]. To avoid a repetition of how the fully rabetted stem came about, Fig 42 has been restricted to show some British examples.

It should then be sufficient to discuss only those solutions that have been used after these earlier methods proved to be workable. This is a stempost, which as well as accommodating the rabbet and plank end fastenings, has to have enough material to hold its shape, provide a knee and take the rough and scuff of use. In the simplest form all of this can be done with one carefully chosen and shaped piece of wood. Carving one calls for skill, whether it is done by eye or drawing. As the figure shows, composite stemposts are more common. Stemposts are better for sharp entries, as finding enough wood for plank fastenings gets more difficult as the angle between the sides increases. Some hulls are sharp below but roomy above the water and this is why aprons are often included in the upper parts of a fully rabbeted stempost (Fig 42).

Room aft gives space for the helmsman clear of those working forward, reserve of buoyancy to prevent swamping by overtaking waves and a wider sheeting base. All combine to give more boat for the same length and are an inducement to make a pointed stern full above the water. A good example of this was to be seen on the west coast of Scotland, where the sterns of the skiffs have almost semi-circular gunwales (Fig 43). The difficulty of securing strakes to a blunt end is less when a breasthook or, in its inclined form, the stemhook or stamering is used to hold the sides together in the same way as floors do in the body of the hull. The plank end fastenings then have only the join in the rabbet to keep tight. Even fuller ends can prevent either the plank ends from being forced into place or from staying there in service. In either case the upper strakes of a boat like this spring progressively clear of the sternpost leaving a tulip-shaped opening above the water. Boarded up, this has the appearance of the transom of a gig or galley.

However the transom may have come about, its difference from the square stern is immediately apparent. While a transom alters the shape of the end, a square stern only limits the length of a boat. A transom involves a reverse curve in the section, which is made by working a tuck in one or more seams. Some transoms are much wider and deeper than those of a gig or a galley, and extreme examples can be given where it is hard to tell a transom

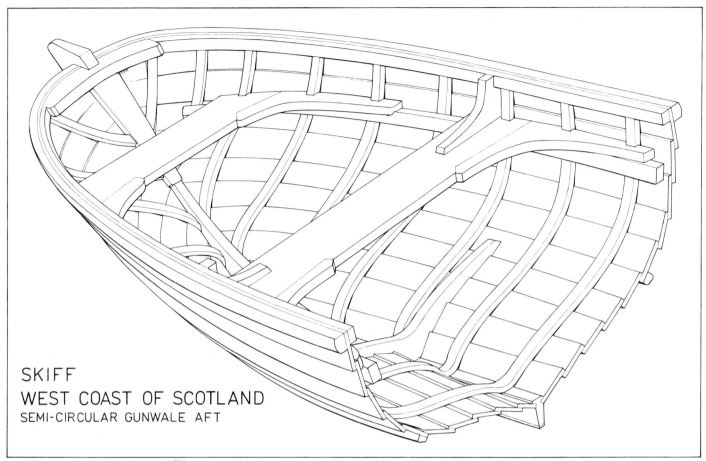

SKIFF
WEST COAST OF SCOTLAND
SEMI-CIRCULAR GUNWALE AFT

Fig 43: Skiff, west coast of Scotland.

from a square stern. When the undersides of the stern spring straight from the keel with little or no reverse curvature it is preferable to call this a 'transom' if there is a sternpost and knee and a 'square stern' if there is not. Lute sterns can be formed on either transom or square sterns, but counters and pink sterns can only be worked on boats with sternposts (Fig 44).

The keel of today is a centreline strength member, which provides an anchorage for many other structural parts. These are, the garboard either side, the stem and sternpost either end and the floors of the frames, directly or indirectly. The keel, now generally thought of as being the most important single item in a plank boat, does not occur in the pure form of the skin boat, raft or dugout at all.

As a skin boat cannot develop beyond a curragh without a framework rigid enough to position planks, it is likely that the keel came from either the raft or the dugout. At first neither source seems more probable; there is no need for a central log in a raft and the one component of a dugout serves every purpose. As both types developed however the situation resolved itself.

In the case of the rafted bottom with a pointed end it is necessary to have a central member to take the fastenings of the post. A longitudinally planked bottom lacks the strength to resist loading, which is downwards from the mast and cargo but upward in the buoyant unloaded sections of the hull. It is undesirable to deepen this member

downwards as this increases draft and attracts all the wear to itself and the chines when aground. If extended upwards, the rungs have to be notched. Apart from an overall increase in scantlings, the way to improve the longitudinal strength of a rafted bottom is to fit a keelson on top of the rungs in way of any loads. The implication of a sprung or dished bottom is that shoal draft is no longer the overriding factor and in any case the centreline component is going to get the brunt of grounding. There is a case here for deepening the central member downwards but this is not a full keel until there is a need to fasten it to the next pair of members outboard.

There is ample evidence to show that as dugouts were extended further the central element grew relatively smaller and less boatshaped. The Norse 'T' or 'Y' section keels retained a vestige of boatshape, though they had by then become a deep web with a flange to which the garboards could be fastened, and looked more like modern keels. Later, when describing an English coble, it will be shown that the web and flange parted to become the keel and the hog of that type. Just as with aprons and rabbeted stems, square and transom sterns, there are hogged and rabbeted keels, which reflect respectively the raft- and dugout-minded solutions to pointed and flat ends and centreline structures. Once again these are signs of seminal methods being re-employed and not signs that they have been in unbroken use throughout the development.

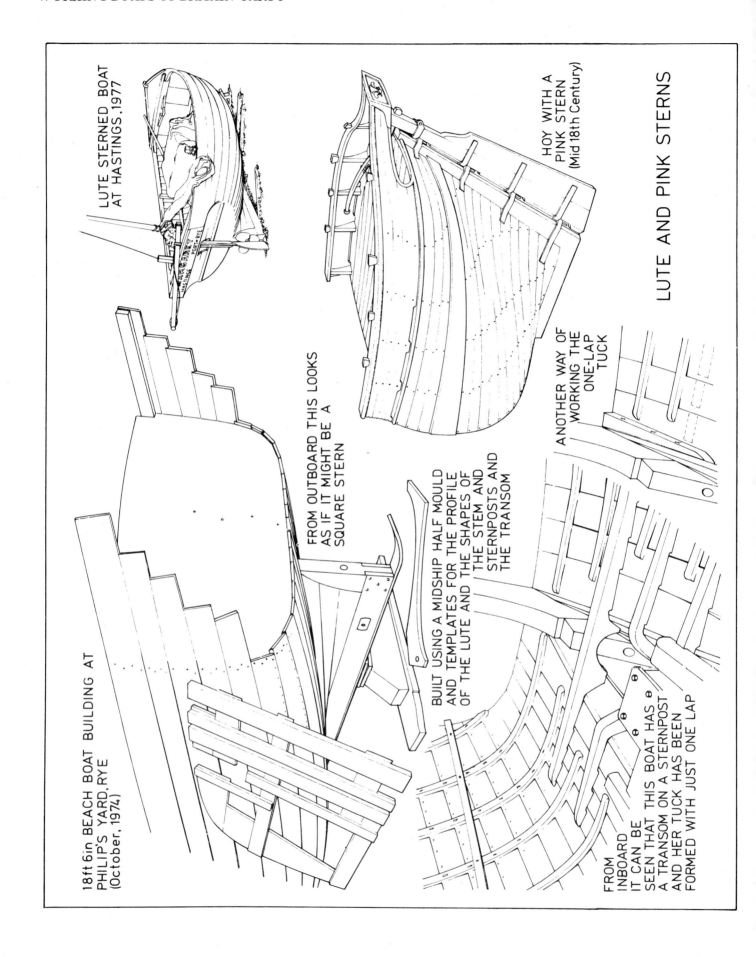

LUTE STERNED BOAT
AT HASTINGS, 1977

HOY WITH A
PINK STERN
(Mid 18th Century)

LUTE AND PINK STERNS

18ft 6in BEACH BOAT BUILDING AT
PHILIP'S YARD, RYE
(October, 1974)

FROM OUTBOARD THIS LOOKS
AS IF IT MIGHT BE A
SQUARE STERN

BUILT USING A MIDSHIP HALF MOULD
AND TEMPLATES FOR THE PROFILE
OF THE LUTE AND THE SHAPES OF
THE STEM AND
STERNPOSTS AND
THE TRANSOM

ANOTHER WAY OF
WORKING THE
ONE-LAP
TUCK

FROM
INBOARD
IT CAN BE
SEEN THAT THIS BOAT HAS
A TRANSOM ON A STERNPOST
AND HER TUCK HAS BEEN
FORMED WITH JUST ONE LAP

Above:
Fig 44: Lute and pink sterns.

Below:
Fig 45: Racking and torsion.

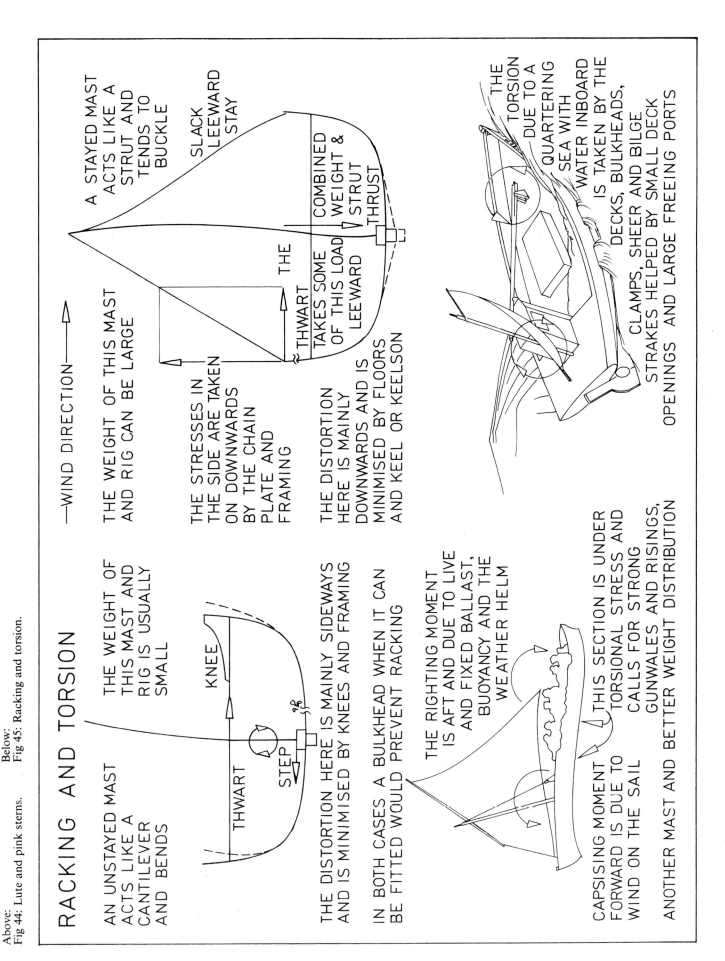

RACKING AND TORSION

—WIND DIRECTION—→

AN UNSTAYED MAST ACTS LIKE A CANTILEVER AND BENDS

THE WEIGHT OF THIS MAST AND RIG IS USUALLY SMALL

A STAYED MAST ACTS LIKE A STRUT AND TENDS TO BUCKLE

SLACK LEEWARD STAY

THE WEIGHT OF THIS MAST AND RIG CAN BE LARGE

COMBINED WEIGHT & STRUT THRUST

THE THWART TAKES SOME OF THIS LOAD LEEWARD

KNEE

THWART

STEP

THE STRESSES IN THE SIDE ARE TAKEN ON DOWNWARDS BY THE CHAIN PLATE AND FRAMING

THE DISTORTION HERE IS MAINLY DOWNWARDS AND IS MINIMISED BY FLOORS AND KEEL OR KEELSON

THE DISTORTION HERE IS MAINLY SIDEWAYS AND IS MINIMISED BY KNEES AND FRAMING

IN BOTH CASES A BULKHEAD WHEN IT CAN BE FITTED WOULD PREVENT RACKING

THE RIGHTING MOMENT IS AFT AND DUE TO LIVE AND FIXED BALLAST, BUOYANCY AND THE WEATHER HELM

CAPSISING MOMENT FORWARD IS DUE TO WIND ON THE SAIL

THIS SECTION IS UNDER TORSIONAL STRESS AND CALLS FOR STRONG GUNWALES AND RISINGS, ANOTHER MAST AND BETTER WEIGHT DISTRIBUTION

THE TORSION DUE TO A QUARTERING SEA WITH WATER INBOARD IS TAKEN BY THE DECKS, BULKHEADS, CLAMPS, SHEER AND BILGE STRAKES HELPED BY SMALL DECK OPENINGS AND LARGE FREEING PORTS

67

Without mutual support between the sides, a framed shell is ill equipped to resist racking and torsional stresses. A racking stress is one that tends to distort the shape of a section. An unstayed mast will do this in one direction and stayed one in another (Fig 45). Torsion occurs when racking in adjacent sections differ in degree or direction. This happens for instance when the mast and the ballast are on different stations, also when lengthy boats are crossing waves at an angle. Although a thwart prevents a section collapsing inwards and upwards when afloat, the corners it makes with the frame must be bracketed to resist racking. In open boats, thwarts laid on risings are the simple practical solution as it allows the knees to be fitted on top. As well as acting as a bench for a rower a thwart can locate a mast, brace a centreboard case or form a bulkhead. A thwart only supports the one or two frames or timbers it spans and few risings are robust enough to act as load spreaders. Horizontal brackets, called lodging knees, are fitted in boats which are beached sideways or are subject to similar treatment. On the north-east beaches of Norfolk the boats make extensive use of lodging knees, not unlike those used to connect deck beams and carlings on eighteenth century gun decks. When a deck is fitted over beams, it helps to distribute uneven end loads, but its weight can increase racking induced by heavy rolling. This is overcome by increasing the strength of the beam shelf and hanging knees. Torsion stresses act mainly on the skin of a vessel, which can be seen to twist in heavy seas. This due to slight slippage in the plank seams, which is acceptable and even, some say, desirable in small light open boats. In a larger vessel the movement is greater and may be enough to strain fastenings and start leaks, unless stiffer planking and framing has been provided.

Boat structures tend towards those that are flexible and light and those that are rigid and heavy. High standards of design, skill and material are essential for the first. The stresses are absorbed by progressive deformation of the structure which, if not taken beyond its elastic limit, springs back into shape as the stress is removed. A light boat responds to an impact sooner than a heavy one and feels it less; she will need fewer oars and less sail and, as a result, be lighter still. Light boats represent a smaller outlay of resources than a heavy one and are easier to beach, especially if kept short. Length is a limitation in a seaway, where the gunwales and keel are subject to alternate tensile and compressive stresses and subsequent failure due to the lightness of the scantlings.

Rowed to windward, a light boat slows down faster than a heavy one during the recovery stroke, unless the oarsmen break stroke, as they do off the Chesil Bank, or shorten and quicken it as they did in Weston-super-Mare Bay. Though not as efficient as a full concerted stroke, this is better than a stop-and-start progress. Similarly the lighter boat under sail has to be sailed freer in critical wave lengths to avoid being halted by successive waves. In a longer wave system a light boat is at an advantage if she handles well and can take a winding course to maintain a steady speed.

Light boats however cannot accept concentrated loads from cargo, ballast, rig or working gear. The structural design of a good light boat is so finely balanced that the failure of any one component generally leads to the overloading of others. Enlargement of the offending part will upset the balance of the design, setting up trouble elsewhere. The development of the sailing trawler is a case study of the inevitability of a rigid structure in this situation. Unless a beam trawl is large and kept moving it does not catch many fish. This calls for a robust trawl attachment, a large sail area in light winds and an easily handled rig to keep the crew small and the share large. All of these lead to a heavier structure and overall decking to allow the boat the stay at sea longer in all weathers. Every weight increase has to be matched by more sail and a larger hull to support it. Although such a boat will have to adopt even heavier scantlings, there is a lot to be gained from sound design, workmanship and materials as a means of cutting out undue weight. A well built rigidly constructed vessel will justify its high initial cost by standing up to heavy work without constant repairs, lasting longer and being more likely to be convertible to other rigs and gear. Development is usually in the direction of bigger and more rigid vessels – ultimately small ships. Unless seaworthiness or speed is essential in working boats or in competitive recreational craft, a flexible structure design tends to be static, representing as it does a near ideal solution in its particular surroundings.

To sum up: a seminal method offers only a limited range of boat designs. To break away, a boatbuilder has to either adopt other seminal techniques or invent new ones. A number of boat components seen today look as if they have been made using the thinking behind these early techniques. It is difficult if not impossible to trace the evolution of these practices back to their origins, but it is evident that what looks like seminal structures are still being used. This is no more evidence of continuity however than a serif on a capital letter is proof that type cutting is an extention of monumental masonry.

6.

Names, shapes and classes of British working boats

NAMES

Names are amongst a boat's more attractive features and one wonders how much they can tell us about individual types. Though these names are as numerous as the shapes, they do not seem to follow definite rules. Sometimes the name is helpful, but is as likely to mislead. To avoid this, one might rationalise the nomenclature and, by devising a standard format indicate the type, location and employment of every type of boat. In this way a Deal cat would be called a second class lugger for hovelling in the Downs, or some abbreviation of this. If this were done, the boatman's terms for his own craft would be forgotten, and convenience alone is not enough reason for this to happen. A boat's name is like the 'bye-name' or 'title' the men gave one another; the reason it was chosen is not clear or has been forgotten. It is necessary to learn the names, like irregular verbs in a foreign language; but once learned, terms like shinerman, doble and sgoth conjure up a sharper picture than synthetic phraseology.

Generally the place name of a boat is used – Ballantrae boat for instance is helpful, as this is in the Firth of Clyde area where many of the boats share similar features. Correctly used a place name will be that of a village, town or river when the boat is a distinct variety of a larger family, known by its estuary, county or coastal zone. The term 'boat' is sometimes omitted as in words like fifie, firthie and wolder, for craft that originated in Fife, the Firth of Clyde and the Norfolk Wolds.

There are names where the prefix indicates the waters in which the boat was used. This helps, as once one knows the limitations of such situations, one has a fair idea of the sort of boat likely to be found there. Names like 'beach boat', 'canal boat' and 'outside barge', though not precise, provide a clue as what to expect. In the same way, a prefix that tells the work of a boat is informative once the nature of the work and gear in a locality is known. Fishing gear, like creel, drift net and stop net, provide many examples[1].

Fishing boats form the largest group of working boat types. As just about any sort of boat can be used for fishing one way or another, the phrase 'fishing boat' says little by itself, but a clearer picture is obtained if the sort of fishing is given – one thinks of crabbers having low topsides to reduce the distance pots have to be lifted inboard. Drifters need to be larger to carry fleets of nets and a lowering mast when lying to them; they should also be fast, so they set large sail areas and have big crews to work sails and nets. Trawlers have to be powerful to keep the gear on the move over the bottom. The smaller trawlers like shrimpers and oyster dredgers need plenty of sail also, which is set on a standing rig with a gaff as there is no call for a lowering mast. Hookers and long-liners cannot be large or they risk parting the warp during recovery unless this is done from smaller boats. Hookers have to be weatherly and handy when picking up end buoys. Like drifters, they have to wait some hours after shooting before hauling again; and these conflicting requirements lead to hookers being both lug- and gaff-rigged. Not all hookers are fishing boats; the Deal hooker grapple and recover slipped anchors and cables in the Downs. The pilchard seine net boat has to be large enough to carry a long net and rowers, yet capable of being launched quickly.

Forms of work other than fishing also gave names to boats. Some, like pilot or ferry boat, are self-evident, but plenty are not. A blobbing boat was an old but still sturdy smack's punt that had been built up to provide some living space, yet was mobile enough to engage in a little trade and seasonal eel fishing in the Humber. A boulder boat was also a makeshift, protected by laths nailed under the lands of her clinker strakes, so she could go ashore under the Sussex cliffs to load flints, which were then taken by sailing coaster and canal boat to the Staffordshire potteries. A boxing fleet boat was a capacious and massively built 17-footer complete with oil and buoyancy tanks. She ferried catches from the trawlers to the boxing fleet carriers that took them back to the Hull market. Foy boat was the name used from the Tweed to the Thames for the boat that tended shipping. From the Downs onwards she would be called a hoveller, if not by some local name. The Blythe and Sunderland foy boat was a small coble, but from the Tyne to Margate a foy boat was a keel boat with a transom not unlike a roomy gig. In the Humber this was a gold-duster's work. This 18- to 21-footer was sprit-rigged on two masts, and her call to work was the yellow quarantine flag of an inward bound ship. It is not agreed how the word 'foy' came about; a derivation from words meaning 'allegiance' or 'fee' have been suggested. The two meanings together however seem to suit a boat that sells her services. The goozieboat was a large Thames wherry that hovelled out of Gravesend, and was rigged with a standing lug foresail and a tiny sprit mizzen. The hovellers off Sussex were called hufflers, and elsewhere there were Spithead wherries, Portsmouth gawlors, Solent ferry punts, Falmouth quay punts and from the Bristol Avon Pill yawls or yaulers. The peter boat was a double-ended

Fig 46: Brighton hog boat.

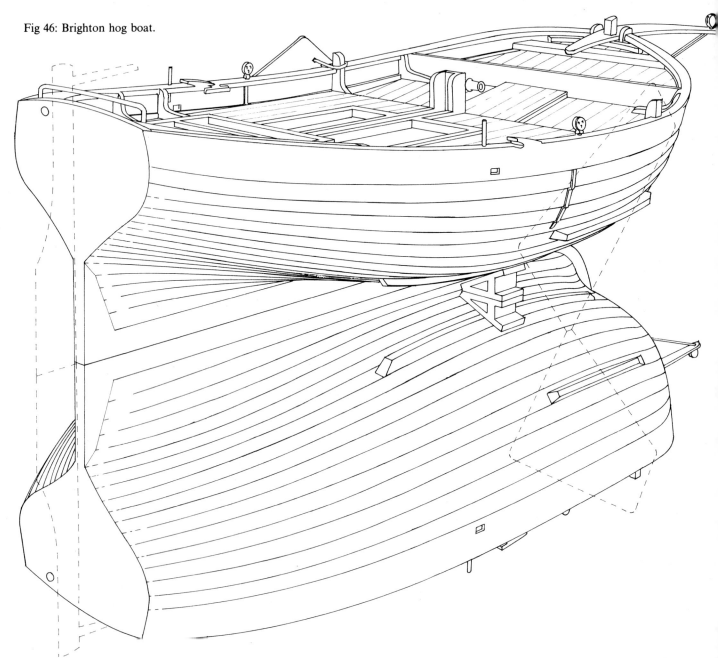

Thames fishing boat with a well. Though normally about 19ft, those above the bridge might be as little as 12ft and those below up to 23ft. The Medway doble was much the same, while the hatch boat was an even larger version not unlike a Norfolk wherry in that it had a sprit mizzen in addition to the loose-footed gaff main. The Thames tilt boat carried passengers or dry goods up and down river, having a tilt or a tent spread over them. The Brighton hog boat or hoggy was an exceptionally beamy sprit-rigged ketch that used to fish off this beach. She was up to 30ft long, clinker-built with a transom and leeboards. Her name which matched her appearance belied her good sailing performance (Fig 46).

There are terms which have changed their meanings over the years or from place to place, due to the word surviving changes in rig, shape, station and work. Even though a local term sounds like a shape, say 'flat', 'punt' or 'skiff', or a rig, say 'cutter', 'ketch' or 'yawl', it is far from safe to assume that this is what is meant. While boats called 'flatners', 'flatties' or 'flats' can often be relied upon to be flat bottomed in construction, not all boats of this sort are so named; the Norfolk canoe (Fig 47) and Fleet trow (p 212) are examples where they were not. The Mersey flat on the other hand was a keel boat with a round bottom. Nor should the term 'trow', which is derived from 'trough', be only associated with flat bottomed vessels, as both the Severn trow and the Tyne trow were round bottomed for a long period before they fell out of use.

The term 'punt' has different meanings from that given by the Concise Oxford Dictionary as 'Flat-bottom shallow boat, broad and square both ends, propelled by a pole thrust against the bottom of the river'. This applies well to the river punts found on the Thames and Severn, but is considerably stretched when used for gun punts, which

Fig 47: Brancaster Staithe flatty or canoe with 15in wire and twine whelk pot.

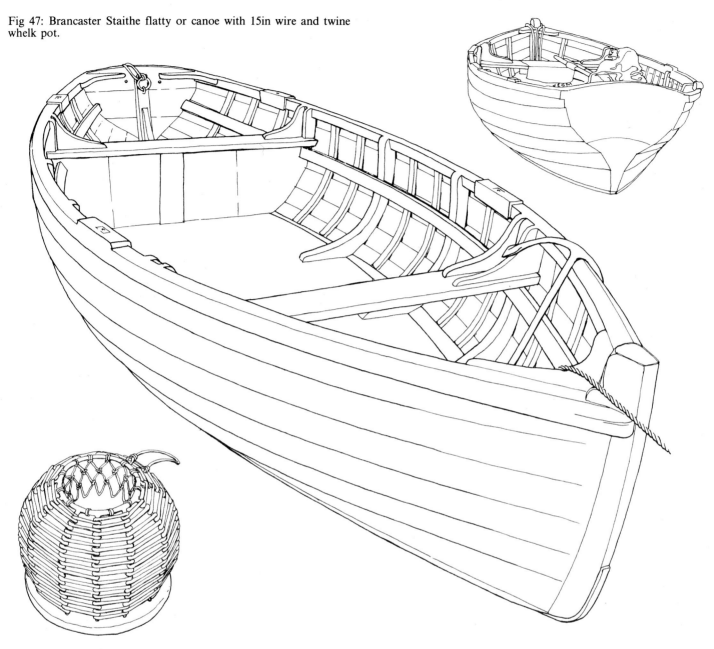

were pointed at both ends and paddled, rowed or sailed. The most usual saltwater meaning of 'punt' is a smaller version of a boat type, the boat used to ferry the crew and their catch ashore or the smaller class in a range of related types being often called a punt. The Weston-super-Mare punt was a small flatner that was used like a yachtsman uses his dinghy, and there are plenty of other examples of this usage along the south and east coasts of England. Deal and Hastings punts were the smallest class of lugger, but at Deal one finds the galley punt is larger than both the galley and the punt found on the same beach. The Solent ferry punt and the Falmouth quay punt were both used as deep water hovellers having deep hulls and good lines, which inspired many designers of small yachts. The Bosham punt (Fig 48) was a small oyster dredger, open with a tall lug, while the Yarmouth beach punt was over 30ft long with a two masted lug rig. The one common factor in all these

boats was that they could all be used as a ferry, either on a river or out to a ship. The copper punt started as a river punt-shaped boat, but kept this name after she changed her structure into one resembling a Tyne trow (p51).

'Skiff' has more than one meaning. In fresh water it is safe to say a skiff is an oared boat, in form and period part way between a wherry and a racing shell. The Ryde and Cowes skiffs were the 15ft waterman's boats, much beamier than the river skiffs. As often was the case with waterman's types there was a naval counterpart, the 16ft skiff, rigged as a gunter lug sloop and rowed randan. In Scotland, the term 'skiff' may indicate a small version of a larger type, for instance a zulu skiff just 25ft long, or this suffix might not be applied at all, as was often the case with the smaller baldies and fifies. On the west coast of Scotland the term skiff is used for a distinct type in some places; the best known of this type was the Loch Fyne skiff that

Fig 48: Mr White and the two Arnolds racing in Bosham punts (from a photo owned by H J Merritt of Wyke Regis).

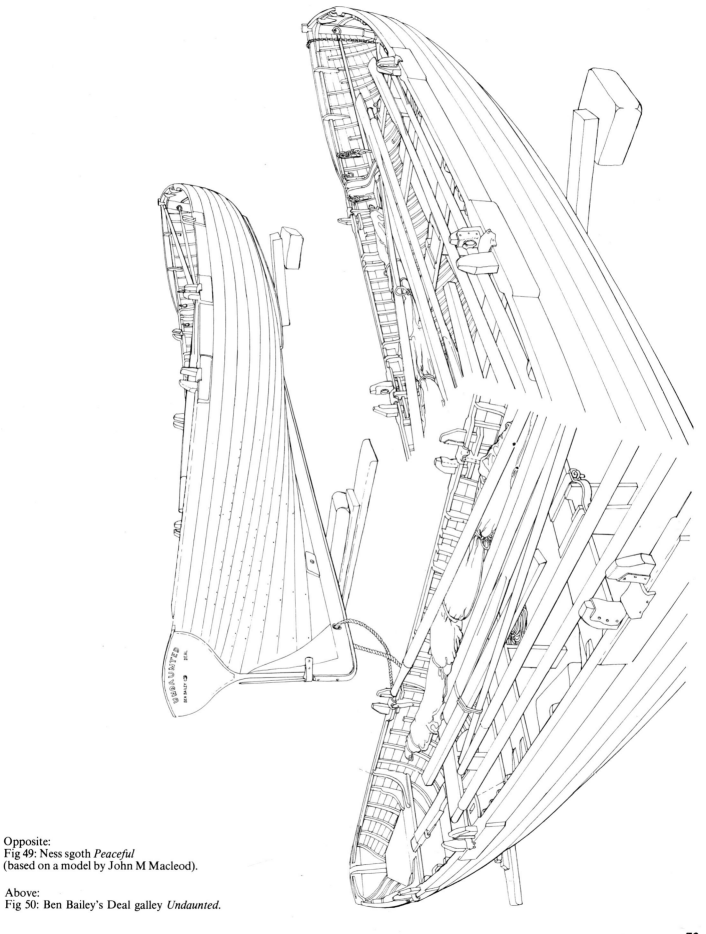

Opposite:
Fig 49: Ness sgoth *Peaceful*
(based on a model by John M Macleod).

Above:
Fig 50: Ben Bailey's Deal galley *Undaunted*.

doubled her length in her transformation from a drifter to a ring net fishing boat, but vanished when her hull was found unsuitable for motorisation. In the eighteenth century there were vessels called Swansea skiffs, which, with crews of three men and a boy, sound like smacks. As the Bristol pilot cutters were also known as skiffs, this may indicate a local meaning of the term that applied once in the Severn estuary. Though the term 'skiff' began by meaning a lighter and faster small boat, this later became blurred.

Some words sound like 'skiff' and may have similar origins; such are the scaith and scaffie of the Moray Firth, both of which were the open fishing boat type that came before the big decked classes of drifter of the last decades of the nineteenth century. The nearly extinct Ness sgoth was one example of the west coast boats like the Skye eather and Outer Isle sgoth, the one from Lewis being from 20 to 30ft long, open with a pronounced standing garboard and overhanging pointed ends (Fig 49).

Gigs and galleys are taken together as they are not easy to tell apart. Both are foremost pulling boats that can be sailed, and were used by both working boatmen and the Royal Navy. The galley was rather larger than the gig, but was associated with the south-east coast, where a few of them, like those from Selsey, were as much as 40ft long with 11 pairs of oars[2]. The gig was found in the extreme south west and was usually close to 30ft long with 5 or 6 oars, but might be a little longer on the north coast of the peninsula; one gig from Appledore was 32ft long with 8 oars. The service galley was this length when she went out of use at the time of the First World War, while the service gig was 30ft long and of diagonal carvel construction when she became obsolete after the Second World War[3]. Like the gigs of Scilly and Cornwall, there are still a few service gigs to be seen, though the latter are now rigged with two gunter instead of dipping lugs. There is still one Deal galley left, Ben Bailey's *Undaunted*, but although all her old gear is kept in place, she is not now put to work (Fig 50). Any light narrow boat with four or more oars and a small high transom is liable to be called a gig, or even a lighthorseman, which used to be disparagingly applied to a boat that was used to pilfer lighters moored in the Thames.

Multi-oared working boats were looked on with suspicion and in 1722 an act was passed ruling forfeit any boats rowing more than four oars along the Dover Straits coast. The clan chieftains on the west coast of Scotland owned galleys and often displayed them in their coats of arms. These emblematic galleys were given the heraldic terms 'lymphad' or 'bior-linn' and were just about as mythical as the heraldic beasts beside them[4].

As has been mentioned above, boats are often called by names of sailing rigs. In a great number of cases, like the Cowes ketch, Humber sloop, Polperro gaffer and Brixham dandy, all is well and the name and the rig correspond. Less general terms, however, like Tyne, Humber, Norfolk and Teign keel are all found to have square sails; and both the Plymouth and Clovelly longboomers did have booms on

the feet of their mainsails. I have not discovered an instance of any lugger rigged in another way. Yawl, sloop, cutter and smack are terms applied to rigs, but applied to a whole boat these terms call for caution, so will be considered one by one.

'Yawl', though well established as a rig, originally referred to a hull type. There are only two known cases where the term actually refers to the rig. The Sussex yawl, which was a large vessel used for pleasure trips before motor boats, and the Devon yawl, an attractive class of recreational dinghy still in use at Salcombe. In the north of Scotland the term 'yawl' indicates that a boat is of yole shape, that is double-ended, with hollow garboards, more or less deadrise, flared sides and raked ends. The Scots yawl is exemplified by the Stroma yole, which is fuller bodied and higher sided than the Fair Isle and Shetland yoles (Fig 51). The terms 'yawl' and 'skiff' are often used loosely for any small boat. Further south the magnificent Norfolk and Suffolk beach yawls, though extinct, were once the East Anglian equivalent of the galleys and gigs. They were larger, twice as long and pulling up to 12 oars, with a legendary sailing performance under two- or three-masted lugger rigs. There was a corresponding service yawl, also 12-oared but beamier and the same length as a galley. A Whitstable yawl was a cutter-rigged oyster dredger, and the Yorkshire yawl was an even larger vessel, 50ft long, clinker-built, with a lute stern and rigged as a gaff ketch in the middle of the last century. The Pill yawl was from 21 to 24ft long, a sprit-rigged open boat. As well as hovelling, she was used by unlicensed pilots. When writing about them, Graham E Farr states, 'Yet another case of an old term used to describe a hull form being taken on to describe a rig of masts'[5]. While in full agreement with this, I cannot see how the term 'yawl' came to be used in this case.

The definitions of the single masted sloop and cutter rigs underwent a change during the nineteenth century. Before then a sloop would have had a fixed bowsprit with a lot of steeve, while the cutter's was more level and could be reefed inboard. Both rigs set more than one headsail. Today a sloop is said to have one headsail and a cutter two, and both may have fixed or reefing bowsprits (Fig 52). There was also a slutter rig, a term which thankfully only had a short life[6]. This shows the care needed with the use of these two terms, as well as with the further refinements of the gaffsail which may have boomed loose feet, long or standing gaffs, and headsails hanked to their stays or set flying.

The term 'sloop' is not a common one for a boat. The Brixham sloop was the largest of the three classes of trawler in this port, the deciding factor being that she had to be over 40 tons. The sloop rig was used initially, but this was found unwieldy in the bigger boats and a two-masted dandy rig was used instead, that is a ketch with a much smaller mizzen than that found in a coaster. An even more involved case occurred with the Norfolk wolder, which was a boat which might be rigged in one of two ways[7]. She

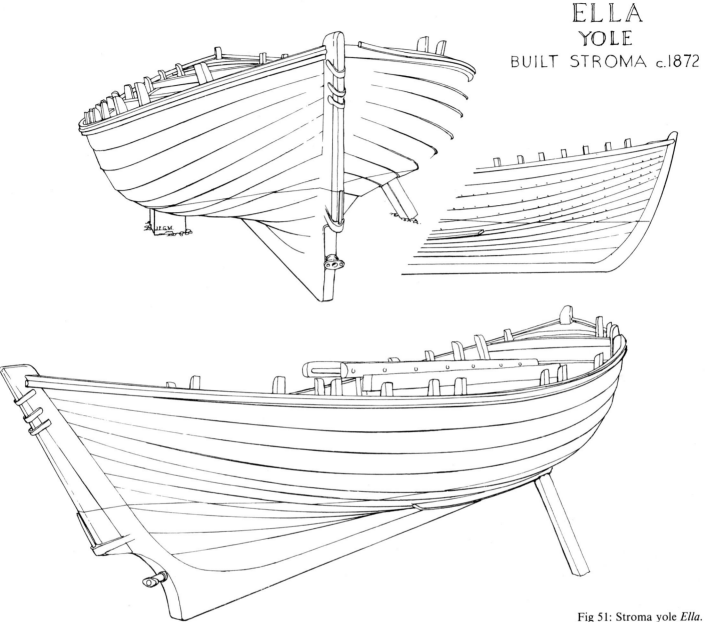

ELLA
YOLE
BUILT STROMA c.1872

Fig 51: Stroma yole *Ella*.

appeared as a lugger when out drifting for mackerel, but as a cutter when trawling; then she was said to have been dandy rigged. What had happened here was that she had started by having the two masted rig, but held on to the name after the mizzen was later removed. The Humber sloop really was a sloop in the modern sense, and it was only her rig that differentiated her from the square-rigged Humber keel. The word 'sloop' sounds like a derivative of the word 'shallop', a light open boat of the seventeenth century or earlier, which was probably itself derived from the French word 'chaloupe'. In Tudor times the shallop was an open boat with two masts, each with one square sail similar in appearance to eighteenth century Cornish fishing boats[8]. Once more it is hard to see how the change from a meaning of form to one of rig came about.

The cutter rig was popular with vessels employed on prevention of smuggling, carrying despatches, packet and pilot work. All of these jobs called for a boat that could stay at sea through bad weather, that could work well to windward and still be fast on other points of sailing. As cargo was not the first aim, she could have fine lines. She had to be able to spread a lot of canvas in a light breeze, yet take it down together with as many spars as possible in a blow. A well stayed mainmast, a fidded topmast and a reefing bowsprit allowed a cutter to do all of this. Even after the schooner rig and, later, steam was used for propulsion, the terms revenue cutter and pilot cutter were retained. In the Navy, apart from the 12 gun cutters, which were hardly distinguishable from the revenue ones, the service cutter was a sturdily built sailing and pulling boat, generally shorter and beamier than a galley or a gig. First appearing early in the eighteenth century, in her final form she was 32ft long, with 12 oars and standing lug sloop rig. The word 'cutter' was also in use on the Thames in the

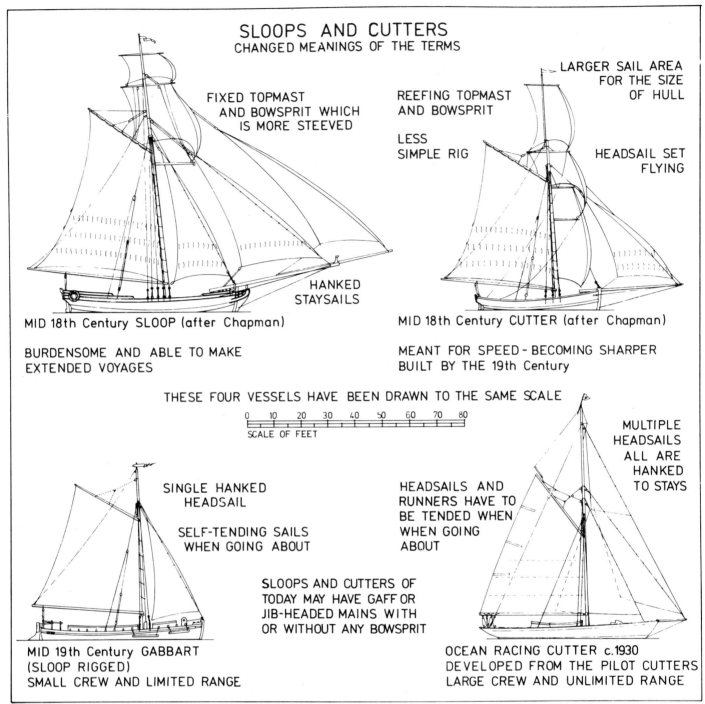

SLOOPS AND CUTTERS
CHANGED MEANINGS OF THE TERMS

FIXED TOPMAST
AND BOWSPRIT WHICH
IS MORE STEEVED

REEFING TOPMAST
AND BOWSPRIT

LESS
SIMPLE RIG

LARGER SAIL AREA
FOR THE SIZE
OF HULL

HEADSAIL SET
FLYING

HANKED
STAYSAILS

MID 18th Century SLOOP (after Chapman)

MID 18th Century CUTTER (after Chapman)

BURDENSOME AND ABLE TO MAKE
EXTENDED VOYAGES

MEANT FOR SPEED – BECOMING SHARPER
BUILT BY THE 19th Century

THESE FOUR VESSELS HAVE BEEN DRAWN TO THE SAME SCALE

0 10 20 30 40 50 60 70 80
SCALE OF FEET

SINGLE HANKED
HEADSAIL

SELF-TENDING SAILS
WHEN GOING ABOUT

HEADSAILS AND
RUNNERS HAVE TO
BE TENDED WHEN
WHEN GOING
ABOUT

MULTIPLE
HEADSAILS
ALL ARE
HANKED
TO STAYS

SLOOPS AND CUTTERS OF
TODAY MAY HAVE GAFF OR
JIB-HEADED MAINS WITH
OR WITHOUT ANY BOWSPRIT

MID 19th Century GABBART
(SLOOP RIGGED)
SMALL CREW AND LIMITED RANGE

OCEAN RACING CUTTER c.1930
DEVELOPED FROM THE PILOT CUTTERS
LARGE CREW AND UNLIMITED RANGE

Fig 52: Sloops and cutters.

nineteenth century, when it was applied to an 8-oared amateur racing boat. In every instance except the service boats, the term implies a turn of speed, but without such prefixes as revenue, pilot or Thames, 'cutter' on its own is vague.

'Smack' was in use by the end of the sixteenth century and has been immortalised by the Beaufort notation for wind strength, in which the behaviour of this type of inshore craft was used to indicate how the wind was increasing – up to Force 8 that is, when, 'Smacks take shelter if possible'. The word has been used so freely it cannot be defined precisely. It is suggested that a smack is rather larger than a boat, being decked with one or two permanently stepped masts with gaffs rather than lug or sprit sails. She might be used for fishing, pilotage or packet work. In the last instance she might well be the size of a small ship yet still be called a boat, a usage which persists for cross-Channel ferry boats of several thousand tons[9]. It is possible to go through the alphabet naming the places with their own sort of smack: Arran, Barking, Colchester, Dover all the way to Yarmouth, with a choice of several alternative places in some cases. Each would differ in some way or other, with a feature a seaman could spot from some way off at sea. Some smacks had special local names like the Leigh and Harwich Bawleys, Ramsgate tosher or Brixham mumble-bee although they were also smacks.

If one excludes the use of the term 'barge' in its meaning of a ceremonial boat used by royalty, flag officers and liveried[10] companies and a medieval class of ship, only the cargo-carrying vessel remains[11]. Prefixes such as 'sailing', 'canal' or 'dumb' give a good idea what the barge might be like, while the addition of the waterway's name will give an exact image. Barges were just as distinctive as the coastal types, whether they were canal barges[12] or sailing barges[13]. Large families of a barge type, like the Thames sailing barge in particular, could have a variety of forms and operate along a long coastline, with may of them being built away from the Thames estuary itself[14]. As a result they developed many sub-types like spritties, boomies, stumpies, mulies and so on, which, though referring to rig, also had marked differences in size and shape of their hulls.

Many boat names give no clue to how they may have come about. The following list though incomplete should be long enough to show what is meant. Some of the words are so outlandish that they are easy to remember:

Baldie, a south east Scottish variety of fifie, which emerged about 1860 when Garibaldi was unifying Italy.

Bog, the small 25ft class of Hastings lugger of 4 to 7 tons. The word may have come from 'bogue', to fall off the wind.

Boggy, a double-ended lugger from the West Coast of Scotland.

Calf, cauf, 12 to 16ft tender to a large coble, mule or yawl. Usually found in the form of a coble.

Coble, one of the family of East Coast boats that have square sterns, plank keels and divide into English and Scottish types.

Doble, 12 to 18ft Medway fishing boat – a double-ender.

Farm, an early five-man boat from Yorkshire.

Folyer, volyer, up to 20ft boat that shot the net that closed the main Cornish pilchard seine. Dialect variation of 'follower'.

Funny, an extreme design of 20 to 30ft Thames racing skiff.

Flash boat, an extreme 4-oared West Country racing shell.

Gabbart, double-ended sailing lighter of the Clyde estuary, about 40ft and able to pass through the Forth/Clyde canal.

Lerret, 4- or 6-oared mackerel seine boat used off Chesil Bank. The name is said to come from *Lady of Loretto*, the prototype.

Mule, Mulie, the under 40-ton class of Brixham trawler, the double-ended coble or the Thames barge with a standing gaff mizzen. Some cross-breeding is implied in all cases.

Mumble-bee, 35 to 40ft, 17-ton Brixham trawler, single-masted with a few ketch conversions. Name said to have been bumble-bee once, but changed when they began to land catches at Swansea.

Nabby, 32 to 34ft open great line luggers of the Clyde estuary that replaced the earlier smacks.

Nobby, large family of 20 to 35ft shoal keel boats, largely decked and cutter rigged, found between Tremadoc Bay and the Solway Firth and used for many purposes (Fig 53).

Picarooner, 15ft fishing lugger from Clovelly. Name of a type of pirate's boat once, but far from relevant any longer.

Pram, a square-ended tender with plank keel, derived from the praam.

Shoe, 20ft box-shaped train barge on Taunton-Bridgwater canal.

Shout, old double-ended flat bottom barge of the Thames and Severn. Name taken from Dutch 'scuit'.

Shinerman, 22 to 24ft part decked mackerel beach lugger from Eastbourne.

Tosher, a one- or two-masted lugger, just under 20ft long at Mevagissey, but a 40ft gaff-rigged smack from Ramsgate. 'Toshing' was taking copper from laid-up warships, a shady term that fitted a class made just short enough to miss harbour dues.

Zulu, 55 to 80ft decked Scottish drifter, with a fifie's plumb stem and a scaffie's raked stern. She had a dipping lug fore and a standing lug mizzen and came out at the time of the Zulu War of 1879.

As well as these fairly recent types, there are some older names, which were recorded in old laws, admiralty accounts, law suits, custom records, logs and letters.

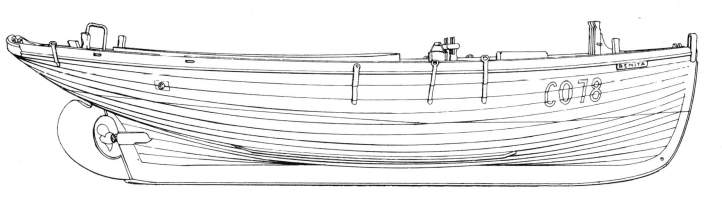

Fig 53: 23ft Tremadoc Bay nobby *Benita*.

CONVENTIONS USED TO DESCRIBE BOATSHAPE
Sheet One
PROFILE

The LENGTH OVERALL (LOA) is the level length of the shell or planked volume of the hull which may have EDGE-FASTENED or -POSITIONED strakes or both

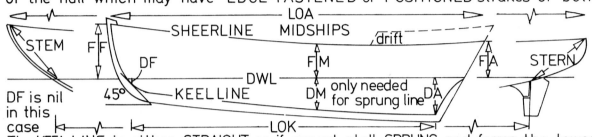

DF is nil in this case

The KEEL LINE is either STRAIGHT or, if curved at all, SPRUNG and forms the lower limit of the shell along the centre line. The LENGTH OF KEEL (LOK) is the level length between any abrupt cut-ups, fwd or aft. If this line is an unbroken curve its limits are taken to be where it rises at 45°, at the DATUM WATER LINE (DWL) or the rudder axis, whichever is inboard. DRAFT FOR'D (DF) and DRAFT AFT (DA) are the amounts that the ends of the keel lie below DWL. The keel is said to be LEVEL unless it slopes more than 1 in 20 (2°), when it has DRAG when the stern, or LIFT when the bow, is the deeper.

DRAFT (TD) may be increased by external features like a ballast keel, fin, skeg or keel. The amount to be applied is given as DEPTH CORRECTION. KEEL LINE STRUCTURES may be:-

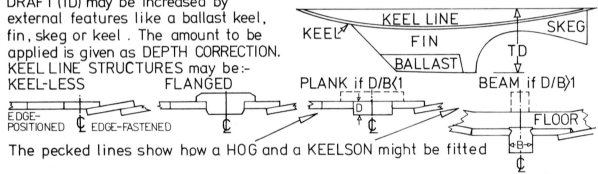

The pecked lines show how a HOG and a KEELSON might be fitted

The SHEERLINE is the upper limit of the shell, and is either at the gunwale of an open boat, the plank sheer in a decked vessel or the rail when the bulwarks increase the heeled size of the hull. The shape of the sheerline is fixed by FREEBOARDS or the heights above DWL of the ends of LOA(FF & FA) and amidships (FM). All stations are measured from the fwd end of LOA. Stations and freeboards at drifts are noted.

The STEM and the STERN are the forward and aft limits of the shell that join the keel line to the sheerline. Their profiles will be STRAIGHT unless the radius of curvature is less than LOA when they may be either CURVED, HOLLOW or REFLEX and be PLUMB or RAKED FORWARD or AFT depending upon the relative positions of the ends

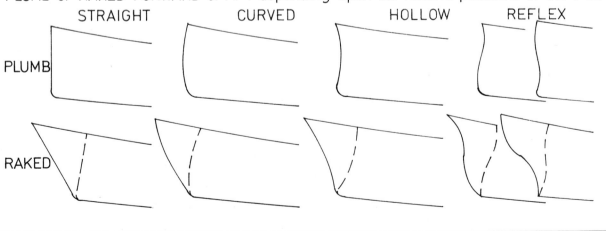

Fig 54: Conventions used to describe boatshape (Sheet 1).

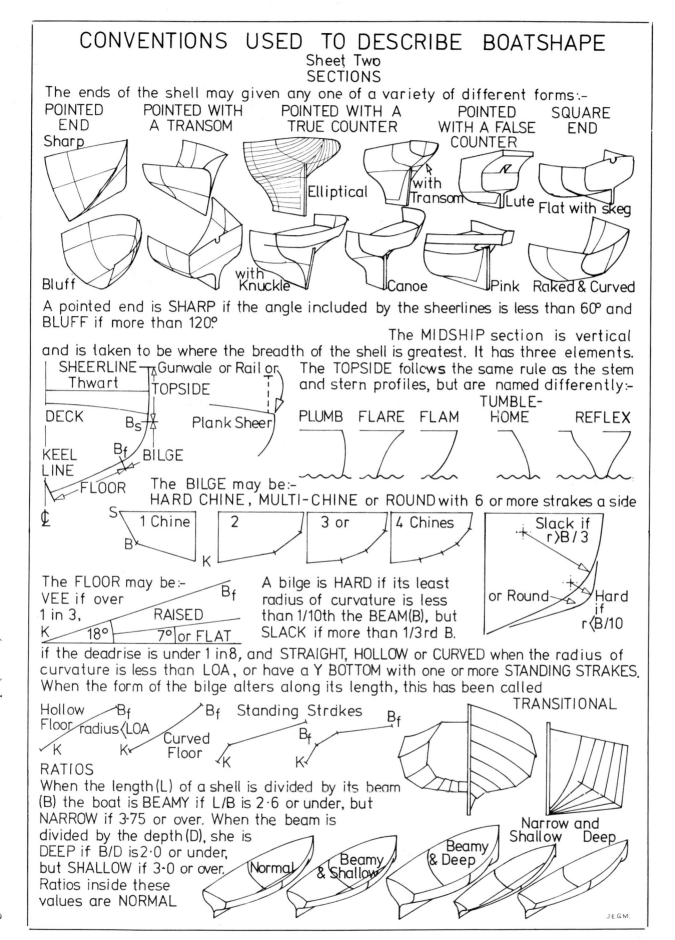

Fig 55: Conventions used to describe boatshape (Sheet 2).

CONVENTIONS USED TO DESCRIBE BOATSHAPE
Sheet Two
SECTIONS

The ends of the shell may given any one of a variety of different forms:-

POINTED END — POINTED WITH A TRANSOM — POINTED WITH A TRUE COUNTER — POINTED WITH A FALSE COUNTER — SQUARE END

Sharp

Elliptical — with Transom — Lute — Flat with skeg

Bluff — with Knuckle — Canoe — Pink — Raked & Curved

A pointed end is SHARP if the angle included by the sheerlines is less than 60° and BLUFF if more than 120°.

The MIDSHIP section is vertical and is taken to be where the breadth of the shell is greatest. It has three elements.

The TOPSIDE follows the same rule as the stem and stern profiles, but are named differently:-

PLUMB   FLARE   FLAM   TUMBLE-HOME   REFLEX

SHEERLINE — Gunwale or Rail or
Thwart — TOPSIDE
DECK — B_s — Plank Sheer
KEEL LINE — B_f — BILGE
FLOOR

The BILGE may be:-
HARD CHINE, MULTI-CHINE or ROUND with 6 or more strakes a side

1 Chine — 2 — 3 or — 4 Chines — or Round

Slack if $r > B/3$
Hard if $r < B/10$

The FLOOR may be:-
VEE if over 1 in 3,   RAISED   B_f
K   18°   7° or FLAT

A bilge is HARD if its least radius of curvature is less than 1/10th the BEAM(B), but SLACK if more than 1/3rd B.

if the deadrise is under 1 in 8, and STRAIGHT, HOLLOW or CURVED when the radius of curvature is less than LOA, or have a Y BOTTOM with one or more STANDING STRAKES. When the form of the bilge alters along its length, this has been called TRANSITIONAL

Hollow Floor   radius < LOA   B_f   B_f   Standing Strakes   B_f
B_f
Curved Floor   K   K
K   K

RATIOS

When the length(L) of a shell is divided by its beam (B) the boat is BEAMY if L/B is 2·6 or under, but NARROW if 3·75 or over. When the beam is divided by the depth(D), she is DEEP if B/D is 2·0 or under, but SHALLOW if 3·0 or over. Ratios inside these values are NORMAL

Normal — Beamy & Shallow — Beamy & Deep — Narrow and Shallow   Deep

J.E.G.M.

Though, as far as it is known, none of the following are in current use, they have been listed as part of the ancestry of our modern boats. By constantly noting in what sense words like 'ballinger', 'buss', 'cock', 'dogger', 'doling', 'hoy', 'owe', 'shotter' and 'tucker' were once used, one can start to know what they really were and became.

New terms and meanings for old ones are coming into use all the time, especially since the introduction of engines. The terms have changed less than the boats, but modern usage is no more rational. To give some recent examples: Honnor Marine build and market on original and admirable range of 18 to 20ft open GRP sailing boats. These are called longboats, drivers, drifters and luggers without regard to their work or rig; Westerly Boats are building a 24ft topsail gaff cutter, which it is a pleasure to say goes well in all weather. Following the established tradition of naming boats in a misleading way, this boat is called a Cornish crabber.

It is simpler to stop trying to read meanings into boat's names, treating them instead like personal names as a means of telling one from another. It would then be as unreasonable to expect all yawls to have two masts and sloops only one, as to wonder if all Winterbottoms stand with their backs to the fire. What is even more certain is boat names can never be the basis of a classification system.

DESCRIPTION OF SHAPE

The study showed that it was essential to be able to describe the shape of a boat clearly and if possible briefly. This would save time by avoiding repetition when giving details of variations of the same type and could very well lead to a method of classifying boats. The system adopted has been illustrated (Fig 55) and it can be seen that though shape has been described using normal nautical words, these have been given actual values, where the amount as well as kind is significant.

The system accommodates all known plank-built working boats in Britain. It would also apply to the majority of foreign boats as long as they have European origins. As the variety of shapes a plank-built boat can assume is finite, it is unlikely that this system would work for bundles, dugouts, inflatables, rafts and skin boats, nor recent man-made materials. The shapes into which these other materials can be fashioned differ from what is possible with planks, so will need to be described separately in relation to their own peculiarities. It is too early to try to devise an overall system, as the evidence is not yet available. Plank boats are only a part of the world's boat population, and I dare say that there are more dugouts south of the Equator than plank boats north of it. When all these and other types have been identified, then will be the time for a comprehensive system. In the meantime we are fortunate in having Dr Rudolph's structural classification for boats to provide a link between plank boats and dugouts[15] and Dr McGrail's morphological code for dugouts[16]. As the system in this work only amplifies those parts of Rudolph's that apply to plank boats which have no major dugout components, there should be no overlap or conflict.

The shape of the hull proper will be described. In nearly all cases, this will be that part of the boat that gives her buoyancy and stability, including what is in reserve as well as what is immersed. In general this can be taken as the planked volume, bounded by the plank edges along the centre and sheer lines. The sheerline is at the gunwale or planksheer, but extended up to the rail of the bulkwarks if these are a fair continuation of the topsides. Features like fins, skegs, gripes, bilge keels and external ballast which affect performance will also be described.

Dr Corlett reminded those present at the Boat Archaeology Symposium at Greenwich in September 1976 that length was the most expensive single dimension of any vessel[17]. It is also the most important in describing shape. As well as conveying an idea of size, length also provides a common factor, with which other dimensions can be compared when saying that a boat is shoal, beamy or fine-lined. In the past, length has been taken on the waterline, along the keel, between perpendiculars and overall, depending upon whether the measurement is to be used for working out displacement, timber requirements, tonnage or the space needed to build or berth her. One cannot always tell which of these dimensions is being quoted and even then between which two points they have been taken.

Length between perpendiculars is concerned more with internal capacity than shape, and as boats can alter their draft and trim so easily, waterline length is too indefinite. In boats the overall length is much the same as that of the shell, as overhanging feature like heads are rare. Two lengths, therefore, will be used in the description of shape: that of the plank volume, *Length* (L) and that of the keel or flat bottom, *Length of Keel* (LOK). These two together give the amounts the ends overhang. The length of a straight or sprung keel is taken between the points where it cuts up at either end. Keels which form an unbroken curve with the stem or stern profile are measured between the slope at 45° forward and cross the axis of the rudder aft, or where the keel line crosses the waterline at either end if this gives a shorter measurement.

The next indication of shapes comes from her profile, which is taken as the line of intersection of the two sides meeting along the centre line. Along the bottom this line can be *straight* or, if at all curved, *sprung* and will be said to be *level* unless the slope is more than 1 in 20 (2°), in which case it will be called *drag*, if deeper, or *lift*, if shallower, aft. Although this line can be *keel-less*, it is more usual to find a *beam keel* or a *plank keel* at this position. The beam keel is a medial strength member that is as deep or deeper than it is wide. The plank keel is one that is wider than it is deep. If there is no medial member thicker than the planking, the structure is keel-less. If a beam keel is reinforced by a separate horizontal member to take the garboard fastenings, this is a *hog*. If there are flanges integral with the keel for the same purpose, this is a *flanged* beam or plank keel.

The *Length of Keel* as determined above is recorded as LOK and its *draft* below datum water level at each end and, if sprung, at the midship station. *Datum waterline* (DWL) is taken at an arbitrary height anywhere between empty and fully loaded, but preferably at a normal working load. Once chosen all other measurements must relate to this loading.

The *midship section* is taken to be vertical at the station where the maximum beam occurs. This section gets its character from three elements of it: the *floor* which starting from the keel line contributes mainly to increasing the breadth of the boat, the turn of the bilge, the *bilge*, which converts the floor into the topsides, and the *side* which rises to the sheer line. Taking these three midship elements separately, their various characteristics can be described.

Depending upon the angle the floor makes with the horizontal at the keel line, it will be described as *flat* if the deadrise is less than 1 in 8 (7°), *raised* if between this and 1 in 3 (18°) and *vee* if more than this. The floor is said to be *curved* or *hollow* if its radius of curvature in the appropriate direction is less than the length of the boat. It will be seen that keel lines and floors between them can give level or inclined bottoms which may be flat or rounded in either or both directions. Any configuration of floor can have a *standing strake* which is a garboard with considerably more deadrise than the strake lying immediately outboard of it, so forming a *Y bottom*.

The bilge element of the midship section can be either *hard chine* if the bottom and side meet at an angle, *multi-chine* if there are two, three or four of these angles, and *round bilge* if there are six or more strakes between the keel and sheerlines. If the radius of curvature of the bilge is under one tenth of the beam it is called *hard* and over one third *slack*. In most designs the bilge characteristic is much the same throughout, but in a few the hard chine amidships becomes a round bilge nearer the ends as in the Thames sailing barge, or a round bilge become a hard chine as in a coble. Such bilges are said to be *transitional* at one or other or both ends.

The side element can have *flare* or *tumblehome* if it leans outboard or inboard of *plumb*, and, like floors, *curved*, *hollow* or *reflex* if the radius is less than the length of the boat.

The maximum width of the complete midship section is *beam* and the height of the sheer above the keel line at this station is *depth*. If length is divided by beam, a quotient of 2.6 and under is *beamy*, but 3.75 and over is *narrow*. If beam is divided by depth, a quotient of 2.0 and under is *deep*, but 3.0 and over *shallow*. When describing the midsection it is said to be *full* if over 85% of the available cross sectional area, if just under *firm*, or if under 70% *easy*.

A boat can end in two ways either as an intersection of the narrowing sides producing a *pointed* end or with the hull cut off or truncated to form a *square end*. Pointed ends are *sharp* if the included angle at the sheerline is less than 60° and *bluff* if over 120°. These angles generally decrease towards the keel line. The pointed end takes one of several forms, and the one pointed all the way up to the sheerline structurally needs a *sternpost* or a *stempost* to which the plank ends can be fastened. One that is pointed part way up, above which the strakes are parted, requires a *transom* to secure their ends. An end in which the upper strakes are both parted from their post and then carried beyond that is a *counter*. Counters are *true* or *false* whether they are watertight with the rest of the hull, or not. True counters may end with *straight* or *curved*, and *raked* or *plumb truncations*, or they can have *unbroken* or *pointed* ends. All of these can have a chine called a *knuckle*. Where the counter ends with a post on the centreline made up of a horn timber or outrigger in its lower part with a further knee on top of that, it forms a *canoe stern* if it rakes aft and a *cruiser stern* if forward. *Lute* and *pink sterns* are false counters.

The truncations or cuts forming square ends may be made *plumb* or *raked*, *straight* or *curved* across the hull. They may also be curved in profile to form an angle or continuation of the keel line. The sternpost of a Bridgwater barge like the 'tombstone' of a dory is the same width as the bottom at its base, but widens upwards. In all these rarer cases, the stations of the measurement points have to be recorded together with the heights above datum waterline and breadth of the sheerline.

The shape of the elevation of a pointed end, its profile, will be that of the rabbet line, where the planks meet the post or each other. The shape and inclination of the end profile modifies the shape of the hull's main body to form the *bow* or the *stern*, the immersed parts of which are the *entry* and *run*. The profile can be *straight*, *curved*, *hollow* or *reflex*. The whole profile may be *raked forward* or *aft* if it is not *plumb*. It will be seen that a clipper bow is a reflex line raked forward and a ram bow one that is raked aft. This line may be angled to an unbroken continuation of the keel line, where they meet at the *toe* forward and *heel* aft.

The effect structure has on shape has to be taken into account. A boat with transverse planking and no floors can hardly have a vee-bottom, for example. As far as structure and shape is concerned, method of planking is the most significant item. Dr Greenhill has tackled this subject and all students of boat structure should read him[18]. He separates shell planks fastened by their edges before the insertion of internal stiffening from planks secured to a pre-erected framework but not to each other. This approach has cleared away the misconceptions inherent in the 'clinker-or-carvel' division.

Minor changes in terms, which follows on from Dr Greenhill's thinking, have been made in this work. The term *edge-joined* will still be used for planks in structures where these fastenings provide the greater part of the structural continuity through the stressed shell. These in effect are hulls that appear to have been built using combinations of techniques that stem from dugout and skin boat practice. Rather than *non-edge fastened*, the term *edge-positioned* will be used where it is the internal framework which provides the structural continuity in the finished hull, which in contrast exhibits signs of refinements of rafted structures. Most hulls are clearly either edge-fastened or edge-positioned but a few are mongrel types which use both sorts of planking, and some where it is hard to say where the main strength continuity lies. A flat bottom boat like a canal boat has such thick transverse planks that she can do without both keel and transverse floors, yet she would probably be classed as edge-positioned. A racing shell with thin edge-fastened strakes depends mostly on her internal structure for strength and is hard to classify. In this sort of exceptional case, it will be taken that the presence of permanent positive fastenings as opposed to temporary locating devices puts the hull into the edge-fastened category. As this is about British boats, the term *clinker* can be safely used, as it is the traditional method used to clench the lapped edges of planks. The poorly defined term *carvel* has been avoided. In hulls which have both edge-fastened and - positioned zones of planking, the Tone withy boat being one example, this will be stated though the method used for the immersed zone has been used for listing.

This section may be summed up thus: an approximation of the size and shape of a boat is given if the following are noted:

Planked volume – Length and if edge-fastened or -positioned

Keel line – Keel-less, plank or beam keel, shape, length, & drafts

Midship section – Shape of floor, bilge & side

Beam and Depth

Sheerline – Shape and freeboards

Ends – Posts

and if with transoms or counters, or square end, with their overhangs, shapes, heights and breadths. Peculiarities not covered by this, like a *coggy boat's* bow being so much fuller than her stern, the height of the deck and combination of keel types, will be commented upon separately. Appendix IV lists a number of boats described by this method. As drawings have been published for all of them it is possible to make direct comparisons with the aid of the references given.

CLASSIFICATION

By no means all the several thousand structurally possible combinations of the available features are found in British working boats. As far as this work goes, about forty of them will cover all the identified types. In a few cases a separate category is required to cover just one distinct type, whilst elsewhere there are categories which apply to many broadly similar types of boat. The situation is not static. At any time, other sorts of boats, which do not match any of the current categories, may be found or invented. For instance, there are no working boats with vee-bottoms and hard chines, a practical arrangement found overseas. This system allows for a boat like this or in many other shapes to be added were they to appear in Britain. Given the data, exclusive systems of classification

can be devised for items subject to natural laws, animal, vegetable or mineral. Artifacts can only be listed within stated limits of period, place, material and use.

In the case of boatshape, the sheer number of types begs for some form of catalogue. The problem has been to decide on which feature to start sorting. The nature of the bottom at the centreline has been chosen, and has worked well enough for the preparation of the text of this book. The use of terms like *genus*, species and variety for the various grades of shape has been avoided as they convey a biological sense; the ease with which one can endow a boat with genetic properties is a pitfall. Although the development of boats often appears to follow a course rather like natural selection and evolution, boats are inanimate. Any new boat may be a copy, improvement or degeneration of a previous model, or she can be an entirely original type. Therefore the boats in this system have been sorted into classes, divisions, sub-divisions and categories.

It also was necessary to find short labels to distinguish the categories conveniently. This label, a taxon, attempts to evoke as near as possible the image of the boats in question, as for example 'mackerel' does for the whole Scomber family.

If a keel can be taken as being a median more robust than the planks on either side of it, then there are three classes of boatshape found in Britain, *keel-less*, *part keel* and *keel boats*. The considerable difference in the shapes associated with these three classes prevents a common method of sorting them into divisions.

Keel-less boats may be either *hard chine* or *round section*. No examples of *multi-chine* hulls have been identified. The hard chine boats which are numerous have had to be subdivided into those with *flat* or *curved sides*, both of which may have completely level or *true*, *sprung* or *dished* (sprung and curved) *flat bottoms*. There are two further categories of flat sided boats which are not found in boats with curved sides, namely where the bottom curves on round to form the end, and where there is a square raked end. These are called *sprung ends* and *swim ends* respectively. In many of the more simple boats, pointed, square and transom stern varieties may be seen lying side by side, having been built like that or modified in their lifetime. No further sub-division has been made when this occurs, beyond noting the fact. Each of the final categories have been labelled and shown on the chart of the system (Fig 56).

Examples of *true*, *sprung* and *dished flatties* (Fig 57) may still be seen all over Britain, wherever there is a stretch of fresh or saltwater big enough to need a boat. The local variety may be called 'canoe', 'trow', or 'punt' rather than 'flatty'. Home- or carpenter-built, they tend to be small and are used for gunning, fishing and transport. The sprung-ended flatties have been labelled *scows* and are exemplified by a wide range of river punts, from the bulky crossing ferries and dugout-like Severn long net salmon punts (Fig 58) to the elegant punts used on the Thames for picnics and racing[19]. The swim-ended flatties were once seen in the form of Thames sailing swim barges, but are

CLASSIFICATION OF SHAPES OF WORKING PLANKED BOATS IN BRITAIN

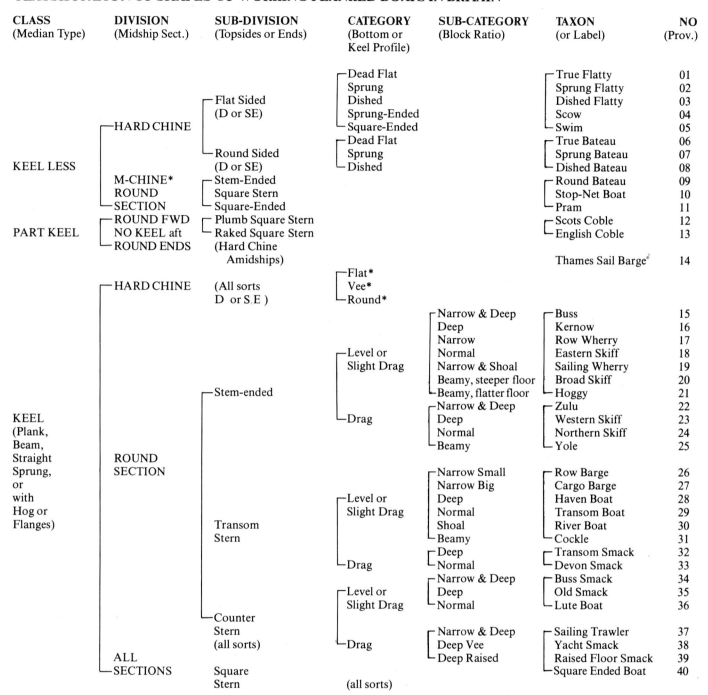

CLASS (Median Type)	DIVISION (Midship Sect.)	SUB-DIVISION (Topsides or Ends)	CATEGORY (Bottom or Keel Profile)	SUB-CATEGORY (Block Ratio)	TAXON (or Label)	NO (Prov.)
			Dead Flat		True Flatty	01
			Sprung		Sprung Flatty	02
		Flat Sided (D or SE)	Dished		Dished Flatty	03
			Sprung-Ended		Scow	04
	HARD CHINE		Square-Ended		Swim	05
			Dead Flat		True Bateau	06
		Round Sided (D or SE)	Sprung		Sprung Bateau	07
KEEL LESS			Dished		Dished Bateau	08
	M-CHINE* ROUND SECTION	Stem-Ended			Round Bateau	09
		Square Stern			Stop-Net Boat	10
		Square-Ended			Pram	11
PART KEEL	ROUND FWD NO KEEL aft ROUND ENDS	Plumb Square Stern			Scots Coble	12
		Raked Square Stern (Hard Chine Amidships)			English Coble	13
					Thames Sail Barge	14
	HARD CHINE	(All sorts D or S.E)	Flat* Vee* Round*			
				Narrow & Deep	Buss	15
				Deep	Kernow	16
				Narrow	Row Wherry	17
			Level or Slight Drag	Normal	Eastern Skiff	18
				Narrow & Shoal	Sailing Wherry	19
				Beamy, steeper floor	Broad Skiff	20
		Stem-ended		Beamy, flatter floor	Hoggy	21
				Narrow & Deep	Zulu	22
			Drag	Deep	Western Skiff	23
				Normal	Northern Skiff	24
KEEL (Plank, Beam, Straight Sprung, or with Hog or Flanges)				Beamy	Yole	25
				Narrow Small	Row Barge	26
				Narrow Big	Cargo Barge	27
	ROUND SECTION		Level or Slight Drag	Deep	Haven Boat	28
				Normal	Transom Boat	29
		Transom Stern		Shoal	River Boat	30
				Beamy	Cockle	31
			Drag	Deep	Transom Smack	32
				Normal	Devon Smack	33
			Level or Slight Drag	Narrow & Deep	Buss Smack	34
				Deep	Old Smack	35
				Normal	Lute Boat	36
		Counter Stern (all sorts)	Drag	Narrow & Deep	Sailing Trawler	37
				Deep Vee	Yacht Smack	38
	ALL SECTIONS			Deep Raised	Raised Floor Smack	39
		Square Stern	(all sorts)		Square Ended Boat	40

D or SE = Double or Single-Ended *= Not Found in British Working Boats.

Fig 56: Classification.

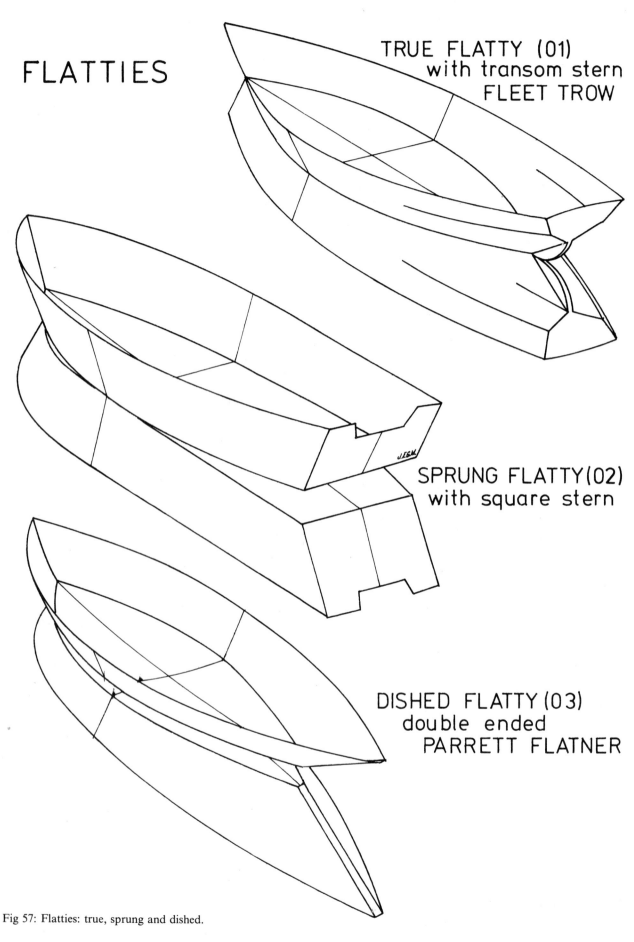

FLATTIES

TRUE FLATTY (01)
with transom stern
FLEET TROW

SPRUNG FLATTY (02)
with square stern

DISHED FLATTY (03)
double ended
PARRETT FLATNER

Fig 57: Flatties: true, sprung and dished.

Fig 58: Scow.

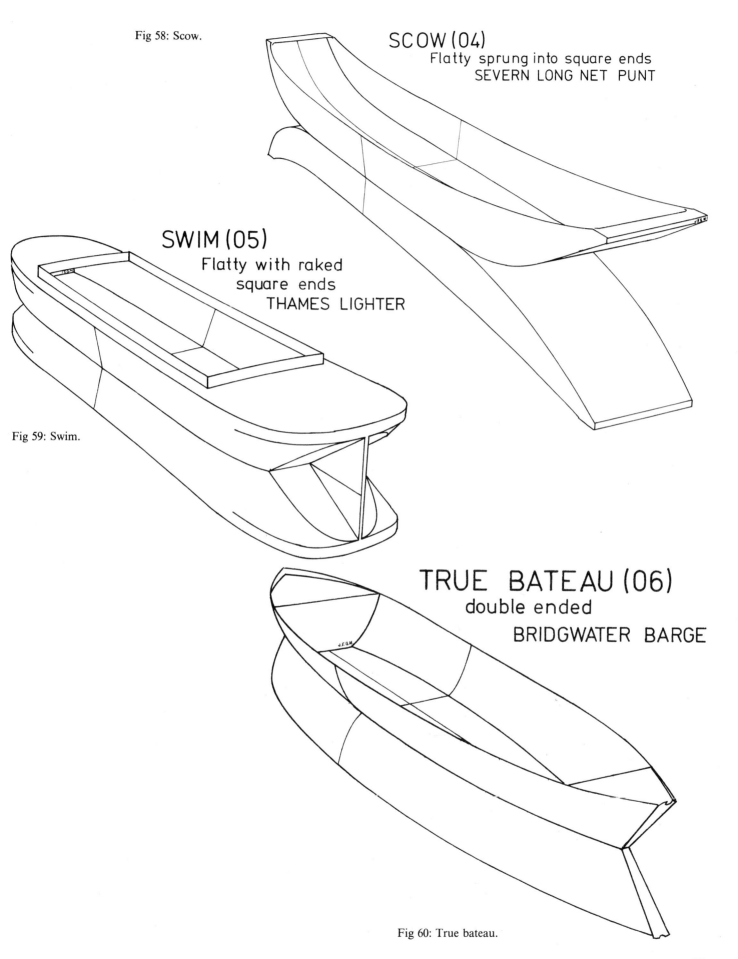

SCOW (04)
Flatty sprung into square ends
SEVERN LONG NET PUNT

SWIM (05)
Flatty with raked
square ends
THAMES LIGHTER

Fig 59: Swim.

TRUE BATEAU (06)
double ended
BRIDGWATER BARGE

Fig 60: True bateau.

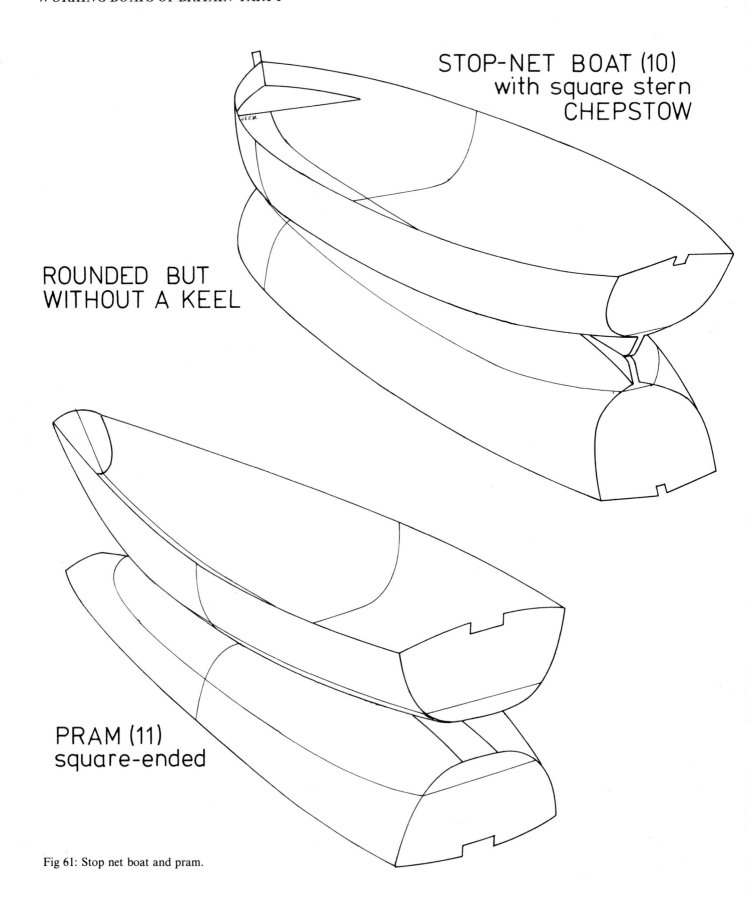

STOP-NET BOAT (10)
with square stern
CHEPSTOW

ROUNDED BUT
WITHOUT A KEEL

PRAM (11)
square-ended

Fig 61: Stop net boat and pram.

still common as dumb lighters, and have been called *swims* (Fig 59).

The French colonial term *bateau* has been used for keel-less boats with hard chines and curved sides. Although this shape has often been used in this country, it was more widely exploited in North America. The shape was used for upper river barge work on the Fens, Parrett, Severn, Teign and Thames, up to the size of vessels, and there were troop landing craft with this shape in the eighteenth century. In the smaller sizes, there is the dished bottom Weston-super-Mare flatner, which was double stemmed, mostly with transoms aft, and used in open water, and also the Norfolk canoe that took advantage of this shape combining shoal draft with a measure of sea-keeping[20] (Fig 60).

There are two sorts of boat that may be anomalous. The first is the Montrose Bay boat (p 114), which is a variety of Scottish coble that has a sprung bottom, hard chines and curved sides with a plumb square stern. The other, the Rye river barge, looks to be a bateau inboard but was planked with rounded bilges outside[21]. On balance with these, it was decided that the structural method was the more significant indication of type. The Bay boats have been placed amongst the cobles and the Rye barges with the bateau.

There are two keel-less types which have fully rounded sections. The first of these is the salmon stop-net boat used at Chepstow on the Wye and Gatcombe on the Severn. They are strongly built, having edge-positioned planks on sawn frames with a stem forward and a square stern aft. The other type is the clinker pram, a foreign introduction built in Britain in wood and GRP for use as a working punt or tender, and also, in a much shorter form, for yachtsmen. Apart from the fact that both the *stop-net boat* and the *pram* are keel-less, they are quite different in shape (Fig 61).

The next class is made up of those that are part keel-less and part keel. There are only two types in this class, which is extremely numerous. The first division consists of the cobles, which are round section and keel-less aft with a keel portion forward. These sub-divide into the *English coble* with a raked square stern and the *Scottish coble* with a plumb square stern. The obsolete mule was a form of English coble which had a keel portion aft as well as forward (Fig 62). The second division was made up of vessels, which combined a keel-less hard chine midships with round section portions both ends. This was the shape of most types of *Thames sailing barge* (Fig 63), excluding the swim barges already listed and the boomy barges, which though they were hard chined amidships, could have keels and counters and be rigged like coasting ketches.

Up to this point, apart from the barges with their unique shapes, the boats have been much of the same size. From here on however, the keeled varieties will be found to vary from small boats up to vessels in size. The effect size makes on shape must now be taken in account. This is scale effect. Doubling the size of a boat does not double all her other

qualities. They are governed instead by the Laws of Comparison, which Froude introduced to relate models in a test tank to full sized ships. Though the change of scale is less in the case of small to large boats, scale effect is still to be reckoned with. If length, breadth and depth is only doubled, areas like sail and wetted surface go up four times and volumes like displacement and induced wave systems by eight. Thus, the relationship between any dimension and an area or volume will also change, and practical problems like the power required and speed expected cannot be solved by doubling either. In particular the righting moment improves twice as fast as the heeling moment due to sails which is why small boats are so much more tender than big ones.

In general working boats have been taken as lying between 14 and 42ft long, a turn down of 3. Some of the types included because they started as boats, like the zulus, can be as long as 84 ft, a turn down of 6. Scale effect will therefore need to be watched, as in any one group of shapes the larger examples may exhibit different characteristics. It is to be expected that vessels that are narrow, deep or both will usually be large, so may differ due to scale effect.

By far the largest class, both in variety and total number, is made up of boats with keels. The main division of these lies between those with hard chines and those with round sections. Apart from recreational craft, there are practically no working keel boats with hard chines of any sort, so our main interest is with those with round sections. Before the arrival of engine propulsion, almost all of these had a stempost forward and a sternport aft, some of which carried transoms and some counters. This gives three sub-divisions: *double-ended, transom stern* and *counter stern*. There were also a relatively few types of boat which had no sternposts, having instead a *square-end*, which cut off the hull shape aft, calling for a fourth sub-division. This last type has grown more popular throughout this century as it lends itself to screw-propulsion.

Each of the other three sub-divisions fall into two categories: those whose keels are level or nearly level with the water line, and those whose keels have a marked degree (more than 1 in 20) of drag. These six categories have to be further sub-categorised before patterns of similar types are evident. This has been done by grouping boats according to their length/beam and beam/depth ratios. What has been taken as narrow, beamy, deep, shallow or normal has been defined and these relate to the distribution of the sample. Though one may think that this amount of sub-division is excessive, without it, a classification into a distinct type of shape would not be obtained.

Taking the level or nearly level keeled double-enders first, five sub-categories are needed to cover the range of these boats. Starting with those that are both narrow and deep (more than 3.75 beams long and more than half the beam deep) we find a group of vessels which include the old herring busses, the Mersey flats and the Humber keels and sloops. This bluff-ended type with its boxy mid-

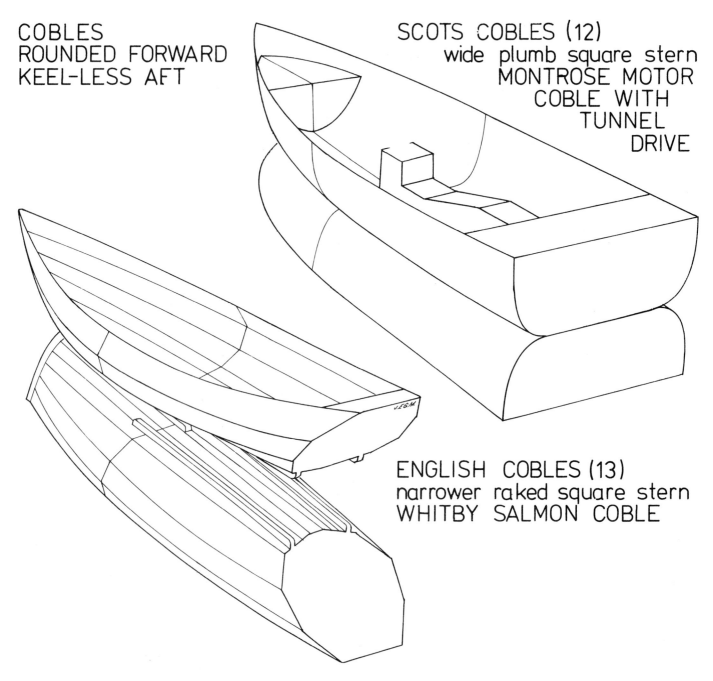

COBLES
ROUNDED FORWARD
KEEL-LESS AFT

SCOTS COBLES (12)
wide plumb square stern
MONTROSE MOTOR
COBLE WITH
TUNNEL
DRIVE

ENGLISH COBLES (13)
narrower raked square stern
WHITBY SALMON COBLE

Fig 62: Cobles – Scottish and English

THAMES SAILING BARGE (14)
TRANSITIONAL
rounded ends with
hard chines
amidships

Fig 63: Thames sailing barge.

Fig 64: Buss.

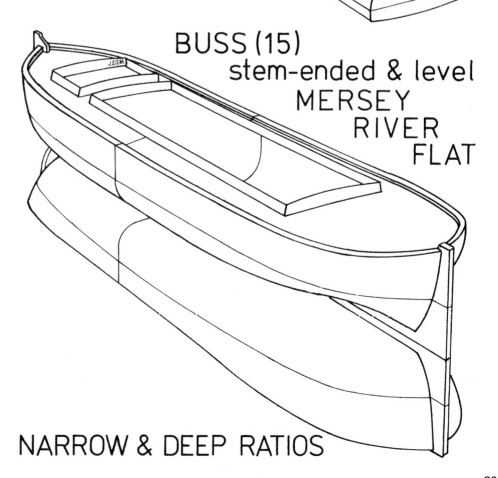

BUSS (15)
stem-ended & level
MERSEY
RIVER
FLAT

NARROW & DEEP RATIOS

sections has been labelled *buss* for convenience when referring to this shape (Fig 64).

Boats which, though normal in length/beam, are otherwise deep make up the next sub-category. These are not so large as the busses and are mainly found to be part-decked fishing boats from the far west of Cornwall or the Isle of Man. Chapman's fully decked hoy or sailing lighter fitted this description[22], though she was almost bluff enough to be regarded as a short buss. The Spithead wherry, a first class hoveller, fits into this group due to her unusual depth for an open boat. This shape, which has an easier but still full-to-firm mid-section, has been named *kernow*, the Cornish for Cornwall (Fig 65).

Boats which are narrow but of normal depth for their beam include the Portsmouth second class and Thames wherries, also the 27ft service whaler, which is a rare example of a sprung keel. All have firm well rounded sections and this shape has been called *row wherry* (Fig 66).

The level double-enders with normal block ratios form a large well spread out sub-category of types centering on the east coast of Scotland, such as the baldies, fifies and scaffies. There are types as well from further afield, the Firth of Clyde, the Solway Firth, the Thames Estuary and the Medway. In addition to these estuary-based boats

there are also the north Norfolk sailing crabbers, which had vee-d floors as opposed to raised curved ones. On the east coast of Scotland these floors were either raised and hollow, or as one further north, had standing garboard strakes. The type was once found as an Aberystwyth beach boat[23] in a form that closely resembled a Maine peapod[24] having the same firm bilges. Had they been within the scope of this study, the almost beamy Shetland boats would have come in this sub-category in spite of their much slighter mid-sections and slack bilges. This shape is still popular and may be seen in the form of the surf and harbour boats in the north east of England, and the small motor creel boats on the west coast of Scotland. This shape has been labelled *eastern skiff*. If a further division of this big group was needed, the rake and the shape of the bow and stern should be taken into consideration (Fig 67).

The narrow and shoal (depth less than one third of beam) sub-category is made up of only two types, quite different from each other in both use and appearance. Both were from Norfolk, the Broads wherry and the beach yawl, and have sweet lines differing in two respects. The yawl was much narrower and sharper in her ends and had a full midship section. The wherry was bluff-ended on deck with an easy mid-section. Unless more examples of either

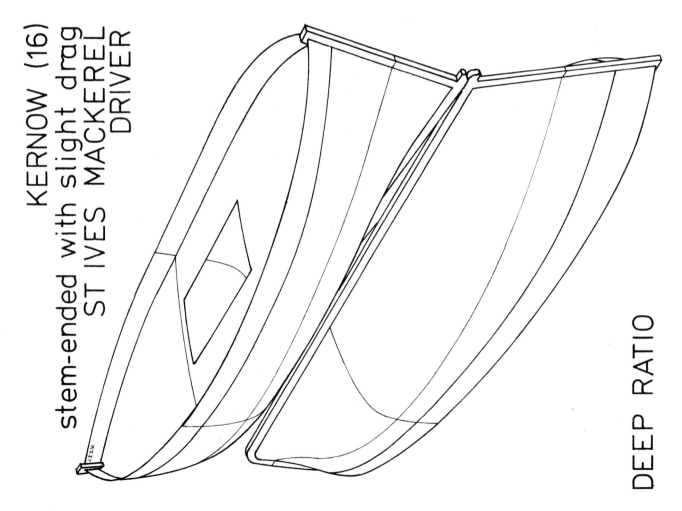

KERNOW (16)
stem-ended with slight drag
ST IVES MACKEREL DRIVER

DEEP RATIO

Fig 65: Kernow.

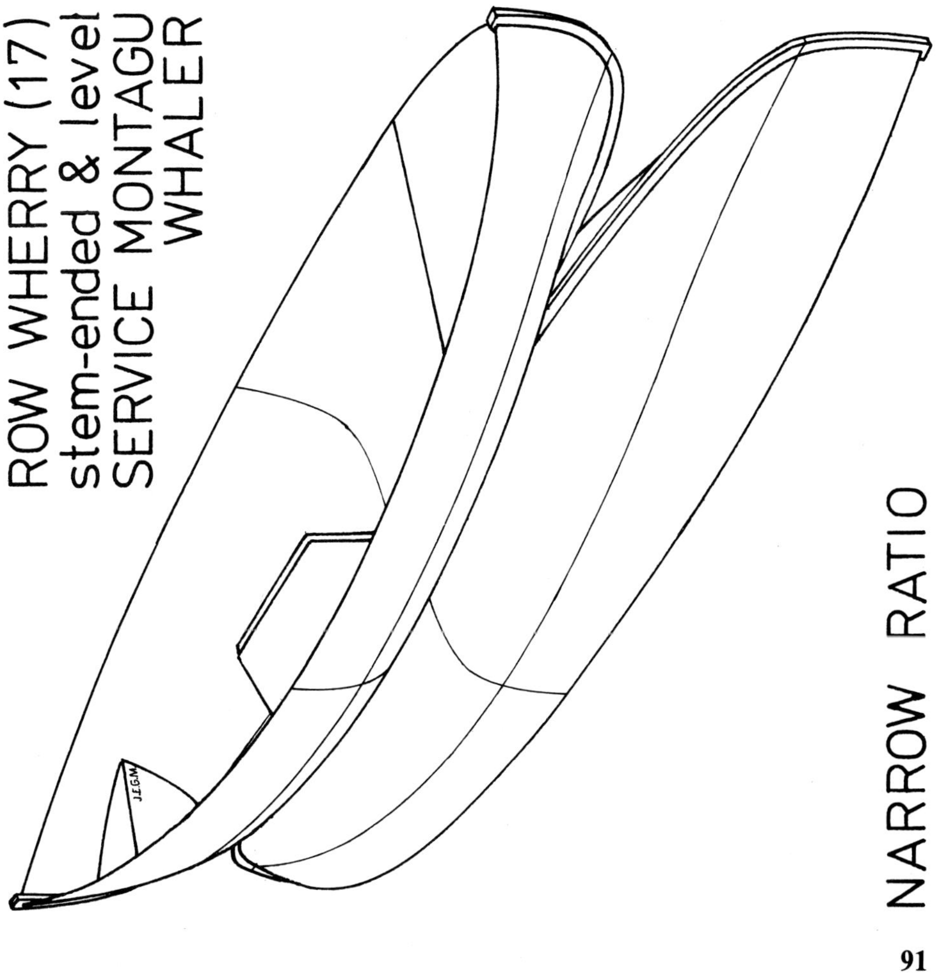

Fig 67: Eastern skiff.

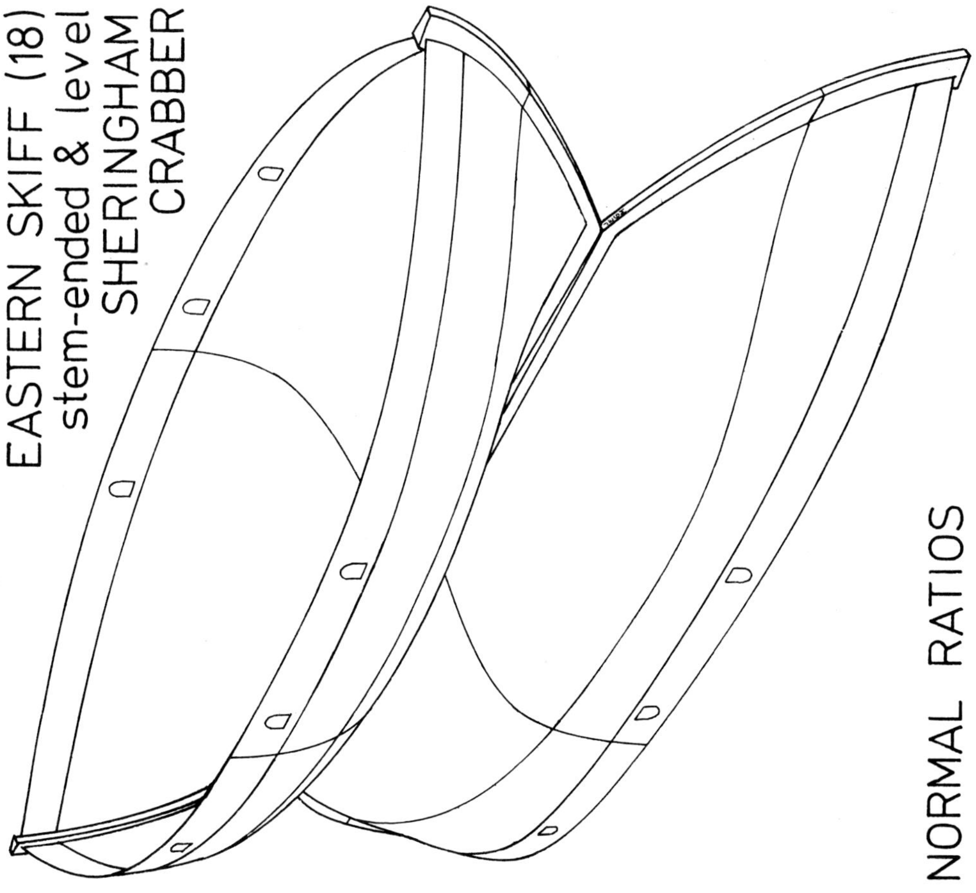

EASTERN SKIFF (18)
stem-ended & level
SHERINGHAM
CRABBER

NORMAL RATIOS

ROW WHERRY (17)
stem-ended & level
SERVICE MONTAGU
WHALER

Fig 66: Row wherry.

NARROW RATIO

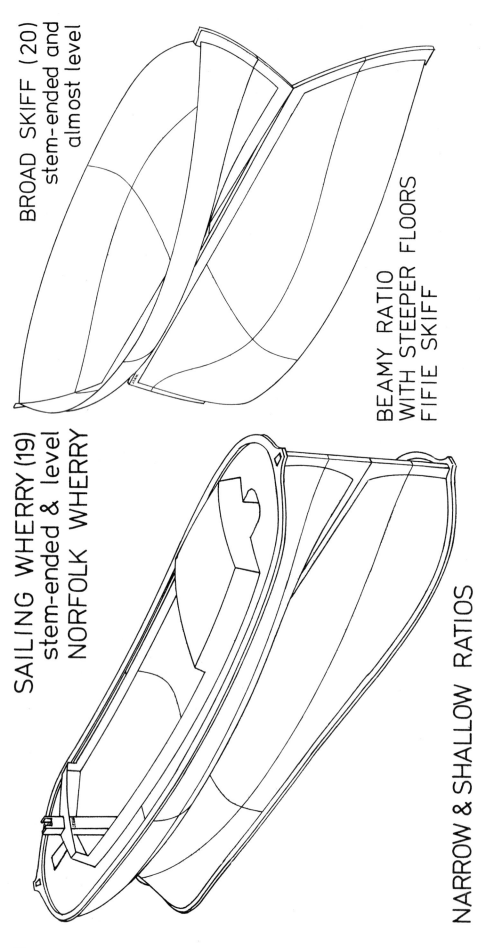

BROAD SKIFF (20)
stem-ended and
almost level

BEAMY RATIO
WITH STEEPER FLOORS
FIFIE SKIFF

SAILING WHERRY (19)
stem-ended & level
NORFOLK WHERRY

NARROW & SHALLOW RATIOS

Fig 69: Broad skiff.

Fig 68: Sailing wherry.

Fig 70: Hoggy.

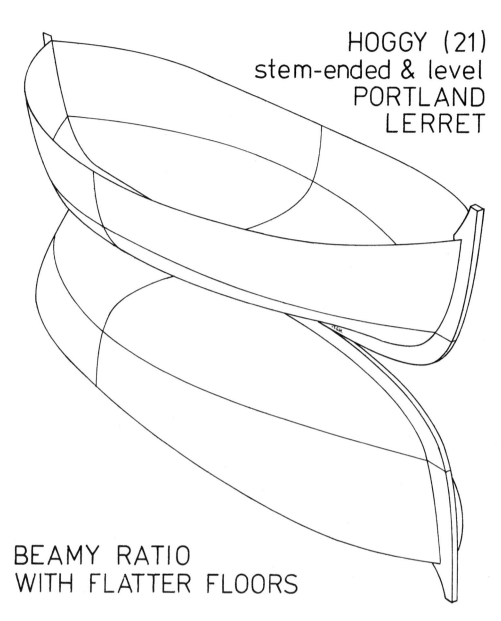

HOGGY (21)
stem-ended & level
PORTLAND
LERRET

BEAMY RATIO
WITH FLATTER FLOORS

variety can be identified – a double-ended Selsey galley for instance – these two are being listed under the label *sailing wherry* (Fig 68).

The last sub-category of the level keel double-ender is for two sorts of beamy (less than 2.6 beams long) boat. Together they are geographically widespread, separated only by the deadrise of their floors. The Portland lerret, the Start Bay seine-netter, two river barges, Chapman's close lighter[25] and the Brighton hoggy all have flat floors and have been given the label *hoggy* (Fig 70). The Scots varieties, illustrated by the boats from Wick, Fraserburgh, and Newhaven in Washington's report, like the more recent fifie type from Rosehearty, have standing strakes in the earlier forms but raised or vee-d floors recently[26]. This group of shapes has been labelled *broad skiff* (Fig 69).

A number of double-ended types have keels which draw a lot more aft than forward, and there are four sub-categories of these. The first consists of boats that are both narrow and deep, but has only one but important instance – the zulu. The type gave rise to vessels of over 80ft down to

the zulu skiffs about half as long. Its success was short, emerging in the 1880s to become obsolescent early in the twentieth century when it was found that the steeply raked sternpost would not accommodate a propeller aperture easily. The firm mid-section had hollow vee-d floors and plumb sides to give a shape that has been labelled *zulu* (Fig 71).

Next are a larger group of types with deep but normal length/beam ratios. In it are various Cornish drivers, Isle of Man nickies and nobbies and the Loch Fyne skiff. An intermediate form of motor fifie can also be included. The sailing boats were alike in most respects, but the motor boats seem to be a separate development. Once faster shaft speeds permitted smaller screws, there was not the need for large draft in motor fishing vessels so this class is vanishing. These boats had firmer mid-sections than the zulu and had raised or vee-d floors, mostly round bilges with flam or plumb sides. This sub-category has been called *western skiff* (Fig 72).

The type with normal block ratios come from the west

Fig 71: Zulu.

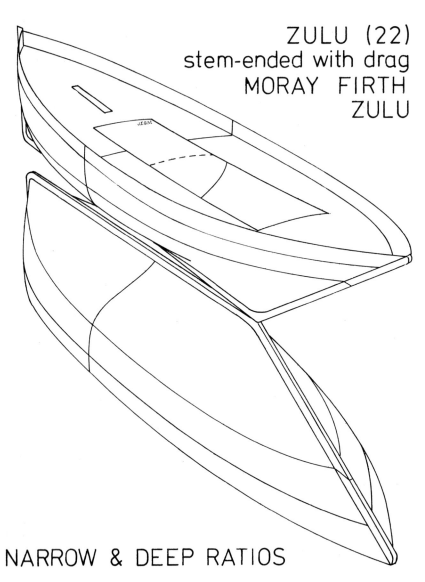

ZULU (22)
stem-ended with drag
MORAY FIRTH
ZULU

NARROW & DEEP RATIOS

and north of Scotland, being similar to the level keeled skiffs apart from the amount of drag and the hollower and steeper floors. The sgoths from the Hebrides and the motor yoles from round Pentland Firth are of this shape, which has been labelled *northern skiff*. The label *yole* has been kept for the beamiest of the Stroma and Orkney yoles. Here the standing strakes, raised floors and flam sides produce an easy mid-section (Fig 73).

Before studying transom sterned boats, consider the effect of the size and the shape of a transom on the afterbody. Small wedge-shaped transoms that only spread a few of the uppermost strakes leave the underwater lines the same as a double-ender. Deep beamy transoms, partly submerged, fill out the whole of the stern of the boat. The width of a transom, both at the sheer and the waterline, has therefore to be noted. As described in the chapter on structure, it can be difficult to tell at a glance a deep transom from a square stern (p 64). Like the double-enders the transom sterned boats are divided into those with level, or almost so, keels and those with drag.

Taking the level keel boats, it is found that there are many examples, which, though narrow, have normal beam/depth ratios. It seems at first that these examples bear little relationship to each other, until one recognises the effect size has in making a split between boats and vessels. The boats include the Cornish harbour and pilot gigs, the east Kent galleys and galley punts, many sorts of waterman's and pleasure boats, all of which had small high transoms clear of the water. The firm mid-sections were made up of straight or curved raised floors, normal bilges and flam sides. All had oars and some had sails. More heavily built with bigger transoms and fuller mid-sections were the oared Cornish pilchard seine-net boats. The vessel-sized examples were bluffer again, and those like the Severn Estuary trow and the Mersey sailing flat had even more ample transoms and mid-sections. Such a wide spectrum in this category required further division to take account of scale effect. As all the types are some form of barge, the labels *row barge* and *cargo barge* have been chosen, the open pilchard seiners being taken as a larger and fuller variety of the row barge (Fig 74).

The next kind of level keeled transom sterned boats is deep with a normal length/beam ratio. In the days of sail this included the bawleys, the Deal luggers, the Falmouth

Fig 72: Western skiff.

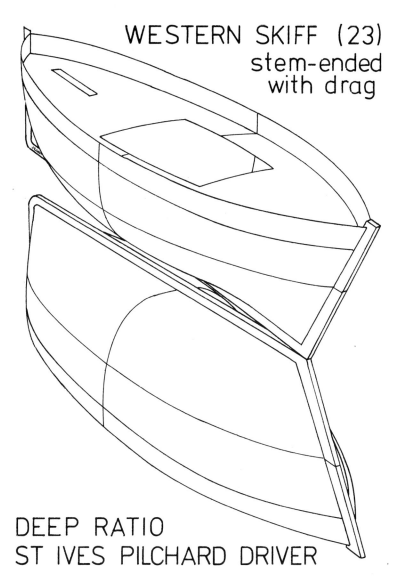

WESTERN SKIFF (23)
stem-ended
with drag

DEEP RATIO
ST IVES PILCHARD DRIVER

quay punt, the Weymouth harbour fishing boat and, only by including her high washstrake, the Sennen Cove crabber. More recently the Mevagissey motor toshers and motor shrimpers from the Wash have joined this list. Apart from the Sennen boat, which might be better in the following sub-category, these are all haven-based with raised or vee-d floors and generally plumb or tumblehome sides. The harbour-based examples tended to have more deadrise and easier midship sections than those that dried out in creeks and leads in open mud or sand flats. These have been labelled *haven boats* (Fig 75).

The level transom boat with normal block ratios is the sub-category of the most common single type in Britain. Though the commonest shape from East Anglia round the south coast to Wales, it is also found in most other places in Britain, but not as the dominant type. Its popularity is due to its versatility, both in the way it is used and propelled. It would be tedious to have to give every example, when a few names like the Yarmouth punt, Cadgwith crabber and the Dover punt should serve. The Portloe crabber, *Rose*, described later (p 184), comes close to be typical of this whole sub-category. She has now

been preserved and may be seen at the National Maritime Museum. These beach boats have less deadrise than the previous group and this gives them full mid-sections. Some harbour-based boats with vee-d floors fall into this group, like those once used for fishing in the Solent and Southampton Water[27]. In the larger sizes there are the service boom boats, the 36ft pinnace and the 42ft launch for instance, and the inside and outside west country sailing barges, which are fuller examples of the same shape. The type accepts both inboard and outboard engine and is the model for many GRP versions. This is the *transom boat*, which has spread further over the world than other British types (Fig 76).

Normal length/beam boats with shallow mid-sections are far less common; only some hire boats and Dee salmon boats have been identified so far. Even these two have greatly different transom widths. Due to their low freeboards this sub-category has been called *river boat* (Fig 77).

The sort of level transom stern types that were beamy but with normal mid-sections were found on the coast: the Aldeburgh sprat boat, the working Itchen ferry, the

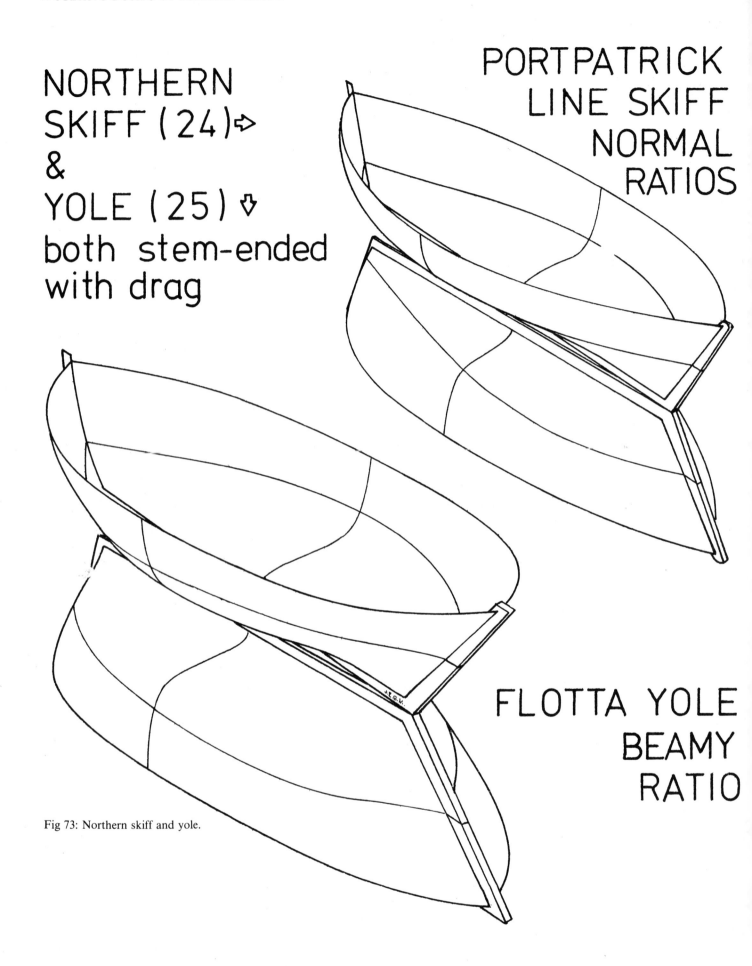

NORTHERN
SKIFF (24)⇨
&
YOLE (25) ⇩
both stem-ended
with drag

PORTPATRICK
LINE SKIFF
NORMAL
RATIOS

FLOTTA YOLE
BEAMY
RATIO

Fig 73: Northern skiff and yole.

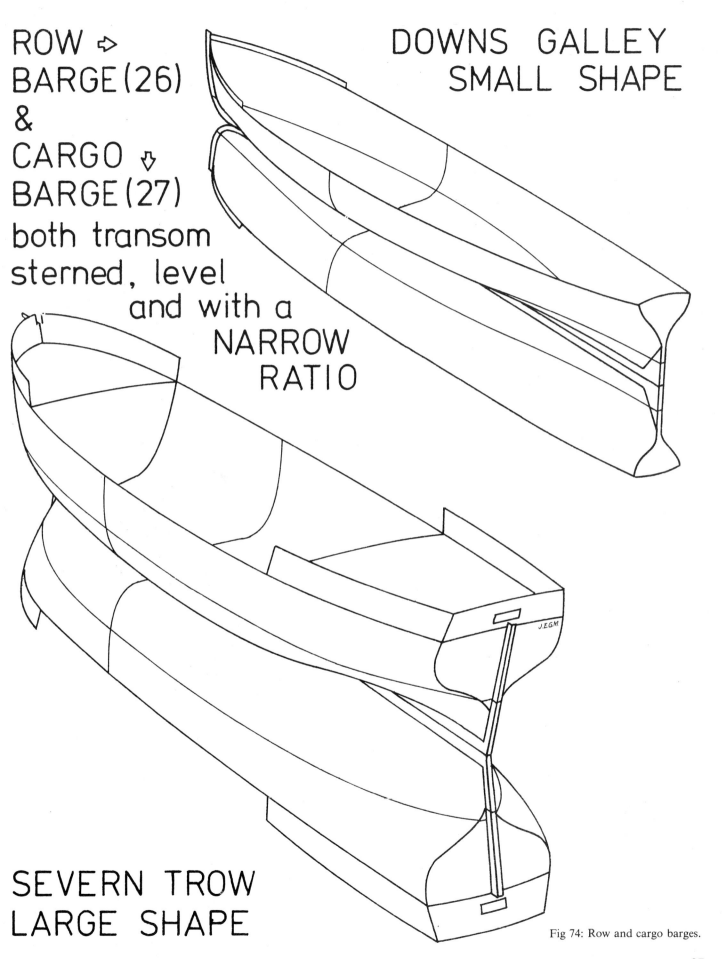

ROW ⇨
BARGE (26)
&
CARGO ⇩
BARGE (27)
both transom
sterned, level
and with a
NARROW
RATIO

DOWNS GALLEY
SMALL SHAPE

J.E.G.M

SEVERN TROW
LARGE SHAPE

Fig 74: Row and cargo barges.

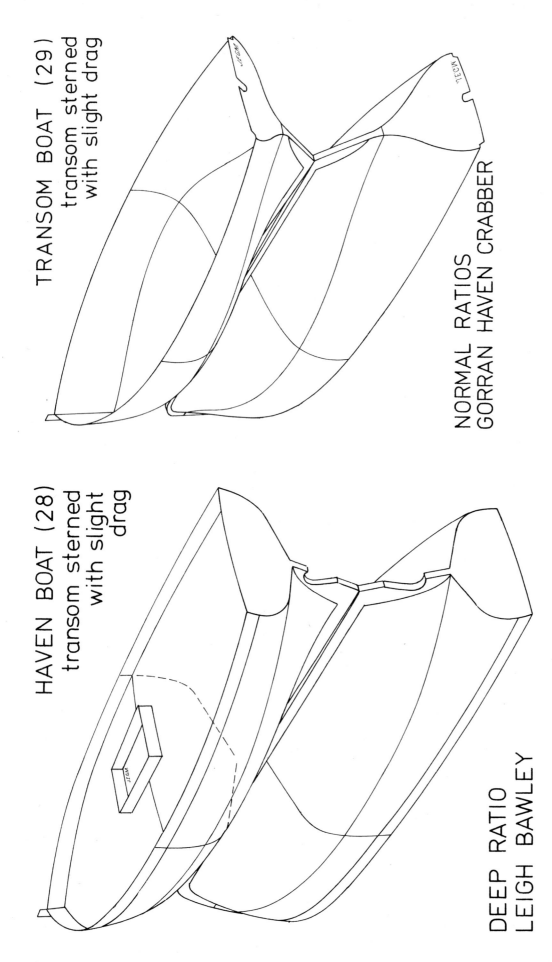

TRANSOM BOAT (29)
transom sterned
with slight drag

NORMAL RATIOS
GORRAN HAVEN CRABBER

Fig 76: Transom boat.

HAVEN BOAT (28)
transom sterned
with slight
drag

DEEP RATIO
LEIGH BAWLEY

Fig 75: Haven boat.

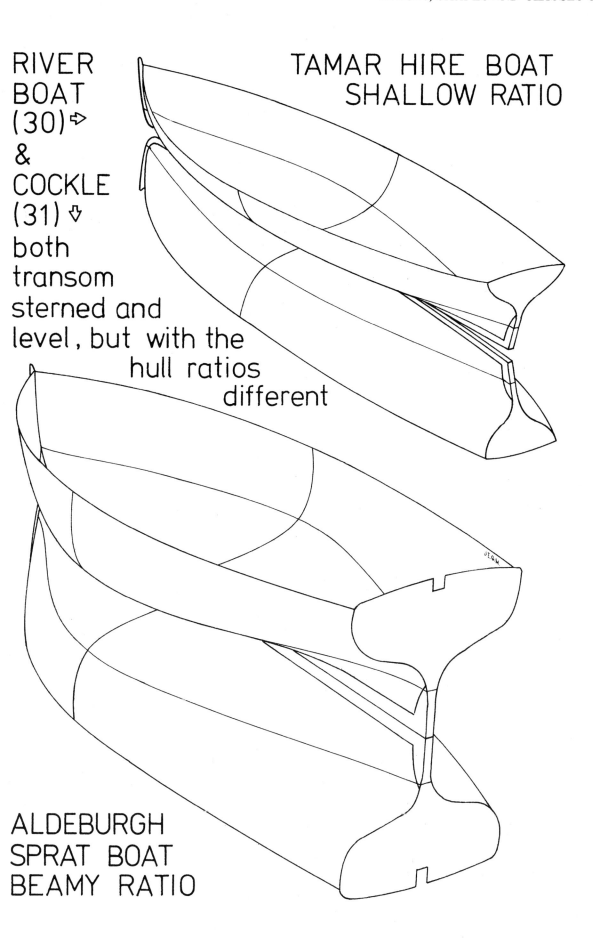

RIVER BOAT (30) ⇨ & COCKLE (31) ⇩ both transom sterned and level, but with the hull ratios different

TAMAR HIRE BOAT SHALLOW RATIO

ALDEBURGH SPRAT BOAT BEAMY RATIO

Fig 77: River boat and cockle.

TRANSOM
SMACK
(32) ⇨
&
DEVON
SMACK
(33) ⇩
both are
transom
sterned
with drag
but have
different
hull ratios

POLPERRO GAFFER
DEEP RATIO

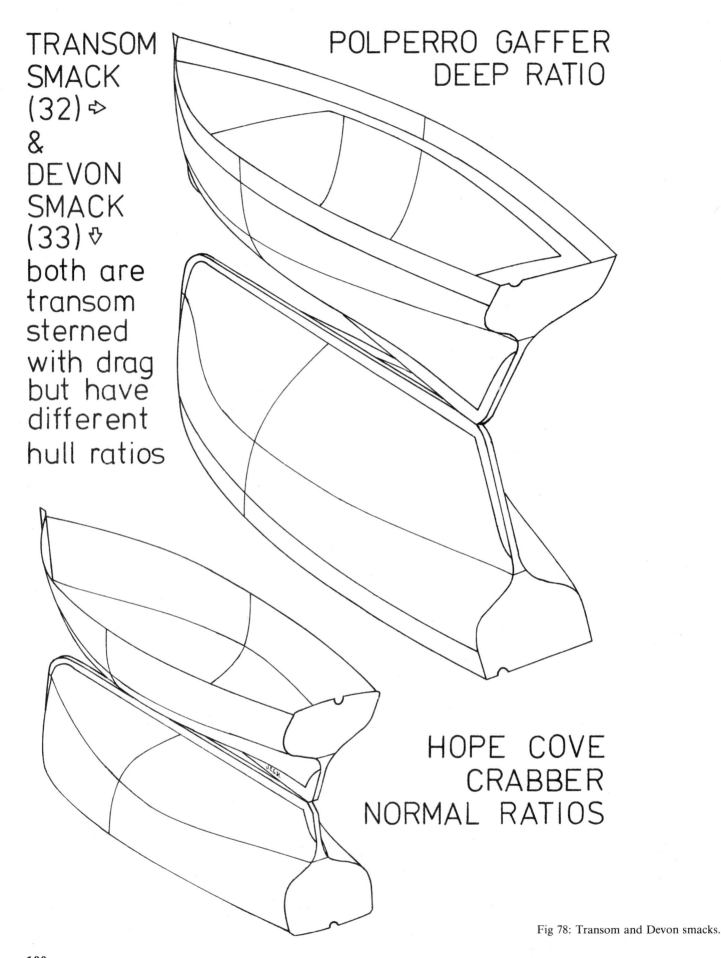

HOPE COVE
CRABBER
NORMAL RATIOS

Fig 78: Transom and Devon smacks.

Hastings punt, the Emsworth lugger, the Hallsand crabber and the Tenby lugger. The motorised versions still being built are not much less beamy. The punts carried by sailing trawlers, the boxing fleet boats, the cock boat of a Mersey flat and the coggie boat of a Humber keel or sloop come into this sub-category, which has been labelled *cockle*.

The transom boats with drag need only two divisions. The deep boats with normal length/beam ratios include the east coast smacks in their simpler forms, the part-decked drivers and hookers from the Start to the Dodman and the Mounts Bay pilchard driver. These boats had raised vee-d floors, round or even slack bilges and flam or nearly plumb sides, combined to give firm mid-sections. The Plymouth hooker exceptionally had a hard turn to her bilge. Though all of these could be and were motorised the shape has not lasted. This shape has been called *transom smack*.

The only boats of this sort with normal block ratios that have been identified were in South Devon in the days of sail, examples being the Beer lugger, the Lympsham hooker, and the Hope Cove Crabber. Since the introduction of engines however, the type has extended into Cornwall. The shape has been called *Devon smack* (Fig 78).

The third sub-division of the keel boat is for those with a sternpost beyond which the hull extends aft. All manner of counters, including the lute, elliptical and obsolete square tuck and pink sterns, have been grouped together. This group mainly consists of deep vessels with decks and a need for working-space aft. The lute differs in this respect; its role is to prevent swamping during beaching and so it is found fitted to small open boats with normal block ratios as well. The same division is made between level and drag keels, with further separation according to the length/beam and beam/depth ratios.

The first sub-category of nearly level keeled craft with counters is for those that are deep and narrow, with the Yarmouth lugger providing an example. The earlier three-masted one, illustrated in Washington's report had a round counter, while the *Gipsy Queen* model Edgar March describes was two-masted and, though built eleven years later, had a lute stern with an open rail above deck[28]. The Lowestoft decked boat, also in Washington's report, was of the same shape apart from a square counter. These vessels had raised and vee-d floors respectively with almost slack bilges in the latter two cases. The underwater level lines were sharp fore and aft. They appear to be a refinement of the herring buss, though this type must have been obsolescent at the time, and are named *buss smack* (Fig 79).

Next are the boats that are deep but have normal length/beam ratios. These are mainly early designs like those above and include the working nobby from the north west of England, the Brixham sloop (forerunner of the trawlers), and two eighteenth century examples: Chapman's smack for flat fish[29] and the *Peggy* of Castletown. There are four different sorts of counter

between them. More recent were the smacks and oyster dredgers from Languard Point to North Foreland. These had counters with raked curved transoms above a knuckle and their easy mid-sections were a combination of raised or vee-d floors with slack bilges. Today this group is still represented by the elliptical and lute sterned beach motor boats of Sussex and the motor nobbies of Lancashire and Cumbria. This shape has been given the name, *old smack* (Fig 80).

The boats of this kind with normal block ratios are only found on the shores of Kent and Sussex. They are small, open and elliphical or lute sterned. They are being built in wood and GRP by at least three firms. In many respects they are like the transom boats, so have been given the label *lute boat* (Fig 81).

Most craft with counters have drag, and those that are deep and narrow form their first sub-category. This includes the classic sailing trawlers from Brixham and Lowestoft, which had vee-d floors, round and even slack bilges and mostly plumb sides. One of the Fal oyster dredgers, *Zigeuner*, was of this type, not that any one boat could be said to be typical of this mixed fleet of still sailing working and racing boats. The label chosen here is *sailing trawler* (Fig 82).

The next group is for those craft that are deep but have normal length/beam ratios. Due to the large numbers it was necessary to distinguish between those that have raised floors and those that are vee-d. The shape with the raised floors originated long ago, yet is still in use, as in, for instance, Steele's fishing hoy of 1804 and modern motor fishing boats. The firm to full midship sections have hardly changed over this time, though motor boats have harder bilges than sailing ones, a few of which like the Brixham mumble-bee could be slack. The counter is where some change has taken place, having progressed from a square tuck barely extending beyond the rudder, through the long counters of the nineteenth century, then on to the stubbier canoe and cruiser sterns of the first generation of motor fishing vessels built as such. More recently the counter has undergone a further change to produce what is termed a transom stern. Here the counter is made even deeper and wider and given a square end. This gives deck space for stern trawling and the buoyancy aft to take a power block[30]. Although the counters and afterbodies vary considerably all these small decked vessels have been labelled *raised floor smacks* (Fig 82).

The vee-d floored variety of the same sub-category is shaped like the long keeled cutter yacht of the turn of the century. In this group are found the Morecambe Bay prawner, the more extreme smacks and dredgers from East Anglia and the later sailing pilot cutters and schooners of the Bristol Channel. Here again the mid-sections changed very little, only the early Bristol pilot skiff of 1808 having slack bilges. The type looked like disappearing until the draft aft was needed again to accommodate the larger screws required by more powerful engines. The transom stern is also fitted here and this with

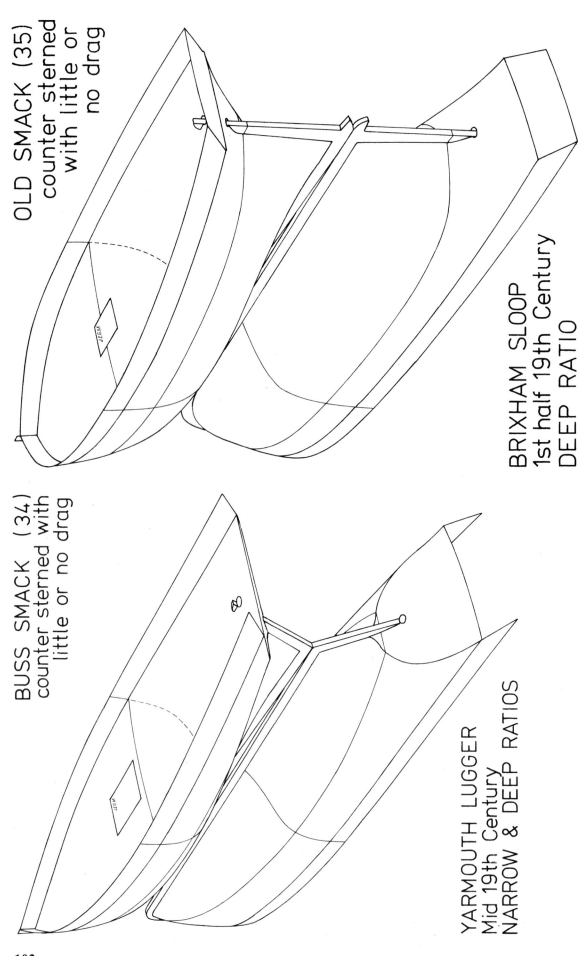

OLD SMACK (35)
counter sterned with little or
no drag

BRIXHAM SLOOP
1st half 19th Century
DEEP RATIO

Fig 80: Old smack.

BUSS SMACK (34)
counter sterned with
little or no drag

YARMOUTH LUGGER
Mid 19th Century
NARROW & DEEP RATIOS

Fig 79: Buss smack.

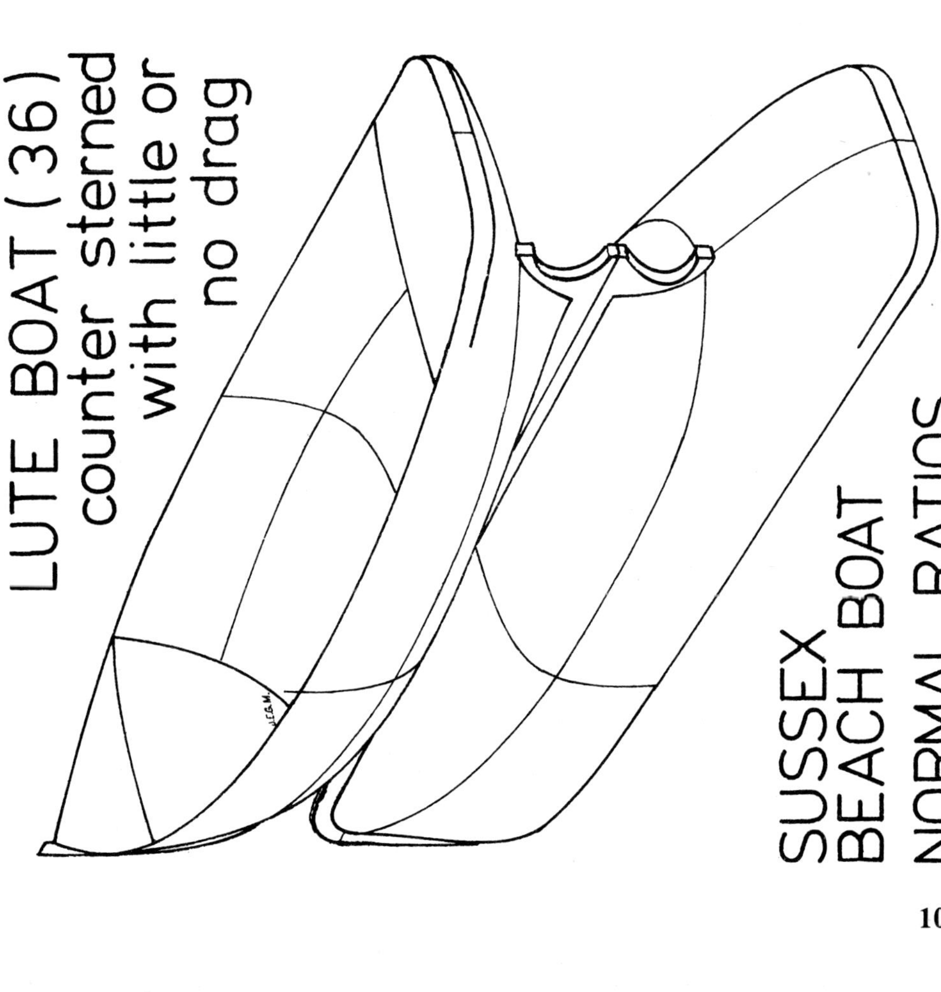
LUTE BOAT (36)
counter sterned
with little or
no drag
SUSSEX
BEACH BOAT
NORMAL RATIOS
J.E.G.M.

Fig 81: Lute boat.

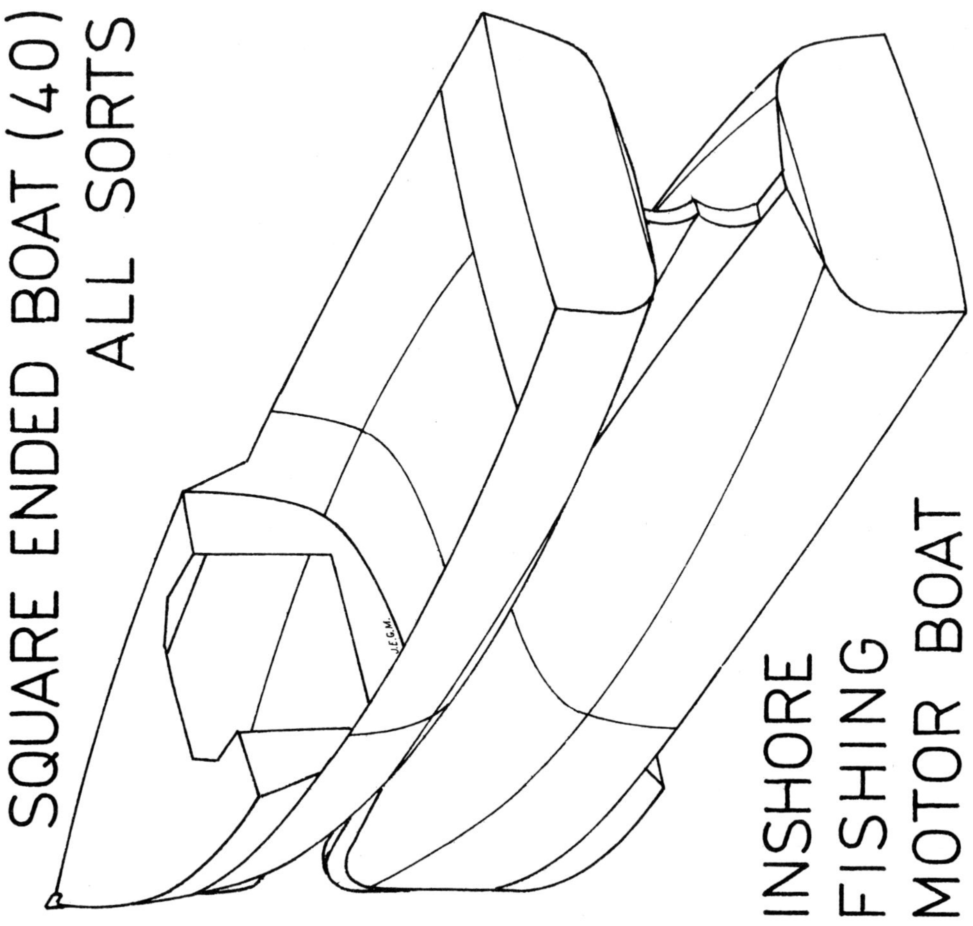
SQUARE ENDED BOAT (40)
ALL SORTS
INSHORE
FISHING
MOTOR BOAT
J.E.G.M.

Fig 83: Square-sterned boat.

COUNTER STERNED CRAFT WITH DRAG

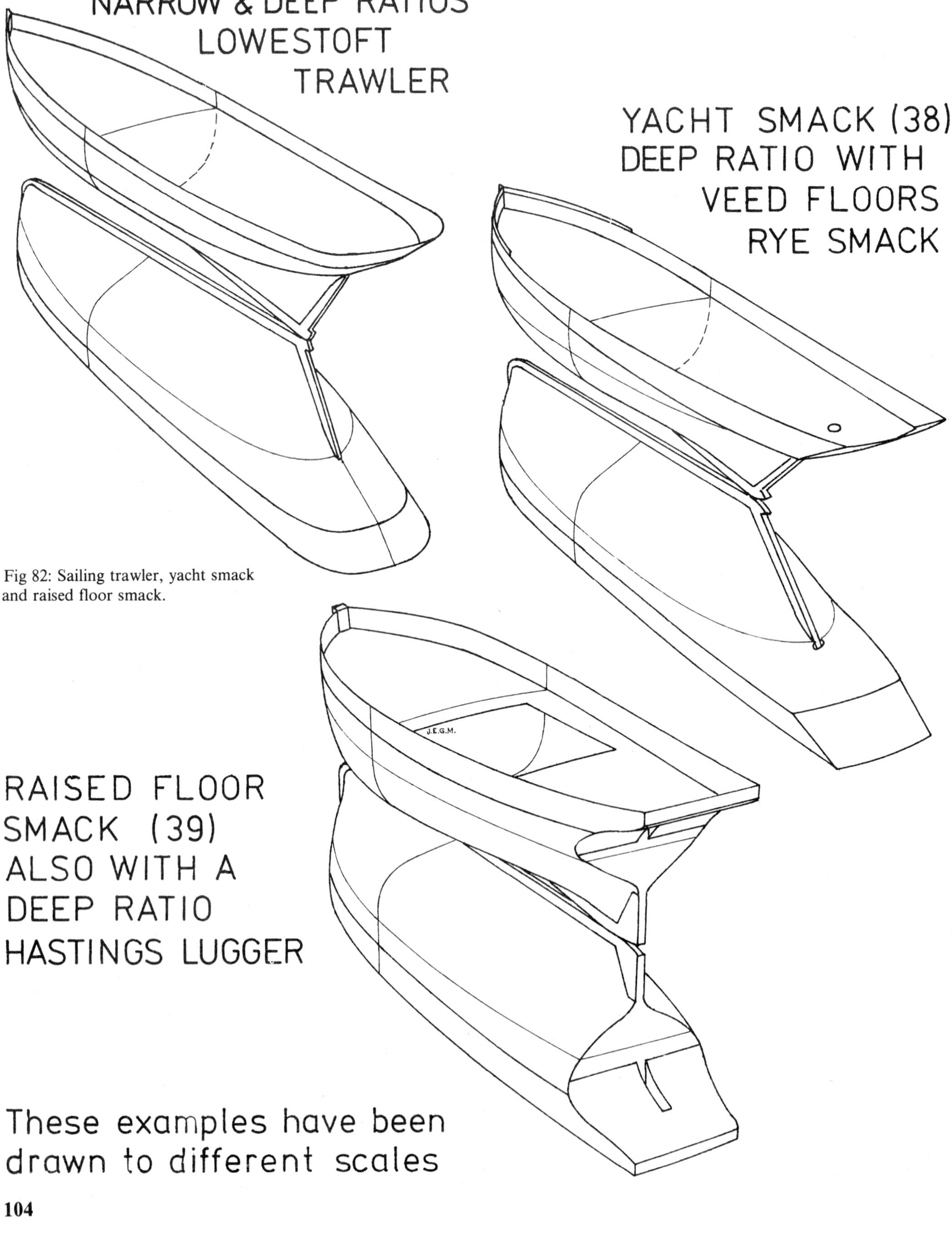

SAILING TRAWLER (37)
NARROW & DEEP RATIOS
LOWESTOFT
TRAWLER

YACHT SMACK (38)
DEEP RATIO WITH
VEED FLOORS
RYE SMACK

Fig 82: Sailing trawler, yacht smack and raised floor smack.

RAISED FLOOR SMACK (39) ALSO WITH A DEEP RATIO HASTINGS LUGGER

These examples have been drawn to different scales

the engine room aft has meant fuller runs. The sections and lines forward retain the easily-driven shape of the earlier boats. This shape has been named *yacht smack* (Fig 82).

The square stern is a truncation of the fair hull, so does not modify the sections as they come aft in the way a transom does. A sprung rabbet line aft is usual as this lifts the bottom up to or above the waterline and minimises turbulence. When afloat, it can be hard to tell if a boat has a square stern or a truncated counter, even though her underwater shape would leave no doubt. There is a draught of a square stern as early as 1706 showing a boat for landing men[31]. This has a full skeg that extends the length of the straight keel right aft, and variations of this design were used in service boats up to the present. Square sterns do not appear to have been adopted in working keel boats so early. Dixon Kemp gives the lines of a Cowes waterman's boat, *c*1880, by which date square sterns were common in tenders and sailing dinghies[32].

Since the 1930s the shape has been developed both for high performance racing sailing boats and a wide range of motor boats. The square stern is popular for small working boats, especially in places where the sailing model had not proved suitable for motorisation. Sometimes the local type has converted well, as in Sussex, where even the old one lap tuck has persisted (Fig 83) when it might seem that a square stern would have been simpler and served as well.

Many varieties of square stern are seen: sprung keels with and without skegs, rudder post and spade rudders, 'A' brackets and shaft logs and plumb or raked, straight or curved sterns. In every case the hull shape is no different, thus sub-division of them at this stage is superfluous. A few keel boats used as tenders have been seen with square bows and sterns, giving them the shape if not the construction of a pram. As they do have keels they have been put in this sub-division, which whatever the drag has been labelled *square stern boat* (Fig 83).

The principal dimensions and characteristics of a boat, coupled to the limits wooden planks can be bent, gives a good idea of her shape. The system outlined above has dealt with the boats listed in Appendix IV. Other boats, new or old, may appear not to fit, but if they are plank boats, any changes to the system should be in the nature of additional sub-categories. This may not be true of new materials, which can be formed into unfair shapes. For the time being GRP and ferro-cement boats are being made to look as wooden as possible and should still fit this system. Once the wider possible range of shapes is exploited this system would be inadequate.

PART II
The Findings of the Study

7.

Realisation of boatshape

Unless he can work from drawings, a boatbuilder has to be able to turn a shape in his mind's eye into reality. As boatbuilding has been practised in Britain for at least 4000 years, it is not unusual to find a builder using an age-old way of doing this, while just up the road another is employing all the most recent techniques. Much depends on the builder. There are those who appear to work entirely by eye, or 'free-arm' as the late Ewing McGruer would say, 'So as to sell every nail driven', whilst others work only from drawings to produce components, whose assembly is a matter of fitting and fastening. In between these extremes there are intermediates, and even builders who adapt their method to suit the boat in mind. Curtis, Frank and Pape of Looe loft and build fine large vessels in their yard, which apart from power tools is out of an earlier century. J & J Harrison of Amble is just as good at building cobles by traditional means as they are MFVs from drawings. L H Walker & Co of Leigh turn out a whole range of mahogany clinker boats on batch production principles, which after the prototype avoid subsequent lofting and spiling. Descriptions of some of these ways of realising boatshape will show how diverse they can be.

No actual measuring may be apparent during the building of a simply shaped boat and there seems to be complete reliance on the eye for both selecting the stock and judging how far each successive operation is taken. Hornell described how a coracle builder spaces out his long withies before interlacing the shorter ones, knowing that the shape can be adjusted before they are bound finally together[1]. In much the same way rafts and dugouts can be formed by initial trial and error. There are some factors which combine to make a boatbuilder exert more control over all stages of his work, such as size of available material, variations in and repeat orders of successful designs, and fixed procedures have been developed to provide this control. Even more astonishing than the ingenuity of these methods is how some of them have been handed down without the help of written or even spoken words. Today when most teaching relies on formal lessons and books, it can be forgotten that knowledge can also be won by imitation alone. An example of this occurs in Alec Blagdon's yard at Mount Wise, Devonport. From time to time a stem or pram dinghy is started to give work when there are gaps in the programme. Anyone or all of the several craftsmen in the yard are seen to work on this boat, taking over and finishing at any stage, sometimes after several days or maybe a few hours. This does not show in the final result, which is a boat typical of this yard. It is not

easy to describe the procedures used to develop the shape of the boat, and even harder to check that the written account is correct, when the boatbuilder himself has not previously had to find words for what he is doing naturally.

As vessels grew in size and complexity, their shape, cutting list, capacity and displacement had to be predicted. While a master boatbuilder could accumulate and recall the proportions and scantlings of a range of designs, it would be a great help to him if he could devise any aid to memory, like a rule-of-thumb[2].

The first example taken will be a turf boat (Fig 84) from the Somerset Flats near Glastonbury, where until recently such boats were used by farmers to get about when the land flooded every winter. There is a replica of one of these boats displayed in the Neptune Hall at Greenwich; she has a flat bottom and acutely flared sides which meet in very raked ends. These boats were built either by the handy man on a farm or by the local carpenter. Mr Stanley Baker, who built the replica, was the woodworker at West Hay, but he, now that flooding had become exceptional, had not built a boat since the Second World War. When asked to build the boat, it took him some time to remember how he used to do it. After a bit, he jotted down some figures in the form of a cross on the back of a cigarette pack (Fig 85). How he went on to build the boat is described by Dr Greenhill so we shall look at how these few figures gave him the shape of the whole boat[3].

The one dimension which controlled the others was the beam of the 'deck' or bottom slab, although it was the half beam of 14in that was used to simplify multiplication. The deck was put with annual rings curved upwards and a centreline was marked down the middle with at least 14in of sound timber on either side of it. Eleven times 14in gave the length of the deck as 154in (12ft 10in); squaring out from the mid-point of this distance he marked 14in either side, and then part-drove a wire nail into each of the four marks at the ends of this cross. Next he bent a $\frac{3}{4}$in square section batten round three of these nails down one side, tacking it in place with two more nails. This curve, he said, was not full enough like this, so he put in two more nails $\frac{3}{4}$in outside the batten and half way out towards the ends from amidships, at the quarters. He then re-sprang the batten over these last two nails as well, as shown in the figure. This curve was pencilled in and another drawn the same way on the other side. This gave the shape of the deck, and, as the angle and height of the side were constant throughout, the shape of the complete boat was established before the first sawcut was made. What Mr Baker

MR STANLEY BAKER'S TURF BOAT 'CROSS' & BATTEN ADJUSTMENT

2' 4"
4' 8"

13'
17'

THE CENTRE LINE NAILS ARE 13' APART AND OUTSIDE THE 3/4" SQUARE BATTEN

INITIAL 3 NAIL LINE

ABOUT 1 1/2"

FINAL
5 NAIL LINE

THE INTERMEDIATE NAILS ARE INSIDE THE BATTEN
WITH THE 1/4" NAILS 3/4" OUTSIDE THE 3 NAIL LINE

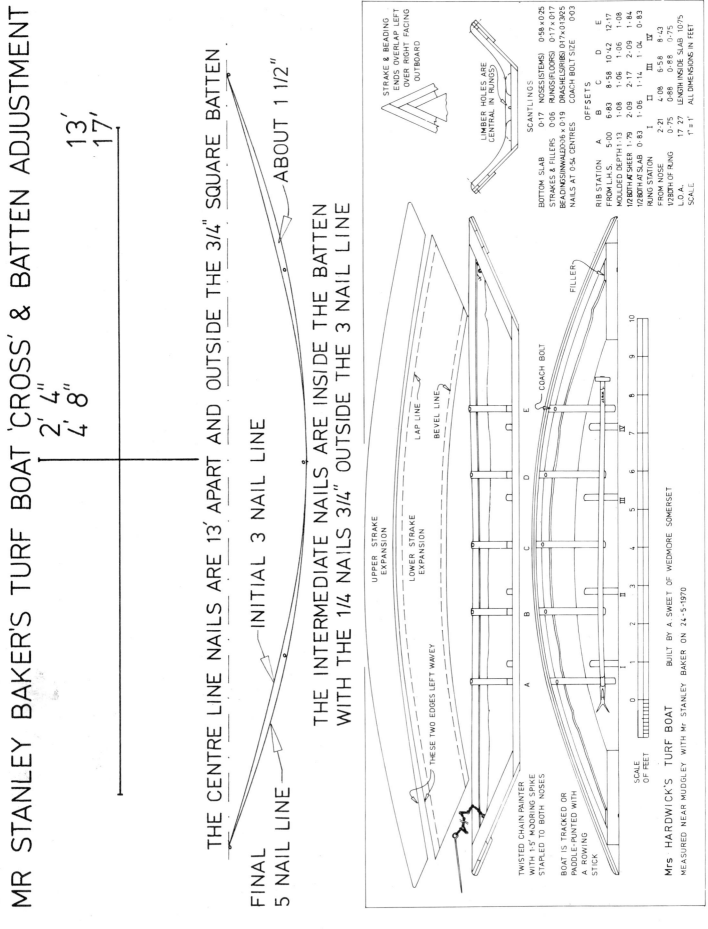

STRAKE & BEADING
ENDS OVERLAP LEFT
OVER RIGHT FACING
OUTBOARD

LIMBER HOLES ARE
CENTRAL IN RUNGS

SCANTLINGS

BOTTOM SLAB	0·58 x 0·25
NOSES (STEMS)	0·17
STRAKES & FILLERS	0·06
RUNGS (FLOORS)	0·17 x 0·17
BEADINGS(INWALE)0·06 x 0·19	DRASHELS(RIBS) 0·17 x 0·13/25
NAILS at 0·54 CENTRES	COACH BOLT SIZE 0·03

OFFSETS

RIB STATION	A	B	C	D	E
FROM L.H.S.	5·00	6·83	8·58	10·42	12·17
MOULDED DEPTH	1·13	1·08	1·06	1·06	1·08
1/2 BOTH AT SHEER	1·79	2·09	2·17	2·09	1·84
1/2 BOTH AT SLAB	0·83	1·06	1·14	1·04	0·83

RUNG STATION	I	II	III	IV
FROM NOSE	2·21	4·08	6·58	8·43
1/2 BOTH OF RUNG	0·75	0·88	0·88	0·75
L.O.A.	17·27	LENGTH INSIDE SLAB 10·75		
SCALE	1"=1'	ALL DIMENSIONS IN FEET		

UPPER STRAKE
EXPANSION

LOWER STRAKE
EXPANSION

LAP LINE

BEVEL LINE

A   B   C   D   E

COACH BOLT

FILLER

THESE TWO EDGES LEFT WAVEY

TWISTED CHAIN PAINTER
WITH 1·5' MOORING SPIKE
STAPLED TO BOTH NOSES

BOAT IS TRACKED OR
PADDLE-PUNTED WITH
A ROWING
STICK

SCALE
OF FEET

0   1   2   3   4   5   6   7   8   9   10

I   II   III   IV

Mrs HARDWICK'S TURF BOAT   BUILT BY A. SWEET OF WEDMORE SOMERSET

MEASURED NEAR MUDGLEY WITH Mr STANLEY BAKER ON 24·5·1970

Below:
Fig 84: Mrs Baker as a girl 'rowing' a turf boat.

Far Left:
Fig 85: Stanley Baker's turf boat 'cross' and batten adjustment.

Left:
Fig 86: Mrs Hardwick's turf boat – lines.

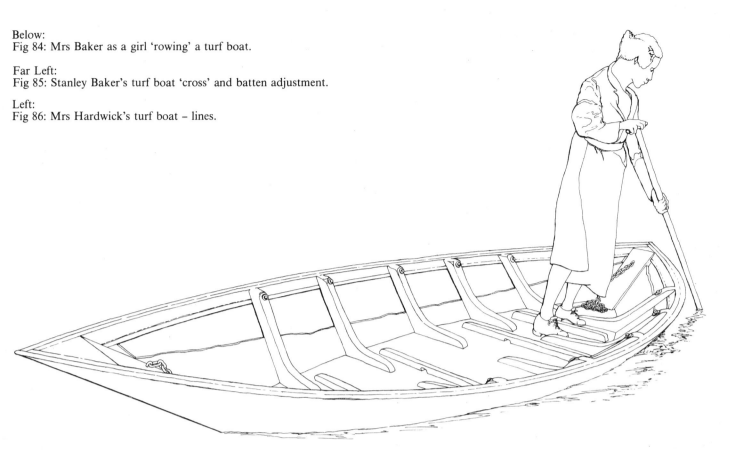

then did to build the boat looked as if he were working by eye, especially as he was constantly looking to see that his curves ran fair and flair angles were regular. However it was the remembered rule-of-thumb which told him the size to make the deck and the internal shape of a turf boat 17ft overall. The boat could have been made proportionately smaller or larger to suit his timber. She would be similar to another turf boat built by someone else anywhere else on the moors – for instance the one built by Mr Sweet at Wedmore, now kept at the Abbey Barn at Glastonbury by the Somerset Rural Life Society (Fig 86).

The straight keeled clinker-built boat with a stem forward and a transom aft is the most universal type found in Britain (Fig 87). Her strength lies mainly in the combination of the backbone with the planking, stiffened where experience had shown it essential for the work she had to do. This particular example has to work off Bucks Mills Ledge in North Devon, and this is why she has twice as many floor timbers than usual. Ewing McGruer, the spar-making member of the great Scottish boatbuilding family, understood the nature and handling of wood as a structural material better than anyone. He described how a 12ft sea-loch boat can be built without lofting, though he does draw a full size mid-section on the back of his shed door. Study of the whole range of this sort of boat establishes that, while there is no fixed relationship between Length (L) and Beam (B), with L varying from (2.6 to 3.75)B, once L is chosen, fractions of it are used to find the stations of the amidships, the mast and the cut-ups, the latter giving the length of the keel. B and Depth

(D) are more closely related, fractions of B often being used to work out the mid, forward and after depths, and the after Beam. Even when they have been calculated all or some of these results are liable to be altered to suit the owner or to make the best use of stock, in particular for the keel and grown crooks for the stem assembly.

The following table gives McGruer's rule-of-thumb with a higher sided boat, which would be better for beaching.

	Length	Beam mid	Depth mid	Depth for'd	Depth aft	Beam aft
	L	B	D	D_{fwd}	D_{aft}	B_{aft}
McGruer's 12ft	(2.67 to 2.75) B	B	$\frac{3}{8}$ B	$\frac{9}{16}$ B	$\frac{7}{16}$ B	$\frac{2}{3}$ B
Beaching 12ft	(2.6 to 2.8) B	B	$\frac{1}{2}$ B	$\frac{3}{4}$ B	$\frac{5}{8}$ B	$\frac{2}{3}$ B

These ratios together with the information given in the chapter on structure are sufficient for a boat to be built, if the backbone and planking are taken separately as follows.

Knowing the general shape, the boatbuilder can decide to fit a rabbet stem and keel if the boat is to be fine forward with vee-d sections, or an apron and hog, if bluff and flat floored. Flare forward generates a raked stem and need for buoyancy aft may call for a fuller transom. He can put the backbone together accordingly, sure that, after the rabbets and bevels have been cut, there will still be enough wood for the plank fastenings (Fig 88).

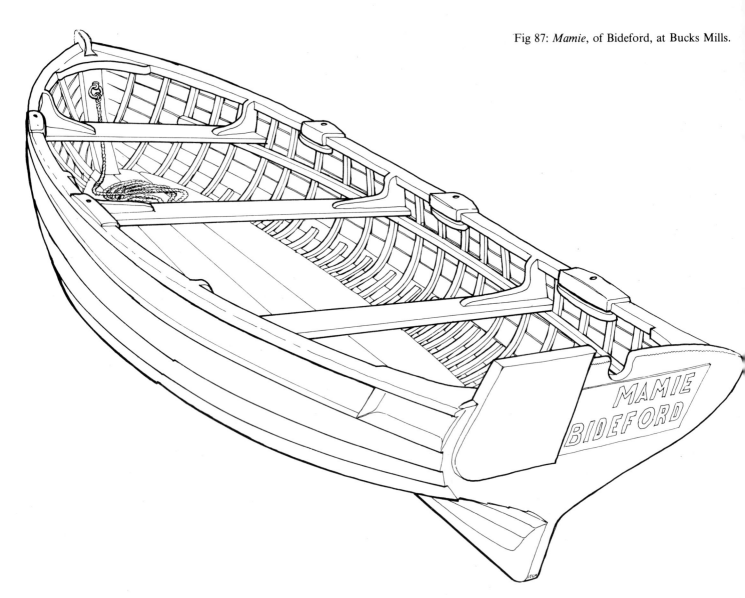

Fig 87: *Mamie*, of Bideford, at Bucks Mills.

With the backbone braced up on a strongback to prevent any movement, the builder can start planking. The first pair of strakes, the garboards, need special care as they have the most twist, a long underwater seam and great influence on the shape of the rest of the hull. Therefore many builders prefer to fit them before working out the run of the other strakes. Normally a thinner 'spiling' batten is used to find the angles of the bearding and the shape of the garboards. This is done by clamping the spiling batten to the keel or hog amidships and twisting it so its ends lie flat along the sides of the stempost and sternpost. The curve made by the upper edge of the spiling batten will be paunchy amidships and meagre either end, just like the batten used by Mr Baker to mark out the turf boat's deck. In the same way the spiling batten has to be sprung out at the quarters to give it a more generous shape. The beardings of the rabbets for the garboard can then be cut to suit and a spiling taken, before the garboards can be made and fitted[4]. For the time being these two strakes will have to be held sprung outwards at the quarters as well.

Ewing McGruer fitted sandstrakes, as they call garboards in North Britain, using a sliding template half as thick and three-quarters the length of the final strake. Each end of the sandstrake is fitted in turn into its rabbet, the midship station being marked each time. The template is set by eye to the desired deadrise along its length 'by memory', though he lets apprentices use a hand-held mould until they have learned to do without it. When fitted, the template will be found to have a convex lower edge. This hollow is avoided by many boatbuilders by sweeping the rabbet upwards towards the sternpost (Fig 89). This in combination with the usually curved rabbet in the stem gives the garboard an almost straight lower edge, which is easier to fit.

Considering the midship section next, the builder works out its girth by adding B to D, takes half this sum for one side and then subtracts the width of the garboard, so as to find out how much he has still left to plank up. He then has to assess how many strakes will be needed to do this. Local practice, width of boards to hand and shape of the transverse sections will tell him whether he will have to use a few broad strakes or many narrow ones, and whether or not

Fig 88: Free-arm clinker building.

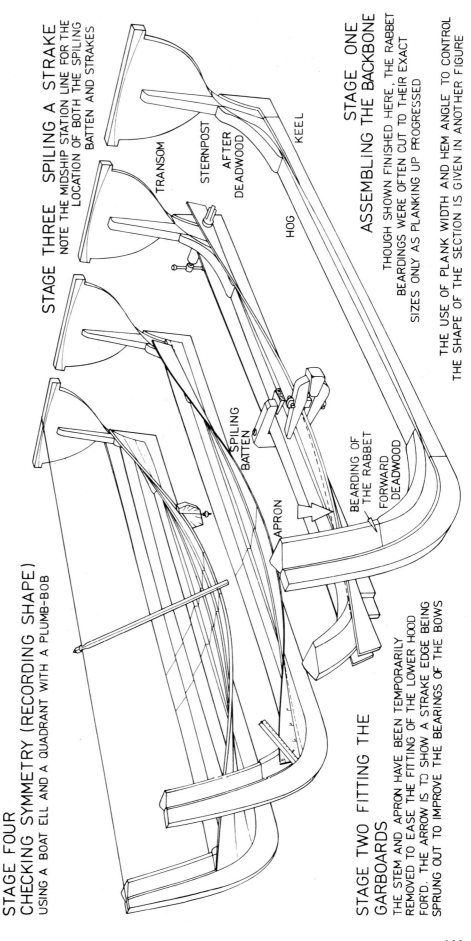

FREE-ARM CLINKER BOATBUILDING
STAGES WHEN SHAPE IS REGULATED

STAGE ONE
ASSEMBLING THE BACKBONE

THOUGH SHOWN FINISHED HERE, THE RABBET BEARDINGS WERE OFTEN CUT TO THEIR EXACT SIZES ONLY AS PLANKING UP PROGRESSED

THE USE OF PLANK WIDTH AND HEM ANGLE TO CONTROL THE SHAPE OF THE SECTION IS GIVEN IN ANOTHER FIGURE

STAGE THREE   SPILING A STRAKE

NOTE THE MIDSHIP STATION LINE FOR THE LOCATION OF BOTH THE SPILING BATTEN AND STRAKES

TRANSOM

STERNPOST

AFTER DEADWOOD

KEEL

HOG

SPILING BATTEN

APRON

BEARDING OF THE RABBET

FORWARD DEADWOOD

STAGE FOUR
CHECKING SYMMETRY (RECORDING SHAPE)

USING A BOAT ELL AND A QUADRANT WITH A PLUMB-BOB

STAGE TWO FITTING THE
GARBOARDS

THE STEM AND APRON HAVE BEEN TEMPORARILY REMOVED TO EASE THE FITTING OF THE LOWER HOOD FOR'D. THE ARROW IS TO SHOW A STRAKE EDGE BEING SPRUNG OUT TO IMPROVE THE BEARINGS OF THE BOWS

THE UPSWEPT RABBET LINE AFT

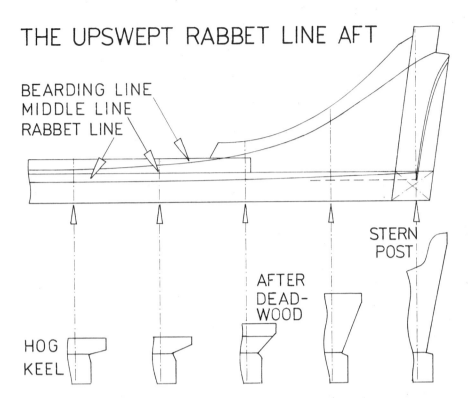

BEARING LINE
MIDDLE LINE
RABBET LINE

AFTER
DEAD-
WOOD

STERN
POST

HOG
KEEL

AS BUILT
A STRAIGHT MIDDLE LINE
GIVES AN UPSWEPT RABBET
LINE AND THE GARBOARD
IS EASIER TO FIT

AS OFTEN DRAWN
A STRAIGHT RABBET LINE
GIVES THE GARBOARD A
HOLLOW LOWER EDGE AFT
THAT IS HARD TO FIT

SECTION AT
ARROWED
STATION

Above:
Fig 89: The upswept rabbet line aft.

Right:
Fig 90: Sectional shape varies with strake width and angle.

they are to be all the same width or vary. Making an allowance for each overlap of normally twice the plank thickness, he gets the widths to use so that this number of strakes will just come up to the sheerline. This is the time to draw out the midship section unless there is a hard and fast local rule like, 'After the garboard, two more out to the bilge, four round this, then two more up to the gun'l'. Either way, he decides when to start turning the bilge and when to stop, keeping in mind that a change in plank angle of more than 20° weakens the joint. A number of sections have been drawn to show how varied they can be made using different plank widths and angles (Fig 90).

With the plank spacing settled amidships, the builder then has to decide how the strakes should finish fore and aft. Strakes that are wide in the middle and narrow each end take up boatlike shapes when their edges are joined. Forward the strakes can generally be spaced evenly up the stem, but aft the run of plank has to be consistent with working any tight curves, especially the reverse curve, or 'tuck', where the transom and sternpost converge. When satisfied, the builder will mark in where the top of each strake is to come and so will have the width of every strake in three places.

Planking is resumed by spiling for and fitting the next pair of strakes made to the desired widths and ending on the marks at the stem and stern. In this method of building the rabbets in the posts, and transom bevel later, are cut as work proceeds. Care is taken to follow the run of strake plan exactly, to ensure symmetry and to maintain the correct fullness of the quarters. As each further pair of strakes is fitted it will be found that the shell stiffens up and the need to constrain the quarters diminishes as the looked-for shape emerges. Ewing McGruer used to stress

three points: that planks must be sawn so as to have neutral grain, that is half way between radial and tangential, that the curve in the plank must follow the line of true growth and that it was essential 'to mind your sheers and beuls'. This last meant that the change in height and breadth of every strake edge should follow 'an economic eye-sweet line' all the way. The ability to achieve this is building by eye. One must be grateful that a practical boatbuilder should have described his own methods so clearly, for, though they differ from others, they demonstrate the common problems all boatbuilders in wood have to solve[5].

Because perspective effects can be more misleading than helpful to the eye, positive means are needed when checking symmetry. To start with this is done by clamping and finishing pairs of strakes together, and then fitting them so that the same amount of overlap is used on both sides. When assembled but not fastened, measurements are taken of the strakes' upper edges, linear ones to the centreline, floor or other datum and angular ones between the inclined surface and a plumbline or spirit level. When it is expected that there is to be another boat built to the same pattern, records are made. As work proceeds templates are made of the stem profile, the transom and the shape of every strake on one side. In addition some of the linear and angular measurements are kept in the form of one or more transverse moulds.

SECTIONAL SHAPE VARIES WITH STRAKE WIDTH & ANGLE

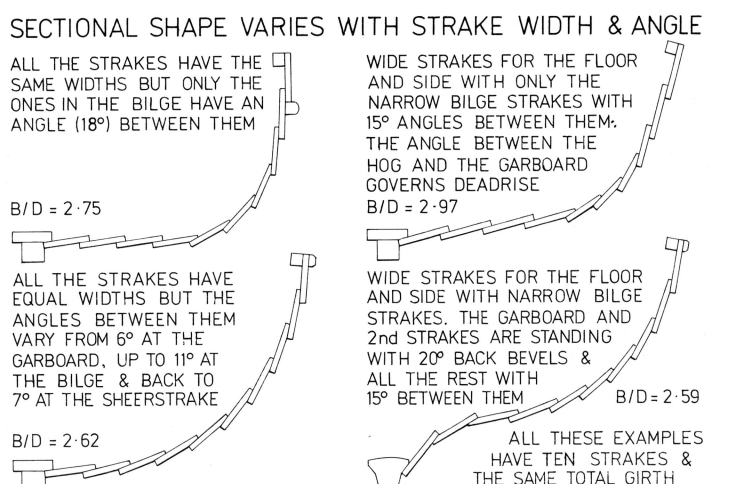

ALL THE STRAKES HAVE THE SAME WIDTHS BUT ONLY THE ONES IN THE BILGE HAVE AN ANGLE (18°) BETWEEN THEM

B/D = 2·75

WIDE STRAKES FOR THE FLOOR AND SIDE WITH ONLY THE NARROW BILGE STRAKES WITH 15° ANGLES BETWEEN THEM. THE ANGLE BETWEEN THE HOG AND THE GARBOARD GOVERNS DEADRISE

B/D = 2·97

ALL THE STRAKES HAVE EQUAL WIDTHS BUT THE ANGLES BETWEEN THEM VARY FROM 6° AT THE GARBOARD, UP TO 11° AT THE BILGE & BACK TO 7° AT THE SHEERSTRAKE

B/D = 2·62

WIDE STRAKES FOR THE FLOOR AND SIDE WITH NARROW BILGE STRAKES. THE GARBOARD AND 2nd STRAKES ARE STANDING WITH 20° BACK BEVELS & ALL THE REST WITH 15° BETWEEN THEM   B/D = 2·59

ALL THESE EXAMPLES HAVE TEN STRAKES & THE SAME TOTAL GIRTH

It is not necessary to follow through the building sequence beyond this point as this does not materially differ from that generally followed in Britain when building with moulds[4]. In any case building without moulds is rare. I have talked to one boatbuilder who, while he was an apprentice in North Devon, saw a man using a taut line and a marked staff in a similar manner to that described by Arne-Emil Christensen[6]. Various types of cobles are still built without drawings, templates or moulds, strake widths and angles being used to control shape[7]. I know of no-one who has used a quadrant and plumbline when boatbuilding, but this instrument is regularly used for measuring angles on ocean racing yachts for rating. It is difficult to get accurate readings from the quadrant as it has to be held square transversely and horizontal on a surface which is inclined to both these planes.

The more a builder can work without reference to drawings or other control devices, the faster and freer he can be. Where similar boats are built in quick succession the dependance on controls decreases and the work becomes habitual. Rightly in this case a standard range of boats should be introduced, as at L H Walker's where there is a comprehensive set of patterns for every component of the boats listed in their catalogue. Except for yards like this and those building one-design racing classes, it is unusual to find that two boats have been built alike in a row, even though repeat orders occur. This encourages the use of moulds, not only as a way of storing previous designs, but as a convenient starting point from which an improvement on an old design can be made. Moulds come in many forms; they can extend the full width of the vessel, or be hinged half way so that they can be swung from one side to the other. Hand-held moulds often stretch from the gunwale to the head of the floor on the other side, to make them easier to hold upright. Not only are moulds altered from time to time, but they are also set up with different spacing to suit other shapes and sizes of boat (Fig 44). The mould is a permanent record of the full size drawing on the shed door, having the added advantage that it indicates the run of strakes. Though moulds can be constructed from a conventional draft, they can also be regarded as a step towards the use of transverse sections as a way of indicating shape. Like moulds, stem and transom templates undergo progressive modifications until they finally fall apart. Strake templates cannot be modified and tend to last longer, but are useless if there are no other templates. If, when building to moulds, the strakes are properly spiled and the laps are correctly hemmed home, the planking will barely touch the moulds as it will be self-formed and supported. In practice it is quite usual to see that considerable gaps have been left between the moulds and planks, though the strake marks have been followed. This is where a boatbuilder has made a change of shape without troubling to alter the moulds.

Amongst the more interesting wooden boats still being built are the English and Scottish cobles. As explained by H O Hill the ways of building the English sort varied from one yard to the next, though the outcome was much the same[7]. Nobody has so far published a full account of how this was done in one of the yards that do not appear to use any moulds or other mechanical aid to controlling shape (Fig 91). There is at least one builder who employs moulds, but though he has told me the full sequence of his work and drawn a strake diagram, he has particularly asked that they should not be published. I believe his reticence must be respected, as it is so much in the tradition of 'Arg' Hopwood of Flamborough, who is said to have dismissed his apprentices if they looked like being able to build a coble on their own. Apart from looking as if all the seminal methods are used in their construction, the coble's shape is complex too. How such a shape can be realised purely by eye, especially when it embodies a propeller tunnel, puzzles me.

The Scottish cobles were built in all sizes for use in rivers and estuaries as well as along the coast. Many of them were and are built in the boat shops that form a part of the major salmon fishing companies. Such shops often undertook work for outside customers as well as for the parent company. At Montrose for instance, at the turn of the century, J Johnston and Co were building at least ten different sorts, varying from 21ft in the ram down to only 10ft (Fig 92). In each case the following dimensions were recorded in case there was another order for the same model: height of stem, breadths of tapered bottom strakes, breadths of parallel side strakes, breadth of bottom, breadth of gunwale, depths at each of three thwarts and length of ram. In only one case was length overall given. This recording of the longest component rather than the length of the finished boat indicates the importance of the size of the material. Nowadays, Mr Tom Easton of this same firm builds two main types, the motor coble with an inboard engine and overall size of $26\frac{1}{2}$ft $\times$ 9ft $\times$ 3ft, and the Bay boat with two outboard engines and overall size of $24\frac{1}{2}$ft $\times$ 9ft $\times$ 2ft 9in, using rather different methods.

The stempost and apron of the motor coble are cut from 2in and 5in oak crooks to the shape of templates, before

Fig 91: 35ft motor coble being built by C A Goodall at Sandsend, near Whitby.

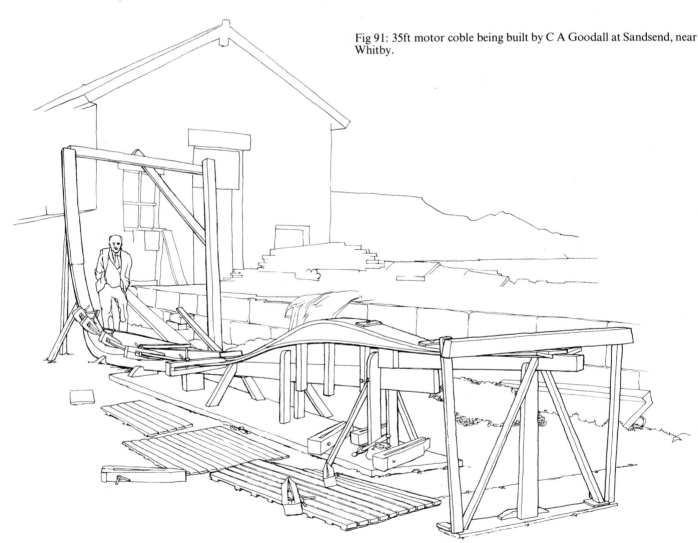

Fig 92: Abstract of coble dimensions from Tom Easton's old notebooks.

ABSTRACT OF COBLE DIMENSIONS FROM TOM EASTON'S OLD NOTEBOOKS

	TRENT SHOT 6 OARED COBLE	4-OARED COBLE	6-OARED COBLE FOR MONTROSE BAY	RIVER COBLE 2-OARS NORTH ESK	4 OARED COBLE ROSSIE	MUSSEL COBLE	6 OARED COBLE (P)	4 OARED COBLE (P)
LENGTH OVERALL	22' 6"	17'	24' 6"	11' 8"	~	22'	24' 3"	22' 4"
LENGTH OF RAM	20'10"	15' 4 1/2"	22' 0"	10' 0"	18' 6"	20' 0"	22'	20'10"
BREADTH OF BOTTOM F.T(haught)	5' 3 1/2"	~	-5' 6 1/4"	2' 7 1/2"(H)	5' 2"	4' 8 3/4"	5' 6"	5' 3"
BREADTH OF BOTTOM M.T(haught)	5' 3 1/2"	~	5' 7"	2' 10 1/2"(I)	5' 0"	5' 2 1/2"	5' 7"	5' 3"
BREADTH OF BOTTOM AFT	5' 1"	~	5' 0"	2' 10 1/2"(J)	4' 8"	4' 7"	5'	5' 1"
DEPTH AT F.T(haught)	2' 10 1/2"	24 1/2"	2' 11"	1' 8"(H)	2' 6"	2' 4"	2' 9 1/2"	2' 8 1/2"
DEPTH AT M.T(haught)	2' 5 3/4"	22 1/2"	2' 6 3/4"	1' 7"(K)	2' 3"	2' 1"	2' 6"	2' 5 1/2"
DEPTH AT AFT	2' 5"(A)	19 1/2"	2' 5 3/4"	1' 8"(J)	2' 2"	2' 6"	2' 3 1/2"	2' 5 1/2"
BREADTH AT GUNWALE F.T(haught)	8' 6 1/2"	5'10 1/2"	8' 9"	4' 10 3/8"(H)	8' 2"	7' 6"	8' 4"	8' 1 1/2"
BREADTH AT GUNWALE M.T(haught)	8' 6"	6' 2"	8' 9"	5' 0"(K)	7' 7"	8' 1 1/2"	8' 9"	8' 6"
BREADTH AT GUNWALE AFT	7' 6 3/4"(A)	5' 11 1/2"	7' 3"	4' 6"(J)	6' 10"	7' 3"	7' 9"	7' 7 1/2"
HEIGHT OF STEM	3' 3"(B)	2' 9"	3' 8 3/4"	2' 6"	3' 0"	3' 2 1/2"	~	~
PLANKING OF SIDES	5"+7"+7"+7" +7"	~	~	~	7 1/2" + 7" + 6 1/2"	~	(Ul)21' 8"	(Ul)19' 0"
BOTTOM PLANKING AT F.T.	6 3/4"	~	~	~	6 5/8"	~	(Uhl)4' 2 1/2"	(Uhl)4' 2"
BOTTOM PLANKING AT M.T.	6 5/8"	~	~	~	6 1/4"	~	(Uhd)3' 0"	(Uhd)3' 0"
BOTTOM PLANKING AT AFT	5 1/2"	~	~	~	6"	~	(Vl)12' 10"	(Vl)11' 6 1/2"
RISE	(C)	~	(F)	(L)	~	~	(Vd) 2 1/2"&1 3/4"	(Vd) 2 1/2"&1 3/4"& 1 3/4"
BREADTH ? AT STERN	~	2' 6"	1' 10"	2' 6"	~	(N)3' 4"	(Vs)3' 11"	(L)
ADDITIONAL NOTES	~	(D & E)	~	(M)	~	(O)	(Q)8'+2"Choke (R,S &T) (W)20' Beech	(Q)6 1/2"×14"×1 1/4" (E)5"HGH & (X) (W)16' 6"Larch

A FORE PART OF BEAM
B HEIGHT OF PLANKING IN CARNOUTIE BOAT-3' 6"
C SAME AS 4-OARED COBLE
D SEA CRAFTS FROM GUNWALES 6" & 5 1/2"
E 2 TIMBER HEADS IN BOW FORE PART OF GUNWALE AT F.T.
F OF RAM-13 3/8,18 3/4,18 5/8,15 1/4,11 3/4, 8 3/4 & 8 1/8
G RIMWELL? F 7 1/2" A 7"
H AT 2nd FLOOR
I AT 5th FLOOR

J AT STERN
K AT 4th FLOOR
L AT BOTTOM FOOT OF STEM -9"
M 5 STREAK
N HEIGHT OF PLANKING AT F.T.
O CAMBER AT
P BUILT AT ABERDEEN, 18 MARCH 08
Q CENTRE BOARD
R MAST STEP 5 1/2" + 3"

CAMBER AT
10 | 11 1/2 | 10   FT

S SEA CRAFTS 2 3/4" + 2"
T BOTTOM FLOORS 3" + 2"
U MAST –
V YARD –
W DOUBLING
X GUNWALE Beech 2"+ 7/8"

LENGTH-Ul. HEEL-Uhl. HEAD-Uhd
LENGTH-Vl, DIAMS-Vd, SLING-Vs

TWO MORE COBLES WERE LISTED – A 2-OARED KINNABER OR WATER COBLE WITH THE SAME DIMENSIONS AS THE RIVER COBLE & A 6-OARED COBLE FROM BUDDIN OR CARNOUSTIE LIKE THE ONE IN THE FIRST COLUMN.

115

MOTOR COBLE FOR DEEP WATER FISHING STATIONS – 26·5′ × 3·0′ × 9·0′

AS BUILT BY THOMAS EASTON OF JOSEPH JOHNSTON & SONS, SALMON FISHERS, MONTROSE

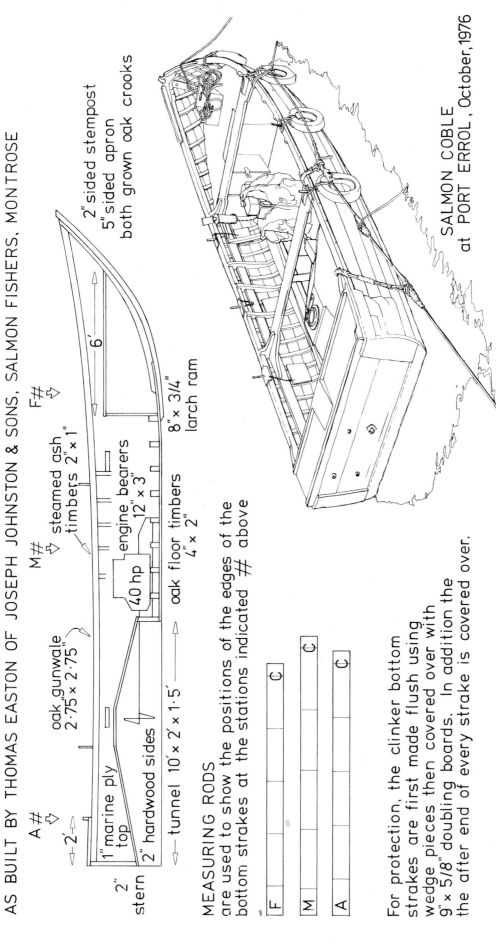

A#

M#

F#

2″ sided stempost
5″ sided apron
both grown oak crooks

oak gunwale
2·75″ × 2·75″

steamed ash
timbers 2″ × 1″

6′

2′

engine bearers
12″ × 3″

40 hp

2″ hardwood sides

2″
stern

1″ marine ply
top

8″ × 3/4″
larch ram

oak floor timbers
4″ × 2″

tunnel 10′ × 2′ × 1·5′

MEASURING RODS
are used to show the positions of the edges of the
bottom strakes at the stations indicated # above

F	℄			
M			℄	
A		℄		

For protection, the clinker bottom
strakes are first made flush using
wedge pieces then covered over with
9″ × 5/8″ doubling boards. In addition the
the after end of every strake is covered over.

SALMON COBLE
at PORT ERROL, October, 1976

Fig 93: Motor coble for deep water fishing stations, 26.5ft × 3.0ft × 9.0.

Fig 94: Bay boat type coble for shallow water fishing stations.

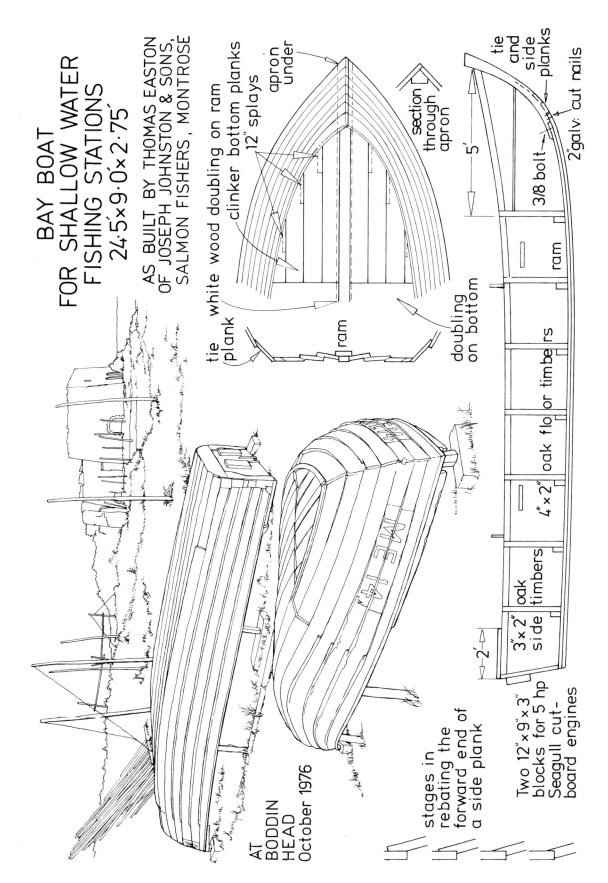

BAY BOAT
FOR SHALLOW WATER
FISHING STATIONS
24·5'×9·0'×2·75'

AS BUILT BY THOMAS EASTON
OF JOSEPH JOHNSTON & SONS,
SALMON FISHERS, MONTROSE

white wood doubling on ram
clinker bottom planks
12" splays

apron
under

tie plank

section
through
apron

ram

doubling
on bottom

tie
and
side
planks

2"galv: cut nails

3/8 bolt

ram

5'

oak floor timbers
4"×2"

3"×2"
oak
side
timbers

2'

AT
BODDIN
HEAD
October 1976

stages in
rebating the
forward end of
a side plank

Two 12"×9"×3"
blocks for 5 hp
Seagull cut-
board engines

117

being bolted on to a 8in × ¾in larch ram secured on top of a jig which gives the shape of the bottom. The bottom is clinker-planked, also in ¾in larch, out to the turn of the bilge. The taper in these planks establishes the shape of the boat. 4in × 2in floor timbers are then fitted every 12in, followed by the side planking up to the required depth (Fig 93). 2in × 1in ash timbers are steamed and bent in for fastening, before the stern is planked up last. The 2¾in square oak gunwales are also steamed before bending into place. The tunnel for the propeller is 10ft long, 2ft high and 1ft 6in wide being rectangular in section with 2in hard wood sides and a marine ply top. The engine bearers are 12ft × 3in and rest on the floors amidships immediately forward of the tunnel. The whole of the underside of the coble up to the waterline is covered with white pine doubling boards to protect the lands of the bottom planking from the rollers on the slipway. At first glance this makes the coble look as if she had flush-laid planks underwater. It will be seen that this coble is built without any moulds at all; her components are cut to shape before they reach the boat, and a marked measuring rod is used for spacing stations.

The Bay boat has a feature not found in any other type of round bottom British boat – a tie plank. Instead of bringing the forward ends of the bottom strakes up and round for fastening to the apron, they end at and are fastened to the tie plank, which is the first strake at the turn of the bilge. This gives a flatter and more buoyant bottom that allows the boat to be beached on gradual beaches. Instead of timbers, the floors are alternately extended into frames using 3in × 2in oak up the sides at 24in centres (Fig 94).

Taking these three cobles together, the English, motor and Bay, there is a variation in type from almost round bottom practice to almost rafted construction in the last. The cobles built for commercial salmon fishing in the Tweed at Spittal are of three sizes, all smaller than those at Montrose, and, if both sides are counted, they have thirteen strakes including the ram. The upriver coble is 14ft long, the cobles 18ft and the boats used in the mouth of the river 21ft. The first five strakes form the bottom with the stem erected on the central one of these. This leaves four more strakes each side, the bottom one of which is called the 'rising strake'. Nearly every part of one of these boats is interchangeable, so that stoppages during the fishing season are kept to a minimum with the help of stocks of spares built up in winter. All new building and regular maintenance takes place out of season. The Lee family has been the main Berwick boatbuilding family for well over a century; the firm is even older than the Berwick Salmon Fisheries Company, which has been in existence since 1856, when it was first incorporated from an older enterprise called The Old Shipping Company[8] (Fig 95).

Shaping a boat with edge-positioned strakes is different from shaping one with edge-fastened ones. In the latter case the shape derives from how each strake in turn is fashioned, with the transverse members having a purely structural purpose. If instead the strakes only have the frames to hold their edges together, it is these members that give the boat her shape. The frames may be cut to shape by eye, rule-of-thumb, or by relying to a greater or lesser degree on templates, drawings, models or combinations of any of these. In every case there has to be a rigid framework of the desired form available before a plank can be put in position.

Boats with edge-fastened and edge-positioned planking have much in common, namely, the wide range of shapes possible and, unless extremely rigid or flexible hulls are wanted, a not dissimilar structural arrangement in the finished boat. They do however differ during construction and in how their shape is realised. There are a number of ways that men building an edge-positioned, or frame-before-plank, boat go about their work, beginning with building mostly by eye and finishing with total dependence on drawings.

Assuming that there are no drawings or other mechanical aids whatever, the builder has no choice but to work from the bottom upwards, once the backbone has been erected. His first thought is how to shape the floor, the first transverse timber fixed on top of the keel and how its and other floors' deadrises should vary from bow to stern to produce either a bawley or baldie in due course.

Knowing what the maximum breadth and depth have to be, some builders will go ahead and build a midship frame, or even a pair of them if there is to be a length of dead-flats amidships. To draw this section he may rely on a rule-of-thumb to get the deadrise and another to blend this line in with the topside, or he may use a flexible spline to find a fair curve from keel to sheerline. The more free-arm builder cuts out only the midship floor, and gives it the correct deadrise. The complete midship frame or floor alone is then set up on that station that will make the boat fuller forward, aft or both ends the same. He then strings or hangs a pair of stout ribbands, one each side, from some way up the stempost, past the floor heads and then on up to some way up the sternpost. There are two adjustments to the shape of a ribband rather like the lath in a coracle. The builder can raise or lower the ends on the posts or he can lengthen or shorten the length of the ribband. If this is not enough, he uses shores, almost as if he was constraining an edge-fastened strake before fastening (Fig 96). His eye will tell him when the curvature of the ribband is fair and the way he wants. This is as an important stage as the first strakes of a clinker boat as it will decide the character of the whole boat.

This done, he can go ahead and fit most if not all of his floors so that their lower sides just touch the ribbands. If some do not reach that far or even extend beyond, it will not concern him very much. Near the bow and the stern the deadwoods will prevent the floors from crossing the keel, but as there is bound to be a lot more deadrise on these stations, the heels of a pair of suitably angled timbers can be bolted through from either side. If instead of a pointed stern there is to be a transom, this is treated in

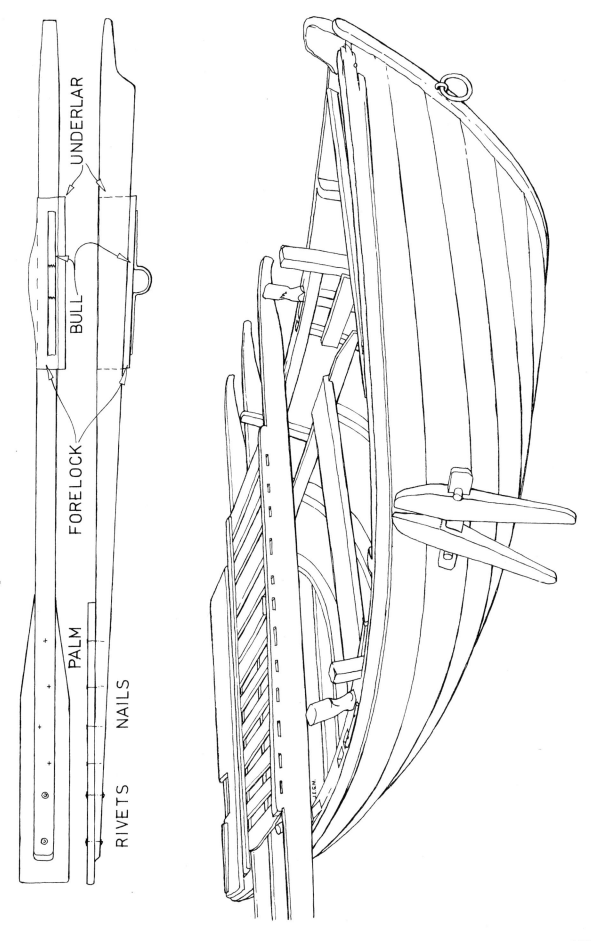

Fig 95: River Tweed up-river coble with oar, net pallet and building tongs.

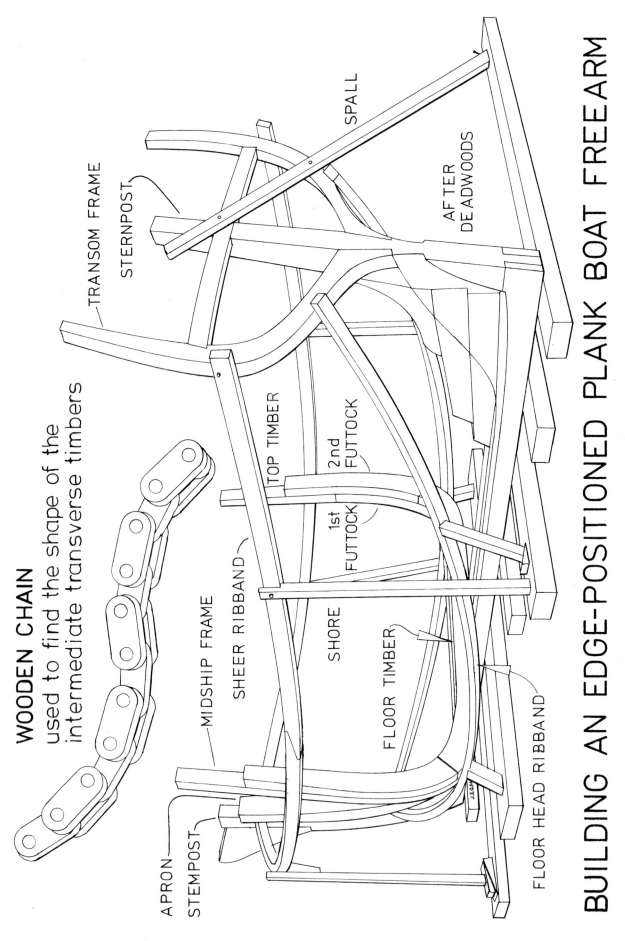

WOODEN CHAIN
used to find the shape of the
intermediate transverse timbers

TRANSOM FRAME

STERNPOST

SPALL

AFTER
DEADWOODS

TOP TIMBER

2nd
FUTTOCK

1st
FUTTOCK

MIDSHIP FRAME

SHEER RIBBAND

SHORE

FLOOR TIMBER

FLOOR HEAD RIBBAND

APRON

STEMPOST

BUILDING AN EDGE-POSITIONED PLANK BOAT FREE ARM

Fig 96: Building an edge-positioned plank boat free-arm and wooden chain.

Fig 97: George Jarvis' 26ft motor fishing boat *Pelagic*.

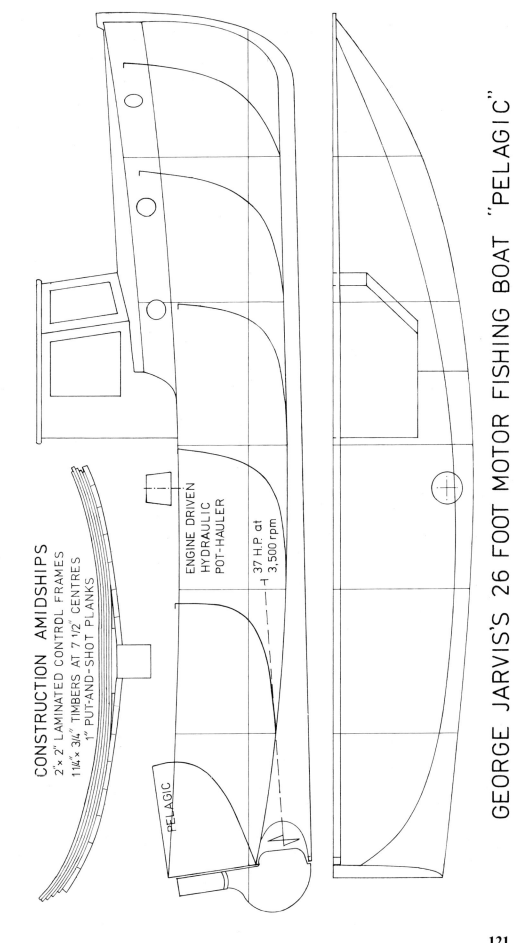

CONSTRUCTION AMIDSHIPS
2" × 2" LAMINATED CONTROL FRAMES
1¼" × ¾" TIMBERS AT 7½" CENTRES
1" PUT-AND-SHOT PLANKS

PELAGIC

ENGINE DRIVEN
HYDRAULIC
POT-HAULER

37 H.P. at
3,500 rpm

GEORGE JARVIS'S 26 FOOT MOTOR FISHING BOAT "PELAGIC"

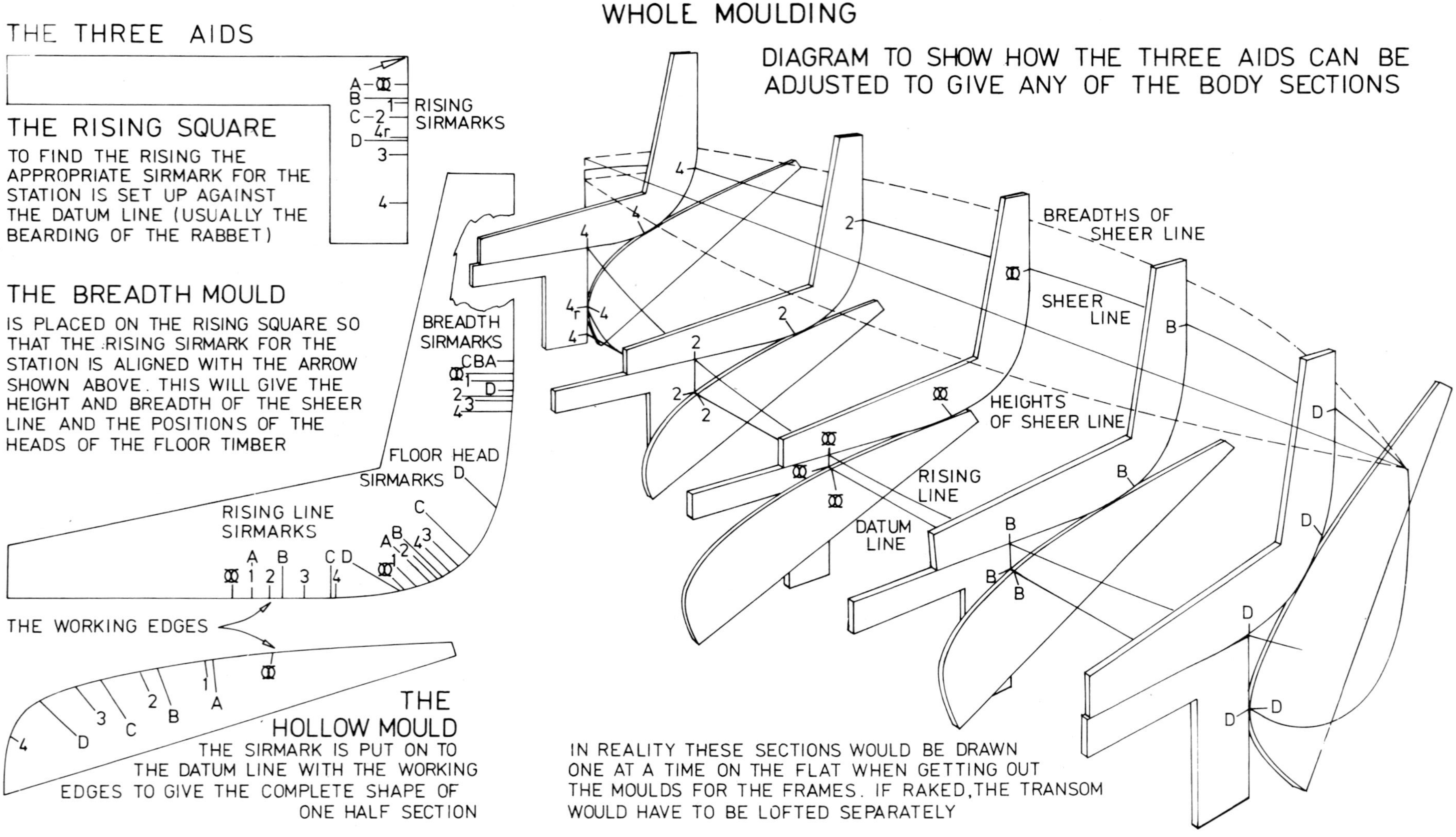

WHOLE MOULDING

DIAGRAM TO SHOW HOW THE THREE AIDS CAN BE ADJUSTED TO GIVE ANY OF THE BODY SECTIONS

BREADTHS OF SHEER LINE

SHEER LINE

HEIGHTS OF SHEER LINE

RISING LINE

DATUM LINE

IN REALITY THESE SECTIONS WOULD BE DRAWN ONE AT A TIME ON THE FLAT WHEN GETTING OUT THE MOULDS FOR THE FRAMES. IF RAKED, THE TRANSOM WOULD HAVE TO BE LOFTED SEPARATELY

THE THREE AIDS

THE RISING SQUARE

TO FIND THE RISING THE APPROPRIATE SIRMARK FOR THE STATION IS SET UP AGAINST THE DATUM LINE (USUALLY THE BEARDING OF THE RABBET)

RISING SIRMARKS

THE BREADTH MOULD

IS PLACED ON THE RISING SQUARE SO THAT THE RISING SIRMARK FOR THE STATION IS ALIGNED WITH THE ARROW SHOWN ABOVE. THIS WILL GIVE THE HEIGHT AND BREADTH OF THE SHEER LINE AND THE POSITIONS OF THE HEADS OF THE FLOOR TIMBER

BREADTH SIRMARKS

FLOOR HEAD SIRMARKS

RISING LINE SIRMARKS

THE WORKING EDGES

THE HOLLOW MOULD

THE SIRMARK IS PUT ON TO THE DATUM LINE WITH THE WORKING EDGES TO GIVE THE COMPLETE SHAPE OF ONE HALF SECTION

Fig 98: Whole moulding: the three aids.

much the same way as if it was a frame, that is to say, by using a complete frame on or close to the sternpost or by building progressively up and out from the floor. Whichever method is used, the final shape of this section should have the same general character as the midship section – if not, the hull will be difficult to fair. The bottom can then be planked up to the first pair of ribbands, which then can be knocked off.

Taking the shape from this bottom the boatbuilder may erect a further pair of full frames or just a number of futtocks, bolting their heels to the planking, either between a pair of floors or alongside one of them. A second pair of ribbands are then strung, this time along the line where the tops of the futtocks will come, generally close to where the bilge and the topside meet. If full frames are being erected a third pair of ribbands can be strung along the sheerline or tops of the frames. If instead, he is not prepared to chance this, he can timber up and plank in easy stages as he goes. Otherwise he will fit a few more intermediate frames to his second and third ribbands. He can then plank down from the sheer, fitting the remaining timbers as and when it suits him to do so, using a 'chain' to find what shape to make them (Fig 96).

In this method the builder has control over the emerging shape throughout, guided partly by experience, but also by the ribbands to keep his boat fair. From time to time he will have to check that both sides are coming out the same. In the case of the ribbands this is a matter of taking comparative measurements. For the frames, the components on one side can be used as patterns for those on the other if a symmetrical arrangement is used, otherwise further measurements are needed. No formal drawings are needed and what happens is very much like what seem to be taking place in Rålamb's Fig 2 (Fig 34). This method of control is suitable when the floors spring straight from the rabbet in the keel, but not where there are floors on a rising line with reverse curves down to this rabbet.

I have never seen this method used, though it was described to me by Mr Atwell, the foreman of F J Carver's Yard at Bridgwater, as the method used for coasting ketches and trows up to the First World War. They would construct and erect the complete midship frame first and then work from ribbands without any lofting. I have however been able to watch George Jarvis, the boat shipwright from Devonport Dockyard, who had built *Boleh* with Lt Cdr Kilroy at Loyang, prior to them sailing her round the Cape of Good Hope back to England. This time George was building, mostly single handed, a 26ft edge-positioned motor fishing boat at Devonport.

He started with a $\frac{1}{12}$th scale drawing, so that scaling up was a matter of reading inches as feet. The drawing was quite simple, showing the profile, five sections, the sheer and waterlines. There were no reverse curves (Fig 97). He redrew the sections full size on a sheet of plywood to give the shape of his control frames. These were 2in square laminations reaching from gunwale to gunwale. They held their shape well, but were far from rigid, so when set up square on their stations, they adjusted themselves to the sheerstrakes, which were fitted first. Battens were then used to guide the shaping of the rabbets in the stem and the bevels on the frames. The 1in planking was fitted by the west country 'put-and-shot' method, though George did not know this term. This was done by 'putting' on half the strakes leaving a gap, a strake wide, between each one. These strakes were tapered each end and the ones round the bilge were hollowed on the inside. When all the 'put' strakes were in place, no two of them were flush with each other, other than where they crossed a control frame every four feet or so. It looked as if George had taken too many short cuts; however, once all the intermediate timbers had been steamed and fastened in at $7\frac{1}{2}$in centres, all the strakes came into line and the hull was fair and round as anyone could wish. An unshaped plank was then clamped over each gap in turn, marked from the inside, taken off and shaped before being 'shot' into place and fastened. The fit was so good that it was only necessary to caulk a few open seams here and there.

Marmaduke Stalkartt, whose *Naval Architecture* provides the opening quotation of this book, describes whole moulding as, 'a method of forming the principal parts of a vessel by the use of a mould of the midship-bend, and continued as far afore and abaft the same, as the form of the midship bend and the curve of the rising line are suitably disposed to each other, in order to make the body fair'. By the time he had written this in the mid-eighteenth century, this method had been in use for at least a century for all sizes of vessels, but had become outmoded for larger ships. Today, no instances of whole moulding having been used recently can be given, except, and I am grateful to David MacGregor for this suggestion, in the way a ship's curve is adjusted when drawing a body plan (Fig 98). Whole moulding is simple to use and economical in material. It is a stage between building by eye and the preparation of a draft using sweeps, the radii of which change every station[9].

If the same height of floor over the keel is retained over its entire length, the number of shapes the hull can be given is limited. If, instead, a curve is drawn over the centreline of the keel so that it is closest to or touches the rabbet line amidships, yet rises each end, a much wider variety of shapes is possible. If a half mould were then made of the midship section and this were adjusted at each frame station so that it fitted between the rising and sheer lines, a fair canoe-shaped hull would be developed. If, as well, a reverse curve were drawn from the rabbet so as to blend into the canoe body at each station, a shapely hull would emerge.

In its simple form a whole moulded boat needs only three aids. The first is the rising square, which is no more than a batten with the heights of the floors marked in for every station. These markes are called 'rising sirmarks' as they are taken from the rising line. The second aid is the breadth mould and this has the convex shape of the midship section, except that it is usual to extend the lengths

SHAPING A HALF MODEL BY EYE

AS IN SPAR MAKING FAIR LONGITUDINAL LINES HAVE TO BE ESTABLISHED
FROM THE START AND MAINTAINED THROUGH EVERY STAGE FROM SQUARE

| 4-SQUARE | TAPERED | 8-SQUARE | 16-SQUARE | TO ROUND |

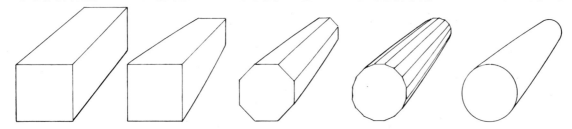

THE BLOCK FOR A HALF MODEL TENDS TO HAVE LIFTS IF THE BOAT IS TO
BE FULLY LOFTED, BUT SOLID AND SAWN ACROSS IF THE FRAMES ARE TO
BE SCALED UP DIRECT FROM THE MODEL

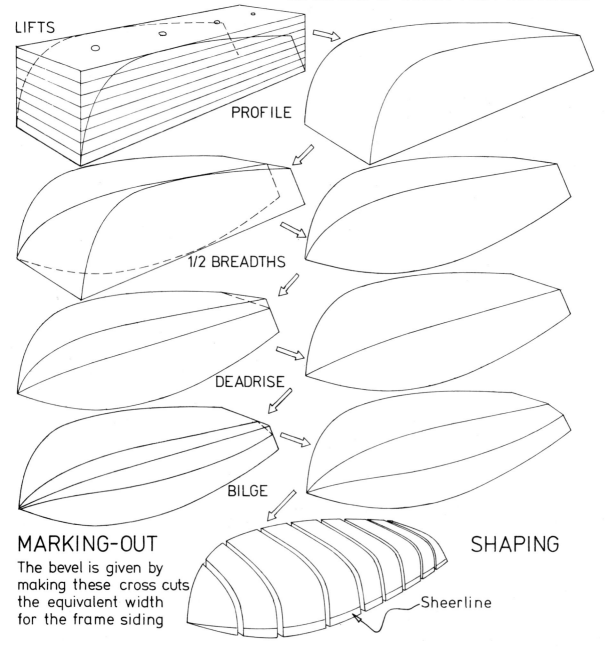

LIFTS

PROFILE

1/2 BREADTHS

DEADRISE

BILGE

MARKING-OUT

The bevel is given by
making these cross cuts
the equivalent width
for the frame siding

SHAPING

Sheerline

of the floor and topside beyond the centre and sheer lines to provide space for further sets of sirmarks. There are three of these: the marks on the first set when aligned with the corresponding rising sirmarks give from one or other of the remaining two sets, the height and half breadth of the sheerline, and the position of the head of the floor timber, for every frame. The third aid, the hollow mould, the sirmarks of which are set on the rabbet line, is then laid tangential to the breadth mould for the reverse curve.

This system may be used to draft the whole hull, altering if thought necessary the curve of the moulds and the placing of the sirmarks until the desired shape is reached. This is a departure from what has been described so far, as it expresses boatshape in terms of the hull sections rather than in the run of planks and ribbands. The three moulds can be used by anyone to get out the frames, which allows the master builder to keep control while others do the manual work. A set of three whole moulding aids can be used to produce a wide range of boats, either by changing the sirmarks or even re-adjusting them by eye. A weakness of the method lies in the shape of the transom having to be the same as part of the midship section, which is not always acceptable. Furthermore, in bluff-ended models square sections are not enough to ensure a fair hull. Therefore some modifications of the system, involving reshaping the ends, by cants or diagonals or even perhaps by eye, are essential.

More elaborate methods of drafting have been used, some of them predating whole moulding. Unless they were used to record an existing boat, they were not at that time, as far as is known, used for small craft, requiring as they do a separate mould for every station. Their offer of a wider choice of designs led to their adoption when fishing boats grew larger and more powerful during the nineteenth century. Traditional clinker practice cannot express shape by the means of frames, whereas well established shipbuilding lofting practice could, especially as, more and more, size favoured the change from edge-fastened to edge-positioned construction.

This is not the place to enter into a detailed account of the various lofting systems. Dr Howard has recently done this[10], and it is evident that they were capable of giving inspired results – combining carrying capacity, shapely underwater bodies, sea-keeping and windward performance. Some were still tied by rule-of-thumb; the *Treatise of Shipbuilding* c1620, for instance, lays down that a ship's depth could be anything from a half to a third of the beam, which is as wide a tolerance any designer might wish[11]. It goes on to say that it is best to use a proportion of 3 to 7. Eventually hard and fast methods and ratios were abandoned in favour of more freely drawn curves. This was replaced in the course of the nineteenth and twentieth centuries by a series of new systems, which in their times

were as firmly believed as the earlier ones, but in this case because they were said to be based on scientific principles. Two theories, that of the curves of immersed areas and the metacentric shelf, have been popular recently. The progress since has not been spectacular, however, as tank testing, however systematic, is a form of trial and error, and computerised fairing and calculation does not help the designer draw the right shape in the first place.

Few small boatbuilders can run a drawing office or spare the space to loft full size, so one of the more popular ways of realising shape has to make a half model first. Sections could then be taken off the model and enlarged to control the shape of the full sized hull. This model might be made from a set of drawings, as Alexander Noble has described, or it might be made freehand almost like shaping the outside of a dugout, except there would be no need to achieve symmetry[12].

Carving a half model from a block by eye called for a disciplined approach if the surface was to be free of bumps and hollows (Fig 99). This drawing shows the process stage by stage with a short description of each. The block itself was generally made up of horizontal boards known as lifts, which, after the finished model was taken apart, gave the vessel's level lines. These then could be scaled up at each station to show the shape of the frames directly, or be used as the point to start a full size lofting. Gerald and Bill Worfold of King's Lynn used half models made up of tranversely cut blocks, so were able to get the shape of their control frames evenly more directly. In spite of this they looked to ribbands to fair and bevel the frames once they were in place.

The method used at Crossfield's at Arnside and by others was an adaptation of the transverse method. They would cut out the profile of the projected nobby from 1in stuff. After marking in the rabbet line they would sink a number of evenly spaced slots down to it. Four of these slots would be square with the waterline and the fifth would follow the angle of the sternpost. Half transverse sections cut roughly to shape would then be inserted in the slots and pared carefully down to their final shape using battens to check fairness. These sections were then taken out and scaled up to provide the control frames for the nobby. This sounds very much like the method George employed on page 123 except here it is being applied to a model and not a full sized vessel. Models are useful when the builder and the owner wish to discuss what the final shape should be, as it is easier to alter a model than the completed boat (Fig 100).

When building from scale drawings and models errors are multiplied. These can raise bumps and hollows, the correction of which can misinterpret the designer's intentions. Re-drawing the lines full size on the mould loft floor under the eye of or even by, the designer himself removes this source of error. Due to perspective effects, full sized boats and drawings look different from scale models and drawings, so there is still a possibility of changes during lofting, if the loftsman lacks experience.

Left:
Fig 99: Shaping a half model by eye.

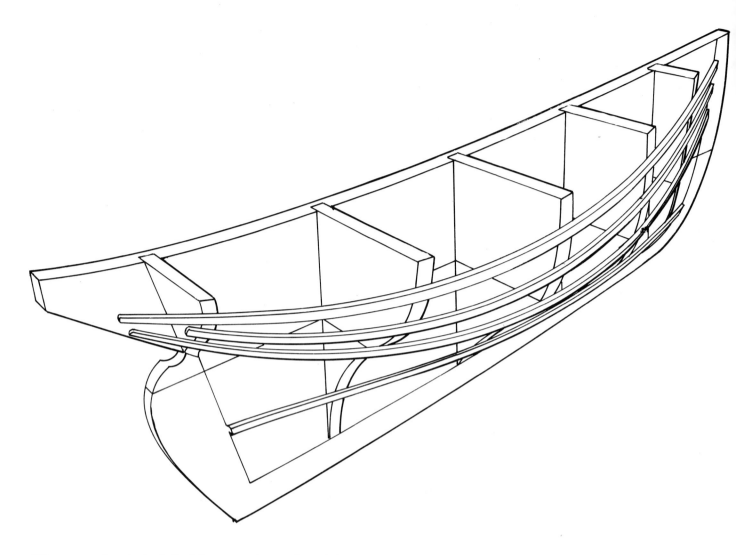

Above:
Fig 100: Skeleton half model used by Crossfield's of Arnside.

Opposite:
Fig 101: Picking up devices.

When completed, the lofted lines may be used to pick up a full set of moulds for the backbone assembly, all the frames and any other components that might be hard to shape correctly in place. Unless picking up is accurate the trouble of lofting is wasted. A great deal of ingenuity is applied to picking up methods. In addition to the method described and illustrated by Alexander Noble there are others including the device used at Miller's Yard at St Monance for doing this (Fig 101).

As well as giving a more accurate result, moulds save far more labour and material on the building site than went into their actual manufacture. Once a boat has been framed up, some large boat builders store their moulds in case of a repeated order, as they represent an expenditure of resources which they would prefer to spread over several boats. Individual tastes and technical advances combine to thwart this aim, until lack of storage space and risk of fire makes it impractical to keep them any longer. To guard against the loss of a design like this a loftsman will draw up a table of offsets and scantlings at the time of lofting. These are tabulations of the lines in figures, examples being given in this book. He will also list the amounts of materials, fastenings and fittings used to assist the re-ordering of stocks. With this done, the floor can be

cleaned off or repainted so that the next lofting can start.

Scale drawings are also a means of showing how a boat is shaped to those who neither want to build her nor are necessarily trained naval architects. The traditional ship draught, showing how the sections in various planes are inter-related, grew out of having to frame before planking, this being as essential step in the development of this order of work. Once faired, a set of lines is comprehensive; not only can the shape of any component however oriented be obtained from them, but also the raw data for displacement and stability calculations. Care is needed when looking at drawings as, for instance, unevenly spaced sections appear to distort shape. Nevertheless this system has been in use for two hundred and fifty years, during which time most vessels, if they have been recorded at all, used this method.

It was seen that a clinker boatbuilder can record shape by making patterns of the stem, transom and strakes on one side, and that this is all that is needed to ensure an

PICKING UP DEVICES
NAILING METHODS

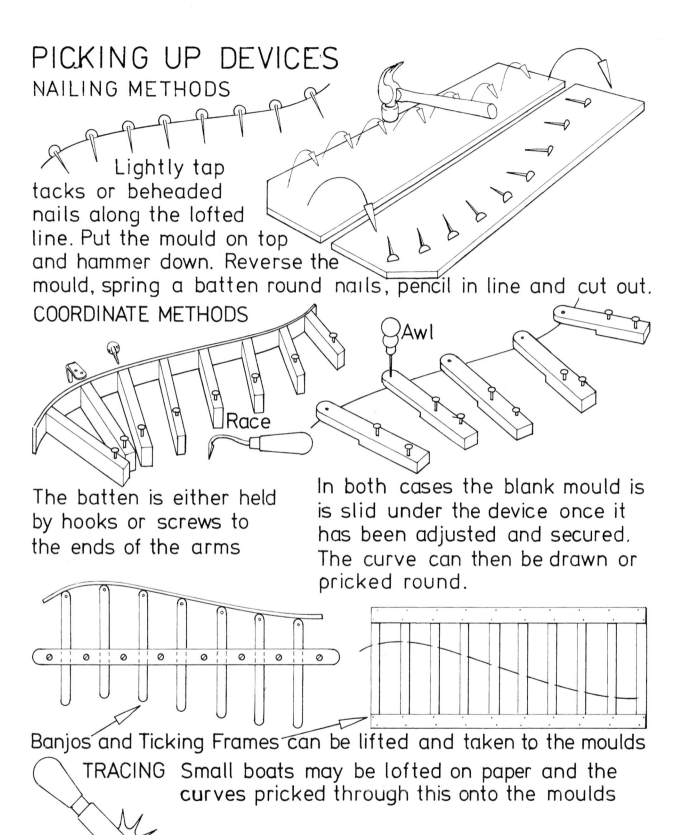

Lightly tap tacks or beheaded nails along the lofted line. Put the mould on top and hammer down. Reverse the mould, spring a batten round nails, pencil in line and cut out.

COORDINATE METHODS

Awl

Race

The batten is either held by hooks or screws to the ends of the arms

In both cases the blank mould is is slid under the device once it has been adjusted and secured. The curve can then be drawn or pricked round.

Banjos and Ticking Frames can be lifted and taken to the moulds

TRACING Small boats may be lofted on paper and the curves pricked through this onto the moulds

IN ALL CASES DATUM AND REFERENCE LINES CROSSING A MOULD SHOULD BE MARKED IN

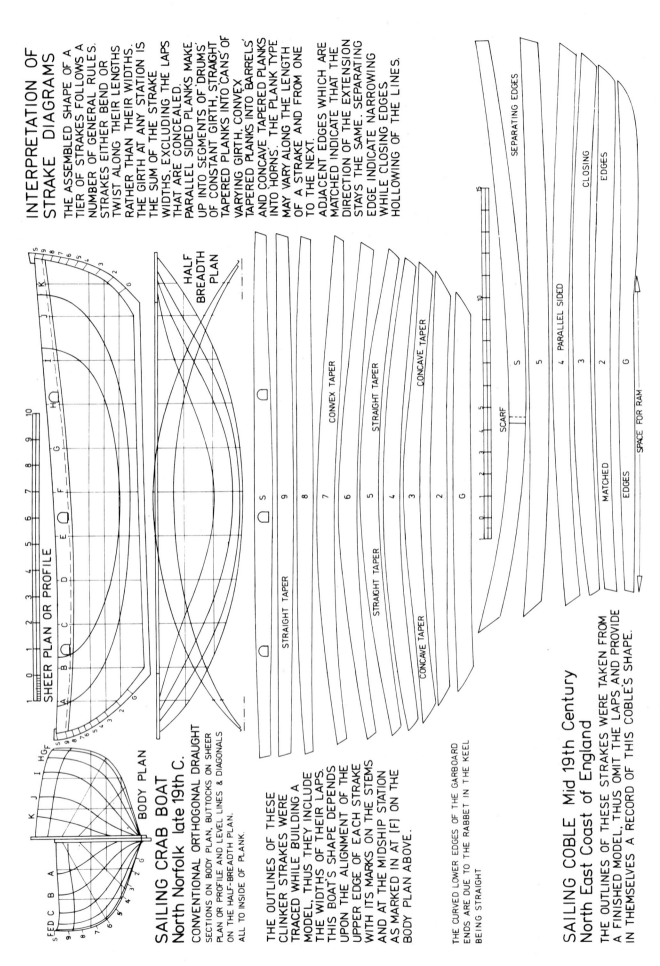

INTERPRETATION OF STRAKE DIAGRAMS

THE ASSEMBLED SHAPE OF A TIER OF STRAKES FOLLOWS A NUMBER OF GENERAL RULES. STRAKES EITHER BEND OR TWIST ALONG THEIR LENGTHS RATHER THAN THEIR WIDTHS. THE GIRTH AT ANY STATION IS THE SUM OF THE STRAKE WIDTHS, EXCLUDING THE LAPS THAT ARE CONCEALED. PARALLEL SIDED PLANKS MAKE UP INTO SEGMENTS OF 'DRUMS' OF CONSTANT GIRTH, STRAIGHT TAPERED PLANKS INTO 'CANS' OF VARYING GIRTH. CONVEX TAPERED PLANKS INTO BARRELS' AND CONCAVE TAPERED PLANKS INTO 'HORNS'. THE PLANK TYPE MAY VARY ALONG THE LENGTH OF A STRAKE AND FROM ONE TO THE NEXT.

ADJACENT EDGES WHICH ARE MATCHED INDICATE THAT THE DIRECTION OF THE EXTENSION STAYS THE SAME. SEPARATING EDGE INDICATE NARROWING WHILE CLOSING EDGES HOLLOWING OF THE LINES.

SHEER PLAN OR PROFILE

HALF BREADTH PLAN

BODY PLAN

SAILING CRAB BOAT
North Norfolk late 19th C.

CONVENTIONAL ORTHOGONAL DRAUGHT

SECTIONS ON BODY PLAN, BUTTOCKS ON SHEER PLAN OR PROFILE AND LEVEL LINES & DIAGONALS ON THE HALF-BREADTH PLAN. ALL TO INSIDE OF PLANK.

THE OUTLINES OF THESE CLINKER STRAKES WERE TRACED WHILE BUILDING A MODEL, THUS THEY INCLUDE THE WIDTHS OF THEIR LAPS. THIS BOAT'S SHAPE DEPENDS UPON THE ALIGNMENT OF THE UPPER EDGE OF EACH STRAKE WITH ITS MARKS ON THE STEMS AND AT THE MIDSHIP STATION AS MARKED IN AT [F] ON THE BODY PLAN ABOVE.

THE CURVED LOWER EDGES OF THE GARBOARD ENDS ARE DUE TO THE RABBET IN THE KEEL BEING STRAIGHT

STRAIGHT TAPER

CONVEX TAPER

STRAIGHT TAPER

STRAIGHT TAPER

CONCAVE TAPER

CONCAVE TAPER

SCARF

PARALLEL SIDED

SPACE FOR RAM

SEPARATING EDGES

CLOSING

EDGES

MATCHED

EDGES

SAILING COBLE Mid 19th Century
North East Coast of England

THE OUTLINES OF THESE STRAKES WERE TAKEN FROM A FINISHED MODEL, THUS OMIT THE LAPS AND PROVIDE IN THEMSELVES A RECORD OF THIS COBLE'S SHAPE.

Fig 102: Profile and strake diagram – interpretation.

exact copy. Laid out together, a scale drawing of these patterns would express the shape of this particular boat. This is a quick and accurate way of measuring an existing boat or an ancient find, especially as the patterns can be used to construct both a model and a set of conventional drawings[13]. This approach gives an idea of how the boatbuilder thought and worked and is altogether a valuable research tool. The profile and strake diagram is not a practical way of communicating shape generally, as it requires a mental re-orientation of the pattern of lines made by flat components before one can envisage how they will look when curved and fitted together (Fig 102). While the profile and strake diagram is probably the best way of recording an edge-fastened boat, there is a better way of showing just what she looked like.

The edges of the strakes of a clinker-built boat in the round can by themselves tell us her shape, but only that bit of her can be seen at any one time. If she is an open boat these lines will be visible inside as well as out. Some of the drawings in this book, a few of which are perspective projections of orthogonal draughts, are meant to demonstrate this. Ewing McGruer, recognising that the conventional draught was not of relevance to a clinker boat, as it employed planes at right angles to each other, published designs which only showed the inside plank edges in both the plan and side elevations[5]. Providing one clears one's mind of thinking that these are not the usual buttock and level lines, the sheers and beuls give an excellent idea of the boat's shape. Offsets can be taken directly from these lines to construct a transverse mould with the strake marks on it. In an open boat, it is these lines that are the most convenient to measure when taking off her lines, and her timbers and frames normally indicate the best stations to use. Some of the book's drawings show the run of plank on the outside of the boat, that is to say the lower edges of the outside of the strakes, which is not the same thing.

It is thought that there should be only one method of communicating the shapes of vessels, and that this should still be the conventional sheer, body and half breadth layout. This does not restrict the way one takes off lines or records, which depend upon the vessel and the site. To amplify the information given by the conventional draught it will often be necessary to employ further forms of presentation, run of strakes or profile and strake diagram, perspective projection, dimensioned sketch, or whatever is appropriate. The camera is an aid to memory, which in combination with photogrammetry promises to give accurate conventional draughts[14]. Even when there is insufficient data to complete a set of lines, the conventional draught is a convenient framework for indicating what has and has not been actually recorded.

In conclusion, it seems as if in recent times British boatbuilders have rarely relied on eye alone to realise boatshape. There controls, like rules-of-thumb and mechanical aids, vary, due more to the personality of the individual than his locality. In so far as it can be separated from shape, structure is more regional in nature. Controls help to establish a design and so provide a basis for further improvement. Where design is static, repetition encourages a man to depend less on controls and work more by habit than intention. Without even a change of model occasionally, this could be less creative than a job on a car assembly line. Creative boatbuilding can be instinctive or reasoned, though never an occult craft. The instinctive builder has the flair to build inspired designs within a certain range. The more rational worker has a wider scope and the ability to interpret the designs of others. The former tends to avoid complications like drawings and calculations that do not seem to add anything tangible to a boat; he is therefore less likely to take up new techniques, materials and shapes than his more rational colleague.

8.

Propulsion and steering

Transportation is the function of all boats; given stable flotation, the other essential is mobility, the product of speed and direction. Before considering how a boat's solid shape might be involved, her draft has to be taken into account. This single dimension limits the places she can visit and from whence she can be regularly operated. If, because of this, a boat has to be shoal drafted she may have to forgo features which in other circumstances might have given her better hydrodynamic qualities – for example, for the same length and weight of cargo, a boat with pointed ends will draw more water than one with square ends.

There are four sources of power for boat propulsion; gravity, muscle, wind and fuel. Tides and currents are manifestations of gravity and though generally predictable they are not always convenient in their direction or duration. One of the other sources of power is needed to overcome these shortcomings. Though animals, usually a man or a horse, have to be fed from time to time, this does not have to be an unbroken process like the combustion of fuel under a boiler or inside a cylinder. Fuel-powered engines,

unlike animals, need no rest. Wind is unreliable as a source of power – it can blow too hard, in the wrong direction or not at all. This has made sailing rigs the most adjustable of all propulsion engines and the most demanding of the shape of the hull below.

GRAVITY

No apparent force is needed to propel a boat that is able to wait for the tide. She must however have the ability to turn and stop. In the first instance she must be able to secure herself from being moved by adverse currents, by anchoring, tying-up or by the temporary use of stakes driven into the bed of the waterway. Once under way, she must be able to position herself in the best part of the stream that takes her in the right direction clear of obstacles. If her destination is short of where the tide would naturally take her, she must be able to regulate her speed by dragging some form of ground tackle and then moving alongside or to an anchorage. What seems to be a simple form of propulsion turns

Fig 103: Bridgwater barge – perspective projection and reflection.

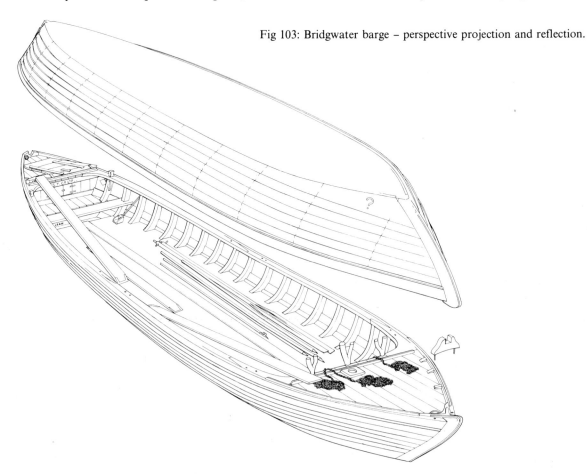

out to require special gear and tidal knowledge to succeed.

All of this is demonstrated in the way the Bridgwater barge was handled in the River Parrett when engaged in the Bath brick trade. These striking looking dumb barges (Fig 103) lightered coal out of coasters lying on the river quays at Bridgwater, and took it to whichever of the brick kilns owned them. It took two men to work and load a barge. On the tide the bargemen directed the barge by two sweeps, one shipped forward in a portable oarlock called a 'monkey' and the other in the groove cut in the top of the sternpost. The rudder was never shipped in the river, only when under tow in the canal to Taunton. If it were necessary to propel the boat the sweeps were pivotted on tholes put in the holes in the sheer clamps. Progress was regulated by 'riding the bottom'. This was done by varying the length of the chains being towed over the side, being turned up to the 'livers' forward and the 'ballards and clinks' at the quarters. On arrival the coal was unloaded using barrows trundled over gangplanks through tunnels cut through the river wall to the kiln. The empty barge would then take an ebb tide down river to between Dunball and Steart. Here there were both reservoirs formed along the river banks and wide areas left uncovered by the tide. These acted as catchments for the 'slime', the raw material for Bath brick, being a mixture of mud and sharp silt brought down by the rivers. The men moored the barges by thrusting their 'geds' (iron pointed poles) into the mud. When the falling tide had sewed the barge entirely, the bargemen would load her with slime. Depending on the season the tide would rise in the normal manner or be delayed while an 'eager' formed. This was a 2ft to 3ft tidal bore which swept up the river, followed by an unusually short time between low and high water. The sharp rake ends and flared sides kept the eager from swamping the barge, which was propelled up river using her chains again to the loading staithe. The unloaded slime would be ground and hand formed into bricks, which, after baking, were dressed and individually wrapped in paper, mainly by women and boys. The barges then took the bricks, 8 million in 1856, back up to Bridgwater for shipment by rail or sea all over the world for scouring, polishing and knife cleaning[1]. As these tidal barges were loaded for 2 or 3 trips out of 4, and their crews were kept busy under way and alongside, they were an economical form of transport.

There were barges relying almost entirely on the current on the tidal stretches of most British rivers. For most of the time there was no relative velocity between the hull and the water, a little when manoeuvring but most when stopped in a tideway. Therefore the shape of a drifting boat, as long as she can be turned and will not swamp, is of small consequence and she can be as beamy and deep as the channels allow. More important is that her crew can move freely and have platforms from where they can work their gear vigorously, even if only for short bursts, when stopping, starting and turning.

MUSCLE

There is a story that a member of the Royal Corps of Naval Constructors once said, 'Unless there is something sticking out of her, a vessel can't be moved through the water'; and bollards, oars, masts and propellers are instances of this. Which one or more of these are chosen will effect the shape of the boat involved, starting with those extensions that require muscle.

The most effective way of moving a boat is to push or pull in exactly the same direction as she is supposed to go. This is harder to arrange than say, once the vessel is any distance from firm ground. Apart from tugs, the only actual example that comes to mind is an illustration showing a string of barges being towed by a horse walking on a sunken path up the middle of the Backs at Cambridge[2].

Tracking from a tow path on the river bank is more usual. If the tow is taken from right forward, a partly sideways pull is exerted on the barge and the source of power, tending to bring the one into the river bank and the other into the water. Leave the latter to find his own salvation, as we have to consider the boat. If available, a rudder or a sweep would stop the barge grounding, but would need a man aboard to operate it when he might be better employed on the tow-rope instead of adding to its load. If the attachment of the tow is moved aft, the sideways force gets less until it starts to pull in the other direction. If unchecked this causes the barge to ram the far bank or re-immerse the horse. When the rope is set to act through the point about which the boat's resistance to motion also acts, she will run in a straight line (Fig 104). This point is for all practical purposes, the Centre of Lateral Resistance (CLR), providing that the barge has not already yawed a long way off course.

If the hull is relatively long, as most inland waterway craft are, the force needed to move her forwards will be far less than that needed to traverse her sideways or rotate her on to a new course. Such a hull is said to have good directional stability and will tend to go the way she points. With this quality, a point of attachment that develops a slight movement towards the tow path is preferred, as actual impact is deadened by the cushion of water the barge builds up between herself and the bank, to which she is running parallel. Lengthening the tow also reduces sideways pull, but may be impractical round bends.

As the point of attachment is on the vessel's centreline, it has to be high enough for the rope to clear the cargo and gear on board, and even high up on a mast if there are bushes and boats to be passed along the water's edge. In the less elaborate turf boat (Fig 86) and withy boat (Fig 105) the towing attachment is on the gunwale as the centreline is obscured when loaded. In boats like these, the tow can be from either end, as it is often impossible to turn the boat end-for-end in a narrow canal, rhine or drainage ditch. It is desirable that the CLR should stay in the same place whether empty or loaded. This means the ends should have the same character, avoiding, for example, a lot of

TRACKING- THE POINT OF ATTACHMENT OF THE TOW-ROPE

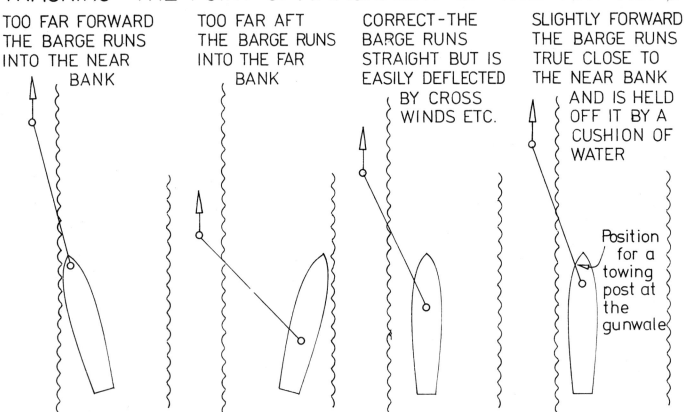

TOO FAR FORWARD THE BARGE RUNS INTO THE NEAR BANK

TOO FAR AFT THE BARGE RUNS INTO THE FAR BANK

CORRECT - THE BARGE RUNS STRAIGHT BUT IS EASILY DEFLECTED BY CROSS WINDS ETC.

SLIGHTLY FORWARD THE BARGE RUNS TRUE CLOSE TO THE NEAR BANK AND IS HELD OFF IT BY A CUSHION OF WATER

Position for a towing post at the gunwale

THE LENGTH OF THE TOW-ROPE MAY BE USED AS AN ADJUSTMENT AND THE POINT OF ATTACHMENT TAKEN OFF CENTRE (AT THE GUNWALE FOR EXAMPLE) ON THE SAME LINE OF PULL

Fig 104: Tracking – the point of attachment of the tow rope.

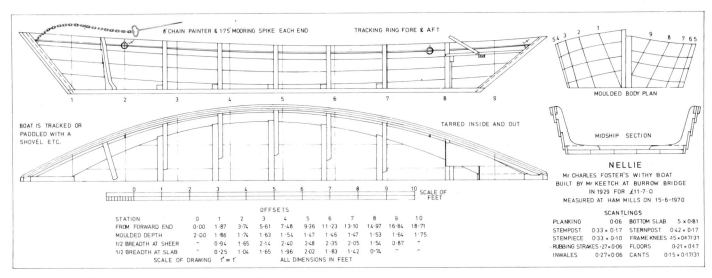

Fig 105: *Nellie*, Mr Charles Foster's withy boat – lines.

Opposite
Fig 106: Some barge rudders.

SOME BARGE RUDDERS
showing how their immersed areas compare with those of their hulls

Not to the same scale

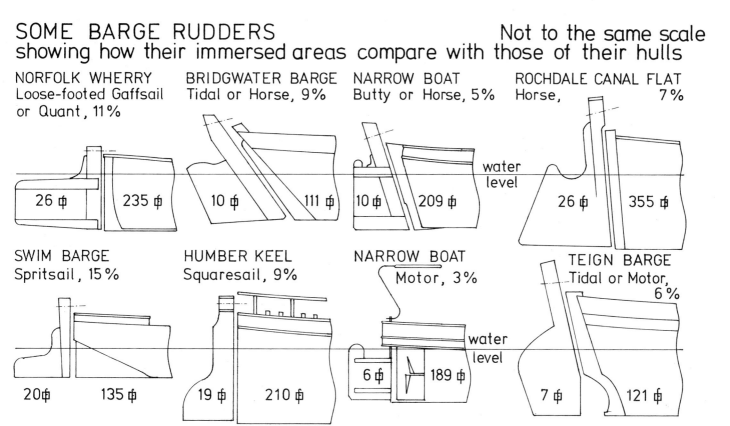

NORFOLK WHERRY
Loose-footed Gaffsail
or Quant, 11%

26 ⌀   235 ⌀

BRIDGWATER BARGE
Tidal or Horse, 9%

10 ⌀   111 ⌀

NARROW BOAT
Butty or Horse, 5%

10 ⌀   209 ⌀

ROCHDALE CANAL FLAT
Horse,   7%

26 ⌀   355 ⌀

water level

SWIM BARGE
Spritsail, 15%

20 ⌀   135 ⌀

HUMBER KEEL
Squaresail, 9%

19 ⌀   210 ⌀

NARROW BOAT
Motor, 3%

6 ⌀   189 ⌀

TEIGN BARGE
Tidal or Motor,
6%

7 ⌀   121 ⌀

water level

flare one end with wall sides at the other. In the past artists have included tracked barges in their landscapes, and some of these are to be described later.

In very narrow or busy waterways the tow-rope alone is not enough for safe steering, especially where there are locks and oncoming barges to be passed. Here a rudder is essential. As speeds and drafts are low, it has to be large; the percentage of the immersed lateral area of the rudder to that of the hull lies between 5 and $8\frac{1}{2}$%, with 7 as a fair working figure. Most rudders are quadrilateral, wider than deep and unbalanced, being pivoted along their forward edge (Fig 106).

Sooner or later a tracked barge will run out of tow path, either because of a tributary, a difficult landowner or because the waterway has widened into a lake, estuary or marsh. She must then have some way to propel herself. The most adaptable single item in a working boat is a stout pole, preferably with a hook or cross-piece at one end. Apart from grabbing and fending off, this can be a temporary mooring post, a spar to extend the peak or clew of a sail, a ridge-pole for a tilt or a depth gauge to find out if there is enough water to float, yet not too much for the barge to be poled along.

A pole can be used to punt or quant. In the first case the user stands still, facing forward with his feet apart. He then lowers one end of the pole, normally on the port side, down to the bottom, rather astern of where his hands are grasping the pole, at a height where a pull can be exerted. This forces the foot of the pole aft and the boat forward, so he takes up the slack, hand over hand to the top of the pole, which is then recovered for the next cycle. The punted boat has to have an ample working platform and bearings aft, so that a man's weight does not spoil the trim. Punting is suitable for fast or long trips in light boats having square sterns, but not for long hauls in heavy vessels, which are better quanted (Fig 107).

To quant the bargee starts at the bows, and, after finding bottom with his pole, sets his shoulder against the other end and walks steadily aft. On reaching the stern he recovers the pole and takes it forward again. To do this, the barge must have a clear walk as straight as possible for as much of her length as possible. She also needs to be large and heavy enough to keep her trim as the bargee moves fore and aft, and to keep going between each thrust. Both punt poles and quants are prone to sticking in the bed of the waterway, and various methods are used to get over it, such as having forks or cleats at the foot and handles or buttons at the top. In both these methods the boatman has a chance of seeing where he is going, and as the pole can be used to alter course, there is no need of a rudder.

When it gets too deep for poling, it is still possible to keep boats moving if the pole is used, still standing, as a paddle. Row-punting like this occurs in both Fleet trows and turf boats and is a more effective form of propulsion than reason alone suggests, though well short of properly-formed paddles, sweeps and oars.

Hardly any traditional boats used paddles, and those that did only in a limited way. In the Teifi coracles the paddle could either be operated with one arm over the side to impart a feathering action to the blade or two handed

PROPULSION BY POLING
PUNTING

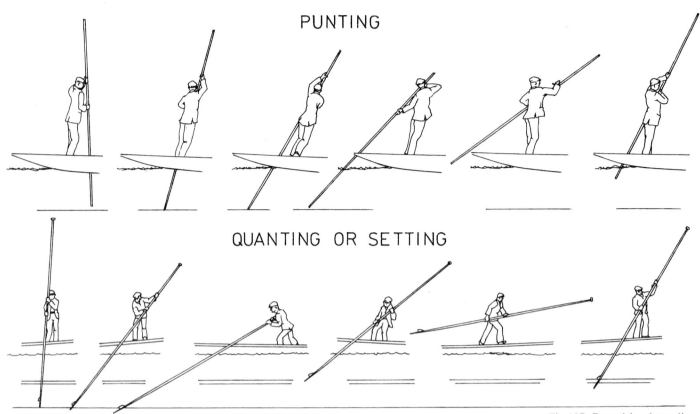

QUANTING OR SETTING

Fig 107: Propulsion by poling.

THE GEOMETRY OF AN OARSMAN

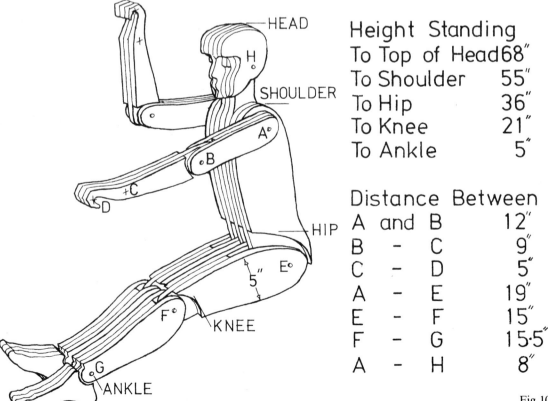

Height Standing
To Top of Head 68"
To Shoulder   55"
To Hip   36"
To Knee   21"
To Ankle   5"

Distance Between
A and B   12"
B - C   9"
C - D   5"
A - E   19"
E - F   15"
F - G   15·5"
A - H   8"

Fig 108: Geometry of an oarsman.

over the bow as a normal paddle[3]. The Severn punt is equipped with paddles, which, though nowadays used like pivoted oars, were previously used as paddles (p 29). The old shape has been kept, so that the paddles can still be used for bailing.

Sculling over the stern is a frequent form of propulsion for boats fitted with transoms or square sterns. The action is a little harder to master than rowing, but better for short trips and when there are obstacles that restrict the use of rowed oars. The action of the blade of a sculled oar is like the blade of an oscillating propeller, changing its handing every stroke. Given bearings aft any boat can be sculled, though heavy ones zig-zag less, so go better.

Propulsion by oars and sweeps, standing and sitting, facing forward and aft, with varying numbers of hands on each oar or men in the boat, needs a book to itself to describe adequately. Oars are as practical today as they were thousands of years ago. In spite of rowing being an easy manoeuvre, the mechanics of it are not self-evident, nor has the geometry been recorded systematically in the past. Even the terms are confusing, as they differ in salt and fresh water. In salt water a man is said to be rowing when he is working a pair of oars, one in each hand, but pulling if he is working with both hands on one oar. A thwart is single-banked if there is only one man on it pulling, but as rowers can only be single-banked, they do not get this designation. (A double-banked thwart is one with two men, both pulling separate oars.) In fresh water, the waterman rows with one oar and sculls with a pair of sculls, only state barges being double-banked. This may be why scholars, who are more likely to be wet-bobs than salts, persist in writing about 'rowing' in sea-going oared vessels, one thing that could not have been done.

Oar length, blade shape, types of pivot and rowing styles are varied to suit the boat, the waters and the work being done. One factor is nearer to being constant than any other and that is the man that does the work. Dr McGrail has recently proposed a classification for the mechanics of rowing[4], but omits the hydrodynamic, bio-mechanic and physiological aspects, which have also to be considered, as indeed they have been at a symposium some years ago[5].

Though men vary in height and build, it has been remarked already how often, even today, men using oars regularly are larger than average in every way. Shaking hands with one of them is like being given the end of an oar to grasp. An $\frac{1}{8}$th scale model was made for this study, 5ft 8in being taken as the average height of an oarsman, with the other limbs in proportion (Fig 108). When the rowing geometry looked cramped or roomy for this model, further checks were made for men 6in taller and shorter than average.

Excluding racing shells, almost any part of which can be made to fit the oarsman, we are concerned with boats with only the stretcher for the feet adjustable. Properly designed for the job and surroundings, this is all that is needed to accommodate most shapes and sizes of man without harming performance, which in most cases is not of the highest order. Oars in a working boat can be anything from the primary source of movement to the last resort. In the first instance, there is a need for sustained power, as, for example, in gigs, galleys and watermen's boats, and every care seems to have been given to obtaining the most effective installation of man and oar to achieve this. In the middle situation, which was that of most sailing beach boats, great power and reliability was essential to get clear of broken water. In the last case, the boatman might have to put up with discomfort, say when using a sweep in a partly decked boat, just to keep moving

Fig 109: Oar lengths in open boats.

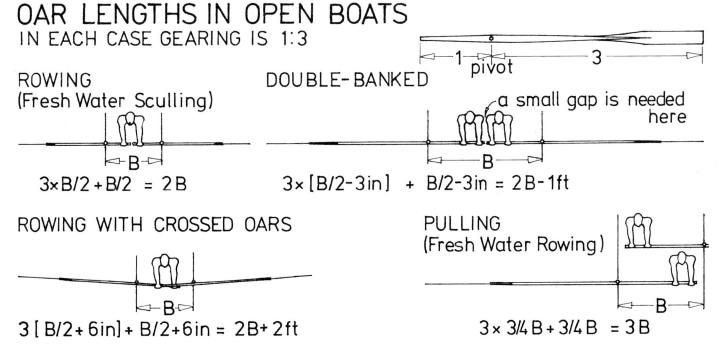

OAR LENGTHS IN OPEN BOATS
IN EACH CASE GEARING IS 1:3

ROWING
(Fresh Water Sculling)

3 × B/2 + B/2 = 2B

DOUBLE-BANKED

a small gap is needed here

3 × [B/2 − 3in] + B/2 − 3in = 2B − 1ft

ROWING WITH CROSSED OARS

3 [B/2 + 6in] + B/2 + 6in = 2B + 2ft

PULLING
(Fresh Water Rowing)

3 × 3/4 B + 3/4 B = 3B

until a breeze came up or the tide turned. A comparison of the boat's rowing and oarsman's geometries will almost always show which of these courses had been chosen.

The rowing arrangements of a number of British working boats, when studied, also suggest the limits of what is or is not workable. The length of the oar is limited inboard by the boat's beam and outboard by what is manageable. The ratio between the length inboard of the pivot and that outboard of it is known as the gearing. Most rowers can manage a gearing of 1:3, but tire more quickly if this is exceeded, even when the oar is counter-balanced inboard. This is thought to be due to the effort wasted in preventing the oar working inboard. If the oar has a device to absorb this force, like being pivoted on a single thole pin, gearings as high as 1:4 can be used for a period. Therefore if the best use is to be made of the space available inboard

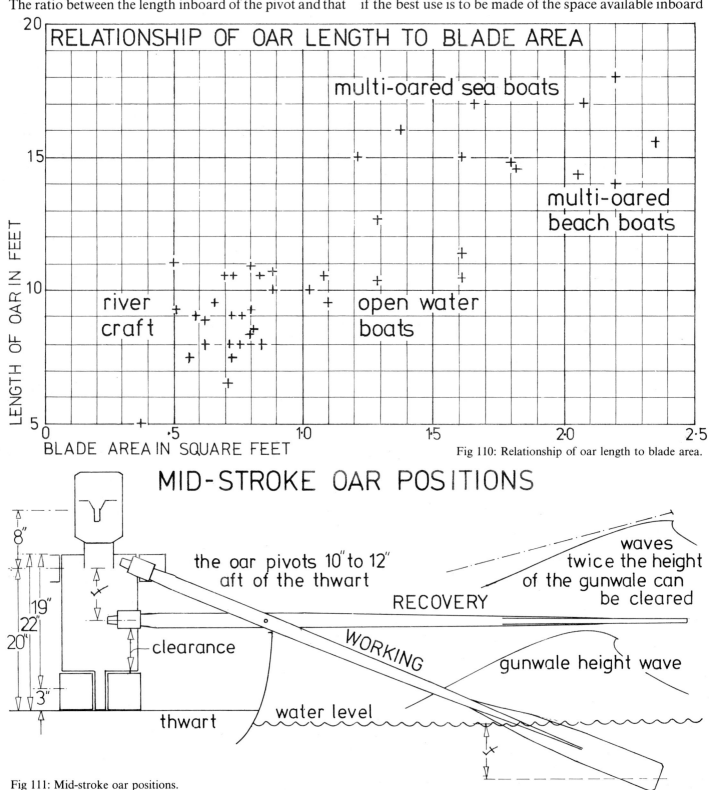

Fig 110: Relationship of oar length to blade area.

Fig 111: Mid-stroke oar positions.

to swing the loom of an oar, certain rules governing its overall length are better followed: twice the beam if rowed, rather less if double-banked and three times when pulled (Fig 109). In practice it is now found that oars are usually to the nearest foot or half foot below the calculated fractional amount. Though these rules compare well for the last hundred years, this may not always have been so. The tables given in the oar making section of an early nineteenth century manual of sparmaking recommend multipliers of $2\frac{1}{2}$ and $3\frac{1}{2}$ the beam respectively, which would give oars a modern boatman might find hard to control for long[6]. Most oars found in boats vary between 7ft and 17ft overall, and require an extra 2–3lbs at their inner end to balance them in their pivots. It is the lack of this balancing weight that gives an oar its necessary 'feel', without which the oar blade would have to be forced to submerge at the start of the working stroke.

An oar blade is like the top of a piston, in so far as the combination of its area, applied force, length of stroke and rate of striking gives the power developed. If the blade areas of an assortment of oars are plotted against their lengths, it is found that the points tend to have a close relationship (Fig 110). It has not been possible to find enough data on rate of striking and numbers of men employed to discover if there are regular relationships here also. However after discussions with boatmen, it seems that above about 15ft in length of oar the striking rate decreases, but the number of men increases. Below this length, there is considerable diversity in whether an oar is rowed or pulled in rough or calm water and as to the size of the blade. In the lower zone oar blades in working boats are about 1sq ft in area, while non-competitive ones are $\frac{3}{4}$sq ft, with a generous margin for personal preference in each.

The ideal shape of blade varies from calm to rough water. In the former a short wide spoon blade will ensure that the same amount of water is taken every stroke and the paths of both the working and recovery strokes are kept as flat as possible. When this happens, the oarsman can concentrate on improving his style so as to get optimum performance. In rough water the immersed area of the blade must be variable, and a long narrow blade without the complication of a back and a front is better for this. More or less power can be generated at will without breaking stroke. Freshwater blades work out to be one fifth the total length of the oar, saltwater ones a quarter down to a third where conditions are unusually rough. Spoon blades are seen in working boats used for ferrying and hovelling and also jobs where extra power is needed, such as seining and dredging, but only as far as their fragility is acceptable.

When a sea oar is at the middle of a working stroke, the hand is the same height above the pivot as the tip of the blade is below the surface (Fig 111). At this point the hands should be an inch or two lower than the shoulders. When the hand is pressed down until the oar is horizontal, the feathered blade just clears the top of a wave high enough to slop over the side. In weather of this roughness, the oarsman must keep his blade clear of the sea during the recovery, so he can start another stroke. When the boat rolls, the hand must be lowered further until the man's own thighs get in the way. Making the height between the pivot and the thwart 10in to 12in, which is twice that of the thigh, or having the oarsman in an almost upright stance with his feet on about the same station as the pivot, will avoid this species of crab being caught. The pivot is put 10in to 12in abaft the thwart's after edge, so that the oar is square to the side at mid-stroke.

If an oarsman is to spend much time at work he must have most of his weight on the thwart and use his powerful leg muscles to increase his pull. If his heels are more than 24in lower than the thwart, not only will he be almost standing up, but unable to exert a worthwhile horizontal push with his legs. As the height between the thwart edge and the heels is reduced the horizontal distance between them must be increased to keep the legs nearly straight. Pairs of these figures for our man are:

Vertically, thwart to heel – 20in 16in 12in or less
Horizontally, thwart to heel – 28in 32in 36in

In the last column the legs are fully extended. Up to and including this point, one notes that the sum of the two figures is 48in, an amount that increases to 52in for a man 6in taller, but decreases to 44in for one 6in shorter than our average. To allow for this variation, stretchers for heels and footspars for insteps are made adjustable to 3in or 4in either side of the average height suited to the size of the boat and her service. More upright arrangements are found where the going is rough. As an added safeguard the bottom boards are fitted lower again when size permits, so that the oarsman can stand down on them to clear his oar (Fig 112). With the same sea running, the hand has to be raised by an amount equal to a third of the freeboard if the blade is to be kept fully immersed in the trough between two waves. If this brings the hand above eye level when seated not much pull can be exerted, and the oarsman may again have to stand to get in a good stroke. He cannot do this quickly enough if his legs are stretched out almost horizontally in front of him, like those of a regatta man.

There is a difference between the styles of rowing adopted in calm and rough water, even in the one boat, let alone boats specially intended for one or other of these conditions. A long stroke with an unhurried recovery makes the best use of the oarsman's energy, reducing the amount the oar is raised and lowered and increasing muscular recuperation. The short deep stroke with a snap recovery, though mechanically less efficient, is effective when the more stylish stroke would risk a series of crabs. As an approximate guide the following gives the distance through which the hands move for various stroke types:

Type of Stroke	Long	Medium Long	Medium	Short
Fore and Aft	26in	24in	22in	20in
Up and down	4in	6in	8in	10in

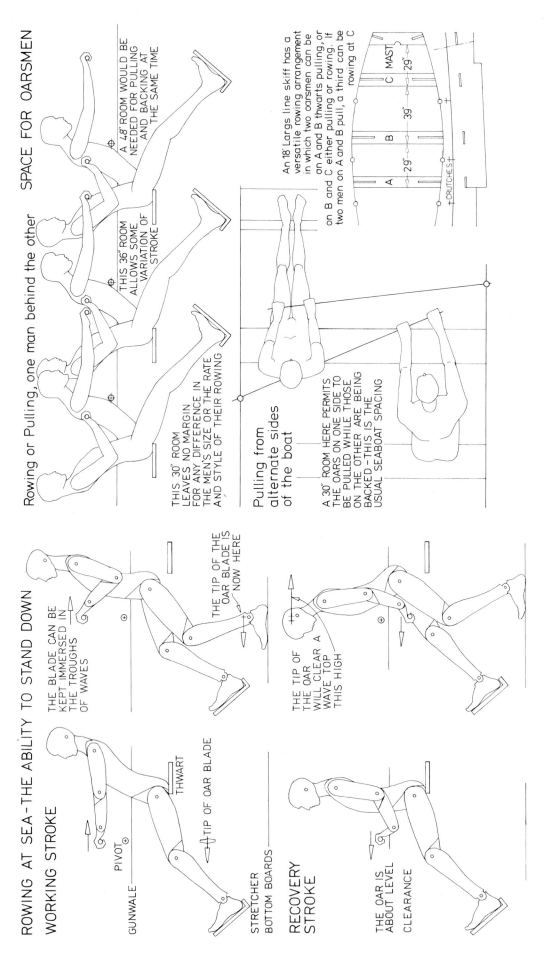

SPACE FOR OARSMEN

Rowing or Pulling, one man behind the other

A 48' ROOM WOULD BE NEEDED FOR PULLING AND BACKING AT THE SAME TIME

THIS 36" ROOM ALLOWS SOME VARIATION OF STROKE

THIS 30" ROOM LEAVES NO MARGIN FOR ANY DIFFERENCE IN THE MEN'S SIZE OR THE RATE AND STYLE OF THEIR ROWING

Pulling from alternate sides of the boat

A 30" ROOM HERE PERMITS THE OARS ON ONE SIDE TO BE PULLED WHILE THOSE ON THE OTHER ARE BEING BACKED – THIS IS THE USUAL SEABOAT SPACING

An 18' Largs line skiff has a versatile rowing arrangement in which two oarsmen can be on A and C either pulling or rowing, or on B and B thwarts pulling, or on A and B pull, a third can be rowing at C

C MAST

29"

39"

29"

CRUTCHES

Fig 113: Space for oarsmen.

ROWING AT SEA – THE ABILITY TO STAND DOWN

WORKING STROKE

THE BLADE CAN BE KEPT IMMERSED IN THE TROUGHS OF WAVES

THE TIP OF THE OAR BLADE IS NOW HERE

GUNWALE

PIVOT

THWART

TIP OF OAR BLADE

STRETCHER

BOTTOM BOARDS

RECOVERY STROKE

THE TIP OF THE OAR WILL CLEAR A WAVE TOP THIS HIGH

THE OAR IS ABOUT LEVEL

CLEARANCE

Fig 112: Rowing at sea – the ability to stand down.

The amount the blade tip will move at the same time can be worked out by applying the gearing ratio to these figures.

The next consideration is how close the thwarts may be spaced if several rowing or pulling stations are wanted. This decides how many oarsmen can be fitted into a boat or how much space is left over for other gear or cargo. In rowing boats and those pulling boats that are so narrow that the men have to sit in a direct line behind one another, a spacing of 36in is needed if a long stroke is contemplated, but correspondingly less for the shorter ones. This distance has to be increased if the wave pattern is likely to interfere with a synchronised stroke. In single-banked pulling boats wide enough for the oarsmen to be disposed on alternate sides, the thwarts can be pitched 30in apart with no risk of interference, even when the men on one side are backing water while those on the other are giving way. When the thwarts are spaced even closer than this, it is generally with the intention of providing a choice of oar stations. The boatmen can use them to trim his boat to suit different working lay-outs (Fig 113). Very much wider spacings are also found: up to 4ft in curraghs, and this and over in the cobles of the north-east coast of England.

The figures given above are not invariably followed. Where boats are seen to ignore them, a careful examination of her other features will often show why a different spacing from normal has been used. This may be for extra transverse stiffening, space to step a mast or stowage space for creels or nets. In the past oar arrangements have had far less attention than sailing rigs, the length and number of oars being omitted though every detail of rig was recorded.

A sweep is a large oar pulled or pushed by one or more men working on either or both sides of it. More often than not this is done standing up. Before fuel powered engines, sweeps provided an auxiliary means of propulsion when the wind failed. In ships these might be up to 52ft long. As has been said earlier, in barges and lighters sweeps were often the only means of making any progress or changing direction in deep water. Barges' sweeps were from 16ft to 28ft long, the two carried in the Bridgwater barge being 25ft. Various styles of working the sweep were used, but in general a few steps were taken, back and forth, in the course of each stroke. Above 24ft or so, sweeps have lower gearings than oars: between 1.25 and 1.50, that of the Bridgwater barge being 1.4. As sweeps shorten the gearing increases, until at about 16ft they are the same as that of an oar. In addition to this difference in geometry, a sweep required more clear working space inboard.

Oars can turn a boat more quickly than any rudder. Indeed there would be little need for rudders if only British oarsmen faced the way they were going. In most working boats however they fact aft; and though this does not reduce the ability to use the oars directionally, it is harder to know when and by how much. A lone rower can see enough to keep out of trouble, by turning his head now and again and taking back bearings. The lack of positive direction grows with the number of oars and men. This can be overcome in two ways, both putting an extra man onboard, sitting aft where he can see all the crew and ahead. This man, the cox'n, can either regulate the output of the oars on either side, by which means he can start, stop or turn the boat, or he can use a rudder, which though better at holding a course is less effective for manoeuvring. Some working boats, like lerrets, relied entirely on oars for steering, while gigs and galleys normally shipped rudders. Many types of boats had an oar station, from which the cox'n could push an oar, as much for warmth as progress, while he was steering with a rudder.

List is deplored in a boat under oars, primarily because few boats run straight when heeled, but also because rowing is tiring when the geometry is different either side. Output on both sides becomes less than ideal and by differing amounts. Correcting this imbalance of direction and power, either by reducing the output of the stronger side or a permanent rudder angle, slows the boat down even more. A professional waterman will be seen to correct heel carefully before starting to row, moving his own weight to one side or asking his passengers to do so.

Oars are a most versatile form of propulsion and they can be adapted to almost any boat, if a suitable oar and geometry is chosen. Outside recreation, oars are not often the prime mover any longer, but continue to be the cheapest and surest stand-by.

WIND

Much of the work round a boat, like loading cargo, launching up and down and hauling fishing gear, is tiring, so more muscular effort like tracking, poling and rowing for any time is undesirable. When the tide does not help, the wind can. Observation of boat types undergoing development shows that a new task or condition affects the method of propulsion before the shape of the hull, which has to wait until a new boat is built. This is also true of sailing boats, whose rig and shape should be matched.

Where the addition of a sail is no more than an improvisation to take advantage of a following wind, there is no change other than in the form of steering. Many small barges on minor rivers did this, especially where the prevailing wind was upstream against the flow. Three types of sail were used, lug on the Stour, sprit on the Arun and the Fens and square on the Teign and the Tyne (Fig 114). The sprit was also popular on small oared crossing ferries, as this is the easiest and quickest rig to set and drop. All these sails draw if trimmed to the wind on the quarter to round river bends. There is no sign that any attempt was made to get any of these craft to point much better, as a short spell of exertion would put them in the next favourable reach.

On the wider rivers and inland waterways, this was not enough and improved forms of the same three rigs gave more power and windward performance. To benefit from a sail improvement the hull must be modified too, preferably without loss of ability to carry loads in shallow water and under bridges.

EFFECT OF WIND ACROSS THE BEAM AND A FEW REMEDIES

INCREASE the resistance to sideways movement by adding to or deepening the lateral area.
DECREASE the resistance to forward movement by hull shape & less top hamper ADOPT a more efficient sail and rig.

LEEWAY

DRIFT
COURSE STEERED
COURSE MADE GOOD
DRIFT
WIND

IMBALANCE

ARDENCY
The boat still bears up with full weather helm

LEEWARDNESS
The boat still falls off with full lee helm

REDUCE distance between the centres of exposed and immersed areas by setting or taking in sail, altering trim and making use of centre or leeboards. Heel also generates a yawing arm that acts to windward [see diagram below]

WIND PRESSURE

RESISTANCE TO LEEWAY

TENDERNESS
THE LACK OF POWER TO CARRY SAIL

THE DESIGNER CAN INCREASE the Righting Moment by adding to the area of the water plane [the beam of it especially], the buoyancy of the topsides, lowering the CG REDUCE the Heeling Moment - adopting less sail area and a lower rig.

THE CREW CAN INCREASE the Righting Moment by moving the cargo, ballast or men to windward.
REDUCE the Heeling Moment by setting less sail lower down.

WIND
CE
EFFECT
YAWING ARM

CENTRES OF
EFFORT
GRAVITY
LATERAL RESISTANCE
BUOYANCY
UPTHRUST
RIGHTING ARM
HEELING ARM [height above CLR]
CG [CH+CB above CLR]
TOTAL WEIGHT

THE BOAT WILL HEEL OVER UNTIL THE RIGHTING AND HEELING MOMENTS ARE THE SAME OR SHE SWAMPS OR CAPSIZES

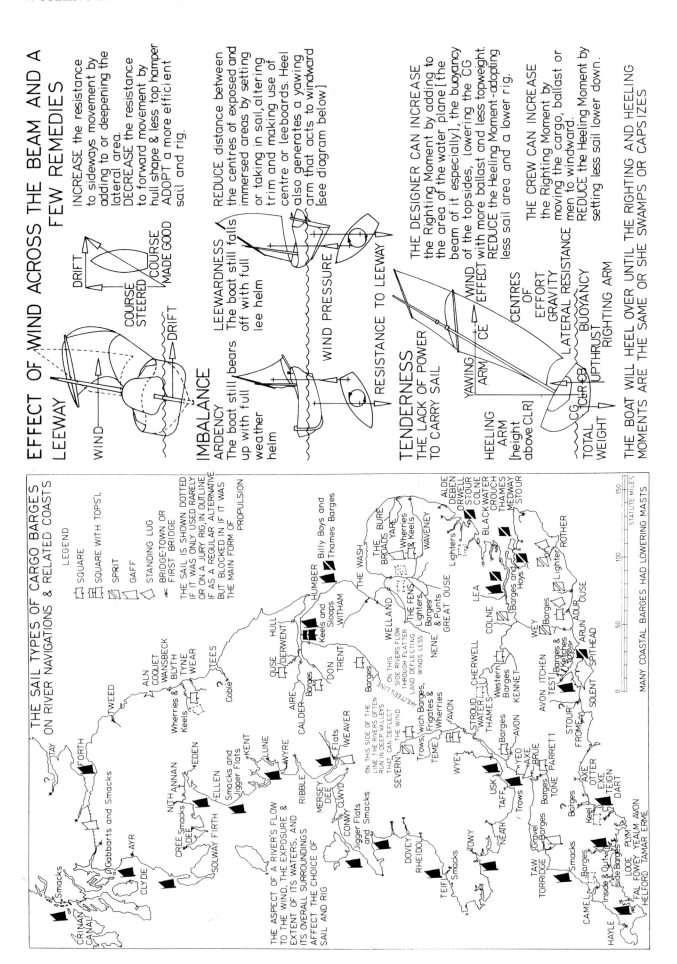

Fig 115: Effect of wind across beam and a few remedies.

THE SAIL TYPES OF CARGO BARGES ON RIVER NAVIGATIONS & RELATED COASTS

LEGEND

- SQUARE
- SQUARE WITH TOPS'L
- SPRIT
- GAFF
- STANDING LUG
- BRIDGE-TOWN OR FIRST BRIDGE

THE SAIL IS SHOWN DOTTED IF IT WAS ONLY USED RARELY OR ON A JURY RIG, IN OUTLINE IF AS A REGULAR ALTERNATIVE BUT BLOCKED IN IF IT WAS THE MAIN FORM OF PROPULSION

THE ASPECT OF A RIVER'S FLOW TO THE WIND, THE EXPOSURE & EXTENT OF ITS WATERS, AND ITS OVERALL SURROUNDINGS AFFECT THE CHOICE OF SAIL AND RIG

ON THIS SIDE OF THE LINE THE RIVERS OFTEN RUN IN DEEP VALLEYS THAT CAN DEFLECT THE WIND

ON THIS SIDE RIVERS FLOW THROUGH FLATTER LAND DEFLECTING WINDS LESS

W.E./TEES LINE

MANY COASTAL BARGES HAD LOWERING MASTS

STATUTE MILES
0   50   100   150

Fig 114: The sail types of cargo barges.

Within the limitations of the cloth used, any shape of sail can be made to point higher by taking the tack forward of the clew, tightening the luff and then finding what clew position will make the sail draw best. Too far off and the sail will not pull, not far enough and it flaps. The luffs of square, lug and staysails are tightened by hoisting or pulling down the tack to stop this edge of the sail wrinkling or sagging down wind as much as possible. It is the mast that holds this edge of gaff, sprit and jib-headed sails up to its work, but interferes with the flow of air over the sail.

The relative position between the sail as a whole and the points of attachment of the tack tye and sheet to the hull is the sheeting base. The way these two ropes and two points are adjusted sets and trims the sail for different directions and strength of wind. If the sheeting point is too far aft the leech of the sail will start to shake before the foot, but if too far forward it will be the foot that shakes first. In light winds it pays to move the sheeting point outboard, but inboard in a blow. Not many working boats could trim their sails with this precision. Instead the hull or its outriggers gave a sheeting base that was a working compromise. The addition of yards under square and booms under fore-and-aft sails transferred the sheeting base from the hull to these spars, which then required the same care in the choice of length and adjustment.

Poor sheeting on any point of sailing makes less than full use of the whole sail area, but does nothing to reduce the windage of the topsides, rigging and spars, all of which are doing their utmost to upset the boat and make her drift down wind. As a result, not only does a badly drawing sail pull less, but the course made good will be further off the wind. Weatherliness is not such a concern for sailing ships on a trade wind route as it is for boats inshore and barges in confined waters, where safety and success frequently rest on doubling headlands and in making as few changes of tack as possible.

There is hardly any problem with a down wind sail. It is pulling in the same direction as the boat wants to go, only slightly off centre if it is other than square and with no risk of it pitchpoling the boat end over end. This carefree situation ends once the sail is made to point across the wind. The boat drifts down wind of the set course, bears up into the wind or runs off out of it and heels over (Fig 115). In every way it shows that the hull does not match the new rig. She is making leeway, is out of balance and does not have the power to carry sail into the wind. These faults can be corrected by modifying the rig or the hull or both.

Boats are longer than broad, so easier to move forward than sideways. Any change in hull shape that improves this quality reduces sideways motion or leeway, and the obvious way is to increase length and reduce beam without altering size. This solution was chosen by gigs, galleys and Norfolk beach yawls, all of which also wanted plenty of oarsmen. This is most effective if the hull is already achieving its maximum speed for wavemaking, but is only practical in competitive working boats where speed matters most. It might seem increased draft on its own would not

make much difference, as this dimension is common to both lateral and transverse areas. In practice it is found that boats drift sideways more readily light than loaded, due to deep shapes offering relatively more resistance to leeway than shallow ones.

Even more effective are better formed entries and runs and reduced midship sections as these lower the resistance to forward motion and may slightly raise it to leeward. This better shape is not necessarily a matter of sharper level lines, but rather the achievement of a smooth flow of water past the hull. Increase of lateral area alone, especially if there is a sharp corner like a chine or a narrow width like a fin keel, gripe, skeg, rudder or bilge keel, reduces leeway. In shallow water a boat's retractable areas like centre, dagger and lee boards does the same thing. When the sailing designs are discussed later, it will be seen which of these features have been adopted. Though invented here boards in cases have not proved as popular in this country as they were in North America[7] because they were prone to jam up with stones or leak in boats which have to take the ground regularly. Leeboards were common on the east coast where they were fitted to the Humber sloops and keels and to the Thames sailing barges, but not on the west coast estuary barges, nor on the Clyde, Mersey or Severn. Some smaller working boats had retractable boards – service boats, Cowes skiffs, Cadgwith and Penberth crabbers and the Somerset flatners – but even if all of these were taken together these are only a small fraction of the whole. The Norfolk wherry probably had the most elegant hull form of any working barge, her lines letting the water pass under rather than round her and her deck arrangement having long straight walkaways for quanting (Fig 116). The wherry could also ship a false keel. Deep rudders on raked sterns were used on the English cobles and the Parrett flatners to combat leeway, but in combination with a deep stem in the coble and a leeboard or a daggerboard in the flatner. In both cases the boats had a bad reputation of broaching when running fast downwind.

The forces exerted by a set of sails on a vessel behave as if their total acted through a single point known as the centre of effort (CE). In much the same way, the forces resisting leeway are said to act through the centre of lateral resistance, the same CLR that affected tracking. If CE and CLR are above one another, the sails do not turn the vessel off course into or out of the wind, and such a boat is said to be balanced. If not, the rudder has to be used to oppose any bias towards luffing or bearing away. The proper task of the rudder is to hold or alter course, and using it to correct a permanent imbalance slows down the vessel. A well balanced boat can be sailed to windward with the rudder unshipped or the tiller lashed, just by moving around.

In fact slight weather helm or tendency to luff up is desirable on the wind. This gives some feel to the tiller, so, when let go, the boat will bring herself up into the wind, taking the pressure out of the sail and stopping – a useful

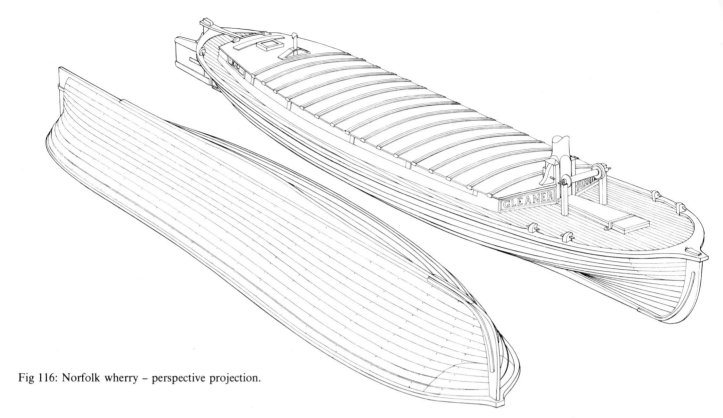

Fig 116: Norfolk wherry – perspective projection.

virtue in a working boat. Boats like this turn through the eye of the wind on to the other tack more surely. Lee helm is disliked, as if the tiller is left unattended, the boat starts to run off down wind, pressing herself harder, picking up speed and giving away weather gauge.

The exact positions of CE and CLR cannot be worked out, as they are constantly on the move as the waves pass, the sails are adjusted and the strength and direction of the wind varies. As a working convention, they are taken as being located at the centres of the areas of the sail plan and the immersed lateral plane. To take account of the assumptions involved, designers set the two apart by amounts their experience has shown will give slight weather helm. If it is found lee or weather helm is excessive, weights have to be moved forward or aft or the rig altered to regain balance. Care was taken to get this right in wooden sailing warships and their success is seen in the small size of their rudders. By way of contrast, the rudder of an eighteenth century frigate was 2% of her lateral area, a Brixham trawler 3¾%, a Thames spritsail barge 3½%, a Yarmouth yawl 5% and a Norfolk wherry 10%.

The position of CE can be adjusted by moving the mast. This was rarely practical in decked boats with standing rigging, but was done in open boats. The Northumbrian cobles could vary the rake their masts, but this was done to suit the point of sailing[8]. It was more usual however, to alter the shape and number of sails set.

Starting with just one sail set, it was necessary to retain balance in all wind states, from a gentle breeze to a fresh gale, by which time all the boats in this book should have taken shelter. With most hulls the CLR moves forward as the heel increases, and though boats ought not to be sailed with great angles of heel, a larger angle is usually accepted as the wind speed rises. That is due to postponing sail

shortening so as to keep the power, especially to windward, needed to get through the waves and not be stopped by them. To preserve balance in a single sail rig the CE should move forward when reefed.

With square sails the theoretical position of CE stays on the same station however much it is reefed. In fore-and-aft sails the position changes when reefing. The different types of sail behave differently in this respect, as follows:

CE Movement Forward on Reefing		CE Movement Aft on Reefing	
Gaff, long boom	5%	Gaff, short foot	22%
Standing Lug	7%	Dipping lug	6%
Jib-headed main	19%		

The amounts are the total movement expressed as a percentage of the foot of the sail – from full sail to reefed right down. The mast is upright in all cases.

These figures need amplification, as though some forward movement may help a great deal it may cause lee helm. The length of foot relative to total area must also be considered. In the case of the modern Bermudian rig the foot of the jib-headed main is much shorter than those of the working headsails, and this main is hardly ever set without headsails. The large movement aft with the short-footed gaff sail is countered to some extent in the Norfolk wherry by a high peak, but would be unmanageable in a cat. The gaff cat rig was not otherwise used in Britain, though the short-footed gaff was popular in working boats with more than one sail. This was due to the nearly vertical leach and loose foot being kinder to those on deck than a sloping leach or a boom. This sail was set on a standing gaff in hoys and bawleys, which could shorten sail by brailing as well as reefing. When fitted with brails, this sail, which is similar in shape to the spritsail of a Thames barge, reduces from aft to forward, easing sail pressure during a squall by destroying its efficiency, while the other sails keep pulling.

In its smaller sizes the spritsail was a common single sail for a small open boat, and is still occasionally seen. Its main worth is its simplicity, but its main drawback is the difficulty of arranging more than one reef without complexity. Nor was there a need for a second reef in a sail, whose area could be halved by unshipping the sprit and tying the peak down to the foot of the mast. Though clumsy, this was enough to get a boat home in a squall from a safe sector (Fig 117).

The dipping lug was also used on its own in working boats. This was provided with many rows of reef point, more so than other types, as, unlike the standing lug, it could be reefed right up to its yard. The masts of luggers were often raked to counteract the movement aft of the CE. The sail drew well and worked well to windward, but required a strong skilful crew when changing tacks. For this reason the sail is not found on other than open coastlines. This shortcoming could be partly overcome by bring the tack of the sail to the mast, thereby converting it into a standing lug, which then had to be sheeted much further aft. The standing lug was set on its own in skiffs on the west coast of Scotland and some cobles, but only those that were too small to want any headsail.

Working the principal sail in conjunction with a second one either before the same mast or set on a second one gives control over the position of CE, and the feel of the tiller will tell which to reduce first. In a sloop with one headsail this would mean reefing the mainsail first to lighten a heavy tiller or setting a smaller headsail if the boat was trying to run off. In the latter case, the double headsail (now called cutter) rig is only a matter of dropping the outer sail, and, if fitted, running in the bowsprit to get snug for a blow. Sail reduction without having to heave to is one of the main advantages of multi-sail rigs, and an essential one when clawing off a lee shore or hurrying home threatened by deteriorating weather.

Multi-sail rigs on several masts are even more adaptable than on a single mast. In this country boats as small as 14ft frequently had two masts for the versatility this brought. With a wardrobe of four sails made up of three sizes of lug and a jib, it was possible to have eight sail arrangements to chose from when setting out, without having to tie a single reef point. If, however, the weather looked as if it might be moderate later, larger reefed sails would be set with a view to shaking them out in due course. If stronger winds were predicted the boatman had a choice between reefing and

Fig 117: Reduction of spritsail area.

REDUCTION OF SPRITSAIL AREA

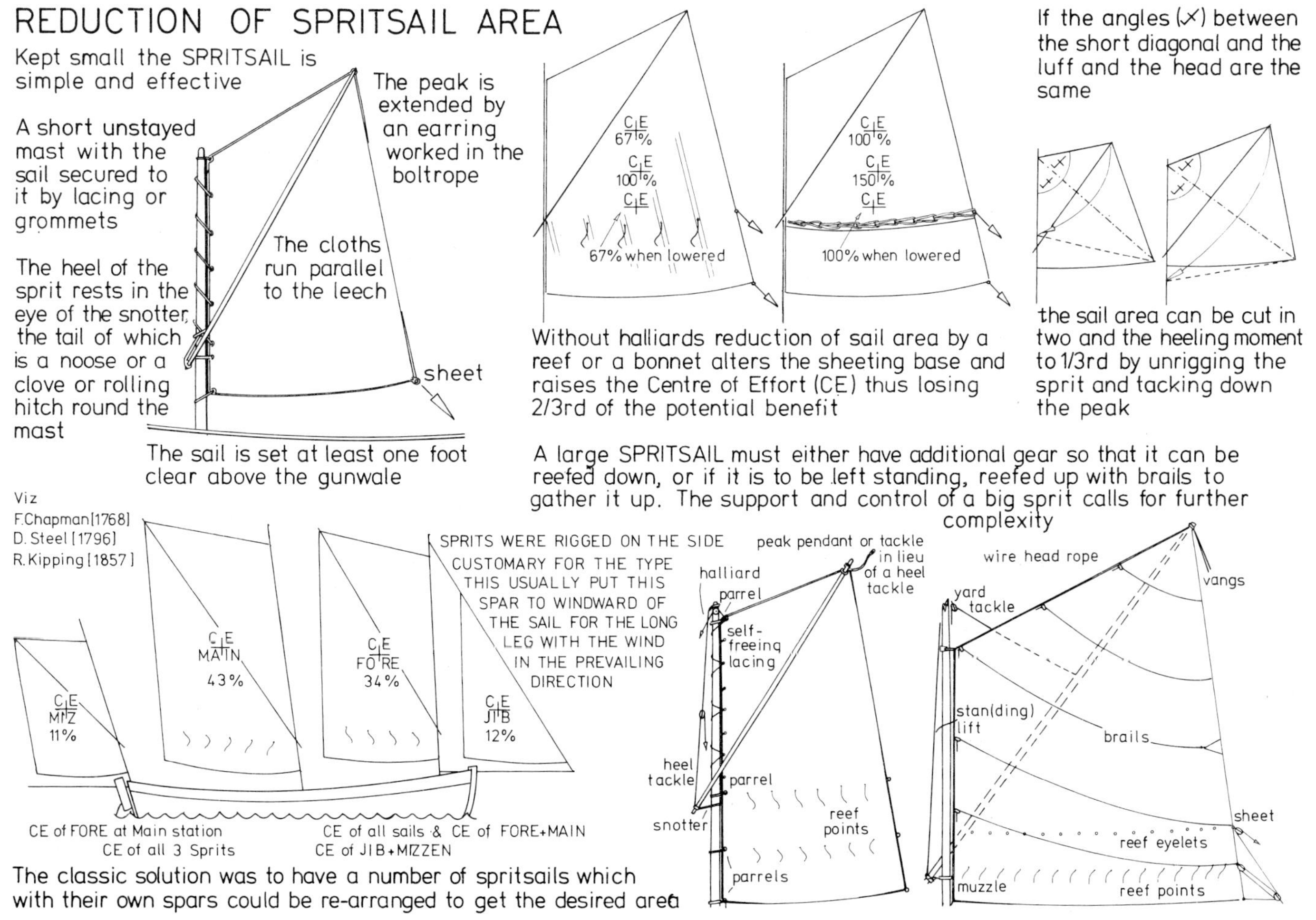

taking down some of the sails altogether. The Mevagissey lugger *Erin* provides an example of this, using the actual dimensions of her first set of sails made by Chesterfield's in 1912 (Fig 118). Here there are eleven sail arrangements with five sails and one of these single reefed.

Multi-mast rigs were liked in open boats as they kept the CE lower than if the same sail area had been set on a single mast. Furthermore only the spars and rigging in use showed above the gunwale. When lying to nets, the mizzen was set alone keeping the boat's head into the wind and preventing some of the rolling. Motor boats in the southwest, like steam drifters and trawlers, kept this sail. Beach boats rigged this way could be quickly unrigged for beaching through surf with nothing to get in the way of the oarsmen, and yet rerigged just as fast after launching and clear of broken water again.

Three-masted boat rigs, as far as contemporary paintings can be trusted, were popular everywhere at the start of the nineteenth century. With more intensive fishing gear and attendant large catches to be handled, the middle or main mast became a hindrance. In general this mast was eliminated and the other two, keeping their old names, made larger to make up for the sail area lost. This did not happen all at once. Three-masted luggers continued at Brighton until the middle of the century, twenty years behind Yarmouth. They were kept at Beer right up to the time engines took over, in the early years of this century. In single-masted rigs, where increasing size had made a second mast essential, the terms 'main' and 'mizzen', 'jigger' or 'dandy' were used, thus supplying a clue to how the two-masted rig had developed.

The adjustments described so far have been to do with the handling of sails and the preservation of balance between the rig and the hull. The next effect felt by a vessel sailing across or into the wind is the one that tries to push her over. This is due to a combination of wind strength, sail size and the height of the CE above a point which may be taken as being CLR. Even when very slight this force will list a vessel as when she is upright there is nothing acting to right her in that position. As she heels the position of a boat's centre of gravity (CG) stays in the same place, but the centre of buoyancy (CB) moves to leeward to suit the new shape the boat is making in the water (Fig 119). As the weight of the boat continues to act downwards and the displaced water upwards, a couple is set up acting so as to right the boat. The boat will go on heeling until the forces trying to capsize her and right her are equal, after which she will stay at this angle. This angle increases with the wind until either the gunwale of an open boat goes under and she swamps, or the CG is brought above the CB, when all boats capsize. The onset of either of these mishaps may be delayed at the design stage by

Fig 119: Stability.

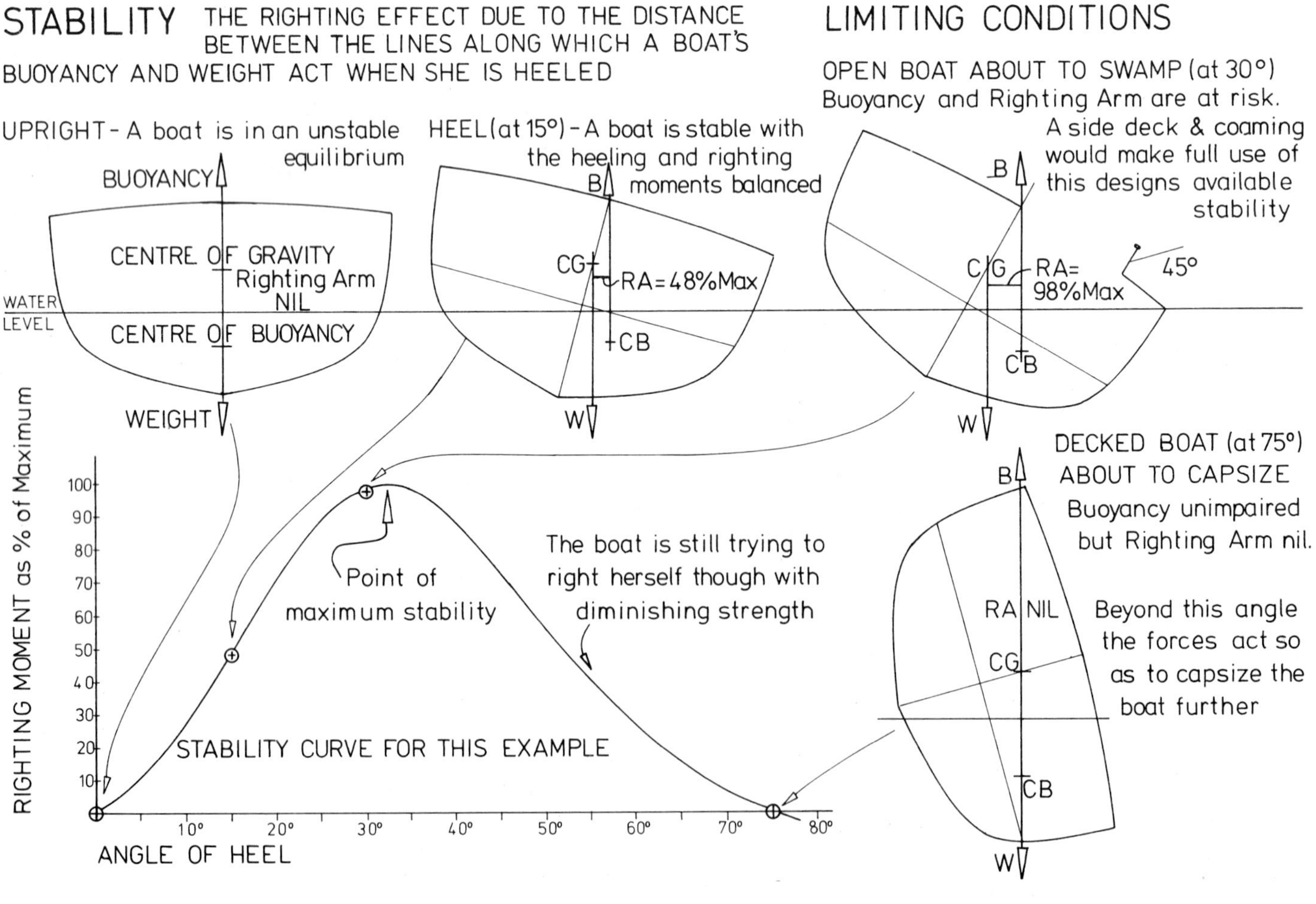

STABILITY
THE RIGHTING EFFECT DUE TO THE DISTANCE BETWEEN THE LINES ALONG WHICH A BOAT'S BUOYANCY AND WEIGHT ACT WHEN SHE IS HEELED

LIMITING CONDITIONS

UPRIGHT - A boat is in an unstable equilibrium

HEEL (at 15°) - A boat is stable with the heeling and righting moments balanced

OPEN BOAT ABOUT TO SWAMP (at 30°) Buoyancy and Righting Arm are at risk.

A side deck & coaming would make full use of this designs available stability

RA = 98% Max   45°

DECKED BOAT (at 75°) ABOUT TO CAPSIZE Buoyancy unimpaired but Righting Arm nil

Beyond this angle the forces act so as to capsize the boat further

Point of maximum stability

The boat is still trying to right herself though with diminishing strength

STABILITY CURVE FOR THIS EXAMPLE

RIGHTING MOMENT as % of Maximum

ANGLE OF HEEL

Fig 118: Sail arrangements to give areas that suit the wind strength – *Erin*.

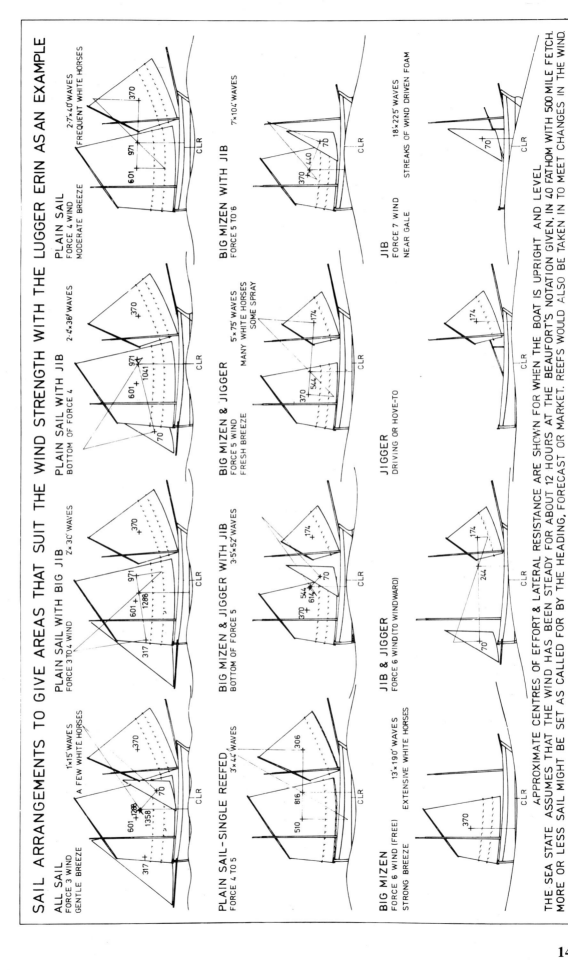

SAIL ARRANGEMENTS TO GIVE AREAS THAT SUIT THE WIND STRENGTH WITH THE LUGGER ERIN AS AN EXAMPLE

ALL SAIL
FORCE 3 WIND
GENTLE BREEZE
1×15' WAVES
A FEW WHITE HORSES

PLAIN SAIL WITH BIG JIB
FORCE 3 TO 4 WIND
2×30' WAVES

PLAIN SAIL WITH BIG JIB
FORCE 3 TO 4 WIND
2·4×36' WAVES

PLAIN SAIL
FORCE 4 WIND
MODERATE BREEZE
2·7×40' WAVES
FREQUENT WHITE HORSES

PLAIN SAIL WITH JIB
BOTTOM OF FORCE 4

PLAIN SAIL–SINGLE REEFED
FORCE 4 TO 5
3×44' WAVES

BIG MIZEN & JIGGER WITH JIB
BOTTOM OF FORCE 5
3·5×52' WAVES

BIG MIZEN & JIGGER
FORCE 5 WIND
FRESH BREEZE
5×75' WAVES
MANY WHITE HORSES
SOME SPRAY

BIG MIZEN WITH JIB
FORCE 5 TO 6
7×104' WAVES

BIG MIZEN
FORCE 6 WIND (FREE)
STRONG BREEZE
13'×190' WAVES
EXTENSIVE WHITE HORSES

JIB & JIGGER
FORCE 6 WIND (TO WINDWARD)

JIGGER
DRIVING OR HOVE-TO

JIB
FORCE 7 WIND
NEAR GALE
18'×225' WAVES
STREAKS OF WIND DRIVEN FOAM

APPROXIMATE CENTRES OF EFFORT & LATERAL RESISTANCE ARE SHOWN FOR WHEN THE BOAT IS UPRIGHT AND LEVEL THE SEA STATE ASSUMES THAT THE WIND HAS BEEN STEADY FOR ABOUT 12 HOURS AT THE BEAUFORT'S NOTATION GIVEN, IN 40 FATHOM WITH 500 MILE FETCH. MORE OR LESS SAIL MIGHT BE SET AS CALLED FOR BY THE HEADING, FORECAST OR MARKET. REEFS WOULD ALSO BE TAKEN IN TO MEET CHANGES IN THE WIND.

FORM STABILITY

THE EFFECT OF BUOYANT TOPSIDES IN THE SECTIONS AT EITHER END

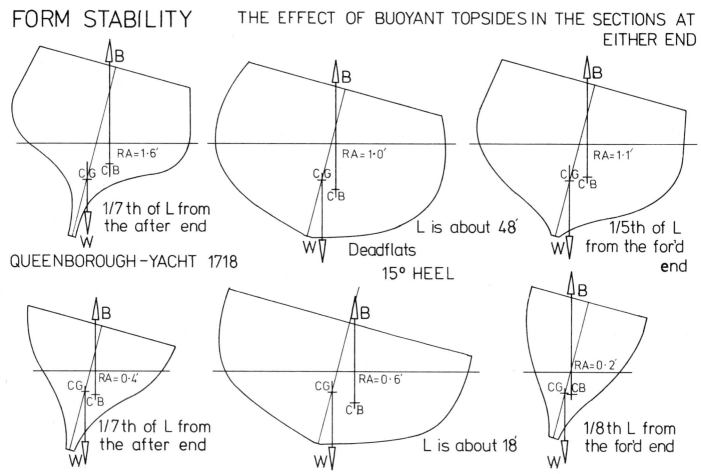

Fig 120: Form stability.

altering the shape of the submersible portions of the hull, re-arranging the weights lower down in the hull or reducing the amount and height of the sails at any time. The use of hull form, ballast and sail area adjustments to ensure satisfactory propulsion, though linked in reality, can be more easily discussed if taken one at a time.

Hull form has to be discussed first as this is fixed during building and cannot be changed easily afterwards. The hull's shape alone can give stability. In plain words this is done by having a hull shaped so that more of it goes into the water on the leeward side than comes out to windward. It is this that moves the CG out from under the CG and sets up a righting moment in opposition to the sails. Given the correct shape it is possible within limits to design a boat, flared out above and cut back below the waterline, that is stable without ballast. She will be of low displacement and likely to swamp unless the topsides are raised until windage and the higher CB become limiting factors. While more beam improves initial stability, capsize is complete and sudden when CG passes to leeward of CB.

Seventeenth and eighteenth century warships adopted an almost circular midship section, with the upright and heeled waterlines nearly passing through the centre of this circle. Unless drastic ballasting had lowered the CB well below this point, this looks like an example of that classic unstable form – the log. However, there were large reserves of buoyancy above the waterline, yet little displacement below in both bow and stern. On heeling, it was these topside volumes that immersed and resisted capsize (Fig 120). Many beach boats adopt the same idea as, having to keep down weight, they cannot rely so much on ballast, nor can they have heavy items like decks or tall masts. The Sheringham crabber is an example which combines a stable midship section with even more stable ends. The canoe form too, in which the turn of the bilge is full and rises clear above the waterline, gives good form stability. This combines well with fine underwater lines to give an easily driven hull, which has ample reserves of stability and buoyancy when pressed under sail. Such a hull can be made to go fast with small sail areas, but hasn't the space for cargo or the power to trawl. A vessel relying on her ends for stability will yaw when heeled in the long seas that form in open water, as when only one of the ends is immersed, the other swings out of the wind.

While light boats like this are ideal for short trips offshore, light fishing gear and speedy transport of people and their trappings, they are not enough for voyages lasting beyond the foreseeable weather. The protection and safety of the crew needs a deck, and the higher all-up weight calls for more sail area, beyond the power of the shape alone to carry.

Ballast low down in the hull will bring the CG lower down than the CB, particularly if it is fastened below the keel like a yacht, in which case there will still be a righting moment when the boat is on her beam ends. To prevent swamping and filling, a side or full deck is desirable in any ballasted vessel which is likely to be sailed with her gunwale awash. Most working open boats carried portable ballast in the form of bags of sand or shingle, large stones or iron pigs. This let an otherwise light boat carry more sail on the way out to her pitch, with the option of dumping the contents of the bags before the trip home in compensation for the weight of the catch and the wet nets. Large stones, much less iron pigs, were not expendable and were normally only found in a boat that had a predictable return load, like a pilot, crabber or tripper. As a boat's weight was much increased by her ballast, some if not all of it, together with all the other loose gear, might have to be unloaded and carried up the beach before she could be hauled up. This was often done every day on open beaches, but in sheltered ones only when laying up over Sunday or in the face of a bad weather spell. In narrow fast boats, ballast was moved up to windward while changing tacks as well as the weight of the crew being used as live ballast. This was safe with the large crew of a multi-oared boat, where the men had little else to do than trim the sails and bail; but most small working boats were short handed and too occupied handling the boat and her gear to shift ballast. Exceptionally, the sprit-rigged Gorran Haven crabber was a 16ft to 18ft open beach boat whose crew found time to do this. Fore and aft trimming of ballast, cargo and catch was essential for the effect it had on the balance, weatherliness and speed of a sailing boat, especially if she had a long, level, straight keel.

Ballast in a boat with a deck and a ceiling was mostly semi-permanently fixed, so properly called kentledge. While stone, scrap and cast iron might be used and only taken out from time to time for cleaning and re-tarring, it was often cemented permanently in place. Strangely, this helped to preserve the wood underneath, and I have yet to hear that cement has been the cause of rot. External ballast though a more effective way of lowering CG, suffers from leakage, keel bolt corrosion and keel decay. A few working boats fitted external ballast – the Annan whammel-net boat and the Fal sailing oyster dredger for example. Towards the end of working sail, more boats like the northwest nobbies, pilot cutters and smacks became yacht-like and fitted iron under their keels. As far as is known lead external keels were never fitted in classes of working boats as a whole.

One of the drawbacks of the shallow types of boats that were developed to work from beaches was the lack of depth of keel to reduce leeway. The performance of boats like these is so much better with some form of centreboard, it is astonishing how few classes adopted them. Perhaps even stranger was that of the now 188-year-old *Peggy* of Castletown IOM, where the three Captain Schank type daggerboards with which she was once fitted were actually taken out. Deadrise lessened leeway but made beaching more difficult. There is insufficient data to say how close the level keel boats without centreboards sailed. A recent trial in a replica of a Gorran Haven crabber gave rather better results than might have been predicted. This boat was built by Mr M Thomas of Stithians in 1979, and was based on P E Oke's drawings of the *Cuckoo*[9]. This 16½ft boat has 12° of deadrise and sailed rather better than a point above a broad reach in calm water (Fig 121). This might also be expected in rougher conditions when more experience has been gained in setting and trimming her sprit sails. It could hardly have been much better than this in fact. Gorran Haven is a partly sheltered inlet on a stretch of exposed shore, from which boats could not be taken out into any sector without regard to what the wind was and was likely to do. A last point of interest about this and other types of boat on this stretch of coast was that the floors became flat once centreboards were adopted.

The last hundred years under sail saw an increase in power, initially to meet increased demand for it and then to compete with early steam. Once again sail change preceded hull change; big improvements were followed by larger sail areas. Fore-and-aft sail area can be added more conveniently aft than forward. This is because a mast can be stepped closer to a stern than a stem, more sail can be set aft of a mast than forward of it, length for length an outrigger can extend more sail area than a bowsprit and the mainsail foot can be boomed. A headsail can be clubbed but this limits its foot, makes the foredeck dangerous, and was not used in working boats (Fig 122). In the majority of cases an increase of sail area brings the CE aft, so the CLR needs to come aft to restore balance. Within limits, this can be done by trimming by the stern using the existing ballast. Once done, this can bring a number of benefits without any more displacement. As the boat now drew more she made less leeway and the hull was a little stiffer, the lower freeboard aft helped the handling of fishing gear over the side, the greater freeboard forward kept the decks drier and the deeper rudder and new lateral profile combine to make her a little quicker in stays. Even when each of these amounted to only a fractional improvement it would show up at once against a fleet of similar boats. New boats had the trim built in, either in the form of a finer run or deeper sections aft. The single dimension draft still depended on the nature of the boat's home base and was a limit of the design's potential.

Exploitation of drag carried a penalty, particularly with sailing trawlers. The combination of fine level lines forward to improved speed to windward and a wide deck aft for the trawl beam gave a hull shape known as the double-wedge[10]. This form progressively lost balance as it heeled, because the reserve of buoyancy aft was so much more

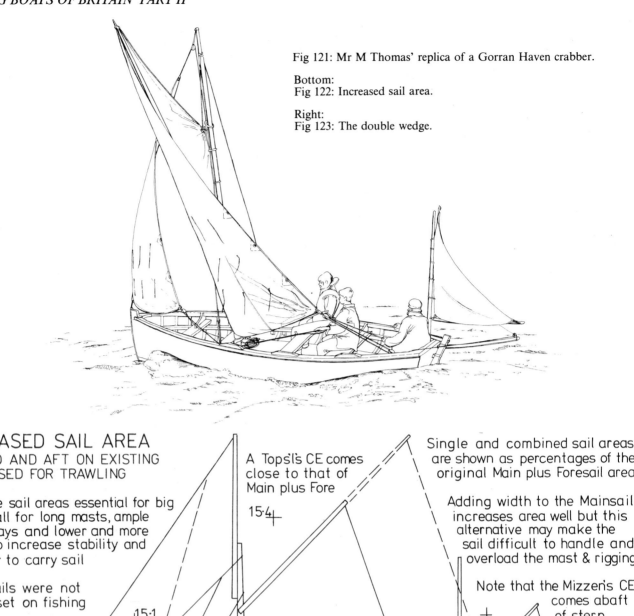

Fig 121: Mr M Thomas' replica of a Gorran Haven crabber.

Bottom:
Fig 122: Increased sail area.

Right:
Fig 123: The double wedge.

INCREASED SAIL AREA
FORWARD AND AFT ON EXISTING HULLS USED FOR TRAWLING

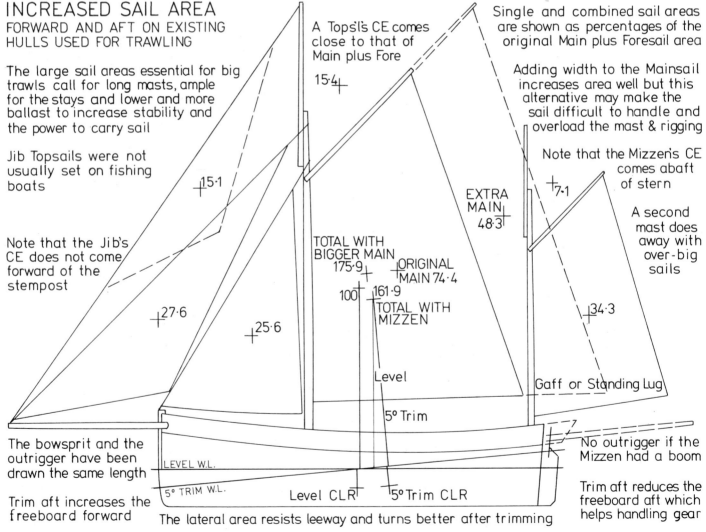

The large sail areas essential for big trawls call for long masts, ample for the stays and lower and more ballast to increase stability and the power to carry sail

Jib Topsails were not usually set on fishing boats

Note that the Jib's CE does not come forward of the stempost

A Topsl's CE comes close to that of Main plus Fore

15·4

15·1

27·6

25·6

Single and combined sail areas are shown as percentages of the original Main plus Foresail area

Adding width to the Mainsail increases area well but this alternative may make the sail difficult to handle and overload the mast & rigging

Note that the Mizzen's CE comes abaft of stern

A second mast does away with over-big sails

EXTRA MAIN 48·3

7·1

34·3

TOTAL WITH BIGGER MAIN 175·9

ORIGINAL MAIN 74·4

100

161·9 TOTAL WITH MIZZEN

Level

5° Trim

Gaff or Standing Lug

The bowsprit and the outrigger have been drawn the same length

LEVEL W.L.

5° TRIM W.L.

Level CLR

5° Trim CLR

No outrigger if the Mizzen had a boom

Trim aft increases the freeboard forward

Trim aft reduces the freeboard aft which helps handling gear

The lateral area resists leeway and turns better after trimming

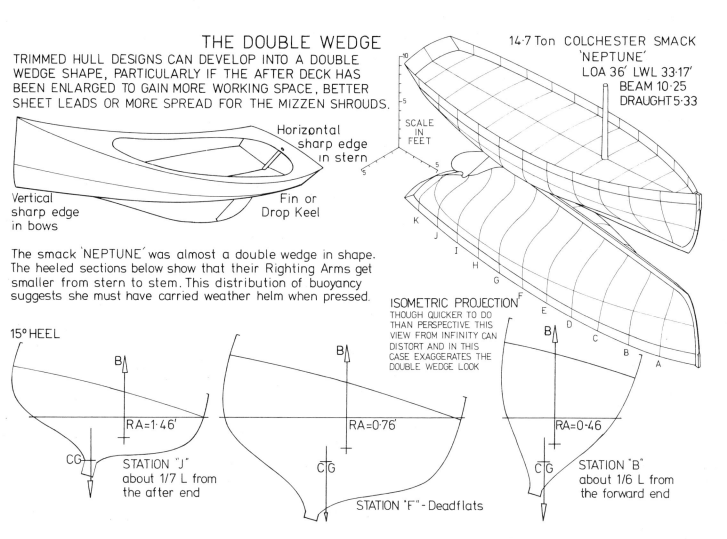

THE DOUBLE WEDGE

TRIMMED HULL DESIGNS CAN DEVELOP INTO A DOUBLE WEDGE SHAPE, PARTICULARLY IF THE AFTER DECK HAS BEEN ENLARGED TO GAIN MORE WORKING SPACE, BETTER SHEET LEADS OR MORE SPREAD FOR THE MIZZEN SHROUDS.

14·7 Ton COLCHESTER SMACK 'NEPTUNE'
LOA 36' LWL 33·17'
BEAM 10·25
DRAUGHT 5·33

Horizontal sharp edge in stern

Vertical sharp edge in bows

Fin or Drop Keel

The smack 'NEPTUNE' was almost a double wedge in shape. The heeled sections below show that their Righting Arms get smaller from stern to stem. This distribution of buoyancy suggests she must have carried weather helm when pressed.

SCALE IN FEET

ISOMETRIC PROJECTION
THOUGH QUICKER TO DO THAN PERSPECTIVE THIS VIEW FROM INFINITY CAN DISTORT AND IN THIS CASE EXAGGERATES THE DOUBLE WEDGE LOOK

15° HEEL

RA=1·46'
STATION "J" about 1/7 L from the after end

RA=0·76'
STATION "F" - Deadflats

RA=0·46'
STATION "B" about 1/6 L from the forward end

than that forward (Fig 123). This produced gross weather helm, a vice which was corrected but not cured by larger rudders, rig changes, long tillers and relieving tackles.

Apart from the hard-mouthed boats like these and the risk of broaching in deep ruddered boats like cobles and flatners, steering did not seem to have been a source of difficulty in sailing boats. A rudder pivoted on a stern post enjoyed a good flow of water and protection from damage. Counters gave more protection, and rudders on square sterns and transoms could be unshipped before beaching or fitted on raked sternposts for mooring in crowded harbours.

There is one last topic, before leaving the subject of the effect sails have on the shape of boats and this is due to the stresses they set up and furthers what has been written on structure. Masts may be set up anywhere in a boat, from well forward to right aft, and the way they are rigged load them and the boat in different ways. Some like the lug act at only one point on the mast and others like the jib-headed main act along most of its length. The mast itself resolves most of these stresses so that their effect is only felt by the hull where the mast or its stays touch. These points have to distribute these forces to the rest of the hull without permanently distorting it.

A mast can be unstayed or held up by its rigging,

running or standing, each method stressing the hull differently. The unstayed mast is a beam fixed rigidly at its lower end for only a fraction of its length, which leverage multiplies the forces due to the sail. The sail tries to push the mast forwards or sideways, depending on the point of sailing. Most masts are held at two points: the foot and where it passes through a thwart or a deck. At the foot the force from the sail acts in the opposite direction from that of the sail, and there is also a downwards force due to the weight of the rig and pull of the tack and the halliard (Fig 124). As unstayed masts are mainly used with small sail areas, the resultant force at the foot can be taken by a mast step spanning a pair or more of floors or timbers. These spread the load to the keel and planking. At the thwart or deck, the force set up by the sail is taken in the same direction out to the sides, pulling on the windward and pushing to leeward. Planking by itself is not suitable to resist this, and rising, knees and gunwales are used to spread these stresses. Unstayed mast are not made thick enough to be rigid, as some springiness decreases the shock transmitted to the hull by a sudden squall. The Norfolk wherry provides an example of a much larger mast without any shrouds, which was pivoted for lowering in a massive tabernacle located by a system of beams and knees. There was a forestay for hoisting and lowering the mast (Fig 125).

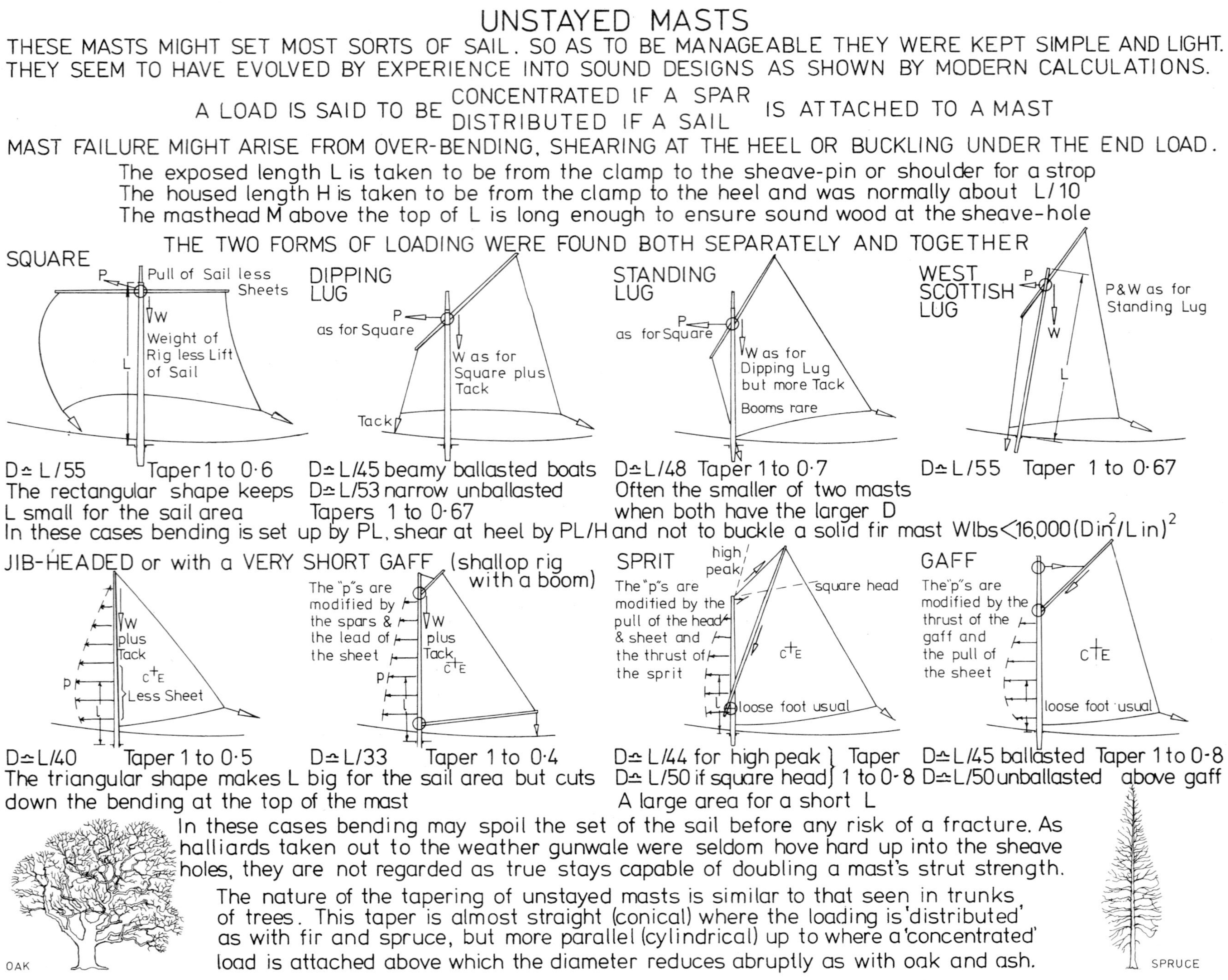

UNSTAYED MASTS

THESE MASTS MIGHT SET MOST SORTS OF SAIL. SO AS TO BE MANAGEABLE THEY WERE KEPT SIMPLE AND LIGHT. THEY SEEM TO HAVE EVOLVED BY EXPERIENCE INTO SOUND DESIGNS AS SHOWN BY MODERN CALCULATIONS.

A LOAD IS SAID TO BE CONCENTRATED IF A SPAR IS ATTACHED TO A MAST DISTRIBUTED IF A SAIL

MAST FAILURE MIGHT ARISE FROM OVER-BENDING, SHEARING AT THE HEEL OR BUCKLING UNDER THE END LOAD.

The exposed length L is taken to be from the clamp to the sheave-pin or shoulder for a strop
The housed length H is taken to be from the clamp to the heel and was normally about L/10
The masthead M above the top of L is long enough to ensure sound wood at the sheave-hole

THE TWO FORMS OF LOADING WERE FOUND BOTH SEPARATELY AND TOGETHER

SQUARE

P Pull of Sail less Sheets
W Weight of Rig less Lift of Sail
L

$D \simeq L/55$ Taper 1 to 0·6
The rectangular shape keeps L small for the sail area
In these cases bending is set up by PL, shear at heel by PL/H

DIPPING LUG

W as for Square plus Tack
P as for Square
Tack

$D \simeq L/45$ beamy ballasted boats
$D \simeq L/53$ narrow unballasted
Tapers 1 to 0·67

STANDING LUG

W as for Dipping Lug but more Tack
P as for Square
Booms rare

$D \simeq L/48$ Taper 1 to 0·7
Often the smaller of two masts when both have the larger D and not to buckle a solid fir mast Wlbs<16,000(Din²/L in)²

WEST SCOTTISH LUG

P&W as for Standing Lug
P
W
L

$D \simeq L/55$ Taper 1 to 0·67

JIB-HEADED or with a VERY SHORT GAFF (shallop rig with a boom)

The "p"s are modified by the spars & the lead of the sheet
W plus Tack
c †E

$D \simeq L/40$ Taper 1 to 0·5
The triangular shape makes L big for the sail area but cuts down the bending at the top of the mast

$D \simeq L/33$ Taper 1 to 0·4

W plus Tack
c †E
Less Sheet
P

SPRIT

The "p"s are modified by the pull of the head & sheet and the thrust of the sprit
high peak
square head
c †E
loose foot usual

$D \simeq L/44$ for high peak } Taper
$D \simeq L/50$ if square head } 1 to 0·8
A large area for a short L

GAFF

The "p"s are modified by the thrust of the gaff and the pull of the sheet
c †E
loose foot usual

$D \simeq L/45$ ballasted Taper 1 to 0·8
$D \simeq L/50$ unballasted above gaff

In these cases bending may spoil the set of the sail before any risk of a fracture. As halliards taken out to the weather gunwale were seldom hove hard up into the sheave holes, they are not regarded as true stays capable of doubling a mast's strut strength.

The nature of the tapering of unstayed masts is similar to that seen in trunks of trees. This taper is almost straight (conical) where the loading is 'distributed' as with fir and spruce, but more parallel (cylindrical) up to where a 'concentrated' load is attached above which the diameter reduces abruptly as with oak and ash.

SPRUCE

OAK

Fig 124: Unstayed masts.

NORFOLK WHERRY
MAST TABERNACLE
L-425" H-66" T-36"
D-11" Taper 1 to 0·8

LODGING KNEES
P & S

The 'Rightups' (coamings) have been
excluded also the deck and the
ceiling from the starboard side

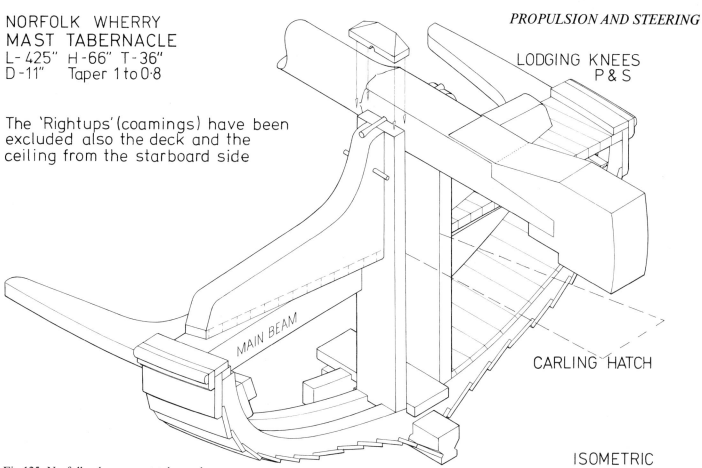

MAIN BEAM

CARLING HATCH

ISOMETRIC

Fig 125: Norfolk wherry: mast tabernacle.

The normal way of staying the mast for a lug sail was to use the halliard as a stay to windward, changing sides when dipping. The British dipping lug was slung by the third, or close to that. With this amount of sail forward of the mast, it generally paid to pass the whole sail round forward of the mast when changing tack, and this allowed the halliard to be passed across to the other side. A dipping lug did not draw as well aback and in strong winds there was a risk of breaking the mast or straining the hull. Another stay was needed with large lugs, partly to permit sailing aback safely, but also to avoid having to pass the halliard. This was the burton, a mast head stay set up on the opposite side to the halliard and named for the purchase it used. On the French side of the Channel, lugs were slung at the quarter and drew well enough aback to be set on opposite sides on two-masted rigs[11].

On the wind a stay turns a mast from a beam into a strut. This increases the thrust down on the step, but reduces the bending moment on the mast and the side loading of the deck or thwart. Though it is possible to do away with all restriction here, the mast is stronger when held. This shortens the strut, a benefit proportional to its square, while firm housing makes a strut four times as strong. In practice the full extent of these benefits are not realised, as fits are never perfect and the structure flexes under load. Nevertheless, both mast and hull can be made lighter when correctly stayed and housed. The attachment of a stay to the hull gives less problems with timbered clinker planks, which are able to take stresses tangential to the surface, than with edge-positioned planks, which needs a plate

spanning several strakes through fastened to frames.

Struts become weak if bent. This can occur if they are too thin for their length, a safe rule being not more than 50 diameters when stayed and 40 diameters unstayed, or when a side load is applied to an unstayed length, most of all mid-way. This means that a yard or gaff close up to the hounds bends the mast less, than when reefed and part lowered, even though the smaller sail in the stronger wind is exerting the same heeling moment.

Boats carrying large loads, towing trawls or, like pilot cutters and packets, have to perform well in light winds, must have large sail areas. From mast step up, the amount and complexity of the timber, metal and cordage increases rapidly with area, all of which generates far greater hull stresses than the simple rigs so far discussed. The mast itself may have to be made in more than one, though rarely more than two in boats, length each with safe strut sizes and stays. This added top weight can set up racking stresses when rolling in a dead calm which are greater than those due to the wind in a storm.

A stay is at a disadvantage in a narrow part of a boat, so a mast here is better treated as if it were unstayed and the hull strengthened accordingly. Even when sailing balance is preserved with a similar area at the other end, it is hard to provide a satisfactory sheeting base without beam. Weights a long way from the CG encourage pitching, which slows a boat down and can stop her if the wave and boat frequencies are the same. A sail set on a stay seems to offer a light method of increasing sail area, but this is only true down wind. On the wind, a luff has to be taut and this extra pull has to be taken by some form of backstay. This put up the end-loading of the mast as a strut, which then must be thicker and require more support from the hull.

The cost of more power is always more weight, not only in rig but also in ballast, which absorbs some of the added power. In the end, a hull which is being driven beyond its economical speed by virtue of a great spread of canvas may be a glorious sight, but it is a sad one as it foretells its own end. Whether the vessel was a clipper scooping the tea market or a working cutter winning the town cup at a regatta, a great deal of extra sail would have had to be set for what would be a small gain in speed, but a great deal more stress and strain above and below deck. This again is an example of technology being taken past its reasonable limit of development. Such sights were a clear sign that wind as a form of propulsion for working boats was due for replacement by a more potent if less romantic method.

FUEL

Power, in the form of coal-fired steam engines, first came to sea in sailing boats in the form of winches to work net warps. Before then drifters took on capstan-men at the pier head, casual pulley-hauley labour for the donkey work, but with no claim to be seamen or fishermen. This extra manpower could also tail on a rope when working large dipping lugs. Once the steam winch or capstan had done away with capstan-men, some lug-rigged drifters, those of Lowestoft in particular, turned to the more easily worked gaff rig or fitted steam main engines to ensure fast trips out and back from the fishing grounds. Trawlers took to steam so that the trawl size could be increased. The dependability of steam to keep moving in calm weather allowed the introduction of the otter trawl, which required less effort to recover than the beam. Nevertheless, the hull shape that suited a sailing rig was not the ideal one for a propeller driven by a fuel burning engine.

The most fundamental difference between the hull of a motor boat and of a sailing boat is that the source of power in the former does not try to capsize the hull or turn it off course. Sailing boats which had the beam, stability and draft to prevent the wind doing this were unlikely to convert directly into efficient power boats. Yet in the early days, with a few exceptions, mechanical propulsion generally meant converting what had once been a sailing boat. Only the largest of these were able to take the weight and afford the space for steam machinery, followed, very much later, by the smaller ones that had wait for the development of the internal combustion engines before they could have power. The steam fishing vessels started to appear in the early 1880s, but motor boats not until just before the First World War; the small ones were not seen in any large number till the early 1920s, when the development of hull shapes specifically for motors really started.

Even after the first conversions had taken place, the phase took about twenty-five years to complete, and longer if the local type was particularly suitable for conversion and was durable. After that all the boats in a given place would be built as motor boats, normally without any reliance on sail beyond one for riding. Other types of sailing boats did not take at all kindly to conversion, because either their shape or their structure or both were unsuitable. Places with boats like these had to look elsewhere for designs if the local boatbuilder was unable to produce a suitable alternative himself.

Apart from a few paddle tugs in the late 1870s, which were turned into trawlers or used to tow sailing fishing boats in or out of harbour, the paddle wheel was not much used in boats. They tended to get snarled up in the fishing gear, were hard to steer when rolling but too fragile to take the ground on a hard or a beach on an open shore. The propeller was the only practical means of propulsion for a boat.

Screw propulsion of working boats made its first inroads where the need for more power had made the sailing rigs elaborate and hard to handle. This could not happen until the engines were compact, reliable and economical on fuel. The trawlers were the first to change, followed by the drifters in the first years of this century. Both grew larger than when under sail, the trawlers to an average of 120ft LOA and the drifters to about 80ft. The Science Museum has a most interesting model of one of the early steam trawlers. This schooner-rigged vessel was 87ft LOA and 83 tons gross register and her compound engine would have developed just about 100hp. What is remarkable is that she should have the hull of a steamer and not a sailing boat. The Doughty Museum at Grimsby has a fine collection of full and half models of steam trawlers built between 1889 and the 1950s, but not one of the *Zodiac*, the first purpose-built steam trawler, built in 1881.

For a sailing boat to be convertible, her hull had to be large enough to hold not only the engine and boiler, but about 60 tons of coal as well. Even then the capital required for a new or converted steamer could only be justified when the fishing grounds were some distance from base, as on short hauls a sailing vessel, which then cost from a quarter to a fifth as much, still gave a better return for outlay. The sailing trawlers lost even this advantage as the nearby grounds were fished out and the steamers took over further afield. In spite of this trawling under sail persisted in a small way, and there were two Lowestoft trawlers, *Ivan* and *Gleam*, working out of Sutton Pool at Plymouth in the early months of 1940.

As coal-fired steam vessels, mostly newly built, became rapidly more common in the 1880s, the number of sailing ones fell correspondingly (Fig 126). The numbers of first class steam fishing vessels reached their peak by 1914. During the war years the statistics were complicated by the large numbers of drifters and trawlers engaged in war service, but after 1920 their numbers dropped steadily, partly due to the availability of suitable internal combustion engines, alternative fishing methods, the rising price of coal and also because the boats were growing still larger. There were just over 2000 English and Welsh

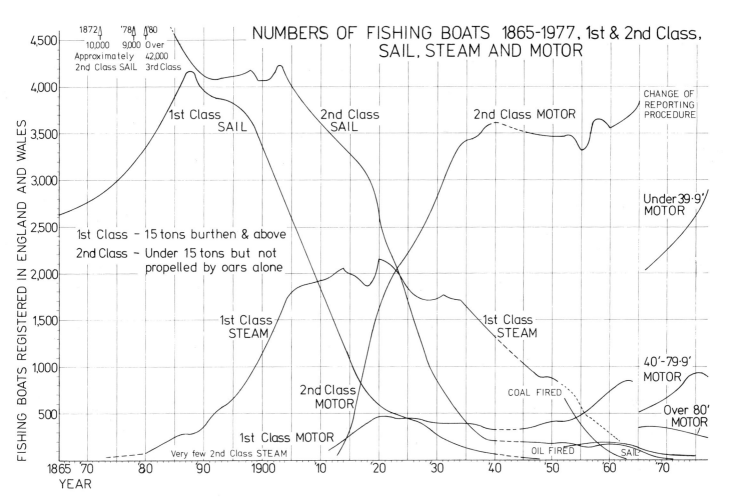

NUMBERS OF FISHING BOATS 1865-1977, 1st & 2nd Class, SAIL, STEAM AND MOTOR

Fig 126: Numbers of fishing boats 1865-1977, First and Second Class sail, Steam and Motor.

trawlers averaging 75 tons each in 1914. By 1964 the number of vessels over 80ft LOA had fallen to just under 500 but as the average size had risen to 430 tons each, representing a 43% increase in the total gross tonnage. In 1974 the numbers had fallen further to 240, with an average size of 475 tons bringing the total tonnage to below the 1914 figure. The situation was broadly similar in Scotland, except that here the fleet was about as half as big. What these figures show is these vessels which started by being large boats have now turned into small ships. The history of this change has been given in detail by John Dyson and Colin Elliott[12] [13] [14]

The sailing vessel numbers had dropped even faster. At the outbreak of the Second World War, there were less than a hundred in the first class. Since this war, it has been difficult to estimate their true number as, until recently, the official returns included some privately-owned fishing vessels that were not being operated commercially.

The use of marine internal combustion engines came much later than steam, although the first Priestman's Otto cycle engine was installed in a 28ft boat as early as 1888. The countries round the Baltic took to internal combustion engines more rapidly than Britain, preferring semi-diesels or hot-bulb engines. Compared with this country, which by 1912 had 131 motorised boats, Denmark had over 2000, with 4000 in Norway. The British fleet was made up of 84 drifters averaging 27 tons each and

30 liner/drifters, but hardly any of the balance were listed as trawlers. The number of these first class motor boats had reached almost 500 after the First World War, then fell slowly to half this number by the end of the Second World War. Since then there has been a steady rise until there were 750 by the mid-1960s.

Internal combustion engines underwent major technical advances in both World Wars. In the first of these, aeroplane, submarine and road transport engines were all improved in terms of weight, efficiency, cost, size and reliability, but most of all they became better known and understood. There was a general move away from the slow heavy but dependable semi-diesels towards diesels that were much more like the larger petrol lorry engine. The introduction of solid, in place of blast-injection of the, fuel greatly simplified the task of the driver-maintainer, which was what the engineman in a boat had to be. The *Fishery Report* of 1922, which covered the war years, expressed the view that this preference for engines which the local garage mechanic could deal with was the reason for semi-diesels failing to achieve the popularity in this country which they enjoyed in the Baltic. Having an automotive type of engine guaranteed that there would be one member of the crew who was prepared to lavish the attention and care that these early temperamental machines needed, however much the rest of the crew might have resented the passing of the old knowledge and skills.

If the First World War established the medium speed diesel, it was the second one that proved the high speed engines which powered the invasion fleets of the Mediterranean, Atlantic and Pacific. There was also a revolution in the method of engine maintenance, which now depended upon the replacement of worn parts by standardised spares, rather than by the adjustment and re-fitting of the old ones, as was customary with steam engines. Even some steam engines, those made by Lobnitz for instance, were totally enclosed and positively lubricated. The new generation of internal combustion engine was more compact and could be removed completely for replacement by a spare should a lengthy overhaul become necessary.

Sheer weight and cost had between them prevented early motors from being installed in the smaller boats of the second and third classes, *ie* those under 15 tons and those propelled only by oars. As late as 1912, the Board of Agriculture and Fisheries reported that, 'The motor for fishing purposes can hardly be said to have passed beyond the experimental stage'. But in the following year the same authority was able to write, 'The application of the internal combustion engine to fishing craft has made considerable progress round the British Isles'. A Yorkshire coble, a Sheringham crabber and a Cornish lugger had all been motorised, but it was in the south-west that the longest strides were being made. The Devon Local Fishing Committee was granted £2000 to experiment with motors. At the end of the First World War, there were just under 200 second class motor boats as compared with over 3000 sailing boats. A year before this in February 1917, the Motor Loan Committee had been set up under Cecil Harmsworth to further the use of motors, by providing object lessons to overcome the doubts of fishermen and their reluctance to borrow money. With a staff of 16 at the most, 152 loans amounting to £28,350 had been made in the first two years. Of these, 21 had been repaid, amounting to £3950, and a further £1757 had been repaid in excess of dues, while the arrears had been insignificant. These loans averaged less than £200 each, and it was claimed that once converted, a boat could catch two or three times as much fish as a sailing boat. These facilities were withdrawn at the end of 1921, though the accounts continued until 1924 as the earlier good record of repayment declined. The object lesson had been learned, as by that year there were equal numbers of motor and sailing boats, 2000 of each.

By 1934 small open boats had established a common range of standard inboard engine horsepowers for their different sizes, the exact horsepower used being fixed more by the marine engine available than by any calculations. In this way, one expected to find a boat between 14ft and 18ft powered by a 3½hp Stuart Turner, from 18ft to 22ft a 6 or 7hp engine and from 22ft to 26ft as much as 12hp. Once

above 26ft the horsepowers would rise more rapidly.

There were less than 200 sailing boats working at the start of the Second World War, but once more the inclusion of yachts registered as fishing boats confuse the postwar figures. By the mid-1960s the total number of second and third class motor boats stood at just under 4000. It will be seen from this how little the total number of these smaller boats has changed during this century. There are, as might be expected, very few steam boats in the second class – the greatest number being 17 in 1919 – as the installation of a steam engine in a boat of less than 15 tons left very little room for nets, fish or accommodation.

Knowing the advantages of powered capstans and winches from the experience with steam, it was not long before attempts were made to power those fitted in motor boats. The early methods were disappointing, but two solutions were found. In decked vessels the winch drive was taken from a pulley on the forward end of the main engine crankshaft by means of a flat belt up to deck level and the winch, which was usually amidships just in front of the wheelhouse. A wide variety of hauling mechanisms were manufactured, largely in Scotland, to meet the requirements of seining, trawling, long lining etc, some of them coiling down the ropes and lines as they came inboard. The smaller boats could not carry such heavy gear, but still wanted to lighten the work of hauling lines and pots. Some most ingenious devices, often with differentials and half-shafts from old cars, were installed with the help of a smith (Fig 127). Since the middle of this century, hydraulic winches and capstans have been developed with can be installed in the smallest boats. These take the form of a V-belt driven pump or 'A' end sited close to the main engine, and a motor or 'B' end wherever

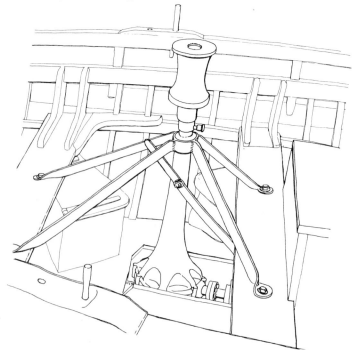

Fig 127: Pot hauler take-off using a car's differential in *IH 51* at Southwold.

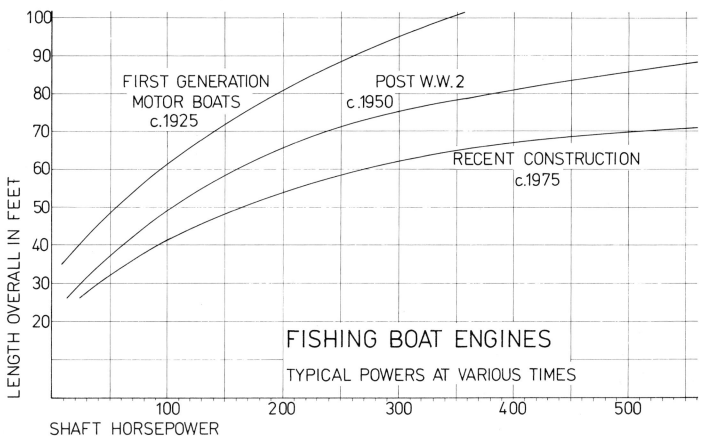

Fig 128: Fishing boat engines – typical powers at various times.

it is needed. The two are linked by a pair of flexible hoses. The hauling device is coupled to the 'B' end, whose speed and direction can be changed at will without altering the rotation of the drive. The power block is a more recent development, being an articulated hydraulically operated arm-like small crane, at the end of which is a large sheave powered by a 'B' end. The sheave is shaped so that it can handle nets as well as warps.

Power blocks have been seen fitted to boats as short as 20ft LOA, where they are potentially dangerous as the weight of a wet net full of fish can raise the CG considerably. This has capsized one boat, which brought her catch inboard over the side instead of over the stern. The added top weight of a great deal of other modern equipment together with the gantry and wheelhouse on which to mount them, is currently making it necessary for the Department of Trade and Industry to impose stricter controls. New boats are now tested for stability by carrying out inclining experiments, but it is harder to screen thousands of older boats that may be fitting more up-to-date equipment inadvisably. Whatever the power take off employed, all these new services required the main engine to be kept running continuously at sea. This results in high fuel consumptions for petrol engines, high rates of wear in diesels and the possibility that a semi-diesel may stop cold.

Whatever the type of the main engine, the power needed to drive the hull through the water at a given speed is much the same. The call for more speed, larger gear and greater

auxiliary loads has combined to increase the horsepowers of main engines. Three curves have been drawn to show this (Fig 128). The first curve is for 1925, which was just after the time when the number of motor boats exceeded that of the sailing boats. What nowadays seem to be modest power installations were then adequate to compete sucessfully with sail and superannuate it. At that time only a middle range of boats could be fitted with diesel engines, say those between 40ft and 75ft LOA. Smaller than this the diesels were too heavy and petrol/paraffin engines had to be used instead while larger vessels still relied upon steam. The second curve refers to 1950, when the fishing industry was beginning to feel the benefits of the experience gained with high speed diesel during the war. This shows up in the manner the new boats were being engined and the old ones re-engined more powerfully than before, without increasing the size of the engine-rooms. The final curve shows the state of affairs in 1975. Together the three curves in the diagram indicate that power had almost doubled in the first twenty-five year period, and more than doubled in the second.

The range of sizes of boat that can be powered by diesel engines has steadily increased until now it includes everything that can be called a boat. Both petrol and steam engines are now rare. The following table illustrates how the weights of appropriate diesel engines have decreased over the last fifty years:

Year	LOA	shp	Specific Weight lb/shp	Engine (lb)	Weight (tons)
1925		200	100	20,000	8.9
1950	100ft	350	60	21,000	9.4
1975		600	25	15,000	6.7
1925		60	100	6000	2.7
1950	60ft	100	22	2200	1.0
1975		210	14	3360	1.5
1925		45	120	5400	2.4
1950	40ft	90	25	2250	1.0
1975		120	12	1440	0.6
1925		12	75	900	0.4
1950	20ft	15	35	526	0.23
1975		20	18	300	0.16

Having settled what shp is appropriate for a new boat, with regards both to performance and available space and displacement, a prospective owner has to consider what type of engine he should have. The choice is a wide one, not only over the fuel to be used, but also the running speed of the engine. The convention is to call engines that run between 75 and 500rpm, slow speed, 900 and 1750, medium speed, 1800 and 2600, high speed, and very high speed when between 2900 and 3600 in the case of diesels, but up to 4000rpm for petrol engines. For design reasons, it is not usual to find any marine diesel operating in either the 500 to 800rpm or 2600 to 2900rpm brackets.

In the early days, internal combustion engines were all slow running, therefore heavy, as every part of them had to be made bigger to make up for the slow rate of firing. To offset this, most of them were two-stroke engines which fired twice as often as a four-stroke turning at the same speed. They were also made taller rather than longer so as not to encroach too far into the fish hold. Two-strokes were preferred because of their short fore and aft length as they needed no space for reduction or reverse gears.

Faster engine speeds brought weight reduction, but this meant more cyclinders to give a more even distribution of torque and reduce the weight of reciprocating masses. A great number of problems had to be overcome before trustworthy reversing gear boxes, torsional vibration-free crankshaft, fast combustion in diesels and salt water-proof electrics for spark ignition were fit for unqualified enginemen in small boats. This took many years, and it was road transport engines that showed the way and proved these faster speeds. It was the improved road transport that took the fish traffic from the railways, closing down the branch lines and making more use of lorries. These lorries now serve both the places the railways have left and fishing stations which previously had only indirect access to the markets. While marinised versions of lorry petrol engines did well enough to start with, driving beach capstans as well as boats, they fell far short of the specially designed marine diesels that appeared after the Second World War. These are rejuvenating the inshore fishing industry and have started a period of change, which is still taking place during the course of this study.

One example of how this is taking place may help to illustrate this. At Beesands near Start Point the traditional pattern of fishing has been to use seine nets off the open beach to catch the bait for pots laid in Start Bay. Two distinct types of beach boats were used for this, the seiners, described on p189 and the crabbers, like the ones from Hallsands drawn by P J Oke, and these were fitted with inboard engines [15] [16]. There being no railway, the crabs and lobsters were collected and taken to the Solent by well smacks in the days of sail and to London by lorry more recently, with a refrigerated chamber put up by the road to store the catch whilst awaiting transport. In 1973, the 150-year-old Exmouth firm of Dixon & Sons completed a wooden 40ft motor crabber for Beesands. This powerful edge-positioned planked boat was unlike either the old seiners or crabbers and much too large to be used from this beach. She was taken instead eight miles away to Kingswear, where there is a fish market at a railhead. The younger fishermen of Beesands now drive themselves into Dartmouth in the early morning to work their new boat, returning at midday or early afternoon. The old men then take over, having come by bus, which takes the younger men home, and clear the catch through the market, buy bait if the price is right, bait the pots and then drive home taking any bait left for storage in the freezer. Though there is no longer any regular commercial fishing at Beesands, there are still fishermen there and the Dart is a little busier. There has also been a complete break from the old local boat designs.

The requirements for a hull propelled by an engine are quite different from those of one by sails. In most cases the motor boat will have to go faster and directly into the wind and the waves. In all but confused formations, a sailing boat can be taken through large waves if she is kept moving on a winding course. Although heeled to the gunwale, she will be kept dry by the raised weather side. Even if it is squally, a sailing boat is under control, as easing the tiller or sheet or both will see her through the puffs. The apparent advantage of a motor boat's ability to go straight into the wind is lost if she pitches and ships so much water that safety forces her to slow down or take a less ardent course. Most motor boats need more freeboard forward, or more deck space if they are open, than a sailing boat of the same size. A fine entry helps speed, but has to be coupled with buoyant topsides to slow down pitching and throw off as much water as possible.

Because their greater speed makes motor boats wetter and colder than sailing boats, their crews, who have less to do to keep warm, need more shelter. In decked vessels this is usually sited aft above the engine room, which is warm. This provides a good view of what is taking place on deck and keeps the leads to the engine and the rudder short. In smaller open boats the shelter is provided forward as the helmsman is generally involved in handling the gear. Shelters, fore or aft, means a change from tiller to wheel steering.

The time it took to motorise working boats indicated which types required next to nothing in the way of alteration of hull shape and those that were beyond conversion. In between these two extremes were other types where experience with the conversions showed what and how much change of shape and structure were needed when building the first true motor boats. Where this happened, the local type, though somewhat changed in shape, has kept its traditional identity. In Scotland, in particular, there have been several stages in the changeover, and it is getting hard to see how the most recent shapes can have developed from the sailing ones. Nevertheless the general appearance and style of finish of these boats is still unique.

Travelling from one fishing station to the next, it is possible to get a fair idea of how each one reacted to the introduction of motors, by looking at the boats now in use. In a few places, where oars and, in one instance, sails are still used, the boats have not been motorised at all and have not changed. In other places such as stations in Cornwall, Sussex and Yorkshire, the motor boat hulls still look very like those of the earlier sailing boats, even where imported designs of motor boat have been introduced. Other havens, though busy, are found to contain a variety of boats from different sources, some not even in Britain. These are the places where not only was the sailing boat beyond conversion, but the local boatbuilder could not find a way to reshape the design (Frontispiece). In stations like this the boat owners have had to find replacements elsewhere, but have not yet settled on a single suitable type. Lastly, there are many stations that have stopped operating altogether as working beaches or harbours. This may have been for other reasons than difficulties over finding suitable shapes for motor boats, and are as likely to be due to depopulation, better jobs ashore or failure of inshore fishing grounds.

With the possible exception of the Admiralty range of 45ft, 62½ft, 75ft and 90ft motor fishing vessels, there has been little sign that a scientific approach has played a part in the development of working boat designs[17]. As Stalkartt has pointed out, design is still in the capable hands of practical builders. This is not to say that there has not been a degree of research and development of the individual components that go to make a boat, but not on the integrated design. Just as in the days of sail, results have been achieved by trial and error, coupled to a keen observation by the boatmen, who are not slow to take up ideas which it will pay them to adopt. One often hears that boatmen are conservative, but that is not the way to describe them. Once they appreciate, as they did over motorisation, the benefits of an innovation, they will adopt it as fast as their limited resources permit. If the motorisation of boats has dragged its feet more than that of road transport, it has been due to the lack of capital or the boatman's fear of losing his independence if he were to borrow.

The structural design of wooden hulls has undergone less change than one might expect from the different stresses set up by sails and propellers. The reason for this is not hard to see: the largest forces exerted on a boat arise from her own weight, when she is thrown about in heavy weather. These far exceed the relatively steady thrust of propulsion. However, because a power boat can be forced faster through the sea she experiences more violent shocks from waves, and needs to be stronger all over to withstand them. The need to locate and design out any useless weights is even more important in motor than sailing boats. The power unit imposes its own weight, propeller thrust and torque, and vibration on the hull in a more localised manner than a sailing rig. This concentration of forces is transmitted to the rest of the hull by the engine bearers, two sister keelsons which extended beyond the extremities of the engine and bolted through the frames or floors which they cross. These joints are bracketed in larger craft to deal with the torsional stresses.

The steadily increasing power of working boats has made vibration a more serious problem. This is set up by either a poor propeller installation or the reciprocating weights of pistons and connecting rods. These cause concern if parts of the boat's structure vibrate with the same frequency, as this could shake the boat to pieces if steps were not taken to detune either the engine or the hull. Prevention is better than cure, but it is not always convenient to avoid the critical engine running speeds and even less likely the engine can be modified to run smoothly. There are a number of detuning devices which can be fitted to the crankshaft or flywheel, if the space and money is available. It is more usual to find more weight has to be added to the structure in the form of stiffening, but extra weight in a boat is hardly an elegant solution. A great deal has and is being done to reduce engine vibration at the design stage and during installation. Better propellers, damped flywheels and rigid/resilient engine mountings which do not upset shaft alignment all further this. Wood as a structural material has good damping properties, unlike some of the more recent ones like foam sandwich, ferro-cement, steel, plywood and GRP, which if used in the form of large thin panels can transmit and amplify vibration.

Wood has a drawback when used in the vicinity of an engine in that it dries out, particularly at the deckhead above and in way of the exhaust, where there is an added risk of fire. This drying-out opens joints and seams starting leaks and rot. To avoid this steel or aluminium structures are often used in these warm areas.

A propeller acts like a pump, which sucks water from forward and discharges it aft. For the pump to work well this water must have a free passage and be relatively free of air bubbles. Propellers cannot work properly astern of bulky sterns and wide sternposts or if they are close to the surface. Many sailing boats had fine runs and ample draft, which met these flow and immersion requirements, but over fine runs raised snags.

If the suction zone of the propeller coincided with the

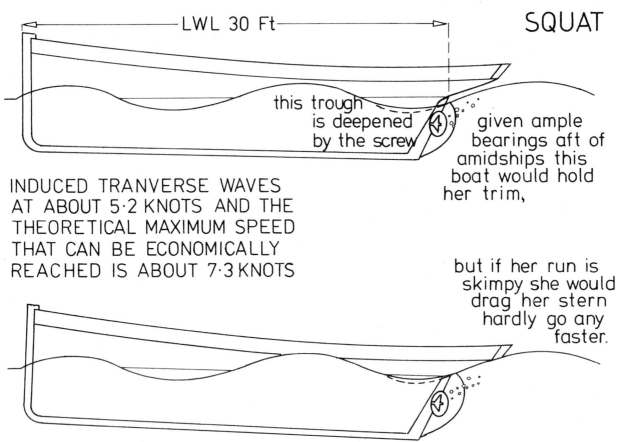

SQUAT

LWL 30 Ft

this trough
is deepened
by the screw

given ample
bearings aft of
amidships this
boat would hold
her trim,

INDUCED TRANVERSE WAVES
AT ABOUT 5·2 KNOTS AND THE
THEORETICAL MAXIMUM SPEED
THAT CAN BE ECONOMICALLY
REACHED IS ABOUT 7·3 KNOTS

but if her run is
skimpy she would
drag her stern
hardly go any
faster.

The lower of the hulls may perform well trawling at lower speeds

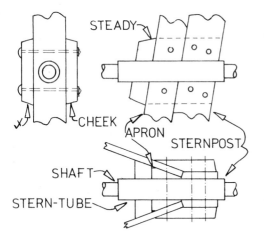

STEADY

CHEEK

APRON STERNPOST

SHAFT

STERN-TUBE

STERNPOST WITH TOO LITTLE
SIDING BRACED WITH CHEEKS

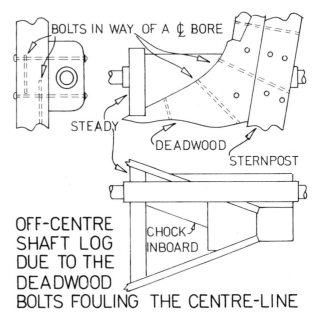

BOLTS IN WAY OF A ₵ BORE

STEADY

DEADWOOD

STERNPOST

OFF-CENTRE
SHAFT LOG
DUE TO THE
DEADWOOD
BOLTS FOULING THE CENTRE-LINE

CHOCK
INBOARD

OFFSET
SHAFT THROUGH PLANKING WITH
SHAFT LOGS INBOARD & OUTBOARD

INSTALLATION OF
STERN-TUBES IN
HULL BUILT FOR SAIL

Top:
Fig 129: Squat.

Bottom:
Fig 130: Installation of stern tubes in hull built for sail.

trough of the induced wave, the stern dropped into its wake. The extra drag set up could stop a free-running boat from going any faster, however much more power was applied, even though the same installation was satisfactory when towing a trawl at lower speeds (Fig 129).

Slow-running propellers apart from being large have to be given thicker shafts than faster turning ones of the same power. As a shaft has to be supported in bearings and provided with a watertight gland where it passes through the hull, a bigger hole than the shaft has to be made, either through the sternpost or the planking. A shaft passing through the planking needs extra support, usually by fitting internal and external shaft logs together with additional transverse frames. To reduce the yaw from this offset thrust, the line of the shaft should pass through the point about which the boat herself turns. An offset shaft was placed on the opposite side to the one used for working gear, as it was more prone to fouling than one on the centreline.

Asymmetrical installations are practicable when there is more than one engine and powers are low. When converting from sail there had to be enough wood left in the sternpost after boring to take the shaft stresses. With only sailing qualities in mind the sternpost would have been made as thin as possible and bolts driven across the intended line of a shaft hole. Devices like cheeks either side of the post could not restore the lost strength in the zone between the two rabbets, where the siding of the sternpost is at its least (Fig 130).

However installed propellers have a bad effect on sailing performance, unless they are small, two bladed and in a close fitting aperture. All these features lower propeller efficiency, and attempts to find a balance between sail and power have not in general met with success. Satisfactory results have however been realised when using mainly sail or power, backed up by relatively small amounts of the other.

Very fine runs do not provide the right amount of space inboard for an engine. There is neither the buoyancy to take the engine weight aft or room for the engine and its fuel tanks unless some of the hold is taken. In some conversions and modern designs the engine is sited forward with a very long shaft. This gives a good deck lay-out for those modern fishing methods that like to work over the stern. Moving the wheelhouse and accommodation right forward adds to the working space and protection for the men on deck.

Another conversion problem was finding the room for an adequately sized aperture on the centre line, especially if the sternpost was well raked and its moulded depth was small (Fig 131). In both cases a common solution was to cut some of the aperture out of the rudder, weakening it considerably and reducing its steering efficiency much more than could be put down to lost area.

In small beach boats the chance of installing central propellers was even less. Even if the sternpost had enough siding it was improbable that there would be the height for an aperture in the short distance between the heel and the tuck. One way out of this was to fit a false sternpost wide enough to form the aperture and then rehang the undamaged rudder astern again of this (Fig 131), and examples can often be seen in use right round the coast. Shaft logs bolted directly to one side or other of the sternpost, like the *Witch of Worbarrow* (p198) are also popular. Though the yawing effect of this slightly off centre thrust was negligible, it interfered with the security of the end fastenings of a number of strakes, which together with vibration were a source of weakness, leakage and decay.

Boats with square sterns, sprung keels and skegs aft lent themselves to motorisation in shape as well as structure. The English and Scottish cobles were like this in many respects, the broad stern of the latter being a feature in modern creel boat design. Before the benefits of this hull form could be appreciated by boats using beaches and drying out harbours, a way of protecting the propeller had to be devised. This is done by fitting tunnels for inboard driven screws if not outboard engines. This type of hull gives a good water flow, ample buoyancy to counter squatting and enough beam aft to fit more than one engine. It lacks the space inboard under the shaft line for a slow-running engine. This drawback was overcome once high speed engines with cranked reduction gearboxes brought the line of the driving flange lower than that of the crankshaft. This type of hull (provisional number 40) developed into one of the main lines of working motor boats, especially in the medium to smaller sizes.

The design of propellers was well advanced by the time that boats got round to fitting them. Then and now their design is a complicated process and largely empirical. Some knowledge of how this process is done is necessary, not so much as to know exactly how to work out trouble-free and efficient power transmissions, but more to get an idea of the inter-relationship between the shape of the propeller and that of the hull. It has been shown already that the shape of the hull can limit the size of a propeller. Conversely the size of the propeller can dictate some of the hull sizes at the design stage. In either case a few sums can get good results without resort to trial and error later on.

The first requirement is that as much of the power available as possible gets converted by the propeller into motion of the boat. If the propeller is too small to absorb all the power, an over-heavy and expensive engine has been fitted. If, on the other hand, the propeller is too big, the engine will begin to labour below its designed operating speed and so fail to give its full power. The blade area of the propeller has to be right for the engine.

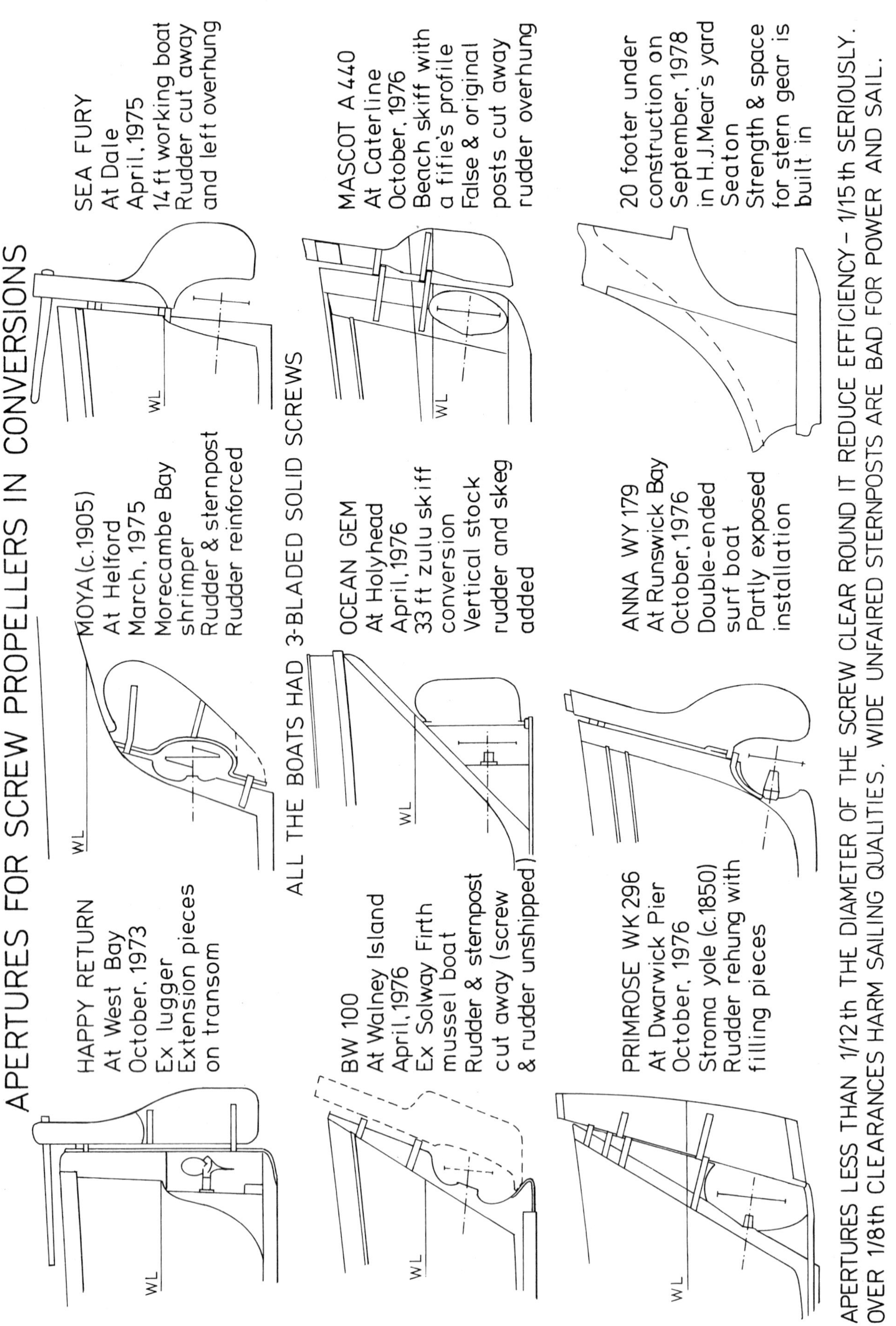

APERTURES FOR SCREW PROPELLERS IN CONVERSIONS

SEA FURY
At Dale
April, 1975
14 ft working boat
Rudder cut away
and left overhung

MASCOT A 440
At Caterline
October, 1976
Beach skiff with
a fifie's profile
False & original
posts cut away
rudder overhung

20 footer under
construction on
September, 1978
in H.J.Mear's yard
Seaton
Strength & space
for stern gear is
built in

HAPPY RETURN
At West Bay
October, 1973
Ex lugger
Extension pieces
on transom

MOYA (c.1905)
At Helford
March, 1975
Morecambe Bay
shrimper
Rudder & sternpost
Rudder reinforced

ALL THE BOATS HAD 3-BLADED SOLID SCREWS

OCEAN GEM
At Holyhead
April, 1976
33 ft zulu skiff
conversion
Vertical stock
rudder and skeg
added

BW 100
At Walney Island
April, 1976
Ex Solway Firth
mussel boat
Rudder & sternpost
cut away (screw
& rudder unshipped)

ANNA WY 179
At Runswick Bay
October, 1976
Double-ended
surf boat
Partly exposed
installation

PRIMROSE WK 296
At Dwarwick Pier
October, 1976
Stroma yole (c.1850)
Rudder rehung with
filling pieces

APERTURES LESS THAN 1/12th THE DIAMETER OF THE SCREW CLEAR ROUND IT REDUCE EFFICIENCY – 1/15th SERIOUSLY.
OVER 1/8th CLEARANCES HARM SAILING QUALITIES. WIDE UNFAIRED STERNPOSTS ARE BAD FOR POWER AND SAIL.

Fig 131: Apertures for screw propellers in conversions.

For any given shaft speed there is an ideal blade area that can absorb a given amount of power. The faster the shaft the greater the power absorbed. There is however a limit to the thrust intensity or blade loading, above which the blade is said to cavitate. This only absorbs power uselessly and in time can waste away the blade. High tip speeds and entrained air encourage cavitation, which can be taken as a sign that the water's ability to transmit power is being overtaxed. The point at which a propeller will cavitate can be estimated with some accuracy if the loading of the blade and its tip speed is known. The design can then go ahead assuming that the shaft will be run rather slower than would cause this.

In most cases it is usual to keep propeller diameter in boats small, as this reduces both draft and tip speed. The blade area is then made rather more than the amount at which any cavitation will occur, when shaft speed, horsepower, boat's forward speed and propeller location are all taken into account. This tends to produce narrow leaf-shaped blades for slow turning screws but wider-than-circular blades for those that are fast. The total desired area is shared between several blades, the widest ones just failing to overlap. Two blades are chosen for auxiliary sailing vessels, so that the drag from them is slight when held upright in their aperture. This is not a sound idea for a propeller that is to be used a lot, as the two-bladed screw loses power and vibrates each time the blades are masked as they pass through the vertical. Three blades are usual in free-running craft, but four or even five for those that have to tow. The actual profile of the blade does not seem to be critical, but the blades most commonly seen approximate to an ellipse whose width lies between a third and a quarter of the propeller diameter.

Once the blade area is known, pitch is the next consideration. In its simplest form a propeller is a screw which would advance through the water as if it were a solid by the amount of its pitch for every full turn. For practical manufacturing reasons, a screw is made with a constant pitch all over the working or after face of the blades. Any hull moving through water takes some of the surrounding water along with it. The speed of this, the wash, is considerable where it meets the propeller, which finds itself working in water that is already flowing in the same direction as it wants to go. To take advantage of this the propeller is given more pitch than it would need if it were to be a screw working in a stationary solid. The amount of extra pitch, called slip, varies a lot depending upon the shape of the hull, the immersion of the propeller and whether it is to be for free running or towing. Figures of 10% to 20% are quoted in text books, but in practice slips as much as 33% are found. In spite of continuous practical experience, experimental testing and theoretical reasoning, the design of a propeller calls for much judgement. In so far as working boats are concerned, reliance is first placed on what the other boats are finding satisfactory, then what the enginemaker recommends and, lastly, and rarely, on calculations.

Variable pitch propellers and those working in nozzles are being used successfully in the largest sizes of boat. They are however an addition to the first cost and a mechanical complication subsequently. They seem to be justified in vessels over 80ft LOA, where the fuel savings are considerable. The use of feathering and reversible pitch propellers is less common in this country for small boats than in Scandinavia.

Normally, inshore boatmen would be back home before lack of food reduced their ability to work. Such men would not take on board more food and water than the amount needed to stave off the discomfort of hunger, thirst and cold, if kept out a bit longer than usual. The introduction of machinery that depended on fuel to keep going brought a factor that previously had never concerned boatmen. Up till then endurance only applied to a man's ability to put up with adverse conditions without wilting. Now that fuel had to be bought and never allowed to run short, something had to be known about it. There were three fuels to choose from diesel, petrol and petrol/paraffin. How do they compare for consumption?

Diesel engines run close to their economical best over a wide range of outputs. The specific consumption for this can be taken as being half a pound of fuel for every horsepower produced for the duration of one hour, or 0.5lb/hp hour. Although 0.4lb/hp hr is obtainable, it is usual to take the larger value, which gives a generous safety margin to allow for bursts of high power, long idling periods and contrary weather – all in a boat's day's work. Thus a 10hp diesel running comfortably at 8hp may be expected to use 8 x 0.5lb of fuel hourly. As diesel weighs 8.8lb/gallon this is the same as $4 \div 8.8 = 0.45$ gal/hour.

Petrol and petrol/paraffin engines run most efficiently with their speed well up, but are wasteful when idling. This is a fact acknowledged by car drivers when comparing mileage per gallon on long trips and in city traffic. Specific consumptions here vary between 0.7 and 0.5lb/hp hour, but 0.6lb/hp hour may be taken as the working figure. Reworking the calculation of the previous paragraph for these two fuels, one gets consumptions for petrol weighing 7.4lb/gal, of 0.65gal/hour and paraffin weighing 8.3lb/gal, of 0.58 gal/hour. This gives a ratio of 1:1.44:1.29 between the consumption of diesel, petrol and paraffin in this example.

It would be ridiculous to suppose a boatman would begin to work things out like this, even if the data were available. Instead he would know fairly well how much fuel the other boats in his harbour were using daily or weekly, which sort of engine suited his work best and, most important of all, how large a tank was required to see him through a working period.

The costs of marine internal combustion engines relate quite closely to the weight of metal that goes into them, providing that a large number of the engines do not include elaborations like vee cylinder blocks, superchargers, sleeve valves or high grade materials normally only found in aero engines. If the engine were very simple and massive, like the early hot bulb semi-diesels, then the cost per lb might be less. The cost rate applicable to an engine depends on to which of three zones it belongs, and an attempt to show this has been made in the form of a graph (Fig 132). This is based on a sample of about 120 British marine engines available in the mid sixties. While there is consistency in Zones 1 and 2, there is a more random spread in the upper zone. This was thought to be due to a wide disparity between the designs involved. As a rough guide only, one would then have expected to pay £0.7/lb for an engine in Zone 1, and £0.5/lb for one in Zone 2. Such a cost exercise is only true for a short period as factors other than the manufacturing cost, like slumps and competition, can cause abrupt fluctuations. Also, for these prices to be significant, they have to be related to horsepower, which in turn depends on engine speed, fuel and design.

The first zone includes all engines which weighed between 100 and 500lb regardless of fuel used but excluded semi-diesels, partly because there were too few to give reliable data but also because they were too low powered to have been of any use in a boat. In order to withstand higher cylinder pressures diesel engines have to have more robust parts than petrol engines of equivalent power. As this makes them heavier they are more costly. There were a large number of engines in Zone 1, and, as they were in close competition with each other, prices were low. In general it can be seen the petrol engines developed up to 50hp and diesels up to 40hp. There was also a small sample of petrol/paraffin engines in this zone developing up to 45hp.

The second zone takes in engines from 400 – 1400lb and is made up almost entirely of diesel engines. The overlap with some of Zone 1 is due to a few heavily-built petrol engines at the bottom of Zone 2, all of which were outmoded for the period. The engines in this zone ran at 1800–2800rpm and developed from 10 up to 100hp.

The third zone includes engines upwards to 44 tons, developing up to 1000hp. While most of these were medium speed engines, some of the lower powered ones were high speed. There was no way of assessing the cost of many of these engines, as the manufacturers did not publish them for their larger models, but where they did there were bigger cost variations than for Zone 2.

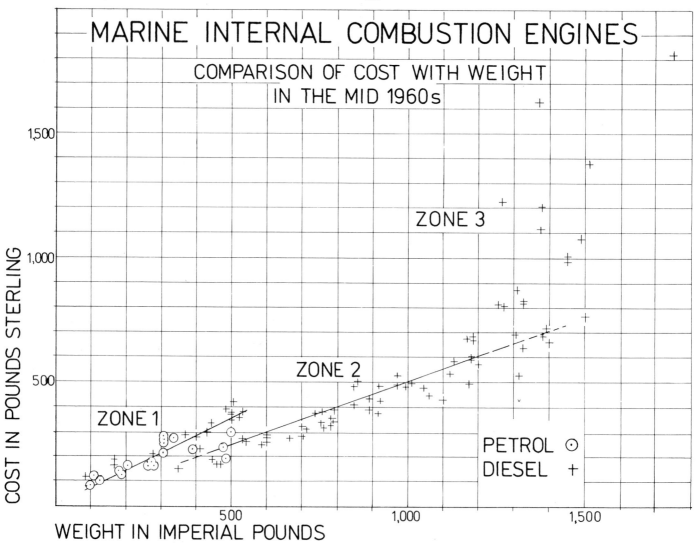

Fig 132: Marine ICEs mid-1960s – comparison of cost with weight.

Fig 133: Marine ICEs mid 1960s – comparison of power with weight.

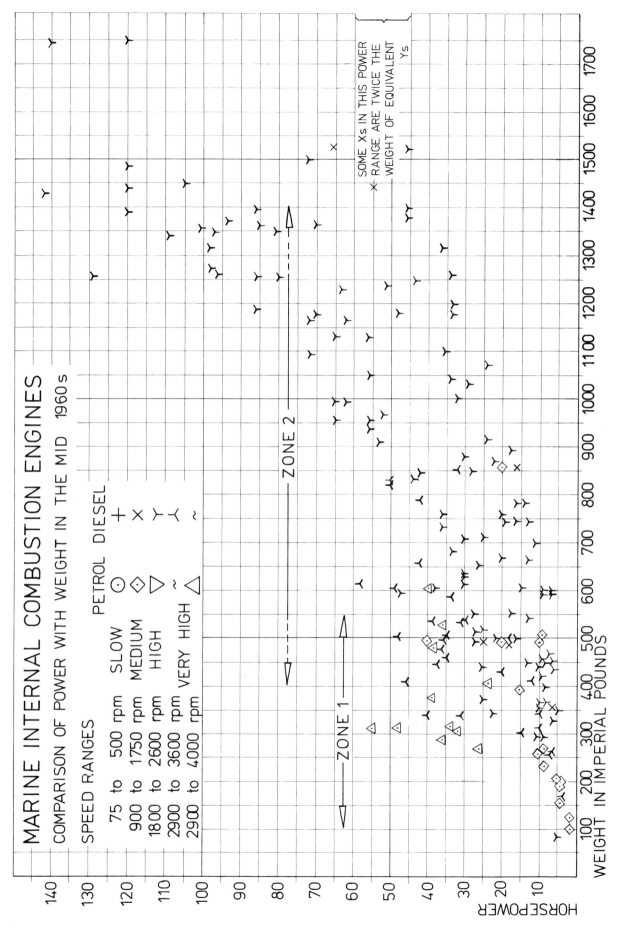

MARINE INTERNAL COMBUSTION ENGINES

COMPARISON OF POWER WITH WEIGHT IN THE MID 1960s

SPEED RANGES

PETROL DIESEL

			PETROL	DIESEL
75	to	500 rpm	SLOW	⊙	+
900	to	1750 rpm	MEDIUM	◇	×
1800	to	2600 rpm	HIGH	▽	Y
2900	to	3600 rpm	VERY HIGH	~	⅄
2900	to	4000 rpm	VERY HIGH	△	~

ZONE 2

ZONE 1

SOME Xs IN THIS POWER
RANGE ARE TWICE THE
WEIGHT OF EQUIVALENT
Ys

HORSEPOWER

WEIGHT IN IMPERIAL POUNDS

Using the same sample, a graph was drawn to see how the weight and horsepower of these engines compared (Fig 133). In the first zone the weight per hp varied from 50lb/hp for medium speed diesels developing 10hp and upwards, down to 30lb/hp for both petrol and diesel engines at the top of the high speed range. There are hardly any engines in this zone that run slower than half way down the high speed range. Very high speed diesels are found to be 20lb/hp at the low end and 12 to 15lb/hp at the top of this range. Petrol engines are even lighter and faster, being only 8 to 10lb/hp at the top of this range. Both types develop from 20 to 45hp.

In the second zone all the engines are high speed. At the slower end the engines weigh from 28 to 40lb/hp and 12 to 20lb/hp at the top end. These engines develop up to 120hp.

To help compare these marine engines to the two extremes of internal combustion piston engine design, it may be said that modern slow-running semi-diesels developing about 75hp per cylinder weigh about 100lb/hp, whereas an 800rpm 4-stroke diesel weighs about 85lb/hp. At the other end of the scale, this can be compared with piston aero engines, which, to suit their airscrews, run at the middle of the high speed range, and weigh as little as 1.25lb/hp for a 1000hp air cooled radial up to 2.5lb/hp for a 120hp in line. This means the heaviest type of marine diesel weighs about 80 times as much as the aero engine developing the same horsepower.

The choice of fuel for a boat was not only a technical one, but also a matter of cost. The cost of fuel varies for reasons other than price of production and distribution, and at any time this may affect the choice of a new engine differently. When the following problem was worked out, a boatman would have paid 75p for a gallon of petrol, 50p for diesel and 47p for paraffin. If one adds the first cost of an engine to its running cost it is possible to discover which engine will have proved the cheapest after any period of time.

Running costs are fuel bills plus maintenance, which can be taken as being similar for all three types of engine. Let us assume that we have a 10hp engine fitted in a small pot boat, which expects to run at 8hp for 50 hours a week, 35 weeks a year, or 1750 hours a year. As a petrol/paraffin engine runs at about 90% power when on paraffin a 11hp engine would have to be bought for this combination fuel. The first cost choice lies between a £290 petrol engine, £320 petrol/paraffin and a £385 diesel. Assuming the fuel consumptions will be the same as those worked out before, a year's fuel usage and cost would be: petrol 1137.5 gals at £853, paraffin 1015 at £477 and diesel 787.5 at £394. This represents a total outlay at the end of the first year of £1143, £797 and £779 respectively, and at the end of the second £1996, £1274 and £1173 respectively. This shows that, on the figures quoted in this case of a heavily-run boat, the diesel engine proved cheapest. In this manner, even the Chancellor of the Exchequer can affect the shape of a boat.

If, however, the initial funds are scarce, a new owner might opt for the cheaper petrol engine with the higher running cost, with the intention of setting this off against the proceeds of his fishing. If he is borrowing from the White Fish Authority and the EEC he may have to follow their recommendations when making this decision.

Apart from the initial and subsequent running costs, there were further factors which had to be considered when choosing a fuel. Until recently it has been difficult to find low power lightweight diesels. Petrol is avoided for its tendency to develop leaks and the risk of fire. A high tension electrical system for ignition is less reliable than compression ignition in a salt-laden atmosphere. In order to make the calculations above, it was assumed that the boat was being run steadily. This is not always the case, as fishing boats habitually go at top speed – out to get the best pitches, and back to get the best markets. In between the engine is kept ticking over to power the winch. This is costly on petrol and wears out the cylinders of diesels. Semi-diesels have similar consumptions to diesels, but cannot be idled for long, as if the hot bulb cools off the engine will stop.

The low efficiency of petrol engines at low speeds was appreciated from the first, and was overcome when motorising Cornish fishing boats by installing two or even three engines each with its own shaft and propeller. This is still being done today in spite of diesels being used. Normally a large engine is placed on the centreline for use when free-running at speed, and a much smaller unit offset for whiffing and while hauling lines or pots. This arrangement, in addition to saving fuel, cuts down wear and spreads maintenance and replacement costs, as well as ensuring a return home should one of the engines fail. Occasionally one finds both a diesel and a petrol/paraffin engine fitted in the same boat, a proliferation of fuels that it would be hard to justify.

Even on a steady course the function of a rudder in a motor boat differs from that in a sailing boat, even more so when manoeuvring. In a sailing boat it is the set of the sails that decide the course, the rudder being used to correct any imbalance between them and the hull. The sails and rudder are used together to change course. In a motor boat, screw thrust and hull resistance act along the same line as the boat's course, so the rudder only has to correct yaw set up by other forces and alter course. The rudder, lying as it does behind the screw, benefits from its wash, which makes it more effective. Most single screws are right-handed, turning clockwise to go ahead as seen from astern. The small thrust to starboard from this is overcome by small rudder angles when under way. When manoeuvring however the effect of the rudder is harder to predict than in a sailing boat. Starting from a steady course and speed, application of rudder turns a motor boat in the desired direction, but on a wider circle than she is heading. This is most evident at the start of the turn. As there are many combinations of boat direction, screw rotation and rudder setting possible, a table has been drawn to show how motor boats with a right-handed screw will usually behave in calm conditions (Fig 134). The actual manoeuvring characteristics of boats can vary from this. The size and type of rudder, distance and direction of screw, size of aperture, shape of the run, speed and area of the screw determines whether at any moment the screw or the rudder will have the greater effect. When a boat behaves consistently, her skipper can use what looks like foolhardiness to a landsman to wriggle her into a crowded berth, quickly and without a scratch.

It has been seen that the change from wind to fuel power has cut down the number of distinct working types because many old designs were unsuitable for conversion. The rest have undergone more or less modification, and where there have been several stages of development, similarity to the original sailing boat may be hard to see. Traditional styles and finishes have lasted and these can indicate origins better than shapes. Development has come from practical experience rather than scientific theory. In the course of change, sailing boat features like deep draft, deadrise, high heeled stability, fine underwater ends and ability to turn sharply have given way to higher sides, space on deck, high initial stability, fuller lines and broad sterns. Distribution of displacement along the length is tuned to the engine and not the rig. As the situation is still fluid no firm conclusion can be made, though it looks as if there are several satisfactory designs in so far as seakeeping and propulsion are involved. It is, however, the fishing that is the problem – modern methods are so good that they run down the stocks of fish they have been designed to catch. This forces a move to a new species, a new fishing method and even a new shape of boat. At present therefore boats which can be adapted to new gear stand the best chance of survival.

Fig 134: Effects of rudder position and screw direction when manoeuvring in calm conditions.

SCREW	BOAT'S DIRECTION					RUDDER
	Steady ahead	**Moving off ahead**	**At rest**	**Moving off astern**	**Steady astern**	
AHEAD	Normal acting rudder	Stern kicks less and starts to move to Port	Stern kicks to Starboard	Stern moves to Starboard as way is lost	Stern moves to Starboard	PORT
		Kick decreases until nil		Sometimes sterns move to Starboard	?	AMID-SHIPS
	(but see text)	Head moves to Starboard	Heading doesn't change	Stern moves to Port as way is lost	Sterns kicks to Port	STAR-BOARD
STOP	Rudder acts normally			Rudder acts normally		P or S
ASTERN	Head pauses then swings to Starboard	Head moves to Port then to Starboard as way is lost	Stern kicks hard to Port	Stern swings to Port	Stern kicks to Port	PORT
	?	Head to Starboard as way is lost	Stern kicks to Port			AMID-SHIPS
	Head pauses then swings to Port	Head pauses then falls off to Port		Swing checked; sterns of some boats will move to Starboard	Stern may swing slightly to Starboard	STAR-BOARD

9.

Some examples of British boats

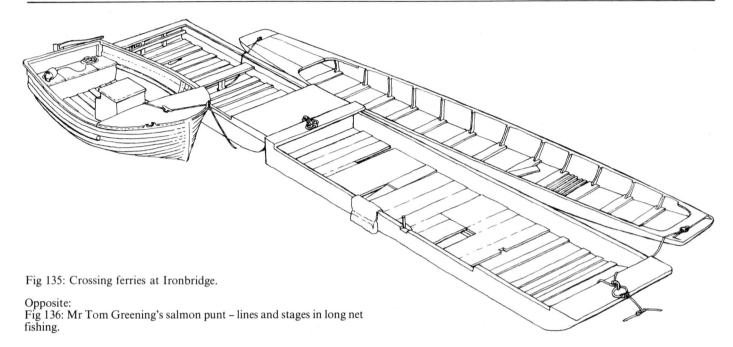

Fig 135: Crossing ferries at Ironbridge.

Opposite:
Fig 136: Mr Tom Greening's salmon punt – lines and stages in long net fishing.

It would not be possible in a single book to describe every type of boat in Britain, especially if the author tried to explain how and why each had developed its particular shape. Much has been done already in this direction by both researchers and contemporary writers, but, even if all of their work were to be put together, there would still be gaps in the types and periods that would need attention. The writers who have dealt with Britain as a whole have been able to make comparisons and draw conclusions about the trends and origins. They could not have done this without the numerous studies in depth that have been made by local amateurs. Such men are well placed to study a distinct type. It takes time to be accepted by boatmen and builder, to watch boats at work in all seasons and weather, in all stages of building and repair, and to uncover the old accounts, pictures and models without which research is incomplete. The uneven manner in which this has been inevitably done accounts for much of the shortfall in our knowledge.

This study has clearly shown how rapidly one type can change or vanish while another develops gradually. This presents a constant risk of missing the first in the course of a few years and failing to detect the second over a longer period. Local men observing, recording and reporting what their own boats and boatmen are doing should reduce this occurrence.

To fill a few of the gaps left by previous writers, this chapter will describe a number of boats whose shape can be attributed to some of the factors outlined in the first part. Wherever possible the boats chosen are of a type which have had insufficient attention given to them in the past. It has been said that a boat does not change in shape and structure without some compulsion. The Severn punt, a scow (04 – numbers in brackets refer to Appendix IV), is probably the most primitive looking type still in use. At first sight, she looks very much as if she had been shaped out of a single tree (Fig 12), as she might once have been when the trees in the Forest of Dean were big enough. Though she is now put together with boards, she has not changed her scow shape since 1807, when six of them appeared together in a drawing of shipping at Tewkesbury. Her relationship with the lightly-built pleasure punts of the Thames is seen more clearly through the more workaday punts used as crossing ferries (Fig 135). There are several examples of Severn punts afloat, though only one of these is now used for long net salmon fishing. The stages in the cycle of working one of these unusually long seines is shown by diagrams (Fig 136). It can be seen that two boats are needed: the larger punt for the net and the smaller one to ferry the muntle man across the river. The smaller boat can be of any handy type, but in this instance was a solidly-built clinker boat of cockle shape(31), such as one might see on the deck of a coaster. The same figure gives the lines of the punt, which has considerable carrying capacity. Her cross-section does not give her much stability, which is reduced even further by

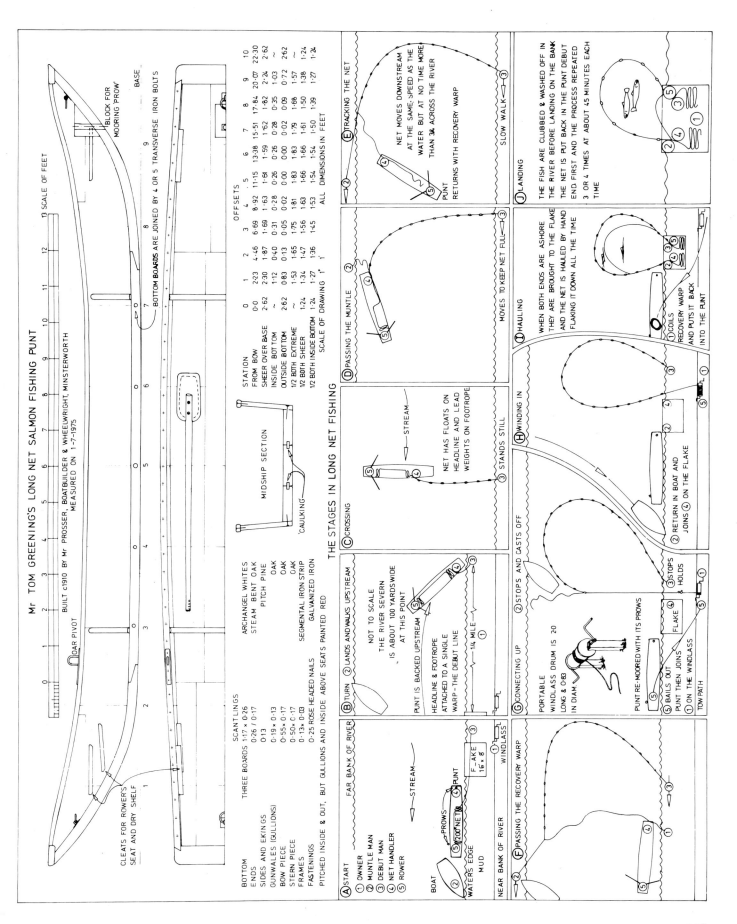

the free water that drains out of the net when it is inboard. This water is shot back over the side using one of the paddles like a shovel; this makes an effective bailer even if it does not sound so. The method of mooring the boat with stakes, called prows, is unusual especially as one of them passes right through the end of the punt.

The boat measured was built at Minsterworth by an uncle of Mr Prosser, who is the present master of a yard capable of any iron- or woodwork involved in the building of a house or cart, but no longer the 'fishing boats' as the punt and cockle were called. A Severn punt is made up of a bottom, two ends and two sides, but has no frames unless as an afterthought for stiffening or repair. The bottom is put together from three 3in Archangel whites, pine boards once imported at Sharpness or Gloucester, and held together by four or five iron bolts running from one side to the other. The plank joins are formed by grooving the edges, inserting a tongue and then caulking at a later stage. The thick bottom took the wear caused by bailing and gave strength to the corners of the box-like sections. The

two ends are oak, bent to the shape of a template, before being scarfed and riveted to each end of the bottom. The 1¾in sides are pitch pine, eked out at either end to gain the height of sheer, and fastened to the ends and bottom by 3in galvanised iron cut nails. In earlier times there were several other punt builders up and down the river, and it was said that their punts could be distinguished by the amount of flare or some other peculiarity.

The shallow draft of these punts allowed them to come close into the bank for many stages of the fishing. It was of interest to find at Newnham, further down the Severn, a Scottish coble being used in place of a punt for this sort of fishing. She was said to have been built by Macpharson and Wishard and shipped down on a lorry. A coble like this has ample bearings aft and her upswept bows would be able to ride the bore better than most other boats.

The long nets are made up on the river bank close to where they are to be used, the owner or an employee doing the work. First an 8ft high row, half as long as the net, of poplar stakes are cut and driven in along the edge of the

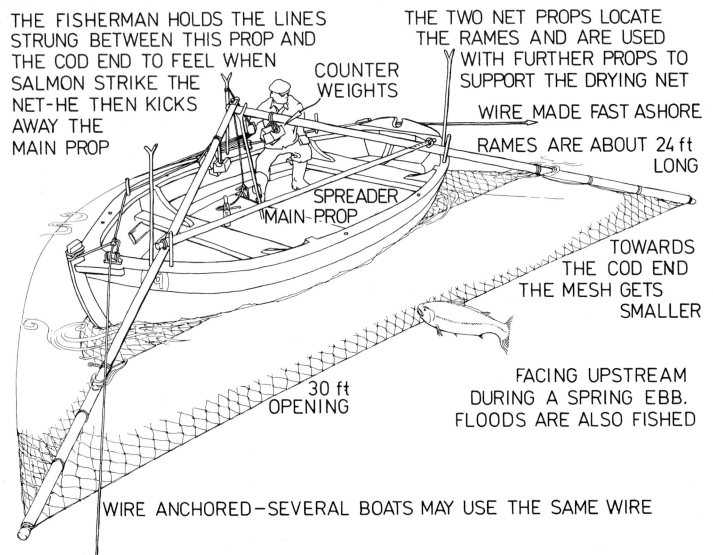

THE FISHERMAN HOLDS THE LINES STRUNG BETWEEN THIS PROP AND THE COD END TO FEEL WHEN SALMON STRIKE THE NET-HE THEN KICKS AWAY THE MAIN PROP

COUNTER WEIGHTS

SPREADER
MAIN-PROP

THE TWO NET PROPS LOCATE THE RAMES AND ARE USED WITH FURTHER PROPS TO SUPPORT THE DRYING NET

WIRE MADE FAST ASHORE

RAMES ARE ABOUT 24 ft LONG

TOWARDS THE COD END THE MESH GETS SMALLER

30 ft OPENING

FACING UPSTREAM DURING A SPRING EBB. FLOODS ARE ALSO FISHED

WIRE ANCHORED—SEVERAL BOATS MAY USE THE SAME WIRE

STOP NET FISHING ON THE SEVERN NEAR GATCOMBE

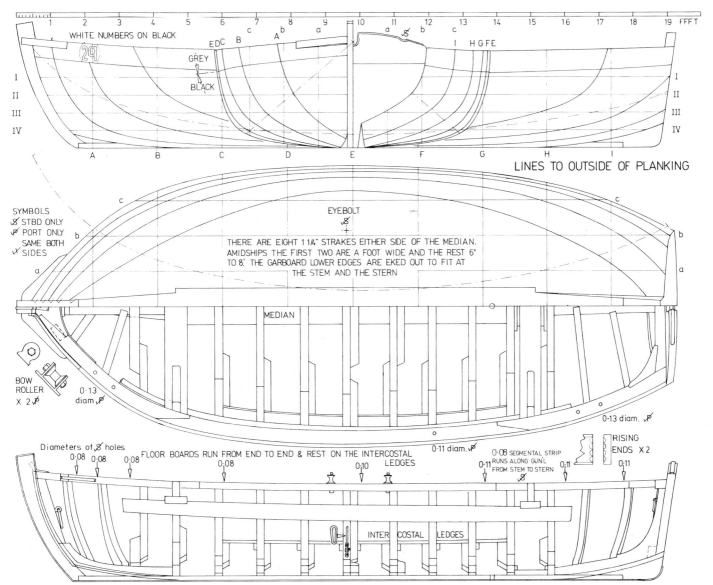

MRS BAYLISS'S STOP NET BOAT No. 29 – MEASURED AT GATCOMBE ON 26th Sept 1976

Left:
Fig 137: Stop net fishing on the Severn near Gatcombe.

Above:
Fig 138: Mrs Bayliss' stop net boat No 29 – lines and construction.

towpath. The head and foot ropes are doubled round and temporarily stopped to these stakes, while the nets, floats and weights are tied into place. The stakes often take root and grow into one of the lines of poplars that form part of this river's landscape, a reversal of the landscape forming the boat. The Severn punt is an example of a boat that has not changed because she is just right for her job, although difficulty in finding a replacement has made one owner shop away from the Severn.

Seven miles down river 'the silver darlings', the salmon, are taken in putchers, basketwork funnels supported on stakes, in lave-nets, worked by waders like shrimp-nets, and in stopping-nets, which are like big lave-nets, spread

and worked by poles attached to special boats moored across the stream[1]. As shown in the diagram the fishing gear is heavy, and the strain put on the boat by the net when it is lowered into a strong current is considerable (Fig 137).

The stop-net boats(10) are worked out of Gatcombe, where there are three belonging to Mrs Bayliss, and twelve miles further down at Chepstow, where the Wye River Authority owns upwards of a dozen more. These boats are very robust, smooth-skinned with stems forward and square sterns. Though the planks are edge-positioned on strong frames, examination shows that there is no keel. Only one man is needed to work each boat, two or three of which fish together in echelon to cover as wide a swath of river as possible. The boats are moved by sculling a single 10ft to 12ft oar with a 3ft to 4ft straight narrow blade, over the stern. The boats are all old – the senior one at Chepstow was said to be 84 years old in 1975 – and they are kept going by taking out any damaged parts and making

169

Fig 139: Wye salmon stop net fishing boats.

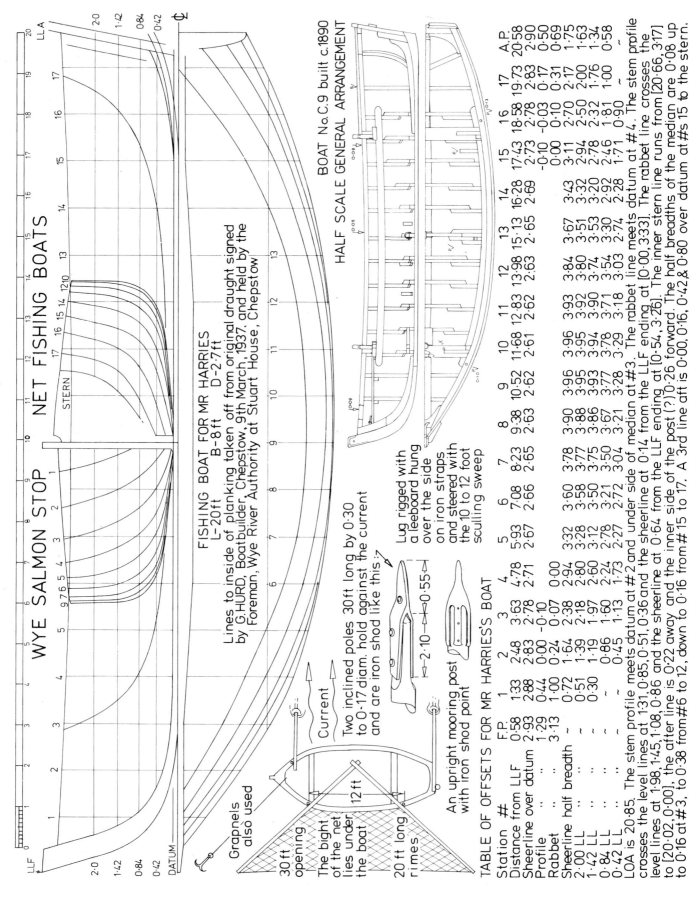

WYE SALMON STOP NET FISHING BOATS

FISHING BOAT FOR MR HARRIES
L–20ft B–8ft D–2·7ft

Lines to inside of planking taken off from original draught signed
by G. HURD, Boatbuilder, Chepstow, 9th March, 1937, and held by the
Foreman, Wye River Authority at Stuart House, Chepstow

BOAT No. C.9 built c.1890

HALF SCALE GENERAL ARRANGEMENT

Current

Two inclined poles 30ft long by 0·30
to 0·17 diam. hold against the current
and are iron shod like this :-

An upright mooring post
with iron shod point

Lug rigged with
a leeboard hung
over the side
on iron straps
and steered with
the 10 to 12 foot
sculling sweep

30ft
opening

The bight
of the net
lies under
the boat

20 ft long
rimes

Grapnels
also used

TABLE OF OFFSETS FOR MR HARRIES'S BOAT

Station #	F.P.	1	2	3	4	5	6	7	8	9	10	11	12	13	14	15	16	17	A.P.
Distance from LLF	0·58	1·33	2·48	3·63	4·78	5·93	7·08	8·23	9·38	10·52	11·68	12·83	13·98	15·13	16·28	17·43	18·58	19·73	20·58
Sheerline over datum	2·93	2·88	2·83	2·78	2·71	2·67	2·66	2·65	2·63	2·62	2·61	2·62	2·63	2·65	2·69	2·73	2·78	2·83	2·90
Profile	1·29	0·44	0·00	–0·10	–0·07											–0·10	–0·03	0·17	0·50
Rabbet	3·13	1·00	0·24	0·07	0·00											0·00	0·10	0·31	0·69
Sheerline half breadth		0·72	1·64	2·38	2·94	3·32	3·60	3·78	3·90	3·96	3·96	3·93	3·84	3·67	3·43	3·11	2·70	2·17	1·75
2·00 LL		0·51	1·39	2·18	2·80	3·28	3·58	3·77	3·88	3·95	3·95	3·92	3·80	3·51	3·32	2·94	2·54	2·00	1·63
1·42 LL		0·30	1·19	1·97	2·60	3·12	3·50	3·75	3·86	3·93	3·94	3·90	3·74	3·53	3·20	2·78	2·32	1·76	1·34
0·84 LL		~	0·86	1·60	2·24	2·78	3·21	3·50	3·67	3·77	3·78	3·71	3·54	3·30	2·92	2·46	1·81	1·00	0·58
0·42 LL		~	0·45	1·13	1·73	2·27	2·72	3·04	3·21	3·28	3·29	3·18	3·03	2·74	2·28	1·71	0·90	~	~

LOA is 20·85. The stem profile meets datum at #2 and under side of median at #4. The stem profile crosses the level lines at 1·31,0·85,0·51,0·36 and the sheerline at 0·14 from the LLF ending at [0·00,3·33]. The rabbet line crosses the level lines at 1·98, 1·45, 1·08, 0·86 and the sheerline at 0·64 from the LLF ending at [0·54, 3·26]. The inner stern line runs from [20·66, 3·17] to [20·02, 0·00], the after line is 0·22 away and the inner side of the post (?)0·26 forward. The half breadths of the median are 0·08 up to 0·16 at #3, to 0·38 from #6 to 12, down to 0·16 from #15 to 17. A 3rd line aft is 0·00, 0·16, 0·42 & 0·80 over datum at #s 15 to the stern.

exact copies, which are then used to replace the damaged parts. The men who work and maintain the boats and their gear are employed by the owners, though Mr Bayliss fishes one of his wife's boats. There are slight differences in the boats and the manner of fishing in the two places.

No-one remembered how the boats at Gatcombe came to be built, and the drawings here were taken off by measuring one of them (Fig 138). This fishing station is completely self-supporting, even the blacksmith work is done on site and Mrs Bayliss, who is a full-time teacher, knits the nets. Making firewood and cider using a horse-power press are amongst the employments during the off-season for salmon. When fishing, these boats moor on wire ropes permanently rigged for the season.

The Chepstow boats were built either from half models or drawings, the Wye River Authority having examples of both. They were built in the local shipyard, almost as if they were small coasters, with a central plank that would not have looked out of place in a trow. The lines given here were traced from the builder's original drawing (Fig 139). At one time the boats here had sails. The Beachley boat, which was larger than the rest (22ft × 7.25ft instead of 20ft × 7ft) had a lug on a 13ft yard set on a 10ft mast and a dagger board case. The rig of the smaller boats was in proportion and a leeboard was hung on straps over the side. Some years ago a conventional clinker boat was obtained from H Ford of Appledore, but she proved unsatisfactory and was sold again recently. These boats moor with an upright pole at the stern, a grapnel upstream from the bows and two slanting poles pointing downstream to starboard from each end.

Though these boats are evidently most suitable for their purpose, they will eventually disappear for the want of a builder. In the meantime, the high price of salmon pays for a laborious form of upkeep. No normal wooden construction could stand up to the shocks from this heavy gear; if this gear is to stay in use it may mean that some other material such as ferro-cement or steel will have to be tried.

The Thames was once one of London's main thoroughfares, not only for lighters fetching cargoes from ship to shore, but also for ferrying passengers across or up and down the river. The principal type of boat used for this was the wherry(26), which appears so often in seventeenth and eighteenth century views of the river that she hardly now needs to be described. She could either be sculled by one man, sculled or rowed by two or, in a larger size, built for three men, rowed randan or have three pairs of sculls. These row wherry types were recognisable at once by their exceptionally long straight overhung bows, which helped passengers to get ashore reasonably dry shod in places where there was no jetty. The sternpost were generally plumb with a full almost circular gunwale aft. E W Cooke's etching of 1823 of four of these wherries, the *Laura*, *Will O' The Wisp*, *Victory* and *Rose In June* at Richmond have more upright and curved stems than the earlier boats[2]. *Laura* and *Will O' The Wisp* were licensed to

carry four passengers each, while *Rose In June* looks longer than the others, and may well be an example of the three-man type.

There is a convincing model of a wherry at the National Maritime Museum[3]. This is 27$\frac{1}{2}$in long and 8in broad, which, if built to a scale of one inch to the foot, represents one of the larger size of wherry. This can be compared with another model at the Science Museum, dated 1781, the full-size version of which was 26ft long and 5.8ft beam[4]. Wherries like these were fitted to take a mast forward, but though wherries were reported as having completed long coastal voyages, from London to Bristol for instance largely under sail, it is not likely that these were of the same sort[5]. Instead, a type more like a hatch boat, in which some writers have noted a resemblance to the Norfolk wherry, would have been more suitable.

The building of bridges, railways and steam boats soon put professional wherries out of business, and the last one of these is illustrated in a book published in 1888[6]. Long before then boating and rowing had become fashionable for recreational outings and competitive amateurs. A wide variety of boat types came and went, starting with the clinker-built wager wherries, funnies and cutters, all made as slender and light as possible, and ending up with today's smooth-skinned shells, eights down to single sculls, some made of GRP further strengthened with carbon filaments. The wherry's place was taken by the skiff for both work and play. Once again Cooke has drawn for us a working skiff hanging in slings from a wharfside crane at Blackwall[7]. There is no need to look back to find out what they were like, as there are still Thames lightermen's skiffs to be seen (p45).

On the recreational side, the skiff developed from about 16ft until she was almost as long as a wherry, so that she could accommodate a sizeable picnic party. She had less overhang to the bow, which had a pleasing curvature, and a raking sternpost with a small transom that flared out the topsides aft to give more room for the sternsheets. The lines of the 24ft skiff given here were taken off from one of Mr W A B Hobbs' boats at Henley (Fig 140). She is no longer hired out but is still raced at regattas by her owner. A better known boat of this type from the same yard starred in a television version of Jerome K Jerome's novel *Three Men in a Boat*. A great number of skiffs, on other rivers and waterways as well as the Thames, were real working boats, in so far as they earned their living by being taken out by those who could not have had this enjoyment otherwise. Boats like this and the river punts were not always built in permanently sited boatyards, but by travelling boatbuilders who would contract to build a number of boats on the premises of a boat hire firm. The work was competitive and the two men working together on a punt would have to pace each other down the two sides, if they were to make a profit.

The rowing arrangement and structure of the wherries and skiffs are interesting. Here the oar, the only means of propulsion practically speaking, was developed to a high

Fig 140: W A B Hobb's skiff, Henley-on-Thames.

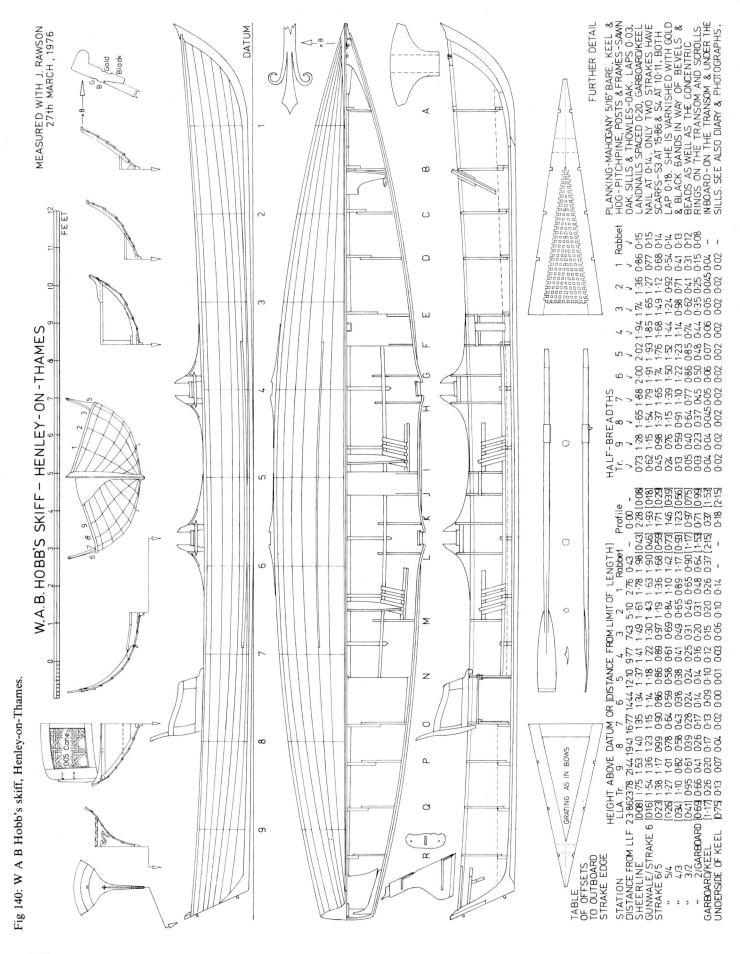

MEASURED WITH J. RAWSON
27th MARCH, 1976

W.A.B. HOBB'S SKIFF – HENLEY-ON-THAMES

FEET

DATUM

GRATING AS IN BOWS

FURTHER DETAIL

PLANKING-MAHOGANY 5/16" BARE, KEEL &
HOG - PITCHPINE, POSTS &FRAMES-SAWN
OAK, SILLS & THOWLES-OAK, LAPS 0·03,
LANDNAILS SPACED 0·20, GARBOARD/KEEL
NAIL AT 0·14. ONLY TWO STRAKES HAVE
SCARFS–S3 AT 15·86 & S4 AT 10·11, BOTH
LAP 0·18. SHE IS VARNISHED WITH GOLD
& BLACK BANDS IN WAY OF BEVELS &
BEADS AS WELL AS THE CONCENTRIC
RINGS ON THE TRANSOM AND SCROLLS
INBOARD. ON THE TRANSOM & UNDER THE
SILLS, SEE ALSO DIARY & PHOTOGRAPHS.

TABLE
OF OFFSETS
TO OUTBOARD
STRAKE EDGE

STATION	LL	A	Tr.	9	8	7	6	5	4	3	2	1	Rabbet	Profile	
HEIGHT ABOVE DATUM OR [DISTANCE FROM LIMIT OF LENGTH]															
DISTANCE FROM LLF	23·86	23·78	21·44	19·41	16·77	14·44	12·10	9·77	7·43	5·10	2·76	0·43	~	0·00	~
SHEERLINE	[·08]	1·75	1·53	1·40	1·35	1·34	1·37	1·41	1·49	1·61	1·78	1·98	[0·43]	2·28	[0·08]
GUNWALE/STRAKE 6	[·016]	1·54	1·36	1·23	1·15	1·14	1·18	1·22	1·30	1·43	1·63	1·90	[0·46]	1·93	[0·18]
STRAKE 6/5	[·023]	1·38	1·17	0·99	0·90	0·86	0·89	0·97	1·19	1·36	1·68	[0·59]	1·71	[0·29]	
" 5/4	[·26]	1·27	1·01	0·78	0·64	0·59	0·58	0·61	0·69	0·84	1·10	1·42	[0·73]	1·46	[·039]
" 4/3	[·34]	1·10	0·82	0·58	0·43	0·38	0·38	0·41	0·49	0·65	0·89	1·17	[0·93]	1·23	[0·56]
" 3/2	[·41]	0·95	0·61	0·39	0·28	0·24	0·25	0·31	0·46	0·65	0·90	[1·17]	0·97	[·075]	
GARBOARD/KEEL	[0·69]	0·66	0·41	0·26	0·17	0·14	0·14	0·16	0·20	0·31	0·48	0·64	[1·53]	0·71	[0·99]
2/GARBOARD	[1·17]	0·26	0·20	0·17	0·13	0·10	0·09	0·12	0·15	0·20	0·26	0·37	[2·15]	0·37	[1·53]
UNDERSIDE OF KEEL	[0·75]	0·13	0·07	0·04	0·02	0·00	0·01	0·03	0·06	0·10	0·14	~		0·18	[2·15]

		Tr.	9	8	7	6	5	4	3	2	1	Rabbet
HALF-BREADTHS												
		0·73	1·28	1·65	1·88	2·00	2·02	1·94	1·74	1·36	0·86	0·15
		0·62	1·15	1·54	1·79	1·91	1·85	1·68	1·65	1·27	0·77	0·15
		0·45	0·98	1·37	1·65	1·76	1·76	1·68	1·49	1·12	0·68	0·14
		0·24	0·76	1·15	1·39	1·50	1·44	1·24	0·92	0·54	0·14	
		0·13	0·59	0·91	1·10	1·22	1·23	1·14	0·98	0·71	0·41	0·13
		0·05	0·40	0·64	0·77	0·86	0·85	0·74	0·62	0·41	0·31	0·12
		0·03	0·23	0·37	0·45	0·50	0·48	0·44	0·35	0·25	0·15	0·08
		0·04	0·04	0·04	0·05	0·06	0·07	0·06	0·045	0·05	0·04	~
		0·02	0·02	0·02	0·02	0·02	0·02	0·02	0·02	0·02	0·02	~

Gold
Black

0·05 Cane

Fig 141: *Nancy*, Thames waterman's skiff – oarlock details.

NANCY–Thames Waterman's Skiff of 1873
Her easily maintained wooden oarlock

PUT TOGETHER

TAKEN APART

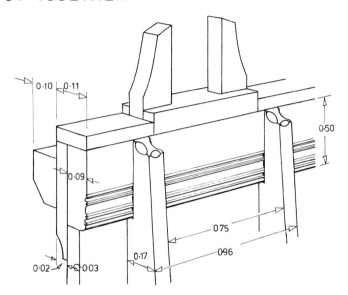

order of efficiency, which was taken ultimately even further by the addition of outriggers and sliding seats. But even without these refinements, these Thames boats were taking full advantage of spreading the oarlocks as far apart as possible, while minimising the waterline beam. They adopted spoon blades and designed out weight even down to the oarlocks. The design of the thowles of the waterman's skiff *Nancy* of 1873 in the National Maritime Museum is an example of fine engineering, not only from the aspect of stressing, but also from practical maintenance and upkeep. Because of the small scantlings brought about by weight reduction, the tholes and the sills in between wore rapidly and became prone to breakage. It is impressive to find that all the parts of these oarlocks are interchangeable and the time taken to make a replacement is negligible (Fig 141).

The structures of the wherry and the skiff are much alike, both employing edge-joined strakes and a disconnected system of framing. In the six-strake wherry model only the main body has floors, which reach out to the third strake. Spaced in between each of these are the futtocks spanning the bilge from the second to fifth strakes. Above that again are pairs of top timbers for each of the oarlocks, once more on separate stations to the other timbers (Fig 41). The frames of the skiff at Hobbs is a bit different. At each end of this boat the floors and futtocks lie side by side, though not directly fastened together. Amidships, there are fewer floors than futtocks, all on different stations. There are no top timbers, some of the futtocks being sited and extended to give support to the oarlocks and thwarts where this is needed. The futtocks are sawn to shape and span the second to fifth strakes.

There are other minor variations as well as these in Thames estuary and river boats. All in all the impression is that the use of sawn rather than grown timbers for disconnected framing is general. Without full knowledge of all the intermediate stages these boats have passed through, it is impossible to be certain. However on balance, it would seem that what originally may have been a combination of dugout and rafting practices have, under the pressures to lighten these lovely boats, taken their structures to the limits of possibility with wood.

If one travels south then west from the mouth of the Thames a gradual change in framing methods is seen (Fig 142). At Rye, a 15-strake clinker beach boat was being built at Philip's yard. This boat's floors were framed partly with grown timbers and partly with fabricated 'leaf spring' ones reaching out to the lap of seventh and eighth strakes. The cants for'd and aft and the intercostal futtocks were steamed timbers spanning from the fifth strake to the gunwale. At Newhaven a similar sized 15-strake boat was building at Lowers, but with an elliptical, in place of a lute, stern. Here only grown floors were used, out to the lap of the sixth and seventh strakes. The intercostal futtocks were steamed timbers from the lap of the second and third strakes up to the gunwale. These were stationed off centre to pick up one of the two rows of fastenings between floors (Fig 143). In both these Sussex-built boats, massive stringers are bolted through the floor heads to support the beaching bilge keels outboard. Further west at Lyme Cobb on the Dorset and Devon border, the 14-strake *Swan* built of wych elm at Beer in 1957 had gunwale to gunwale steamed timbers with grown floors three or four

173

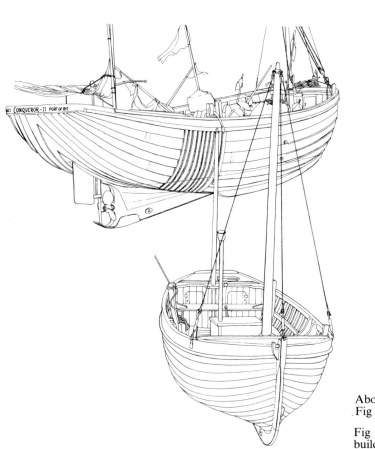

Above:
Fig 142: East Sussex beach boats built by R Lower & Son of Newhaven.

Fig 143: Variations in the framing worked by two East Sussex boat-builders

VARIATIONS IN THE FRAMING WORKED BY TWO EAST SUSSEX BOATBUILDERS

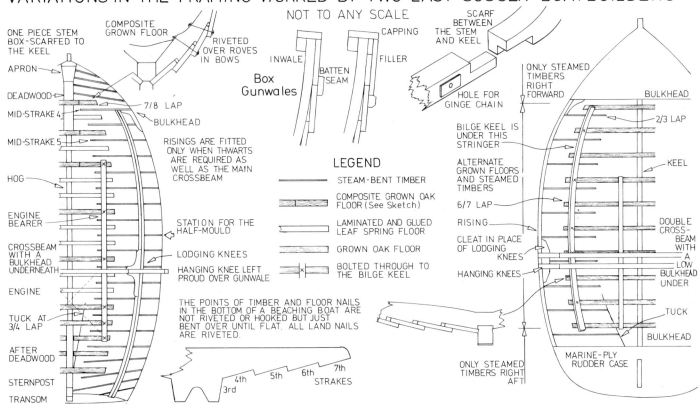

NOT TO ANY SCALE

ONE PIECE STEM BOX-SCARFED TO THE KEEL

COMPOSITE GROWN FLOOR

RIVETED OVER ROVES IN BOWS

APRON

DEADWOOD

MID-STRAKE 4

MID-STRAKE 5

7/8 LAP

BULKHEAD

HOG

RISINGS ARE FITTED ONLY WHEN THWARTS ARE REQUIRED AS WELL AS THE MAIN CROSSBEAM

ENGINE BEARER

CROSSBEAM WITH A BULKHEAD UNDERNEATH

STATION FOR THE HALF-MOULD

LODGING KNEES

ENGINE

HANGING KNEE LEFT PROUD OVER GUNWALE

TUCK AT 3/4 LAP

AFTER DEADWOOD

STERNPOST

TRANSOM

CAPPING

INWALE

BATTEN SEAM

FILLER

Box Gunwales

SCARF BETWEEN THE STEM AND KEEL

HOLE FOR GINGE CHAIN

ONLY STEAMED TIMBERS RIGHT FORWARD

BULKHEAD

2/3 LAP

KEEL

BILGE KEEL IS UNDER THIS STRINGER

ALTERNATE GROWN FLOORS AND STEAMED TIMBERS

6/7 LAP

RISING

CLEAT IN PLACE OF LODGING KNEES

HANGING KNEES

DOUBLE CROSS-BEAM WITH A LOW BULKHEAD UNDER

TUCK

BULKHEAD

MARINE-PLY RUDDER CASE

ONLY STEAMED TIMBERS RIGHT AFT

LEGEND

	STEAM-BENT TIMBER
	COMPOSITE GROWN OAK FLOOR (See Sketch)
	LAMINATED AND GLUED LEAF SPRING FLOOR
	GROWN OAK FLOOR
	BOLTED THROUGH TO THE BILGE KEEL

THE POINTS OF TIMBER AND FLOOR NAILS IN THE BOTTOM OF A BEACHING BOAT ARE NOT RIVETED OR HOOKED BUT JUST BENT OVER UNTIL FLAT. ALL LAND NAILS ARE RIVETED.

3rd 4th 5th 6th 7th STRAKES

18.5 Foot LUTE STERNED BOAT WITH 15 STRAKES A SIDE, BUILDING AT PHILIPS' YARD, RYE, OCTOBER 1974

BOTH ARE BUILT ON ONE HALF-MOULD

20 Foot ELLIPTICAL STERNED BOAT WITH 15 STRAKES A SIDE, BUILDING AT R. LOWER & SONS, NEWHAVEN, OCTOBER 1974

Fig 144: Perth-built rod fishing coble No 1.

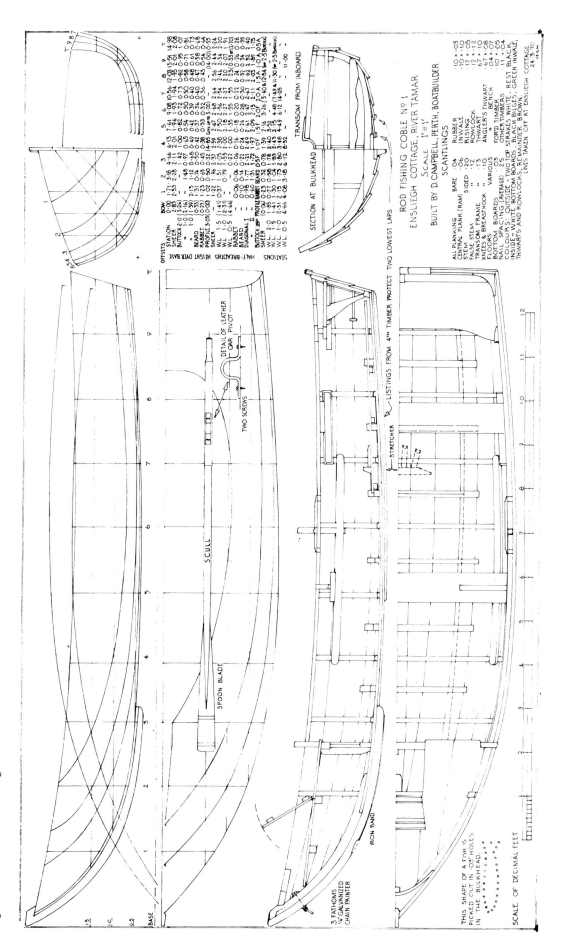

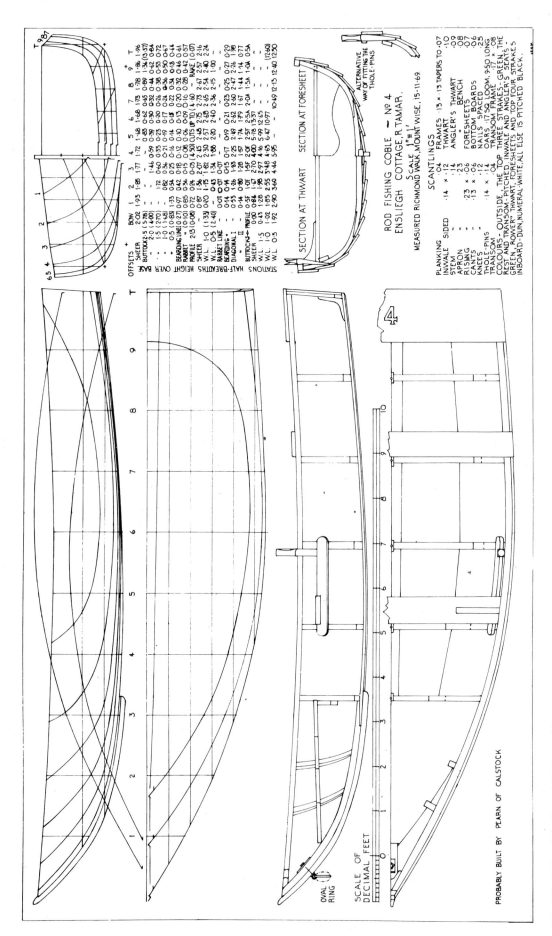

Fig 145: Calstock-built rod fishing coble.

timbers apart. As boats can dry out in shelter and not have to beach at the Cobb, the bilge keels are only supported by a few short internal cleats. In all these three motor boats the midship thwart, no longer needed as a seat, has been kept in the form of a stout beam secured at each end to the rising by a pair of lodging knees. Further west, especially in Cornwall where more and smaller boats have edge-positioned planking, a number of control frames with several steamed timbers between each are found.

No clear progression from sawn through grown to steamed timbers is evident northwards from the Thames. Essex has become an area of dormitories and yachts, which, though many fine barges and smacks have been re-stored here, has lost the identity of all but a few of the working boats. This is not true of the Suffolk and Norfolk coasts, where the motor boats working off the beaches and out of the rivers still look like their sailing forerunners. Timbers are steam bent with occasional continuous frames in the larger boats. The round bateau-shaped Norfolk canoe (07) also has this frame arrangement (Fig 47).

The Scottish coble(12) is distributed over an even wider area than the English variety. She is mainly found from Berwick-on-Tweed to Dornoch Firth, but also in well separated places on the coast of Scotland, Portree and Dunnet Bay for instance, as well as on the rivers and fresh water lochs. The type has been introduced into England, on the Severn (p168) and the Tamar (p166). Nowhere in Scotland is the coble the dominant type or as numerous as the English cobles are in Northumbria.

The usual work for Scottish cobles is commercial salmon fishing, which makes them a seasonal type that works from May to August and lays up for the rest of the year. Salmon are taken by seine-nets off shore and by stake, bag, drift and set-nets off the coast, all of which methods require the use of a coble. The coble is also used for private rod fishing as the beamy net-board aft makes an ideal angler's seat. The Duke of Bedford brought one or more of these boats to his fishing estate, Ensliegh Cottage, on the Tamar. These have been copied locally. Drawings of both are included as examples of a type that have moved from one set of surroundings to another as there was nothing suitable on this English river (Figs 144 & 145).

The forms of the English and Scottish cobles are similar – their plank keels, sharp stems, truncated sterns and a 'deck' right aft[8]. There are also distinct differences in their appearance, the Scottish ones being more box-like aft and abruptly upswept forward. Peter Anson included many of these boats in his views of Scottish fishing villages[9]. They are so much part of the everyday scene, he has rarely drawn them with the detail he gives to the sailing boats and steamers, except for two at Balintore. In the summer of 1929 his drawings show cobles at Ross, Burnmouth, Cock-burnpath, Usan, Catterline, Portlethen, Port Errol and Rockfield, which look even more like the shorter and simpler Donegal curraghs than English cobles. The Scots coble shape is able to take a load of wet nets and stay afloat and dry in shallow water and surf. They vary from thirty foot down to twelve foot in overall length, and even less when used as a tender to a larger coble out on a mooring.

The Scottish coble is primarily a rowing boat using a bull oar and a single tholepin, much the same as an English coble, Irish curragh and Chesil Bank lerret. Many of the larger cobles today have inboard engines driving a propeller in a tunnel or one or two, often powerful, outboard engines clamped to brackets on the square stern.

The ancient salmon companies that operate by employ-ing fishermen in cobles build them for themselves and for sale to others. The Berwick Salmon Fisheries Co Ltd. had been trading for nearly a century before its incorporation in 1854. At the end of the eighteenth century the Tweed salmon fisheries were employing 300 fishermen; nowadays this one company employs 90 fishermen, which represents about half the total in this area. The men are formed into crews of 7 each with two cobles. The seine-nets are from 40 to 50 fathoms long with the depth to suit the water being fished. Such a crew can make 8 'drags' an hour or 30 drags in a fishing tide of about 4 hours. Counting those laid up out of season in 1976, there were not less than 28 cobles at Spittal. All these boats are built and maintained here since they moved from Berwick a few years ago. George Lee the great-great-grandfather of the present boatbuilder, David Lee, built the coble Grace Darling and her father took out to the steamer *Forfarshire* when she ran aground in the Farne Islands in 1838. A coble which is claimed to be the same one is on view at the Grace Darling Museum at Bamburgh, and she is a fine example of an $21\frac{1}{2}$ft English coble of the sort that was used for salmoning and foying (Fig 146). There would seem to be a discrepancy here; unless the Lees were building the English sort of coble one hundred and fifty years ago, one has to wonder what sort of boat the Darlings actually used here on the present borderline between the two types.

Scottish cobles are now being built of GRP as well as wood. The well established firm of J & D R Sellar Ltd. of Macduff makes a 30ft glass coble and Newhailles Plastic of Trenant does a 15 footer. The Scottish coble is an example of a type that has stayed the same for a long time, as it fulfilled the needs of salmon fishing in a large area where there were other sorts of boats fulfilling other activities. The introduction of motors has shown the suitability of the broad stern for screw propulsion, especially if combined with more conventional bows with stems.

It is an open question whether or not the plank keel cobles have an Irish origin, and would require more research to answer. There can be little doubt however that the more widely distributed and numerous classes of Scottish boats which have or had standing sandstrakes can look to Norway for their origin, particularly those that have no rabbets cut into their keels. The Shetlands, Fair Isle and the Orkneys might have provided examples of this feature had they not fallen outside the study limits. However, the islands of Lewis and maybe Stroma once had boats that were more Scandinavian than British, in shape and structure.

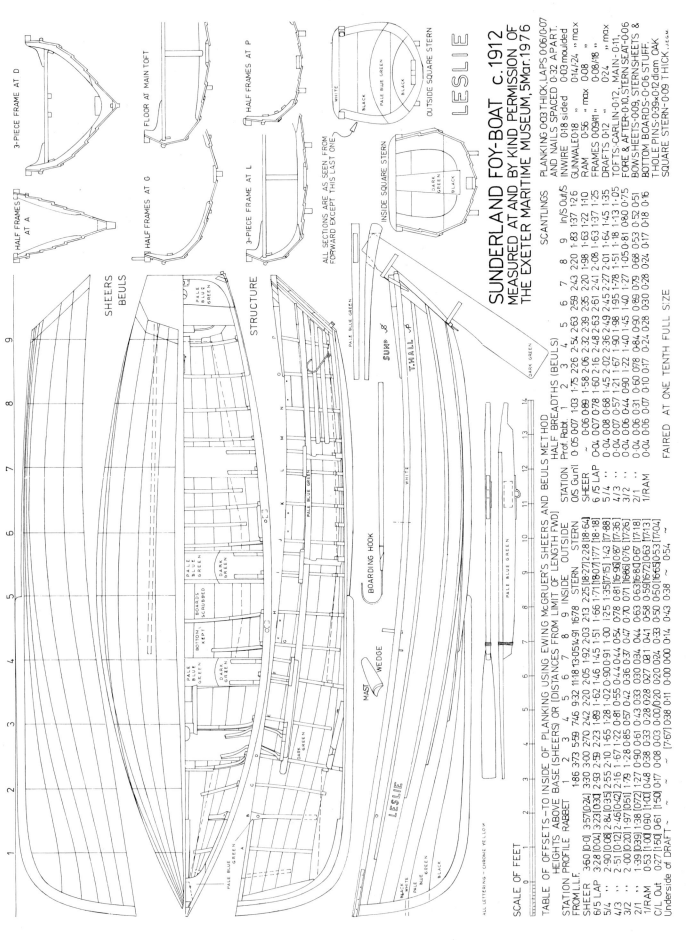

Fig 146: *Leslie*, Sunderland foy boat – lines.

The sandstrake, as the first strake out from the keel is called in North Britain, is said to be standing if it has a lot more deadrise than the ones immediately outboard. This produces a marked reverse curve in the floor of the mid-section, like one sees in modern sailing yachts (Fig 147). Unlike most garboards in Britain, the standing strake has much less twist, nor is there the need to locate its edge in a rabbet. This last is due to the small angle this almost upright strake makes with the vertical surfaces of the sides of the backbone. No British boats have been found that eliminate rabbets altogether but some of the old Scottish open boats, Captain Washington's example from Aberdeen for instance, might well have been of this kind. It is safe to say that the further south one comes down the east coast of Scotland the less noticeable the Norse influence becomes until it re-occurs with the Danish colonisation of Northumbria. The forward end of the garboard in an English coble is like that of a standing strake.

John Murdo Macleod, Senior Lecturer in the Building Department at Lews Castle College, Stornoway, is descended from the one and only surviving boatbuilding family that used to build the sgoth Niseach. This is the Gaelic name for the skiff that worked out of the Port of Ness, a man-made harbour a bare mile south-east of the Butt of Lewis, the northernmost head of the Outer Isles. He has been good enough to enlarge upon two articles he has written about these boats[10].

Before the harbour wall was built in 1836, smaller mainly rowing boats were enough for hand line fishing for local needs. The sgoth then developed into a distinct type which reached a peak of 30 boats during the last twenty years of the nineteenth century. She was a double-ender, 30-31ft over all, 21ft on the keel, 11ft beam and from 4.3 to 4.7ft deep. The 6-man crew pulled oars or set a single dipping lug. She had a curved raked stem and a straight raked sternpost, with a slight drag to the keel. There were 12 clinker strakes a side, the first three of which formed the reverse in the mid-section. This made her fine underwater, rather fuller aft than forward. The hull flared out above water so she looked somewhat bluff-ended, chiefly at the sheerline aft. The principal fishery was for ling, much of which was cured, being brined and air dried, for sale in Ireland. That these open boats were able to work out in the Atlantic and the Minch, which could be worse, tells of their seaworthiness (Fig 49). This century saw a decline of the ling fishery, the fleet only numbered four in 1910 and nothing by 1920. The last sgoth of this size was the *Dell* (SY 455), built in 1918 by John Macleod's grandfather. She was

Fig 147: Standing strakes, using Captain Washington's Aberdeen fishing boat as an example.

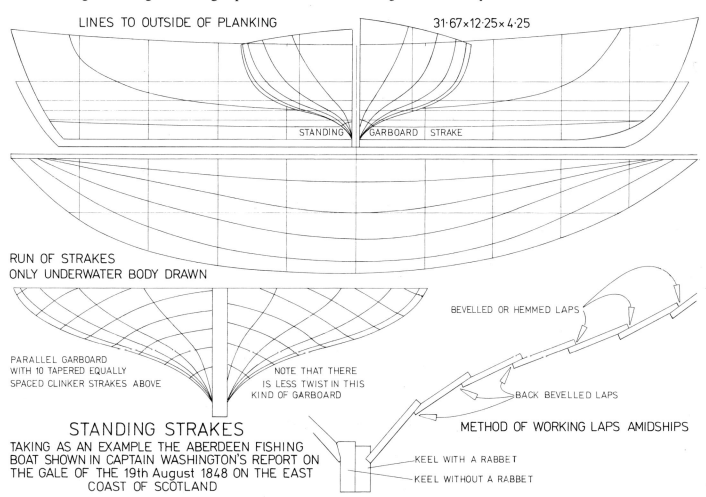

LINES TO OUTSIDE OF PLANKING

31·67 × 12·25 × 4·25

STANDING GARBOARD STRAKE

RUN OF STRAKES
ONLY UNDERWATER BODY DRAWN

PARALLEL GARBOARD
WITH 10 TAPERED EQUALLY
SPACED CLINKER STRAKES ABOVE

NOTE THAT THERE
IS LESS TWIST IN THIS
KIND OF GARBOARD

BEVELLED OR HEMMED LAPS

BACK BEVELLED LAPS

METHOD OF WORKING LAPS AMIDSHIPS

STANDING STRAKES
TAKING AS AN EXAMPLE THE ABERDEEN FISHING
BOAT SHOWN IN CAPTAIN WASHINGTON'S REPORT ON
THE GALE OF THE 19th August 1848 ON THE EAST
COAST OF SCOTLAND

KEEL WITH A RABBET
KEEL WITHOUT A RABBET

a sailing boat until 1925 and with an engine last went to sea in 1934. A smaller but in most respects similar variety was then built. This measured 25–26ft long, 16–17ft on the keel and 9ft beam and was more suited for inshore work, mainly for haddock and herring.

In 1910 it took two men 8 weeks to build a sgoth for about £35 without the sail and rigging. Building took place outside as well as indoors, the order of work being much like the rest of Britain. Planking proceeded ahead of framing. The floors were inserted as soon as the bilges were reached, and the rest of the frames after planking was finished. The sandstrakes were tapered in section, having been sawn out of a 7in × 2½in baulk using a partly diagonal cut. Each was then back soled to give a 2in fay of the proper bevel all along its length. They were then fastened to the rabbetless keel. Rabbets were cut into the stem and sternpost, extra bearding being obtained by deadwoods fitted where the posts met the keel. The second strakes were also back soled and had to be in place before the two shadow moulds, one forwards and one aft, could be used to control shape. The nearly circular sheer strake aft, characteristic of the Scottish west coast, had to be steam-bent or boiled into place.

The framing arrangement, starting from forward was as follows: two cant frames joggled to the laps, floors 4in moulded 2in sided at 14in centres to amidships, then 3½in moulded 2in sided at 24in centres. Forward the frames have their futtocks side-butted to their floors, but aft of that the futtocks were intercostal between the floors. There were two more cants aft. The heads of all the cants and futtocks were checked over the 2¼in moulded 2½in sided inwales. The risings and shelves were notably sturdy being 1¼in moulded 7in sided and 9in moulded 3in sided respectively. The risings spanned the plumb frames, while the shelves went no further than the frames next beyond the thwarts, which were 11in × 3in. The scantlings of the sgoth's midship structure are not thought to be exceeded by any other boat type in Britain (Fig 41). It can be seen that the framing is concentrated in the middle third of the boat, where the thwarts, risings and shelves combine to share out the stresses set up by a fully laden and hard pressed hull. The fore end had to be free of obstruction for stepping the mast, which was only up when under sail. The starboard after end was kept for shooting and hauling fishing gear.

The sgoths, *Peaceful* (SY31), *Jubilee* and *Oigh Niseach* (SY56) show boatbuilding skills being handed down within a family, and each of them was wholly built by one person. The first was built by John Macleod's grandfather in 1913 and was last at sea in 1947. She survived until 1972 when she was vandalised beyond repair. After grandfather's death, the father John F Macleod built the *Jubilee* in 1935 which worked under sail until she was engined in 1947. In 1979 a few enthusiasts of the Ness Historical Society launched an appeal to buy and restore her (Fig 148). Thanks to private and public donations and the acceptance of the restoration by the Manpower Services

Commission as a Special Temporary Employment Programme, this sgoth went to sea under sail again in 1980. 18 months before, John Macleod had started to build a new sgoth, the *Oigh Niseach* for Garry Gualach, a private outdoor adventure centre at Invergarry. The third generation worked only during holidays and weekends without taking any time off teaching, using all his forbear's methods, save that he had to use copper seam nails as galvanised ones were unobtainable. She was almost the same as the *Jubilee* and quite by chance the two boats were launched at the same time and on at least one day they sailed in company (Fig 149). The *Oigh Niseach* was then taken 200 sailing miles to Loch Hourn, the nearest sea loch to the centre, by her owner Captain Grey and a guest crew. It is earnestly hoped that John Macleod will publish in full what he knows about the sgoths, which without his efforts would have vanished thirty years ago.

The men of Lewis have had a long tradition of crewing in ocean-going ships, but Stornoway is also the base of a fleet of modern middle distance fishing boats, some of which are built of ferro-cement at Scrabster. There are numbers of crofter's boats, copies of Norwegian prams or imported from the mainland as there are no full time boatbuilders in the Outer Isles any longer.

At Devonport, where the two naval yards stretch almost three miles along the east bank of the Tamar, there used to be colonies of watermen at Moon Cove, North Corner, Torpoint and Mutton Cove. The boats they used were up to 18ft, clinker-built, fine forward and roomy aft. They were rowed by one waterman using 10ft spoon bladed oars pivotted in pairs of tholepins (Fig 150). Apart from the 100-year-old *Parson Gay* and *Emma* still afloat in Tamar Canal Quay and taking part in regattas, there other examples of watermen's boats to be seen. One of these is the *Isis* at the National Maritime Museum, 12 strakes a side, 16ft long, 5ft beam and 2ft deep. Her timbers are spaced at 9in intervals which is light for a working boat. The arrangement of land nails – two hooked with a roved one between – suggests that she started with single roved nails, which after a time were not enough, and so the hooked nails were added later. This boat was converted to take a sail, by the addition of a centreboard case and a deck forward of the mast, but this was not usual. There is no work for watermen now but there is for these boats. Some like the *Isis* have been turned into recreational sailing boats, others motorised for amateur fishing, while a few are still working on the upper reaches of the Tamar, seine-

Top:
Fig 148: Sgoth *Jubilee* before restoration.

Middle:
Fig 150: Tamar waterman's boat on Torpoint Hard. Shape of stemhead suggests she was built by Norris.

Bottom:
Fig 149: Sgoth *Jubilee* after restoration.

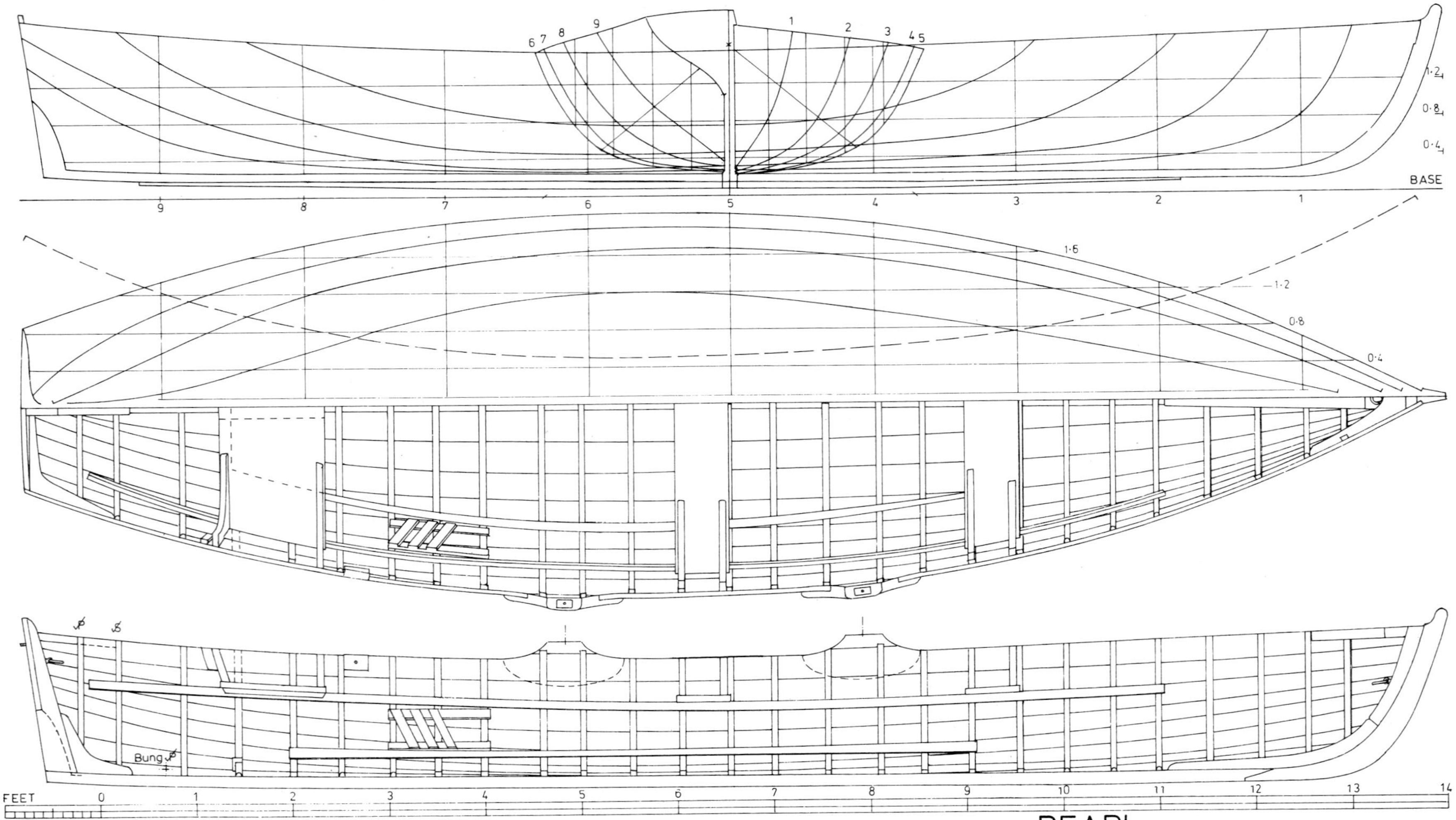

PEARL

ONE OF ALEC BLAGDON'S HIRE SKIFFS BUILT BY MR KESSEL AT MOON COVE, MORICE TOWN IN DEVONPORT IN 1904 FOR £8/10/- INCLUDING TWO 8' SPOON BLADED OARS

MAXIMUM SCANTLING SIZES

KEEL	OAK	0·13m × 0·12s	RISING	TEAK	0·04m × 0·08s
STERNPOST	"	× 0·16s	THWARTS	"	0·06 stuff
STERNPOST	"	0·23m × 0·12s	SHEERSTRAKES & PADS	"	0·045 & 0·12stuff, 0·065 lap
Fwd DEADWOOD	"	× 0·23s	PLANKING	ARCHANGEL WHITES 0·035 "	0·075 "
Aft "	"	× 0·14s	TIMBERS	CANADIAN ROCK ELM	0·05m × 0·03s
BREASTHOOK	"	× 0·09s	" " "		0·06m × 0·04s
HANGING KNEES	" various	× 0·07s	2/3 BILGE-KEEL #8-22 GREENHEART		0·05m × 0·05s
QUARTER "		× 0·09s	3/4 " 10-21 "		0·07m × 0·06s
APRON "		0·12m × 0·23s	FALSE KEEL		0·08m × 0·12s
TRANSOM	ELM	0·055 stuff	SKIRT RAIL	MAHOGANY	0·03m × 0·12s

One land-nail between timbers. Boat is varnished outboard down to the 3/4 laps then green, and down to 6/7 laps inboard then pale ochre. Measured with N. Bradley at Richmond Walk on 27th Dec.1977. The rudder, bottom-boards, back-board with wrought iron wings, oars and crutches were not available.

TABLE OF OFFSETS – Conventional Draught to Inside of Plank

STATION #	Fwd Profile	Rabbet	1	2	3	4	5	6	7	8	9	Aft Profile
Distance to LLF	[0·00]		1·48	2·96	4·44	5·92	7·41	8·89	10·33	11·85	13·33	~ 14·81
Heights over Base 1·6 BUTTOCK	1·81	[0·03]	1·74	1·67	1·62	1·58	1·54	1·40	1·64	1·74	1·90	1·67 [14·79]
0·8	1·63	4·21	1·67	1·62	1·45	0·88	0·75	0·93	1·40			1·67 [12·43]
0·4	1·67	[2·78]			1·49	0·65	0·54	0·47				1·79 [13·78]
1·2	1·73	[1·82]			0·65	0·44	0·36	0·32	0·33	0·53	0·83	1·46 [14·76]
0·8	1·77	[0·94]			0·82	0·37	0·27	0·30	0·28	0·26	0·27	0·35 0·62 0·99 1·40 [14·71]
RABBET LINE	~	~	0·26	0·23	0·22	0·22	0·22	0·24	0·25	0·27	0·33	1·40 [14·33]
Underside KEEL	~	~	0·15	0·14	0·13	0·13	0·14	0·15	0·16	0·18	0·23	[14·55]
FALSE "	~	~	[2·73]	0·12	0·03	0·04	0·08	0·08	0·04	0·08	0·14	[13·55]
Bths ½ SHEERLINE	0·03	[0·03]	0·06	[0·27]	0·61	1·25	1·66	1·92	2·04	1·95	1·72	1·36 0·86 [14·77]
0·4 LEVEL LINE	0·02	[0·20]	0·07	[0·44]	0·55	1·11	1·52	1·77	1·89	1·90	1·77	1·50 1·02 0·10 [14·67]
0·8	0·02	[0·38]	0·07	[0·64]	0·39	0·92	1·29	1·53	1·67	1·65	1·51	1·18 0·59 0·04 [14·48]
1·2	0·02	[0·70]	0·07	[1·11]	0·13	0·47	0·74	0·99	1·19	1·00	0·56	0·14 0·04 [14·34]
½ Base DIAGONAL	0·08	[0·31]	0·08	[0·08]	0·67	1·20	1·49	1·65	1·73	1·74	1·65	1·41 1·02 0·40 [14·73]

LINES FAIRED AT 1/10th FULL SIZE

FEET 0   1   2   3   4   5   6   7   8   9   10   11   12   13   14

Fig 151: Alec Blagdon's *Pearl* – lines.

netting commercially for salmon. The differences between these and the Thames waterman's boat though distinct are superficial.

Together the waters of the Tamar, Plym and Sound have given the people of Plymouth the pleasures of bathing, boating and fishing. Nowhere are there more public open air sea water pools. These were made by walling up the small harbours the trading smacks and barges once used. For those that did not own boats there were firms with a number of rowing and sailing boats to be hired by the hour. The requirements of the watermen and the hire firms gave work to many small boatbuilding concerns scattered along the 26 miles of shore between Saltash and Laira. Some details of a few of these firms show their general nature.

William Blagdon first came to Richmond Walk, Mount Wise, as a coasting skipper experiencing a set-back in trade in 1860. Acting first as a shipkeeper for laid-up vessels, he took up letting out boats for hire. This firm operated from two sites on land owned by the St Aubyn estate on the Devonport side of Stonehouse Creek as well as afloat on the old Cremyll horse ferry, none of which involved either title deeds or rents. This changed when the city acquired the water frontage in 1934 with the intention of building a marine drive through to Mutton Cove. This project was baulked by the Admiralty, but not before Blagdon's yard was, so to speak, put on the map. At that time the yard was run by the grandfather of the present owner, Alexander Blagdon, operating a fleet of 20 to 25 rowing boats and a number of sailing boats up to 5 tons Thames measurement. In addition to keeping all these boats repaired, they built a few of their own boats themselves. The *Pearl*(30) is one they bought (Fig 151). She was built in 1904 by Mr Kessel of Moon Cove along with her sister *Ina*. Each boat with a pair of spoon blade oars cost £8 0s 0d. Of the few other boats surviving from this fleet, Mr Blagdon's grandfather built the 12 footers *Nellie Dean* and *Rosette* while Ted Rogerman of Laira built the *Freddie* in 1905 using Archangel white and teak, taken from the Blagdon's own stocks, for the planking, seats and backboard. Norris,

another Moon Cove boatbuilder, also worked for the Blagdons, but in a heavier style than Kessel's, whose boats could always be picked out by Alec as they looked to him as though they were laughing. Another builder, Chant, worked both on the Barbican as well as Moon Cove.

Alec picked up boatbuilding as a boy from his grandfather, but learned the finer points from his uncle, Harry Blagdon, who built and operated boats from an establishment at West Hoe Pier, close to the present site of the Royal Western Yacht Club. Alec lost his grandfather in 1936 after a fall from the roof of a shed, and was then called up into the Royal Artillery for the war. Though no longer a young woman, 91 years old in 1954, his grandmother ran the firm in his absence, while his uncle built whalers and cutters for the Navy. Back from the war, Alec built his first boat in 1947. She was the 11ft 3in long *Alec* (Fig 152). Under his management, the yard went ahead, concentrating now on laying up and repairing yachts. Though he no longer hires out boats, Alec still builds a small clinker stem or pram dinghy from time to time.

The drawings of the *Pearl* illustrate a type part way between the extremely light and delicate skiff and a boat able to stand up to the rough and tumble of inshore fishing. Nonetheless she had to take the treatment she might get from anyone who hired her. Special boats like this, however, would not be let out to any newcomer, but only to those whose sensible behaviour had been established. Great care was taken of the boats and they were never ever dragged up the slipway on their keel, even though a greenheart false keel was fitted. They had to be carried. After three quarters of a century this boat is still useable, reflecting equal credit on builder and owner. The lines while fine fore and aft are not at the cost of skimped bearings. The flared sides help to give the required width of pivot for the oars, but this is increased by fitting the row cleats externally. She is structurally interesting in that, although deep deadwoods and an apron are fitted, rabbets are cut into the stem and sternpost. The open gunwale gives her a rather unfinished look, but in a lightly stressed hull like this an inwale and capping would only put up

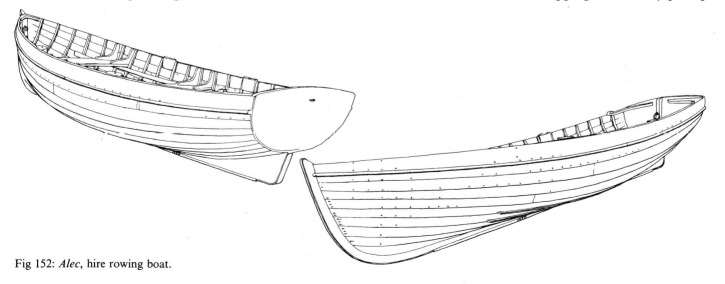

Fig 152: *Alec*, hire rowing boat.

weight, hold moisture and start rot. The obsolescence of this kind of boat would be reversed if rowing became popular again.

Cawsand Bay is at the western entrance to Plymouth Sound, sheltering in the lee of Rame Head and Penlee Point. It is wide and shallow, so was suitable for pilchard seine-netting, which fishery has lasted from at least the sixteenth century until these fish went away after the First World War[11].

This manner of fishing calls for big capital outlays, to buy the huge net, its boats and the fish curing cellars. Most of all plenty of quickly-available labour is essential, from July through to September, when the shoals were expected. Sometimes this was managed by the fishermen forming companies to obtain and operate the gear. However, the independent nature of the men did not take to co-operative enterprises, and at Kingsand and Cawsand it was the landlords of eight public houses who owned and controlled the pilchard companies by the turn of this century. The fishermen bound themselves to one of these establishments in return for which he was given off-season credit for groceries and drink. When the pilchards arrived all credit would stop until the accumulated debt had been worked off at the fishery.

The seine-net boat was quite large, about 30ft, pulling six oars, but of little other use beyond shooting a seine. For this reason they hardly outlasted the pilchards. The volyer, about 22ft, and the larker, the 18ft master seiner's boat, could be put to many other uses and survived for as long as they held together. The nearly 17ft *Two Sisters*, which spent a great part of her later life crabbing, was built as a larker in 1918 by Algernon (Algee) Marks and his brother-in-law (Fig 153).

She is an example of a boat that is part way between an open beach boat and an open river boat, like the *Pearl*. As the solid-looking Jacky Nicholls suggest, she normally lay at a mooring, but would be brought ashore if the wind turned easterly, when it gets very nasty in this bay. She was propelled in a variety of ways during her working life. She was rigged at first with two masts, both with sprits, the fore stepped through the foremost thwart and the mizzen on the transom. At a later date, she was fitted with a centre-board case, a single mast stepped at the midship thwart and given a sheet horse across the transom. Next a Stuart Turner inboard petrol engine was fitted, and when that wore out an outboard over the stern. Under power the sprit mizzen was brought back. As a larker she would have had a play-thwart so she could be pulled with four oars, but under power now she has just a pair of 9ft spoons. This may seem short for $5\frac{1}{2}$ft of beam, but enough for the short distance she had to be rowed. When new, she was finished bright using a precise mixture of varnish and resin. Too much varnish was said to over harden and crack off, while too much resin never dried. However, this boat has been painted white for so long that she is now known as the 'white boat'. Though still in a fair condition this 61-year-old boat is hardly ever used.

This 12 strake boat had her sheerstrakes $1\frac{1}{4}$in higher when she was built, the gunwale being boxed in when she was cut down. The pecked line on the drawing shows the original sheerline and explains why the transom now lacks 'ears'. The floors are flat for much of her length, yet the ends have been kept fine. The bilges are so hard that the limiting hemming angle of 20° must have been exceeded in places – she would not have been an easy boat to plank. She would have drawn very little empty and have accommodated her five-man crew under oars with ease. The propeller, which could not have been more than 8in in diameter, was on the centreline. This leads one to wonder if the builders had not anticipated fitting an engine at a later date by careful placing of the fastenings aft. The transom is fully formed with a tuck, and this gives ample space aft for the helmsman under sail and later on the outboard without spoiling the boat's trim. It is felt that even with a centreboard the *Two Sisters* did not sparkle under sail.

The *Rose* of Portloe is now at the National Maritime Museum. She is smaller than the last boat, just under $14\frac{1}{2}$ft long and 5ft beam. A little background explains why such a lightly built boat came to be working in South Cornwall. Portloe is the only haven in Veryan Bay, and is on the more sheltered western coast. The nearest refuges are Portscatho in Gerrans Bay, 5 miles to the west round Nare Head, and Gorran Haven, 7 miles to the east round the Dodman, neither easy passages in a blow. Portloe creek is shaped like the figure 7, the top end of which dries out at low tide and was exceptional as being the only place around there to have clinker boats. This has changed to the more usual Cornish pattern at present, whereby the larger boats are edge-positioned and the smaller edge-fastened when they are not GRP.

The *Rose* was built for Mr Benjamin Blamey Johns in 1904 or 1905 by Arthur Johns, the Portloe boatbuilder, for £7. She was built as a small crabber, which were two-man boats, luggers 14ft to 17ft long, and there were about 18 of them at Portloe at that time. It looks as if this particular boat did not work pots, as the half round protection strip had been taken off her starboard gunwale, but from the way the port gunwale aft has been scored, that she had been used for whiffing instead. Mr B B Johns died in 1911 and the *Rose* was stored in a cellar at Tretheake Manor until 1972, so she has stayed almost unchanged from the day she was built. She was built for sailing (Fig 154). Her rig can be deduced as one with two unstayed masts. The fore had a dipping lug and the mizzen a sprit or a standing lug, both with outriggers. As the lines show, she has marked deadrise increasing towards her ends so that she has a much shorter floor than the boat from Cawsands. The bilges are also slacker, with the result she will be more weatherly under sail. Care has been taken to keep down her weight. Though the timbers are spaced the same as the larker, only half of the *Rose*'s are taken beyond the rising up to the gunwale. The method of securing the capping to the timbers is unique in so small a boat, so has been shown

Fig 153: *Two Sisters*, Cawsand pilchard larker – lines.

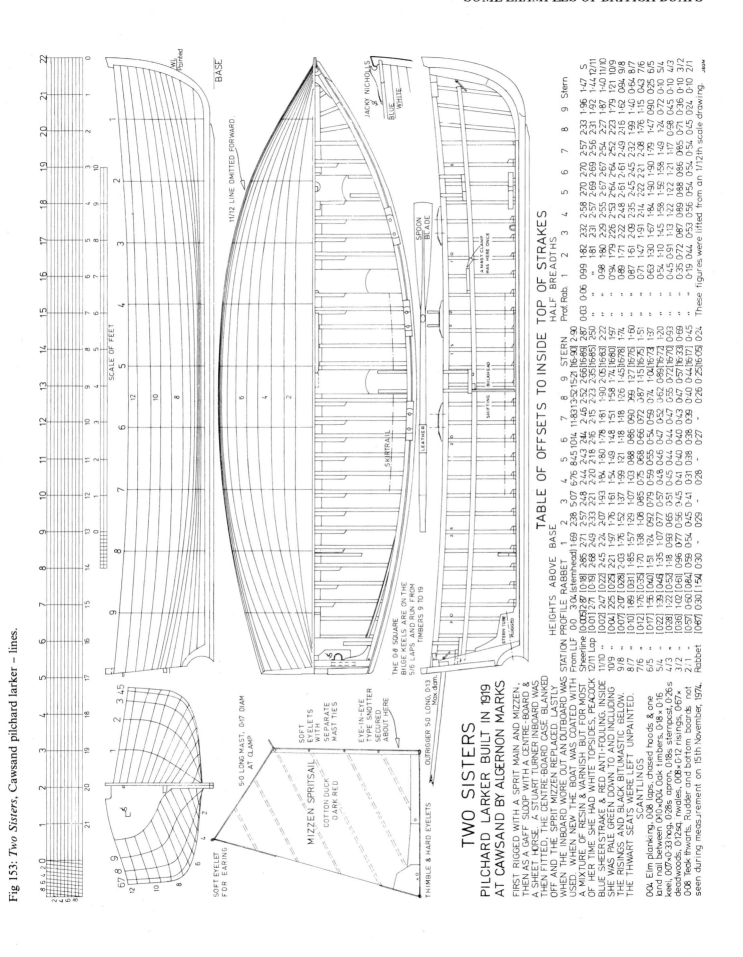

TWO SISTERS

PILCHARD LARKER BUILT IN 1919
AT CAWSAND BY ALGERNON MARKS

FIRST RIGGED WITH A SPRIT MAIN AND MIZZEN,
THEN AS A GAFF SLOOP WITH A CENTRE-BOARD &
A SHEET HORSE. A STUART TURNER INBOARD WAS
THEN FITTED, THE CENTRE-BOARD CASE BLANKED
OFF AND THE SPRIT MIZZEN REPLACED. LASTLY
WHEN THE INBOARD WORE OUT AN OUTBOARD WAS
USED. WHEN NEW THE BOAT WAS COATED WITH
A MIXTURE OF RESIN & VARNISH BUT FOR MOST
OF HER TIME SHE HAD WHITE TOPSIDES, PEACOCK
BLUE SHEERSTRAKE & RED ANTI-FOULING. INSIDE
SHE WAS PALE GREEN DOWN TO AND INCLUDING
THE RISINGS AND BLACK BITUMASTIC BELOW.
THE THWART SEATS WERE LEFT UNPAINTED.

SCANTLINGS

0·04 Elm planking, 0·08 laps, chased hoods & one
land nail between 0·10×0·04 Oak timbers, 0·18 × 0·16
keel, 0·07×0·33 hog, 0·28s apron, 0·18s sternpost, 0·26s
deadwoods, 0·12sq nwales, 0·08×0·12 risings, 0·67×
0·08 Teak thwarts. Rudder and bottom boards not
seen during measurement on 15th November, 1974.

SOFT EYELET
FOR EARING

THIMBLE & HARD EYELETS

5·0 LONG MAST, 0·17 DIAM
AT CLAMP

MIZZEN SPRITSAIL

COTTON DUCK
DARK RED

SOFT
EYELETS
WITH
SEPARATE
MAST TIES

EYE-IN-EYE
TYPE SNOTTER
SECURED
ABOUT HERE

OUTRIGGER 5·0 LONG, 0·13
Max. diam.

SCALE OF FEET

WL
Painted

BASE

11/12 LINE OMITTED FORWARD

THE 0·8 SQUARE
BILGE KEELS ARE ON THE
5/6 LAPS AND RUN FROM
TIMBERS 9 TO 19

SKIRTRAIL

LEATHER

SPOON
BLADE

A MAST CLAMP
WAS HERE ONCE

SHIFTING
BULKHEAD

STERN TUBE
PLUGGED

JACKY NICHOLLS
BLUE
WHITE

JGM

TABLE OF OFFSETS TO INSIDE TOP OF STRAKES

HALF BREADTHS

	Prof. Rab.	1	2	3	4	5	6	7	8	9	Stern
	0·06	0·99	1·82	2·32	2·58	2·70	2·57	2·33	1·96	1·47	S
	"	"	1·81	2·31	2·57	2·69	2·56	2·31	1·92	1·44	12/11
	"	0·98	1·80	2·29	2·55	2·67	2·54	2·27	1·87	1·40	11/10
	0·94	1·79	2·26	2·53	2·64	2·52	2·23	1·79	1·21	10/9
	0·89	1·71	2·22	2·48	2·61	2·49	2·16	1·62	0·94	9/8
	0·87	1·61	2·09	2·35	2·45	2·32	1·99	1·40	0·64	8/7
	0·71	1·47	1·91	2·14	2·22	2·21	1·76	1·15	0·43	7/6
	0·63	1·30	1·67	1·84	1·90	1·90	1·47	0·90	0·25	6/5
	0·54	1·10	1·45	1·59	1·58	1·49	1·24	0·72	0·10	5/4
	0·45	0·91	1·13	1·22	1·21	1·17	0·98	0·45	0·10	4/3
	0·35	0·72	0·87	0·89	0·86	0·85	0·71	0·36	0·10	3/2
	0·19	0·44	0·53	0·56	0·54	0·54	0·45	0·24	0·10	2/1

These figures were lifted from an 1/12th scale drawing.

HEIGHTS ABOVE BASE

STATION	PROFILE RABBET	1	2	3	4	5	6	7	8	9	STERN
From LLF	0·0	3·04 (stemhead)	1·69	2·38	5·07	6·76	8·45	10·44	11·83	13·52	15·21	16·90	2·90
Sheerline	[0·005]	2·87	[0·18]	2·85	2·71	2·57	2·48	2·44	2·43	2·46	2·52	2·66	[16·89]	2·87
12/11 Lap	[0·01]	2·71	[0·19]	2·68	2·49	2·33	2·21	2·18	2·16	2·15	2·23	2·35	[16·85]	2·50
11/10	[0·02]	2·47	[0·22]	2·45	2·24	2·07	1·93	1·84	1·80	1·81	1·90	2·05	[16·83]	2·22
10/9	[0·04]	2·25	[0·25]	2·23	2·01	1·76	1·61	1·54	1·49	1·48	1·51	1·74	[16·80]	1·97
9/8	[0·07]	2·07	[0·28]	2·03	1·76	1·52	1·37	1·29	1·21	1·18	1·26	1·45	[16·78]	1·74
8/7	[0·10]	1·89	[0·31]	1·85	1·57	1·29	1·07	1·03	0·88	0·90	0·99	1·27	[16·76]	1·60
7/6	[0·12]	1·76	[0·35]	1·70	1·38	1·08	0·85	0·75	0·68	0·66	0·72	0·87	[16·75]	1·51
6/5	[0·17]	1·56	[0·40]	1·51	1·24	0·92	0·79	0·68	0·55	0·59	0·74	1·04	[16·73]	1·37
5/4	[0·22]	1·39	[0·46]	1·35	1·07	1·07	0·77	0·57	0·52	0·47	0·62	0·99	[16·72]	1·20
4/3	[0·28]	1·22	[0·52]	1·18	0·93	0·65	0·51	0·45	0·44	0·44	0·55	0·72	[16·70]	0·93
3/2	[0·36]	1·02	[0·61]	0·96	0·77	0·56	0·45	0·41	0·40	0·43	0·47	0·57	[16·33]	0·69
2/1	[0·57]	0·60	[0·84]	0·59	0·54	0·45	0·41	0·31	0·38	0·38	0·39	0·44	[16·17]	0·45
Rabbet	[0·87]	0·30	[1·54]	0·30	0·29	—	0·28	—	0·27	—	0·26	0·25	[16·05]	0·24

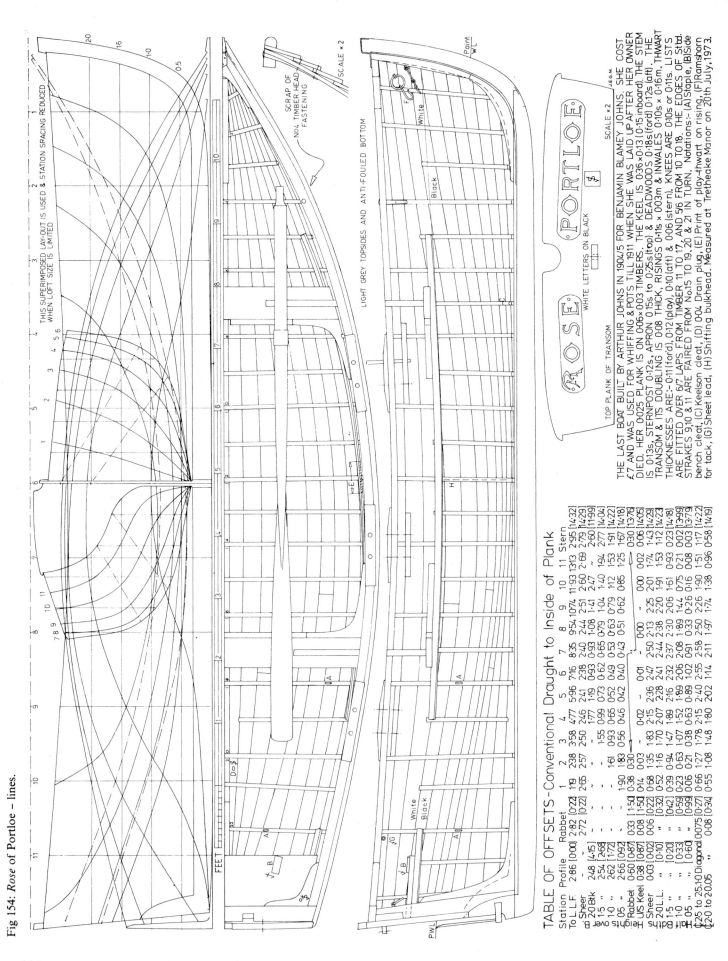

Fig 154: *Rose of Portloe* – lines.

in a scrap on the drawings. In general, it looks as if this were a rather special boat built for an older man to suit his accumulated experience.

Benjamin Johns in addition to farming owned and operated other fishing boats, for which he kept an account book from 1881 to 1890. This has survived and is in the keeping of Mr R J Julyan of Tretheake Manor, a descendant. Appendix V is an abstract of the original, in which the *Rose* referred to is an earlier and larger boat than the one above. The fortunes of this small fleet can be condensed further, boat by boat yearly. The catch is indicated by the letter 'P' for pilchards and 'M' for Mackerel, using drift-nets in both cases. Losses have been shown in brackets.

	Rose	Cock	Mary	Olga	Total
1881	21 15 0 P	35 16 3 P	45 18 6 P	–	£103 9 9
1882	32 10 6 P	32 0 6 P	89 0 2 M&P	93 13 6 M	247 4 8
1883	–	81 15 6 P	82 1 2 M&P	22 10 4 M	186 7 0
1884	43 2 0 P	(4 1 3)	24 11 9 M	27 19 10 M	91 0 7
1885	12 3 9 P	18 16 2 P	(5 15 0)	4 2 7 M	29 7 6
1886	9 3 11 P	28 2 6 P	–	60 7 0 M	97 13 5
1887	24 7 9 P	5 11 2 P	31 8 6 M	(3 13 7)	57 13 10
1888	15 11 8 P	22 8 9 P	24 8 2 M	–	62 8 7
1889	13 6 9 P	16 18 11 P	–	–	29 15 8
1890	–	–	–	27 17 2 M	27 17 6
	£172 1 4 P	236 6 9 P	291 3 3 M&P	232 17 2 M	932 18 6

Though at that time these accounts would have been clear to Mr Johns, this is not so today. It seems that he used accounts as a means of investigating his various enterprises, and kept changing his system to this end. The entries become more vague towards the end of the period and there were more arithmetical slips. Nevertheless they give an idea of how these boats were employed over a decade. It can be seen that *Rose* and *Cock-of-the-West* were pilchard drivers, *Olga* was a mackerel driver, and *Mary Ann* was used as both.

The fishery returns show that there was one first class vessel at Portloe, nine second class vessels engaged in drift-net fishing for mackerel and pilchards and fourteen unregistered pilchard drivers[12]. It was stated that the larger boats landed their catches at Falmouth, Mevagissey and Plymouth. Only *Olga*, the mackerel driver, never showed a credit at Plymouth in the account book. As mackerel drift-nets were usually made up of 30-mesh net till a mile long compared with the half mile long 45-mesh pilchard drift-net it is likely that, though *Rose* and *Cock* may have been smaller, all four boats were of the second class, *ie* under 15 tons and permanently rigged sailing vessels. 1882 was the only year all of them were in use together, it being usual to lay up one of them in succession annually. The reports said that 1888 had been a slightly better year, except that the smaller boats had not been able to do much fishing.

At Portloe there were 43 unregistered boats. These lined, set trammel-nets, and laid pots for different periods from January through to November. The whole population of the village was only 300, out of which 77 men and 9 boys fished, leaving about a dozen active males for other work. The small boats alone, with crews of one or two, could have accounted for nearly all the fishermen. The

second class boats would need 3 men for pilchard and 4 men for mackerel driving, so many of the men would have to have worked in more than one boat. It is evident from the accounts that mackerel could be more rewarding than pilchards, but varied by ten to one between good and bad weeks. The whole fishery fluctuated too, but over the decade this group of boats made an average profit of about £100 a year.

Nowhere is mention made of fishermen's wages, though carters, sweepers, shipwrights and men and women curing fish all get paid. It looks as if the accounts refer to the share due to the owner of the nets and boats after running costs have been met. Fishing took place from February to October with a break in early summer between the mackerel and pilchard seasons. It cannot be told if the men worked in only one boat or moved from one to the other, nor how many men in all were involved. There were periods when no fishing occurred, so the boat's crews may have worked on the farm or taken on other work.

One year, probably 1884, Mr Johns kept a detailed account of the costs of curing fish.

Paid women	5 8 0	Receipts for curing	21 12 0
Paid men	2 6 0	Sales of 'oill'	5 12 6
Casks	8 17 6	Sales of salt	1 17 0
Salt & barrels	6 9 0	Furnace	4 6
5 barrels	12 6		£29 6 0
Cellar rent	3 8 0		
Sundries	15 0		
	£27 16 0		

This does not seem to be a very profitable venture; except that on the next page there is a list of 16 more transactions with persons, who, with names like Duke, Trudgeon, Blamey and Johns, all sound like locals. These deals add up to 284 gallons of an unspecified liquid at about 1s 6d a gallon. This could only have been the train oil that was pressed out of the pilchards during curing, and which was used for lamps and dressing leather. On top of this there were further credits for items such as 'boats', 'barrels' and 'carig', which brought in a futher total of £31 7 9. If the interpretation is correct then the profit made on fish curing that year was 118% on the outlay.

The cost of some of the individual items that re-occur can be isolated. New nets cost about £1 each but would then require 4s for head rope, 2s for norsels and 2s for corks to make up. No mention was made of lead sinkers, so perhaps stones were used. Together these came to 28s per net in a made up fleet of nets. *Cock* had a deck which cost 3s to caulk and a new mast for £1 4s 6d. A stove for *Rose* cost £1 and a new mizzen sail for *Olga* cost £2 2s 0d. Salt in 1885 was 19s 6d a ton, exclusive of transport and handling. Mr Johns bought in 14 tons of this, selling off nearly 3 tons of it in about ½ ton amounts to local buyers, amongst whom was the Reverend W C Bird. One deduces that some people were curing fish for themselves as the accounts occasionally record the sale of small amounts of fish to such persons.

Though the economic aspect has little effect on a

boat's shape, it has on size. Even if the lack of financial reserves did not make it hard for an independent fisherman to support his family over a slack period, it is unlikely that it would allow him to acquire the capital for a larger boat and her gear. Even nowadays with a large proportion of a boat's first cost being available through White Fish Authority and EEC loans, there are so many uncertainties in the future of fishing that the purchase of a new boat is a hazardous undertaking for a single individual.

Though there has been only one main line Cornwall has been well served by the railways in the past. The peninsula is narrow and no fishing station is more than twenty miles from a railway. In spite of this, shortening this distance is beneficial. Information sent to Commander Hill in 1934 by Mr W H Barrow, the Fishery Officer for the Cornwall Sea Fishery District, covers 29 places from which sailing crabbers once operated. In general terms, the further away from the railway the smaller the crabbers became, but not much under 15ft[13]. This is reasonable as a large catch of shellfish was hard to sell in a remote place. In the last days of the sailing crabber the main stations were at Gorran Haven with 30 crabbers, Sennen with 24, St Mawes and Port Isaac with 20 each, Portloe and Looe with 18 each and Porthleven with 15. All except the last two were porths or sheltered beaches.

By 1934 nearly all crabbers were motorised. Instead of 292 boats averaging 18ft long, there were 218 Cornish boats averaging 21ft. This represented a tonnage increase of more than a half. The number of fishermen dropped from 631 down to 460 as both propulsion and pot-hauling called for less manpower. The increase in size was most noticeable in the larger sizes. 30ft motor crabbers now becoming usual, together with a shift from beach to harbour bases. The main stations in 1934 were at St Ives with 34 boats, Looe with 21, Porthleven and Port Isaac with 18, then Cadgwith, Gorran Haven, and Polperro all with 14. Better roads and lorries have made distance from railways less important, while in summer the demand for fish by the tourist trade is so large that it has to be met by imports to supplement the local catch.

Changes like this have been noticed round the coast, with a more recent development which has been seen at Selsey and Beer. These are fleets of boats, too large to be beached, that anchor off for a season. In this way a boat normally harbour based can cut down the distance to her grounds and save fuel costs, which have abruptly become a major factor in the fishing economy.

A further idea of the relationship that existed between the owner of the boat and nets and the men that operated

Below:
Fig 155: 4-oared lerret – typical construction and scantlings.

Opposite:
Fig 156: *Freetrader*, Beesands seiner.

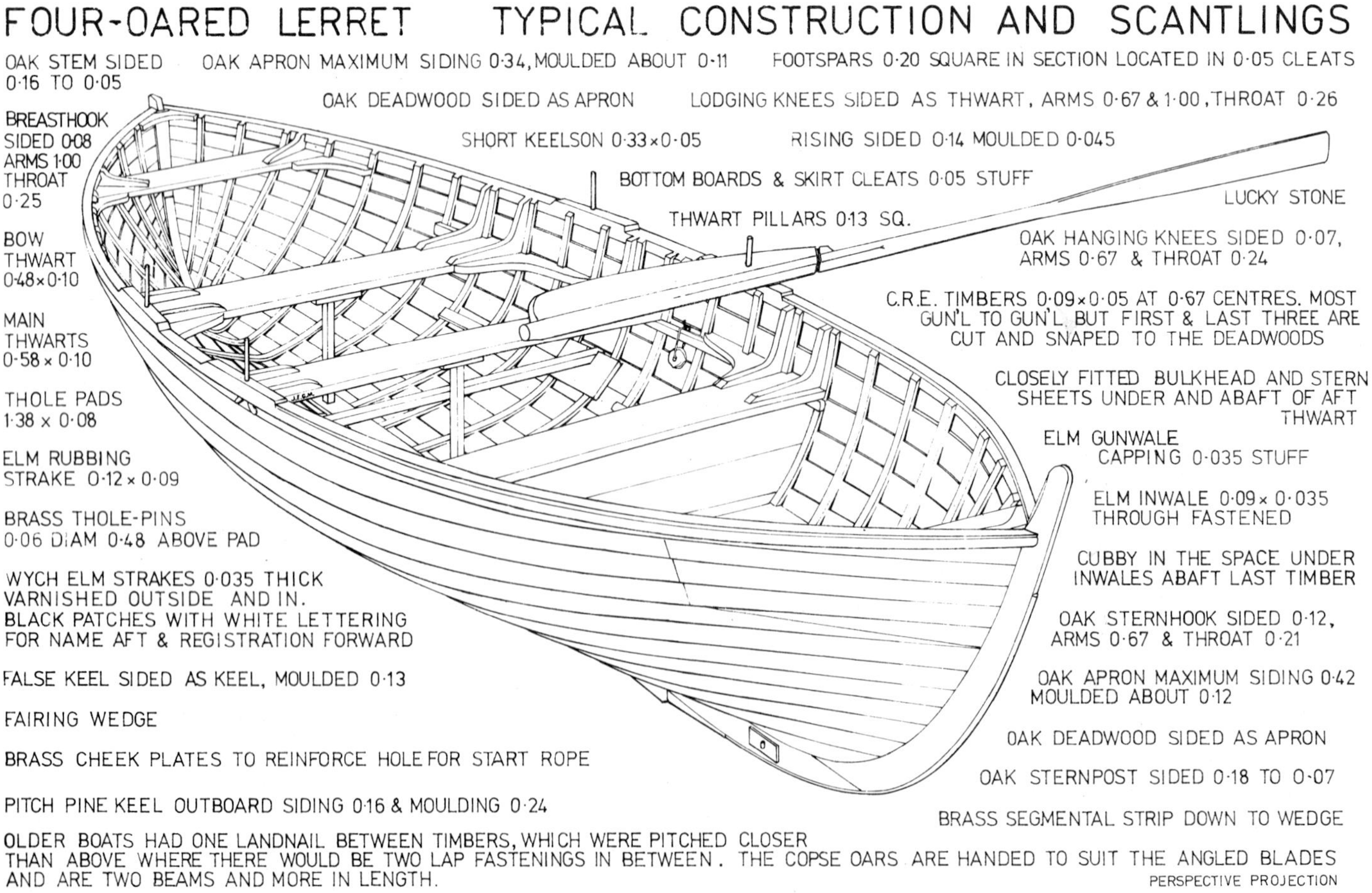

FOUR-OARED LERRET   TYPICAL CONSTRUCTION AND SCANTLINGS

OAK STEM SIDED 0·16 TO 0·05   OAK APRON MAXIMUM SIDING 0·34, MOULDED ABOUT 0·11   FOOTSPARS 0·20 SQUARE IN SECTION LOCATED IN 0·05 CLEATS

OAK DEADWOOD SIDED AS APRON   LODGING KNEES SIDED AS THWART, ARMS 0·67 & 1·00, THROAT 0·26

BREASTHOOK SIDED 0·08 ARMS 1·00 THROAT 0·25

SHORT KEELSON 0·33 × 0·05   RISING SIDED 0·14 MOULDED 0·045

BOTTOM BOARDS & SKIRT CLEATS 0·05 STUFF

THWART PILLARS 0·13 SQ.

LUCKY STONE

BOW THWART 0·48 × 0·10

OAK HANGING KNEES SIDED 0·07, ARMS 0·67 & THROAT 0·24

MAIN THWARTS 0·58 × 0·10

C.R.E. TIMBERS 0·09 × 0·05 AT 0·67 CENTRES. MOST GUN'L TO GUN'L BUT FIRST & LAST THREE ARE CUT AND SNAPED TO THE DEADWOODS

THOLE PADS 1·38 × 0·08

CLOSELY FITTED BULKHEAD AND STERN SHEETS UNDER AND ABAFT OF AFT THWART

ELM RUBBING STRAKE 0·12 × 0·09

ELM GUNWALE CAPPING 0·035 STUFF

BRASS THOLE-PINS 0·06 DIAM 0·48 ABOVE PAD

ELM INWALE 0·09 × 0·035 THROUGH FASTENED

WYCH ELM STRAKES 0·035 THICK VARNISHED OUTSIDE AND IN. BLACK PATCHES WITH WHITE LETTERING FOR NAME AFT & REGISTRATION FORWARD

CUBBY IN THE SPACE UNDER INWALES ABAFT LAST TIMBER

FALSE KEEL SIDED AS KEEL, MOULDED 0·13

OAK STERNHOOK SIDED 0·12, ARMS 0·67 & THROAT 0·21

FAIRING WEDGE

OAK APRON MAXIMUM SIDING 0·42 MOULDED ABOUT 0·12

BRASS CHEEK PLATES TO REINFORCE HOLE FOR START ROPE

OAK DEADWOOD SIDED AS APRON

PITCH PINE KEEL OUTBOARD SIDING 0·16 & MOULDING 0·24

OAK STERNPOST SIDED 0·18 TO 0·07

BRASS SEGMENTAL STRIP DOWN TO WEDGE

OLDER BOATS HAD ONE LANDNAIL BETWEEN TIMBERS, WHICH WERE PITCHED CLOSER THAN ABOVE WHERE THERE WOULD BE TWO LAP FASTENINGS IN BETWEEN. THE COPSE OARS ARE HANDED TO SUIT THE ANGLED BLADES AND ARE TWO BEAMS AND MORE IN LENGTH.

PERSPECTIVE PROJECTION

SCANTLINGS

ELM GARBOARDS AND SHEERSTRAKES 0·04 THICK
  ,,   KEEL   0·18s × 0·30m
  ,,   HOG   0·36s × 0·08m
OAK STEMS   0·22 to 0·06s × 0·30m
  ,,   DEADWOODS 0·38s × about 0·20m
  ,,   BREASTHOOK 0·14s, ARMS 1·05 & THROAT 0·30
  ,,   KNEES-'UPRIGHT' 0·09s, ARMS 0·82 & THROAT 0·33
INWALES 0·13s × 0·16m CAPPING AFT 0·20 × 0·04
BOW THWART   0·58 × 0·06
TIMBERS   0·12s × 0·06m, GUN'L TO GUN'L
BILGE RAILS FASTENED TO 3/4 AND 5/6 LAPS

REMAINING STRAKES ELM 0·03 THICK
0·14 DIAM. HOLE FOR COD ROPE AT AFTER END
HOLLY FALSE KEEL HELD ON BY SQUARE PEGS
OAK APRONS 0·38s × about 0·21m
TOE AT No6 TIMBER FORWARD & No20 AFT
OAK STERNHOOK 0·13s, ARMS 1·75 & THROAT 0·21
'LAY' 0·06s, ARMS-IN 0·86 & AFT 1·00, & THROAT 0·33
'REASONS' (RISINGS) FWD APRON TO No18 0·12s × 0·06m
MID AND AFTER THWARTS 0·67 × 0·12
EXCEPT Nos 1,2,3 & 25 SNAPED TO DEADWOOD
HOLLY OR APPLE 'WAYS' USED FOR LAUNCHING UP
            THE NET SHELF IS
            NOT IN PLACE

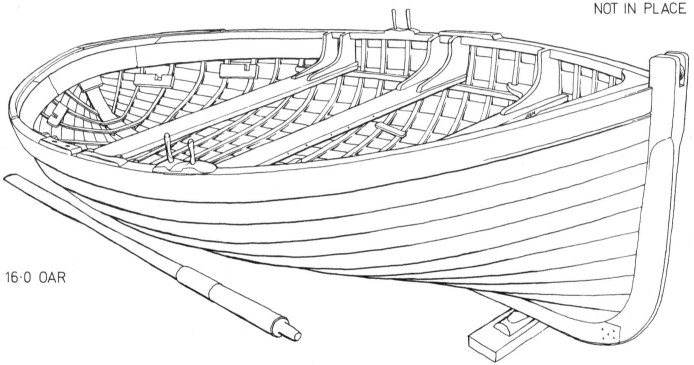

16·0 OAR

FREETRADER   BEESANDS   SEINER   17·0 × 6·2 OVERALL

them can be had from an agreement that was drawn up at Park Wall on the East Fleet near Weymouth, as far back as 1792. Mr Levi Northover, who operates lerrets on this stretch of the Bank, has been kind enough to let me copy this, which is given in full in Appendix VI. Once one has become accustomed to the absence of commas, it is reasonably easy to follow.

The boats that were involved in this fishery were the 6-oared lerrets, seining for mackerel off the exposed Chesil Bank. The 'Backwater Boatts' were the Fleet trows(02) that ferried crews and catches between the Bank and the mainland. The 6-oared lerret(21) is obsolete as a working boat, so it was only possible to make drawings of the more recent 4-oared variety (Fig 155). Recently Mr Northover has presented one of his, the *Pleasure*, to the Weymouth and Portland Museum for preservation. This is the boat wrongly named *Treasure* in my article[14]. The lerret has to be afloat in as short a time as possible and then carry the

combined weight of her large crew and net through the surf without swamping, before she can start to fish. What appears to be a simple canoe form is a successful compromise between buoyancy and power, and a shape that was adopted for most ships' lifeboats.

55 miles away, across Lyme Bay on the east side of Start Point, is another shingle beach stretching north from where the village of Hallsands used to be, for some 5 miles to Slapton. This beach is divided into three: Hallsands, Beesands and Slapton Sands, by Tinsey Head and Dun Point. Both of these were vantage points for spotting shoals and directing the seine fishing. Like Chesil there are lagoons behind these beaches; these wild fowl sanctuaries are known as leys and are not large enough to need boats to cross them. The drawing shows the type of boat used for seining off Beesands up till recently (Fig 156). The similarity of the landscapes and the boats of these two places is remarkable. There could not have been any direct

contact between the two fishing stations, and the main difference of the low sheer of the Devon boat is probably due to Beesands being a lee shore most of the time.

In the north-east of England the coasts of Northumberland, Durham and Yorkshire are populated for the most part by two distinct types of boat. These are the cobles and the double-ended keel-boats. The peculiarity here is that examples of both types may be found being used both out of harbours and off beaches with little apparent difference in their shape or structure.

The cobles(13), possibly the most distinctive of all the British boat types, should hardly need any description, as nearly every local boat writer has given one[8]. They have some extremely interesting features, which hint at plank, skin and dugout origins, but, as far as I know, these have yet to be investigated conclusively. Like the British race, the coble has a mongrel extraction and is an adaptable breed. Her buoyant shallow square stern was developed for launching and beaching stern to shore, and though able to windward under sail, she has been motorised successfully when given more beam, topside and a deck or a shelter forward. As cobles were and are still built almost entirely by eye, authentic drawings of them are rare, as are models with reliable structural details. To partly fill this

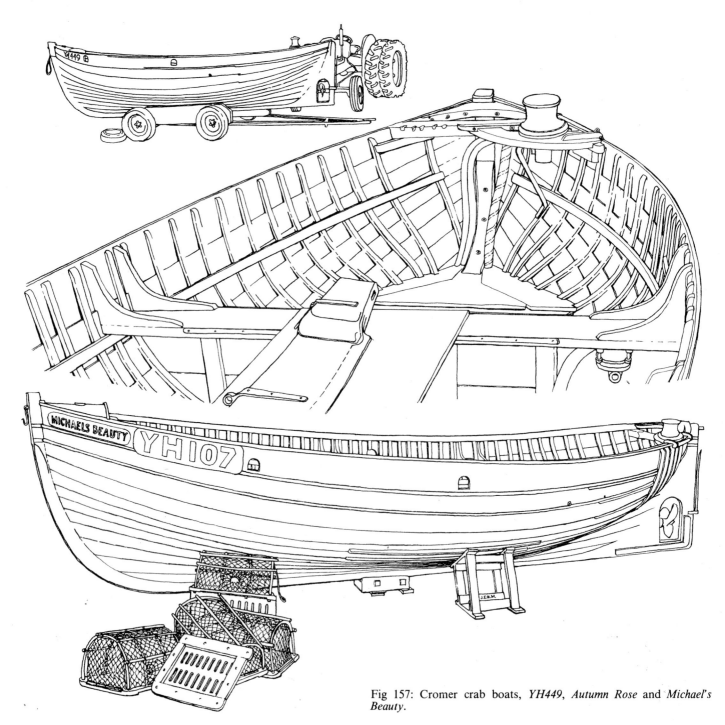

Fig 157: Cromer crab boats, *YH449*, *Autumn Rose* and *Michael's Beauty*.

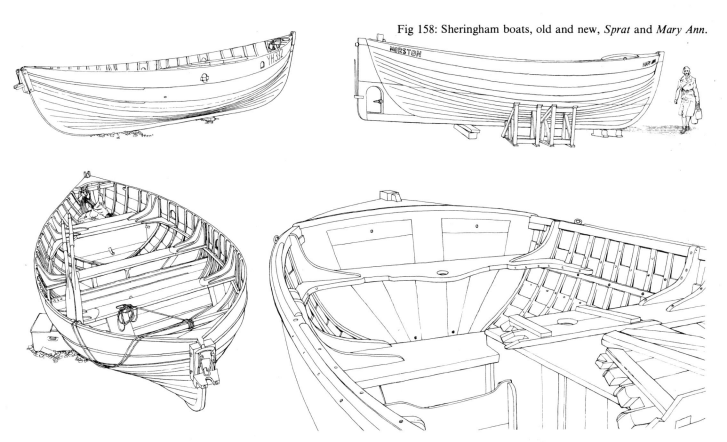

Fig 158: Sheringham boats, old and new, *Sprat* and *Mary Ann*.

gap, the lines and construction of a small coble have been included (Fig 146). She is the *Leslie*, a foyboat from Sunderland, and can be seen at the Exeter Maritime Museum. She is similar in most respects to the *Sunshine* at the National Maritime Museum. Though motor cobles continue to be built, the sailing ones have gone. A few, like Hector Handyside's *Sweet Promise*, Joe Gelsthorpe's *Pebble*, David Wharton's *Gratitude* and J Seymour's *Willy Nilly*, though well cared for by enthusiasts, are no longer working boats.

The English type of coble was used as far south as Yarmouth in E W Cooke's time, and it seems that the term 'coble' lasted in Norfolk within living memory. Nevertheless the southern limit of the coble has been receding, and her place has been taken by boats similar to, if not identical to, the Cromer and Sheringham crab boats (18) (Fig 157). These double-enders have kept their identity in spite of motorisation, largely due to the invention of thicker sternposts by the Sheringham boatbuilder, Harold Emery[15]. The motor crabbers have flatter floors and higher sides than the sailing ones, but still have 'arruk' holes – oar ports with Norman arches – and the characteristic abruptly-formed entry and run. The sailing crabbers came north and there were colonies of them at Withernsea and Hornsea at the beginning of this century; these were called 'sheringhams' to distinguish them from cobles [16]. Drawings of both sailing and motor crabbers have been shown together so that the change of shape can be compared (Fig 158). The motor boat is two or three foot longer now that they can be hauled out by tractor and do not have to be bumped up the beach and lifted out by the men.

These sturdy double-enders did not penetrate very far up the Yorkshire coast. Instead, a much finer and lighter double-ender is seen in almost every beach and harbour station. Examples have been sketched at Runswick Bay, Filey, Scarborough and Redcar (Fig 159). They have also been seen at Bridlington, Staithes, Whitby and Saltburn in considerable numbers, but were not seen at either of the Flamborough landings or north of the Tees in the course of my tours. All manner of names are given to these boats: surf boat, skiff, canoe, wop, jolly-boat and even coble. Even if these names follow local variations they are, like those of a coble, relatively minor. Most of the harbour-based boats were hired out for pleasure, being oar-propelled. Some of these have ornamental wooden galleries abreast the stern sheets. The beach boats are motorised by inboard or outboard engines. These boats are not like cobles at all. They have keels, many more strakes and steamed timbers. They are launched and beached bows to shore, and because of this often have a washstrake to increase the freeboard aft. Though these boats are replacing the smaller sizes of coble, this is not true for boats more than 18-20ft long. In the larger sizes the coble is competing with two further types. The first of these is the keel-boat, which is a locally built hybrid different again from the obsolete mule, and the second the motor fishing vessel(38) built in a Scottish yard (Fig 160), collectively referred to as fifies in this part of England. The small double-ended surf boats are popular with both amateur and professional part-time fishermen.

It should not be thought that beach boats have to be

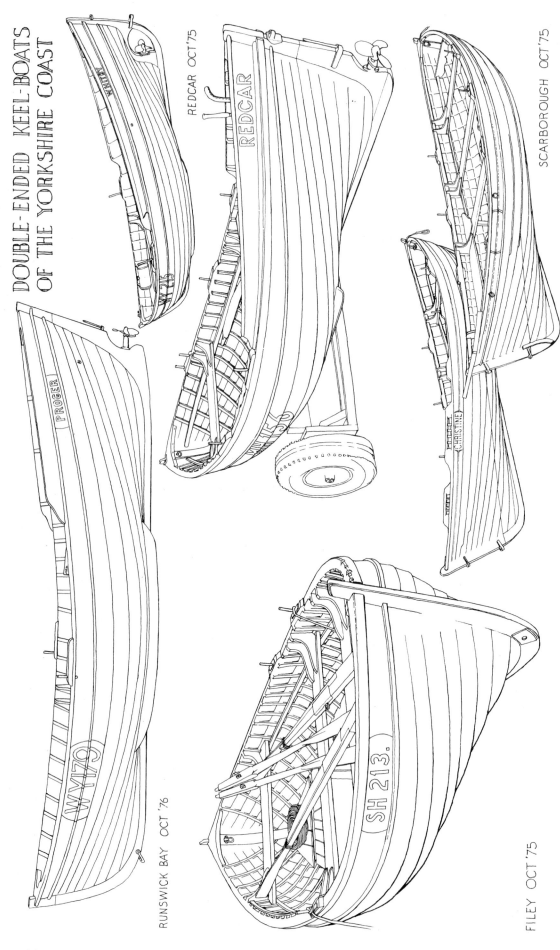

DOUBLE-ENDED KEEL-BOATS
OF THE YORKSHIRE COAST

REDCAR OCT'75

REDCAR

SCARBOROUGH OCT'75

PROGER

CHRISTINE

WY79

RUNSWICK BAY OCT '76

SH 213.

FILEY OCT '75

Fig 159: Double-ended Yorkshire keel boats.

NORTH BERWICK
SEPT. '76

Fig 160: Canoe-sterned motor fishing vessel and large double-ended keel.

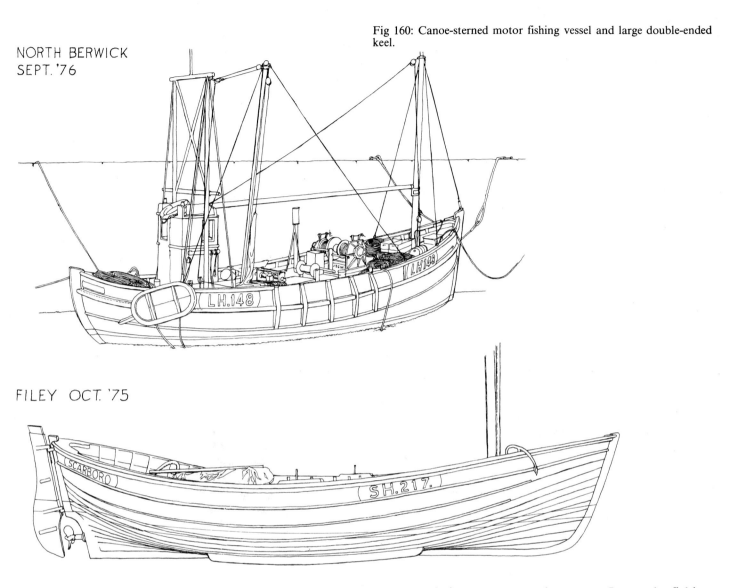

FILEY OCT. '75

short and light if they are to be manhandled ashore through surf. Some beach boats were, like the heroic Norfolk yawls, as much as 60-70ft long. As described, the East Kent galleys and Cornish gigs though smaller were by no means short boats. All these long narrow boats had large crews and so the manpower to lift them if needs be. Motorised cobles have become increasingly heavy with smaller crews. The ones that have to be beached depend upon wheeled trolleys pulled by tractors or capstans to get them in and out of the water. Much larger boats, even small ships, beach, to unload cargo, like the 50ft or more Yorkshire yawl, but were not hauled up and down.

The real home of the large beach boat was and still is Sussex. The shingle beaches here are steep and even the smaller boats need a beach capstan to haul them up the slope. To a lesser extent this is true all along the South Coast as far west as the Exe. Originally these capstans were man- or horse-powered, but nowadays they are diesel, petrol and electric motor driven winches. Only Budleigh Salterton has kept their hand capstans working (Fig 161). At the start of our period Brighton was an important fishing station, but commercial fishing and seaside holiday accommodation are not good partners. It was the fishing that declined at Brighton and the hoggy(21), the beamiest of the beamy Sussex beach boats, disappeared (Fig 46). In Hastings and Eastbourne the residential and fishing stretches of beach are well apart, so the visitors can but are not forced to take an interest in fish. The Sussex boats are clinker-built and the luggers from Hastings were decked and up to 48ft long at the time of Washington's report, though nearer 30ft by the time they were being motorised. Though built as keel boats with flat floors, they also had deep bilge runners to hold them upright and to act as skids during movement ashore. Beaching, even in fair weather, is worth watching. The boat drives inshore bows first fast enough to get the foot of the stem clear of the water up the beach. A hand then climbs down the stem using a permanent step on the port side of the stem at the waterline. Ashore, he hooks the fall block from the capstan onto the strap stem chain or bridle which is permanently rove through the ginge hole in the forward end of the keel. Almost before the boat comes to rest, the capstan starts to haul the boat, either to the crown of the beach if she is to be relaunched shortly or up over it onto

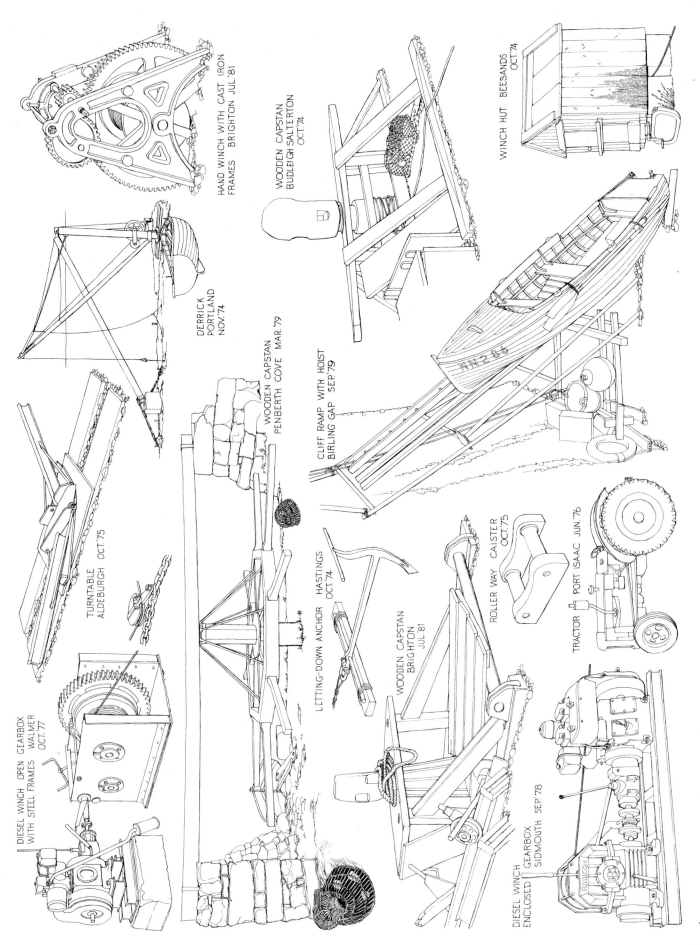

HAND WINCH WITH CAST IRON FRAMES BRIGHTON JUL.'81

WOODEN CAPSTAN BUDLEIGH SALTERTON OCT.'74

WINCH HUT BEESANDS OCT.'74

DERRICK PORTLAND NOV.'74

WOODEN CAPSTAN PENBERTH COVE MAR.'79

CLIFF RAMP WITH HOIST BIRLING GAP SEP.'79

TURNTABLE ALDEBURGH OCT.'75

LETTING-DOWN ANCHOR HASTINGS OCT.'74

WOODEN CAPSTAN BRIGHTON JUL.'81

ROLLER WAY CAISTER OCT.'75

TRACTOR PORT ISAAC JUN.'76

DIESEL WINCH OPEN GEARBOX WITH STEEL FRAMES WALMER OCT.'77

DIESEL WINCH ENCLOSED GEARBOX SIDMOUTH SEP.'78

Fig 161: Beach boat handling gear.

the level if there is to be bad weather or repairs.

The modern Sussex motor boats of all sizes are similar in character to their sailing predecessors, many of them having the old lute stern. A lute is structurally simple to build. All that has to be done is to run the upper strakes on beyond the transom to form a platform aft (Fig 44). Even small beach skiffs are given lute sterns and those turned out by L H Walker of Leigh are found far beyond the immediate coasts of Essex, Kent and Sussex. The elliptical form of stern has been gaining favour. Once again the strakes are run on past the transom, not only the upper few, but all that are above the tuck. The lower strakes are extended until they meet the ones from the other side of the centreline, but once the sheerline is reached the strakes are cut off flush with it. There are two views of which is the better arrangement: the elliptical stern is said the have better sea-keeping qualities while the lute stern gives better protection in surf. Being easier and cheaper to build, a lute stern gives a bigger boat for one's money. Nevertheless one sees elliptical sterns much further afield than lute sterns, possibly because the latter look old fashioned to strangers

to Sussex.

In bad weather the boats often hit the beach hard and this has given rise to a practice which anywhere else might be called poor fastening. The points of the nails holding the planks to the timbers are only turned and never hooked or riveted over roves. The reason for this is a heavy landing will only straighten and perhaps draw turned nails, whereas a more positive fastening would break a timber. Any strained nails can be seen at once and turned back over or replaced if they get brittle and break. The lerrets also used turned nails.

The Sussex boats are similar in many ways to those of Berck, France, in shape, build, rig and use of lee or centreboards, even the curved timbers of the 'mast cast' resemble each other[17]. Parallels like this on either side of the Channel are rare; the only other which comes to mind is the one that exists between some of the Cornish luggers and those of Lannion in North Brittany (Fig 163).

The beaches stretch westwards from Hastings with only a few breaks. The boats on them are never as large, partly because there are harbours offering shelter for bigger

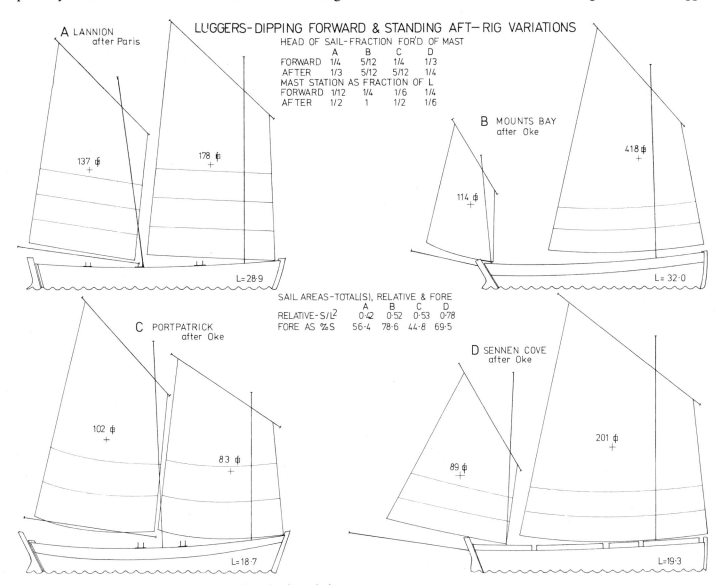

Fig 162: Luggers – dipping forward and standing aft: rig variations.

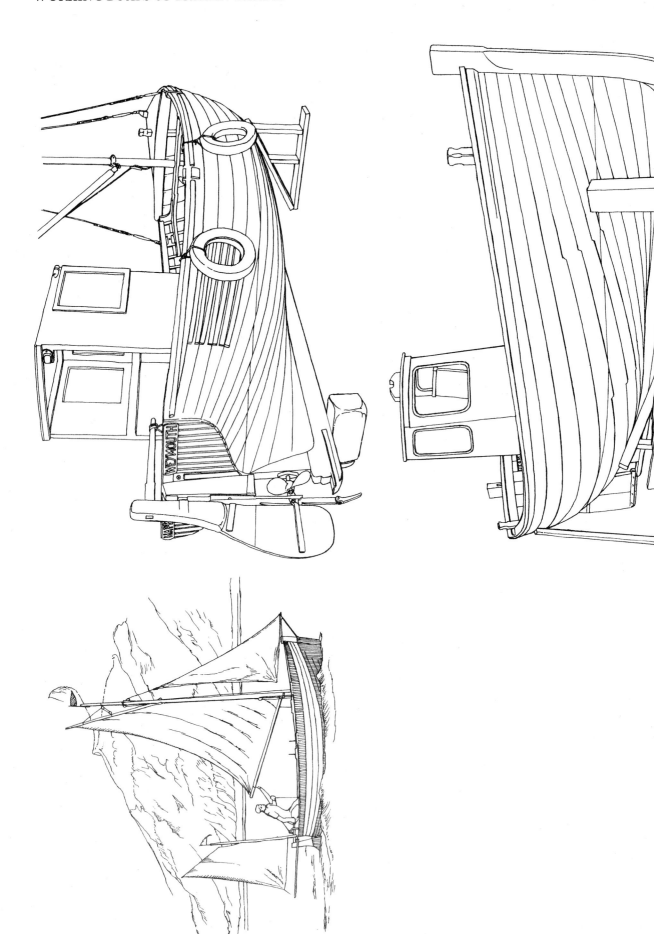

Left:
Fig 163: *Witch of Worbarrow* under sail.

Right:
Fig 165: Two Weymouth-registered boats, *Happy Return* at West Bay and a converted Weymouth harbour fishing boat.

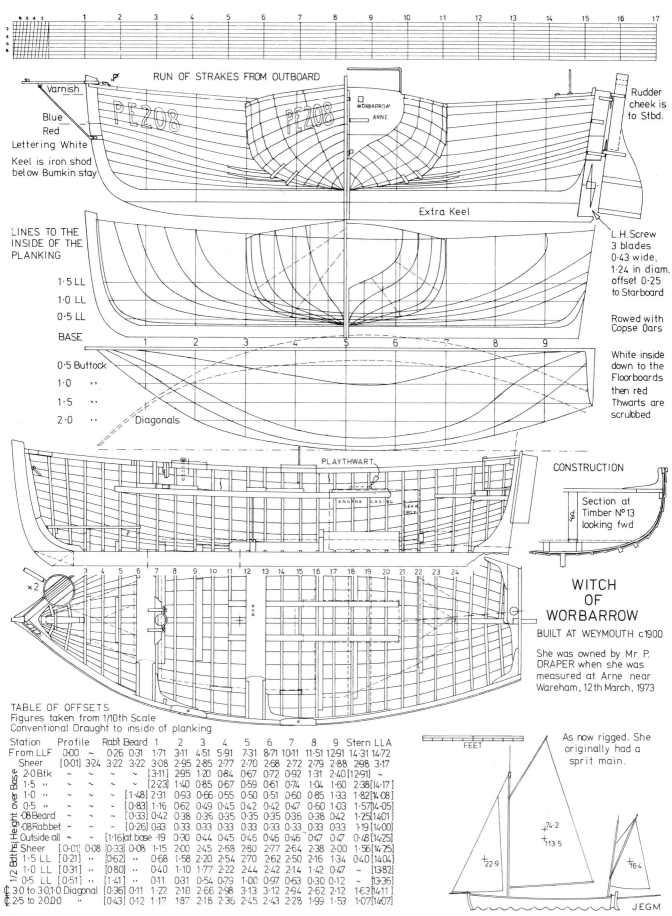

Fig 164: *Witch of Worbarrow* – lines.

boats. The nature of these harbour differ. Some of them are sited on river mouth: Rye on the Rother, Newhaven on the Ouse, Shoreham on the Adur and Littlehampton on the Arun. All these ports have had long deep-water histories and their rivers have carried trade well inland. From Selsey Bill to the Isle of Purbeck there are a series of landlocked waters inland from the shoreline: the harbours of Chichester, Langstone and Portsmouth, Spithead, Southampton Water and the Solent inside the Isle of Wight, then Christchurch and Poole Harbours. Except for Weymouth, Torbay and the Dart there are no safe all-weather havens between St Albans and the Start. Those at Bridport, Exmouth and Teignmouth in particular have treacherous approaches. Most of the boats of Lyme Bay can only work from one of the numerous beaches.

The *Witch of Worbarrow* (Fig 163) is an example of the sort of boat from a bay in the Isle of Purbeck. She is similar to, though smaller than, the harbour-based fishing boats that once worked out of Weymouth, where she was built in the early 1900s for work as a crabber. Though gaff-rigged now, she was originally sprit-rigged on both masts. In her conversion from a working into a pleasure craft she was re-engined with an off-set installation and had the false keel added, but apart from that has kept her old appearance. She lay on a mooring in Poole Harbour near to Shipstall Point, only laying up ashore there every winter. Her owner, the late Philip Draper, left her to the National Maritime Museum, where she is now (Fig 164).

The *Witch* exhibits many of the characteristics of a boat, which though harbour-based can still be beached. If she were to have been kept entirely at Weymouth, not only would she have been larger but the floors would have had more deadrise, like the unnamed 18-footer at Weymouth or the *Happy Return* at West Bay, Bridport (Fig 165).

Leaving Dorset for Devon, the representative sailing type along the east coast of Lyme Bay was the Beer lugger, though even the motorised version has been replaced by much larger boats on moorings rather than having to be hauled out on the common chain described by Commander Hill[18]. These luggers were of exceptional

Fig 166: East Lyme Bay boats *WH191*, *Dorset Lad* and *E219* at Seaton, and *Swan* at Lyme Cobb.

interest as they held on to their third mast right up till they were motorised in 1917. The boats seen on the East Devon beaches today are built by H S Mears of Seaton, Dixon or Lavis of Exmouth, or occasionally from Dartmouth or even Salcombe. The smaller beach boats have a strong resemblance to the Beer type, wych elm frequently being used for the planks. The larger tripping motor launches, those at Lyme Cobb for instance, show the same heritage (Fig 166).

Many working boats and barges have been preserved through having been turned into yachts, houseboats or museum exhibits. Inevitably they lose part of their nature when this happens. They gain a lease of life instead, and as more of their owners show more interest in achieving reality in preference to show or comfort, the more valuable their contribution becomes. One of these boats is the lugger *Erin* (32), built as the *Ibis* for Mr Lakeman in 1904 by W Frazier of Mevagissey. Her first name was transferred to a larger boat built for Mr Lakemen a few years later. *Erin* was probably one of the earlier boats to have been motorised under the so-called Cornish Loan (p154), which operated shortly before the First World War. Not only has she survived after a long working life which lasted into the 1970s, but so too have the details of her first set of sails cut for her by Mr G M Chesterfield, also of Mevagissey (Fig 168). Details of her construction and lines were taken off in 1977, while she was lying in Mr C Tom's yard at Polruan being restored for M & Mme G Cey, who planned to live on board her at Paimpol. She is by no means a wallflower, as she crossed the Channel twice in 1978, once to collect a new mainsail from Penrose, the sailmakers at Falmouth and the second time to take part in the Old Gaffer's Rally in Plymouth Sound. Conversion in her case has meant decking over the top of the coaming around the open fish hold, but this comes no higher than her bulwarks. Apart from that the alterations have been restricted to restoring her as nearly as possible to her sailing rig, taking out the wing engine and fitting a new centreline engine.

In *Erin* we have an example of a boat which had to work out of a drying-out harbour. She was a drifter that was only partly decked, leaving a large opening into the fish and net holds. There was a deep midship beam, called a thwart, to preserve the transverse strength. Before any engines were fitted there must have been accommodation aft as the companion is quite elegantly finished. The cuddy was forward with a scuttle to let the mast lower for lying to nets. The total area of sail set could be considerable and this was achieved by extending the tack of the jib with a bowsprit and the clew of the mizzen by a bumkin. The chapter on sails has described the variety of sail areas obtainable by setting the sails on different masts as well as by reefing (p143).

The mid-section of *Erin* differs from that of the unnamed 1906 lugger shown by Edgar March[19]. The latter has a deadrise of about 35° as compared with the 20° of the slightly older boat. It is hard to account for so much dif-ference. In spite of much flatter floors, *Erin*'s fuller lines are still shapely, giving her an easily driven hull without stinting her capacity for her nets and her catch. The square-cut ends of boats like these always seem to make them look boxier than they actually are (Fig 167).

The term 'nobby' in Britain refers to the hull shape found on the lee and exposed shores between Cardigan Bay and the Solway Firth. There are many shallow tidal bays and estuaries throughout this coast, which, though rich in sea-food, is a maze of shoals and banks and tricky to navigate. The north-west coast nobby came in a variety of sizes and was mainly used for shrimping, potting and yachting under sail but has now survived in a motorised but modified form. The Manx nobby was of a different type altogether having developed from the Cornish driver for deep water work.

The mainland nobby was essentially a shoal but weatherly sailing boat. As she had to carry enough sail to tow a trawl and work closely to windward, she had fine lines, ample beam and ballast. The best known class of nobby is the variety used for shrimping in Morecambe Bay. Though originally rightly described as a shrimper by Holdsworth[20] this boat had popularly become known as a prawner by the 1920s. This is misleading as prawns are generally taken in pots. Though other firms built these boats, the best known name of all is that of Crossfield's of Arneside. This 125-year-old yard has now changed hands, but the name has been retained. There have been Crossfields at Hoylake since 1908, and there still are at Conway, though the present firm is a yacht chandlery. The shape of the nobbies from these yards were so similar that it would be hard to say from which one of them any Crossfield-built boat came (Fig 169).

The nobby owed her fine lines to her deadrise rather than her profile, although this became more rounded in keel and forefoot as the design advanced. As a boat draws less water when heeled than upright, deadrise helps to avoid grounding and to refloat a boat that finds a bank instead of a channel. The introduction of outside ballast and sprung keels improved handling under way as well as making it easier to swing a grounding boat into the best aspect for refloating. Shrimp trawls bring a lot of water and debris onboard, and this affects deck lay-out. Side decks and coamings helped to keep the water out of the boat and provided a table for sorting the catch.

Benita (CO 78) is a Tremadoc Bay nobby, a 23ft (Fig 53) clinker boat built at Criccieth in 1908. She is still in use, partly as a yacht but also for working lobster pots commercially. This boat, apart from the refinement of an elliptical counter, comes close to being a nobby in one of her earlier forms, with a transom counter or just a plain transom stern. She has moderate depth and deadrise, drawing not much more aft then forward. She is rigged with a gaff mainsail on a pole mast and has a running bowsprit. By way of comparison *Moya* is a typical Morecambe Bay prawner, built with edge-positioned planking by Crossfield at Arneside in 1905 (Fig 170). This

199

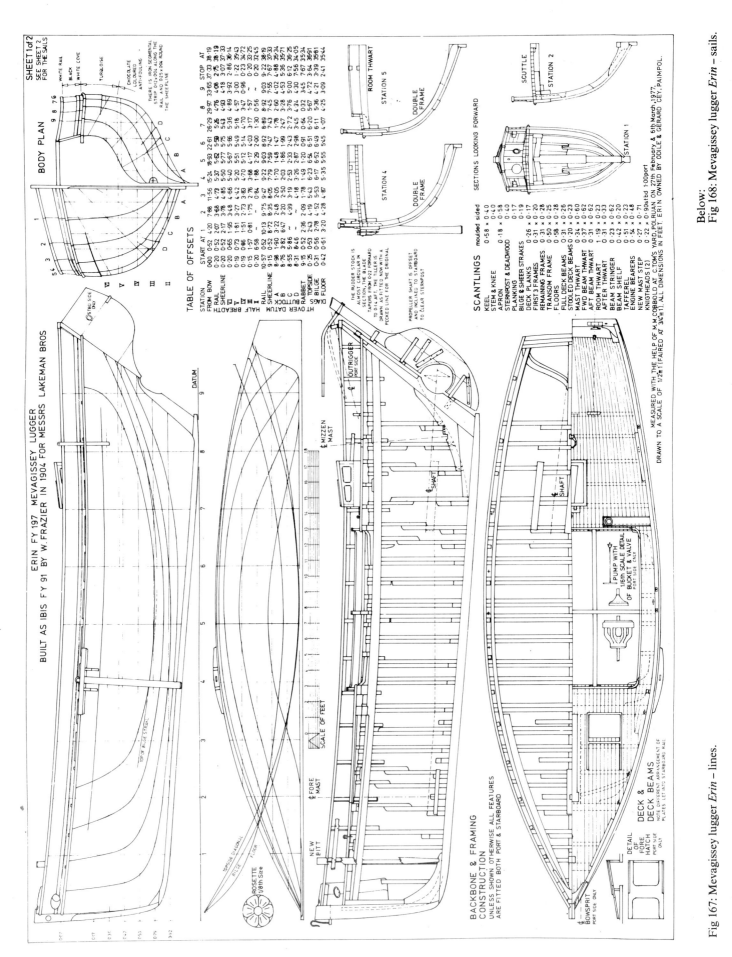

SHEET 1 of 2
SEE SHEET 2
FOR THE SAILS

BODY PLAN

THERE IS IRON SEGMENTAL
STRIP OF 1/2 × 0.04 ALONG THE
RAIL AND 0.25 × 0.04 ROUND
THE SHEERLINE

WHITE RAIL
BLACK
WHITE COVE
TURQUOISE

CHOCOLATE
COLOURED
ANTI-FOULING

TABLE OF OFFSETS

SECTIONS LOOKING FORWARD

ROOM THWART
STATION 5

DOUBLE FRAME
STATION 4

DOUBLE FRAME

SCUTTLE
STATION 2

DOUBLE FRAME
STATION 1

SCANTLINGS

	moulded	sided
KEEL	0·58 ×	0·40
STEM & KNEE	0·58 ×	0·40
STERNPOST & DEADWOOD	0·18 ×	0·58
PLANKING		0·17
BILGE & SHEER STRAKES		0·19
DECK PLANKS	0·26 ×	0·17
FIRST 3 FRAMES	0·31 ×	0·20
REMAINING FRAMES	0·31 ×	0·28
TRANSOM FRAME	0·50 ×	0·25
FLOORS	0·58 ×	0·28
FULL DECK BEAMS	0·31 ×	0·26
STOOLED DECK BEAMS	0·20 ×	0·23
MAST THWART	0·34 ×	0·60
FWD BEAM THWART	0·37 ×	0·62
AFT BEAM THWART	0·31 ×	0·62
ROOM THWART	1·19 ×	0·23
AFTER THWART	0·31 ×	0·33
BEAM STRINGER	0·23 ×	0·62
BEAM SHELF	0·42 ×	0·20
TAFEREL	0·51 ×	0·23
ENGINE BEARERS	0·54 ×	0·48
NEW MAST STEP	0·27 ×	0·71
KNIGTHEADS (12)	0·22 × 0·90 stbd 1·00 port

THE RUDDER STOCK IS
ALMOST CIRCULAR IN
SECTION, THE BLADE
TAPERS FROM 0·22 FORWARD
TO 0·14 AFT. THE TILLER IS
DRAWN AS FITTED NOW WITH A
PECKED LINE FOR THE ORIGINAL.

PROPELLER SHAFT IS OFFSET
AND INCLINED TO STARBOARD
TO CLEAR STERNPOST

ERIN FY 197 MEVAGISSEY LUGGER
BUILT AS IBIS FY 91 BY W. FRAZIER IN 1904 FOR MESSRS LAKEMAN BROS

℄ FORE MAST

SCALE OF FEET

℄ MIZZEN MAST

℄ SHAFT

OUTRIGGER
PORT SIDE

DATUM

TOPSIDE BILGE STREAK

ROSETTE 1/8th Size

TOPSIDE DIAGONAL
BILGE

NEW BITT

BACKBONE & FRAMING
CONSTRUCTION

UNLESS SHOWN OTHERWISE ALL FEATURES
ARE FITTED BOTH PORT & STARBOARD

PUMP WITH 1/6th SCALE DETAIL
OF BUCKET & VALVE
PORT SIDE ONLY

℄ SHAFT

BEAM SHELF

MEASURED WITH THE HELP OF M.M.CORBOLD AT C.TOM'S YARD, POLRUAN ON 27th FEBRUARY & 6th MARCH 1977.
DRAWN TO A SCALE OF 1/12 = 1 (FAIRED AT 3/4 = 1). ALL DIMENSIONS IN FEET. ERIN OWNED BY ODILE & GERARD CEV, PAIMPOL.

DETAIL
OF
FORE
HATCH
PORT SIDE
ONLY

DECK &
DECK BEAMS

NOTE DIFFERENT ARRANGEMENT OF
PLATES, LET IN STARBOARD RAIL

℄
BOWSPRIT
PORT SIDE ONLY

Fig 167: Mevagissey lugger *Erin* – lines.

Below:
Fig 168: Mevagissey lugger *Erin* – sails.

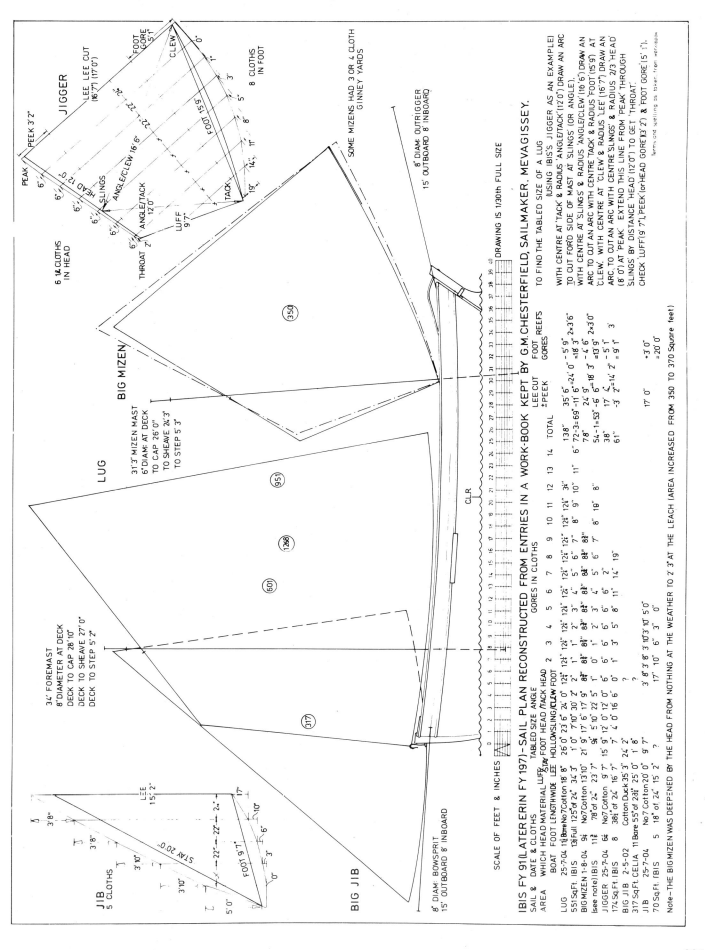

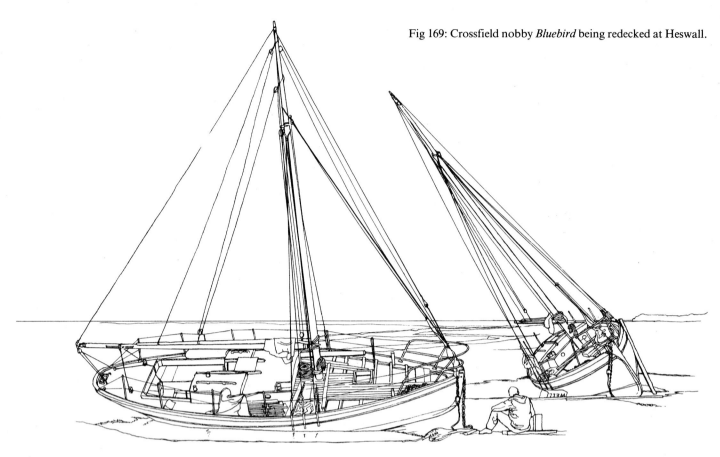

Fig 169: Crossfield nobby *Bluebird* being redecked at Heswall.

working boat is 34ft long, 28ft on the water line, 10.25ft beam and 3.75ft draft. It can be seen how easily this type (35) could be converted into a yacht, though in the pursuit of comfort and safety, their appearance was often altered by the addition of high coach roofs and toe-rails along the deck edge.

Subsequently the type adopted hollow floors and lost its identity as they became more like the conventional yachts of their time. Some of the old shrimpers are still about, with motors and their rigs partially or totally cut down. New motor nobbies are being built, some reverting to the plain transom stern once more. With the disappearance of masts, asymmetrical deck lay-outs are frequent, with the wheelhouse to one side and a broad sorting side deck on the other (Fig 171).

The general form of the nobby is found under other names and rigs in other English estuaries. The east coast Bawleys and smacks and the Solent ferry or fishing boats are examples. Largely because their excellent qualities have inspired many yacht designs, they have been adequately described by such gifted writers as Folkhard, Kemp, March and Leather. Happily, excellent examples have been saved from scrapping and have been restored so that they can now be used again. Over and above those in John Lewis's classic on the restoration of elderly boats, there are others like the *Joseph* of Maldon, *Mayflower* of Colchester and the *Wonder* (31) of Southampton still about[21]. J W Holness, the owner of the latter, has written about a range of five Solent ferry boats, varying from a lug-rigged 14ft centreboard boat up to the 19ft *Wonder*,

which has hollow garboards and an outside ballast keel to hold her up to her gaff cutter rig[22]. This article well illustrates how what is thought of as a single class of boats may be made up of a number of different sizes and variations. Sometimes in the past the performance of a certain vessel or the existence of drawings of another has established a more precise image of the type than careful research can confirm. All these shoal-drafted classes could be taken into deep water, which traditionally calls for deep hulls. Whether they are for fishing or pilots deep hulls must have proper harbours, in which they can stay afloat or be sheltered enough to bump half afloat without harm four times a day.

The English and Scots developed deepwater designs starting from local boats, not without problems and with different results. The nursery for this development was in the south west in England and the north east of Scotland, giving rise in the main to the gaff-rigged trawling ketch and lug-rigged drifters from the south and the much larger lug-rigged zulus and fifies from the north of Britain. All of these large classes together with their derivatives stopped working when steel and steam replaced wood and sail, but the effects of this change were felt differently in the two countries. In England the main deepwater fishing centres moved away from the south and the east to the north west and north east, closer to steel shipbuilding and coal mines. The size and number of wooden boats and boatyards dropped all over the country. In Scotland though some of the old ports grew dramatically, in general the boats and yards stayed largely where they have always been. Scottish

Top:
Fig 170: Morecambe Bay prawner *Moya* at Helford.

Below:
Fig 171: Motor nobbies at Silloth.

boatbuilding has continued, turning out wooden motor vessels of up to 80ft long, every bit as large as the biggest sailing boats that preceded them. This survival has been due to the continuing availability of good boatbuilding timber in Scotland.

The broad development of both the English and Scottish deepwater boats can be traced at least up to the point that they become ships rather than boats. As this stage is reached the local features become blurred and tend to merge into a standard type. While an expert can still tell the difference between a British and a German motor trawler, he would have to look at the registration letters to say from which port she came. Even these can be misleading as boats do not always change their registration when passing into new ownership at another port, and many deep sea boats come now from foreign yards.

The harbours along the deepwater nursery coasts of England and Scotland were broadly similar. They were not, as might be expected, either the large natural harbours like those formed by the drowned river valleys of the Tamar and Fal, nor the artificial ones the Victorians built at many railheads to cater for growing demands and catches. The start was made in small sheltered havens, which were only improved much later by the addition of quays, breakwaters and covered fish markets. Though numerous, some of the more successful early ones in England were at Brixham, Plymouth, Penzance and St Ives. The first two of these saw the rise of the sailing trawlers, which in turn had a powerful influence on the development of the fisheries at Ramsgate, Lowestoft, Yarmouth, Grimsby and Hull, until the steam driven steel vessels took over. A spread north took place in much the same way from the last two ports of sailing drifter designs to the Isle of Man and Fleetwood, once again till power took over. In Scotland the first fishing stations also grew from small coastal havens, which had been progressively provided with protection from the dominant north-north-westerly winds.

Here, as Washington's report of 1849 makes clear, the protected harbours were in a decrepid state and the local open boats were, as proven by the loss of life from Eyemouth to Wick, unable to withstand this summer gale long enough to see it out or regain the doubtful safety of their ill maintained home-ports. Captain Washington's recommendation that the Scottish fisherman should adopt decked designs like those in England were not acceptable to the Secretary to the Board of Fisheries in Scotland, much greater cost per vessel being the reason given. In fact as the Scots have pointed out, a great number of English boats were still undecked at that time.

Nevertheless the Scots repaired and improved their harbours and began to deck over the larger sizes of their local designs, concentrating on luggers for herring drifting rather than trawlers. The development has been told often enough, but was briefly as follows. The scaffie came first, an East coast skiff, double-ended, clinker-built, with raking sternpost and cutaway forefoot. She was based on the Moray Firth herring boat from Buckie, which was 41ft long and 13ft beam in Washington's report, and then entirely open. She had a standing sandstrake and the firm bilges that are still liked for the way they cut down rolling when lying to nets.

The scaffie was replaced by the larger fifie which had almost vertical stem and sternposts, less hollow floors and the same transverse sections fore and aft. The zulu combined the bow of a fifie with the stern of a scaffie, giving a longer boat for a given length of keel. The fifie and zulu co-existed, both having a two-masted lug rig in which the dipping fore lug was far the larger sail. On the introduction of the screw it was the fifie that was converted as her upright sternpost and rudder accepted an aperture without weakness. Alexander Noble's account of the subsequent development of the powered fishing boats brings the Scottish ones up to the present day[23].

Peter Anson showed the difference in the need for boats on the west and east coasts of Scotland[24]. Broadly speaking the east coast fisheries are concerned with marketing fish, while on the east coast fishing provides part of a crofter's diet. There have been and still are attempts to encourage commercial fisheries on this coast, by building better harbours and installing fish processing plants. Some of these enterprises, like those at Ness and Castlebay, have flourished, but only for a short time. Others, like those at Ullapool, Stornoway and Mallaig, have survived, though at the time of writing these too are experiencing a set-back due to restrictions aimed at conserving stocks of herring. Though the men of the west have consistently shown themselves to be excellent naval and mercantile seamen and by necessity steadfast part-time inshore boatmen, they do not seem to produce many full-time inshore fishermen.

There are several reasons for this. Primarily a crofter has to be self-supporting and self-dependent. Even if the weather permitted all-the-year-round fishing, a crofter could hardly live on fish alone; he had to farm a patch and keep sheep or cattle as well. This meant that there were few local funds and a reluctance to accept external influence. The distances from worthwhile markets make local processing essential. While ling and herring were cured in this way, the taste for salt fish has not lasted. Canning and freezing has encouraged steady fishing once again, particularly for valuable catches like crab and lobster. The plants have had to be funded by outside capital so remain as economically precarious as the earlier attempts to promote a fishing industry on the west coast. Lastly there is less boatbuilding timber north-west of the Caledonian Canal, so that it is often cheaper to import timber in the form of a boat than in that of logs and planks. Though there have been excellent boatbuilders all along the west coast and in the Outer Isles, the imported types of boat are most in evidence today.

Until this has been realised, the variety and random distribution of the boat types seen is confusing. The boats

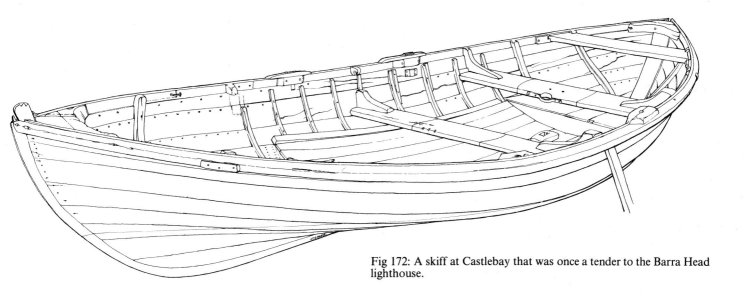

Fig 172: A skiff at Castlebay that was once a tender to the Barra Head lighthouse.

here reflect the contacts that have existed. It would be fitting if one were able to say that leather boats were still in evidence to reflect the once strong Celtic influence on this coast. All that can be seen is the occasional use of Scottish cobles, and that they are currently being built at Portree. The probability here is that the design has been brought back from the east coast. The evidence from the islanders' personality is inconclusive. There are signs of Neolithic origins. The Celtic influence is strong, with Gaelic still freely spoken and Catholicism in the south. Yet there is Calvinism in the north. The place names are often Norse, while the clan names follow the old geographical pattern. It is no wonder that the boats are such a mixture of alien types.

Two sorts of boat of Norse origin are seen, the pram quite a lot and the skiff more rarely. These are probably fairly recent arrivals. The carpenters of timber-importing ships from Scandinavia built prams and sold them over here long before the cheap Rana boats were imported in large numbers. L Harris has told me that a Harris boat-builder has been building prams as replacements for imported ones. A more common type seen in the creeks serving crofts are similar to the smaller types seen on the East Coast of Scotland. Since the opening of the Caledonian Canal in 1822, the east coast fishermen have been able to work on either coast without having to brave the Pentland Firth. As these boats grew larger they needed small boats which were sold to the islanders before returning home.

The 40-70ft long inshore fishing boats are of the motor fishing vessel type with cruiser, canoe or transom sterns, arranged for trawling or ring netting in the larger sizes and lining or potting in the smaller. More recently the wheelhouse has been moved forward for scallop dredging rigs and large fleets of pots. The majority of the boats above boats are wooden and were built on the east coast or south west of Scotland. John Jefferis and Tom Swansom of Scrabster, as well as repairing wooden boats,

build fishing boats up to 65ft long in ferro-cement. A smaller size is popular with the crofters on the west coast because of this material's ability to stand up to harvesting seaweed. Clinker creel boats up to 40ft long built in the Orkneys are used for the commercial pot catch. James Duncan of Burray and J W McKay of Stromness build these in GRP as well as wood, while Halmatic of Kirkwall build only in GRP. These powerfully engined boats are large and fast enough to work lobster pots on the Atlantic side of the Outer Isles in the summer from the eastern facing ports like Castlebay, Lochboisdale, Tarbert in Harris and Stornoway, but work closer to home in the Minches during the spring and autumn.

The boats of the Firth of Clyde and Loch Fyne are using waters better thought of as a northern extension of the Irish Sea than part of the Atlantic Coast of Scotland. The fishing boats and small traders of these relatively sheltered but gusty seas between Campbeltown in Kintyre and Portpatrick in Galloway have been recorded in the past[24]. Instead of a large number of small fishing stations, the fisheries nowadays, concentrate on fewer places, like Campbeltown, Tarbert in Kintyre, Ardrossan, Ayr and Girvan. Even these are mainly home bases and one is just as likely to see some of these modern well-equipped boats landing mackerel in Newlyn, Falmouth or Plymouth as lying in their home-port.

At the start of the nineteenth century the common sort of boat was the Clyde nabbie. She would appear to have been an extension of the Irish Sea nobby, having transom or square counter sterns and gaff rig. In the middle of that century they were replaced by double-ended and fine lines forward. The lines aft had a fuller appearance, especially the topsides where the gunwale was almost circular in plan view. The masts were given more than usual rake and the standing lug was preferred to the dipping lug. Jibs were set on running bowsprits.

P J Oke took off the lines of many of the varieties of this

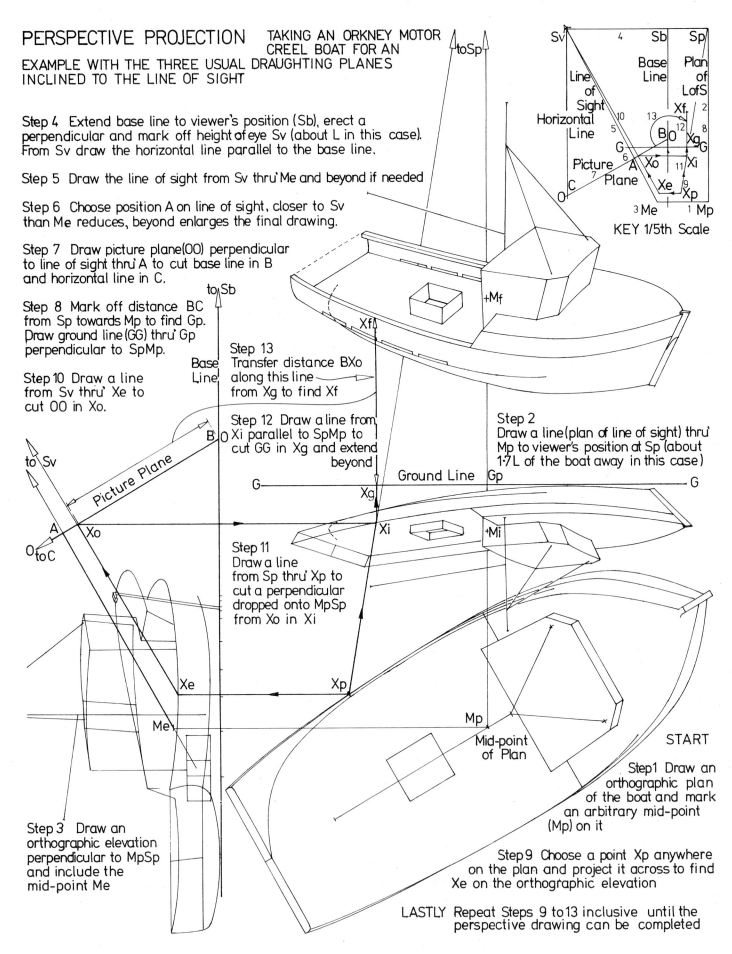

PERSPECTIVE PROJECTION TAKING AN ORKNEY MOTOR CREEL BOAT FOR AN EXAMPLE WITH THE THREE USUAL DRAUGHTING PLANES INCLINED TO THE LINE OF SIGHT

KEY 1/5th Scale

Step 4 Extend base line to viewer's position (Sb), erect a perpendicular and mark off height of eye Sv (about L in this case). From Sv draw the horizontal line parallel to the base line.

Step 5 Draw the line of sight from Sv thru' Me and beyond if needed

Step 6 Choose position A on line of sight, closer to Sv than Me reduces, beyond enlarges the final drawing.

Step 7 Draw picture plane(OO) perpendicular to line of sight thru' A to cut base line in B and horizontal line in C.

Step 8 Mark off distance BC from Sp towards Mp to find Gp. Draw ground line (GG) thru' Gp perpendicular to SpMp.

Step 10 Draw a line from Sv thru' Xe to cut OO in Xo.

Step 13 Transfer distance BXo along this line from Xg to find Xf

Step 12 Draw a line from Xi parallel to SpMp to cut GG in Xg and extend beyond

Step 2 Draw a line (plan of line of sight) thru' Mp to viewer's position at Sp (about 1·7 L of the boat away in this case)

Step 11 Draw a line from Sp thru' Xp to cut a perpendicular dropped onto MpSp from Xo in Xi

Step 3 Draw an orthographic elevation perpendicular to MpSp and include the mid-point Me

Ground Line

Base Line

Picture Plane

Mid-point of Plan

START

Step 1 Draw an orthographic plan of the boat and mark an arbitrary mid-point (Mp) on it

Step 9 Choose a point Xp anywhere on the plan and project it across to find Xe on the orthographic elevation

LASTLY Repeat Steps 9 to 13 inclusive until the perspective drawing can be completed

later type for the Coastal and River Craft committee of the Society for Nautical Research. Starting with the Annan whammel-net boat, whose full sections suggest a mixture of English and Scottish influence, he went round the coast to draw the Portpatrick line boat's slightly hollow floors and unusual schooner lug rig, with dipping fore and standing main. There are still a few remaining beach skiffs at Ballantrae and those Oke drew at Ardrossan and Largs got shallower further up the Clyde. Though these were initially small boats, some were being built as long as 45ft by the end of the century and continued to be

built up to the early 1920s. A distinctive detail on all these west coast standing lug-rigged boats was the short horse for the tack on the sailing thwart, a little forward of the mast. This horse had a sliding tack hook, which gave a better set to the sail on either tack. The 18ft skiff *Gylen* that Oke measured at Oban was even more pear-shaped than the Clyde estuary types, but had hardly any hollow in her floors. The circular gunwale aft can still be seen in a few of the older boats in the vicinity of the Firth of Lorne.

Two related features of Scottish boats stand out: how the old sailing types have disappeared almost completely, and how well the motor boats have advanced. In every respect these boats have taken advantage of up-to-date machinery and fishing gear, using old or new materials with equal success. The boatyards in England are smaller and far more numerous. They are more traditional in their methods and this has preserved many of the old local characteristics in the motor boats they are now building.

Left:
Fig 173: Perspective projection, taking an Orkney creel boat as an example.

Below:
Fig 174: Standing lugs: fixed and sliding tacks.

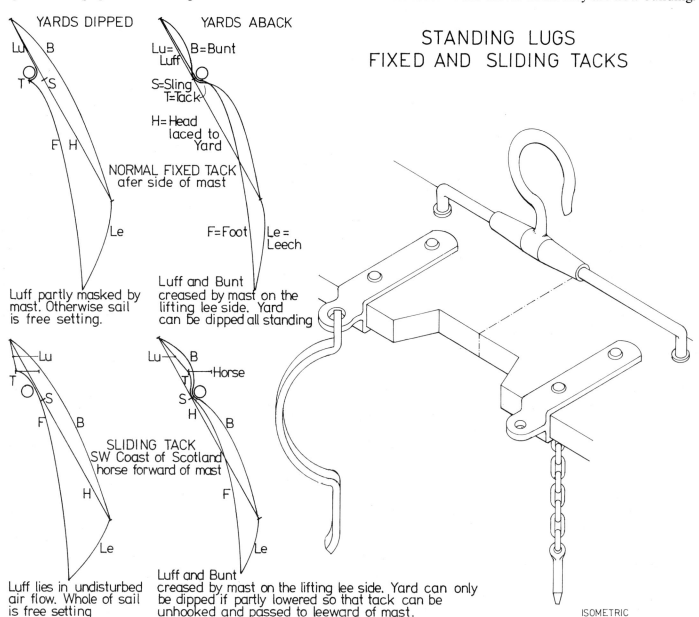

STANDING LUGS FIXED AND SLIDING TACKS

10.

Distribution patterns

The manner in which a distinct boat type is distributed in relation to her task and surrounding can be complex, especially when it is constantly changing. As these distribution patterns tell a great deal about a type's capability, some space must be given to them. A group of boats can be said to belong to a distinct type, if all of them share cognate features that are alike in origin, appearance or structure by an amount that differentiates them from any other group of boats. A boat that does not belong to any distinct type is indeterminate. If these definitions are accepted, it will be seen that more careful study may show that there is a need to regroup some distinct types and that some boats, previously regarded as indeterminate, belong to a distinct group. This is especially true today when geographical separation of similar types is more common.

It is not easy to decide what matters, in terms of overall numbers, range of size or period of existence, when choosing boats to be typed. It would be equally unsatisfactory if there was only one designation for a numerous, persistent but variable type like the flatties, as to have a distinct type with only one known example. If, in a large fishing station, like Brixham at the start of the century, there were three well represented classes of sailing trawler, which were classed by tonnage only, this would merit three sub-divisions of a grade of related types. If they had also differed (which they did not) in some of their cognate features, in that one class was flat-bottomed, another double-ended and the third class was the only one to be clinker built, then three distinct types are evident. Unlike ships, the number of masts in a boat is a less significant indication of type than whether those masts carry square, gaff or lug sails, as this may determine whether she is lightly- or heavily-built, decked or undecked, and shoal-drafted or deep-keeled. If quite a small group of boats have features, which come from an ancient tradition and lead on to a recent one, this type might be regarded as distinct. Ultimately, the chief purpose of classification is to aid comprehension of what might otherwise be confusing. Too much of it is as bad as too little.

At any one period, examples of a distinct type may be found in a number of different situations, which may spread alone a coastline or be found dotted all over the place. These distribution patterns are the outcome of very much the same factors that determine the shape of the boat: task, skills, seascape and so on. The pattern is an additional indication of what that kind of boat is capable of doing in a wider field than the immediate surroundings that first saw her. There are more patterns possible than could be conceivably identified. The important variables seem to be: suitability of work, from specialised to general,

adaptability to locale, from just one place to anywhere, and coverage, from a single type meeting all the boat work in one place to fulfilling the needs of only one grade in the full range of boat work. There is also the singularity in the way requirements are met – some being exclusive to just one design whilst others may permit several solutions. The salmon stop-net tends towards a one-design boat, while the salmon seine-net is known to have several. The extreme cases may be illustrated in the form of a diagram:

The only boat suitable for some specialised work in a certain place	A versatile type of boat capable of all sorts of general work in most places
One of a choice of boat types all able to do part of the work in a certain place	One of a range of boats that together are able to do most of the work in most places

Such extreme cases are rarely met, so provision has to be made for the distribution patterns that come between. If, as a means of showing what these patterns are, we sort them into five kinds of distribution and five situations, a matrix can be constructed with twenty-five different definitions. Before the individual definitions, the various distributions and situations involved have to be described.

When a boat type is found in only one place in the whole of Britain, this is called an *isolated* distribution. If the same type occurs in several places separated by areas populated by some other boat type, the distribution is called *interrupted*. If the type is found all along a stretch of coast, there is a *continuous* but *limited* distribution, when there are only slight changes in the tasks and surroundings; but *continuous* and *extended*, when there are considerable variations in both. If the boat type can be found all over Britain, this is called *universal* distribution. The distributions of the following types, which are described on the page indicated, would be as follows under this system:

Severn punt – isolated.
Orkney creel boat – interrupted
E. Devon beach boat – continuous limited
Scottish coble – continuous extended
Stem keel boat with transom – universal.

In all these distributions it is possible for a boat to be in any of the following situations. The type may occur all by itself, in what is called a *solitary* situation. The type can also occur as one of the grades of boats that together perform all the boat work in that place. This may happen in four ways. All the grades in the range may be related with similar cognate features, so the boat may be said to be in a *related grade*, which is *arrested* if, for whatever reason, it is found that the type has not developed for some time. It is *functional* however, if the type is being actively developed to keep abreast of changing requirements, but without loss of cognate features. If instead the type in question is different from the other types that make up the range in that place, this is called an *unrelated grade*. Lastly if in the one grade more than one distinct type is employed then this is a *mixed grade* situation. Specific exampes may help to illustrate this:

Dunwich beach boats – solitary
Motorised Hastings luggers – related arrested grade
Motorised Filey keel boats – related functional grade
Bridlington rowing boats – unrelated grade
Inshore fleet at Abersoch – mixed grade

When both distributions and situations are brought together they create the twenty-five definitions of the available patterns which appear as in Appendix VII. The working of the system is more straight-forward than it might seem at first. It can be better demonstrated if an imaginary example is taken before several actual ones.

Assume the discovery of a group of similar boats, which are unlike any other type yet read about or seen. Talks on site backed up by old picture postcards show that this has been the only type used in the cove for about a century. It looks as if this is a case of an isolated solitary type of boat. Further research shows that a larger station in the next bay once used this class of boat for winter fishing, but depended on a bigger and better documented type in the summer. The features of the two types had little in common, indicating that in the larger station the newly-discovered type had been of the interrupted unrelated grade. After hearing a talk at the local university town and port, a retired boatbuilder shows his work books dating back to the 1880s. These leave no doubt that boats of a similar type had once been built for stations all along this coast, especially as the old boatbuilder was able indicate a derelict example to ensure the same sort of boat was being talked about. It would now seem that, unless further examples turned up further afield, that in its heyday the type was of the limited but continuous unrelated grade in the larger station, though it had so fallen in numbers today as to have become an isolated solitary type in the cove. It will be seen that the category changes as time passes and from place to place. It is these changes that matter and prompt a search for reasons. In this example there may have been difficulties over motorisation or even failure of the winter fishing.

The system only applies to distinct types, for today's harbours are populated with many boats, which have to be taken as indeterminate until they have been properly recorded, examined and sorted. This is a large task which depends upon an agreed method of describing boats so that they can be compared. The system described in Chapter 6 was devised so that this book could be written. No more claim is made for it other than as a place from which to start. Without some common system there can be

no real progress towards classifying plank boats. Some case studies of existing or recent boats in actual situations are given to show the use of distribution patterns.

In the flat central plain known as the Somerset levels, which lie inland of the coast between Watchet and Clevedon (E10 & S9, IV12 – see Appendix I) as far as the Mendips in the east and the Quantocks in the west, there were until recently various types of flat-bottomed keel-less boats, which between them performed all the boat work other than acting as tenders to the coasting vessels. Although the different types had distinctive names and features, and did vary considerably in size, they all seem to be related to one another. Starting with the most simple, they were:

Turf boat

A true flatty (1) used on inland waters for farm transport and commerce on the River Brue. Recently obsolete. Single slab flat bottom, hard chine to flat 45° flared edge-joined 2-strake sides, which meet in raked and pointed ends with internal posts. Widely spaced rungs and inter-costal side knees, inwales. 17–35ft long. Pole/paddled or tracked. Identical ends. (p107)

Withy boat

A true flatty (1) used on inland waters for osier farming on Rivers Parrett and Tone. A few still used. Edge-positioned multi-strake flat bottom, hard chine to flat 20° flared edge-joined 4-strake sides, which meet in raked and pointed ends with internal posts and a false stem for'd. Less widely spaced rungs and knees overlap either side of the same stations, inwales and rubbers at sheerline. 18–19ft long, poled, paddled or tracked with a few with outboard engines. A pair of canted knees forward and a stowage box aft tell the bow from the stern (p131).

Bridgwater barge

A true bateau (6) used on inland waters as a river lighter, a canal barge and for the collection of the ingredients of Bath brick, from Start Point to Langport on the River Parret and to Taunton on the River Tone and the Bridgwater & Taunton Canal. Recently obsolete. Edge-positioned multi-strake flat bottom, 45° hard chine to curved edge-joined multi-strake sides, which meet at a curved raked pointed rabbet stem forward and a raked tombstone sternpost aft. Short decks each end with boxed gunwales between. Close-fitted ceiling above rungs. Up to 52ft long (limit of canal locks is 54 × 13ft), moved by tide, tug or tracking, steered by sweeps or rudder. Bow fuller than stern (p31).

Parrett flatner

A dished flatty (3) used in Bridgwater Bay and the lower reaches of the River Parrett as a farm's fishing boat. A few modified examples remain. Edge-positioned 5-strake sprung and cambered bottom, hard chine to 30° flared flat sides (single-strake butt scarfed just aft of midships)

Fig 175: Parrett flatner – 19ft bay boat, perspective projection.

meeting at a slightly curved raked two-part stem and raked tombstone aft. Well spaced frames with overlapped rungs and knees. Inwales. 17–22ft long, sail or oar; one unstayed mast with spritsail and jib, lee or dagger board and deep narrow rudder when sailing, double thole pins for two pairs of oars. Recently square sterns for outboards have been fitted. (Fig 175).

Watchet flatty
A dished flatty (3) built at Combwich and like the Parrett flatner except the bottom was protected by an external layer of rough boards because of the rough ledges over

which she worked. Recently obsolete.

Weston-super-Mare flatner
A dished bateau (8) used out of Weston Bay as far as Steep and Flat Holm for fishing and tripping. The few remaining are privately owned. Single or double thickness slab bottom, sprung and cambered, hard chine to 60° edge-joined multi-straked curved flared sides, which meet at a raked rabbet stem for'd and sternpost aft, with or without transom. Closely spaced rungs with wider spaced futtock knees overlapping occasional rungs. Later boats employed steamed timbers. 10–23ft long, sail or oar; one unstayed

mast for spritsail and jib, case took two dagger boards in tandem, normal depth rudder, double thole pins or crutches for one or two pairs of oars. Late examples have outboard or inboard engines and are fuller in shape (Fig 176).

Clevedon boat
Almost certainly a dished bateau (8) but not fully identified. Reputed to have been a 16ft class of Weston flatner and used in both places. Included as being the furthest north these types are found.

The main features of these boats have been set out in the form of a table to help comparison (Fig 177). It can be seen from this that the five main types share the following cognate features, namely:

Keel-less, with flat or almost flat bottoms, rung stiffened

Hard chines, flared sides meeting at pointed ends fore and aft

Clinker side planks, where there is more than one strake

The features that tell them apart are aspects of differences in work and surroundings. The up-river boats, which have to be shoal, are true flatties, while the coastal boats, which have to be launched over stretches of mud, are dished. The Weston flatner has closely spaced rungs to stand bumping on the tide at Knightstone, as has the barge, which also has to take the ground as well as concentrated loads. The close

Fig 176: Weston-super-Mare flatners.

THE FLAT-BOTTOMED BOATS OF NORTH SOMERSET COMPARATIVE TABLE

Type	**TURF BOAT**	**WITHY BOAT**	**BRIDGWATER BARGE**	**PARRETT FLATNER**	**WESTON-S-MARE FLATNER**
Taxon	True Flatty (01)	True Flatty (01)	True Bateau (06)	Dished Flatty (03)	Dished Bateau (08)
Length	17–35 ft	18–19 ft	Up to 52 ft	17–22 ft	10–23 ft
Waterway	Inland	Inland	Inland	River and Estuary	Estuary
Builder	Carpenter	Carpenter	Shipbuilder	Owner or Carpenter	Owner or Boatbuilder
Propulsion	Pole and Track	Pole and Track	Drift, Tow and Track	Sail and Oar	Sail and Oar
CONSTRUCTION					
Plank	Slab	Edge-position	Edge-position	Edge-position	Slab (2)
Bottom					
Frame	Spaced rungs 2-strake	Spaced rungs 4-strake	Close rungs Multi-strake	Spaced rungs One-strake	Close rungs Multi-strake
Plank	Edge-joined	Edge-joined	Edge-joined	Two planks	Edge-joined
Sides					
Frame	Intercostal	Overlapping	Overlapping	Overlapping	Overlapping
Stem	Internal post	Internal post + false stem	Rabbet stem	2-piece stem	Rabbet stem
Ends					
Stern	Internal post	Internal post	Tombstone	Tombstone	Sternpost +/− transom

Fig 177: Comparative table of flat-bottom boats of north Somerset.

spacing of the barge's side knees withstand both this loading and knocks alongside when lightering. The curved sides of the Weston flatner and the barge help to keep these open boats dry, out in the chop of the estuary for the flatner, but for the barge when she is deeply loaded in the river when the eager runs. The various propulsion methods are clearly attuned to each class's job and locale, and all the tracked boats are towed from asymmetric positions.

This group of boats between them present an almost Darwinian progression of forms. Within the limitations of a flat bottom design, which are actually advantages in the Somerset surroundings, each type has developed up to a point where the local requirements have been met to perfection. The inspiration towards improvement seems to have been largely internally generated. There are two evident exceptions, both being where the communications with the rest of Britain were better: at Weston-super-Mare where transom sterns were found, and at Bridgwater where the barges share features with the nineteenth century up-river barges and trows[1]. Improved land drainage, better roads, the decay of the port of Bridgwater, softer scouring powders than 'Monkey Brand' and difficulty of engining flat-bottom pointed stern boats, all combined to superannuate this range of boats. In recent times only basket-making gives work to a few withy boats. Since the Second World War, Harold Kimber of Highbridge built a few 16ft Weston flatners, some with inboard engines. Though his modified design suited these shallow choppy waters, it is unlikely to compete with much cheaper, batch-built GRP boats. Turning back to the first quarter of this century when all of these boats were in active use, they formed a clear distribution pattern in North Somerset. The distribution was 'continuous and extended' and the situation was that of an 'arrested related range'. Written out in full any one of these types were: 'developed no further than needed to provide one of the related grades in places over an extended area or stretch of coast, with much variation in task or surroundings or both, and where a range of boats is necessary'.

Fifty miles south-east of Bridgwater is Weymouth on the Dorset coast (L2 & E4, 116). Here the pattern is quite different. Within a mile of each other there are three unrelated types of boat: the lerrets on Chesil Bank, the trows on the Fleets and the fishing boats that were once peculiar to Weymouth Harbour. Though they are so close together, the work and surroundings differ so much that they appear to have only one common feature, the single-pin copse oar. Even then the trow is mostly poled and not rowed. Otherwise they do not seem to have had any influence on each other's designs.

Lerret

A hoggy (21), used for mackerel seining off Chesil Bank between East Beckington and Chesiltom, with a long standing record of lifesaving, salvage and freetrading[2]. Some are still in use and one builder recently active. Keel boat, edge-joined, flat floored, round bilged, slightly flam sides meeting at raked 2-piece stems both ends. Steamed timbers with inwales and rubbers. Beam to length ratio 3:1 or less, 16–21ft long. 4- or 6-oared, one man to each. Simple sailing rigs were once used for longer trips. (p188).

Fleet trow or Backwater boat

A dished flatty (3) used on the Fleets to transport the lerret's crew and catch as well as for fishing and wildfowling. Still in use and being built. Edge-positioned multi-strake bottom, very slightly dished with well-spaced rungs and intercostal frames. Hard chine to 25° flared flat edge-joined 3-strake sides meeting at raked one- or two-piece stems at either end. As many trows have transom sterns as not. Breasthooks and quarter knees are fitted to suit. The top strakes are blocked under the cleats for the thole pins, but no other stiffening for the gunwales. 15–18ft long, pole paddled or up to three pairs of oars (Figs 178 & 179).

Weymouth Harbour Fishing boat

A haven boat (28), was harbour based and used for trawling and handlines in Weymouth Bay and along the Isle of Purbeck Coast to Lulworth Cove. There are one or two motorised examples left. Straight level keel, edge-joined multi-strake, raised floor, round bilge and plumb sides. The stem is almost upright with a round forefoot below the waterline and an upright sternpost with a generous transom clear of the water. She is decked forward of the mast with narrow side and short after decks. 18–20ft long, they were propelled by sail, copse oars and later inboard engines, to which they converted readily. The rig was gaff main and topsail, small bumkin for the tack of the head sail and a boomed out jib-headed mizzen (Fig 180).

None of these types existed in isolation at Weymouth, as each had their variations elsewhere. The square-ended pot boat is still an active sub-type of the lerret, found mainly near Portland, some being derricked over the edge of a cliff in and out of the sea (Fig 161). These liners and crabbers are seen anywhere between Burton Bradstock and Lulworth Cove. 14–16ft long, they are propelled by outboard motor and copse oar, and are distinct from boats

with sternposts and transoms elsewhere along this coast as they are square-ended boats (40). There are all kinds of flat bottom boats on most inland waters from Abbotsbury to Mudeford. At Wareham there are 18½ft sprung flatties (2) used for cutting reeds for thatching. These are 17ft along the edge-positioned 5-plank bottom, with 10° flared edge-joined sides and pointed at both ends. They are propelled by oars working in crutches. In Christchurch Harbour there are punts used primarily for commercial salmon fishing but also for hiring out to visitors. There are also sprung flatties (2), but with square sterns and larger with a more elaborate construction. Both thole pins and crutches are seen, with some of the hire boats being GRP copies. Very like the Weymouth Harbour fishing boat was the small open crabber once used all the way along the Purbeck Coast. These like *Witch of Worbarrow* (p198) were built at Weymouth, generally about 14ft long and sprit-rigged with oars.

The three principal types co-existed until the 1940s when the harbour fishing boats were the first to go, being replaced by a mixture of unrelated motor boats, which have been further complicated by the introduction of owner fitted out standard GRP hulls. The lerrets are much

Fig 178: Two fleet trows on Chesil Bank, opposite Park Wall, a new transom-sterned boat and an older double-ender.

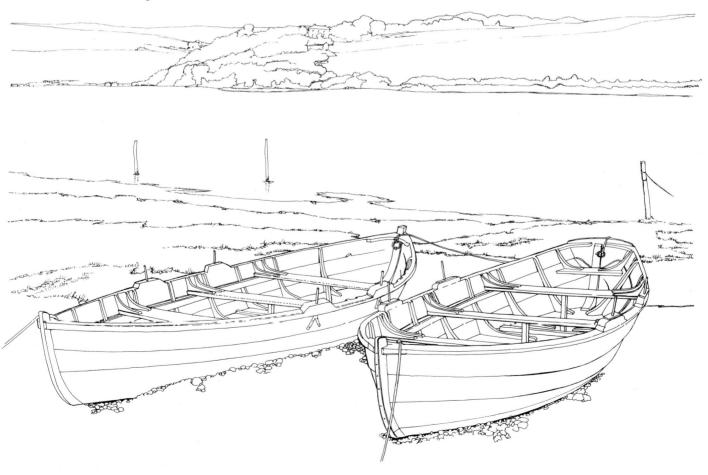

FLEET TROWS OR BACKWATER BOATS

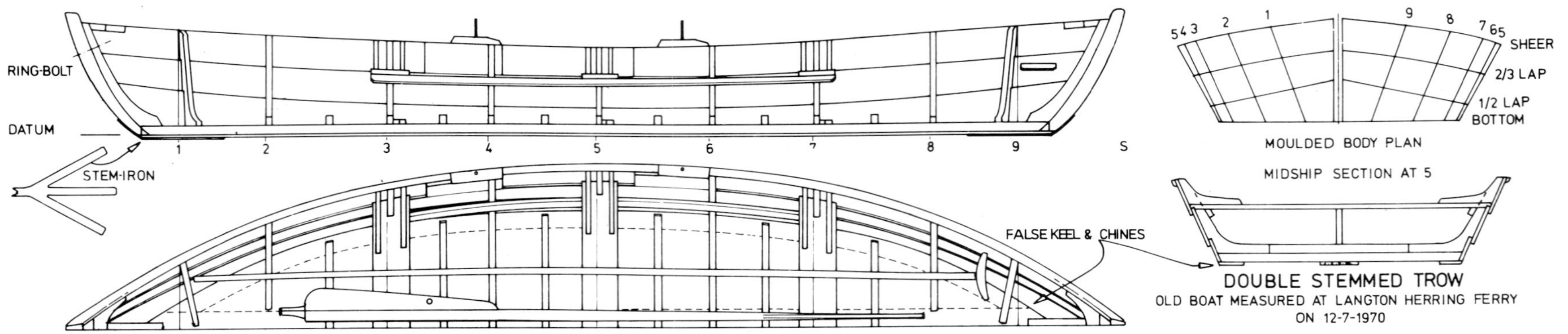
RING-BOLT
DATUM
STEM-IRON
1 2 3 4 5 6 7 8 9 S
5 4 3 2 1 9 8 7 6 5
SHEER
2/3 LAP
1/2 LAP
BOTTOM
MOULDED BODY PLAN
MIDSHIP SECTION AT 5
FALSE KEEL & CHINES

DOUBLE STEMMED TROW

OLD BOAT MEASURED AT LANGTON HERRING FERRY ON 12-7-1970

OFFSETS OF D.S. TROW

STATION	F	at	1	2	3	4	5	6	7	8	9	at	S
FROM FOR'D	0·00	~	1·58	2·80	4·50	5·92	7·39	8·94	10·43	11·94	13·23	~	14 78
1/2 BDTHS SHEER	0·06	0·22	0·94	1·54	2·00	2·17	2·26	2·17	2·00	1·55	0·93	14·57	0·06
1/2 BDTHS 2/3 LAP	0·06	0·39	0·77	1·34	1·80	1·95	2·04	1·97	1·80	1·37	0·80	14·37	0·06
1/2 BDTHS 1/2 LAP	0·06	0·59	0·62	1·16	1·60	1·73	1·79	1·76	1·60	1·17	0·63	14·16	0·06
1/2 BDTHS BOTTOM	0·06	1·05	0·44	1·02	1·46	1·63	1·69	1·67	1·48	1·04	0·45	13·77	0·06
FROM DATUM SHEER	1·60	0·22	1·48	1·40	1·31	1·28	1·22	1·26	1·31	1·41	1·50	14·57	1·60
FROM DATUM 2/3 LAP	1·17	0·93	1·07	0·96	0·86	0·81	0·78	0·81	0·85	0·96	1·07	14·37	1·17
FROM DATUM 1/2 LAP	0·74	0·59	0·62	0·51	0·40	0·37	0·35	0·37	0·41	0·51	0·62	14·16	0·74
FROM DATUM BOTTOM	0·12	1·05	0·12	0·12	0·12	0·12	0·12	0·12	0·12	0·12	0·12	13·77	0·12
FROM DATUM	0·00	0·25	0·50	0·75	1·00	1·25	1·50	1·60	1·75				
STEM PROFILE	0·99	0·71	0·52	0·37	0·25	0·15	0·06	0·04	0·00				
STEM RABBET	1·21	0·93	0·73	0·58	0·48	0·36	0·29	0·23	~				
STEM APRON	1·34	1·30	0·90	0·73	0·58	0·47	0·38	0·33	~				
STERN PROFILE	0·99	0·71	0·52	0·37	0·25	0·15	0·06	0·04	0·00				
STERN RABBET	1·21	0·97	0·77	0·61	0·49	0·36	0·29	0·23	~				
STERN STERN KNEE	1·34	1·34	0·96	0·78	0·65	0·50	0·40	0·33	~				

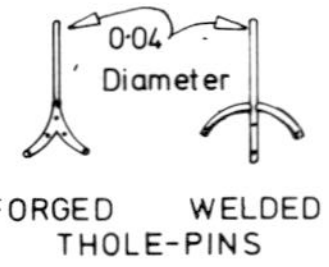
0·04
Diameter

FORGED WELDED
THOLE-PINS

OFFSETS OF T.S. TROW

F	at	1	2	3	4	5	6	7	8	9	at	S
0·00	~	1·69	2·94	4·45	5·96	7·47	8·98	10·94	12·00	13·27	~	14·92
0·05	0·27	0·95	1·53	1·99	2·24	2·28	2·22	2·03	1·72	1·36	~	0·82
0·05	0·38	0·82	1·38	1·80	2·02	2·07	2·00	1·81	1·49	1·11	14·83	0·61
0·05	0·46	0·62	1·22	1·62	1·80	1·87	1·79	1·57	1·22	0·75	14·56	0·06
0·05	0·93	0·49	1·09	1·51	1·70	1·76	1·66	1·43	1·03	0·49	14·11	0·06
0·00	0·27	0·12	0·20	0·29	0·33	0·37	0·36	0·31	0·22	0·12	~	0·00
0·43	0·38	0·56	0·66	0·71	0·78	0·80	0·77	0·73	0·66	0·57	14·83	0·43
0·79	0·46	0·96	1·07	1·19	1·24	1·25	1·23	1·20	1·08	0·96	14·56	0·97
1·47	0·93	1·47	1·49	1·50	1·51	1·51	1·50	1·50	1·49	1·47	14·11	1·47
0·15	~	0·00	0·30	0·55	0·80	1·05	1·30	1·55				
0·00	~	0·04	0·10	0·16	0·22	0·31	0·46	0·76				
0·27	0·11	0·28	0·34	0·39	0·46	0·57	0·75	1·02				
~	~	0·39	0·45	0·51	0·60	0·72	0·93	1·14				
~	~	0·00	0·06	0·11	0·17	0·25	0·40	0·83				
~	~	0·07	0·13	0·18	0·24	0·33	0·54	0·83				
~	~	0·13	0·26	0·33	0·43	0·55	1·06	1·40				

OLDER BOATS ARE PITCHED BLACK ALL OVER BUT NEW ONES ARE VARNISHED

SCANTLINGS	D.S.	T.S.
BOTTOM	0·13	0·10
PLANKING	0·04	0·03
CANTS	0·07	0·08
KNEES	0·08	0·07
FRAMES	0·07	0·08
FLOORS	0·10×0·08	0·13×0·10
THWARTS	0·50×0·06	0·50×0·08
STEMS	0·10	0·17
APRONS	0·19	0·25
STERN KNEE	~	0·17
RISING	0·13×0·06	0·13×0·08
GUNWALE	0·10×0·07	0·10×0·08
TRANSOM	~	0·07
FALSE CHINE	0·06	0·06
FALSE KEEL	0·06	0·06

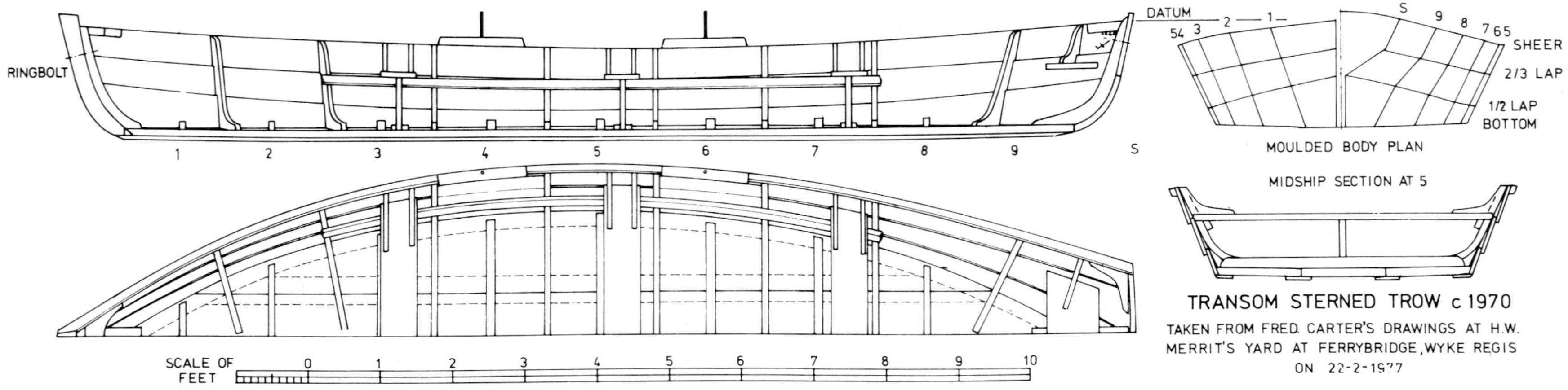
RINGBOLT
1 2 3 4 5 6 7 8 9 S
DATUM
5 4 3 2 1 S 9 8 7 6 5
SHEER
2/3 LAP
1/2 LAP
BOTTOM
MOULDED BODY PLAN
MIDSHIP SECTION AT 5
SCALE OF FEET
0 1 2 3 4 5 6 7 8 9 10

TRANSOM STERNED TROW c 1970

TAKEN FROM FRED. CARTER'S DRAWINGS AT H.W. MERRIT'S YARD AT FERRYBRIDGE, WYKE REGIS ON 22-2-1977

Fig 179: Fleet trows or backwater boats – lines and constructions.

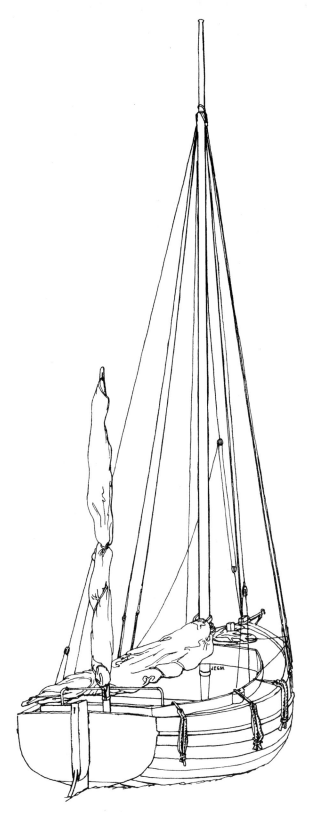

Fig 180: Weymouth harbour fishing boat.

reduced in numbers, though the pot boats and trows flourish. Even in a small station like Lulworth Cove today, there are no two boats of the same type. In the 1920s however, these three main types made up an unrelated range of grades, which between them met all the needs for boats in that vicinity.

A visit to Kingsdown, Walmer and Deal (W12, III4) at the end of the last century would have shown yet another distribution pattern. Old photographs show the astonishing number of sailing vessels that could accumulate, while waiting for a favourable wind, here in the Downs, which must have been the best known anchorage the world has known. The three miles of steep weather beach lying to the south of the anchorage might rank equal for the fame of its boats and boatmen. Although the boats formed a complete related range and shared many cognate features, the size and proportions of each grade in the range was distinct and suited certain tasks and weather conditions. Before all else these boats were for looking after ships, outward and homeward bound. Although there were three lifeboats manned by the men of these three villages, the next important work was rescue and salvage when vessels were in difficulties, generally on the Goodwins. Next there was fishing, mainly for local consumption; and finally clandestine traffic with the nearby continent.

In general all the types had the following in common: they were clinker and, with one exception, open boats, having straight keels with a small amount of drag. Amidships there was some lift to the floors, firm bilges and nearly plumb sides. The stems fore and aft were almost upright. For'd the forefoot profiles were rounded, and aft the sternpost had a narrow vee-d transom well clear of the sea. All classes had the same shaped curve on the after edge of their rudders, which drew several inches less than the heel. All the boats could be pulled or sailed as luggers. The differences between the classes arose either from the size or which of the forms of propulsion was the more important. The boats were beached and launched bows first, but the larger and narrower boats were bumped up when the tide was rising and the wind offshore. Capstans, matched to the boat's size, were used to haul them clear of the high tide mark and to turn them around. The boats were built of English elm planks, which 'slept' away with the repeated wetting and drying, and ash timbers.

The grades and classes can be listed, but it is not clear how far they were all in existence at any one time. Further there is contradiction over whether or not there were two or three classes of galley punt, and whether the half boat was not one of these galley punt classes rather than a small lugger. In addition to the related classes, there were other rigs and types employed entertaining summer visitors.

The first grade was the lugger, all classified as haven boat (28), of which there were three classes:

Forepeaker

Was the largest of the luggers, having a crew of 8 to 11 men when she went searching for homeward-bound ships to put a man aboard before entering compulsory pilotage waters. This might mean working as far west as out of the River Fal. Otherwise they worked at the recovery of slipped anchors or supplying extra ones to ships dragging in the Downs. As the forepeakers had a carrying capacity of about 10 tons they were large enough to carry enough ground tackle for any sailing ship. The forepeaker could be up to 46ft long, but 38–40ft was more usual, with 12 to 12½ft beam and 7½ft depth, 1½ft drag and 22 strakes to the side. This class was decked over for the first 15ft to give a cuddy where 4 or 5 men might stretch out at a time. Early in the nineteenth century these luggers, in common with many other local craft, had three masts and topsails, but by the 1830s the main mast was excluded, though the tabernacle for it was kept until the middle of the century. The foremast was rigged with a dipping lug, the mizzen with a standing lug and a jib was set with its tack run out on a traveller on a short reefing bowsprit. A big lugger like this would have an extensive wardrobe of sails consisting of 3 fore lugs, 3 jibs, 2 mizzen lugs and a mizzen topsail, to meet every occasion, summer and winter, off the Lizard and at regattas. The mizzen was stepped right aft, straight up like the sternpost, and her outrigger was almost horizontal. This made the Kent lugger distinguishable at sea from a Cornish one, whose mizzen was inboard raking forward, with the outrigger steeved well up. When under oars, the men stood up facing forward, pushing on their oars. These were heavy boats, the hull alone weighing 3 or 4 tons, to which 6 more tons of ballast were added. A ten bar capstan was needed to haul one of them to the top of the beach, and they were among the largest beach boats to have been built in Britain.

Cat-boat

This lugger was not much smaller, but was entirely open, having a portable caboose which could be fitted amidships to give some shelter for 3 or 4 men at a time, when the space was not needed for ground tackle. She would not normally search much further west than Beachy Head, when she would have a 6 or 7 man crew. Cat-boats were about 35ft long, 10ft beam and built with 18 strakes to each side.

Half boat

Was as her name suggests about half the size of a first class lugger, but was used for fishing rather than hovelling. Apart from the foresail and mizzen rig and an iron lamp bracket forward, it must have needed a practiced eye to distinguish her from the second class of the next sort of boat.

There were three classes of galley punt, or mackerel boat, all of which can be classed as row barges (26), being small. These were able sea boats and could be used for hovelling or fishing in most weathers, and were generally chosen by pilots and shipping agents when getting on and off shore. They were rigged with a dipping lug on a single mast amidships, and to save time going about, it was customary to carry a second sail on the other side of the mast and then hoist that. The second sail would be the smaller winter sail, for which there was a smaller mast, which also stepped amidships in a blow. There was a further mast position forward of the first thwart which allowed both these sails to be set together in light airs. As

the need arose, the whole rig could be set up and taken down quickly, and this was essential as when lying alongside a rolling square-rigger a hoveller with a mast up was in danger of being struck under. The galley punt was a lot lighter built than a lugger, needing only a six bar capstan on the beach, and she had a fine reputation for being a fast safe boat in a blow. The different classes were:

First class galley punt

The largest ever of these was the *Falcon* of Walmer and she was lost just in the way as described above. She was 35ft long, the same as a lugger, but the usual size was between 29–32½ft long, 6.8 to 7ft beam, with 16 strakes to the side and a 3 man crew. They were said to have had a cod's head and mackerel tail stern.

Second class galley punt

These were between 22½–26ft long, and 6.5–6.8ft beam. The crew could be 2 or 3, but 'hooking on' to a steamer under way was thought to be too risky with only two men in the boat. The *Happy-go-Lucky*, drawn by P J Oke, was one of this class.

Third class galley punt

Was the two-handed boat, under 22ft long, 6–6½ft beam.

There were two further grades of boat here, quite distinct from each other and those already described:

Galley

Was originally a 6 or 8-oared boat. The *Blue Jacket* was one of the latter and was possibly built with a little freetrading in mind. The later boats, of which there is still the *Undaunted* remaining, were 5-man boats, which is to say the crew pulled four oars and the cox'n a fifth if he had the mind to. At 28–30ft long, 5½ft beam and 2ft deep, these long fast boats are classed as row barges (26) though more light and slender than the galley punts. They were mainly fine weather boats, when oars rather than sail would get a hoveller to a ship before anyone else. They were rigged in a similar way to the galley punts, and their length made it safer to knock them up the beach sideways than launch them up straight on (p71).

Punt

Or foresail-and-mizzen boat, was not unlike a small lugger to look at, though only 12–16ft long and 6ft beam. They were general purpose work boats, and one or more were to be found at each of the lugger stations along the beach. They class as transom boats (29).

North along this coast is the harbour of Ramsgate and the protected beach at Broadstairs, with deep-keeled boats and luggers once in the former and some Deal type luggers and punts in the latter, these last fishing and foying for the most part. To the west are found punts in St Margaret's Bay, and a full if not so numerous range of luggers, galleys

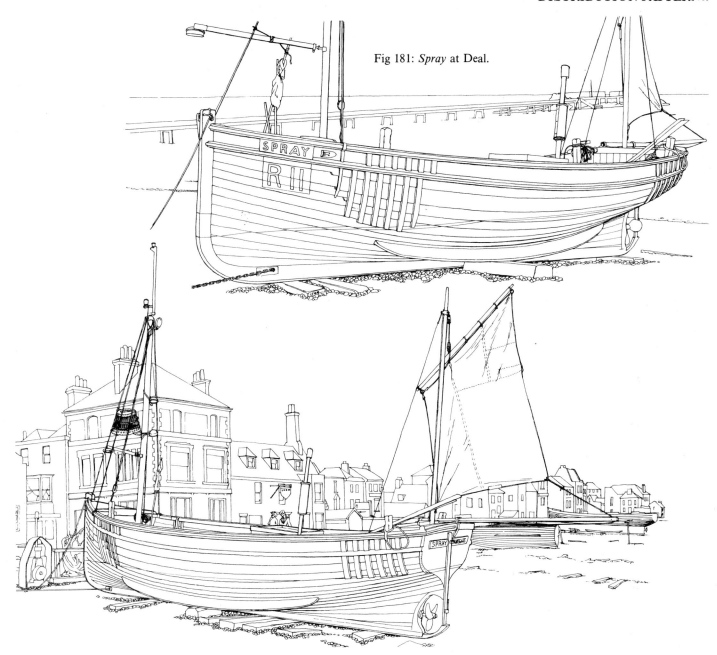

Fig 181: *Spray* at Deal.

and punts at Dover. A little further west and one finds there were luggers from both Cornwall and Sussex in the harbour at Folkestone. Altogether it looks as if at Deal eighty years ago there was a range of related fully functional boats, distributed in a limited but continuous manner. Close by, isolated examples of Deal types would be found making up mixed ranges with other types.

The internal combustion engine changed all that. Nevertheless there is still a well populated working beach at Deal and Walmer today, though the boats are different. The task for boats has changed, the Downs hardly serves as an anchorage and sea fishing, much of it recreational, has taken pride of place. The modern boats are motorised, most of them having been built as such. A few still have the appearance of the old punts or galley punts, and one, the *Spray* of Ramsgate, looks like a half boat (Fig 181). The remaining boats are of all sorts, some with lute and some with elliptical sterns, presenting overall an isolated distribution of a mixed grade of boats all employed in much the

same way.

There must have always been boats in Barra, the southernmost of the Outer Isles. Nowadays, these are all fishing boats, but before 1851 and David McBrayne's steamers, they were needed for transport and in earlier rowdier times for plunder and survival[3]. The island's heritage is distinct if mixed. The people are of the clan McNeil, speaking both English and Gaelic, being mainly Roman Catholic and showing the charm and cheer of the Celt rather than the gloom and tabus of the straiter-laced race in the northern island. For the most part Barra has a crofter economy based on cattle and sheep. The meat rather than the wool has been exported, but the crofters in their well spaced out properties have been mainly self-supporting. The eastern crofts, which have access to the indented and more sheltered shore (S15, VIII/Outer) have the advantage of being able to fish as well as farm.

Fishing is partly for food locally and partly for export, the former by crofters and the latter by full-timers working

217

boats out of Castlebay and North Bay. The crofter's one or two-man boat is generally of the eastern skiff (18) type and is used to set lines and creels. She is a double-ended clinker boat, 15–17ft long, and looks as if she had come from the Moray Firth, having a nearly plumb stem well rounded into a level keel with a curved raked sternpost (p40). She has standing sandstrakes giving a wine glass mid-section. Most still have their masts and tack hooks both on the stem head and the sailing thwart, so the lug can be set dipping or standing. Most crofter's boats now have inboard engines and just a few with outboards, but all with at least one pair double thole pin oarlocks. These boats were either brought by larger fishing boats or came all the way afloat through the Caledonian Canal from where they were built.

The full-time fishing boats are larger and of two sorts, the creel boats and the ring-netters. About half a dozen of the former large square sterned (40) type were Orkney built (p205), but in spite of their name, these creel boats use the inkwell shape, known here as Devon pots, which are not often seen north of Anglesey or Aldeburgh. There are a like number of ring-netters, fine examples of Scottish built wooden keelboats with cruiser or canoe sterns of varying sizes. They are of the raised floor smack type (39). Commercial fishing was encouraged by James Methuen's herring curing station at Castlebay. This operated from the 1860s till the 1930s and is now derelict. While this benefited visiting fishing fleets and employed local labour, it did not do much for local boats. There is now a modern freezing and packing plant at North Bay processing the catches of the local boats.

The situation now at Barra is that excluding all the visiting fishing boats from Stornoway, Campbeltown and Fleetwood that frequently come in for a night's shelter, there are two grades of boat. The crofters' boats, which are all of the same arrested type, but well able to do all that is asked of them, and the large fishing boats, made up of two functional types, each of which are distributed in an almost continuous manner over much of North Britain.

During the last days of sail the distribution patterns were either only changing slowly or in a few types were static. The arrival of the screw increased the rate of change everywhere except where there was no need for it, either because the type was arrested, motorisation proved impossible or engines were banned in the interests of conservation. Where a local type could conveniently and profitably be converted from sail to power, and the boatmen realised this, there was no problem. The cobles, the Norfolk crab boats, the Sussex beach boats and the Cornish porth boats were instances of this. The local boatbuilder and motor mechanics were kept busy first converting the old then building new motor boats. The more enterprising firms accepting orders from places with unconvertible types of boats and boatbuilders.

Several things could happen in a place like this. The station would try to carry on under sail, and being unable to compete, run down and fail. This almost happened at

Brixham, where without close access to steel and coal the change to steam trawlers was too great a step. Nor did the deep wooden hulls convert well into motor boats. It took nearly fifty years for the Brixham fishermen to shop around elsewhere for new and second-hand boats after the local boatbuilders closed or turned over to yachts. Now there is a flourishing cooperative marketing system and a full range of boats, made up a mixture of British and Continental types. Elsewhere the local boatbuilder has learned to build in the new manner, as they did at Hull, or they developed in several stages new shapes of boats, as they have done in Scotland. Where this happened, the local harbours are still populated with related ranges of boat, even though different from those that relied on sail.

Other busy places show no uniformity of type at all. In places like Bridlington, where it might be expected that cobles would still dominate, it is only in the medium sizes. Scottish keel boats make up the majority of the larger grade, and the double-ended skiffs provide the boats for hire. Apart from the boats that have converted well already mentioned there are other types which are beginning to be seen all over Britain. The Orkney creel boats, Lancastrian motor nobbies, decked East Devon boats with transom sterns and a growing variety of standard GRP models moulded by firms that have specialised in working boats, *ie* Brooks Marine, Cheverton, Halmatic, Aqua-Star and many more. There are two more kinds worth mention for the frequency with which they are seen. There is the ship's lifeboat conversion, which properly done can be excellent for shrimping, and a bluff double-ended import from Scandinavia, which is seen widely distributed in ones or twos. This foreigner, together with the pointed and square sterned Rana boat, are so universal as to make one wonder if they will be an influence on future British boatshape.

New ways of fishing have accelerated the revolution in boatshape. Blindfold capture by methods like the long line, drift-net and trawl are being outdated by visually aided fly-dragging, mid-water trawling and purse-seining, while larger fleets of pots are being handled by bigger winches and boats. There has been a move towards handling more gear, old and new, over the stern. This favours square sterns or buoyant counters with wide transoms, and forward wheelhouse for maximum space aft for gantries and power blocks. Fish capture is so competitive that it challenges the survival of the smaller inshore classes, unless they are made up of efficient well laid out boats equipped with modern fish-finding and handling gear. In spite of the reputation that British boatbuilders and boatmen have for being individualistic and conservative, there is a move towards financing, owning, building, and operating the larger sizes of inshore boat in a way that was previously only associated with the deep-sea fishing fleets. As a result of all these changes, one finds fewer distinct types of boat distributed more widely in Britain today than there were in the days of wood and sail.

11.

Conclusions

I have known many boats overseas – a shore boat at Alexandria, an outrigger fishing canoe in Ceylon, a trading junk at Chinwangtao, a beetle cat at Bar Harbour, a Hwangpu wharf boat, a sprit-rigged extended dugout at Roseau, a Singapore twakow, a Sydney harbour 18-footer, a square-rigged drifter in Tokio Bay and an outrigger sailing canoe at Ulithi. After such exotic craft, the discovery that British boats and their surroundings are just as interesting and varied has been one of the most rewarding aspects of this Caird research fellowship.

Conversely, it was sobering to discover how much of the currently available skill and energy is still being spent on researching and re-assessing the sailing period. In spite of the considerable changes that have been taking place since the disappearance of sail, there is very little to show that these are being studied.

Where it has been possible to reach conclusions, specific subjects have been summed up at the end of the appropriate chapter. There are a few more general topics. It had been expected at the outset that there was a link between a boat's work and, in the widest sense, her surroundings and her shape. If so, this could well account for the wide variety of British boat types. This has proved to be only partly true, and the way a type is distributed can show why. The shape and build of isolated types in solitary situations, like the Severn stop-net boat (10) and less remote examples, like the lerret (21) are almost entirely governed by their work and surroundings. I cannot think of any other type that might replace them satisfactorily. However, the shapes of the widespread types like the transom boat (29) and the modern multi-purpose motor fishing boats (39) or (40) concede very little to what they are doing or where it is done. It seems that as working boat designs move towards more general purpose craft, their variety must decrease. Though such boats cost more, they will survive changes in fishing methods better.

Even at the risk of being obvious, there are two more conclusions I have reached. The first is the conviction that to study properly one must live close and long enough to the boats and the boatmen to be accepted as part of the scenery. The second realisation is that if the study is to be useful, its findings must be in a form that can be integrated with those about other boats elsewhere. As far as this fellowship was concerned, a study in depth of all British types was out of the question. Instead, an attempt has been made to meet the second requirement, namely developing a common system for describing and classifying the shapes of boats more precisely. These proposals are in their infancy. They need to be tested and, no doubt, adjusted. If they can be looked at in this light, a step forward is possible.

Since the Coastal and River Craft Committee of the Society for Nautical Research was wound up, there has not been any administrative framework through which the study of working boats could be furthered. Either this committee, which did so well in the 1930s, should be revived, or sections of the National Maritime Museum and the regional and local Maritime Museums should consider making a concerted move in this direction.

Most museums of this type have greatly improved in the last ten years or so. The limitations of national and local organisations are not unlike those given in my two obvious conclusions above. Inability to work in depth over a wide front in the former case, and the inefficiency of random work in the latter. In each case the limits of what can be achieved in isolation must be near, and further advance depends upon the willingness to join forces.

Local researchers and museums are best placed to carry out detailed research, but generally lack specialists of one sort or another. Here the staffs of regional and national Museums could help, if only to give advice and direction. This is not a move towards more centralisation. What is now wanted is a free association of these establishments, publicly or privately funded, mutually assisting each other to discover and display evidence of boat-lore in keeping with their nature.

The improvements in professional standards and academic performance of nautical research has also been outstanding. Essential as this is, there are dangers. The shift to shelf rather than field work eventually leads nowhere, but what is more immediate is making the best use of the foretold increase of leisure time. Amateur workers must be encouraged and not under valued on account of their lack of academic status. This book has tried to show that the study of boats needs many kinds of practical and scientific talent, not the least of which is seamanship. Given some administration, some academic disciplines and a broadly based work force, it should not take long to make up the backlog in our knowledge of what has happened to our boats in the last fifty years.

12.

Further reading

There are several bibliographies which may prove useful. The National Maritime Museum's *The Development of the Boat* by Michael Sanderson, the list of books given by John Dyson in *Business in Great Waters* and for its list of official reports from 1758 to 1914, J T Jenkins' *The Sea Fisheries*. Out of all the books listed, there have been a few which I could not have done without. Holdsworth's *Deep Sea Fisheries and Fishing Boats*, mainly for the text, but also because he was covering the same field as myself exactly a century ago and because he also drew his own illustrations. The Science Museum's *British Fishing Boats and Coastal Craft*, being E W White's revision of G S Laird Clowe's work is the most compact and complete account of them available. There is no definitive work on this subject. The well indexed articles and reviews in *The Mariner's Mirror*, the Journal of the Society for Nautical Research, are invaluable.

The text includes references to many recent excellent books and articles about various types and classes of boats, but the overall coverage is patchy. The National Maritime Museum holds several collections of photographs and research material, much of it hardly tapped; those of H O Hill have been particularly helpful to me. Local sources are generally fruitful. Apart from newspapers, county magazines, town guides, topographical handbooks and the proceedings of provincial societies, there has been a wave of books more directly concerned with the boats and their work in the vicinity. Possibly because so many of the authors are women, their role in fishing communities has had the interest it deserves. Taken from a much longer list, the following few may give some idea how well spread the studies are:

Easter Ross: *Down to the Sea* by Jessie Macdonald & Anne Gordon.
North Norfolk: *Fishermen* by Sally Festing.
North Cornwall: *The Story of Port Isaac* by Monica Winstanley.
South Ayr: *Fisherfolk of Carrick* by Catherine Czerkawska.
Argyll: *Men and Herring* by Naomi Mitchison.
One of the few writers about modern fishing boats is also a woman, Gloria Wilson. Her *Scottish Fishing Craft* and *More Scottish Fishing Craft* are regularly seen on the shelves of fishing skippers.

H H Lamb's *Climate, past, present and future* (Vols 1 & 2) together with the Meteorological Office's, *Weather in Home Waters* (Vol II part 1) provide a full description of our most variable weather. J A Steer's *The Coastline of England and Wales*, read in conjunction with the relevant *Pilot* (Channel part 1, West Coast of England, West Coast of Scotland parts 1 & 2 and North Sea parts 2 & 30) do much the same for our coastal waters.

F M Davis' *An Account of the Fishing Gear of England and Wales* (4th Ed 1958) while being the most comprehensive work on traditional fishing methods, needs the inclusion of modern methods. David Thompson's *The Seine Net* makes good this shortfall to some extent, and has a valuable chapter describing the boats and gear now being used. Willy Elmer's *The Terminology of Fishing* (No 19 of the English Dialect Series) is a recent and most helpful survey of English and Welsh inshore fishing.

Almost every one of the books mentioned has a bibliography of its own. Together they offer a much wider range of books to read than I could put together.

Appendices

APPENDIX I FETCH IN MILES OVER OPEN SEA AT VARIOUS PORTS IN BRITAIN

PLACE	CODE rock	shore	PORT TYPE	FETCH IN MILES IN VARIOUS DIRECTIONS (* = Inland, † = more than 1000 miles)							
				N	NE	E	SE	S	SW	W	NW
Deal	III4	W12	SOB	18	200	55	25	25	*	*	*
Whitstable	III8	S28	ITF	30	420	100	*	*	*	6	20
Leigh-on-Sea	III10	E24	TF	*	*	*	12	5	2	1	*
Aldeburgh	III10	S26	SOB	*	385	115	87	90	*	*	*
Cromer	III11	S25	GOB	†	560	148	*	*	*	*	70
Grimsby	I1	W8	AHF	4	7	10	*	*	*	*	14
Bridlington	III13	W8	AHT	*	*	335	220	*	*	*	*
Filey	III14	W8	GOB	2	370	360	8	*	*	*	*
Newbiggin	V6	W8	MOB	*	345	330	290	*	*	*	*
Dunbar	V7	W8	NHI	42	350	410	*	*	*	*	16
Anstruther	V8	S22	AHT	*	360	410	395	12	25	*	*
Stonehaven	V10	S21	AHT	*	330	390	380	120	*	*	*
Buckie	V11	S20	AHT	74	360	*	*	*	*	5	62
Cromarty	V13	S18	NHI	4	450	16	*	*	*	6	4
Wick	V16	S17	NHI	*	700	350	480	73	*	*	*
Scrabster	V16	S16	AHT	†	16	8	1	*	*	*	†
Ullapool	VII3	E20	NH	*	*	2	1	2	2	2	50
Stornoway	VIII	W13	NHI	*	*	*	35	*	*	*	*
Mallaig	VII4	E20	AHT	12	*	*	*	*	15	16	5
Oban	VII7	E20	NHI	8	*	*	*	*	3	1	6
Campbeltown	VII8	W3	NH	*	*	32	*	*	*	*	*
Ballantrae	VII12	E19	IOB	53	*	*	*	*	35	42	27
Portpatrick	VII13	L13	NHI	*	*	*	6	200	24	24	†
Whitehaven	VI16	E18	AHT	22	*	*	*	*	35	77	20
Morecambe	VI13	E17	TF	8	4	*	*	*	72	12	6
Fleetwood	VI14	E17	NHI	15	8	1	3	2	*	133	77
Lytham	VI14	E17	TC	*	*	2	3	4	43	*	*
Rhyl	VI12	S12	TC	72	22	*	*	*	*	12	70
Holyhead	VIII	L10	AHT	50	8	4	*	*	*	62	76
Pwllheli	VI9	S11	NHI	*	*	12	18	46	7	*	*
Aberystwyth	VI8	E15	TCI	11	*	*	*	*	27	95	38
Fishguard	VI7	S10	NHI	190	56	2	*	*	*	*	75
Solva	VI7	L8	TC	*	*	*	5	8	†	60	*
Tenby	VI5	E13	NHI	*	8	20	45	66	*	*	*
Barry	VI1	E11	NHI	*	*	15	18	16	22	*	*
Weston-S-Mare	I5	E10	IGOB	12	*	*	*	2	2	†	10
Ilfracombe	IV12	S9	NHI	26	17	*	*	*	*	†	42
Clovelly	IV10	S8	IMOB	52	12	6	*	*	*	*	130
Port Isaac	IV9	E8	NHI	73	3	*	*	*	*	†	150
St Ives	IV9	E8	NHI	285	22	3	3	*	*	†	155
Sennen Cove	IV8	L5	IMOB	295	3	1	*	*	†	†	170
Newlyn	IV8	S7	NHI	*	3	5	125	450	*	*	*
Mullion	IV6	L4	IMOB	*	*	*	*	450	†	†	8
Polperro	IV5	E7	NHI	*	*	13	160	120	†	6	*
Hope Cove	IV4	E6	NHI	*	*	*	*	*	†	42	*
Brixham	IV3	S5	NHI	4	27	220	82	110	*	*	*
Lyme Cobb	II7	E5	IMOB	*	*	7	100	130	†	*	*
Chesil Bank	II6	L2	SOB	*	*	*	*	130	†	350	*
Swanage	II5	S3	IGOB	*	*	26	120	60	*	*	*
Littlehampton	II3	E2	NHI	*	*	*	85	100	90	*	*
Hastings	II2	E2	ISOB	*	*	42	50	75	118	*	*

Abbreviations

TF	Tidal Flat	AHT	Artificial Harbour Tidal	SOB	Steep Open Beach
TC	Tidal Creek	AHF	Artificial Harbour Floating	MOB	Medium Open Beach
NH	Natural Harbour	DWC	Deep Water Creek	GOB	Gradual Open Beach

In all cases 'I' indicates the addition of a sea-wall or other civil engineering works

APPENDIX II A SUMMARY OF THE COASTAL STRUCTURE OF BRITAIN (see Fig 7)

This is in eight sections. The quaternary estuaries have been taken together first and the islands close to the coast of Britain including the Outer Isles last. The remaining six are made up of the coasts either side of Dungeness, one northward to the Tees and one westward to the Axe in Dorset. Beyond the Tees/Axe line, the western limit of Jurassic rocks, there is a section north again to Strathy Point, and another west again round to Stolford in Bridgwater Bay. The rest of the West Coast is divided in two by the Solway Firth.

SECTION I – QUATERNARY ESTUARIES

Code	Estuary	Limits and Coastal Mileage	Landscape	Coastline	Seascape	Miles from 25fm 50fm	Spring Tide Range
I/1	Wash to Humber	Hunstanton/Sunk Island 130 miles	Flat, not more than 300ft high	Beach and low cliff or dunes	Shallow and shoals offshore	more than 10m 25m	21ft Hull
I/2	Yare	Horsey Mere to Yarmouth 12 miles	Very low, with with flooding	Dunes and groyned beaches	Shallow and shoals offshore	more than 10m 25m	8ft Y'mouth
I/3	Thames/ Medway	Canvey to Sheppey Is 85 miles	Very low and tidal creeks	Low cliff or dyke & groyned beaches	alternate shoals and deep leads or channels	more than 10m 25m	19ft Chatham
I/4	Crouch	Shoebury Ness/Sale Pt 20 miles	Low with deep tidal & river creeks	Sea-walls, mud flats and saltings, marshes	Shoals, bars and deep channels	more than 10m 25m	16ft Burnham
I/5	Severn	Stolford to Penarth 95 miles	Mainly low sloping to hilly interior	Dunes, low cliffs or sea-walls	Deep leads with sand & mud banks drying out	more than 10m 25m	41ft Avon- mouth
I/6	Upper Firth of Forth	Bo'ness to Culross 20 miles	Flat with easy slopes	Low walls or cliffs	Shallow	more than 10m 25m	19ft Grange- mouth
I/7	Moray Firth	R Spey to Sutors of Cromarty 55 miles	Coastal plain with interior Highlands	Beach and low cliff or dunes	Gradually deepening water	6m 25m	16ft Nairn
I/8	Solway Firth	R Nith to Maryport 48 miles	Coastal plain with interior Highlands	Saltings, flats or beaches	Vast areas of sand at low water	more than 10m 25m	27ft Silloth

Approximate total length of coast – 465 miles

SECTION II – DUNGENESS TO RIVER AXE, DORSET

Code	Limits and Coastal Mileages	Rock	Landscape	Coast see Appendix III	Seascape	Miles from 25fm 50fm	Spring Tide Range
II/1	Dungeness 12	4	Reclaimed land, marshes and saltings	L1 & E2	Shoal bay shelves to 18fm channel	more than 10m 25m	26ft Rye Bay
II/2	Winchelsea 23	2, Cr Weal-den	Flat with low hills near the shore	E2	Shelving with shoals inshore	10m 25m	23ft Hastings
II/3	Eastbourne 40	2, Cr Chalk	500ft Downs run close to shore but gets flat near R Arun	E2	Shelving	8m 25m	19ft Brighton
II/4	Littlehampton 73	3, Olig	Mainly flat, one 400ft ridge near coast	E2, E3 & E4	Shallow, land locked waters, some deep channels	8m 25m	17ft Selsey Bill
II/5	Studland Bay 4	2, Cr Complex	500ft ridge near the coast	S3	Shallow and shelving gradually	8m 25m	6ft Swanage
II/6	Swanage 56	2, Ju Oolite	Rollings hills up to 700ft close to shore Chesil Bank & Fleets	S3, E4, L2 & E5	10fm close in to land except the Shambles off Portland	8m 25m	12ft West Bay
II/7	Eype, near Bridport 13	2, Ju Lias	Scarps and deep valleys	E5	Shallow off Lyme Regis, the rest shelves	8m 25m	12ft Lyme Cobb
	R Axe						

221

SECTION III – DUNGENESS TO RIVER TEES

Code	Limits and Coastal Mileages		Rock	Landscape	Coast see Appendix III	Seascape	Miles from 25fm 50fm		Spring Tide Range
III/1	Dungeness	14	4	Reclaimed land marshes and saltings	S1 & E1	Shallow inshore with shoals	more than 10m	25m	24ft East Roads
III/2	Hythe	4	2, Cr Wealden	400ft range of hills run down to shore	E1	17fm channel lies 4m. off shore	more than 10m	25m	–
III/3	Folkestone	6	2, Cr Greensand	400ft range of hills run down to shore	E1	Steep to 8 fathoms close in to shore	more than 10m	25m	21ft Folkestone
III/4	Dover	9	2, Cr Chalk	Hilly first then flat near Walmer & Deal	W12	The Downs and Goodwin Sands	5m	25m	22ft Dover
III/5	Deal	9	4	Flats, marshes and meanders of the R Stour	W12	Shallow bay that largely dries out	8m	25m	18ft Deal
III/6	Ramsgate	12	2, Cr Chalk	Isle of Thanet, 200ft	W12 & S28	Rock platforms under cliffs and offshore shoals	more than 25m	25m	17ft Ramsgate
III/7	Margate	6	4	Slight hills	S28	Extensive areas of shallows	25m	25m	16ft Margate
III/8	Reculver	13	3, Eocene	Hillocks falling to marshes	S28	Very shallow with little or no gradient	25m	25m	16ft Whitstable
III/9	Thames/ Medway	8	3	Marshy isles and tidal channels	S27	Tidal mud and shingle banks offshore	25m	25m	19ft Southend
III/10	Crouch Estuary	78	3	Undulating low land cut by rivers, inlets and broads	S26 & W10	Shifting banks offshore	25m	25m	15ft Bright- lingsea
III/11	Yare Estuary	37	3 lower	Undulating low hills and marshes	W10 & S25	Shifting banks offshore	25m	25m	7ft Great Y'mouth Roads
III/12	Sheringham	19	3 lower	Low hills inland with flats to shore	S25	Shifting banks offshore shallow	25m	25m	17ft Wells Bar
III/13	Wash/Humber	66	2, Cr Chalk	Level and low near coast Wolds inland	W8	Slight shelving south of Flamboro' then steeper-to	5m	25m	18ft Bridlington
III/14	Filey	28	2, Ju Oolite	Moors up to 1000ft cut by deep valleys down to coast	W8	Shallow bays, rock ledges off cliffs, and then steep-to	4m	2m	17ft Scar- borough
III/15	Whitby R Tees	22	2, Ju Lias	High moors turning to low flats near Tees	W8	As above with bars offshore in the North	4m	2m	16ft Staithes
		331							

SECTION IV – RIVER AXE TO STOLFORD (SEVERN ESTUARY)

Code	Limits and Coastal Mileages		Rock	Landscape	Coast see Appendix III	Seascape	Miles from 25fm 50fm		Spring Tide Range
IV/1	River Axe	17	2, Cr MM Complex	Steep hills up to 500ft cut by river valleys	E5 & S5	Shelving out to 25fm line	more than 10m	25m	
IV/2	Straight Point	22	1 Perm Red SS	Hills up to 500ft out to shore & valleys	S5	Shallow in bays	7m	25m	13ft Torquay
IV/3	Paignton	16	1, Dev ORS	400ft hills to shore except Slapton bank and lagoon (Ley)	S5	Shoals and shallow in Start Bay, then steps sharply	4m	25m	16ft Dartmouth
IV/4	Torcross	13	Arch MM	300ft plateau to cliff edge reduced bank and ley	S5 & E6	Shelves steeply	3m	25m	17ft Salcombe
IV/5	Hope Cove	88	1, Dev ORS	300ft plateau & undulating hills cut by drowned valleys	E6, L3, E7 & S6	Shallow bays, steep-to off headlands & a few off-lying rocks	2m	25m	18ft Plymouth
IV/6	The Manacles	17	Arch Ig/In	300ft flat downs out to shore	S6 & L4	Steep-to with some off-lyers	2m	22m	17ft Coverack
IV/7	Mullion Cove	17	1, Dev ORS	Land 600ft high inland slopes right down to coastline	L4 & S7	Shallow and gradually shelving Mounts Bay	more than 6m	25m	18ft Porthleven
IV/8	Penzance	31	Arch Ig/In	800ft heights steeper on the North and West	S7, L5 & E8	Steep-to with many off-lying rocks	2/6m	25m	29ft St Ives
IV/9	St Ives	58	1, Dev ORS	Hills over 1000ft drop to 200ft on coast, some valleys steep near Bodmin	E8	Steep-to with many off-lying rocks	4m	25m	23ft Newquay
IV/10	Boscastle	48	1, Carb Upper	Rolling uplands up to 700ft and shallow valleys	E8 & S8	Steep-to off headlands but beaches gradual	5/9m	25m	27ft Bideford Bar
IV/11	Bideford Bar	52	1 Dev ORS	600ft to 1000ft close to shore with higher moors in land	S9	Shallow in bay, but steep-to on North Exmoor shore	more than 10m	25m	29ft Ilfracombe
IV/12	Minehead	17	MM, Ju & Lias Complex	Slopes more gradually down from Exmoor and shallow valleys	S9	Rock platforms run further out becoming mud flats towards start of estuary	10m	25m	36ft Bridgwater Bar
	Stolford	396							

SECTION V – RIVER TEES TO PORTSKERRA SUTHERLAND

Code	Limits and Coastal Mileage	Rock	Landscape	Coast see Appendix III	Seascape	Miles from 25fm 50fm	Spring Tide Range
V/1	Redcar 11	2, Tr Keuper	Tees Bay & low valley, river meanders	W8	River bar with little depth outside	more than 8m 25m	16ft Hartlepool
V/2	Hartlepool 19	1, Perm MgLim	Rolling plain up to 300ft falls to low cliffs	W8	Shelving to medium depths offshore	5m 25m	15ft Seaham
V/3	Sunderland 33	1, Carb Coal M	Low coastal plain 1000ft highlands well inland	W8	Shelves steeply at first to no great depths	2m 25m	15ft Blythe
V/4	Amble 4	1, Carb Upper	High ground sloping gradually down to the shore	W8	Shelves steeply at first to no great depths	3m 25m	15ft Coquet Bar
V/5	Alnmouth 36	1, Carb CLim Ig/In	Coastal plain 2500ft range inland Rocky outcrops	W8	Reefs and low islands offshore	3/5m 25m	16ft Holy Island
V/6	River Tweed 14	1, Silur	High ground sloping to cliffs at shore	W8	Very rocky & indented Steep-to	1/3m 25m	15ft Berwick
V/7	St Abbs Head 65	1, Carb CLim Ig/In	Flat with 1500ft high ground well inland	W8 & S23	Mainly shallow especially in bays	more than 10m 25m	18ft Leith
V/8	Bo'ness/ Culross, Firth of Forth 55	1, Carb CLim Ig/In	Low shoreline rising slowly to uplands	S22 & W7	Shallow in the Firth, steep-to off Fifeness	10m 25m	15ft Crail
V/9	St Andrews 18	4	Flat with a few low hills	S21	Shallow especially in Firth of Tay	10m 25m	16ft St Andrews
V/10	Wormit, Firth of Tay 53	1, Dev Basalt In	Rolling foothills falling towards shore	S21	Becoming steep-to as one goes further north	3/8m 25m	16ft Montrose Bar
V/11	Stonehaven 98	Arch MM Ig/In Complex	Coastal plain widens to the north but narrows in Moray Firth	S21, W6 & S22	Shallow between Aberdeen and Port Errol, steep-to off Kinnaird Head	1/6m 5/13m	12ft Fraserburgh
V/12	Buckie 4	1, Dev	Narrow coastal plain then slopes up to 1000ft	S21	Shelves into deep water	8m 25m	12ft Lossie-mouth
V/13	River Spey/ Sutors of Cromarty, Moray Firth 42	1, Dev	Low hills sloping down to the shore	S18 & W4	Shallow in Firths shelving gradually off Tarbat Ness	8m 25m	13ft Portmaho-mack
V/14	Dornoch 21	4	Coastal plain narrows to become very steep	S17	Inshore rocky shelves more deeply	more than 10m 25m	13 Golspie
V/15	Helmsdale 14	Arch Ig/In	2000ft highlands close to shore	S17	Shelves more steeply into deep water	6m 25m	12ft Helmsdale
V/16	Berriedale 92	1, Dev	Low plain rising in West to high slopes & valleys	S17 & S16	Very steep-to off the headlands	1/3m 5m	10ft Wick
	Portskerra 579						

SECTION VI – PENARTH TO MARYPORT, SOLWAY FIRTH

Code	Limits and Coastal Mileages		Rock	Landscape	Coast see Appendix III	Seascape	Miles from 25fm 50fm		Spring Tide Range
VI/1	Penarth	38	2 Ju Lias	Flat with some low hills and cliffs	E11 & L6	Shallow with shoals offshore	more than 10m	25m	36ft Barry
VI/2	Port Talbot	14	1 Carb Coal M	Ground up to 900ft slopes steeply to shore	E12	Shallow with large mud flats at low water	10m	25m	29ft Swansea
VI/3	Mumbles	32	1, Carb & Dev Complex	Hilly but not above 400ft	E12	Steeper-to but to no great depth of water	10m	25m	–
VI/4	Gower	42	1, Carb Coal M 4 in estuaries	Hilly close to shore	L7 & E13	Extensive sand and mud flats in bays & inlets	10m	25m	26ft Llanelly
VI/5	Saundersfoot	56	1, Carb & Dev Complex	Hilly with low plateau inland	E13 & L8	Deep near headlands, many rocks and islands but shallow in bays	5m	25m	25ft Milford Haven
VI/6	Broad Haven	6	1 Carb Coal M	200ft plateau falls steeply at coastline	L8	Shallow gradual sloping bottom	more than 10m	25m	18ft Solva
VI/7	Newgate, St Brides Bay	112	1, Ord Ig/In	Land getting higher & steeper to the north, deep valleys	E14 S10, & E15	Deep off St Davids Head, but shallow in Bay with bars off rivers	2m	12m	13ft Fishguard Quay
VI/8	Towyn	36	1, Camb	Mountains up to 3500ft close to coast, steep sided valleys	E15 & S11	Shallow inshore with bars across river mouths	10m	25m	16ft New Quay
VI/9	Criccieth	34	1,Ord Ig/In	400ft uplands slope to coast	S11 & L9	Shallow inshore but steep-to off Bardsey Island	3m	18m	17ft Portmadoc
VI/10	Bardsey Sound	45	Arch MM Camb & ORS Complex	High ground lies closer to shore getting higher to the north	L9 & E16	Shelving bay with tidal sand banks in the Menai Strait	more than 10m	25m	17ft Caernarvon
VI/11	Bangor	18	1, Ord & Camb	Mountains & Conway valley slope to shore	S12	Shallow strait and Conway merge and deepen	more than 10m	25m	23ft Conway Entry
VI/12	Great Ormes Head	18	1 & 2 Complex	Foothills on coast with mountains inland	S12	Steep-to off headlands but to no great depth	10m	25m	24ft Rhyl Quay
VI/13	Rhyl	44	2, Tri Bunter	Flat low coastal strip	S12 & E17	Silted-up Dee estuary but deeper off Flint and Hoylake	10m	25m	29ft Liverpool
VI/14	Bootle	61	2 Tri Keuper	Flat and low well inland	E17	gradually shelving offshore	10m	25m	30ft Fleetwood Bar
VI/15	Pilling, Lune Estuary	78	1 & 2 Complex mainly CLim	Flat and low along coast rising to over 2000ft inland	E17 & L11	Very shallow bays and river estuaries	10m	25m	29ft Barrow Docks
VI/16	Haverigg Point	30	2, Tri Bunter	Mountains up to 3000ft cut by deep valleys slope to shore	L11	Silted landlocked inlets, steep-to off coast, but to no great depth	10m	25m	26ft Whitehaven Outer Quay
VI/17	Whitehaven	13	1, Carb Coal	Coastal flats with high ground inland	E18	Shelving gradually	10m	25m	27ft Working-ton
	Maryport	677							

SECTION VII – PORTSKERRA TO RIVER NITH, SOLWAY FIRTH

Code	Limits and Coastal Mileage	Rock	Landscape	Coast see Appendix III	Seascape	Miles from 25fm 50fm		Spring Tidal Range
VII/1	Portskerra 28	Arch MM	Ground rising with inlets to the west. 3000ft interior	S16	Shelves to medium depths islands and rocks offlying	4m more than 25m		15ft Tongue
VII/2	Whiten Head 11	1, Camb	Foothills not high on coast. Deep lochs and small sandy bays	S16	ditto, but steep-to off Faraid head	2/6m25m		15ft Rispond
VII/3	Kyle of Durness 183	Arch MM & PreCamb	2000ft to 3500ft ridges run into coast with lochs between	E20	Offlying rocks and islets, some deep water close into the shore	0/5m2/16m		16ft Ullapool pier
VII/4	Kyle of Lochalsh 118	Arch MM Ig/In on point	Ridges & lochs as above but getting lower to the south	E20	Deep passages and sounds sheltered by offshore islands	0/3m2/16m		14ft Mallaig
VII/5	Ardnamurchan Point 12	Arch MM	Rolling heights up to 2000ft follow coast	E20	Steep-to lochs and sound in the lee of Is of Mull	0/1m 25m		14ft Tobermory
VII/6	Morvean 17	Arch Ig/In	Less steep up to 1800ft ridges parallel to shore	E20	Steep-to lochs and sound in the lee of Is of Mull	0/1m 25m		14ft Lochaline
VII/7	Lochaline 336	Arch MM	Less steep up to 1800ft ridges parallel to shore	E20, L15 & W3	Very long deep narrow sea-lochs with offshore isles	0/4m1/10m		8ft Campbeltown
VII/8	Kilkreggan 14	1, Dev	Rolling 1000ft foothills slope down to Clyde	E20	Mainly shallow estuary with deep channel	10m 25m		12ft Dumbarton
VII/9	Old Kilpatrick 16	1, Carb CLim	Low plain rising to boggy upland in south	E20	Steep to ship channel	1/8m25m		11ft Greenock
VII/10	Inverkip 29	1, Dev	Uplands revert to low plain to the southward	L14	Shallow inshore with islands to seaward	2/7m6/?m		9ft Ardrossan
VII/11	Irvine Bay 13	2, Ju Oolite	Wide coastal plain with foothills well inland	E19	Shelving into deep water, Is of Arran 18m	6m 12m		10ft Ayr
VII/12	Ayr 30	1, Dev	Foothills to the coast with some valleys	E19	Water deepens gradually with shoals offshore	1/7m 25m		9ft Girvan
VII/13	Ballantrae 39	1, Ord with Ig/In	1400ft hills east of Loch Ryan and 200ft plateau to west	E19 L13	as above but steep-to on North Channel side of Mull of Galloway	2m 4m		9ft Stranraer
VII/14	Portpatrick 96	1, Sil with Ig/In	Ridges getting higher to the east, separated by shallow bays	L13 W1, W2, L12 & S13	Shallow with extensive sand flats at low water	3/?m4m then more than 25m		21ft Garliestown
VII/15	Kirkudbright Bay 46	1, Carb CLim	Hills up to 1800ft form points, but higher interior, many rivers in valleys	S13	Shallow with even larger low water flats	more 10m than 25m		23ft Kirkudbright
	R Nith							
	988							

SECTION VIII – ASSOCIATED ISLANDS INCLUDING THE OUTER HEBRIDES

Code	Limits and Coastal Mileage	Rock	Landscape	Coast see Appendix	Seascape	Miles from 25fm 50fm	Spring Tidal Range
VIII/ IOW, N	Isle of Wight, Foreland 25	3, Olig	Gradual slope to shore	S2	Ship channels and mud flats	more 10m than 25m	14ft Cowes
VIII/ IOW, S	Isle of Wight, Needles 30 Isle of Wight, Foreland	2, Cr Chalk	Hills up to 700ft near to coast	S2, E3	Shelves steep to 10fm	10m 25m	12ft Bembridge
VIII/ Ang	Anglesey 92	Arch & 1, Complex	Low & flat to south, higher to the north	L10 & S12	Shallow to S & NE. Steep-to to the west	6m 16m	16ft Holyhead
VIII/ Skye 1	Skye, Loch Sliachan 141	Arch Ig/Vol	Steep mountains up to 3000ft divided by lochs and valleys	E20 & L16	Deep sounds & rocky islets offshore	1/? 2/?m	16ft Uig Bay
VIII/ Skye 2	Skye, Loch Seavaig 10	2, Ju Oolite	Rounded shoulder of 3200ft peak forms headland	E20 & L16	Shelving into deep water	1/4m5/10m	–
VIII/ Skye 3	Skye, Loch Slapin 54	1, Camb mainly, Complex	Low hills to the south, steep up to 2500ft in north	E20 & L16	Shelves steeply into deeps but not in narrows	1m 2m	see VII/4
VIII/ Skye 4	Skye, Loch Ainort 8	Arch Ig/In	2400ft steep mountain sides	E20	Shallow lochs and sound formed by islands	more than 10m 25m	–
VIII/ Mull	Isle of Mull 127	Arch Ig/Vol & /In	Mountains up to 3000ft, deep glens on all sides	E20	Steep-to except to west – shallow & offlying islets	1/9m3/7m	see VII/5
VIII/IJ1	Isles of Islay & Jura, Port Askaig 135	Arch MM	Separate peaks up to 2500ft	E20	Steep-to in the Sound of Jura	1m 4m	7ft Port Askaig
VIII/IJ2	Isles of Islay & Jura, Bowmore 37 Isles of Islay & Jura, Port Askaig	Arch Precamb	Low with central ridge	E20	Shallow, shelves gradually west	5/10m25m	4ft Bowmore
VIII/ Arran 1	Isle of Arran, Glen Sannox 21	1 & 2 MMDev Complex	Mountains up to 2800ft sides & glens slope to sea	E20 W3	Steep-to into deeps	1m 4m	10ft Loch Ranza
VIII/ Arran 2	Isle of Arran, Machrie Bay 36 Isle of Arran, Glen Sannox	2, Bunter Ig/In	Highlands up to more gradual slopes	E20 W3	Shelving into medium depths further south	0/3m3/4m	12ft Brodick Bay

VIII/ Outer   The Outer Isles – Lewis/Harris, North & South Uist, Benbecula and Barra etc, are except for some Ig/In on the NW Coast of Lewis MM rocks. The Coastal mileage is 225 miles. See Appendix III, E21, E22, E23, S14 & S15, for description of coast.

Total mileage of Section VIII is 941 miles approximately

Total mileage for all 8 sections is 4598 miles approximately

Abbreviations used to describe Rock Formations above.
ARCH – ARCHAEAN ERA
   PreCamb – Pre-Cambrian, Ig – Igneous, Vol – Volcanic,
   In – Intrusive.
1 – PRIMARY ERA
   Camb – Cambrian, Ord – Ordovician, Sil – Silurian,
   Dev – Devonian, ORS – Old Red Sandstone
   Carb – Carboniferous, CaLim – Carboniferous Limestone,
   Coal M – Coal Measures, Perm – Permian, Red SS – Red Sandstone
   MgLim – Magnesian Limestone

2 – SECONDARY ERA
   Tr – Trias, Ju – Jurassic, Cr – Cretaceous

3 – TERTIARY ERA
   Olig – Oligocene

4 – QUATERNARY ERA

APPENDIX III TYPES OF SHORES IN BRITAIN

LEE SHORES (Face the SW wind, from one close reach to the other)

Code	Limits & Direct Miles		Coastline	General Features
L1	Dungeness/ R Rother	9	Shingle beach	Access to Rye
L2	Portland Bill/ West Bay	19	Shingle beach with cliffs at each end	Chesil Bank with the Fleets behind
L3	Rame Head/ Looe	17	Mainly gradual sand beaches with cliffs at each end	Improved beach at Portwrinkle and an open one at Downderry
L4	Lizard/ St Michaels Mount	17	Cliffs, coves, rocky foreshore & a long sandy beach	Coves at Kynance and Prussia, improved beach at Mullion Cove and an artificial harbour at Porthleven
L5	Lands End/ Cape Cornwall	8	Cliffs and rock falls, bay with beach	Improved beach at Sennen Cove
L6	Nash Point/ R Neath	21	Low cliff, rocky shingle foreshore	River mouth ports at Ogmore, Port Talbot and Neath
L7	Porteynon Point/R Towy	17	Low cliff, beaches & sand or mud flats at river mouths	Access to Llanelly, Kidwelly and Carmarthen
L8	St Gowans Head/ St Davids Head	31	Cliffs, coves and sandy beaches	Access to large natural harbour at Milford Haven, improved inlets at Porth-clais & Martin's Haven and open beaches at Little Haven, Broad Haven & Newgate. Quays in Solva creek
L9	End of Lleyn Peninsular	9	Cliffs, inlets with beaches	Open beach at Aberdaron
L10	Menai Strait/ Carmel Head	22	Beaches with sand dunes	Improved natural harbour at Holyhead, creeks to Maltraeth-Yard & Aberffraw
L11	Walney Head/ St Bees Head	37	Tidal inlets with beaches and some low cliffs	Ship harbour at Barrow-in-Furness, tidal creek havens at Millom, Haverigg and Ravenglass
L12	Borrow Head/ Glenluce	22	Rocky low foreshores	Small artificial harbour at Port William
L13	West Coast of Galloway	28	Rocky foreshores with small coves	Creek at Port Logan, improved natural harbour at Portpatrick
L14	Irvine/ the Cumbraes	13	Beaches & low cliffs	River mouth port at Irvine, artificial harbour at Ardrossan
L15	The ends of Arran & Kintyre	14	Low cliffs, rocky foreshores with some beaches	
L16	West Coast of Skye	44	Deep lochs, cliff headlands	Crofters slips and havens, beaches at heads of the lochs
LEE ACCESS				
	Brean Down/ Lavernock Pt	8		Approach to Severn Estuary and docks at Avonmouth, Sharpness, Gloucester, Chepstow, Newport, Cardiff & Penarth

336

EXPOSED SHORES (Close reach to down wind)

Code	Limits & Direct Miles		Coastline	General Features
E1	S Foreland Dymchurch	18	Groyned beaches and cliffs	Port complexes at Dover and Folkestone
E2	R Rother Gosport	86	Groyned beaches, cliffs, river exits and land-locked harbours	Beach stations at Hastings, Eastbourne, Brighton and Selsey. River ports at Newhaven, Shoreham, Littlehampton and tidal harbours of Pagham, Chichester, Langstone and Portsmouth.
E3	St. Catherines Point Poole Harbour	30	Cliffs, shallow bays with beaches and land-locked harbours	Access to the West Solent and the tidal harbours of Christchurch and Poole.
E4	Durlstone Head Weymouth	22	Steep-sided hills, cliffs, small bays and coves	Beach stations at Worbarrow, Kimmeridge and Lulworth. River mouth port of Melcombe Regis/Weymouth.
E5	West Bay Sidmouth	23	Beaches, broken by steep-sided hills, cliffs and mouths of small rivers	Improved river port at West Bay (Bridport). Artificial harbour at Lyme Cobb, beach stations at Chideock, Charmouth, Seaton, Beer, Branscombe and Sidmouth.
E6	Start Point Rame Head	31	Large bays with rocky inlets, some beaches & medium cliffs	Access to Salcombe and Plymouth Sound, Hope Cove and rivers Avon, Erme and Yealm.
E7	Looe Pendennis Point	34	Cliffs, deep bays & river ports	Access to Carrick Roads, river harbour at Looe, Fowey, Par & Falmouth, with improvements at Polperro, Mevagissey, Charlestown, Gorran Haven, Port Loe and Portscatho. No open beach stations.
E8	Cape Cornwall Hartland Point	84	High indented cliff with rock-falls, bold headlands and long gradual beaches	Improved Beaches at St. Ives, Newquay & Port Isaac, river ports at Padstow & Hayle, artificial harbours at Bude and Portreath, improved creek at Boscastle and beach inlet at Port Gaverne.
E9	Westward Ho Morte Point	12	River mouth with beaches and salting. Some cliffs with rocky foreshores	Access to Tawe/Torridge estuary, quays at Appledore, Bideford & Barnstaple.
E10	R Parett Brean Down	9	River mouth with vast tidal mud and sand flats & dunes. Headland with cliff	Access to Highbridge and Bridgwater.
E11	Lavernock Pt Nash Pt	18	Shingle beaches with low cliffs	Dock complex at Barry.
E12	R Neath Porteynon Pt	18	Mud flats, beaches & dunes in bays & some cliffs	Dock complex at Swansea, drying out haven at Oystermouth.
E13	R Towy, St Govans Head	27	River mouth, long sandy beaches, low and high cliffs. Islands offshore	River port at Laugharne, improved haven at Saundersfoot, and improved natural haven with beach at Tenby.
E14	St Davids Head Strumble Head	18	Indented cliffs with small creeks and beaches	Small havens with beach and quay at Abereiddy and Porthgain, both difficult to enter
E15	New Quay Head Portmadoc	48	Mainly cliffs, but sand flats and lagoons at rivers	River ports at Aberystwyth, Barmouth & Portmadoc, improved havens at New Quay & Aberavron, and beach station at Borth.
E16	Bardsey Sound Menai Strait	32	Low cliffs, rocky shore with small coves & beaches	Improved haven at Trevor. River port at Caernarvon
E17	Wallasey R Kent	48	Deep river mouths, sand & mud flats backed by dunes	Access to rivers Mersey, Ribble, Lune and Kent. Docks at Liverpool, Fleetwood, Glasson & Heysham. Tidal creeks in Morecambe Bay, Lytham, etc. dry out.
E18	St Bees Head Silloth	27	Low rock strewn foreshores, river mouths and some low cliffs and beaches	Docks at Whitehaven, Workington, Maryport and Silloth.
E19	Corsewall Pt. Irvine	47	Cliffs & rocky foreshores, river mouths with sandy beaches	Access to Loch Ryan. River Ports of Girvan & Ayr. Improved havens at Ballantrae, Maidens, Dunure & Troon.
E20	Mull of Kintyre Cape Wrath	216	Deeply indented steep high ground with offshore archipelagoes	Access to quays and dock works at Oban, Mallaig, Fort William, Portree and Ullapool. Many smaller ports at West Tarbert, Crinan etc and crofters' slips.
E21	Barra Head Pabbay	75	Cliffs or rocky headlands with long beaches, sounds between islands	Small havens for crofters' boats.
E22	Pabbay Gallan Head	35	Deep lochs & sounds	as above
E23	Kebock Head Sound of Harris	32 / 32	Deeply indented, low cliffs and rocky foreshores	as above
E24	Shoeburyness Canvey Island	11	Long beaches with tidal mud & sand flats to seaward	Tidal channels run along coast to Leigh-on-Sea and South Benfleet. Boats take the ground on flats at low tide.

1001

SHIELDED SHORES (Down wind to 6 points off)

Code	Limits & Direct Miles	Coastline	General Features
S1	Dymchurch Dungeness 8	Groyned shingle beach	Once gave access to old port of Romney.
S2	Gosport St Catherines 22	Tidal mud flats & inlets, some cliffs	Access to Spithead and Bembridge.
S3	Poole Harbour Durlstone Head 8	Shingle beaches split by cliffs	Improved beach at Swanage.
S4	Weymouth 8 Portland Bill	Gravel spit and cliffs	Artificial docks and harbour at Portland, boat derricks at the Bill
S5	Sidmouth Start Point 37	Cliff headlands with beaches and river mouths in bays	Access to rivers Teign, Exe & Dart. Docks at Exmouth & Teignmouth. Beaches at Budleigh Salterton, Dawlish & Start Bay. Improved harbours at Torquay, Paignton, Brixham and Dartmouth.
S6	Pendennis Pt. The Lizard 15	Cliff headlands and creeks with beaches. River.	Access to Helford River. Improved beaches at Porthallow, Porthousestock, Coverack and Cadgwith.
S7	St Michaels Mt Lands End 11	Beaches, then cliffs with small creeks	Docks or wharves at Penzance, Newlyn & Mousehole. Improved coves at Lamorna and Porthcurno.
S8	Hartland Pt Westward Ho 12	Cliffs with rocky fore-shores, then becoming beaches	Improved beach at Clovelly, narrow landing at Bucks Mills.
S9	Morte Point R Parrett 54	High cliffs with occasional bays then rock ledges further east & flats	Improved natural harbours at Ilfracombe, Lynmouth, Porlock Weir, Minehead & Watchet. Beach at Combe Martin & landing at Kilve.
S10	Strumble Hd New Quay Hd. 35	Cliffs with shoal bays and river mouths	Improved harbour at Fishguard & Aberporth. Beach at Parrog, river quays at Cardigan and St Dogmaels.
S11	Portmadoc Bardsey Sound 28	Land steep at coast. Spits at river mouths	Docks at Portmadoc, improved harbours at Criccieth, Pwllheli & Abersoch and a beach at Llanbedrog.
S12	Carmel Head Wallasey 64	Cliffs & rocky heads with creeks & beaches, getting longer as tidal flats appear to the eastward	Improved harbour at Camaes Bay, Amlwch, Beaumaris, Conway, Deganwy, Rhos-on-Sea and river port of Rhyl. Access to Menai Strait & Dee estuary.
S13	Annan 45 Garlieston	Deep inlets with tidal flats, rocky fore-shores to heads	Bridge ports at Annan, Dumfries, Kirkudbright, Gatehouse of Fleet, Newton Stewart. Many minor landings.
S14	Gallan Head Butt of Lewis	High & low cliffs indented with lochs and smaller creeks.	Crofters' landings.
S15	Sound of Harris Barra Head 68	Maze of lochs, headlands, creeks and islands	Improved natural harbours at Lochmaddy, Lochboisdale, & Castlebay; numerous small quays and crofters' landings.
S16	Cape Wrath Duncansby Hd. 73	Cliffs with inlets, beaches in creeks & some river mouths	Improved havens at Rispond, Fresgoe, Castletown, Dunnet. Docks at Scrabster. Many minor landings in lochs and creeks.
S17	Duncansby Hd. Dornoch 65	Mainly steep with some cliffs. Flat in the north	Improved natural harbours at Wick, Lybster, Helmsdale, Dundeath, Keiss & Freswick. Beaches at Golspie & Bora.
S18	Tarbat Ness Fort George 22	Lochs with long shingle beaches in between	Access to Firths of Cromarty & Beauly and Loch Ness (Caledonian Canal). Beaches at Rockfiel, Hilton, Avoch and Balintore.
S19	Fort George Lossiemouth 31	Sandy fore-shore with bars off river mouths	Improved harbours at Nairn, Burghead, Hopeman & Lossiemouth. Undeveloped natural harbour at Findhorn.
S20	Port Gordon Kinnaird Hd 38	Cliff headlands with many inlets, rivers & beaches	Improved harbours at Port Gordon, Buckpool, Buckie, Findochty, Portnockie, Cullen, Portsoy, Whitehills, Banff, Macduff, Gardenstown, Crovie & Rosehearty. Beaches at Portessie, Sandend, Pennan, Sandhaven and Pitulie.
S21	Buchan Ness Out Head 90	Cliffs in North to Hacklie Head, beach to Aberdeen, cliff to Milton Ness then sand to St Andrews	Improved harbours at Boddam, Port Errol Cove, Caterline, Stonehaven, Gourdon, Auchtmithie & Johnshaven. Docks at Aberdeen, Montrose & Arbroath. Access to Newburgh, Esk & Tay estuaries. Creeks at Bullers of Buchan, Whinnyfold, Collieston & Beach at Portlethen.
S22	Fife Ness Culross 47	Low cliffs with rocky fore-shores, beaches in bays	Improved harbours at Crail, Cellardyke, Anstruther, Pittenweem, St Monance, Largo, Buckhaven, Kirkaldy, Kinghaven & Aberdour. Docks at Burntisland. Access to Firth of Forth.
S23	B'oness N Berwick 33	Low with rocky foreshore, beaches or saltings in bays	Improved harbours at Cramond, Cockenzie and North Berwick. Docks at Granton, Newhaven and Leith.
S24	Gibraltar Pt. R Welland 18	Low with sand & mud flats out to sea	Access to River Witham for Boston and Lincoln.

231

Code	Limits & Direct Miles		Coastline	General Features
S25	Great Ouse Cromer	45	Low cliffs with marshes or dunes and beaches	Access to Kings Lynn & tidal harbours of Brancaster, Wells & Blakeney, beach stations at Sheringham & Cromer.
S26	Lowestoft Colne Point	60	Mainly beaches & dunes, some low cliffs. River outlets	Access to Rivers Waveney, Blyth, Alde, Deben, Orwell and Stour. Beach station at Kessingland, Southwold, Dunwich, Aldeburgh, Docks at Lowestoft, Felixstowe & Harwich.
S27	Foulness Pt Shoeburyness	11	Low with tidal channels between islands. Vast flats	Access to River Roach.
S28	Canvey Island North Foreland	38	Large inlets in between low land, flats to seaward & few low clffs	Access to Thames, Medway and Swale. Docks at Sheerness. Improved beaches at Whitstable and Margate.
		1018		

WEATHER SHORES (6 points off on either tack)

Code	Limits & Direct Miles		Coastline	General Features
W1	Garlieston Barrow Hd	8	Low lying shore with sand flats	Improved havens at Garlieston & Isle of Whithorn.
W2	Glenluce Mull of Galloway Hd.	16	Some low cliffs, sand or gravel beach & rocky fore-shores	Drying out havens at Sandhead, Ardwell, Terally, with a sea-wall at Drummore.
W3	East Coasts of Arran & Kintyre	33	Low cliffs, sandy bays & natural harbours	Improved harbour at Campbeltown. Access to Loch Fyne, piers at Brodick, Lamlash & Whiting Bay. Landing at Corrie.
W4	Dornoch Tarbat Ness	9	Sea loch with tidal sand & mud flats	Access to Dornoch Firth, improved beach at Portmahomack.
W5	Lossiemouth Portgordon	11	Long beach with very high dunes. River mouth with spit	Access to River Spey.
W6	Kinnaird Head Buchan Ness	18	Sand & gravel beaches separated by steep headlands, small rivers	Docks at Fraserburgh and Peterhead. Improved harbour at Buchanhaven, beach at Inverlochy/Cairnbulg, St Combs.
W7	Out Head Fife Ness	12	Cliffs & headlands sand & gravel beaches	Improved Harbour at St Andrews.
W8	North Berwick Gibraltar Point	235	Broken cliff and offshore rocks down to border. Lowlands with medium cliffs, bays and rivers to R. Tees. Bigger cliffs & bays to Flamborough. Rest low & shallow	Improved harbours at Dunbar, St Abbs, Eyemouth, Burnmouth, Seahouses, Craster, Scarborough, Bridlington. Beaches at Holy Island, Beadnall, Boulmer, Newbiggin, Cullercoats, Redcar, Filey, Hornsea, Withernsea. River ports at Berwick-on-Tweed, Alnmouth, Amble, Staithes & Whitby. Landings at Runswick & Robin Hood's Bays, Sandsend and N & S Flamborough. Docks at Blyth, Sunderland, Seaham, Hartlepool, Grimsby & Immingham. Access to Rivers Tyne, Wear, Tees, and Humber.
W9	R Welland Great Ouse	16	Low with river outlets, flats to seaward	Access to R Nene and Wisbech.
W10	Cromer Lowestoft	39	Beaches backed by dunes or saltings. Bars off river mouths and Broads	Beaches at Happisburgh, Sea Palling, Caister-on-Sea and Great Yarmouth. River wharves at Yarmouth & Gorleston.
W11	Colne Point Foulness Point	13	River outlets and tidal flats	Access to rivers Blackwater, Crouch and Colne, and many riverside ports.
W12	North to South Foreland	18	Long beaches with cliffs at each end. River mouth	Improved harbour at Broadstairs. Docks at Ramsgate. Access to ancient port of Sandwich. Beaches at Deal, Walmer & Kingsdown.
W13	Butt of Lewis Kebock Head	41	Mainly low shoreline with deep bays or lochs, cliff headlands	Improved harbours at Ness & Stornoway.
		469		

TOTAL DIRECT MILEAGE = 336 + 1001 + 1018 + 469 = 2824 miles

Note: This gives a much shorter distance than by Coastal Mileage.

APPENDIX IV – EXAMPLES OF BRITISH BOAT TYPES CLASSED BY SHAPE   Sheet 1

Nº TAXON   MAIN FEATURES   THE ABBREVIATIONS ARE LISTED AT THE END OF THE APPENDIX

PLACE & TYPE   NAME OR NUMBER   BUILDER & DATE   DRAWING REFERENCE   DEPTH CORRECTION
GENERAL DETAILS – WORK, DECK, PROPULSION ETC.
PLANKING   BOTTOM LINE   SHEER LINE   MID·SECTION   FORWARD   RATIO   AFT
BOT/SIDE   TYPE   TYPE   FLOOR   BILGE   SIDE   TYPE PROFILE & GROUP   TYPE PROFILE

L	LOK	DF	DA	FF	FM	FA	#	Bmax	BWL	Bsh	Depth	#	BF	BWF	L/B	B/D	#	BA	BWA
00·0	00·0	0·0	0·0	0·0	0·0	0·0	00·0	00·0	0·0	00·0	0·0	00·0	0·0	0·0	0·0	0·0	00·0	0·0	0·0

01 TRUE FLATTY   FLAT BOTTOM, FLAT SIDES, POINTED ENDS WITH OR WITHOUT TRANSOMS, NO KEEL

MEARE TURF BOAT   SWEET c1930   MᶜKEE ✳   NIL
FARM TRANSPORT, OPEN, TRACKED AND POLE-PADDLED
SLAB/E-F   KEEL-LESS   VERY SLIGHT   FLAT   H/C 45° Fᶜ   SHARP RAKED   3·7   SHARP RAKED
17·3   12·0 0·5 0·5   0·7 0·5 0·7   08·7 04·5 3·3 04·5 1·0   02·6 0·0 0·0   S 4·5   14·6 0·0 0·0

HAM MILLS WITHY BOAT, NELLIE   KEETCH 1929   MᶜKEE ✳   NIL
OSIER CROPPING, OPEN, TRACKED
E-P/E-F   KEEL-LESS   NORMAL   FLAT   H/C 20° Fᶜ   SHARP RAKED   3·6   T.S. RAKED
18·7   14·6 0·5 0·5   1·4 0·9 1·4   09·4 05·2 4·2 05·2 1·6   02·1 0·0 0·0   S 3·3   16·7 0·8 0·2

MANY OTHER WIDELY DISTRIBUTED EXAMPLES IN FLAT COUNTRY SUBJECT TO FLOODING. GUN-PUNTS & DITCH CLEARING.

02 SPRUNG FLATTY   FLAT SPRUNG BOTTOM, FLAT SIDES, POINTED ENDS WITH OR WITHOUT TRANSOMS, NO KEEL

MANNINGTREE GUN-PUNT   PORTER 1951   LEWIS, 'VINTAGE BOATS', p.97   ADD ·14 FOR SPRING
WILD-FOWLING, END AND SIDE DECKS, 2-STRAKE SIDE, ROWED, PADDLED, LUG OR SPRIT SAIL
E-P/E-F   KEEL-LESS   FLAT   FLAT   H/C 6° Fᶜ   SHARP RaCu   5·4 N   SHARP RAKED
16·8   15·8 0·0 0·0   0·9 0·9 0·9   09·4 03·1 2·9 03·1 1·1   00·5 0·0 0·0   S 4·4   16·3 0·0 0·0

FLEET TROW   F. CARTER c1950   MᶜKEE ✳   ADD ·04 FOR SPRING
FERRY, OPEN, 3-STRAKE SIDE, POLE-PADDLED AND ROWED WITH SINGLE THOLES
E-P/E-F   KEEL-LESS   NORMAL   FLAT   H/C 27° Fᶜ   SHARP RaCu   2·8   TRNSM Ra CUT
14·8   13·3 0·3 0·3   1·3 0·9 1·3   07·7 05·0 3·7 05·0 1·2   00·9 0·0 0·0   S 4·1   14·2 1·9 0·0

ALSO WAREHAM REED FLATTY

03 DISHED FLATTY   CAMBERED & SPRUNG BOTTOM, FLAT SIDES, POINTED ENDS WITH OR WITHOUT TRANSOMS, NO KEEL

PARRETT FLATNER   MᶜKEE M.M. VOL. 56, p.233   ADD 0·4 FOR DISH
FISHING - STAKE AND DIPPING NETS, OPEN, SPRITSAIL & JIB AND ROWED WITH PAIRED THOLES, DAGGER OR LEE-BOARD
E-P/E-F   KEEL-LESS   LIVELY   CURVED   H/C 30° Fᶜ   SHARP RaCu   3·5   SHARP RAKED
18·7   13·6 0·5 0·5   2·0 0·8 1·9   09·3 05·3 4·5 05·3 1·7   02·0 0·0 0·0   S 3·1   15·7 0·0 0·0

ALSO CHRISTCHURCH HARBOUR SALMON PUNT

04 SCOW   FLAT BOTTOM SPRUNG INTO THE ENDS, FLAT SIDES, NO KEEL

MINSTERWORTH LONG-NET PUNT   PROSSER c1910   MᶜKEE ✳   NIL
SALMON SEINER, OPEN   ROWED WITH PADDLES IN STAPLE SHAPED PIVOT
E-F/EKED   KEEL-LESS   NORMAL   FLAT   H/C 5° Fᶜ   SQUARE RaCu   6·0 N   SQUARE RaCu
22·3   11·0 0·5 0·5   2·0 1·1 2·0   11·1 03·7 3·2 03·7 1·5   05·6 3·0 3·0   2·5   16·6 3·0 3·0

ALSO MANY ENGLISH RIVER PUNTS, SOME CROSSING FERRIES

05 SWIM   FLAT BOTTOM, FLAT SIDES, RAKED SQUARE ENDS, SKEGS FOR RUDDERS, NO KEEL

THAMES CHALK BARGE   c1765   CHAPMAN A.N.M. L.13
ESTUARY SAILING LIGHTER, END DECKS, LOWERING SPRIT SLOOP RIG, LEE-BOARDS, BUDGET STERN   NIL
E-P   KEEL-LESS   NORMAL   FLAT   H/C 17° Fᶜ   SQUARE RAKED   3·7   Sq Ra AND Sq TRNSM
56·3   35·3 1·0 1·0   8·2 6·7 8·2   28·0 15·3 13·0 15·3 5·2   12·0 6·2 6·1   2·9   37·3 7·5 7·5

ADMIRALTY SWIM BARGE   c1803   CARR 'SAILING BARGES' p.38   NIL
STORES LIGHTER, DECKED WITH HATCHES, SPRIT RIGGED WITH BOWSPRIT & MIZZEN ON RUDDER, LEE-BOARDS
E-P   KEEL-LESS   NORMAL   FLAT   H/C 14° Fᶜ   SQUARE RaCu   3·15   Sq RaCu & Sq TRNSM
56·7   36·7 4·7 4·7   3·3 1·6 2·8   26·4 18·0 16·5 18·0 6·0   07·5 5·4 8·5   3·0   44·2 6·0 8·3

L	LOK	DF	DA	FF	FM	FA	#	Bmax	BWL	Bsh	Depth	#	BF	BWF	L/B	B/D	#	BA	BWA

APPENDIX IV–   SHEET 2

Nº TAXON   MAIN FEATURES

PLACE & TYPE	NAME OR NUMBER		BUILDER & DATE		DRAWING REFERENCE		DEPTH CORRECTION		
GENERAL DETAILS – WORK , DECK , PROPULSION									
PLANKING	BOTTOM LINE	SHEER LINE	MID-SECTION		FORWARD		RATIO	AFT	
BOT/SIDE	TYPE	TYPE	FLOOR	BILGE SIDE	TYPE PROFILE		& GROUP	TYPE PROFILE	
L	LOK DF DA	FF FM FA	#	B_{MAX} B_{WL} B_{SH} DEPTH	#	BF BWF	L/B B/D	#	BA BWA

05 SWIM (Cont.)

THAMES SWIM BARGE   1840 – 1890   CARR 'SAILING BARGES' p.70   NIL
ESTUARY SAILING LIGHTER , DECKED WITH HATCHES , SPRIT RIG WITH BOWSPRIT & TOPS'L & MIZZEN ON RUDDER , LEEBOARDS

E-P	KEEL-LESS	SLIGHT	FLAT	H/C	14° FF	SqRa Round Foot	4·4 N	SqRa & SqTransom	
71·0	36·7 4·0 4·0	3·5 2·0 2·5	35·0	16·0 14·4 16·0 6·0	12·0	15·0 14·0		2·7	60·0 14·0 13·0

ADMIRALTY SWIM BARGE   ANT   DEPTFORD YARD 1819   CARR 'SAILING BARGES' p.40   NIL
SAILING STORES LIGHTER , DECKED WITH HATCHES , SISTER VESSEL WAS GAFF CUTTER WITH BOWSPRIT, TOPS'L & SQUARESAIL, LEEBOARDS

E-P	KEEL-LESS	NORMAL	FLAT	H/C	13 FF	Square Raked	3·4	SqRa & Sq Transom	
72·0	38·5 2·0 2·0	8·2 6·7 8·2	28·4	21·0 17·8 21·0 8·4	16·5	15·6 6·0		2·5	55·0 15·2 6·0

ALSO DUMB BARGES & LIGHTERS

06 TRUE BATEAU   FLAT BOTTOM , CURVED SIDES , POINTED ENDS WITH OR WITHOUT TRANSOMS , NO KEEL

BRIDGWATER BARGE   S.T. Co. Ltd.   CARVER c 1900   GREENHILL 'ARCH. OF THE BOAT' Fig. 184   NIL
DUMB LIGHTER , DECKED ENDS , TIDE & TRACKED , RUDDER SHIPPED IN CANAL

E-P/E-F	KEEL-LESS	NORMAL	FLAT	H/C	FLAM	POINTED RaCu	4·1 N	T.S. RAKED	
52·6	45·7 1·4 1·0	3·8 2·7 3·8	23·3	12·7 10·8 12·7 4·0	03·2	0·0 0·0	S 3·2	48·9 1·6 0·6	

FENLAND BARGE   IVY   DUNN - N.M.M. No 14 & 69   NIL
WATERWAY BARGE , OPEN APART FROM SHORT END DECKS & WIDE PLANKSHEERS , TRACKED

E-F	KEEL-LESS	SLIGHT	FLAT	H/C	FLAM	POINTED RaTh	4·8 N	BLUFF RaTh	
47·5	38·2 1·0 1·0	4·6 3·3 3·5	25·0	10·3 10·3 09·8 4·5	05·0	0·0 0·0	2·1	43·2 0·0 0·0	

TEIGN GRAVEL BARGE   TWO BROTHERS   UPHAM 1924   McKEE ✷
RIVER BARGE , ENDS DECKED , INBOARD ENGINE , TIDE AND PERHAPS A SMALL MAST   NIL

E-P	KEEL-LESS	SLIGHT	FLAT	H/C	FLAM	POINTED RaCu	3·0	TRANSOM RaCut	
40·6	37·3 3·0 3·0	2·5 1·5 2·3	20·9	13·4 12·8 13·4 4·5	05·0	0·0 0·0	S 3·0	37·8 5·0 2·3	

ALSO   OTHER INLAND WATERWAY CRAFT INCLUDING ROTHER LIGHTERS

07 SPRUNG BATEAU   FLAT SPRUNG BOTTOM , CURVED SIDES , POINTED ENDS WITH OR WITHOUT TRANSOMS , NO KEEL

FENLAND PUNT   DUNN · N.M.M. No 57
LIGHT RIVER TRANSPORT , OPEN , CHINE DEEPER THAN THE CENTRE-LINE , POLED OR TRACKED   ADD 0·25 FOR SPRING

E-F	KEEL-LESS	SLIGHT	INVERTED CURVE H/C	PLUMBCu	POINTED Th/RaCu	3·5	POINTED Th/RaCu	
15·7	12·2 0·7 0·7	0·8 0·5 0·8	06·7 04·5 4·5 04·3 1·4	01·8 0·0 0·0		S 3·2	14·0 0·0 0·0	

ALSO BRANCASTER STAITHE CANOE

08 DISHED BATEAU   CAMBERED SPRUNG BOTTOM, CURVED SIDES , POINTED ENDS WITH OR WITHOUT TRANSOMS , NO KEEL

WESTON-S-MARE FLATNER   SILVER SPRAY   WATTS 1903 REBUILT 1920   M.M. VOL. 57 p. 28   ADD 0·2 FOR DISH
FISHING & TRIPPING , OPEN , INBOARD ENGINE , SPRITSAIL & JIB AND ROWED WITH PAIRED THOLES , DAGGERBOARDS

E-P/E-F	KEEL-LESS	NORMAL	CURVED	H/C	FLAM	SHARP RaCu	3·2	TRANSOM RAKED	
22·3	20·1 0·8 0·8	2·3 1·6 2·1	11·0	07·0 6·0 07·0 2·7	01·4	0·0 0·0	2·6	21·5 1·4 0·0	

ALSO

09 ROUND BATEAU   ROUNDED SECTIONS WITH POINTED BUT NO KEEL

10 STOP-NET BOAT   ROUNDED SECTIONS , POINTED BOW & SQUARE STERN , NO KEEL

CHEPSTOW STOP-NET BOAT   HURD 1937   McKEE ✷   NIL
SALMON DIPPING , OPEN , ROWED (SOME WITH LUG SAIL)

E-P	KEEL-LESS	SLIGHT	FLAT	ROUND	FLAM	POINTED RaCu	2·5 B	SQUARE RAKED	
20·0	16·5 1·0 1·0	2·0 1·8 2·0	10·0	08·0 7·5 08·0 2·7	02·9	0·0 0·0	S 3·0	19·4 3·5 1·2	

| L | LOK DF DA | FF FM FA | # | B_{MAX} B_{WL} B_{SH} DEPTH | # | BF BWF | L/B B/D | # | BA BWA |

APPENDIX IV   SHEET 3

Nº TAXON   MAIN FEATURES

PLACE & TYPE   NAME OR NUMBER   BUILDER & DATE   DRAWING REFERENCE   DEPTH CORRECTION
GENERAL DETAILS - WORK, DECK, PROPULSION
PLANKING BOTTOM LINE   SHEER LINE   MID-SECTION   FORWARD   RATIO   AFT
BOT/SIDE   TYPE   TYPE   FLOOR BILGE SIDE   TYPE PROFILE & GROUP   TYPE PROFILE
L   LOK DF DA   FF FM FA   # Bmax BWL Bsh Depth   # BF BWF   L/B B/D   # BA BWA

10 STOP-NET BOAT (CONT.)

GATCOMBE STOP-NET BOAT MARGARET   McKEE ✶   NIL
SALMON DIPPING, OPEN, SCULLED TO & FROM FIXED MOORING FOR THE SEASON
E-P   KEEL-LESS   SLIGHT   FLAT   ROUND FLAM   POINTED RaCu   2.4 B   SQUARE RAKED
19.0   16.0 1.0 1.0   1.9 1.7 1.9   09.0 07.8 7.2 07.8 2.7   01.6 0.0 0.0   2.9   18.6 4.2 1.5

11 PRAM ROUNDED SECTIONS, BOTH ENDS SQUARE, NO KEEL

IMPORTED OR COPIED WORK BOAT FROM NORWAY, TENDERS TO LARGER CRAFT, OPEN, ROWED. FERRY TUG

12 SCOTS COBLE   ROUND SECTIONS, POINTED BOW WITH STEM, SQUARE STERN, PART KEEL.

ENSLIEGH COTTAGE COBLE Nº1   CAMPBELL, PERTH   McKEE ✶   NIL
ROD FISHING ON TAMAR, OPEN, ROWED WITH SINGLE THOLE-PIN OARS
E-F   SPRUNG CENTRAL PLANK NORMAL   CURVED   ROUND FLAM   POINTED RaCu   2.7   SQUARE RAKED
14.7   12.0 0.3 0.0   1.8 1.0 1.1   08.3 05.5 4.7 05.5 1.6   02.4 0.0 0.0   5 3.4   14.2 4.6 4.3

TWEED SALMON COBLE   LEE, 1951   HILL JOURNAL 3 p.1   NIL
SEINING IN RIVER MOUTH, OPEN, ROWED WITH SINGLE THOLE-PIN OARS
E-F   SPRUNG CENTRAL PLANK NORMAL   FLAT   ROUND FLAM   BLUNT RaCu   3.2'   SQUARE PLUMB
17.0   13.3 0.5 0.2   1.6 1.1 1.3   08.5 05.3 ? 05.3 1.7   03.7 0.0 0.0   5 3.1   17.0 5.2 4.0

ALSO VARIETIES FROM 8' TO 30' LOA, MAINLY ALONG E. COAST OF SCOTLAND (INCLUDES BODDIN HEAD 'BAY BOAT')

13 ENGLISH COBLE   ROUNDED SECTIONS FORWARD TO RAKED SQUARE STERN WITH CHINE, PART KEEL

YORKSHIRE COBLE ELIZA   BLAKE Y.M. Vol.56 p.192   ADD 0.4 FOR FOREFOOT
FISHING BEACH BOAT, OPEN, ROWS 4 OARS ON SINGLE THOLE-PINS, LOWERING MAST, LUG SAIL   ADD 4.0 FOR RUDDER
E-F   RAM PLANK, LIFT   NORMAL   FLAT   ROUND Cu WITH TH   POINTED RaCu   3.7   SQUARE RAKED
25.7   19.2 1.0 0.0   3.8 2.5 2.9   10.8 06.9 5.5 06.2 3.2   03.3 0.0 0.0   2.2   22.3 2.9 2.1

NORTHUMBERLAND COBLE EGRET   HARRISON 1962   HOLNESS FEB. 1965   ADD 0.6 FOR FOREFOOT
RECREATIONAL FISHING, OPEN, ROWED WITH SINGLE THOLE-PIN OARS, LUG ON LOWERING MAST, DAGGER BOARD   ADD 3.1 FOR RUDDER
E-F   RAM PLANK, LIFT   NORMAL   FLAT   ROUND Cu WITH TH   SHARP RaCu   3.7   SQUARE RAKED
22.7   14.3 1.1 0.1   3.2 1.8 2.5   13.7 06.1 5.7 05.6 2.4   06.8 0.0 0.0   2.4   20.7 3.5 2.8

NORTHUMBERLAND MOTOR COBLE   HARRISON   N.M.M. Nº286   ADD 1.0 FOR FOREFOOT
FISHING BOAT, DECKED OVER FOREWARD OF AMIDSHIPS, DIESEL MAIN ENGINE ALSO POWERS CAPSTAN   ADD 1.6 FOR RUDDER
E-F   TUNNEL RAM, LIFT   REFLEX FWD   FLAT   ROUND Cu WITH TH   SHARP RaCu   3.7   SQUARE RAKED
30.3   21.0 1.4 0.0   4.8 2.8 3.4   15.6 08.3 7.7 07.4 3.4   06.3 0.0 0.0   2.4   27.3 4.0 3.8

SUNDERLAND FOY BOAT LESLIE   McKEE ✶   ADD 0.3 FOR FOREFOOT
ASSIST SHIPPING, OPEN, ROWED & SAILED, MAST LOWERS, DIPPING LUG   ADD 2.2 FOR RUDDER
E-F   RAM PLANK, LIFT   NORMAL   RAISED   ROUND Cu WITH TH   SHARP RaCu   3.6   SQUARE RAKED
18.5   14.0 0.4 0.0   2.7 1.6 2.0   10.0 05.2 4.1 04.7 1.9   02.7 0.0 0.0   2.7   16.7 2.9 2.6

MOTOR COBLES ARE NOW SEEN ELSEWHERE THAN IN N.E. ENGLAND (INCLUDES DOUBLE-ENDED COBLES (MULES))

14 THAMES SAILING BARGE ROUND SECTION ENDS, FLAT BOTTOM & SIDES WITH HARDCHINE AMIDSHIPS, SOME WITH KEELS

THAMES SAILING BARGE   1865   CARR 'SAILING BARGES' fig 20   NIL
ESTUARY FREIGHT, DECKED WITH HATCES, SPRIT RIGGED ON MAIN & MIZZEN (ON RUDDER), BOWSPRIT, LEEBOARDS
E-P   KEEL-LESS (KEELSON)   NORMAL   FLAT   H/C 6°FC   TRANS TO BLUFF PLUMB 4.5 N   TRANS TO TRANSOM
74.5   71.5 4.0 4.0   5.1 1.4 3.6   37.0 16.7 16.3 16.7 5.4   03.0 0.0 0.0   5 3.1   74.5 11.0 4.4

THAMES MULE BARGE   1895   CARR 'SAILING BARGES' fig 22   ADD 1.0 FOR KEEL
COASTER, DECKED 1.6 BELOW SHEER, WITH HATCHES, SPRIT MAIN, GAFF MIZZEN, TOPS'L, BOWSPRIT, LEEBOARDS
E-P   BEAM KEEL DRAG   NORMAL   FLAT   H/C 14°FC   TRANS TO BLUFF PLUMB 4.3 N   TRANS TO PLUMB TRNSM
91.8   87.2 6.0 7.0   5.8 3.0 4.8   45.5 21.5 21.0 21.5 9.4   04.6 0.0 0.0   2.3   91.8 14.0 1.6

L   LOK DF DA   FF FM FA   # Bmax BWL Bsh Depth   # BF BWF   L/B B/D   # BA BWA

APPENDIX IV

Nº TAXON   MAIN FEATURES

PLACE & TYPE   NAME OR NUMBER   BUILDER & DATE   DRAWING REFERENCE   DEPTH CORRECTION
GENERAL DETAILS – WORK, DECK, PROPULSION
PLANKING   BOTTOM LINE   SHEER LINE   MID-SECTION   FORWARD   RATIO   AFT
BOT/SIDE   TYPE   TYPE   FLOOR   BILGE   SIDE   TYPE PROFILE   & GROUP   TYPE PROFILE
   L   LOK   DF   DA   FF   FM   FA   #   B$_{MAX}$ BWL   B$_{SH}$ DEPTH   #   BF   BWF   L/B   B/D   #   BA   BWA

14 THAMES SAILING BARGE (CONT.)

THAMES TOPS'L BARGE (CHAMPION CLASS) 1895   CARR 'SAILING BARGES' F$_{ig}$ 21   ADD 1·4 FOR SPRING
ESTUARY FREIGHT, DECKED WITH HATCHES, SPRIT MAIN & MIZZEN, TOPS'L & BOWSPRIT, LEEBOARDS

BOT/SIDE	TYPE			TYPE			FLOOR	B$_{MAX}$	BWL	B$_{SH}$	DEPTH	#	BF	BWF	L/B	B/D	#	BA	BWA
E–P	KEEL-LESS, SPRUNG			NORMAL			FLAT	H/C	6°F$_\ell$	TRANS TO POINTED	P$_B$	4·5	N				TRANS TO RAKED TRANSOM		
85·0	82·5	2·8	3·2	5·0	1·4	3·8	42·5	18·7	18·0	18·7	6·2	01·2	0·0	0·0		2·3	83·7	11·8	1·8

15 BUSS   KEEL, ROUNDED SECTIONS, STEMS BOTH ENDS, LEVEL WITH NARROW AND DEEP RATIOS

HERRING BUSS   c 1765   CHAPMAN A.N.M. P$_\ell$. LIX 2   ADD 1·1 FOR KEEL
DRIFTER, DECK 2·8 BELOW SHEER, SHORT DECK AFT IS FLUSH, 2 MASTS, SQUARE MAIN, BOWSPRIT, RIDING SAIL ON MIZZEN

E–P	BEAM KEEL			NORMAL			RAISED	ROUND	T'HOME	BLUFF RAKED CURVE	4·0	N				BLUFF RAKED, PINK		
67·5	57·2	6·5	6·5	9·2	6·5	8·8	33·8	17·0	17·0	15·4	13·0	06·0	0·0	0·0	D 1·3	63·2	0·0	0·0	

MERSEY RIVER FLAT   M.M. 58 ⱷ 259   ADD 0·1 FOR KEEL
RIVER FREIGHT, DECKED WITH HATCHES, GAFF SLOOP

E–P	BEAM KEEL			EASY			FLAT	HARD	PLUMB	BLUFF RAKED CURVE	4·1	N				POINTED R$_A$C$_U$		
82·7	70·4	8·6	8·6	5·6	1·6	2·0	41·8	20·0	20·0	20·0	10·2	10·0	0·0	0·0	D 2·0	80·4	0·0	0·0	

HUMBER KEEL (SHEFFIELD SIZE)   LATE 19TH C.   HUMBER YAWL CLUB, 1901 ⱷ.16   ADD 0·3 FOR KEEL
ESTUARY & WATERWAY FREIGHT, DECKED WITH HATCHES, SQUARE MAIN & TOPS'L, LEE-BOARDS

E–P	BEAM KEEL			EASY			FLAT	HARD	6°F$_\ell$	BLUFF PLUMB	3·9	N				BLUFF PLUMB		
60·0	56·0	4·0	4·0	4·5	3·4	4·1	30·0	15·3	15·3	15·3	7·8	04·0	0·0	0·0	D 2·0	60·0	0·0	0·0	

HUMBER SLOOP   LATE 19TH C.   HUMBER YAWL CLUB, 1903 ⱷ.2   ADD 0·6 FOR KEEL
RIVER FREIGHT, DECKED WITH HATCH, GAFF SLOOP, LEE-BOARDS

E–P	BEAM KEEL			NORMAL			FLAT	HARD	5°F$_\ell$	BLUFF PLUMB	3·8	N				BLUFF PLUMB		
68·0	64·2	2·8	2·8	8·8	6·2	8·2	34·0	17·3	17·3	17·3	9·0	03·8	0·0	0·0	D 1·9	64·2	0·0	0·0	

16 KERNOW   KEEL, ROUNDED SECTIONS, STEMS BOTH ENDS, LEVEL, WITH DEEP RATIO

ST IVES FISHING BOAT   PAYNTER c.1848   WASHINGTON ⱷ$_\ell$ 5   ADD 0·8 FOR KEEL
DRYING-OUT HARBOUR, FOC'SL DECKED, DIPPING FORE & STANDING LUG MIZZEN, BOWSPRIT, OUTRIGGER

E–P	BEAM KEEL			NORMAL			FLAT CURVED	ROUND	PLUMB	POINTED R$_A$C$_U$	3·2					POINTED RAKED		
39·5	33·4	4·7	5·0	3·4	2·5	4·7	17·0	12·3	12·3	12·3	7·7	03·7	0·0	0·0	D 1·6	37·1	0·0	0·0	

PEEL FISHING BOAT <u>DOVE</u>   GRAVES c.1848   WASHINGTON ⱷ$_\ell$ 6   ADD 1·0 FOR KEEL
DRIFTER, DRYING-OUT HARBOUR, FOC'SL DECKED, SMACK RIGGED WITH MIZZEN

E–F	BEAM KEEL			EASY			HOLLOW VEE	ROUND	PLUMB C$_U$	POINTED R$_A$C$_U$	3·5					BLUFF RAKED		
39·4	31·2	4·2	4·5	3·4	3·3	3·4	20·6	11·8	11·7	11·7	7·5	04·8	0·0	0·0	D 1·6	36·0	0·0	0·0	

ST IVES MACKEREL DRIVER <u>EBENEZER</u> SS 340 PAYNTER 1869   N.M.M. Nº 99 A, B & C   ADD 0·6 FOR KEEL
DRIFTER, DRYING-OUT HARBOUR, DECKED 1·6 BELOW SHEER, DIPPING FORE & STANDING LUG MIZZEN, TOPS'L ON FORE.

E–P	BEAM KEEL			NORMAL			RAISED CURVE	ROUND	FLAM	SHARP RAKED C$_U$	3·4					POINTED RAKED		
48·0	42·5	3·1	5·0	6·0	4·3	5·2	20·5	14·0	13·3	14·0	8·7	02·4	0·0	0·0	D 1·6	44·9	0·0	0·0	

HOY OR LIGHTER   c 1765   CHAPMAN A.N.M. P$_\ell$ LI 1   ADD 0·6 FOR KEEL
SAILING LIGHTER, DECKED 0·8 BELOW SHEER, SINGLE MAST, STANDING GAFF & LOOSE FOOTED MAIN, 2 HEADSAILS, BOWSPRIT

E–P	BEAM KEEL			LIVELY			RAISED	ROUND	T'HOME	BLUFF RAKED C$_U$	3·1					BLUFF R$_A$ WITH PINK		
51·8	42·5	6·7	7·3	7·5	3·2	6·0	23·0	16·8	16·8	15·8	9·9	06·0	0·0	0·0	D 1·7	63·2	0·0	0·0	

SPITHEAD WHERRY <u>WOODHAM</u>   N.M.M. (S.N.R.)   ADD 0·8 FOR KEEL
ATTENDING SHIPS, OPEN, SPRIT KETCH WITH STAYSAIL ALL INBOARD, 6 PAIRED THOLES

E–F	BEAM KEEL			NORMAL			RAISED CURVE	ROUND	FLAM	SHARP RAKED	3·3					POINTED RAKED		
27·0	22·5	1·5	2·2	4·4	3·2	3·4	15·8	08·2	6·8	08·2	5·0	02·7	0·0	0·0	D 1·7	25·2	0·0	0·0	

ALSO OTHER CORNISH FISHING BOATS

   L   LOK   DF   DA   FF   FM   FA   #   B$_{MAX}$ BWL   B$_{SH}$ DEPTH   #   BF   BWF   L/B   B/D   #   BA   BWA

APPENDIX IV   SHEET 5

Nº TAXON   MAIN FEATURES

PLACE & TYPE   NAME OR NUMBER   BUILDER & DATE   DRAWING REFERENCE   DEPTH CORRECTION
GENERAL DETAILS – WORK , DECK , PROPULSION
PLANKING   BOTTOM LINE   SHEER LINE   MID-SECTION ·   FORWARD   RATIO   AFT
BOT/SIDE   TYPE   TYPE   FLOOR   BILGE SIDE   TYPE PROFILE & GROUP   TYPE PROFILE
   L   LOK DF DA   FF FM FA   # Bmax BWL Bsh Depth   # BF BWF L/B B/D   # BA BWA

17 ROW WHERRY   KEEL , ROUNDED SECTIONS , STEMS BOTH ENDS , LEVEL WITH A NARROW RATIO

THAMES WHERRY   c 1765   CHAPMAN A.N.M. Pℓ L9   ADD 0·2 FOR KEEL
RIVER PASSENGER FERRY , OPEN , 4 OARLOCKS , SAXBOARDS
E - F   BEAM KEEL   EASY   RAISED CURVE ROUND FLAM   SHARP RAKED Cu   5·0 N   BLUFF RAKED
  25·2   20·0 1·0 1·0   1·8 1·0 1·4 14·5 05·0 4·6 05·0 2·0   04·0 0·0 0·0   2·5 24·0 0·0 0·0

SERVICE WHALER (MONTAGU)   FIRST HALF 20ᵀᴴ C.   ADMIRALTY   ADD 0·3 FOR KEEL
SEABOAT, OPEN , PULLS 5 OARS IN CRUTCHES, STANDING LUG MAIN , JIB-HEADED MIZZEN , STAYSAIL , LEEBOARDS
E - F   SPRUNG BEAM WITH HOG NORMAL   FLAT CURVE ROUND FLAM   POINTED Ra Cu   4·1 N   POINTED Thome
  26·4   21·0 1·4 1·4   2·3 1·3 2·0 15·0 06·4 5·5 06·4 2·6   02·7 0·0 0·0   2·5 23·7 0·0 0·0

PORTSMOUTH 2ᴺᴰ CLASS WHERRY BIRD OF FREEDOM   c 1910   N.M.M. 273   ADD 0·2 FOR KEEL
ATTENDING SHIPS , OPEN , 6 PAIRED THOLES , SOME SET SMALL SPRIT OR LUG , OTHERS AS SPITHEAD WHERRY (16)
E - F   BEAM KEEL   NORMAL   RAISED CURVE ROUND FLAM   POINTED Ra Cu   3·8 N   POINTED RAKED
  22·2   18·0 0·8 0·8   2·1 1·2 2·1 12·0 05·8 4·8 05·8 2·0   03·6 0·0 0·0   2·9 21·6 0·0 0·0

ALSO A FEW OTHER WATERMEN'S BOATS

18 EASTERN SKIFF KEEL , ROUNDED SECTIONS , STEMS BOTH ENDS , LEVEL WITH BOTH RATIOS NORMAL

PETERHEAD FISHING BOAT   BOOTH c. 1848   WASHINGTON'S Pℓ 2   ADD 0·6 FOR KEEL
HERRING DRIFTER , DRYING-OUT HARBOURS , OPEN , ROWED OR 2-MASTED LUG-RIG
E - F   BEAM KEEL   NORMAL   RAISED HOLLOW ROUND FLAM   POINTED Ra Cu   2·7   POINTED Ra Cu
  36·7   30·7 2·6 2·6   4·7 3·3 3·7 21·0 13·5 10·6 13·5 5·7 02·8 0·0 0·0   2·4 33·5 0·0 0·0

SHERINGHAM CRABBER STAR OF PEACE   EMERY 1912   N.M.M. 1 & 289   ADD 0·2 FOR KEEL
BEACH BOAT , OPEN , ROWED WITH 6 THURROCKS OR SAILED USING SINGLE DIPPING LUG
E - F   BEAM KEEL   NORMAL   VEE   ROUND FLAM   POINTED Ra Cu   2·7   POINTED Ra Cu
  18·3   12·8 1·5 1·6   2·3 1·5 1·8 10·2 06·8 6·3 06·8 3·2   04·0 0·0 0·0   2·1 16·8 0·0 0·0

MEDWAY DOBLE   LOUISE R.R.28   EARLY 20ᵀᴴ C.   N.M.M. 94   ADD 0·8 FOR SPRUNG KEEL
FISHING BOAT WITH WELL, DECKED APART FROM FISH HOLD, SPRIT MAIN HAS A BOOM, JIB SET FLYING, DAGGER PLATE IN WELL, 2 OARS
E - F   SPRUNG BEAM KEEL NORMAL   RAISED CURVE SLACK FLAM   POINTED Ra Cu   2·8   POINTED Ra Cu
  18·0   15·2 0·7 0·6   2·1 1·3 1·7 09·0 06·4 5·5 06·4 2·5   01·5 0·0 0·0   2·6 16·7 0·0 0·0

WEST COAST FIFIE   BOUNTY U.L.217   GAMRIE BAY 1880   N.M.M. 63   ADD 0·6 FOR KEEL
LOCH & COASTAL FISHING , OPEN , SINGLE LOWERING MAST WITH VARIABLE RAKE , DIPPING LUG , 4 PAIRED THOLES
E - F   BEAM KEEL   NORMAL   RAISED HOLLOW ROUND FLAM   POINTED Ra Cu   2·8   POINTED Ra Cu
  23·2   21·5 1·5 2·0   2·7 1·4 1·7 12·0 08·4 7·7 08·4 3·2   08·0 0·0 0·0   2·6 22·4 0·0 0·0

ANNAN WAMMEL-NET BOAT DORA   WILSON 1900   N.M.M. 118 A & B   ADD 0·7 FOR BALLAST KEEL
SALMON DRIFTER , DECKED ALL BUT A SMALL COCKPIT, MAST LOWERS, BOOMED STANDING LUG, ROWS 2 OARS IN CRUTCHES
E - P   BEAM KEEL   NORMAL   RAISED   ROUND FLAM   POINTED RAKED   2·9   POINTED RAKED
  18·7   16·4 1·0 1·4   2·7 1·8 2·1 09·6 06·4 5·4 06·4 3·2   00·7 0·0 0·0   2·0 17·1 0·0 0·0

PORTKNOCKIE SCAFFIE YAWL GRATITUDE B.C.K. 252 INNES 1896   N.M.M. 10 , 62 A & B   ADD 0·3 FOR KEEL
HERRING DRIFTER , DECKED 0·5 BELOW SHEER, WELL CLOSED BY HATCHES, MAST LOWERS, DIPPING LUG, JIB ON BOWSRIT, 2 OARS
E - F   BEAM KEEL   NORMAL   FLAT   ROUND FLAM   POINTED Ra Cu   2·9   POINTED RAKED
  25·1   14·0 2·1 2·4   3·2 2·0 2·6 12·3 08·6 8·0 08·6 4·3   04·4 0·0 0·0   2·0 17·4 0·0 0·0

ST. MONANS SMALL FIFIE   MILLER 1865   N.M.M. 64 A   ADD 1·0 FOR KEEL
DRIFTER , DRYING-OUT HARBOUR , (DRAWING TAKEN FROM HALF MODEL), BULWARK HEIGHT TO BE ADDED TO FREEBOARDS
E - P ?   BEAM KEEL   NORMAL   VEE HOLLOW ROUND PLUMB Cu   POINTED PLUMB   3·0   POINTED RAKED
  28·6   27·1 2·0 2·0   3·7 2·7 3·4 14·2 09·4 8·6 09·4 4·8   00·0 0·0 0·0   2·0 27·3 0·0 0·0

   L   LOK DF DA   FF FM FA   # Bmax BWL Bsh Depth   # BF BWF L/B B/D   # BA BWA

APPENDIX IV   SHEET 6

Nº TAXON   MAIN FEATURES

PLACE & TYPE   NAME OR NUMBER   BUILDER & DATE   DRAWING REFERENCE   DEPTH CORRECTION
GENERAL DETAILS – WORK, DECK, PROPULSION
PLANKING   BOTTOM LINE   SHEER LINE   MID-SECTION   FORWARD   RATIO   AFT
BOT/SIDE   TYPE   TYPE   FLOOR BILGE SIDE   TYPE PROFILE & GROUP   TYPE PROFILE

L	LOK	DF	DA	FF	FM	FA	#	Bmax	BWL	Bsh	Depth	#	BF	BWF	L/B B/D	#	BA	BWA

18 EASTERN SKIFF (Cont)

MORAY FIRTH OR BUCKIE HERRING BOAT   BOOTH c.1848   WASHINGTON Pℓ.8   ADD 0·8 FOR KEEL
DRIFTER, DRYING-OUT HARBOUR, OPEN, 2 LUG SAILS
E-F   BEAM KEEL   EASY   RAISED SS ROUND   FLAM   POINTED RaCu   3·0   BLUFF RAKED

| 40·0 | 29·0 2·9 2·9 | 4·2 2·8 3·0 | 23·4 | 13·0 | 11·2 | 13·0 5·7 | 05·5 0·0 0·0 | 2·3 | 34·5 0·0 0·0 |

ABERDEEN FISHING BOAT   HALL c.1848   WASHINGTON Pℓ.7   ADD 0·4 FOR KEEL
HERRING DRIFTER, HARBOUR, OPEN, 2 MASTED.
E-F   BEAM KEEL   EASY   RAISED SS ROUND   FLAM   POINTED RaCu   3·0   POINTED RaCu

| 38·5 | 27·8 3·0 3·0 | 3·4 2·2 2·8 | 20·0 | 12·5 | 11·2 | 12·5 5·0 | 07·0 0·0 0·0 | 2·5 | 34·8 0·0 0·0 |

Sᵀ MONANS FIFIFE   TRUE VINE M.L.20 INNES 1905   N.M.M 217 A, B & C   ADD 0·7 FOR KEEL
DRIFTER, DECKED 1·2 BELOW SHEER, FOREMAST LOWERS, DIPPING FORE & STANDING LUG MIZZEN, JIB ON BOWSPRIT, STEAM CAPSTAN
E-P   BEAM KEEL   NORMAL   VEE HOLLOW ROUND FLAM   SHARP PLUMB   3·2   POINTED RAKED

| 70·0 | 67·0 5·0 7·7 | 8·8 5·8 6·6 | 31·5 | 22·0 | 22·0 | 22·0 11·2 | 00·8 0·0 0·0 | 2·0 | 67·2 0·0 0·0 |

ABERYSTWITH BEACH BOAT   WILLIAMS c.1900   M.M.Vol.41 p.155   ADD 0·2 FOR KEEL
TRIPPING & OFF-SEASON FISHING, OPEN, ROWED WITH 2 OARS IN CRUTCHES, STANDING LUG MIGHT BE SET OFF THE WIND
E-F   BEAM KEEL   NORMAL   FLAT   ROUND FLAM   POINTED Ra Cu   3·2   , POINTED RaCu

| 17·4 | 11·6 0·6 0·6 | 1·7 1·2 1·6 | 09·0 | 05·5 | 5·2 | 05·5 1·8 | 02·0 0·0 0·0 | 2·9 | 13·7 0·0 0·0 |

SHETLAND SIXERN   WATERWITCH   BEFORE 1881   MARCH, I.C. of B. Vol.1 p.65   ADD 0·5 FOR KEEL
DEEP WATER LINES, OPEN, BEACH & COVE BOAT, ROWS 6 OARS WITH 8 GROMMED KABES, MAST LOWERS, DIPPING LUG
E-F   BEAM KEEL   NORMAL   RAISED SS SLACK FLAM   POINTED RaCu   3·2   POINTED Ra Cu

| 29·2 | 20·9 1·2 1·5 | 3·4 1·7 2·4 | 14·7 | 09·0 | 6·6 | 09·0 3·0 | 05·5 0·0 0·0 | 3·0 | 26·4 0·0 0·0 |

SHETLAND SIXERN   OLD TIMES 2866 L.K.   N.M.M. 7, 8 & 9   ADD 0·4 FOR KEEL
AS WATERWITCH ABOVE
E-F   BEAM KEEL   NORMAL   RAISED SS SLACK FLAM   POINTED RaCu   3·4   POINTED RaCu

| 29·4 | 20·0 1·9 2·5 | 3·7 1·7 2·3 | 15·0 | 08·7 | 7·1 | 08·7 3·4 | 05·2 0·0 0·0 | 2·6 | 25·2 0·0 0·0 |

WINDEMERE BOAT No 1   18th C.   Y.M.58 p.180-6   ADD 0·5 FOR KEEL
PLEASURE?, SIDES & ENDS DECKED, STANDING LUG & JIB, ROWS 2 OARS IN CRUTCHES
E-F   BEAM KEEL   LIVELY   RAISED SS ROUND FLARED BLUFF RAKED CURVE 3·5   POINTED Ra Cu

| 21·2 | 16·6 1·1 1·8 | 2·2 0·9 1·8 | 11·0 | 06·1 | 5·5 | 06·1 2·4 | 02·8 0·0 0·0 | 2·5 | 19·4 0·0 0·0 |

LARGS LINE SKIFF   BOAG c.1890   N.M.M. 115 A & B   ADD 0·2 FOR KEEL
BEACH BOAT, OPEN, ROWS 6 OARS IN CRUTCHES, MAST LOWERS, STANDING LUG, JIB ON BOWSRIT
E-F   BEAM KEEL   NORMAL   RAISED CURVE ROUND FLAM SHARP RAKED CURVE 3·5   POINTED RAKED

| 17·6 | 15·7 0·3 1·0 | 2·1 1·3 1·7 | 10·0 | 05·1 | 4·0 | 05·1 2·0 | 00·8 0·0 0·0 | 2·1 | 20·7 0·0 0·0 |

ALSO SKIFFS FROM W. & SW COASTS OF SCOTLAND AND THE OUTER ISLES, DOUBLE-END SURF & HARBOUR BOATS OF YORKSHIRE

19 SAILING WHERRY   KEEL, ROUNDED SECTIONS, STEMS BOTH ENDS, LEVEL WITH NARROW & SHOAL RATIOS

YARMOUTH YAWL   BITTERN   1892   N.M.M. 233   ADD 0·6 FOR KEEL
RESCUE & SALVAGE, BEACH BOAT, OPEN, BOTH MASTS LOWER, DIPPING FORE & STANDING LUG MIZZEN, 16 OAR PIVOT IN OARBEDS
E-F   BEAM KEEL NORMAL-SOME REFLEX FWD FLAT   ROUND Cu THOME SHARP PLUMB   4·9   SHARP RAKED

| 47·1 | 15·7 0·6 0·6 | 4·2 2·5 3·6 | 23·8 | 09·6 | 7·7 | 09·0 3·1 | 01·4 0·0 0·0 | 3·1 | 46·1 0·0 0·0 |

NORFOLK WHERRY   GLEANER (ORION) ALLEN 1894   Y.M. 54 pp 193-5   ADD 0·2 FOR KEEL
BROADS TRAFFIC, DECKED WITH COAMINGS, MAST LOWERS, LOOSE FOOTED MAIN WITH GAFF, QUANT   ADD 1·3 FOR SLIPPING KEEL
E-F   BEAM KEEL NORMAL-SOME REFLEX F.&A. RAISED HOLLOW ROUND FLAM POINTED RaCu 4·0   BLUFF PLUMB CURVE

| 56·0 | 53·0 2·5 2·5 | 3·6 1·7 3·0 | 27·3 | 14·0 | 13·0 | 14·0 4·2 | 02·5 0·0 0·0 | 3·3 | 55·6 0·0 0·0 |

ALSO PROVISIONALLY THE NORFOLK KEEL, THOUGH SHE HAD A NARROW TRANSOM OR SQUARE STERN

L	LOK	DF	DA	FF	FM	FA	#	Bmax	BWL	Bsh	Depth	#	BF	BWF	L/B B/D	#	BA	BWA

APPENDIX IV   Sheet 7

NO TAXON   MAIN FEATURES

PLACE & TYPE   NAME OR NUMBER   BUILDER & DATE   DRAWING REFERENCE   DEPTH CORRECTION
GENERAL DETAILS – WORK , DECK , PROPULSION
PLANKING   BOTTOM LINE   SHEER LINE   MID-SECTION   FORWARD   RATIO   AFT
BOT/SIDE   TYPE   TYPE   FLOOR   BILGE SIDE   TYPE PROFILE & GROUP TYPE PROFILE
L   LOK DF DA   FF FM FA   # Bmax BWL Bsh Depth # BF BWF   L/B B/D   # BA BWA

20 BROAD SKIFF   KEEL , ROUNDED SECTIONS , STEMS BOTH ENDS , LEVEL WITH BEAMY RATIO. (STEEPER FLOOR)

NEWHAVEN FISHING BOAT   ROSE c.1848   WASHINGTON Pℓ.7   ADD 0·6 FOR KEEL
LONG-LINER & DRIFTER , OPEN , BEACHES , 6 PAIRS OF THOLES , 2 LUGSAILS
E–F   BEAM KEEL   NORMAL   RAISED HOLLOW ROUND FLAM   POINTED RaCu   2·6 B   BLUFF RAKED Cu
  34·6   24·0 2·7 2·7   4·1 2·3 3·3   16·8 13·3 11·7 13·3 5·0   05·4 0·0 0·0   2·7   29·4 0·0 0·0

WICK FISHING BOAT   BREMNER c.1848   WASHINGTON Pℓ.5   ADD 0·5 FOR KEEL
DRIFTER , DRYING-OUT HARBOUR , OPEN , 2 LUGSAILS
E–F   BEAM KEEL   NORMAL   RAISED S.S. ROUND FLAM   POINTED RAKED   2·6 B   POINTED RaCu
  33·4   27·3 3·0 3·2   3·7 2·3 3·0   16·5 13·0 12·0 13·0 5·3   03·3 0·0 0·0   2·5   30·6 0·0 0·0

FRASERBURGH HERRING BOAT   WEBSTER c.1848   WASHINGTON Pℓ.8   ADD 1·2 FOR KEEL
DRIFTER , OPEN OR FORECASTLE DECK , 2 LUGSAILS
E–F   BEAM KEEL   EASY   VEE S.S.   SLACK FLAM   POINTED RaCu   2·6 B   BLUFF RAKED Cu
  35·4   31·7 2·8 3·0   4·5 3·4 4·1   17·3 13·5 11·2 13·5 6·3   02·2 0·0 0·0   2·1   33·0 0·0 0·0

ROSEHEARTY FIFIE FLOWER OF POLBAIN U.L.320 1882   N.M.M.64   ADD 0·2 FOR KEEL
DRIFTER , OPEN , MAST LOWERS , DIPPING LUG ,
E–F   BEAM KEEL   NORMAL   RAISED   ROUND FLAM   POINTED RaCu   2·5 B   POINTED RaCu
  16·7   15·1 0·7 1·0   2·2 1·3 1·6   09·0 06·6 5·5 06·6 2·3   00·8 0·0 0·0   2·9   15·9 0·0 0·0

ALSO SOME YOLES FROM THE NORTH OF SCOTLAND

21 HOGGY   KEEL , ROUNDED SECTIONS , STEMS BOTH ENDS , LEVEL WITH BEAMY RATIO (FLATTER FLOOR)

HALLSAND SEINE BOAT   CHANT 1905   N.M.M. 77   ADD 0·3 FOR KEEL
POT BAIT , OFF BEACH , OPEN , 6 PAIRS OF THOLE-PINS , PLATFORM DECK AFT FOR NETS
E–F   BEAM KEEL & HOG   LIVELY   FLAT HOLLOW ROUND FLAM   POINTED RaCu   2·6 B   BLUFF RAKED CURVE
  17·2   11·0 1·0 1·0   2·5 1·3 1·5   08·6 06·6 6·1 06·6 2·3   03·3 0·0 0·0   2·9   14·3 0·0 0·0

PARKWALL LERRET   A BLESSING   WILLS 1960   M.M. 63 p.42   ADD 0·2 FOR KEEL
MACKEREL SEINER OFF BEACH , OPEN , PULLED WITH 4 SINGLE THOLE-PIN OARS
E–F   BEAM KEEL   NORMAL   RAISED   ROUND FLAM   POINTED RaCu   2·5 B   POINTED RaCu
  15·5   10·0 0·4 0·5   2·6 1·9 2·6   07·8 06·2 4·9 06·2 2·4   02·8 0·0 0·0   2·6   12·8 0·0 0·0

CLOSE LIGHTER   c.1765   CHAPMAN A.N.M. LII 2   ADD 0·8 FOR KEEL
LOCK-UP GRAIN LIGHTER , DECKED WITH HATCHES , DUMB WITH SWEEPS
E–P   BEAM KEEL   LIVELY   FLAT   ROUND PLUMB   BLUFF RAKED CURVE 2·4 B   BLUFF RAKED CURVE
  45·0   39·0 5·0 5·6   6·4 3·9 4·7   19·2 18·7 18·7 18·7 9·0   05·0 0·0 0·0   2·1   44·0 0·0 0·0

TYNE KEEL   19th C.   M.M. 28 p.161   ADD 1·2 FOR KEEL
COAL BARGE , DECKED , MAST LOWERS , SQUARE , LUG , THEN SPRIT RIG WITH JIB , ROWED & PUNTED
E–F THEN E.P. BEAM KEEL   FLAT   FLAT   SLACK FLAM   BLUFF RAKED CURVE 2·1 B   BLUFF RAKED
  40·8   33·1 4·0 4·0   3·1 3·1 3·1   21·0 19·0 16·0 19·0 7·1   05·9 0·0 0·0   2·7   39·0 0·0 0·0

PORTLAND LERRET   PUSSYFOOT   N.M.M. 59   ADD 0·4 FOR KEEL
AS FOR A BLESSING ABOVE
E–F   BEAM KEEL   LIVELY   FLAT   ROUND FLAM   POINTED RaCu   2·4 B   BLUFF RAKED CURVE
  17·2   13·5 0·6 0·6   2·9 1·8 2·7   08·6 07·4 5·6 07·1 2·5   01·6 0·0 0·0   2·8   16·1 0·0 0·0

BRIGHTON HOG BOAT   MID 19th C.   N.M.M. 254   ADD 0·7 FOR KEEL
MACKEREL DRIFTER , BEACHED , STEPPED DECKS , ALL BELOW SHEER , DANDY SPRIT RIG , PLANK BUMKIN FOR JIB , LEEBOARDS
E–F   BEAM KEEL   LIVELY   FLAT HOLLOW SLACK FLAM   BLUFF RAKED CURVE 1·7 B   TRANSOM PLUMB CUT.
  27·0   20·0 2·4 2·4   5·2 3·2 4·3   10·5 16·2 15·0 16·2 5·6   04·0 0·0 0·0   2·9   25·4 0·0 0·0

ALTHOUGH SHE HAS A TRANSOM , THIS BOAT HAS BEEN PUT HERE ON ACCOUNT OF HER EXCEPTIONAL BEAM , SEE ALSO TAXON NO 31

L   LOK DF DA   FF FM FA   # Bmax BWL Bsh Depth # BF BWF   L/B B/D   # BA BWA

APPENDIX IV   SHEET 8

Nº TAXON   MAIN FEATURES

PLACE & TYPE   NAME OR NUMBER   BUILDER & DATE   DRAWING REFERENCE   DEPTH CORRECTION
GENERAL DETAILS – WORK , DECK , PROPULSION
PLANKING   BOTTOM LINE   SHEER LINE   MID-SECTION   FORWARD   RATIO   AFT
BOT/SIDE   TYPE   TYPE   FLOOR   BILGE SIDE   TYPE PROFILE & GROUP   TYPE PROFILE
   L   LOK DF DA   FF FM FA   #   Bmax BWL Bsh Depth   #   BF BWF   L/B B/D   #   BA BWA

22 ZULU   KEEL , ROUNDED SECTIONS , STEMS BOTH ENDS , DRAG WITH NARROW & DEEP RATIOS

PORTESSIE ZULU   FIDELITY B.F. 1479   McINTOSH 1904   N.M.M. 91 A,B & C   ADD 0.7 FOR KEEL
HERRING DRIFTER , DECKED 1.1 BELOW SHEER , MASTS LOWER, DIPPING FORE & STANDING LUG MIZZEN , JIB ON BOWSRIT, STEAM CAPSTAN, SWEEPS
E-P   BEAM KEEL WITH HOG NORMAL   VEE HOLLOW ROUND PLUMB   SHARP PLUMB   3.9 N   POINTED RAKED
  79.0   56.0 6.2 9.5   10.2 4.5 5.6 43.0 20.3 19.8 20.3 13.0 02.8 0.0 0.0   D 1.6 58.0 0.0 0.0

23 WESTERN SKIFF   KEEL, ROUNDED SECTIONS , STEMS BOTH ENDS , DRAG WITH DEEP RATIO

LOCH FYNE (ZULU) SKIFF   BONNIE JEAN T.T. 177   HENDERSON c 1895   N.M.M. 113 A & B   ADD 0.6 FOR KEEL
DRIFTER , OPEN , DECKED FWD , STAYED MAST LOWERS , STANDING LUG, JIBS ON BOWSPRIT , 4 PAIRED THOLE-PINS
E-F   BEAM KEEL   NORMAL   VEE   ROUND PLUMB Cu SHARP RAKED CURVE   3.1   BLUFF RAKED
  34.4   24.0 1.8 4.2   4.6 3.2 3.8 15.0 11.1 10.2 11.1 6.5 03.1 0.0 0.0   D 1.7 27.1 0.0 0.0

LOCH FYNE AUXILIARY SKIFF   MILLER 1923   DESIGN Nº 372   ADD 0.5 FOR KEEL
RING NETTER , DECKED , STANDING LUG & JIB ON BOWSPRIT , 2.5 APERTURE FOR SCREW
E-P   BEAM KEEL   NORMAL   RAISED HOLLOW HARD FLARE POINTED RaCu   3.1   BLUFF RAKED
  39.0   26.0 1.8 4.0   5.6 3.7 4.5 22.0 12.0 12.5 12.5 6.8 05.0 0.0 0.0   D 1.8 31.0 0.0 0.0

GIRVAN MOTOR FIFIE   LINES TAKEN BY A.NOBLE FROM A HALF MODEL FOR M.M.& R.31 fig IV   ADD 0.7 FOR KEEL
LINES OR SCOTTISH SEINE , DECKED 0.8 BELOW SHEER , 2.0 APERTURE FOR SCREW IN FALSE STERNPOST
E-P   BEAM KEEL   NORMAL   VEE   ROUND PLUMB   POINTED RAKED   2.8   BLUFF RAKED
  36.7   29.8 3.0 4.7   5.8 3.6 4.3 18.8 13.2 13.2 13.1 7.4 03.0 0.0 0.0   D 1.8 32.8 0.0 0.0

MANX NOBBY GLADYS P.L. 61   1901   N.M.M. 90 A & B   ADD 0.5 FOR KEEL
DRIFTER , DECKED 1.1 BELOW SHEER , OPEN WELL , 2 STANDING LUGS , HANKED STAYSAIL , JIB ON BOWSPRIT
E-P   BEAM KEEL   NORMAL   RAISED HOLLOW ROUND PLUMB   POINTED RaCu   3.1   BLUFF RAKED
  37.4   29.0 2.9 5.3   6.6 4.0 4.3 20.0 12.0 12.0 12.0 8.4 03.6 0.0 0.0   D 1.4 32.6 0.0 0.0

PENZANCE FISHING BOAT   MATTHEWS c 1848   WASHINGTON Pl.1   ADD 0.9 FOR KEEL
DRIFTER , DRYING-OUT HARBOUR , HALF DECK FWD & HATCHES , DIPPING FORE & STANDING LUG MIZZEN , BOWSPRIT & OUTRIGGER
E-P   BEAM KEEL   EASY   FLAT CURVE ROUND FLAM   POINTED RaCu   3.2   POINTED RAKED
  38.6   29.3 3.0 5.0   5.2 3.6 3.9 20.0 12.0 11.0 12.0 7.5 05.1 0.0 0.0   D 1.6 34.4 0.0 0.0

ST IVES PILCHARD DRIVER GODREVY SS.92   AT PORTHLEVEN c.1898   N.M.M. 33, 85A & B, 270   ADD 0.6 FOR KEEL
DRYING-OUT HARBOUR , DECKED 1.6 BELOW SHEER , FOREMAST LOWERS , DIPPING FORE & STANDING LUG MIZZEN
E-P   BEAM KEEL   NORMAL   RAISED CURVE ROUND FLAM   POINTED PLUMB   3.2   POINTED RAKED
  34.8   29.2 2.3 4.7   5.7 4.5 5.1 16.3 11.0 10.5 11.0 7.8 01.3 0.0 0.0   D 1.4 30.5 0.0 0.0

MANX NICKIE EXPERT C.T. 55   c.1881   S.N.R.   ADD 0.7 FOR KEEL
DRIVER , DECKED 1.7 BELOW SHEER , OPEN WELL , FOREMAST LOWERS , DIPPING FORE & STANDING LUG MIZZEN WITH TOPSL , STEAM CAPSTAN
E-P   BEAM KEEL   EASY   RAISED CURVE ROUND PLUMB   POINTED PLUMB   3.3   POINTED RAKED
  51.5   44.2 3.0 6.4   7.7 5.0 5.6 25.0 15.6 15.6 15.6 9.6 02.0 0.0 0.0   D 1.6 46.4 0.0 0.0

MOUNTS BAY MACKEREL DRIVER BOY WILLIE P.Z. 602   PEAKE 1897   N.M.M. 51, 84 A & B   ADD 1.0 FOR KEEL
HARBOUR AT NEWLYN , DECKED 2.2 BELOW SHEER , FOREMAST LOWERS , DIPPING FORE & STANDING LUG MIZZEN WITH TOPSL , STEAM CAPSTAN
E-P   BEAM KEEL   EASY   VEE   SLACK FLAM   SHARP RAKED   3.5   POINTED RAKED
  51.8   45.2 3.7 6.5   6.5 4.7 5.0 24.6 14.9 14.5 14.9 9.8 02.1 0.0 0.0   D 1.5 47.3 0.0 0.0

ALSO

24 NORTHERN SKIFF   KEEL, ROUNDED SECTIONS , STEMS BOTH ENDS , DRAG WITH BOTH RATIOS NORMAL

PORTPATRICK LINE BOAT   BROTHERS B.A. 318   MACDOWELL 1898 N.M.M. 112 A & B   ADD 0.4 FOR KEEL
DRYING-OUT HARBOUR , OPEN , MASTS LOWER , MAST STEP FOR RUNNING , DIPPING FORE & BOOMED STANDING LUG MAIN , 4 PAIRED THOLE-PINS
E-F   BEAM KEEL   NORMAL   RAISED HOLLOW ROUND FLAM   POINTED RAKED   2.7   POINTED RAKED
  18.4   15.4 0.9 1.4   2.6 1.6 2.0 10.0 06.8 5.5 06.8 2.8 01.3 0.0 0.0   2.4 16.7 0.0 0.0

   L   LOK DF DA   FF FM FA   #   Bmax BWL Bsh Depth   #   BF BWF   L/B B/D   #   BA BWA

APPENDIX IV   SHEET 9

Nº TAXON   MAIN FEATURES

PLACE & TYPE   NAME OR NUMBER   BUILDER & DATE   DRAWING REFERENCE   DEPTH CORRECTION
GENERAL DETAILS ~ WORK, DECK, PROPULSION
PLANKING   BOTTOM LINE   SHEER LINE   MID-SECTION   FORWARD   RATIO   AFT
BOT/SIDE   TYPE   TYPE   FLOOR BILGE SIDE   TYPE PROFILE & GROUP TYPE PROFILE
   L   LOK DF DA   FF FM FA   # Bmax BWL Bsh Depth   # BF BWF   L/B B/D   # BA BWA

24 NORTHERN SKIFF (Cont.)

OBAN SKIFF   GYLEN   O.B.5   MACDONALD AT PORTBEG c.1886   N.M.M. 109 A&B   ADD 0.5 FOR KEEL
INSHORE FISHING & PLEASURE, VARYING RAKE & LOWERING MAST, STANDING LUG & JIB ON BOWSPRIT, 4 PAIRED THOLE-PINS
E-F   BEAM KEEL   NORMAL   RAISED HOLLOW ROUND FLAM   SHARP RAKED Cu   3.0   BLUFF RAKED
  17.7   14.0 0.4 1.1   2.2 1.6 2.0 10.9 06.0 4.4 06.0 2.4 01.0 0.0 0.0   2.5 15.1 0.0 0.0

GIRVAN SKIFF JEAN MORGAN B.A.472   AT GIRVAN c.1890   N.M.M. 111 A&B   ADD 0.3 FOR KEEL
GENERAL FISHING, OPEN, VARIABLE RAKE MAST LOWERS, STANDING LUG, JIB ON BOWSPRIT, 4 PAIRED THOLE-PINS
E-F   BEAM KEEL   NORMAL   VEE HOLLOW SLACK FLAM   POINTED Ra Cu   3.2   BLUFF RAKED
  22.1   18.4 0.7 1.8   2.7 2.0 2.4 11.2 07.0 5.4 07.0 3.3 01.3 0.0 0.0   2.1 19.7 0.0 0.0

ALSO MOTOR YOLES ON THE NORTH COAST OF SCOTLAND, ORKNEY & STROMA, SGOTHS

25 YOLE KEEL, ROUNDED SECTIONS. STEMS AT BOTH ENDS, DRAG WITH BEAMY RATIO

FLOTTA YOLE   K.284   SIMPSON 1923   N.M.M. 205   ADD 0.4 FOR KEEL
GENERAL FISHING, OPEN, SCHOONER SPRIT RIG, JIB ON BOWSPRIT
E-F   BEAM KEEL   NORMAL   RAISED S.S. ROUND FLAM   POINTED Ra Cu   2.2 B   BLUFF RAKED
  16.0   12.4 0.8 1.6   2.2 1.2 1.5 09.0 07.2 6.5 07.2 2.3 01.4 0.0 0.0   S 3.1 13.5 0.0 0.0

26 ROW BARGE KEEL, ROUNDED SECTIONS, TRANSOM STERN, LEVEL WITH NARROW RATIO (SMALLER)

ST MAWES GIG   SHAH   PETERS 1873   G&C of the I of S   ADD 0.2 FOR KEEL
PILOTAGE & SALVAGE, OPEN, TWO LUGS, PULLS 6 OARS IN PAIRED THOLE-PINS
E-F   BEAM KEEL   NORMAL   RAISED CURVE ROUND FLAM   SHARP RAKED Cu   6.1 N   TRANSOM NEARLY PLUMB
  30.0   28.3 1.0 1.0   2.0 0.9 1.6   3.5 04.9 4.8 04.9 2.0 01.5 0.0 0.0   2.5 29.8 1.4 0.0

DOVER GALLEY   PRINCESS   NICHOLAS 1880   N.M.M. 214 A&B   ADD 0.3 FOR KEEL
ASSISTANCE TO SHIPPING, OPEN, WASHBOARD FWD, MASTS LOWER, 2 DIPPING LUGS, 6 OARS IN 7 PAIRED THOLES
E-F   BEAM KEEL   EASY   FLAT CURVE ROUND FLAM   SHARP RAKED Cu   5.4 N   TRANSOM Ra CUT
  29.0   26.3 0.3 0.5   2.5 1.7 2.2 14.0 05.4 4.8 05.4 2.2 01.8 0.0 0.0   2.5 28.1 1.8 0.0

SERVICE 30 FT. GIG   LATE 19th TO MID 20th C.   ADMIRALTY   ADD 0.2 FOR KEEL
CEREMONY & RECREATION, OPEN, WASHBOARD FWD, MASTS LOWER, 2 DIPPING LUGS, PULLS 6 TO 8 OARS IN CRUTCHES
E-F   BEAM KEEL+HOG,SPRUNG EASY   FLAT CURVE SLACK FLAM   SHARP PLUMB TO RaCu 5.1 N TRANSOM PLUMB CUT
  29.5   26.5 1.1 0.4   2.0 1.2 1.8 15.5 05.8 5.5 05.8 2.5 03.0 0.0 0.0   2.3 29.5 3.0 0.6

DEAL GALLEY PUNT HAPPY GO LUCKY   NICHOLAS 1883   N.M.M. 219 A&B   ADD 0.4 FOR KEEL
ASSISTANCE TO SHIPPING, OPEN, MAST LOWERS, 2 POSITIONS, DIPPING LUG, 6 PAIRED THOLES
E-F   BEAM KEEL   EASY   RAISED Cu ROUND FLAM   POINTED RAKED   4.4 N   TRANSOM RaCut
  28.3   26.5 1.0 1.0   2.5 2.0 2.5 11.2 06.5 5.6 06.5 3.0 00.8 0.0 0.0   2.2 27.3 3.2 0.0

ST IVES GIG   N.M.M. 88 A&B   ADD 0.4 FOR KEEL
PILOTAGE & SALVAGE, OPEN, BOTH MASTS LOWER, DIPPING FORE & STANDING LUG MIZZEN, 5 PULLING THWARTS & ROOM FOR PLAY THWART
E-F   BEAM KEEL   EASY   RAISED CURVE ROUND FLAM   SHARP RAKED Cu   4.1 N   TRANSOM Ra CUT
  26.4   24.3 0.7 1.8   2.3 1.4 1.5 14.4 06.4 6.1 06.4 2.6 00.9 0.0 0.0   2.5 25.4 2.4 0.4

PORTHSCATHO SEINE BOAT OLIVE   PASCOE c.1900   N.M.M. 222   ADD 0.3 FOR KEEL
PILCHARD SEINER, OPEN, PULLS 6 OARS IN PAIRED THOLE-PINS, CAPSTAN FOR WARP, NET ROOM AFT
E-P   BEAM KEEL & KEELSON   EASY   FLAT CURVE ROUND PLUMB Cu SHARP RAKED Cu 4.0 N   TRANSOM Ra CUT
  31.2   26.4 0.4 1.1   2.9 2.2 2.8 16.1 07.8 6.8 07.7 2.9 02.5 0.0 0.0   2.7 28.9 4.2 0.0

CADGWITH SEINE BOAT MOSELLE   ROBERTS c.1900   N.M.M. 79   ADD 0.5 FOR KEEL
PILCHARD SEINER, OPEN, PULLS 6 OARS, CAPSTAN FOR WARP, NET & FISH ROOM AFT
E-P   BEAM KEEL   EASY   FLAT   ROUND FLAM   POINTED Ra Cu   3.9 N   TRANSOM RAKED CUT
  38.7   32.2 2.1 2.1   2.4 2.1 3.1 22.8 10.0 9.0 10.0 3.5 06.0 0.0 0.0   2.9 38.2 5.0 0.0

   L   LOK DF DA   FF FM FA   # Bmax BWL Bsh Depth   # BF BWF   L/B B/D   # BA BWA

APPENDIX IV   SHEET 10

NO TAXON   MAIN FEATURES

PLACE & TYPE   NAME OR NUMBER   BUILDER & DATE   DRAWING REFERENCE   DEPTH CORRECTION
GENERAL DETAILS - WORK, DECK, PROPULSION
PLANKING   BOTTOM LINE   SHEER LINE   MID-SECTION   FORWARD   RATIO   AFT
BOT/SIDE   TYPE   TYPE   FLOOR   BILGE SIDE   TYPE PROFILE   & GROUP TYPE PROFILE
   L   LOK DF DA   FF FM FA   #   Bmax BWL Bsh Depth   #   BF BWF   L/B B/D   # BA BWA

26 ROW BARGE (CONT.)

EAST KENT LONGSHOREMAN'S BOAT   c.1918   J.W.HOLNESS Nov.1968   ADD 0·2 FOR KEEL
HIRING & INSHORE FISHING, OPEN, ROWS 4 OARS IN CRUTCHES, DIPPING LUG SET OCCASIONALLY

| E-F | BEAM KEEL | EASY | | RAISED CURVE | ROUND | FLAM | SHARP PLUMB | | 3·8 N | | TRANSOM RAKED Cut. |
| 17·0 | 15·6 0·7 0·7 | 1·4 1·1 1·2 | 08·1 | 04·5 3·8 04·5 1·8 | 00·7 0·0 0·0 | | 2·5 | 16·3 2·0 0·0 |

GRAVESEND WATERMAN'S WHERRY   WARNER 1932   N.M.M. 226   ADD 0·4 FOR KEEL
ATTENDING SHIPS, OPEN, 4 PAIRED THOLE-PINS, STANDING LUG MAIN & STAYSAIL

| E-F | BEAM KEEL | NORMAL | | FLAT CURVE | ROUND | FLAM | SHARP RAKED Cu | | 3·8 N | | TRANSOM RAKED |
| 20·3 | 18·2 0·6 0·6 | 2·5 1·5 1·9 | 11·0 | 05·4 4·5 05·4 2·2 | 01·8 0·0 0·0 | | 2·5 | 20·0 2·7 0·0 |

PENZANCE PILOT GIG   EVELYN   SIMMONS 1888   N.M.M. 98 A & B   ADD 0·3 FOR KEEL
OPEN, BOTH MASTS LOWER, DIPPING LUG FORE & SPRIT MIZZEN, ROWS RANDAN WITH 4 PAIRED THOLE-PINS

| E-F | BEAM KEEL | NORMAL | | RAISED CURVE | ROUND | FLAM | SHARP RAKED Cu | | 3·8 N | | TRANSOM RAKED Cut. |
| 19·0 | 17·5 0·6 0·8 | 2·2 1·5 1·8 | 10·5 | 05·0 4·5 05·0 2·2 | 00·9 0·0 0·0 | | 2·3 | 18·4 2·1 0·0 |

ALSO HAMOAZE WATERMAN'S BOAT, ILFRACOMBE TRIP BOAT AND CONWAY SALMON & MUSSEL BOATS

27 CARGO BARGE   KEEL, ROUNDED SECTIONS, TRANSOM STERN, LEVEL WITH NARROW RATIO (LARGER)

MERSEY CANAL FLAT (BRIDGEWATER TYPE)   M.M. 58 p.289   ADD 0·1 FOR KEEL
ESTUARY & WATERWAY FREIGHT, FLUSH DECK WITH HATCHES, MAST LOWERS, GAFF SLOOP RIG, TRACKED & TOWED

| E-P | BEAM KEEL | NORMAL | | FLAT | HARD | PLUMB | BLUFF RAKED Cu | | 4·5 N | | TRANSOM RAKED Cut. |
| 64·3 | 58·1 4·5 4·5 | 4·5 1·1 3·0 | 32·5 | 14·5 14·5 14·5 5·6 | 04·8 0·0 0·0 | | 2·6 | 62·9 11·8 4·5 |

SEVERN TROW   NORAH   AT BRIDGWATER 1868   M.M. 32 p.88   ADD 1·0 FOR KEEL
ESTUARY TRADER, OPEN, WITH DECKS BOTH ENDS, FULLY RIGGED GAFF KETCH WITH TOPMAST & BOWSPRIT, SIDE-CLOTHS

| E-P | BEAM KEEL & KEELSON | NORMAL | | FLAT | ROUND | PLUMB | BLUFF RAKED Cu | | 3·9 N | | TRANSOM RAKED |
| 74·5 | 68·0 7·0 7·0 | 5·0 2·0 3·0 | 40·0 | 19·0 19·0 19·0 9·0 | 05·4 0·0 0·0 | | 2·1 | 73·0 12·0 2·5 |

ALSO

28 HAVEN BOAT   KEEL, ROUNDED SECTIONS, TRANSOM STERN, LEVEL WITH DEEP RATIO

SENNEN COVE CRABBER   SILVER STREAM PZ.168   1892   N.M.M. 26,27 & 86   ADD 0·4 FOR KEEL
OPEN, PERMANENT WASHSTRAKES, MASTS LOWER, DIPPING FORE & STANDING LUG MIZZEN, ROWS 4 OARS FROM FWD POSITIONS

| E-P | BEAM KEEL | NORMAL | | FLAT CURVE | ROUND | FLAT | POINTED RAKED Cu | | 2·9 | | TRANSOM RAKED |
| 22·3 | 19·5 1·1 2·7 | 3·2 2·2 2·4 | 11·0 | 07·8 7·6 07·8 4·1 | 01·0 0·0 0·0 | | D 1·9 | 21·5 3·6 2·5 |

THAMES AUXILIARY BAWLEY   M&S in E&A p.182 (Y.M.) ADD 0·9 FOR KEEL AFT
ESTUARY STOW-NETTER, DECKED 0·2 BELOW SHEER, STANDING GAFF CUTTER, LOOSE-FOOTED MAIN, 2·1 APERTURE FOR SCREW

| E-P | BEAM KEEL | EASY | | RAISED | ROUND | PLUMB Cu | POINTED PLUMB | | 2·8 | | TRANSOM RAKED Cut. |
| 31·5 | 24·5 3·0 3·2 | 4·0 2·9 3·2 | 16·0 | 11·3 11·2 11·2 6·1 | 04·5 0·0 0·0 | | D 1·9 | 29·0 5·8 0·0 |

DEAL LUGGER   HAYWARD c.1848   WASHINGTON Pl.2   ADD 0·8 FOR KEEL
FISHING & ATTENDING SHIPPING, BEACHES, OPEN-FOC'S'L DECKED, 3 LOWERING MASTS WITH LUGS

| E-F | BEAM KEEL | NORMAL | | RAISED | ROUND | FLAM | POINTED R.Cu | | 3·0 | | TRANSOM RAKED Cut. |
| 37·0 | 32·0 2·9 3·6 | 5·0 3·4 4·0 | 18·0 | 12·3 11·3 12·3 6·4 | 03·8 0·0 0·0 | | D 1·5 | 35·8 6·2 0·0 |

MEVAGISSEY MOTOR TOSHER   MITCHELL 1927   N.M.M. 5   ADD 0·3 FOR KEEL
INSHORE POTS & LINES, OPEN, SOME HAVE SHORT DECK FWD, VARIOUS LUG OR CUTTER RIGS, 1·6 APERTURE FOR SCREW

| E-P | BEAM KEEL | NORMAL | | VEE | ROUND | Thome | SHARP ALMOST PLUMB | | 2·7 | | TRANSOM RAKED Cut. |
| 18·8 | 14·2 1·8 2·4 | 2·8 1·9 2·1 | 10·5 | 06·8 6·2 06·4 3·9 | 02·5 0·0 0·0 | | D 1·7 | 16·7 3·4 0·2 |

FALMOUTH QUAY PUNT   PRIDE OF THE PORT   THOMAS c.1880   Y&BS 10th Ed Pl.58   ADD 1·8 FOR BALLAST KEEL
ATTENDING SHIPPING, OPEN-FOC'S'L DECKED, LOOSE FOOTED GAFF MAIN, JIB TACKED TO SHORT BUMKIN, JIB-HEADED JIGGER, 2 OARS IN CRUTCHES

| E-P | BEAM KEEL | EASY | | VEE HOLLOW | ROUND | Thome | SHARP PLUMB | | 3·2 | | TRANSOM RAKED Cut |
| 26·4 | 22·4 3·0 3·0 | 3·7 2·6 2·5 | 14·4 | 08·3 8·0 8·0 6·0 | 02·0 0·0 0·0 | | D 1·4 | 24·4 4·7 0·0 |

   L   LOK DF DA   FF FM FA   #   Bmax BWL Bsh Depth   #   BF BWF   L/B B/D   # BA BWA

APPENDIX IV   Sheet 11

Nº TAXON   MAIN FEATURES

PLACE & TYPE   NAME OR NUMBER   BUILDER & DATE   DRAWING REFERENCE   DEPTH CORRECTION
GENERAL DETAILS — WORK , DECK , PROPULSION
PLANKING   BOTTOM LINE   SHEER LINE   MID-SECTION   FORWARD   RATIO   AFT
BOT/SIDE   TYPE   TYPE   FLOOR   BILGE SIDE   TYPE PROFILE & GROUP   TYPE PROFILE
  L   LOK DF DA   FF FM FA   #   Bmax BWL Bsh Depth   #   BF BWF   L/B B/D   # BA BWA

28 HAVEN BOAT (Cont)

THAMES BAWLEY   MAY FLOWER L.O. 190   STONE LATE 19th C.   Y & B.S. 10th Ed. Pf. 61   ADD 0·7 FOR KEEL
ESTUARY STOW-NETTER , DECKED 0·3 BELOW SHEER , LOOSE-FOOTED STANDING GAFF CUTTER
E-P   BEAM KEEL   EASY   VEE   ROUND PLUMB Cu   POINTED RAKED Cu   2·8   TRANSOM RAKED Cut.
  31·2   25·6 3·0 3·3   4·0 3·0 3·0   16·2 11·3 11·0 11·0 6·2   04·0 0·0 0·0   D 1·8   29·6 6·0 0·0

ALSO BOSTON SHRIMPER , WEYMOUTH HARBOUR FISHING BOAT ,

29 TRANSOM BOAT   KEEL , ROUNDED SECTIONS , TRANSOM STERN , LEVEL WITH BOTH RATIOS NORMAL

ITCHEN FERRY PUNT NELLIE   HATCHER 1862 , REBUILT BY LUKE 1886   N.M.M. 73   ADD 0·8 FOR KEEL
FISHING, HOVELLING & PLEASURE , SIDE & FORE DECKS OPEN AFT , POLE-MASTED GAFF CUTTER WITH TOPS'L & BOWSPRIT
E-P   BEAM KEEL & HOG SPRUNG   EASY   VEE HOLLOW ROUND PLUMB Cu   POINTED RAKED Cu   2·7   TRANSOM RAKED Cut
  21·3   17·7 1·4 1·8   2·8 2·2 2·1   11·6 07·8 7·4 07·4 3·7   02·0 0·0 0·0   2·1   19·7 4·7 0·0

YARMOUTH PUNT Nº 2   TEASDEL c. 1848   WASHINGTON Pf. 1   ADD 0·8 FOR KEEL
HERRING DRIFTER , OPEN BUT SOME HAD DECKS , 2 MASTED LUGGER
E-F   BEAM KEEL   EASY   RAISED Cu   ROUND FLAM   POINTED RAKED Cu   2·7   TRANSOM RAKED Cut.
  36·6   33·0 2·3 3·3   5·4 3·7 4·1   21·5 12·3 12·0 12·3 6·3   02·6 0·0 0·0   2·0   35·6 6·0 0·0

GORRAN HAVEN CRABBER   CUCKOO   PILL 1881   N.M.M. 95 & 87   ADD 0·2 FOR KEEL
OPEN , 2 LOWERING MASTS BOTH WITH SPRITSAILS , HANKED STAYSAIL , PAIRED THOLE-PINS - RANDAN
E-P   BEAM KEEL   NORMAL   RAISED   ROUND FLAM   POINTED RAKED   2·8   TRANSOM RAKED Cut.
  16·2   14·4 0·7 1·5   2·2 1·6 1·6   09·4 05·8 5·1 05·7 2·6   00·8 0·0 0·0   2·2   15·2 3·0 0·0

CORNISH COASTING SMACK   MARY   STEPHENS 1875   M.M. 46 p. 82   ADD 0·5 FOR KEEL
COASTER , DECKED 1·3 BELOW SHEER , GAFF CUTTER RIG , SWEEP OCCASIONALLY , CONVERTED TO MOTOR BARGE
E-P   BEAM KEEL   NORMAL   RAISED   ROUND FLAM   POINTED RAKED Cu   3·2   TRANSOM RAKED Cut.
  49·5   44·6 4·8 6·2   4·2 2·0 2·4   25·0 18·0 17·5 18·0 7·8   02·4 0·0 0·0   2·0   47·0 11·0 0·0

CADGWITH CRABBER   WATERFALL F.H. 26   WHITBURN 1884   N.M.M. 28 & 81   ADD 0·5 FOR KEEL
INSHORE POTS & LINES , OPEN , MASTS LOWER , DIPPING FORE & STANDING LUG MIZZEN , CENTREBOARD , 3 PAIRED THOLE-PINS
E-P   BEAM KEEL   EASY   RAISED   ROUND FLAM   SHARP RAKED CURVE   2·9   TRANSOM RAKED Cut
  19·1   17·0 1·1 1·8   2·2 1·4 1·1   10·5 06·6 6·4 06·6 2·8   00·8 0·0 0·0   2·4   17·9 3·8 0·0

DOVER PUNT   ARGONAUT DR. 56   NICHOLAS c. 1880   N.M.M. 216 A & B   ADD 0·8 FOR KEEL
POTS & SPRATS , OPEN , FOREMAST LOWERS , DIPPING FORE & STANDING LUG MIZZEN , 6 PAIRED THOLE-PINS
E-F   BEAM KEEL   EASY   RAISED   ROUND PLUMB   SHARP RAKED Cu   3·0   TRANSOM RAKED Cut.
  15·4   14·0 0·5 0·7   2·2 1·7 1·9   07·1 05·2 4·4 05·2 2·3   01·8 0·0 0·0   2·3   14·8 2·8 0·0

TAMAR BARGE   FLORA MAY   HAWKE 1897   N.M.M. 20, 21 & 23   ADD 0·8 FOR KEEL
RIVER FREIGHT , DECKED 1·5 BELOW SHEER , BALD GAFF CUTTER WITH BOWSPRIT , BOOM UNDER LOOSE-FOOTED MAINSAIL
E-P   BEAM KEEL & KEELSON NORMAL   FLAT   ROUND PLUMB   POINTED RAKED HOLLOW 3·2   TRANSOM RAKED
  49·5   45·5 5·0 5·5   3·2 1·8 2·5   25·0 15·5 15·5 15·5 7·0   02·0 0·0 0·0   2·2   47·5 0·0 0·0

SERVICE 36 Ft MOTOR PINNACE   MID 20th C.   ADMIRALTY   ADD 0·6 FOR KEEL
SHIP/SHORE BOOM BOAT , OPEN WITH CANOPIES , 12 OARS IN ROWBEDS , DE HORSEY 'B' RIG ON SAILING TYPE , LOOSE-FOOTED GAFF SLOOP
E-F (DIAG.) BEAM KEEL & HOG   EASY   RAISED   ROUND PLUMB   POINTED PLUMB   3·3   TRANSOM RAKED
  35·0   33·6 2·0 2·2   3·3 2·3 2·6   18·0 10·5 10·0 10·5 4·2   02·7 0·0 0·0   2·5   34·1 5·4 0·5

SERVICE 42 Ft SAILING LAUNCH (AUX. MOTOR)   LATE 19th to EARLY 20th C.   ADMIRALTY   ADD 0·7 FOR KEEL
SHIP/SHORE BOOM BOAT , OPEN , 18 DOUBLE-BANKED OARS IN ROWBEDS , DE HORSEY 'A' RIG , LOOSE-FOOTED GAFF SLOOP
E-F (DIAG.) BEAM KEEL & HOG   EASY   RAISED   ROUND PLUMB   POINTED PLUMB   3·6   TRANSOM RAKED
  41·0   39·0 2·3 2·3   4·2 3·4 3·8   20·4 11·5 11·5 11·5 5·4   00·8 0·0 0·0   2·1   39·8 6·6 0·7

ALSO MANY TYPES OF SMALL S. COAST PUNTS & MOTOR BOATS, SALMON BOATS, LUNE WAMMEL NET BOAT & SMALL CUMBRIAN SHRIMPER

  L   LOK DF DA   FF FM FA   #   Bmax BWL Bsh Depth   #   BF BWF   L/B B/D   # BA BWA

APPENDIX IV   SHEET 12

Nº TAXON   MAIN FEATURES

PLACE & TYPE   NAME OR NUMBER   BUILDER & DATE   DRAWING REFERENCE   DEPTH CORRECTION
GENERAL DETAILS — WORK , DECK , PROPULSION
PLANKING   BOTTOM LINE   SHEER LINE   MID-SECTION   FORWARD   RATIO   AFT
BOT/SIDE   TYPE   TYPE   FLOOR   BILGE   SIDE   TYPE   PROFILE   & GROUP   TYPE   PROFILE
   L   LOK DF DA   FF FM FA   #   Bmax BWL Bsh Depth   #   BF BWF   L/B B/D   #   BA BWA

30 RIVER BOAT KEEL , ROUNDED SECTIONS , TRANSOM STERN , LEVEL WITH SHOAL RATIO

TAMAR SKIFF   PEARL   KESSEL 1904   McKEE ✱   ADD 0·1 FOR KEEL
HIRE , OPEN , ROWS 4 OARS IN CRUTCHES , EXTERNAL ROW-CLEATS
E-F   BEAM KEEL SPRUNG   EASY   RAISED CURVE SLACK   FLAM   SHARP RAKED Cu   3·6   TRANSOM RAKED Cut.
  14·6   12·8 0·2 0·2   1·3 1·1 1·3   07·8 04·1 2·8 04·1 1·3   01·4 0·0 0·0   5   3·1   14·2 1·7 0·0
ALSO DEE SALMON BOAT

31 COCKLE KEEL , ROUNDED SECTIONS , TRANSOM STERN , LEVEL WITH BEAMY RATIO

ALDEBURGH SPRAT BOAT   OSSIE I.H.77   CRITTEN 1893   N.M.M. 68   ADD 0·3 FOR KEEL
BEACH PUNT , OPEN , FOREMAST LOWERS , DIPPING FORE & STANDING LUG MIZZEN , SHORT IRON BUMKIN FORE-TACK , 8 PAIRED THOLE-PINS
E-F   BEAM KEEL   EASY   RAISED CURVE ROUND Thome   POINTED RAKED Cu   2·4 B   TRANSOM PLUMB Cut.
  15·0   13·0 0·7 0·7   2·1 1·8 1·8   05·3 06·3 5·5 06·2 2·4   01·4 0·0 0·0   2·6   14·4 3·5 0·0

BRIXHAM TRAWLER'S PUNT   ¼ FORSETI   c. 1900   N.M.M. 224   ADD 0·3 FOR KEEL
FLEETING CATCH TO CARRIER , OPEN , PULLS 4 OARS IN PAIRED THOLE-PINS
E-F   BEAM KEEL   NORMAL   FLAT CURVE ROUND   FLAM   POINTED RAKED Cu   2·2 B   TRANSOM RAKED Cut.
  14·0   10·7 1·1 1·1   1·8 1·4 1·7   07·5 06·3 5·8 06·3 2·4   01·0 0·0 0·0   2·6   11·7 3·4 1·2

ITCHEN FERRY PUNT   WONDER S.O.120   HATCHER 1860   J.W. HOLNESS 1966   ADD 1·3 FOR BALLAST KEEL
FISHING & PLEASURE , DECKED , POLE-MASTED GAFF CUTTER WITH TOPS'L & BOWSPRIT , HANKED FORESAIL TACKED TO BUMKIN
E-P   BEAM KEEL   EASY   VEE HOLLOW ROUND Thome   POINTED PLUMB   2·2 B   TRANSOM RAKED Cut.
  18·6   17·2 2·1 1·9   2·7 2·0 1·8   10·0 08·3 8·1 07·8 4·4   03·5 0·0 0·0   2·3   17·7 5·0 1·8

EMSWORTH LUGGER   MATILDA   1945   N.M.M. 275 , 275 A & B   ADD 0·4 FOR KEEL
OYSTER DREDGER , OPEN , FLUSH DECK FWD & 1·8 BELOW SHEER AFT , DIPPING LUG WITH VARIABLE TACK , 4 PAIRED THOLE-PINS , SKEG
E-F   BEAM KEEL SPRUNG AFT   NORMAL   RAISED S.S. SLACK   FLAM   POINTED RAKED Cu   2·4 B   TRANSOM RAKED
  15·4   13·4 1·2 0·2   1·7 1·0 1·7   08·3 06·3 5·6 06·3 2·2   00·6 0·0 0·0   2·9   14·7 3·4 0·3

HALLSAND CRABBER   SILVIA D.H. 60   DORNOM 1921   N.M.M. 19 & 82   ADD 0·3 FOR KEEL
BEACHED , OPEN , MAST LOWERS , SPRIT RIG , JIB ON SHORT BOWSPRIT , 8 PAIRED THOLE-PINS , ROUNDED HEEL TO KEEL
E-F   BEAM KEEL & HOG   EASY   RAISED   ROUND   FLAM   POINTED RAKED Cu   2·5 B   TRANSOM RAKED Cut.
  16·2   14·0 0·8 1·5   2·0 1·5 1·5   08·0 06·6 5·9 06·6 2·6   01·1 0·0 0·0   2·5   15·1 3·5 0·0

HASTINGS PUNT   HAPPY THOUGHT R.X. 53   M.M. 24 p.39   ADD 0·7 FOR KEEL
SEASONAL INSHORE FISHING , OPEN , FOREMAST LOWERS , DIPPING FORE & STANDING LUG OR SPRIT MIZZEN , JIB ON BOWSPRIT , DAGGERBOARD , 6 CRUTCH CLEATS
E-F   BEAM KEEL   EASY   FLAT   ROUND   PLUMB Cu POINTED RAKED Cu   2·6 B   TRANSOM RAKED Cut.
  14·6   13·1 0·5 1·1   2·0 1·4 1·5   07·3 05·6 5·3 05·6 2·2   00·7 0·0 0·0   2·5   13·8 3·5 1·5

TENBY LUGGER   SEAHORSE M. 170   NEWT 1886   M.M. 44 p.102   ADD 1·1 FOR KEEL
INSHORE LINES , DRYING HARBOUR , OPEN WITH DECK FWD , FOREMAST LOWERS , DIPPING FORE & SPRIT MIZZEN , JIB ON BOWSPRIT , 4 PAIRED THOLE-PINS
E-F   DEEP BEAM KEEL   NORMAL   FLAT   ROUND   FLAM   POINTED PLUMB   2·6 B   TRANSOM RAKED Cut.
  23·2   19·4 1·3 1·9   3·5 2·3 2·6   12·3 09·0 8·0 09·0 3·8   01·4 0·0 0·0   2·4   20·6 5·0 0·6

ALSO HUMBER KEEL'S COGGIE BOAT , BRIGHTON & SHOREHAM LUGGERS (SEE TAXON 21) , BOSHAM OYSTER DREDGER)

32 TRANSOM SMACK KEEL , ROUNDED SECTIONS , TRANSOM STERN , DRAG WITH DEEP RATIO

MALDON OYSTER SMACK   BOADICEA C.K. 213   WILLIAMSON 1808 (REBUILDS)   LEWIS, 'VINTAGE BOATS' p.22   ADD 0·8 FOR KEEL
ESTUARY , DECKED 1·2 BELOW SHEER , BALD GAFF CUTTER RIG WITH BOWSPRIT , BOOM UNDER LOOSE-FOOTED MAINSAIL , SWEEP
E-P   BEAM KEEL   EASY   RAISED Cu   ROUND   FLAM   POINTED RAKED Cu   2·7   TRANSOM RAKED
  30·3   24·8 1·1 3·2   5·1 3·9 3·8   15·2 11·2 9·4 11·2 6·0   03·0 0·0 0·0   D 1·9   27·8 5·3 1·1

HARWICH BAWLEY   MAUD 63 H.H.   CANN c 1900   Sc. Mus. Ph. 5325 , 6 & 7   ADD 0·7 FOR KEEL
STOWNET , SHRIMP TRAWL & WHELK POTS , DECKED , FULL STANDING GAFF CUTTER RIG WITH FIDDED TOPMAST & REEFING BOWSPRIT
E-P   BEAM KEEL   NORMAL   RAISED HOLLOW ROUND FLAM   POINTED PLUMB   2·8   TRANSOM RAKED
  37·0   28·4 2·8 4·5   5·2 2·6 2·6   16·5 13·0 12·0 13·0 6·8   02·8 0·0 0·0   D 1·9   31·2 8·0 0·0
   L   LOK DF DA   FF FM FA   #   Bmax BWL Bsh Depth   #   BF BWF   L/B B/D   #   BA BWA

APPENDIX IV   SHEET 13

Nº TAXON   MAIN FEATURES

PLACE & TYPE   NAME OR NUMBER   BUILDER & DATE   DRAWING REFERENCE   DEPTH CORRECTION
GENERAL DETAILS – WORK, DECK, PROPULSION
PLANKING   BOTTOM LINE   SHEER LINE   MID-SECTION   FORWARD   RATIO   AFT
BOT/SIDE   TYPE   TYPE   FLOOR   BILGE SIDE   TYPE PROFILE   & GROUP   TYPE PROFILE
L   LOK DF DA   FF FM FA   # B_{max} BWL B_{sh} DEPTH   # BF BWF   L/B B/D   # BA BWA

32 TRANSOM SMACK (CONT.)

MOUNTS BAY PILCHARD DRIVER   <u>VERACITY</u> PZ.111   BLEWETT 1902   N.M.M. 122 A,B&C   ADD 0·6 FOR KEEL
HARBOUR, SIDE & END DECKS 1·4 BELOW SHEER, FOREMAST LOWERS, DIPPING FORE & STANDING LUG MIZZEN, SWEEPS
E–P   BEAM KEEL   NORMAL   RAISED   ROUND PLUMB Cu SHARP RAKED CURVE 3·0   TRANSOM RAKED Cut.
31·6   22·5 2·2 3·4   5·0 3·4 3·5   16·0 10·4 10·4 10·3 6·3   03·5 0·0 0·0   D 1·7   26·0 5·8 1·2

MEVAGISSEY LUGGER   <u>ERIN</u> F.Y.197   FRAZIER 1904   McKEE ✳   ADD 0·4 FOR KEEL
DRIFTER, DRYING INNER HARBOUR, SIDE & END DECKS 1·3 BELOW SHEER, FOREMAST LOWERS, DIPPING FORE & STANDING MIZZEN, JIB ON BOWSPRIT
E–P   BEAM KEEL   NORMAL   VEE   ROUND PLUMB   POINTED RAKED Cu 3·4   TRANSOM RAKED Cut.
37·7   28·7 2·7 4·9   5·3 3·8 4·0   18·8 11·1 11·1 11·1 7·8   01·5 0·0 0·0   D 1·4   30·2 6·3 2·9

MEVAGISSEY LUGGER   c 1906   MARCH 'SAILING DRIFTERS' p.311   ADD 0·7 FOR KEEL
DECK 1·5 BELOW SHEER, OTHERWISE AS FOR <u>ERIN</u>
E–P   BEAM KEEL   NORMAL   VEE   SLACK FLAM   POINTED PLUMB 3·3   TRANSOM RAKED Cut.
39·5   30·3 3·4 5·4   5·0 3·8 4·0   20·7 12·0 11·3 12·0 8·4   01·5 0·0 0·0   D 1·4   31·7 6·8 1·2

POLPERRO GAFFER   <u>GLEANER</u> F.Y.8   PEARCE 1898   N.M.M. 24,76A & B   ADD 0·4 FOR KEEL
DRIFTER, DRYING HARBOUR, FORE & SIDE DECKS 1·2 BELOW SHEER, STERNSHEETS, BOOMLESS GAFF CUTTER, LONG BOWSPRIT, SWEEPS
E–P   BEAM KEEL Cu   EASY   RAISED CURVE SLACK   PLUMB Cu SHARP RAKED CURVE 2·8   TRANSOM RAKED Cut.
24·8   18·8 2·4 4·0   4·3 3·5 3·2   12·2 08·8 8·4 08·8 6·8   02·2 0·0 0·0   'D 1·3   21·0 4·8 0·5

PLYMOUTH HOOKER   <u>DAYSPRING</u> P.H.339   PEARCE 1893   N.M.M. 22, 70A & B   ADD 0·7 FOR KEEL
HARBOUR, DECKS F.& A. WITH WATERWAYS 1·0 BELOW SHEER, BOOMLESS GAFF CUTTER, TOPS'L & LONG BOWSPRIT
E–P   BEAM KEEL   NORMAL   VEE   HARD   FLAM   POINTED RAKED Cu 3·1   TRANSOM RAKED
30·7   25·5 3·3 5·4   4·5 3·3 3·7   15·2 10·0 9·6 10·0 7·8   02·0 0·0 0·0   D 1·3   28·5 6·0 0·0

ALSO TORBAY HOOKER

33 DEVON SMACK   KEEL, ROUNDED SECTIONS, TRANSOM STERN, DRAG WITH BOTH RATIOS NORMAL

BEER LUGGER   <u>LITTLE JIM</u> E.159   LAVERS 1916   N.M.M. 74 A & B   ADD 0·5 FOR KEEL
DRIFT NETS & LINES, BEACHED, OPEN WITH FORESHEETS, MAST LOWERS, DIPPING FORE & STANDING LUG MIZZEN, IRON BUMKIN, 4 CRUTCHES
E–F   BEAM KEEL   NORMAL   RAISED CURVE ROUND   FLAM   POINTED RAKED 2·7   2·0   20·5 4·8 0·0
22·8   18·0 1·3 2·6   3·6 2·3 2·5   11·3 08·4 8·0 08·4 4·3   02·5 0·0 0·0

LYMPSTONE HOOKER   <u>MERIT</u> E.89   N.M.M. 92 A,B&C   ADD 1·0 FOR KEEL
ESTUARY & INSHORE, FORE & SIDE DECKS 0·3 BELOW SHEER, GAFF CUTTER WITH TOPS'L & LONG BOWSPRIT, 6 CLEATS FOR PAIRED THOLE-PINS
E–F   BEAM KEEL CURVED   EASY   RAISED CURVE ROUND   FLAM   SHARP RAKED CURVE 2·7   TRANSOM RAKED Cut.
20·8   18·3 1·3 2·4   3·1 1·9 1·7   10·7 07·6 7·3 07·6 3·8   00·7 0·0 0·0   2·0   19·0 4·6 3·5

HOPE COVE CRABBER   <u>IRA</u> S.E.25   CHANT 1924   N.M.M. 47 & 80   ADD 0·4 FOR KEEL
PARTLY SHELTERED BEACH, OPEN, SPRIT DANDY RIG, JIB TACKED TO SHORT BUMKIN, 6 PAIRED THOLE-PINS
E–F   BEAM KEEL & HOG   EASY   RAISED CURVE ROUND   FLAM   POINTED PLUMB 2·7   TRANSOM RAKED Cut.
17·8   15·6 0·8 1·7   3·0 2·1 2·0   08·8 06·7 5·7 06·7 3·3   01·2 0·0 0·0   2·0   16·8 3·8 0·7

ALSO MOST MOTOR BEACH BOATS IN LYME BAY

34 BUSS SMACK   KEEL, ROUNDED SECTIONS, COUNTER STERN, LEVEL WITH NARROW & DEEP RATIOS

YARMOUTH LUGGER   <u>GIPSY QUEEN</u> Y.H.56   1859   MARCH 'SAILING DRIFTERS' p.300 ADD 0·8 FOR KEEL
DRIFTER, DECKED 1·7 BELOW SHEER, FOREMAST LOWERS, DIPPING FORE & STANDING LUG MIZZEN WITH TOPS'L, JIB ON LONG BOWSPRIT, SWEEPS
E–F   BEAM KEEL   EASY   VEE   SLACK FLAM   SHARP RAKED CURVE 3·8 N LUTE RAKED POST KNUKLE
65·4   50·0 3·1 5·1   8·8 5·8 5·8   33·0 17·0 14·8 17·0 10·3 04·0 0·0 0·0   D 1·7   54·0 11·1 0·0

YARMOUTH LUGGER   Nº 1   TEASDALE c1848   WASHINGTON Pℓ.3   ADD 0·8 FOR KEEL
DRIFTER, HARBOUR, DECKED 1·9 BELOW SHEER, 3 LOWERING MASTS RIGGED WITH LUGS & TOPS'LS
E–F   BEAM KEEL   EASY   RAISED HOLLOW ROUND PLUMB   POINTED RAKED Cu 4·1 N COUNTER ROUND Ra Knkl
61·3   44·0 4·0 5·4   6·6 4·6 5·4   23·0 14·9 14·9 14·9 9·2   05·0 0·0 0·0   D 1·6   49·0 0·0 0·0

L   LOK DF DA   FF FM FA   # B_{max} BWL B_{sh} DEPTH   # BF BWF   L/B B/D   # BA BWA

APPENDIX IV   SHEET 14

Nº TAXON   MAIN FEATURES

PLACE & TYPE   NAME OR NUMBER   BUILDER & DATE   DRAWING REFERENCE   DEPTH CORRECTION
GENERAL DETAILS — WORK, DECK, PROPULSION

PLANKING	BOTTOM LINE			SHEER LINE	MID-SECTION					FORWARD			RATIO	AFT		
BOT/SIDE	TYPE			TYPE	FLOOR	BILGE	SIDE			TYPE	PROFILE		& GROUP	TYPE	PROFILE	
L	LOK	DF	DA	FF FM FA	#	Bmax	BWL	Bsh	Depth	#	BF	BWF	L/B B/D	#	BA	BWA

35 OLD SMACK   KEEL, ROUNDED SECTIONS, COUNTER STERN, LEVEL WITH DEEP RATIO

BARKING WELL SMACK   SAUCY JACK   AT GRAVESEND c 1836   MARCH, 'SAILING TRAWLERS' p. 311   ADD 1·1 FOR KEEL
FISH CARRIER, DECKED 1·8 BELOW SHEER, GAFF CUTTER

E–P	BEAM KEEL			NORMAL	RAISED CURVE	SLACK	PLUMB			POINTED RAKED Cu.	3·5			COUNTER RAKED POST Tr.Cu.		
55·7	43·8	6·0	7·5	7·5 5·0 5·4	23·0	16·0	16·0	16·0	11·8	06·0	0·0	0·0	D 1·4	49·8	8·0	0·0

LOWESTOFT DECKED BOAT   SPARHAM c. 1848   WASHINGTON Pf. 6   ADD 1·1 FOR KEEL
DRIFTER, DECKED 1·5 BELOW SHEER, 3 MASTED LUGGER WITH TOPS'LS

E–F	BEAM KEEL			EASY	RAISED CURVE	ROUND	FLAM			POINTED RAKED Cu.	3·5			COUNTER RAKED POST TRANSOM		
51·6	36·0	4·0	6·1	5·9 4·0 4·0	22·7	14·8	14·1	14·8	9·0	06·6	0·0	0·0	D 1·6	42·6	7·8	0·0

WHITSTABLE OYSTER DREDGER   F. 62   c. 1870   N.M.M. 225   ADD 0·5 FOR KEEL
ESTUARY, DECKED 1·3 BELOW SHEER, POLE-MASTED GAFF CUTTER, BOOM ON LOOSE-FOOTED MAIN, TOPS'L & BOWSPRIT

E–P	BEAM KEEL			EASY	VEE	SLACK	Thome			POINTED RAKED Cu.	3·5			COUNTER RAKED POST TRANSOM		
46·0	33·2	4·4	5·0	4·2 3·2 3·1	23·0	13·1	12·9	13·1	8·0	03·0	0·0	0·0	D 1·6	36·2	6·8	0·0

COLNE SMACK   STONE 1909   MARCH, 'I.C. of B.' Vol 1 p.208   ADD 0·6 FOR KEEL
SPRATS & OYSTERS, DECKED 1·3 BELOW SHEER, FULL GAFF CUTTER RIG, FIDDED TOPMAST & REEFING BOWSPRIT, SWEEPS

E–P	BEAM KEEL & KEELSON			EASY	RAISED HOLLOW	ROUND	Thome			POINTED PLUMB	3·4			COUNTER RAKED POST TRANSOM		
37·8	22·8	3·2	4·3	4·0 3·0 2·8	18·3	11·0	11·0	10·8	6·6	05·0	0·0	0·0	D 1·7	27·8	4·6	0·0

CASTLETOWN BOAT   PEGGY   c. 1791   N.M.M. 129 C   ADD 0·3 FOR KEEL
PASSAGE TO MAINLAND, OPEN, LOOSE-FOOTED BALD SCHOONER WITH BOOM UNDER MAINSAIL & JIB ON BOWSPRIT, 6 OAR-PORTS, 3 DAGGER-BOARD CASES

E–F	BEAM KEEL			NORMAL	RAISED HOLLOW	ROUND	FLAM			BLUFF RAKED CURVE	3·3			LUTE RAKED POST TRANSOM		
26·0	21·0	2·1	2·1	2·9 2·2 3·3	11·0	07·8	7·0	07·8	2·9	02·3	0·0	0·0	D 1·8	23·3	3·5	1·0

MORECAMBE BAY NOBBY (OLD)   CROSSFIELD-ARNSIDE   MARCH, 'I.C. of B.' Vol 2 p.286   ADD 0·7 FOR KEEL
SHRIMPER, FLUSH DECK, GAFF CUTTER, WITH TOPSAIL & JIB ON BOWSPRIT

E–P	BEAM KEEL			EASY	VEE	ROUND	PLUMB Cu			POINTED PLUMB	3·3			COUNTER RAKED POST ROUND		
40·0	29·3	2·8	3·3	4·4 2·8 3·0	21·8	11·7	12·0	11·7	6·1	03·8	0·0	0·0	D 2·0	33·1	0·0	0·0

ENGLISH SMACK FOR FLAT-FISH   c. 1765   CHAPMAN A.N.M. Pf. LIX, 3   ADD 0·7 FOR KEEL
WELL BOAT, DECKED 1·1 BELOW SHEER, GAFF RIG

E–P	BEAM KEEL			NORMAL	RAISED	ROUND	Thome			BLUFF PLUMB	2·9			SQ TUCK RAKED POST & Tr.		
40·0	30·0	4·4	5·7	7·1 4·4 5·6	12·0	14·0	14·0	13·2	9·5	05·4	0·0	0·0	D 1·5	35·4	5·0	0·0

BRIXHAM SLOOP   CHARLIE D.H.79 UPHAM c.1838   MARCH, 'SAILING TRAWLERS' p. 321 ADD 1·3 FOR KEEL
BEAM TRAWL, DECKED 2·1 BELOW SHEER, FULL GAFF CUTTER RIG, FIDDED TOPMAST & REEFING BOWSPRIT, SQUARE TOPS'L

E–P	BEAM KEEL			EASY	FLAT CURVE	ROUND	FLAM			BLUFF RAKED CURVE	2·7			COUNTER RAKED POST & Tr.Cu.		
46·6	36·0	6·0	7·2	6·0 4·7 5·7	15·0	17·0	17·0	17·0	9·7	06·2	0·0	0·0	D 1·8	42·2	7·4	0·0

ALSO IRISH SEA MOTOR NOBBIES & S.E. COAST MOTOR OTTER TRAWL BOATS, SHOREHAM HARBOUR LUGGER

36 LUTE BOATS   KEEL, ROUNDED SECTIONS, VARIOUS COUNTER STERNS, LEVEL WITH BOTH RATIOS NORMAL

THOUGH NO DRAWINGS CAN BE QUOTED, MOST LUTE & ELLIPTICAL STERNED SUSSEX BEACH PUNTS & BOGS ARE OF THIS SORT

37 SAILING TRAWLER   KEEL, ROUNDED SECTIONS, COUNTER STERN, DRAG WITH NARROW & DEEP RATIOS

BRIXHAM MULE   WILLIAM & SAM   UPHAM 1917   MARCH, SAILING TRAWLERS' p.323 ADD 0·8 FOR KEEL
BEAM TRAWL, DECKED 2·5 BELOW SHEER, GAFF KETCH RIG, FIDDED TOPMAST & REEFING BOWSPRIT

E–P	BEAM KEEL & KEELSON			NORMAL	VEE CURVE	SLACK	FLAM			SHARP RAKED CURVE	4·5 N			COUNTER RAKED POST & Tr.Cu.		
67·0	52·5	3·7	8·6	8·0 4·2 5·0	28·4	15·0	15·0	15·0	11·0	04·5	0·0	0·0	D 1·4	57·0	9·5	0·0

PLYMOUTH TRAWLER   ERYCINA P.H.63   SHILSTON 1882   N.M.M. 223 A, B & C   ADD 0·8 FOR KEEL
BEAM TRAWL, DECKED 2·0 BELOW SHEER, GAFF CUTTER THEN IN 1894 KETCH, STEAM CAPSTAN

E–P	BEAM KEEL & KEELSON			NORMAL	VEE HOLLOW	ROUND	PLUMB Cu.			SHARP PLUMB	4·1 N			COUNTER RAKED POST & Tr.Cu.		
72·2	54·4	5·7	9·2	7·0 3·9 4·8	33·7	17·6	17·6	17·6	12·3	04·8	0·0	0·0	D 1·4	59·2	9·5	0·0

L	LOK	DF	DA	FF FM FA	#	Bmax	BWL	Bsh	Depth	#	BF	BWF	L/B B/D	#	BA	BWA

APPENDIX IV   Sheet 15

Nº TAXON   MAIN FEATURES

PLACE & TYPE   NAME OR NUMBER   BUILDER & DATE   DRAWING REFERENCE   DEPTH CORRECTION
GENERAL DETAILS - WORK , DECK , PROPULSION
PLANKING BOTTOM LINE   SHEER LINE   MID-SECTION   FORWARD   RATIO   AFT
BOT/SIDE   TYPE   TYPE   FLOOR BILGE SIDE   TYPE PROFILE   & GROUP TYPE PROFILE
L   LOK DF DA   FF FM FA   # Bmax BWL Bsh Depth # BF BWF L/B B/D # BA BWA

37 SAILING TRAWLER (CONT)

LOWESTOFT TRAWLER   MASTER HAND L.T.1203   SMITH (RYE) 1920   MARCH,'SAILING TRAWLERS' p.343   ADD 0·9 FOR KEEL
BEAM TRAWL , DECKED 2·3 BELOW SHEER , BOOMED LOOSE-FOOTED GAFF KETCH , TOPS'LS & BOWSPRIT , STEAM CAPSTAN
E-P   BEAM KEEL & KEELSON   EASY   VEE   ROUND   PLUMB   POINTED PLUMB   4·0 N   COUNTER WITH Tr.Cu.
76·0   55·6 5·8 8·7   7·6 4·6 5·1   37·5 19·2 19·2 19·2 12·2   05·3 0·0 0·0   D 1·6 61·9 11·2 0·0

LOWESTOFT SMACK   PURPLE HEATHER L.T.249 REYNOLDS 1908   MARCH,'SAILING TRAWLERS' p.318   ADD 1·0 FOR KEEL
BEAM TRAWL , DECKED 2·3 BELOW SHEER , BOOMED LOOSE-FOOTED GAFF KETCH , TOPS'LS & BOWSPRIT
E-P   BEAM KEEL   NORMAL   VEE   ROUND   PLUMB Cu. POINTED PLUMB   3·9 N   COUNTER,ROUND WITH KNUCKLE
75·0   58·6 4·2 8·8   9·3 5·5 6·0   38·0 19·0 18·8 18·8 11·8   03·6 0·0 0·0   D 1·6 62·2 0·0 0·0

RIVER FAL WORKING BOAT   ZIGUENER F.H.89   FERRIS 1840   N.M.M. 227 A,B&C   ADD 0·7 FOR BALLAST KEEL
OYSTER DREDGER , DECKED 0·7 BELOW SHEER , LARGE COCKPIT , POLE-MASTED GAFF CUTTER , TOPS'L & BOWSPRIT (BUILT ALL CLINKER)
E-P/E-F   BEAM KEEL   EASY   VEE   SLACK FLAM   SHARP PLUMB   3·8 N   COUNTER WITH TRANSOM
32·8   24·0 2·1 4·3   3·8 2·7 2·2   15·0 08·6 7·4 08·6 6·2   01·9 0·0 0·0   D 1·4 25·9 3·7 0·0

38 YACHT SMACK   KEEL , ROUNDED SECTIONS , COUNTER STERN , DRAG WITH DEEP RATIO & VEE FLOOR

MORECAMBE BAY NOBBY (NEW)   CROSSFIELD-ARNSIDE   MARCH,'I.C.of B.' Vol.2 p.286   ADD 1·1 FOR CURVED BALLAST KEEL
SHRIMPS & PLEASURE , FLUSH DECK , LARGE COCKPIT , GAFF CUTTER RIG
E-P   BEAM KEEL   EASY   VEE HOLLOW ROUND FLAM   POINTED RAKED CURVE 3·0   COUNTER ROUND
40·0   20·0 3·4 4·8   4·4 2·8 3·0   21·8 13·5 12·0 12·8 6·8   10·0 0·0 0·0   D 1·9 30·0 0·0 0·0

COLCHESTER SMACK   HARRIET BLANCHE   N.M.M. 231 A,B&C   ADD 0·3 FOR KEEL
OYSTER DREDGER , DECKED 1·1 BELOW SHEER , BOOMED LOOSE-FOOTED GAFF CUTTER , TOPS'L , FIDDED TOPMAST & REEFING BOWSPRIT
E-P   BEAM KEEL   NORMAL   VEE   ROUND FLAM   POINTED RAKED CURVE 3·7   COUNTER WITH Tr.Cu.
37·6   22·9 2·5 4·3   3·9 2·2 2·7   16·0 10·2 10·1 10·2 5·7   02·7 0·0 0·0   D 1·8 25·6 3·5 0·0

GIRVAN M.F.V.   SPINDRIFT B.A.220   NOBLE 1974   M.M.&R. Nº 31 Fig. XVI   ADD 0·7 FOR KEEL
TRAWLER , DECKED 2·0 BELOW SHEER , WHALEBACK FWD , DIESEL
E-P   BEAM KEEL   NORMAL   VEE HOLLOW ROUND PLUMB POINTED RAKED   3·0   COUNTER WITH Tr.Cu.
53·5   42·8 4·2 6·5   9·4 4·7 6·6   28·5 17·8 17·8 17·7 10·3   04·0 0·0 0·0   D 1·7 46·8 13·6 0·0

RYE SMACK   THREE BROTHERS R.X.153   SMITH 1896   N.M.M. 96 A,B & C   ADD 0·9 FOR KEEL
TRAWLER , DECKED 1·9 BELOW SHEER , BOOMED LOOSE-FOOTED GAFF KETCH , TOPS'LS , FIDDED TOPMAST & BOWSPRIT , STEAM CAPSTAN
E-P   BEAM KEEL & KEELSON   NORMAL   VEE   ROUND PLUMB Cu. POINTED PLUMB   3·7   COUNTER WITH Tr.Cu.
56·5   41·5 3·7 7·0   7·3 3·7 4·2   25·0 15·3 15·3 15·1 9·4   03·0 0·0 0·0   D 1·6 44·5 9·0 0·0

LOWESTOFT DRIFTER   STRIVE L.T.766   REYNOLDS c.1898   MARCH,'SAILING DRIFTERS' p.304   ADD 0·8 FOR KEEL
DECKED 2·0 BELOW SHEER , LOOSE-FOOTED POLE-MASTED GAFF KETCH , BOOM ON MIZZEN , JIGGER TOPS'LS , BOWSPRIT , STEAM CAPSTAN
E-P   BEAM KEEL & KEELSON   EASY   VEE   ROUND FLAM   SHARP PLUMB   3·5   COUNTER , ROUND WITH KNUCKLE
63·0   57·2 4·6 8·4   7·0 4·3 4·3   31·0 18·0 17·3 18·0 11·0   02·5 0·0 0·0   D 1·6 59·7 0·0 0·0

BRISTOL PILOT SKIFF   CHARLOTTE   HILLHOUSE 1808   M.M. Vol.39 p.37   ADD 1·3 FOR KEEL
ESTUARY & OPEN SEA , FLUSH DECKED , GAFF CUTTER
E-P   BEAM KEEL   LIVELY   VEE CURVE SLACK Thome BLUFF RAKED CURVE 2·9   COUNTER WITH Tr.Cu.
34·2   21·4 4·7 6·0   4·7 3·0 5·0   16·0 11·6 11·6 11·0 7·7   10·0 0·0 0·0   D 1·5 31·4 5·9 0·0

BRISTOL CHANNEL PILOT CUTTER   HILDA   COOPER 1899   Y.M. Vol VII p.106   ADD 1·0 FOR KEEL
ESTUARY & OPEN SEA , DECKED 1·5 BELOW SHEER , GAFF CUTTER
E-P   BEAM KEEL   NORMAL   VEE CURVE ROUND PLUMB Cu. SHARP PLUMB   3·7   COUNTER WITH Tr.Cu.
49·3   34·4 3·0 7·0   7·0 4·3 4·6   24·4 13·4 13·4 13·3 10·0   05·3 0·0 0·0   D 1·3 30·2 5·0 0·0

SWANSEA BAY PILOT SCHOONER   BENSON S.4 c.1870   N.M.M. 130   ADD 0·8 FOR KEEL
OPEN SEA , DECKED 1·0 BELOW SHEER , SHALLOP RIG WITH BOWSPRIT
E-P   BEAM KEEL   NORMAL   VEE   ROUND FLARE POINTED RAKED   3·7   COUNTER ROUND
50·0   37·0 5·2 9·7   6·8 3·8 4·4   22·3 13·5 13·0 13·5 11·6   04·5 0·0 0·0   D 1·2 41·5 0·0 0·0

L   LOK DF DA   FF FM FA   # Bmax BWL Bsh Depth # BF BWF L/B B/D # BA BWA

APPENDIX IV   SHEET 16

Nº TAXON	MAIN FEATURES			
PLACE & TYPE	NAME OR NUMBER	BUILDER & DATE	DRAWING REFERENCE	DEPTH CORRECTION
GENERAL DETAILS – WORK, DECK, PROPULSION				
PLANKING	BOTTOM LINE	SHEER LINE	MID-SECTION	FORWARD	RATIO	AFT
BOT/SIDE	TYPE	TYPE	FLOOR BILGE SIDE	TYPE PROFILE	& GROUP	TYPE PROFILE
L	LOK DF DA	FF FM FA	# Bmax BWL Bsh Depth	# BF BWF	L/B B/D	# BA BWA

39 RAISED FLOOR SMACK KEEL, ROUNDED SECTIONS, COUNTER STERN, DRAG WITH DEEP RATIO & RAISED FLOOR

SOUTHAMPTON FISHING HOY   STEEL c 1804   Sc.Mus. Photo 7581   ADD 1·1 FOR KEEL
DECKED 1·3 BELOW SHEER, SMACK RIGGED, LOOSE-FOOTED GAFF MAIN WITH BOOM, LONG BOWSPRIT, SHORT TOPMAST

E-F	BEAM KEEL	NORMAL	RAISED CURVE SLACK FLAM	BLUFF RAKED CURVE	2·4 B	SQ. TUCK WITH Tr.Cu.
28·1	15·0 3·2 4·4	5·7 4·0 4·0	13·0 11·8 10·6 11·8 7·7	08·0 0·0 0·0	D 1·5	23·0 6·5 0·0

HASTINGS LUGGER   THWAITES c.1848   WASHINGTON Pℓ. 3   ADD 0·7 FOR KEEL
BEACHED, MACKEREL & HERRING DRIFTER, DECKED 1·4 BELOW SHEER, 3-MASTED LUGGER WITH TOPSLS

E-F	BEAM KEEL	EASY	RAISED ROUND FLAM	POINTED RAKED	2·8	COUNTER WITH TRANSOM
41·5	31·5 3·9 5·5	5·3 4·4 4·4	25·0 14·9 14·5 14·9 9·2	03·4 0·0 0·0	D 1·6	34·9 9·0 0·0

HASTINGS LUGGER INDUSTRY R.X.94   c.1870   M.M. 24 p. 46   ADD 0·5 FOR KEEL
TRAWLING, BEACHED, DECKED 1·6 BELOW SHEER, MASTS LOWER, DIPPING FORE & STANDING LUG MIZZEN WITH TOPS'L, JIB ON BOWSPRIT, LEE OR CENTRE-BOARDS

E-F	BEAM KEEL & KEELSON	NORMAL	FLAT CURVE ROUND PLUMB	POINTED PLUMB	2·7	LUTE RAKED POST Cut.
32·2	25·4 3·0 4·5	4·4 3·2 3·8	15·6 12·0 12·0 12·0 7·0	01·8 0·0 0·0	D 1·7	27·2 5·8 3·5

ADMIRALTY 45' MOTOR FISHING VESSEL   c 1940   T.I.N.A. 1946 p. 300   ADD 0·6 FOR KEEL
HARBOUR TRAFFIC, DECKED 1·4 BELOW SHEER, DIESEL

E-P	BEAM KEEL	NORMAL	RAISED HOLLOW ROUND PLUMB	POINTED RAKED	3·0	BLUFF CRUISER STERN
49·0	37·2 2·8 4·2	8·4 5·4 6·0	26·7 16·2 16·2 16·2 8·5	06·0 0·0 0·0	D 1·9	43·2 0·0 0·0

COLCHESTER SMACK NEPTUNE   N.M.M. 201 A&B   ADD 0·5 FOR BALLAST KEEL
OYSTER DREDGER, DECKED 1·0 BELOW SHEER, GAFF CUTTER RIG

E-P	BEAM KEEL	NORMAL	RAISED HOLLOW ROUND PLUMB	SHARP RAKED CURVE	3·6	COUNTER WITH Tr.Cu.
36·4	23·7 2·7 4·8	4·2 2·2 2·1	20·4 10·0 10·0 10·0 6·5	02·4 0·0 0·0	D 1·5	26·1 6·0 0·0

ADMIRALTY 62½' MOTOR FISHING VESSEL   c 1940   T.I.N.A. 1946 p. 300   ADD 0·7 FOR KEEL
HARBOUR PATROL & TRANSPORT, DECKED 1·7 BELOW SHEER, DIESEL

E-P	BEAM KEEL SPRUNG FWD	LIVELY	RAISED HOLLOW ROUND FLAM	POINTED RAKED	3·6	BLUFF CRUISER STERN
63·7	43·5 4·0 6·0	9·9 5·4 6·5	31·2 17·9 17·9 17·0 10·8	12·0 0·0 0·0	D 1·7	55·5 0·0 0·0

BRIXHAM MUMBLE BEE NISHA B.M.2   UPHAM 1907   N.M.M. 220 A B & C   ADD 0·5 AFT FOR CURVED 0·9 KEEL
TRAWLER, DECKED 2·1 BELOW SHEER, GAFF CUTTER, KETCH LATER, LOOSE-FOOTED MAIN WITH BOOM

E-P	BEAM KEEL & KEELSON	EASY	RAISED Cu. SLACK PLUMB Cu.	SHARP PLUMB	3·7	COUNTER WITH Tr.Cu.
52·5	43·4 3·7 7·0	7·0 5·0 4·0	25·0 14·3 14·3 14·2 10·4	04·5 0·0 0·0	D 1·4	47·9 11·0 0·0

MUMBLES OYSTER SKIFF EMMELINE 14 S.A. PAYNTER c 1865   M.M. 40 p.258   ADD 0·6 FOR KEEL
DREDGER, DECKED 1·4 BELOW SHEER, FULL GAFF CUTTER, BOOMED LOOSE-FOOTED MAIN, FIDDED TOPMAST, REEFING BOWSPRIT, STEAM CAPSTAN

E-P	BEAM KEEL & KEELSON	EASY	RAISED CURVE ROUND FLAM	POINTED PLUMB	3·7	COUNTER WITH Tr.Cu.
39·2	27·7 3·2 6·0	4·5 2·6 2·6	15·0 10·7 10·7 10·8 7·5	02·5 0·0 0·0	D 1·4	30·2 5·0 0·0

ALSO HASTINGS MOTOR LUGGERS, MANY SCOTTISH M.F.V.s INCLUDING THOSE WITH RAISED FOC'SLS

40 SQUARE ENDED BOAT KEEL, ROUNDED SECTIONS, TRUNCATED STERN, ALL KEEL ASPECTS & HULL RATIOS

SERVICE CUTTER - LUG SLOOP D.Z.   1st HALF 20th C.   ADMIRALTY   ADD 0·4 FOR KEEL
SEA BOAT, OPEN, MAST LOWERS, DIPPING LUG & STAYSAIL, PULLS 12 OARS DOUBLE-BANKED IN OAR-BEDS, DROP-KEEL

E-F	BEAM KEEL & SPRUNG HOG	NORMAL	FLAT CURVE ROUND FLAM	POINTED Ra.Cu.	3·6	SQUARE RAKED
32·0	29·0 1·4 0·6	3·4 2·2 2·8	17·0 09·0 8·2 09·0 3·5	02·8 0·0 0·0	2·6	31·8 4·2 1·2

ALSO VARIETIES OF MOTOR BEACH, CREEL & FISHING PARTY BOATS

THIS SYSTEM MAY HAVE TO BE MODIFIED IN STEP WITH FRESH DATA. VIZ:— SUBDIVISION OF Nº 40 & RE-VALUATION OF THE 'NORMAL' HULL RATIOS

ALL DIMENSIONS ARE GIVEN IN FEET

ABBREVIATIONS

B	BEAMY RATIO	E-F	EDGE-FASTENED	M.M.	MARINER'S MIRROR	S	SHALLOW	Th	TUMBLEHOME	Y.M.	YACHTING MONTHLY
Cu.	CURVE(D)	E-P	EDGE-POSITIONED	N.	NARROW RATIO	Sc.Mus.	SCIENCE MUSEUM	Tr	TRANSOM	#	STATION FROM FWD
Cut.	CUTAWAY	Ff	FLARE	N.M.M	NATIONAL MARITIME MUSEUM	Sq	SQUARE	Trans	TRANSITIONAL	✳	SEE INDEX
D	DEEP RATIO	H/C	HARD CHINE	Ra.	RAKED	S.S.	STANDING STRAKE	Ts	TOMBSTONE		

A.N.M.   ARCHITECTURA NAVALIS MERCATORIA   F. H. CHAPMAN
G.& C. of the I. of S.   GIGS & CUTTERS OF THE ISLES OF SCILLY   A. JENKINS
I.C. of B.   INSHORE CRAFT OF BRITAIN   E. MARCH
M.& S. in E. & A.   MAST & SAIL IN EUROPE & ASIA   H. WARINGTON SMYTH
M.M. & R.   MARITIME MONOGRAPHS & REPORTS   N.M.M
T.I.N.A.   TRANSACTIONS OF THE INSTITUTE OF NAVAL ARCHITECTS
Y. B.& S.   A MANUAL OF YACHT & BOAT SAILING   DIXON KEMP

APPENDIX V ABSTRACT OF MR B B JOHNS' ACCOUNT NOTEBOOK

1881

ROSE

Nets & barking	£17: 6: 3	Pilchard driving 16/7-15/10	£32: 18: 0
Repair & maintenance	6: 10: 3	Salt fish	12: 18: 6
Carriage	5: 0		45: 16: 6
Cellar rent	1: 0: 0		
	24: 1: 6	Profit on boat £21: 15: 0	

PRIDE OF THE WEST

Nets & barking	11: 13: 1	Pilchard driving 23/7-15/10	29: 3: 0
Repairs & maintenance	12: 8	Salt fish	8: 16: 6
Cellar rent	17: 0	Plymouth	6: 10: 0
Salt	3: 6	Rec'd for nets	3: 13: 0
	13: 6: 3	45t Op [?]	15: 0
			48: 17: 6
		Profit on boat £35: 11: 3.	

MARY ANN

Nets & barking	15: 10: 0	Pilchard driving 23/7-?/10	40: 10: 6
Cellar rent	17: 0	Salt fish	7: 10: 0
	15: 18: 0	[Blank entry]	11: 0: 0
		45–16 [?]	2: 16: 0
			61: 16: 6
		Profit on boat £45: 18: 6.	

1882

ROSE

13 res nets	5: 0	Pilchard driving 22/7-6/10	26: 19: 6
Store	1: 0: 0	blank entries [2]	7: 13: 0
Cellar rent	17: 0		34: 12: 6
	2: 2: 0	Profit on boat £32: 10: 6.	

COCK OF THE WEST

Nets	16: 11: 0	Richard Pd	5: 11: 6
R & M	3: 6	Pilchard driving 29/7-14/10	34: 0: 6
Cellar rent	17: 0	Plymouth	10: 0: 0
	17: 11: 6		49: 12: 0
		Profit on boat £32: 0: 6	

MARY ANN

Nets [mackerel?]	27: 19: 6	Mackerel driving 18/2-29/4	86: 3: 6
Cellar rent	17: 0	17/6-15/7	16: 4: 0
Nets [pilchard?]	10: 18: 0	Pilchard driving 5/8-6/10	14: 6: 6
[2 blank entries]	1: 4: 4	[2 blank entries]	14: 2: 0
Cellar rent	17: 0		130: 16: 0
	41: 15: 0	Profit on boat £89: 0: 2.	

OLGA

Nets & barking	11: 0: 3	Mackerel driving 18/2-17/5	101: 8: 9
Cellar rent	17: 0	10/6-24/6	4: 2: 0
	11: 17: 3		105: 10: 9
		Profit on boat £93: 13: 6.	

1883

COCK

Nets	2: 2: 6	Money [mackerel?]	48: 6: 3
R & M	2: 15: 0	Pilchard driving 21/7-23/9	33: 8: 0
St Mawes dues	2: 0	Salt fish	18: 15: 0
[Blank entry (cellar?)]	1: 0: 1		100: 9: 3
[Blank entry]	12: 13: 4		
	18: 13: 9	Profit on boat £81: 15: 6.	

MARY ANN
Nets [mackerel?]	20: 4: 0	Mackerel driving 22/3-4/5	44: 2: 6
Cellar rent	17: 0	2/6	1: 4: 0
Nets (pilchard)	13: 11: 4	Pilchard driving 21/7-?/10	48: 10: 0
	34: 12: 4	Plymouth	8: 0: 0
SHARED £24		Salt fish	14: 17: 0
			116: 13: 6

Profit on boat £82: 1: 2.

OLGA
Nets & barking	14: 18: 6	Mackerel driving 22/3-4/5	43: 16: 0
[Blank entry]	5: 9: 2		
Cellar etc.	18: 0	Profit on Boat £22: 10: 4	
SHARED £41: 8: 9.			

1884   ROSE
Sail & rope	3: 17: 6	Pilchard driving 19/7-28/9	32: 18: 0
Drying quay dues	5: 0	Salt fish	5: 15: 0
[2 blank entries]	12: 6	[2 blank entries]	9: 4: 0
	4: 15: 0		47: 17: 0

Profit on boat £43:   2: 0.

COCK
Repairs & maintenance	4: 13: 0	Loss on boat £4: 13: 0.

MARY ANN
Nets etc	13: 0: 9	Mackerel driving 15/3-18/5	38: 9: 6
Cellar	17: 0		
	13: 17: 9	Profit on boat £24: 11: 9.	

OLGA
Nets	13: 10: 6	Mackerel driving 15/3-18/5	44: 1: 3
Cellar	17: 0		
R & M	1: 13:11	Profit on boat £27: 19: 10	
	16: 1: 5		

1885   ROSE
Nets (2)	7: 0: 6	Pilchard driving 18/7-13/10	18: 3: 3
Cellar	17: 0	[2 blank entries]	3: 17: 2
[Blank entry]	1: 19: 2		22: 0: 5
	9: 16: 8	Profit on boat £12: 3: 9.	

COCK
Nets etc	6: 14: 0	Pilchard driving 11/7-17/10	26: 7: 2
Cellar	17: 0		
	7: 11: 0	Profit on boat £18: 16: 2	

MARY ANN
Nets and barking	5: 15: 0	Loss on boat £5: 15: 0.

OLGA
Nets	6: 4: 5	Mackerel driving 21/3-11/4	12: 4: 0
Cellar	17: 0		
R & M (L Johns)	1: 0: 0	Profit on boat £4: 2: 7	
	8: 1: 5		

1886   ROSE
Expense	11: 5: 7	[Pilchard driving?]) 21/3-?/10	18: 2: 0
		Salt fish	2: 7: 6
			20: 9: 6

Profit on boat £9:   3: 11.

COCK
'in bay'	10: 0	[Pilchard driving?] 16/7-?/10	28: 12:11
R & M	1: 11: 8	Salt fish	1: 11: 3
	2: 1: 2		30: 4: 2

Profit on boat £28:   2: 6.

OLGA
Nets	1: 0: 6	Mackerel driving 10/4-1/6	67: 10: 0
Cellar	1: 0: 0		
R. & M.	5: 2: 6	Profit on boat £60: 7: 0.	
	7: 3: 0		

1887	ROSE [Blank entry]	1: 0: 0	[Pilchard driving?] 23/7-?/9 Plymouth Profit on boat £24: 7: 9.	16: 17: 9 8: 10: 0 25: 7: 9
	COCK [Blank entry]	5: 8: 7	[Pilchard driving?] 27/8-?/9 Profit on boat £5: 11: 2.	10: 19: 9
	MARY ANN Nets R & M	4: 4: 9 2: 14: 0 6: 18: 9	Mackerel driving 1/4-27/5 Profit on boat £31: 8: 6	38: 7: 3
1887	OLGA R & M	3: 13: 7	Loss on boat £3: 13: 7	
1888	ROSE Bills	13: 0:10	Pilchards 4/8-13/10 Plymouth Profit on boat £15: 11: 8.	22: 2: 6 6: 10: 0 28: 12: 6
	COCK Bills	9: 10: 3	Summer [pilchards?] Blank entry Profit on boat £22: 8: 9.	28: 3: 0 3: 16: 0 31: 19: 0
	[MARY ANN?] [Blank entry]	10: 5: 6	[mackerel?] 7/4-19/5 [pilchard?] 11/10-17/10 Profit on boat £24: 8: 2.	21: 16: 0 12: 17: 8 34: 13: 8
1889	[ROSE?] Bills	11: 6	[pilchards?] 3/8-?/10 Profit on boat £13: 6: 9.	13: 8: 5
	COCK Bills	11: 9	[pilchards?] ? -12/9 Oil 3/10 Profit on boat £16: 8: 11.	14: 1: 8 2: 19: 0 17: 0: 8
1890	OLGA Bills	9: 18: 9	[mackerel?] 5/4-14/6 Profit on boat £27: 17: 6.	37: 16: 3

APPENDIX VI PARK WALL AGREEMENT

A Coppy of instructions and Rules

of fysshing tacken from Henry Rose William Hardy Thomas Vivian & Co. in the year of Our Lord One thousand seven hundred and 92 directions. First the owner must find a boat seine Backwater Boats two fish baskets and buckett for the use of the boat and every article required for the use

The owner is to chose a man to have the care of the boat and seine to see it properly used and not to geet injured by laying in the boat And to see every man to do his best when thear.

The Captin and owner must ship twelve men whitch is called seine Company and each man that do agre to the number of Twelve to go for the season are so long as convenient according thear husbandry calling in worck and every man to the number of twelve must be paid one shelling each by the Captin or owner whitch is called sheping shelling And not go with any other Companey for the season without some just provocation and then to give the shelling to the owner And if any man after comencing fishing should be ill and not of his own seeking he is entitled to his shear during the time the Company is fishing that shipped but not any others that is on occasion coming whitch have not shiped And if any of the Company cannott go over for wont of a boat at the time the fish being caught they are not to lose thears according to the majorety of the Companey wheather it is on cause of drincking or any other fault of carelessness or thear own And after the first hundred of mackerell is caught the rule is for the Companey to go to lot by putting in each man a peble in a hat that every man must know his own and they must be served out by the Captin that every man may have his day beginnin on Munday whitch it is thear duty to acte as buttlers and not to delay no time when sent and not to give away neither in any way to defraud the Compancy And se that the flagin is always clean and every man acording to his day mist see the ropes brut to the boat after the boat is hulled after shutting And every man acording to the day is entitled to one mackerel each lot that is caught if over a hundred and when fish is caught it is the captains duty to see that the men that understand is appointed to count the number and send to sell sutch men that understand selling and when soald give the sample of mackerell called vresk to the buiers as binding the bargin for sutch fish being soald And every reasonable expence is to be paid to those that go to sell And those men that tacke them to whear they are to be carred And when the monet is colected the owner and

Captin must see the money so earned by the Companey brot forward that every man may see every expence paid for caring and selling the fish and then the thurd part is to be taken for the owner and then the money to be aloued to be paid for drinck and the remainder to be devided among the number acording to whot they have earned of eacg lot And any man that first seea lot of fish stray over one thousand is entitled to one shelling And every man during the time of meals must avoid smocking or causing any interuption of aney sort. The Captin may dismis any won that do not abay the rulles and agreable with the Companey in every way with kindness.

APPENDIX VII **DISTRIBUTION PATTERNS** – Definitions (see Chapter 10)

	ISOLATED	INTERRUPTED	CONTINUOUS BUT LIMITED	CONTINUOUS AND EXTENDED	UNIVERSAL
SOLITARY SITUATION	Type matched only to the task and surroundings of one place, where only one type of boat can be justified	Type matched to minor variations of either task or surroundings or both in separated places where only one type of boat is justified	Type suited to place where only one type of boat can be justified, and in the same area or stretch of coast with no marked variations in either task or surroundings or both	Type able to do the tasks in all the places, where only one type of boat can be justified, and over an extended stretch of coast with much variation of task or surroundings or both	Type can manage all simple tasks in any place in Britain, where only one type of boat can be justified
ARRESTED RELATED GRADE	Type developed no further than needed to provide one of the related grades in just one place where a range of boats is necessary	Type developed no further than needed to provide one of the related grades in separated places with only minor variations in either task or surroundings or both where a range of boats is necessary	Type developed no further than needed to provide one of the related grades in places over a limited area or stretch of coast with no marked variations in either task or surroundings or both, and where a range of boats is necessary	Type developed no further than needed to provide one of the related grades in places over an extended area or stretch of coast with much variation of task or surroundings, and where a range of boats is necessary	Type developed no further than needed to provide one of the related grades in any place in Britain, and where a range of boats is necessary
FUNCTIONAL RELATED GRADE	Type developed to function as one of the related grades in just one place where a range of boats is necessary	Type developed to function as one of the related grades in separated places with only minor variations in either task or surroundings or both where a range of boats is necessary	Type developed to function as one of the related grades in places over a limited area or stretch of coast with no marked variations in either task or surroundings or both, and where a range of boats is necessary	Type developed to function as one of the related grades in places over an extended area or stretch of coast with much variation in task or surroundings or both, and where a range of boats is necessary	Type developed to function as one of the related grades in any place in Britain, and where a range of boats is necessary
UNRELATED GRADE	Unrelated type chosen for its ability to function as one of the grades in just one place where a range of boats is necessary	Unrelated type chosen for its ability to function as one of the grades in separated places with only minor variations in either tasks or surroundings or both, and where a range of boats is necessary	Unrelated type chosen for its ability to function as one of the grades in places over a limited area or stretch of coast with no marked variation in either task or surroundings or both, and where a range of boats is necessary	Unrelated type chosen for its ability to function as one of the grades in places over an extended area or stretch of coast with much variation in task or surroundings or both, and where a range of boats is necessary	Unrelated type chosen for its ability to function as one of the grades in any place in Britain, and where a range of boats is necessary
MIXED GRADE	One of a random collection of boats all able to function in the same grade in just one place where a range of boats is necessary	One of a random collection of boats all able to function in the same grade in separated places with only minor variations in either task or surroundings or both, and where a range of boats is necessary	One of a random collection of boats all able to function in the same grade in places over a limited area or stretch of coast with no marked variation in either task or surroundings or both, and where a range of boats is necessary	One of a random collection of boats all able to function in the same grade in places over an extended area or stretch of coast with much variation in task or surroundings or both, and where a range of boats is necessary	One of a random collection of boats all able to function in the same grade in any place in Britain, and where a range of boats is necessary

Glossary

BEARDING. The surface of a rabbet laying between the middle and bearding lines and in contact with the inside of the plank.

BEARINGS. A boat's immersed volume, the distribution of which determines her ability to carry loads and how she trims.

BEUL. Scots terms for the opening formed by the upper edges of a pair of strakes as seen from above, as opposed to 'sheer' which is the side view of the same edges.

BRAILS. Ropes that draw the *leech* of any loose-footed sail up towards its head so as to stow it or reduce its area.

BROACH. When running down wind, to swing side on to the wind, waves or both, so risking swamping and capsize.

CANT. Most frames lie plumb and square to the keel, but cants, though plumb, are set square or nearly so to one side. Stem rungs though square are out of plumb. Cants and rungs are fitted at each end and need less bevel than square transverse frames.

DEADRISE. The amount a floor rises above the rabbet often expressed as an angle or slope, and most in way of the deadwoods either end.

GINGE HOLE. Sussex term for the hole in the forefoot used when hauling out. Elsewhere other terms are found.

GRIPE, SKEG. Piece added, for'd or aft respectively, to increase the lateral resistance locally or overall. *Skegs* also improve the water flow over and support of a rudder.

JACK(Y) NICHOLLS. A pair of cleats fitted outside between the stem and the gunwales, to give strength and take wear when on moorings. This may also include a thumb cleat on top of the gunwale to prevent the rope or chain sliding aft.

LEECH, LEE. The trailing edge of a fore-and-aft sail, or either of the upright sides of a square one.

NORSELS, OSSELS. Lines that attach a drift net to its headrope, shortening it or setting-in by the proper amount.

RAM. The plank-shaped part of a coble's keel, the length of which is often given as the size of this class of boat.

RHINE. Large open ditch or drain.

SEW. To be grounded or high and dry.

SHORE. Temporary strut for holding timbers in place during building or the complete boat while slipping.

SIRMARK. A mark on a mould that shows where a timber or another mould should go.

SPLINE. A nearly square sectioned batten made of flexible straight grained stuff.

STAITHE. A landing stage or wharf.

TRAMMEL. A set net made up of a fine meshed net sandwiched between two coarse ones. This entangles fish.

TURN DOWN. An indication of by how much the greatest and least values within a group differ.

WET-BOB. One who devotes himself to freshwater boating.

YAW. The amount a vessel deviates from her mean course.

References

CHAPTER 1

1. Noble, A 1978 *The Scottish Inshore Fishing Vessel.* Maritime Monographs and Reports No 31, p2.
2. Kemp, D 1884 *Manual of Yacht and Boat Sailing*, 4th ed.
3. Norton, P 1972 *State Barges.* National Maritime Museum.
4. Cluness, A 1967 *The Shetland Book.* Zetland Education Committee.

CHAPTER 2

1. *Dorset County Magazine* No 13
2. Washington, J 1849 *Report on the Loss of Life and on the Damage caused to Fishing Boats on the East Coast of Scotland in the gale of 19th August 1848.* House of Commons.
3. Lamb, H 1978 *Climate, Past, Present and Future.* Vol 2, p647.
4. Holdsworth, W H 1874 *Deep-Sea Fishing and Fishing Boats.* p298.
5. Pearce, R 1963 *The Ports and Harbours of Cornwall.*

CHAPTER 3

1. Waters, I 1975 *The Town of Chepstow.* p27. Chepstow.
2. Farr, G 1955 'Bristol Channel Pilotage'. *The Mariner's Mirror* No 39, p27.
3. Pike, D 1978 'Fishing Boats and their Equipment'. *Fishing News.*

CHAPTER 4

1. Department of Trade 1976 *Examinations for Certificates of Competency, Skippers and Second Hands of Fishing Boats – Regulations.*

CHAPTER 5

1. McPhee, J 1975 *Survival of the Bark Canoe.* New York.
2. Boczar, M 1966 'The Craft of the Dunajec'. *The Mariner's Mirror* No 52, p211.
3. Hornell, J 1936 'The Curraghs of Ireland.' *The Mariner's Mirror* No 23, p74.
4. Greenhill, B 1976 *The Archaeology of the Boat.* p45.
5. May, W 1974 *The Boats of Men of War.* Maritime Monographs and Reports No 15, p18.
6. Wilson, R 1974 *Boatyards and Boatbuilding.* p13. Corby.
7. Rice, W 1822 *Account of an Ancient Vessel recently found under the old bed of the River Rother.* Sheet 2 of drawings with MSS at National Maritime Museum.
8. Lehmann, L 1978 'The Flat-Bottomed Roman Boat from Druten'. *International Journal of Nautical Archaeology* No 7, p259.
9. Greenhill *op cit*, p211.
10. Rålamb, A 1691 *Skeps Byggerij eller Adelig Öfnungs Tionde Tom.* fig 9.
11. Warrington Smythe, H 1929 *Mast and Sail in Europe and Asia.* p402, 483.
12. Rudolph, W 1974 *Inshore Fishing Craft of the Southern Baltic.* Maritime Monographs and Reports No 14, p5.
13. Greenhill *op cit*, p81.

CHAPTER 6

1. Davis, F 1958 *An Account of the Fishing Gear of England and Wales.*
2. Thurston Hopkins, R 1931 *Small Sailing Craft.* p152.
3. May *op cit*, p16.
4. Woodward *Treatise on Heraldry – Ships in Armoury.*
5. Farr, G 1969 'Pill Yawls'. *The Mariner's Mirror* No 55, p246.
6. Illingworth, J 1949 *Offshore.* p49.
7. Holdsworth *op cit*, p246.
8. Baker, W 1966 *Sloops and Shallops.* Chapter 3.

9. Munro, G 1937 *Leith-London Smack (174 tons).* Marine Models No 10, p16.
10. Norton *op cit.*
11. Burwash, D 1947 *English Merchant Shipping 1460–1540.* p109.
12. Paget Tomlinson, E 1978 *Canal and River Navigations.*
13. Carr, F 1971 *Sailing Barges.*
14. March, E 1948 *Spritsail Barges of the Thames and Medway.*
15. Rudolph *op cit.*
16. McGrail, J F 1978 *Logboats of England and Wales.* British Archaeological Reports, British Series, No 51.
17. McGrail, J F (ed) 1977 *Sources and Techniques of Boat Archaeology.* British Archaeological Reports, Supplementary Series, No 29, p229.
18. Greenhill *op cit*, Chapter 3.
19. Goddard, D 1975 *Exeter Maritime Museum Catalogue.* Item 48.
20. McKee, E 1971 'The Weston-super-Mare Flatner'. *The Mariner's Mirror* No 57, p25.
21. Vidler, L 1935 'The Rye River Barges'. *The Mariner's Mirror* No 21, p378.
22. Chapman, F H 1768 *Architectura Navalis Mercatoria.* Plate L.11.
23. Lloyd, R 1955 'Aberystwyth Fishing Boats'. *The Mariner's Mirror* No 41, p155.
24. Bray, M 1979 *Watercraft.* Mystic Seaport Museum, p146.
25. Chapman *op cit*, PL L11.2.
26. Washington *op cit.*
27. Holness, J 1972 'Itchen Ferry Boats'. *Yachting World Annual*, p11.
28. March, E 1969 *Sailing Drifters.* p42, plan 2.
29. Chapman *op cit*, P1 LIX.3.
30. Noble *op cit*, p29.
31. May *op cit.*
32. Kemp *op cit*, p288.

CHAPTER 7

1. Hornell *op cit*, p27.
2. Leitao, M 1978 *Boats of the Lisbon River.* Maritime Monographs and Reports No 34.
3. Greenhill *op cit*, p37.
4. McKee, E 1972 *Clenched Lap or Clinker.* National Maritime Museum.
5. McGruer, E nd *Engineering in Wood.* Edinburgh.
6. Christensen, A E 1972 'Boatbuilding Tools and the Process of Learning' in Hasslöf, O (ed) *Ships and Shipyards, Sailors and Fishermen.* Copenhagen.
7. Hill, H O 1978 *The English Coble.* Maritime Monographs and Reports No 30.
8. Reed, 1956 *A Salmon Saga – The Story of the Berwick Salmon Fishery Co Ltd 1856 – 1956.*
9. Stalkartt, M 1781 *Naval Architecture or the Rudiments of Shipbuilding.* Book 1.
10. Howard, F 1979 *Sailing Ships of War 1400 – 1860.*
11. Salisbury, W & Anderson, R C 1958 *A Treatise on Shipbuilding.* Occasional Publication No 6, Society for Nautical Research.
12. Noble *op cit*, p17.
13. Fenwich, V (ed) 1978 *The Graveney Boat.* British Archaeological Reports, British Series, No 53, Chapter 9.
14. McGrail, J F 1974 *The Building and Trials of the Replica of an Ancient Boat.* Maritime Monographs and Reports No 11, p14.

CHAPTER 8

1. *Annual Reports, Factories and Workshops* 1888, p80.
2. Wilson, J 1972 *Fenland Barges.* p9. Kettering.
3. Hornell, J 1936 'British Coracles'. *The Mariner's Mirror* No 27, p26.

4. McGrail, J F 1979 'Rowing: aspects of the ethnographic and iconographic evidence'. *International Journal of Nautical Archaeology* No 8, p155.
5. Williams, J et al 1967 *Rowing, a Scientific Approach*. Proceedings of a Symposium.
6. Steele and Goddard 1816 *The Art of Making Masts, Yards and Oars*. p184.
7. Hawkins, C 1969 'The *Lady Nelson*'. *The Mariner's Mirror* No 55, p417.
8. Hill *op cit*.
9. Oke, P 1935 *Cuckoo 1881, Gorran Haven*. Drawing for Society of Nautical Research.
10. Harrison Butler, T 1945 *Cruising Yachts*. p86.
11. Cadoret, B 1978 *Ar Vag*. p6.
12. Dyson, J 1977 *Business in Great Waters*.
13. Elliott, C 1978 *Sailing Fishermen*.
14. Elliott, C 1979 *Steam Fishermen*.
15. Oke, P 1935 *Hallsand Crabber Silvia 1921*. Drawing for SNR.
16. Oke, P 1935 *Hallsand Seiner, Chart Built*. Drawing for SNR.
17. Holt, W 1946 'Admiralty type MFVs'. *Transactions of the Institute of Naval Architects* No 88 p295.

CHAPTER 9

1. Taylor, J 1974 *Fishing on Lower Severn*. p11.
2. Cooke, E W 1829 *Shipping and Craft*. Pl 48.
3. National Maritime Museum Catalogue No F3/129.
4. White, E 1952 *British Fishing Boats and Coastal Craft* Pt 1, No 35.
5. Anon 1911 'Note.' *The Mariner's Mirror* No 1, p129.
6. Widgate, W 1888 *Boating* p142.
7. Cooke *op cit*, Pl 32.

8. Hill *op cit*.
9. Anson, P 1930 *Fishing Boats and Fisher Folk on the East Coast of Scotland*. p238.
10. MacLeod, J 1974 'An Sgoth Niseach.' *Eilean an Fhraoich Annual Fishing in Ness. The Stornoway Gazette*.
11. Noall, C 1972 *Cornish Seines and Seiners*.
12. *Fourth Annual Report of the Inspectors of Sea Fisheries* 1889.
13. Hill, H O 1934 *Unpublished Journal No 7: Cornish Crabbers*.
14. McKee, E 1977 'The Lerrets of Chesil Bank'. *The Mariner's Mirror* No 63, p39.
15. Festing, S nd *Fishermen*.
16. Holmes, G 1908 *Humber Yawl Club Year Book*.
17. Beaudouin, F 1970 *Les Bateaux de Berck*. Institut d'Ethnologie, Paris.
18. Hill, H O 1952 'Lugger of Beer.' *The Mariner's Mirror* No 38, p143. *Unpublished Journal No 2* pp70–104.
19. March *op cit*, p311.
20. Holdsworth *op cit*, p182.
21. Lewis, J 1975 *Vintage Boats*.
22. Holness *op cit*, p11.
23. Noble *op cit*.
24. Anson, P 1950 *Scots Fisherfolk*. Saltine.

CHAPTER 10

1. Farr, G 1956 'Severn Navigation and the Trow'. *The Mariner's Mirror* No 32, p80.
2. Boddy, M 1975 *Dorset Shipwrecks*. Nos 48–50.
3. MacPherson, J 1975 *Tales of Barra*.

Index

(Numbers in italics refer to figure numbers)